Writing with POWER

Contributing Author
Joyce Senn

Senior Consultants
Constance Weaver
Peter Smagorinsky

Language

Composition

21st Century Skills

Perfection Learning®

Editorial

Editorial Director	Carol Francis
Executive Editor	Jim Strickler
Editorial Team	Gay Russell-Dempsey, Terry Ofner, Kate Winzenburg, Sue Thies, Andrea Stark, Paula Reece, Sheri Cooper

Design

Art Director	Randy Messer
Design Team	Tobi Cunningham, Deborah Bell, Emily Greazel, Mike Aspengren, Jane Wonderlin, Dea Marks, Lori Zircher, Jill Kimpston
Illustration/Diagrams	Mike Aspengren, Sue Cornelison
Image Research	Anjanette Houghtaling

Joyce Senn taught both middle and high school before putting her experience and love of language to work in her distinguished career as educational consultant and author. Specializing in grammar, Senn was a pioneer in textbook publishing in her use of themed activities, helping to provide a context for once-isolated grammar, usage, and mechanics practice. Senn's other publications include the acclaimed children's reference book *Quotations for Kids* (Millbrook Press, 1999) and *Information Literacy: Educating Children for the 21st Century* (with Patricia Breivik, National Education Association, 2nd Ed., 1998).

Special thanks to Joan McElroy, Ph.D., for contributions to the research strand of *Writing with Power,* and to David Kulieke, English instructor and consultant, for his review of the grammar, usage, and mechanics chapters.

Copyright © 2012
by Perfection Learning® Corporation
1000 North Second Avenue
P.O. Box 500
Logan, Iowa 51546-0500
Tel: 1-800-831-4190 • Fax: 1-800-543-2745
perfectionlearning.com

4 5 6 7 QG 16 15 14

ISBN 13: 978-1-61563-630-3
ISBN 10: 1-61563-630-7

Senior Consultants

Peter Smagorinsky wrote the activities that form the project-centered "structured process approach" to teaching writing at the heart of the composition units of *Writing with Power*. A high school English teacher for fourteen years, Smagorinsky has also taught in the English Education programs at the University of Oklahoma (1990-1998) and University of Georgia (1998-present). In addition to numerous articles, he has published books through Heinemann (*Teaching English by Design*, 2007, and *The Dynamics of Writing Instruction: A Structured Process Approach for the Composition Teacher in the Middle and High School,* with Larry Johannessen, Elizabeth Kahn, and Thomas McCann, 2010); through Teacher's College Press (*Research on Composition: Multiple Perspectives on Two Decades of Change*, ed., 2006); through Cambridge University Press (*Vygotskian Perspectives on Literacy Research: Constructing Meaning through Collaborative Inquiry*, with Carol D. Lee, 2000); and through the National Council of Teachers of English (NCTE) Press (*Standards in Practice, Grades 9–12*, 1996). For NCTE, he also chaired the Research Forum, co-edited *Research in the Teaching of English*, co-chaired the Assembly for Research, chaired the Standing Committee on Research, chaired the Research Foundation, and served as President of the National Conference on Research in Language and Literacy.

Constance Weaver developed the "power" concept and features for *Writing with Power,* identifying strategies for using grammatical options to add power to writing and thinking as well as developing the "Power Rules," beginning with ten "must know" conventions for success in school and the workplace and expanding into features more relevant for advanced writers. Weaver has shaped English education for more than thirty years, illuminating the relationship between grammar and writing and providing practical, effective teaching guidance, from her earliest works on the subject, the best-selling *Grammar for Teachers* (NCTE, 1979) and the widely acclaimed *Teaching Grammar in Context* (Boynton/Cook, 1996), to her most recent *Grammar Plan Book* (Heinemann, 2007) and *Grammar to Enrich and Enhance Writing* (with Jonathan Bush, Heinemann, 2008). She has also long been a leader in literacy and reading. Her book *Reading Process and Practice* (Heinemann, 1988) is authoritative in its field. In 1996, Weaver was honored by the Michigan Council of Teachers of English with the Charles C. Fries award for outstanding leadership in English education. Weaver is the Heckert Professor of Reading and Writing at Miami University, Oxford, Ohio, and Professor Emerita of English at Western Michigan University, Kalamazoo.

National Advisory Panel

Writing with Power was developed under the guidance of outstanding educators—teachers, curriculum specialists, and supervisors—whose experience helped ensure that the program design was implemented in a practical, engaging way for every classroom.

Middle School

DeVeria A. Berry
Curriculum Specialist
Frank T. Simpson-Waverly School
Hartford Public Schools
Hartford, Connecticut

Marylou Curley-Flores
Curriculum Specialist
Reading/Language Arts
Curriculum and Instruction
San Antonio Independent School District
San Antonio, Texas

Karen Guajardo
Curriculum Specialist
Reading/English Language Arts
Curriculum and Instruction
San Antonio Independent School District
San Antonio, Texas

Tina DelGiodice
English Teacher/Staff Developer (retired)
Jersey City Public Schools
Jersey City, New Jersey

Julie Hines-Lyman
Curriculum Coach
Agassiz Elementary School
Chicago Public Schools
Chicago, Illinois

Marcia W. Punsalan
Language Arts Department Chair
Clay High School
Oregon City Schools
Oregon, Ohio

Melanie Pogue Semore
Director of Upper School
Harding Academy
Memphis, Tennessee

High School

Nathan H. Busse
English Language Arts Teacher
Fox Tech High School
San Antonio Independent School DIstrict
San Antonio, Texas

Joyce Griggs
Instructional Specialist
Peoria Unified School District
Peoria, Arizona

Jill Haltom
English Language Arts/Reading Director
Coppell Independent School District
Coppell, Texas

Lynn Hugerich
Retired English Supervisor
Secaucus Public School District
Secaucus, New Jersey

Linda M. Moore, M.Ed.
English Instructor
Coppell High School
Coppell Independent School District
Coppell, Texas

Debora Stonich
Secondary Curriculum Coordinator of English Language Arts
McKinney Independent School District
McKinney, Texas

Student Contributors

Writing with Power proudly and gratefully presents the work of the following students, whose writing samples—from effective opening sentences to in-depth literary analyses—show so clearly the power of writing.

From Lucyle Collins Middle School
Fort Worth, Texas
Marbella Maldonado
Victor Ramirez

From Evanston Township High School
Evanston, Illinois
Morgan Nicholls

From Sunrise Mountain High School
Peoria, Arizona
Griffin Burns

From Canton South High School
Canton, Ohio
Cody Collins
Marti Doerschuk
Reanna Eckroad
Erica Gallon
Lindsay Kerr
Elise Miller
Katie Smith
Natalie Volpe

CONTENTS IN BRIEF

COMPOSITION

W.5 Develop and strengthen writing as needed by planning, revising, editing, rewriting, or trying a new approach, focusing on addressing what is most significant for a specific purpose and audience.

L.5 Demonstrate understanding of figurative language, word relationships, and nuances in word meanings.

**Common Core
State Standards Focus**

W.4 Produce clear and coherent writing in which the development, organization, and style are appropriate to task, purpose, and audience.

COMPOSITION

**Common Core
State Standards Focus**

W.3 Write narratives to
develop real or imagined
experiences or events using
effective technique, well-
chosen details, and well-
structured event sequences.

**Common Core
State Standards Focus**

W.3 (d) Use precise words and phrases, telling details, and sensory language to convey a vivid picture of the experiences, events, setting, and/or characters.

COMPOSITION

Common Core State Standards Focus

W.3 (a) Engage and orient the reader by setting out a problem, situation, or observation, establishing one or multiple point(s) of view, and introducing a narrator and/or characters; create a smooth progression of experiences or events.

W.2 Write informative/explanatory texts to examine and convey complex ideas, concepts, and information clearly and accurately through the effective selection, organization, and analysis of content.

W.1 Write arguments to support claims in an analysis of substantive topics or texts, using valid reasoning and relevant and sufficient evidence.

COMPOSITION

Common Core State Standards Focus

W.9 Draw evidence from literary or informational texts to support analysis, reflection, and research.

UNIT 3

Research and Report Writing

10 Research: Planning and Gathering Information

Common Core State Standards Focus

W.8 Gather relevant information from multiple authoritative print and digital sources, using advanced searches effectively; assess the usefulness of each source in answering the research question; integrate information into the text selectively to maintain the flow of ideas, avoiding plagiarism and following a standard format for citation.

COMPOSITION

Common Core
State Standards Focus

W.7 Conduct short as well as more sustained research projects to answer a question (including a self-generated question) or solve a problem; narrow or broaden the inquiry when appropriate; synthesize multiple sources on the subject, demonstrating understanding of the subject under investigation.

Common Core
State Standards Focus

L.5 Demonstrate understanding of figurative language, word relationships, and nuances in word meanings.

COMPOSITION

Common Core State Standards Focus

L.4 Determine or clarify the meaning of unknown and multiple-meaning words and phrases based on grades 9–10 reading and content, choosing flexibly from a range of strategies.

**Common Core
State Standards Focus**

S.1 Initiate and participate
effectively in a range of
collaborative discussions
(one-on-one, in groups, and
teacher-led) with diverse
partners on grades 9–10
topics, texts, and issues,
building on others' ideas and
expressing their own clearly
and persuasively.

W.6 Use technology,
including the Internet,
to produce, publish, and
update individual or shared
writing products, taking
advantage of technology's
capacity to link to other
information and to display
information flexibly and
dynamically.

GRAMMAR

**Common Core
State Standards Focus**

L.1 Demonstrate command of the conventions of standard English grammar and usage when writing or speaking.

**Common Core
State Standards Focus**

W.3 (c) Use precise words and phrases, telling details, and sensory language to convey a vivid picture of the experiences, events, setting, and/or characters.

GRAMMAR

Common Core State Standards Focus

W.2 (c) Use appropriate and varied transitions to link the major sections of the text, create cohesion, and clarify the relationships among complex ideas and concepts.

Common Core State Standards Focus

(a) Use various types of phrases (noun, verb, adjectival, adverbial, participial, prepositional, absolute) and clauses (independent, dependent; noun, relative, adverbial) to convey specific meanings and add variety and interest to writing or presentations.

GRAMMAR

Common Core State Standards Focus

(a) Use various types of phrases (noun, verb, adjectival, adverbial, participial, prepositional, absolute) and clauses (independent, dependent; noun, relative, adverbial) to convey specific meanings and add variety and interest to writing or presentations.

Common Core State Standards Focus

L.1 Demonstrate command of the conventions of standard English grammar and usage when writing or speaking.

GRAMMAR

L.1 Demonstrate command of the conventions of standard English grammar and usage when writing or speaking.

**Common Core
State Standards Focus**

L.1 Demonstrate command of the conventions of standard English grammar and usage when writing or speaking.

GRAMMAR

Common Core State Standards Focus

L.1 Demonstrate command of the conventions of standard English grammar and usage when writing or speaking.

**Common Core
State Standards Focus**

L.2 Demonstrate command
of the conventions
of standard English
capitalization, punctuation,
and spelling when writing.

GRAMMAR

Common Core State Standards Focus

L.2 Demonstrate command of the conventions of standard English capitalization, punctuation, and spelling when writing.

**Common Core
State Standards Focus**

L.2 (a) Use a semicolon
(and perhaps a conjunctive
adverb) to link two or more
closely related independent
clauses.
(b) Use a colon to introduce
a list or quotation.

L.2 (c) Spell correctly.

GRAMMAR

**Common Core
State Standards Focus**

L.6 Acquire and use accurately general academic and domain-specific words and phrases, sufficient for reading, writing, speaking, and listening at the college and career readiness level; demonstrate independence in gathering vocabulary knowledge when considering a word or phrase important to comprehension or expression.

Writing with POWER

Language

Composition

21st Century Skills

Perfection Learning®

Unit 1

Style and Structure of Writing

Writing often begins quietly, slowly. You jot down a promising word. You type a sentence. You take a break. At some point, though, as you sit at your desk or brainstorm with others, the ideas and words may begin to grow wildly. This exciting phase may produce pages and pages of writing, some of it overgrowing your original idea. The best writing emerges after stepping away from those first pages and returning later, with editorial "scissors" in hand. In this unit you will learn to work with others to develop and shape ideas. You will learn to find your unique voice. You will also learn to snip and cut like a gardener until only a sound structure, strong ideas, and vigorous words remain.

I believe more in the scissors than I do in the pencil.
—*Truman Capote*

A Community of Writers

The title of this program is *Writing with Power*. Why is it important to learn how to write with power, and what does that even mean? What is it about language and communication in the 21st century that makes writing with power an essential skill? This chapter will begin to answer those questions and lay the foundation for the writing instruction and activities presented in future chapters.

You encounter many written texts every day. Without even knowing why, you can probably tell when one of those communicates with power. Such writing usually

- demonstrates the **six traits** of good writing
- uses **language in varied, interesting ways** to show relationships and provide details
- follows the **conventions** appropriate for the purpose, occasion, audience, and genre

This program will help you learn how to think, communicate, and write with power.

 ## The Six Traits

IDEAS

The foundation of strong writing is a clear idea, message, or theme. Good writing builds on that foundation with well-chosen details that help explain or back up the message and that bring it to life. Powerful writing keeps the focus on the message and avoids unnecessary or off-topic details.

ORGANIZATION

Well-organized writing has a clear beginning, middle, and ending. It presents details in a logical order. Clear and appropriate transitional words and phrases, including those listed in the chart below, show readers the connections among the ideas.

WRITING PURPOSE	ORGANIZATIONAL PATTERNS	COMMON TRANSITIONS
Expository (to explain or inform)	Order of importance	*First, next, most important*
	Comparison/contrast	*Similarly, in contrast, on the other hand*
	Cause/effect	*As a result, for that reason, because*
Narrative (to tell a real or imaginary story)	Chronological (time) order	*First, yesterday, the next day, last year, next, until*
Descriptive	Spatial (location) order	*At the top, near the middle, to the right, on the other side, next to, behind*
Persuasive	Order of importance	*The most important, equally important, in addition, also, in fact*

VOICE

Voice is the quality in writing that makes it sound as if there is a real, live person behind the words. It is the writer's personal and distinctive way of expressing ideas. However, it must also be suited to the writer's audience and purpose. For example, a personal narrative for sharing with the class and an expository essay for a writing contest might call for different voices.

WRITING PURPOSE	WHAT THE WRITER'S VOICE SHOULD CONVEY
Expository and persuasive writing	Genuine interest in the subject, often including personal insights about why the subject is important to the writer and what the reader might expect to gain from it; respect for differing viewpoints; confidence without swagger
Descriptive and narrative writing	A genuine, not phony, personality; often some personal statements that show a willingness to trust readers with sensitive ideas

WORD CHOICE

Good writing uses specific, lively, and natural sounding language. Verbs are mostly in the active voice (see pages 704–705). Nouns and modifiers are precise rather than general or trite. The writing may use, but not overuse, colorful comparisons or figurative language to reinforce meaning. (You will learn more about word choice in Chapter 2.)

SENTENCE FLUENCY

In good writing, one sentence seems to flow smoothly into another with the help of transitions, repeated words, and words such as pronouns that refer back to an earlier word. At times you may need to rearrange the sentences so all of your ideas follow in a logical order. You may need to add transitions and occasionally repeat a key word or replace it with a pronoun, a synonym, or a substitute. (You will learn more about sentence fluency in Chapter 2.)

CONVENTIONS

Good writing is free of errors in spelling, capitalization, and punctuation. Word choice is accurate, and constructions within sentences follow grammar and usage rules. Paragraphing is appropriate. Writing that follows conventions makes a strong positive impression; writing that does not follow conventions loses the respect of readers. (You will learn more about some of the most important conventions on pages 8–10.)

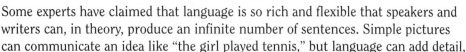

② The Power of Language

Some experts have claimed that language is so rich and flexible that speakers and writers can, in theory, produce an infinite number of sentences. Simple pictures can communicate an idea like "the girl played tennis," but language can add detail, meaning, subtlety, and feeling to that idea in seemingly endless ways: "The strong young girl, soaked in sweat from the heat of the summer and the ferocity of the competition, played the best tennis game of her life while thousands cheered her on, hardly believing that a girl so young could take on the mighty champion."

The ability of language to be used to express so many ideas gives people who are in command of language great power. For this reason, each composition chapter in this program includes a warm-up activity called "The Power of Language" to give you experience in creating interesting and varied patterns that add shades of meaning to your thoughts. Each language strategy has a two-part name. The first part identifies the language concept. The second part following the colon suggests the purpose and function of the strategy. The "Power of Language" strategies in this book are:

- Participial Phrases: Getting into the Action, page 57
- Parallelism: The Power of 3s, page 89
- Appositives: Who or What? page 127
- Adjectival Phrases: Adjectives Come Lately, page 157
- Fluency: Let It Flow, page 184
- Semicolons: Catch and Release, page 223
- Adverbial Phrases: Scene Setters, page 272
- Dashes: Dash It All, page 314
- Adverbial Clauses: Tip the Scale, page 370

> **Learning Tip**
>
> With a partner, take the simple sentence "the girl played tennis" and use your language power to expand it with details and subtlety of meaning. Share your revised sentence with the rest of the class.

Using these strategies will help you transform your writing from "the girl played tennis" to all the detailed, interesting, and original expressions your imagination can create. That ability is language *power*.

③ The Power Rules

Language also has the power to open or shut doors. The language you use—the word choices and the grammar—mark you as members of this or that group or groups. In casual speech and writing, you use the grammar heard in your home and community, or possibly different forms used by your peers. Some of you naturally say, "He doesn't have any," while others naturally say "He don't have none." The language you use depends on the language you hear around you and the language of those with whom you want to identify. Your casual language is the language of power among your friends and family, so you use it comfortably and confidently.

However, your casual language may not be the language of power in the larger society, where "public language" or "mainstream English"—the language of those with decision-making power in mainstream society—is the norm. Its grammar may or may not be close to the casual speech forms you use in your family, culture, peer, or other in-group. However, when you seek success in mainstream society—in school, in the job market, or in college—you increase your chances by using the language of power in those settings. Viewed this way, the grammar you use is not a matter of right or wrong; it's a matter of which choices are best for what circumstances and audiences.

Some studies have identified the language patterns that send up a red flag, or warning signal, to potential employers and academic decision makers who expect adherence to the rules of mainstream English, also called "Standard English." Since these have such an impact on future success, you should edit your work carefully to avoid them. Following are ten of the most important conventions to master—the Power Rules. Always check for them when you edit.

EDITING FOR MAINSTREAM CONVENTIONS: THE POWER RULES

1. **Use only one negative form for a single negative idea.** (See pages 789–790.)

Before Editing	After Editing
They won't bring *nothing* to the picnic.	They won't bring *anything* to the picnic.
There wasn't *nothing* we could do.	There wasn't *anything* we could do.

2. **Use mainstream past tense forms of regular and irregular verbs.** (See pages 684–703.) It's a good idea to memorize the parts of the most common irregular verbs.

Before Editing	After Editing
I already *clean* my room.	I already *cleaned* my room.
Yesterday he *come* to study with me.	Yesterday he *came* to study with me.
She *brung* her new album with her.	She *brought* her new album with her.
I should have *went* along with them.	I should have *gone* along with them.

3. **Use verbs that agree with the subject.** (See pages 750–767.)

Before Editing	After Editing
He / she / it *don't* make sense.	He / she / it *doesn't* make sense.
Carlos always *reach* for the top.	Carlos always *reaches* for the top.
The sisters or Elena *sing* next.	The sisters or Elena *sings* next.
Either Maya or her friends *knows* what happened.	Either Maya or her friends *know* what happened.

4. **Use subject forms of pronouns in subject position. Use object forms of pronouns in object position.** (See pages 716–725.)

Before Editing	After Editing
Her and Morgan always show up together.	*She* and Morgan always show up together.
Him and Jamal went to the same college.	*He* and Jamal went to the same college.
Her and *me* are going to the movies.	*She* and *I* are going to the movies.

5. **Use standard ways to make nouns possessive.** (See pages 895–897.)

Before Editing	After Editing
Do you have the *coach* jacket?	Do you have the *coach's* jacket?
Is that *Deidres* book?	Is that *Deidre's* book?
Josh wrote the *committees* report.	Josh wrote the *committee's* report.
All the *kids* ideas are important.	All the *kids'* ideas are important.

6. **Use a consistent verb tense except when a change is clearly necessary.** (See pages 693–703.)

Before Editing	After Editing
The lake level *rises* when it rained.	The lake level *rose* when it rained.
After she forgot her lines, she *doesn't* want to be in the play.	After she forgot her lines, she *didn't* want to be in the play.

7. **Use sentence fragments only the way professional writers do, after the sentence they refer to and usually to emphasize a point. Fix all sentence fragments that occur before the sentence they refer to and ones that occur in the middle of a sentence.** (See pages 666–671.)

Before Editing	After Editing
One day. The rain finally stopped.	*One day,* the rain finally stopped.
Driving in the city can be difficult. *During the evening rush hour.* So we try to avoid it.	Driving in the city can be difficult *during the evening rush hour,* so we try to avoid it.
I missed the bus today. *The reason being that I took too long at lunch.*	I missed the bus today *because* I took too long at lunch.

8. **Use the best conjunction and/or punctuation for the meaning when connecting two sentences. Revise run-on sentences.** (See pages 672–674.)

Before Editing	After Editing
We went to the *store we* decided to buy ice cream.	*When we went to the store,* we decided to buy ice cream.
Micah drove the *car, Inez* gave him directions from her map.	*While Micah drove the car,* Inez gave him directions from her map.
Then Inez drove for a *while,* Micah slept in the back seat.	Then Inez drove for a while, *and* Micah slept in the back seat.

9. **Use the contraction *'ve* not *of* when the correct word is *have,* or use the full word *have.* Use *supposed* instead of *suppose* and *used* instead of *use* when appropriate.** (See pages 801, 805, and 808.)

Before Editing	After Editing
You should *of* finished your homework.	You should *have* finished your homework.
We might *of* missed the whole show.	We might *have* missed the whole show.
Reggie could *of* let me know.	Reggie could *have* let me know.
Jack was *suppose* to call me.	Jack was *supposed* to call me.
Reggie *use* to be on the team.	Reggie *used* to be on the team.

10. **For sound-alikes and certain words that sound almost alike, choose the word with your intended meaning.** (See pages 796–811.)

Before Editing	After Editing
Mia went *too* her violin lesson. (*Too* means "also" or "in addition".)	Mia went *to* her violin lesson. (*To* means "in the direction of".)
She practiced *to* times today. (*To* means "in the direction of".)	She practiced *two* times today. (*Two* is a number.)
Are these *you're* tickets? (*You're* is a contraction of *you are.*)	Are these *your* tickets? (*Your* is the possessive form of *you.*)
They're new school is very modern. (*They're* is a contraction of *they are.*)	*Their* new school is very modern. (*Their* is the possessive form of *they.*)
I put your books over *their.* (*Their* is the possessive form of *they.*)	I put your books over there. (There means "in that place".)
Its not a good time to bring up that problem. (*Its* is the possessive form of *it.*)	*It's* not a good time to bring up that problem. (*It's* is a contraction of *it is.*)

The proofreading symbols shown on the next page are convenient shorthand notations that writers frequently use to make changes during the editing stage to make sure their writing follows expected conventions, especially those reflected in the Power Rules.

PROOFREADING SYMBOLS

∧	insert	We went on a _fantastic_ journey.
⩟	insert comma	Meg enjoys hiking, skiing and skating.
⊙	insert period	Gary took the bus to Atlanta⊙
ℒ	delete	Refer ~~back~~ to your notes.
¶	new paragraph	¶ Finally Balboa saw the Pacific.
no ¶	no paragraph	no ¶The dachshund trotted away.
⋯	let it stand	I appreciated her ~~sincere~~ honesty.
#	add space	She will be#back in a moment.
⌒	close up	The airplane waited on the run‿way.
t̸	transpose	They only have two dollars left.
≡	capital letter	We later moved to the s̲o̲u̲t̲h̲.
/	lowercase letter	His favorite subject was S̸cience.
ⓈⓅ	spell out	I ate 2 oranges.
ⱽ ⱽ	insert quotes	"I hope you can join us," said my brother.
⩑̄	insert hyphen	I attended a school⸗related event.
ⱽ	insert apostrophe	The ravenous dog ate the cats food.
↷	move copy	I usually on Fridays go to the movies.

Learning Tip

Write the following sentence on a piece of paper, just as it's written here.

   "Did youmiss the bus this mornig Maxs teacher asked

Add proofreading symbols to show corrections. Compare your work with a partner's. Did you find the same errors and mark them in the same way?

Writing in the 21st Century

Nobody knows better than your generation what 21st century writing is all about. You do it every day. You text your friends and family at an average rate of 96 messages a day. You spend about an hour a day on the Internet, using some of that time to update your social-networking page on Facebook or a similar network. You may keep a blog to share your news and thoughts, and you may respond to the writing of others in their blogs or on their profile pages. You post pictures and videos and other illustrations, and viewers often comment on them. Although some of what you post is for anyone to see, often you restrict your postings to a circle of chosen friends. When you write, you are very aware of who will be reading your writing. You chat one-on-one and sometimes have several conversations going on at once.

You also write in school. You keep notes about science experiments, express math problems in words, write formal papers for English and other classes, and answer essay questions on tests.

You write thank-you notes to relatives who give you a present, make lists of things to take with you on your trip, write a script for a silly video you make with your friends, and leave a note for your mom about when you'll be home.

THE RIGHT KIND OF WRITING?

With all these kinds of writing, what is the "right" way to write?

There is no one "right" way to write. The right way to write is the way that's right for the situation you are in, your purpose for writing, and whoever will be reading your writing.

GLOBAL INTERACTIONS

The technology that makes it possible for you to be as connected as you are to others has helped bring about many changes beyond those in writing. Every aspect of life today has a global element: the economy is global; the opportunities for interacting with people of diverse cultures are greatly increased; environmental challenges affect the entire globe.

Facing global challenges and competing effectively in the global economy require **creative thinking** and the ability to **work creatively with others,** including those from a culture different from your own. They require **critical thinking** with sound reasoning and effective **problem-solving.** They require excellent **communication skills** and **expertise in using technology** to find and evaluate information. Writing can develop all of those skills and prepare you for leadership in the 21st century.

Collaborating Through the Writing Process

When you think of the writing process, do you picture a tortured, solitary artist toiling away in an unheated attic, waiting for inspiration to light the way? Certainly some activities during the writing process can be done only by a lone writer. Picture, though, how real-world writing is actually produced. In school, you confer with your lab partners to write up the results of an experiment, maybe even dividing the work of creating the report among group members. In businesses, workers meet often and discuss ideas for new products or better service and then write proposals and other business documents based on those discussions. Writing does have some solitary stages, but it is nonetheless a social act. For the writing in this program, you and your classmates will create and participate in a **community of writers** and work in **collaboration** throughout the writing process. Most often, you will be working in writing groups of three to four students.

Prewriting: Getting Started

STRATEGIES FOR FINDING A SUBJECT

A good subject is one that holds genuine interest for you and your readers. The following strategies will also help you identify possible subjects.

Taking an Inventory of Your Interests A good way to start thinking about possible subjects is to think about your life. Try the technique of self-interview or interview a partner. Make a chart like the one below to record your ideas.

Personal Interest Inventory	
Subjects I know a lot about	
Hobbies	
Unusual experiences I have had	

Keeping a Journal A **journal** is a daily notebook in which you record your thoughts, feelings, and observations. Because you use your journal to write about subjects that interest you, it becomes an excellent source of writing ideas. Be sure to write in your journal every day and to date each entry. You can also use your journal in other ways to get writing ideas.

Reading, Interviewing, and Discussing You can also develop ideas for subjects using the following strategies. In each case, take notes to remember the ideas that surfaced.

Strategies for Thinking of Subjects

- Do some background reading on general topics that interest you. If you are interested in aviation, for example, read some articles about aviation in the library or online.
- Interview someone who knows more about a subject than you do.
- Discuss subjects of mutual interest with members of your writing group or other classmates, friends, and/or family to find interesting and fresh angles on a subject.

Keeping a Learning Log A Learning Log is a section of your journal where you can write down ideas or information about math, science, history, health, or any other subject that interests you. You can use it to capture what you know about a subject and what you still need or want to learn about it. You can also use it to keep track of what you learn about writing.

CHOOSING AND LIMITING A SUBJECT

How can you use the prewriting work you have done so far to find a good subject? The following guidelines will help.

Guidelines for Choosing a Subject

- Choose a subject that genuinely interests and engages you and your readers.
- Choose a subject that you know well or can research in a reasonable amount of time.
- Consider your purpose for writing, the occasion for writing, and the readers of your work. (See the next page for more on purpose, occasion, and audience.) Be sure your topic is appropriate for each of those factors.

When you choose a subject, you will often start with a general topic, such as "sports" or "current events." Those general topics are too broad to cover adequately in a single work, so you need to limit your subject. When you limit a subject, you make it specific enough to cover completely in the amount of space you have for writing. To limit your subject, use one or a combination of the following strategies.

Guidelines for Limiting a Subject

- Limit your subject to one person or one example that represents the subject.
- Limit your subject to a specific time or place.
- Limit your subject to a specific event.
- Limit your subject to a specific condition, purpose, or procedure.

As always, share your thinking with your peers and get feedback from them at each stage of your progress.

PURPOSE, OCCASION, AUDIENCE, AND GENRE

Purpose is your reason for writing or speaking. In successful communication, the purpose of your message is appropriate to both the occasion that prompts it and the audience who will receive it. The following chart lists the most common purposes.

WRITING PURPOSES	POSSIBLE FORMS
Expository to **explain** or **inform;** to focus on your subject matter and audience	**Factual writing** scientific essay, research paper, business letter, summary, descriptive essay, historical narrative, news story
Creative (literary) to **create;** to focus on making imaginative use of language and ideas	**Entertaining writing** short story, novel, play, poem, dialogue
Persuasive to **persuade;** to focus on changing your readers' minds or getting them to act in a certain way	**Convincing writing** letter to the editor, persuasive essay, movie or book review, critical essay (literary analysis), advertisement
Self-expressive to **express** and **reflect** on your thoughts and feelings	**Personal writing** journal entry, personal narrative, reflective essay, personal letter

Occasion is your motivation for composing—the factor that prompts you to communicate. Occasion usually can be stated well using one of the following sentences.

- I feel a need to write for my own satisfaction.
- I have been asked to write this by [name a person].
- I want to write an entry for [name a publication].
- I want to enter a writing contest.

As you plan your writing, you also need to remember the audience you will be addressing, or who will be reading your work. What are their interests and concerns? How can you best communicate to this particular audience?

Audience Profile Questions

- Who will be reading my work?
- How old are they? Are they adults? teenagers? children?
- What do I want the audience to know about my subject?
- What background do they have in the subject?
- What interests and opinions are they apt to have? Are there any words or terms I should define for them?

Your writing will also be influenced by the **genre,** or form of writing, you choose. (See the chart on the previous page for a listing of common forms or genres of writing.) Each genre has characteristics that make it different from the others, and readers expect these characteristics to be present. If you are reading a novel, for example, you expect that there will be narrative and descriptive passages. If instead you find dialogue and stage directions, you wouldn't know what to make of them. In the same way, if you are writing a thank-you note to your grandmother for a gift certificate to a movie theater, she will expect certain characteristics—a greeting, a body, a closing. If instead she finds that you have sent her a bulleted list of reasons you like the gift, without an opening or closing, she is likely to be mystified, even though you are still writing about the gift.

Collaboration in Action

Prewriting

Chelsea, Joaquin, and Rakesh are in a writing group together. It's their first writing activity of the year. They are supposed to come up with topics and choose the purpose and audience for their writing. Here's how their discussion might go:

Chelsea: I don't know what to write about. I'm overwhelmed getting used to high school. How about you guys?

Rakesh: I don't know either.

Chelsea: I just finally got used to middle school and now I have to get used to this.

Joaquin: Maybe you could write about that.

Chelsea: About what?

Joaquin: Adjusting to high school

Chelsea: I guess I could, yeah.

Rakesh: Who would you write it for?

Chelsea: Myself, maybe, or maybe for my younger brother who will start here next year.

Rakesh: What would you say?

Chelsea: I don't know. Maybe that it's very different from middle school, though actually I guess there are some things that are similar.

Joaquin: Sounds like you could talk about just that—the similarities and the differences.

Chelsea: Yeah. Maybe I could focus on just a few of each. I could do that.

Talking and listening help Chelsea focus her thoughts and start to get a good subject. After the group finishes talking about Chelsea's topic, they have a similar conversation about the subjects Joaquin and Rakesh will write about.

Collaboration Practice

Meet with a small group for 10 minutes. Use what you have learned to try to come up with a good writing topic for each member.

② Prewriting: From Ideas to a Plan

DEVELOPING A SUBJECT

After you have chosen and limited a subject and determined your purpose, audience, and occasion, you can flesh out your ideas with supporting details. **Supporting details** are the facts, examples, incidents, reasons, or other specific points that back up your ideas. Following are some strategies for developing supporting details.

Brainstorming **Brainstorming** means letting ideas come to you freely, without judgment. Work with a partner or a group of classmates and freely list all ideas related to your subject as they occur to you.

Collaborating: Guidelines for Group Brainstorming

- Set a time limit, such as 10 minutes.
- Write the subject on a piece of paper and assign one group member to be the recorder. If your group meets frequently, take turns recording ideas.
- Start brainstorming for supporting details, such as facts, reasons, and examples. Since you can eliminate irrelevant ideas later, record any and all ideas.
- Build on the ideas of other group members. Add to those ideas or modify them to improve them.
- Avoid criticizing the ideas of other group members.

When you have finished brainstorming, get a copy of all the supporting details from the group recorder. From that list, select the details related to your own writing task.

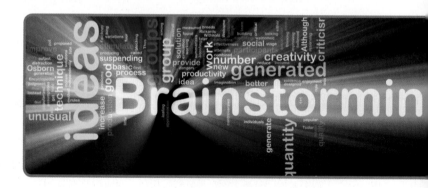

Clustering Another strategy for developing supporting details is **clustering,** a visual brainstorming technique that lets you both record and group your ideas. A cluster looks something like a wheel. At the hub, or center, you write your limited subject. Each idea or detail you think of to develop your subject is connected to the hub like a spoke in a wheel. Sometimes supporting ideas become new hubs with spokes of their own. After her discussion with Rakesh and Joaquin, Chelsea created the following cluster.

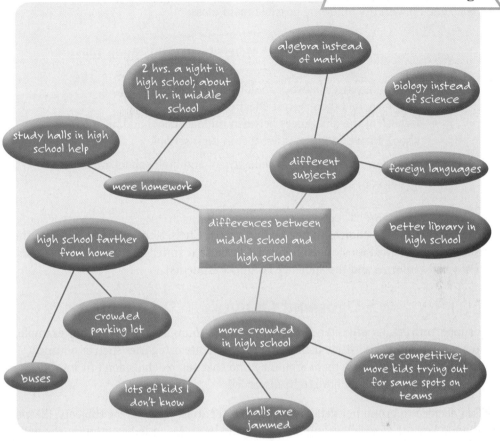

Inquiring Another good way to generate the supporting details you need to develop your subject is to ask yourself questions. Questions that begin *who, what, where, when, why,* and *how* can produce answers that are helpful in developing a subject.

ORGANIZING DETAILS

Focusing Your Subject Before you arrange your ideas logically, decide on a focus, or **main idea,** for your essay. A main idea is also known as a **controlling idea** because all other ideas and details in the text need to relate directly to it.

Guidelines for Deciding on a Focus

- Look over your details. Can you draw meaningful generalizations from some or all of the details? If so, the generalization could be the focus of your writing.
- Choose a main idea that intrigues you.
- Choose a main idea that suits your purpose and audience.

For her composition on differences between middle school and high school, for example, Chelsea came up with the following possible main ideas:

> **MODEL: Possible Main Ideas**
>
> - Of the differences between middle school and high school, three have had the greatest effect on me.
> - Because of the differences between middle school and high school, I have sometimes felt lost in high school.
> - The differences between middle school and high school are all for the best.

After talking over these choices in her writing group, Chelsea chose the first idea as the focus because it seemed most meaningful and because it suited the writing purpose she had chosen (to inform) and the audience (younger students).

CLASSIFYING AND ORDERING DETAILS

Your supporting details will often fall naturally into groups, or categories. For example, if you are explaining good study habits, you might create categories such as advance preparation and time management. You may find that some details don't fit into any category and may eventually have to be discarded.

Chelsea decided to group her details into three categories: (1) different subjects, (2) more homework, and (3) crowded feeling. By presenting her ideas in logical groups, she will help readers understand what she is trying to say.

After classifying your details, place them in an order that will best achieve your purpose and also make the most sense to your reader.

WAYS TO ORGANIZE DETAILS		
Types of Order	**Definition**	**Examples**
Chronological	the order in which events occur	story, explanation, history, biography, drama
Spatial	location or physical arrangement	description (top to bottom, near to far, left to right, etc.)
Order of Importance	degree of importance, size, or interest	persuasive writing, description, evaluation, explanation
Logical	logical progression, one detail growing out of another	classification, definition, comparison and contrast

Chelsea made the following list of organized details. Notice that the list includes only those details from the cluster on page 19 that relate to the main idea and that the details are listed in order of importance. She used this list as a guide when writing the first draft.

MODEL: Ordering Details

Focus (Main Idea): Of the differences between middle school and high school, three have had the greatest effect on me.

Order of Ideas	Reasons
1. Different subjects —math versus algebra —science versus biology —foreign languages	Good to start with because the course schedule is the first you see of high school
2. More homework —1 hour versus 2 hours —study hall	Next in importance and follows logically from above
3. Crowded feeling —halls jammed —kids I don't know —competition	Save for last as the most important difference; makes my point that you have to get used to high school

③ Drafting

When you have some good ideas to work with and a logical organization, you can test your plan by writing a first draft. Unlike your prewriting notes, which are for you and your writing group only, your first draft is targeted for your audience, so your language should be appropriate to the subject and the occasion. As you start to express your ideas in complete sentences, be aware of voice and tone and make sure they, too, are appropriate for the subject, audience, and occasion. (See pages 14–16.)

Strategies for Drafting

- Write an introduction that will capture the reader's interest and express your main idea.
- After you write your introduction, use your organized prewriting notes as a guide. Feel free to depart from those notes, however, when a good idea occurs to you.
- Write fairly quickly without worrying about spelling or phrasing. You will have the opportunity to go back and fix your writing when you revise.
- Stop frequently and read what you have written. This practice will help you move logically from one thought to the next as you draft.
- Return to the prewriting stage whenever you find that you need to clarify your thinking. You can always stop and brainstorm or cluster to collect more ideas.
- Write a conclusion that drives home the main point of the essay.

Following is Chelsea's first draft. Notice the three features identified in the sidenotes:

MODEL: First Draft

> High school was a real surprise for me. I knew it would be different from middle school, but not this different. There were three things especially that made me realize that high school would never be the same.
>
> One difference you notice write away from middle School is the courses you take. In middle school for example you take science and and math. In high school the courses are definately more avanced. In highschool you take Biology in stead of science and Algebra insteadof math. High school offers also foriegn languages which some middle schools don't, I'm taking spanish.
>
> You also find you have more homework in high school. I find I have twice as much homework in high school. In middle school I used to spend about an hour every week

The first and last paragraphs serve as an introduction and conclusion, which give a sense of wholeness to the text.

The draft follows the planned order of ideas (see page 21).

night doing homework. Now that I'm in high school I spend about two hours a night and sometimes even week ends. It does help that high schools have longer study hall periods. In study halls you can get some of your work do during school hours. There should be some way to keep things quieter in study halls at least some of the time.

High school is also much more crowded than middle school. The halls are jammed with students, and I dont even know alot of them. You sometimes feel lost. The other thing about so many students is that high school has a pretty competative atmosphere. There are more kids trying out for the same spots on sports teams, or in other groups. The added competition is a plus because it keeps you on you toes you really have to do your best at all times.

I guess I'm getting used to the idea that high school is a hole new experience. There are a lot of diffrences between middle school and high school and these are only three of them. Such differences can be unsettling at first but you will find that they all have a strong plus side too.

> Chelsea made several mistakes in spelling, grammar, and punctuation. These mistakes will be corrected at a later stage in the writing process.

DRAFTING A TITLE

You may think of a good title at any stage in the writing process. Whenever you come up with a title, however, consider carefully whether it will get your readers' attention. The title should also be appropriate to your subject, purpose, and audience.

HERE'S HOW Guidelines for Choosing a Title

- Choose a title that identifies your subject or relates to your subject focus.
- Choose a title that is appropriate for your purpose and audience.
- Choose a title that will capture the reader's interest.

④ Revising

When you revise, you stand back from your writing and try to look at it with a fresh eye. Following are some strategies you can use to improve your draft. If you can answer *no* to any of the questions in the first column, you can try the fixes suggested in the second.

STRATEGIES	QUICK FIXES
• **Check for Clarity and Creativity** • Are your ideas interesting and fresh, rather than ones that people have heard over and over? Does the text satisfy its purpose?	• Insert a personal experience or example. • Think of an unlikely comparison between your subject and something else. • Talk with others to get ideas.
• **Elaborate by Adding Details** • Does your writing seem fully developed? Are your ideas fully supported? Have you used details that would help bring a scene or idea to life for a reader?	• Explore your subject from someone else's point of view. • Use one of the prewriting strategies on pages 18–19 to come up with lively elaborations. • Get into the action with participial phrases (page 57), tell who or what with appositives (page 127), add scene setters (page 272) and/or add adjectival phrases (page 157) and other descriptive words. • Show, don't tell. • Take a mental snapshot of a scene and write what you see.
• **Rearrange Out-of-Order Items** • Check the organization of your words, sentences, and ideas. Does one idea lead logically into another? • Can any ideas be combined?	• Use your word processor to rearrange and reorganize your sentences or paragraphs so the reader can easily follow your thoughts. • Use transitions to show the relationships between ideas.
• **Delete Unnecessary Words or Details** • Do all of the details in your draft relate clearly to your controlling idea?	• Delete, or remove, them. Also delete any extra or unneeded words and repetitive sentences.
• **Substitute Words and Sentences** • Are all parts of your draft clear enough for a reader to follow easily? Are your words lively and precise?	• Ask a "test reader" to tell you where you need to provide clearer information. • For a dull, general word, find a richer and more vivid synonym.

Using a Six-Trait Rubric

A rubric like the one below can help you determine what you need to do to improve your draft. You can also use it to evaluate the work of your writing group partners. Each row focuses on a specific aspect of writing. Each column describes a different level of quality, with the highest quality traits labeled 4.

Ideas	4 The main idea is clear. Plenty of details such as facts, examples, and anecdotes provide support.	3 The main idea is clear. There is enough support for the main idea to back it up adequately.	2 The main idea could be clearer. There are some supporting details, but more details would be helpful.	1 The main idea statement is missing or unclear. Few examples and facts are provided in support.
Organization	4 The organization is clear with abundant transitions.	3 A few ideas seem out of place or transitions are missing.	2 Many ideas seem out of place and transitions are missing.	1 The organization is unclear and hard to follow.
Voice	4 The voice sounds natural, engaging, and unique.	3 The voice sounds natural and engaging.	2 The voice sounds mostly natural but is weak.	1 The voice sounds mostly unnatural and is weak.
Word Choice	4 Words are specific, powerful, and appropriate to the task.	3 Words are specific and language is appropriate.	2 Some words are too general and/or misleading.	1 Most words are overly general and imprecise.
Sentence Fluency	4 Varied sentences flow smoothly.	3 Most sentences are varied and flow smoothly.	2 Some sentences are varied but some are choppy.	1 Sentences are not varied and are choppy.
Conventions	4 Punctuation, usage, and spelling are correct. The Power Rules are all followed.	3 Punctuation, usage, and spelling are mainly correct and Power Rules are all followed.	2 Some punctuation, usage, and spelling are incorrect but all Power Rules are followed.	1 There are many errors and at least one failure to follow a Power Rule.

Using a Checklist

A checklist like the one below is another tool for improving a draft.

✓ Evaluation Checklist for Revising

- ✓ Did you clearly state your main idea? (pages 19–20)
- ✓ Does your text have a strong introduction, body, and conclusion? (page 22)
- ✓ Did you support your main idea with enough details? (pages 19–21)
- ✓ Do your details show instead of merely telling what you want to say? (pages 19–21)
- ✓ Did you present your ideas in a logical order? (pages 20–21)
- ✓ Do any of your sentences stray from the main idea? (pages 21 and 27)
- ✓ Are your ideas clearly explained? (page 24)
- ✓ Are your words specific and precise? (pages 24 and 46)
- ✓ Are any words or ideas repeated unnecessarily? (pages 64–66)
- ✓ Are your sentences varied and smoothly connected? (pages 55–62)
- ✓ Is the purpose of your text clear? (pages 5–6 and 15–16)
- ✓ Is your writing suited to your audience? (pages 15–16)

Conferencing

You have been **conferencing,** meeting with others to share ideas or identify and solve problems, throughout the writing process. Conferencing is especially helpful during revising when weaknesses in the writing can be addressed. However, offering something that might sound like criticism isn't easy. Yet to help your writing group members, you need to be honest. Use the following for guidance in conferencing.

HERE'S HOW   Guidelines for Conferencing

Guidelines for the Writer

- List some questions for your peer. What aspects of your work most concern you?
- Try to be grateful for your critic's candor rather than being upset or defensive. Keep in mind that the criticism you are getting is well intended.

Guidelines for the Critic

- Read your partner's work carefully. What does the writer promise to do in this text? Does he or she succeed?
- Point out strengths as well as weaknesses. Start your comments by saying something positive like, "Your opening really captured my interest."
- Be specific. Refer to a specific word, sentence, or section when you comment.
- Be sensitive to your partner's feelings. Phrase your criticisms as questions. You might say, "Do you think your details might be stronger if....?"

Collaboration in Action

Revising

Chelsea's writing group has already discussed Joaquin's and Rakesh's drafts. They made notes on their papers about where they could make improvements based on their peers' feedback. Now it is Chelsea's turn to have her paper discussed.

Rakesh: Your ideas are really good. I agree about everything.

Joaquin: Me too. And you presented them in logical order.

Chelsea: Thanks.

Joaquin: One thing I noticed was the last sentence of the third paragraph. It seemed like the idea about keeping study halls quiet didn't quite fit in with your main idea.

Chelsea: Hmm, okay. I'll make a note of that. Maybe I'll cut that.

Joaquin: In your fourth paragraph, do you think you have two different ideas going? The crowded hallways and the competition.

Chelsea: Don't they both fit under the idea of a bigger number of students?

Rakesh: They do, yeah, but it seems your main idea for that paragraph talks about crowding. Maybe you could turn that paragraph into two paragraphs, one about the crowds and one about the competition.

Chelsea: Ok, I see.

Rakesh: I was just thinking maybe you could add more details about the crowded halls to fill out that paragraph.

Joaquin: Yeah, like sights and sounds and even smells.

Chelsea: Yeah, I see how I could do that.

Collaboration Practice

Choose a paper you are working on or have completed previously and make two copies, one for each member of your group. Conference with one another to improve your drafts. Use the rubric on page 25 as a guide. Then try the revision strategies on page 24 to make the changes suggested by your peers.

USING FEEDBACK FROM YOUR TEACHER

Your teacher is a member of the community of writers and both a collaborator and mentor. He or she is probably with you for each stage of the writing process. The chart shows different ways your teacher can provide feedback and how you can use that feedback to improve your writing.

TEACHER FEEDBACK	HOW TO USE FEEDBACK
During prewriting your teacher might • meet briefly with you to discuss and approve your topic • suggest ways you might gather information and other supporting materials • comment on your organization	You can use this feedback to improve your work by • rethinking if necessary to come up with a sharply focused topic • following the suggestions with an open mind • experimenting with different organizational patterns
During drafting your teacher might • move from desk to desk to offer suggestions on your process of drafting (for example, continually going back and rereading what you've written) • offer suggestions or concerns about a direction your draft seems to be taking	You can use this feedback to improve your work by • trying out the suggestions, even if they are uncomfortable at first • saving your work and then coming back to it with a fresh eye to try to see the concerns your teacher raised • asking questions if you don't understand the concerns your teacher has
During revising your teacher might • meet with you to go over some issues face to face • make written comments on your work about ideas, organization, and flow	You can use this feedback to improve your work by • making a good effort to change the things you discussed • using the comments as positive guides rather than negative criticisms
During editing your teacher might • identify errors • offer mini-lessons on challenging points	You can use this feedback to improve your work by • making corrections and adding items to your personalized checklist
During publishing your teacher might • give you presentation ideas • help you reach your audience	You can use this feedback to improve your work by • gaining confidence in sharing your work with readers and being willing to take risks

⑤ Editing and Publishing

EDITING FOR WORDINESS: EDITING STAR

The Environmental Protection Agency works with makers of consumer products to ensure "energy star" efficiency. Products marked with an energy star are proven to get the same results as others like them but with less power. The less power needed to get the job done, the more energy-efficient the product is.

Word power, like other kinds of power, needs to be used efficiently. The fewer words needed to get the job done, the more energy-efficient the writing. Notice how much stronger the efficient version is.

Word Guzzler	Due to the fact that it was my birthday, I decided to treat myself and give myself the gift of seeing two movies in a row, one after the other.
Fuel Efficient	On my birthday I treated myself to two movies in a row.

Throughout the composition chapters in this book, you will see the language arts version of the energy star logo: the editing star. It will accompany a brief activity which can remind you to cut out wordiness.

USING A GENERAL EDITING CHECKLIST

The best way to use a checklist is to go over your paper several times, each time looking for a different kind of problem. For instance, you might look for spelling errors in one reading and comma errors in the next. You might also want to read your essay backward, word by word. You will find that you are able to spot many errors that you might otherwise miss. The following checklist will help you guard against some common errors.

 Editing Checklist

✓ Are your sentences free of errors in grammar and usage?
✓ Did you spell each word correctly?
✓ Did you use capital letters where needed?
✓ Did you punctuate each sentence correctly?
✓ Did you indent paragraphs as needed and leave proper margins on each side of the paper?

CHAPTER 1

USING A MANUAL OF STYLE

As you edit, you may wish to consult one of the following style guides or handbooks to review rules for grammar, usage, and mechanics.

- *The Chicago Manual of Style: The Essential Guide for Writers, Editors, and Publishers.* 15th ed. Chicago: University of Chicago Press, 2003.
- *MLA Handbook for Writers of Research Papers.* 7th ed. New York: Modern Language Association of America, 2009.
- Turabian, Kate. *A Manual for Writers of Research Papers, Theses, and Dissertations.* 7th ed. Chicago: University of Chicago Press, 2007.

CREATING A PERSONALIZED EDITING CHECKLIST

You may want to reserve an eight-page section at the end of your journal to use as a Personalized Editing Checklist. Here you can record errors that you seem to make over and over. Write one of the following headings on every other page: Grammar, Usage, Spelling, and Mechanics (capitalization and punctuation). Use these pages to record your errors. See the index in this book to find the pages on which each problem is addressed. Write the page numbers in your journal next to the error, with examples of the corrected problem. Add to this checklist and refer to it when you edit your work.

PROOFREADING

Proofreading means carefully rereading your work and marking corrections in grammar, usage, spelling, and mechanics. Following are useful techniques.

 Proofreading Techniques

- Focus on one line at a time.
- Exchange essays with a partner and check each other's work.
- Read your essay backward, word by word.
- Read your essay aloud, very slowly.
- Use a dictionary for spelling and a handbook for grammar, usage, and mechanics.

Here's how Chelsea used proofreading symbols to edit a portion of her revised draft.

One difference I notice write away is the courses I am taking which are definately more avanced. In middle school for example I took courses called science and and math. In highschool I take Biology instead of science and Algebra instead of math. High school offers also more subjects than middle school, including foreign languages I find that all the new courses make the

subjects more interesting.

PUBLISHING

Following are just a few ways you could share your writing.

Publishing Options

In School
- Read your work aloud to a small group in your class.
- Display your final draft on a bulletin board in your classroom or school library.
- Read your work aloud to your class or present it in the form of a radio program or video.
- Create a class library and media center to which you submit your work. This library and media center should have a collection of folders or files devoted to different types of student writing and media presentations.
- Create a class anthology to which every student contributes one piece. Use electronic technology to design a small publication. Share your anthology with other classes.
- Submit your work to your school literary magazine, newspaper, or yearbook.

Outside School
- Submit your written work to a newspaper or magazine.
- Share your work with a professional interested in the subject.
- Present your work to an appropriate community group.
- Send a video based on your written work to a local cable television station.
- Create and broadcast a podcast.
- Post your work on your blog or social networking site.
- Enter your work in a local, state, or national writing contest.

Using Standard Manuscript Form   The appearance of your text may be almost as important as its content. A marked-up paper with inconsistent margins is difficult to read. A neat, legible paper, however, makes a positive impression on your reader. The section of this book called *Electronic Publishing* on pages 473–487 offers tips for presenting texts effectively.

Many compositions will use standard manuscript form. The model on pages 32–33 shows how the writer used the following guidelines to prepare her final draft on the differences between middle school and high school.

HERE'S HOW

Standard Manuscript Form

- Use standard-sized 8½-by-11-inch white paper. Use one side of the paper only.
- If handwriting, use black or blue ink. If using a word-processing program or typing, use a black ink cartridge or black typewriter ribbon and double-space the lines.
- Leave a 1.25-inch margin at the left and right. The left margin must be even. The right margin should be as even as possible.
- Put your name, the course title, the name of your teacher, and the date in the upper right-hand corner of the first page. Follow your teacher's specific guidelines for headings and margins.
- Center the title of your essay two lines below the date. Do not underline or put quotation marks around your title.
- If using a word-processing program or typing, skip four lines between the title and the first paragraph. If handwriting, skip two lines.
- If using a word-processing program, indent the first line of each paragraph five spaces. If handwriting, indent the first line of each paragraph 1 inch.
- Leave a 1-inch margin at the bottom of all pages.
- Starting on page 2, number each page in the upper right-hand corner. Begin the first line 1 inch from the top. Word-processing programs allow you to insert page numbers.

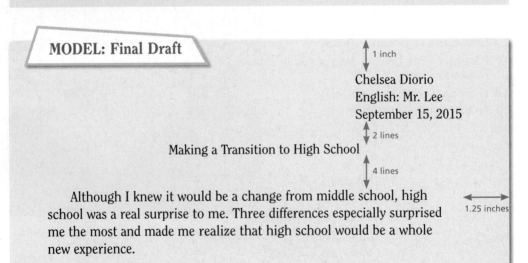

MODEL: Final Draft

1 inch

Chelsea Diorio
English: Mr. Lee
September 15, 2015

2 lines

Making a Transition to High School

4 lines

  Although I knew it would be a change from middle school, high school was a real surprise to me. Three differences especially surprised me the most and made me realize that high school would be a whole new experience.

1.25 inches

One difference I noticed right away is the courses I am taking, which are definitely more advanced. In middle school, for example, I took courses called science and math, while in high school I take biology instead of science and algebra instead of math. High school also offers more subjects than middle school, including foreign languages. I find that all the new courses make the subjects more interesting.

Another surprise was the amount of homework. I find I have twice as much homework in high school. In middle school I spent about an hour every weeknight doing homework, but now I spend about two hours a day, sometimes even on weekends. Longer study hall periods, however, help me to get some of my homework done during school hours. Although the homework takes longer and is harder than before, I usually feel like I'm accomplishing things.

1.25 inches

When I discovered I was having trouble concentrating in study hall, I realized how much more crowded high school is compared to middle school. The halls are jammed with students, many of whom I don't even know. It can be overwhelming.

With so many students, high school has a more competitive atmosphere than middle school. Many kids are trying out for the same spots on sport teams, for example. The added competition does have a positive side, however. It keeps me sharp.

I'm getting used to the idea that high school is a whole new experience. Although the differences between middle school and high school unsettled me at first, I find they all have a strong plus side. The changes, such as the different courses, more homework, and a bigger crowd, become less surprising every day.

1 inch

Collaborating Through the Writing Process   **33**

Keeping a Writer's Portfolio

In addition to publishing your work for others to read, you might want to keep a **portfolio**—a collection of your work that represents various types of writing and your progress in them. The following guidelines will help you make the most of your portfolio.

Guidelines for Including Work in Your Portfolio

- Date each piece of writing so that you can see where it fits into your progress.
- Write a brief note to yourself about why you included each piece—what you believe it shows about you as a writer.
- Include unfinished works if they demonstrate something meaningful about you as a writer.

On occasion, you will be asked to take "Time Out to Reflect." Use your written reflections to think about what you have learned, what you want to learn, and how you can continue to grow as a writer.

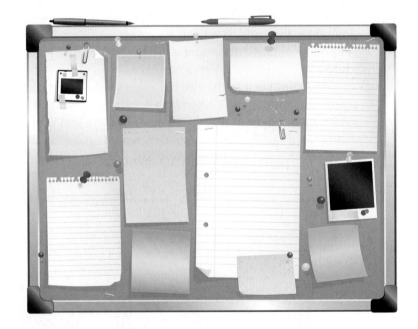

Time Out to REFLECT

After working through the five stages of the writing process, ask yourself how closely this process matches your previous experiences as a writer. What might account for any differences between the writing process as described in this chapter and the writing process as you have previously experienced it? How did the experience of working with your peers affect your writing?

There are times in school, such as during testing, when you will not be able to benefit from collaboration. The more you collaborate when you can, however, the less alone you will feel in those situations. You will no doubt be able to remember things your writing partners have said during your group meetings and then use them in your solo writing as well. For example, you might catch yourself writing a word or phrase that your group members thought was overused and too general. Or you might remember that time after time, your group members reminded you to use transitions to connect ideas. Use these memories to help you do your very best on timed writing tasks.

The following chart shows the stages of a timed writing experience. In each, imagine what your writing partners would be saying to help you.

Working Through Timed Writing Tasks

- Begin by understanding the task. Read the prompt carefully. Identify the key words in the directions: they will tell you what kind of writing to produce. Ask yourself what your audience—the examiners—will be looking for and try to provide it.

- Think about the time you have for the test and make a budget. Leave the most time for drafting, but build in time for planning and revising as well.

- Plan your writing by jotting down ideas, making lists, or using any other format that helps you (such as a cluster diagram). When you have good ideas to work with, arrange them in a logical order.

- Think through how to begin your writing. Begin drafting when you know what your main idea will be and you have ideas for introducing it.

- Use your notes to draft the body of your work. Be sure to use transitions.

- Remember what you have learned about strong conclusions and write a good ending to your work.

- Read over your work. If something seems confusing or out of place, fix it.

- Even though you are under time pressure, take the time to "step it up" and make your writing the best it can be. Look for places where such rhetorical devices as metaphors, similes, and analogies can add subtle meaning to your message.

- Check your work for errors in grammar, usage, mechanics, and spelling. Try to remember the mistakes you have made in the past so that you can avoid them.

Like everything else, writing under time pressure gets easier with practice. Each composition chapter in this book ends with a timed writing activity that you can use to practice.

You can learn more about preparing for timed writing experiences on pages 420–421.

CHAPTER 2

Developing Style and Voice

Your writing style is the distinctive way you express yourself through the words you choose and the way you shape your sentences.

As you develop your own personal writing style, you will also develop a voice that comes through in your writing. (See page 6.) Just as you can make choices to create a style, you can choose the appropriate voice for your purpose and audience.

Voice is the quality in writing that makes it sound as if there is a real and unique person behind the words, a verbal fingerprint.

Writing Project  Memoir

A Lifeline Develop your unique style and voice by writing a memoir about a situation in which someone threw you a lifeline.

Think Through Writing A lifeline is a floatation device attached to a long rope that can be thrown to a drowning swimmer, who can then be pulled to safety. More generally, "lifeline" refers to any help offered to someone in dire need. Think of a situation in which someone "threw you a lifeline"—that is, offered you help when you thought all was lost. Describe what you were struggling with, the person who "saved" you, the kind of lifeline this person threw you, and how you responded to the help. For now, just try to get your thoughts on paper without worrying too much about your spelling, grammar, and other features of writing that you can fix up later.

Talk About It In a group of three to five students, discuss the situations you have each written about. Discuss the sorts of situations that call for lifelines, the kinds of people who throw them, and the changes that a lifeline makes in a person's life. Share your conclusions with the rest of the class.

Read About It In the following passage, Maya Angelou writes about "the lady who threw me my first lifeline." Read it and think about your own situation in light of hers.

I Know Why the Caged Bird Sings

Maya Angelou

For nearly a year, I sopped around the house, the Store, the school and the church, like an old biscuit, dirty and inedible. Then I met, or rather got to know, the lady who threw me my first lifeline.

Mrs. Bertha Flowers was the aristocrat of Black Stamps. She had the grace of control to appear warm in the coldest weather, and on the Arkansas summer days it seemed she had a private breeze which swirled around, cooling her. She was thin without the taut look of wiry people, and her printed voile dresses and flowered hats were as right for her as denim overalls for a farmer. She was our side's answer to the richest white woman in town.

Her skin was a rich black that would have peeled like a plum if snagged, but then no one would have thought of getting close enough to Mrs. Flowers to ruffle her dress, let alone snag her skin. She didn't encourage familiarity. She wore gloves too.

I don't think I ever saw Mrs. Flowers laugh, but she smiled often. A slow widening of her thin black lips to show even, small white teeth, then the slow effortless closing. When she chose to smile on me, I always wanted to thank her. The action was so graceful and inclusively benign.

She was one of the few gentlewomen I have ever known, and has remained throughout my life the measure of what a human being can be. . . .

One summer afternoon, sweet-milk fresh in my memory, she stopped at the Store to buy provisions. Another Negro woman of her health and age would have been expected to carry the paper sacks home in one hand, but Momma said, "Sister Flowers, I'll send Bailey up to your house with these things."

She smiled that slow dragging smile, "Thank you, Mrs. Henderson. I'd prefer Marguerite,[1] though."

---

1 **Marguerite:** Maya Angelou was named Marguerite Johnson at birth.

The comparison of Angelou with "an old biscuit, dirty and inedible," is startling and grabs the reader's attention.

Specific words make Mrs. Flowers easy to picture.

Expressions such as "our side's" make clear that Angelou is an African American in a community sharply divided by race. Part of her voice is her pride in being an African American.

What effect does the phrase "sweet-milk fresh in my memory" have on the reader's expectation of what is to come?

Describing a smile as "dragging" is unusual and fresh.

My name was beautiful when she said it. "I've been meaning to talk to her, anyway." . . .

She said, without turning her head, to me, "I hear you're doing very good school work, Marguerite, but that it's all written. The teachers report that they have trouble getting you to talk in class." We passed the triangular farm on our left and the path widened to allow us to walk together. I hung back in the separate unasked and unanswerable questions.

"Come and walk along with me, Marguerite." I couldn't have refused even if I wanted to. She pronounced my name so nicely. Or more correctly, she spoke each word with such clarity that I was certain a foreigner who didn't understand English could have understood her.

"Now no one is going to make you talk—possibly no one can. But bear in mind, language is man's way of communicating with his fellow man and it is language alone which separates him from the lower animals." That was a totally new idea to me, and I would need time to think about it.

"Your grandmother says you read a lot. Every chance you get. That's good, but not good enough. Words mean more than what is set down on paper. It takes the human voice to infuse them with the shades of deeper meaning."

I memorized the part about the human voice infusing words. It seemed so valid and poetic. She said she was going to give me some books and that I not only must read them, I must read them aloud. She suggested that I try to make a sentence sound in as many different ways as possible. . . .

The sweet scent of vanilla had met us as she opened the door.

> Mouth-watering details make the reader feel right inside the scene.

"I made tea cookies this morning. You see, I had planned to invite you for cookies and lemonade so we could have this little chat. The lemonade is in the icebox." . . .

They were flat round wafers, slightly browned on the edges and butter-yellow in the center. With the cold lemonade they were sufficient for childhood's lifelong diet. Remembering my manners, I took nice little lady-like bites off the edges. She said she had made them expressly for me and that she had a few in the kitchen that I could take home to my brother. So I jammed one whole cake in my mouth and the rough crumbs scratched the insides of my jaws, and if I hadn't had to swallow, it would have been a dream come true.

As I ate she began the first of what we later called "my lessons in living." She said that I must always be intolerant of ignorance but understanding of illiteracy. That some people, unable to go to school, were more educated and even more intelligent than college professors. She encouraged me to listen carefully to what country people called mother wit. That in those homely sayings was couched the collective wisdom of generations.

When I finished the cookies she brushed off the table and brought a thick, small book from the bookcase. I had read *A Tale of Two Cities*[2] and found it up to my standards as a romantic novel. She opened the first page and I heard poetry for the first time in my life.

"It was the best of times and the worst of times. . . ."[3] Her voice slid in and curved down through and over the words. She was nearly singing. I wanted to look at the pages. Were they the same that I had read? Or were there notes, music, lined on the pages, as in a hymn book? Her sounds began cascading gently. I knew from listening to a thousand preachers that she was nearing the end of her reading, and I hadn't really heard, heard to understand, a single word.

"How do you like that?"

It occurred to me that she expected a response. The sweet vanilla flavor was still on my tongue and her reading was a wonder in my ears. I had to speak.

I said, "Yes, ma'am." It was the least I could do, but it was the most also.

"There's one more thing. Take this book of poems and memorize one for me. Next time you pay me a visit, I want you to recite."

> One rhetorical strategy that Angelou uses often is contrasting pairs of words or phrases. In this paragraph, the difference between "little lady-like bites" and "jammed one whole cake in my mouth" reflects her shifting relationship with Flowers.

---

2 **A Tale of Two Cities:** Novel by Charles Dickens.
3 **"It was . . . times":** First sentence of *A Tale of Two Cities*.

I have tried often to search behind the sophistication of years for the enchantment I so easily found in those gifts. The essence escapes but its aura remains. To be allowed, no, invited, into the private lives of strangers, and to share their joys and fears, was a chance to exchange the Southern bitter wormwood[4] for a cup of mead[5] with Beowulf[6] or a hot cup of tea and milk with Oliver Twist.[7] When I said aloud, "It is a far, far better thing that I do, than I have ever done . . ."[8] tears of love filled my eyes at my selflessness.

On that first day, I ran down the hill and into the road (few cars ever came along it) and had the good sense to stop running before I reached the Store.

I was liked, and what a difference it made. I was respected not as Mrs. Henderson's grandchild or Bailey's sister but for just being Marguerite Johnson.

Childhood's logic never asks to be proved (all conclusions are absolute). I didn't question why Mrs. Flowers had singled me out for attention, nor did it occur to me that Momma might have asked her to give me a little talking to. All I cared about was that she had made tea cookies for me and read to me from her favorite book. It was enough to prove that she liked me.

> Angelou draws contrast between the essence and the aura of a memory, and between being allowed and being invited. Like her earlier contrasts, these contribute to her voice, which is one of a careful observer.

---

4 **wormwood:** Something bitter.
5 **mead:** Drink of the Middle Ages made from honey.
6 **Beowulf:** Hero of an Old English epic poem.
7 **Oliver Twist:** Hero of a novel by Charles Dickens.
8 **"It is. . .done":** Line in *A Tale of Two Cities,* spoken by a character who dies so that another may live.

Respond in Writing In your journal, write about the language that Maya Angelou uses in her autobiography. What sort of voice does she have? In other words, what in her method of personal expression makes her unique as a writer? Identify words, phrases, point of view, and any other techniques or personal qualities that stand out when you read her writing.

Develop Your Own Criteria Work with your classmates to develop an understanding of Maya Angelou's writing techniques and the qualities that make her a unique writer.

Small Groups: In your writing group, share the insights from your journal writing. Discuss each person's assessment of Angelou's voice and compile a list of traits that distinguish her as a unique writer.

Whole Class: Report your list to the class. One student should serve as the class recorder, using the board or a projection screen to characterize Angelou's writing voice. When all lists have been reported and recorded, evaluate Angelou's writing style. Do you like it, dislike it, or have mixed feelings about it? Would you want your own writing to take on the qualities that distinguish hers? What can you learn from studying another writer's methods, techniques, and style?

Write About It You will next write about a situation in which someone threw you a lifeline, with attention to how you present your memoir in a unique voice. You might, for instance, produce writing of the sort described in the chart below.

Possible Topics	Possible Audiences	Possible Forms
• a time when you felt nobody cared about you, and someone demonstrated caring toward you • a time when you lacked an essential resource, and someone provided it for you • a time when you needed knowledge or help in performing properly, and someone reached out to share it with you • a time when you did not realize that you lacked something, and someone pointed out what was missing and helped you acquire it	• readers of your social networking Web site • the person who threw you the lifeline • admirers of the person who helped you • readers of your life story	• a text designed to help other young people stay hopeful when times are bad • a letter of thanks • a Web page commemorating this person's life and achievements • a chapter in your memoir or autobiography

CHAPTER 2

1 American Dialects

As you explore and develop your style, you have a very rich language on which to draw. The English language has more than a million words. People in different English-speaking countries and even different regions of the same country often have their own way of pronouncing certain words. In the United States, for example, New Englanders are said to speak with a twang and Southerners with a drawl. The different ways of speaking the same language are called **dialects.** Dialects find their way into writing and help shape voice and style.

American English varies among three main regional dialects: Eastern, Southern, and General American. Each of these dialects contains many subdialects. For instance, the Southern dialect includes distinctive subdialects spoken in Texas and Louisiana.

Dialects can be different from one another in vocabulary, pronunciation, and even grammar. In Columbus, Ohio, for instance, a green pepper may be called a mango, and in parts of New York City, many local residents pronounce *birds* as *boids*. Although dialects vary across the country, none is so different that one group cannot understand another. In fact, dialects add color and richness to American English.

PROJECT PREP *Analyzing* *Identifying Dialects*

With a small group, discuss the dialect that is spoken in your region of the country. Brainstorm examples of the vocabulary, pronunciation, and grammar that characterize the dialect. For example, do speakers of the dialect say *sofa, lounge, davenport, couch,* or *settee?* Do they say *soda, pop,* or *tonic?* Is the dialect influenced by another language, such as Spanish? Make a chart, index, or dictionary of words to introduce your regional dialect to people from other parts of the country.

Soda?
Pop?
Tonic?

2 Standard American English

Dialects have appropriate uses in informal conversation and in creative writing. In a formal speech or informative writing, however, you should use standard English, or mainstream English (see page 8). **Standard English** is the formal English taught in school and used in newspapers, scholarly works, and many books.

(see page 8)

Writing Tip

Use **standard English** when writing for school and for a large general audience.

● Practice Your Skills

Comparing Dialects with Standard English

After you have developed a list of examples of the dialect, compare and contrast them with standard English. Make a T-chart, with the dialect words and phrases in one column and the standard English version in the other.

● Practice Your Skills

Reviewing the Power Rules

Take another look at the Power Rules on pages 8–10. For each one, determine whether or not the dialect you naturally speak conforms to the rule or differs from it. Write a paragraph explaining the results of your analysis.

PROJECT PREP   *Analyzing*   *Identifying Voice*

Return to the writing that you began. In your writing groups, take turns reading a portion of your text aloud, and listen especially to phrasing. Does the speaker sound like you? If not, how can you use your analysis of your local dialect to help express yourself more naturally? For each writer in your group, make suggestions on how to revise the writing so the voice sounds natural, conversational, and unique. Then revise, incorporating the feedback.

③ Colloquialisms, Idioms, Slang, and Jargon

Besides dialect, another source of the richness of English is found in its colloquialisms, idioms, slang, and jargon. Because these types of expressions are informal, they are sometimes not appropriate in your writing.

COLLOQUIALISMS

A **colloquialism** is an informal phrase or colorful expression that is appropriate for conversation, but not for formal writing.

> As soon as Dan and Luis met, **they hit it off.** (got along well together)
>
> For dinner the Hendersons certainly **put out a spread.** (served a generous amount of food)

IDIOMS

An **idiom** is a special type of colloquialism. It is a phrase or expression of a given group of people that has a meaning different from the literal translation of the words. Idioms do not often make sense when taken literally, yet they are quite meaningful to most people who speak a particular language.

> Elise was **beside herself with worry** (very concerned) because she had not heard from Barbara.
>
> When Henry came home that night, **he looked like something the cat dragged in.** (didn't look very good)

SLANG

Slang consists of English expressions that are developed and used by particular groups. Such expressions are highly colorful, exaggerated, and often humorous. Although most slang goes out of fashion quickly, a few slang expressions—such as those that follow— have become a permanent part of the language.

> Simone earned ten **bucks** (dollars) by mowing the Henshaws' lawn.
>
> Sitting and waiting for someone in an airport can be **a real drag.** (tiresome)

JARGON

Jargon is the specialized vocabulary that people within the same profession use to communicate precisely and efficiently with one another. Using jargon to communicate with other experts, such as in an article for a scientific journal, is appropriate. However, using jargon to communicate with a general audience can cause a lack of understanding. The second sentence below would be much clearer to a general audience than the first sentence.

| Jargon | There is no locality similar to a structure that is used exclusively for a permanent residential domicile and/or noncommercial purpose. |
| Translation | There is no place like home. |

● Practice Your Skills

Using Appropriate Standard English

Substitute words or phrases in standard English for the underlined colloquialisms, idioms, jargon, and slang expressions in the following sentences.

1. The gymnastics coach told Midori to go all out in her next routine.
2. It can be difficult and time-consuming to score a part-time summer job.
3. Maria asked her little brother to stop bugging her while she tried to read.
4. Julia would jump at the chance to work for the newspaper during the summer.
5. The library has tons of books, articles, and pamphlets on that topic.
6. Are you going to see them off at the train station tomorrow afternoon?

Writing Tip

Idioms, **colloquialisms**, **slang**, and **jargon** can make the style and voice of your fiction and poetry convincing and lively. They are not, however, appropriate for the formal writing you will do in school and at work.

PROJECT PREP *Revising* *Voice and Audience*

In your effort to sound more "natural," you also need to take into account the expectations of the writing situation. In your writing group, return to the writing that you focused on in the previous Project Prep. Discuss each writer's voice in relation to each writer's choice of audience and form or genre. Is the voice appropriate to the job of communicating effectively with these readers in this setting? If not, how would you modify the style to suit the situation? Make revisions as appropriate.

Choosing Vivid Words

To make writing shine, choose words and expressions that express what you mean specifically.

① Specific Words

Specific words help readers visualize what they read and make a writer's style sparkle. Consider the following example, which describes the same item on a restaurant menu. The first example uses general words that leave only a vague impression. The second uses specific words that whet the appetite.

General   Cooked meat covered with a good sauce, served with tasty potatoes and cooked fresh vegetables

Specific   Barbecued spareribs smothered in a tangy sauce, served with sizzling French-fried potatoes and crisp steamed broccoli

General words may mean different things to different people, but specific words call specific images and feelings to mind. Compare the following general and specific words.

GENERAL AND SPECIFIC WORDS			
	General	Specific	More Specific
Nouns	meat	pork	spareribs
	clothes	pants	blue jeans
Adjectives	uneasy	nervous	jittery
	thin	delicate	fragile
Verbs	went	walked	strolled
	saw	watched	examined
Adverbs	happily	gleefully	exuberantly
	soon	promptly	now

PROJECT PREP   *Revising*   *Specific Words*

In your writing group, read aloud a section of your work in progress. Are your nouns, verbs, and modifiers vivid and memorable? For each writer, make suggestions on how to make the language come alive in ways that are appropriate to the writer's voice, the readers, and the situation. Then revise that section, using fresh, specific words, including any from the second two columns of the chart above that may work.

Denotation and Connotation

All words convey a literal meaning, or **denotation,** the direct, specific meaning found in a dictionary. Many words, however, also stir up emotions or suggest associations; this is called **connotation.** The words *trip* and *vacation,* for example, have similar denotations; but *vacation* has an extra level of meaning. Its connotation brings many feelings to mind: freedom from the usual routine, fun, relaxation, different surroundings.

Understanding connotations is important when you write because some words have similar denotations but opposite connotations.

Positive Connotation	The city was **bustling** with people during the holiday.
Negative Connotation	The city was **mobbed** with people during the holiday.

In these examples the words *bustling* and *mobbed* both mean "filled." *Bustling,* however, suggests a positive feeling of energy and excitement, while *mobbed* suggests a negative feeling of overcrowding, noise, and restricted movement. A word's connotation helps to stir readers' emotions. You can convey subtle meanings by choosing words with connotations that evoke feeling.

● **Practice Your Skills**

Using Connotation to Convey Subtle Meaning

Write the word in each of the following sentences that has the connotation given in brackets.

Example	Ellen is very (frank, blunt). [negative]
Answer	blunt

1. Every October the old maple (paints, litters) the lawn with its falling leaves. [positive]
2. The girl ran (courageously, recklessly) into the flaming barn to save her colt. [positive]
3. We walked at a (leisurely, sluggish) pace. [negative]
4. The rabbit (scrambled, scampered) across the lawn. [positive]
5. Facing his parents' concerned expressions, the boy gathered up his courage and (truthfully, factually) told how the window got broken. [positive]

LOADED WORDS

Subjective words that are interjected into a seemingly objective report of an event are **loaded words.** These words are meant to sway the audience emotionally one way or another without the audience's awareness. You can find loaded words in advertisements, in political campaigns, and on television. Writers use the connotations of loaded words to convey bias while trying to sound objective.

The writer of this news item is using loaded words to get across the point that he or she thinks the school committee is ineffectual; the writer's opinion has crept into the news story. Another writer may have seen the meeting differently.

Loaded Words

The school committee meeting got off to another slow start, with the committee members arguing among themselves. Finally the board settled down to review the budget for the proposed school annex. While the clock ticked, the committee still could not come to a decision.

Practice Your Skills

Using Connotation to Add Meaning

Identify the loaded words in the following version of the school committee report.

(1) Once again, the school committee members tackled the monumental task of sorting out the budget for the proposed school annex. (2) The ten members wrestled with the budget throughout the evening and adjourned, having made significant progress but not yet having brought the matter to a close.

PROJECT PREP *Revising* *Consistent Connotations*

In your writing group, read aloud a section of your writing and listen carefully. Are the connotations of the words you have chosen consistent? Do they convey the subtle meanings you intend? For instance, if you said, "The regal woman scurried over to greet me," you might be implying that the woman was like both a queen ("regal" refers to royalty) and a rat (often described as scurrying). Such conflicting connotations cause confusion in readers. Revise so that your use of connotation creates unified images of the people and situation you are describing.

③ Figurative Language

You can create vivid pictures in your readers' minds not only by using specific words and subtle shades of meaning that connotations provide, but also by using **figurative language.** The two most common types of figurative language are similes and metaphors.

SIMILES AND METAPHORS

These figures of speech stimulate the reader's imagination by expressing a similarity between two things that are essentially different.

Similes state a comparison by using the words *like* or *as*. **Metaphors,** in contrast, imply a comparison by simply saying that one thing is another.

Simile	Her skin was a rich black that would have peeled **like a plum** if snagged. . . .
Metaphor	To be allowed, no, invited, into the private lives of strangers, and to share their joys and fears, was **a chance to exchange the Southern bitter wormwood for a cup of mead with Beowulf or a hot cup of tea and milk with Oliver Twist.**

A woman's skin and the skin of a plum are different things, of course. Maya Angelou suggests that Mrs. Flowers had skin as plump and smooth, and as richly hued, as a plum. By evoking the image of a peeling plum, the author also conveys a sense of how vulnerable to harm that smooth skin might be.

A human life is not like a drink, but the metaphor suggests that to enter the private world of Mrs. Flowers and the literary England of the eighth and nineteenth centuries is sweet nourishment for Marguerite.

● Practice Your Skills

Identifying Similes and Metaphors

Write simile or metaphor to identify each underlined figure of speech in the following sentences.

1. My brother's room <u>is a federal disaster area.</u>

2. With crashing cymbals and booming drums, the symphony <u>was like a thunderstorm.</u>

3. Good friends revolve around Keisha <u>as the planets revolve around the sun.</u>

4. Hope went through me <u>like a faint breeze over a lake.</u> —Antoine de Saint-Exupéry

5. The coach <u>growled</u> when his players quit too soon.

6. Her secret was <u>as dark as her eyes</u>.

7. Hermit crabs, <u>like frantic children</u>, scamper on the bottom sand. —John Steinbeck

8. All the strength went out of me, and I toppled forward <u>like an undermined tower.</u> —Mark Twain

9. Memories <u>poured</u> from every corner of the old house.

10. The <u>black bat, night, has flown.</u> —Alfred, Lord Tennyson

● Practice Your Skills

Identifying Figurative Language

Identify the figurative language in the following passage.

Summer burned the canals dry. Summer moved like a flame upon the meadows. In the empty Earth settlement, the painted houses flaked and peeled. Rubber tires upon which children had swung in back yards hung suspended like stopped clock pendulums in the blazing air.

—Ray Bradbury, "Dark They Were and Golden Eyed"

Figurative language can help you write concise, vivid sentences. Notice how the long, wordy first passage is improved by use of a metaphor in the second. Rewrite the first passage using a different metaphor or simile.

> He was a very important book critic in the literary world. He was a kind and supportive reviewer who would never intentionally want to harm or slow down any writer's career. Any slight criticism from him, though, could cause great damage to a writer's career.

> He was the elephant among book critics: kindly, but with such power that he could cause great damage without meaning to.

Think Critically

Developing Vivid Comparisons

When you write a simile or a metaphor, you are using a thinking skill called comparing. When you **compare,** you tell how two things are similar. Thinking of a fresh comparison to use in a simile or metaphor, however, is sometimes difficult. The following chart illustrates a thinking strategy that will help you develop vivid comparisons.

QUALITIES OF A STRAWBERRY	THINGS WITH SIMILAR QUALITIES
plump	a marshmallow, a baby's cheek
juicy	a watermelon, an orange
red	a ruby, a clown's nose
rough	a cat's tongue; cornmeal

To create a comparison chart, first think about what you want to describe. Then make a list of its most important qualities. Next to each quality list some other things that have the same quality. Stretch your imagination and avoid overused comparisons like "red as a rose." Once you have a list of comparisons, you can select the best one for your simile or metaphor.

Simile Red, ripe strawberries gleamed under the shadowy leaves **like unmined rubies in a gem field.**

Thinking Practice

Use the thinking strategy described above to help you write a fresh simile or metaphor for each of the following items.

1. waves hitting rocks
2. a Ferris wheel at night
3. a stubbornly determined child going up stairs

CLICHÉS

Some comparisons that were once clever and striking have become dull with overuse. Such worn-out expressions are called **clichés.** If you find yourself using a cliché, replace it with a fresh comparison or with specific words.

Cliché	make a mountain out of a molehill
Specific Words	exaggerate unnecessarily; needlessly make more difficult
Cliché	as cool as a cucumber
Specific Words	relaxed; nonchalant
Fresh Comparisons	as calm as a blind man in the dark; as self-possessed as a snail

● **Practice Your Skills**

Revising to Eliminate Clichés

Revise the following personal narrative by replacing each underlined cliché with a fresh simile or metaphor or with specific words.

Everyone told me the tryouts for the school play would be (1) as easy as A, B, C, but by the time I was called to read my lines, I was (2) shaking like a leaf. Somehow I managed to (3) spit out my lines, but after I flubbed I had (4) to start from scratch. This time my voice was (5) as clear as a bell.

TIRED WORDS AND EUPHEMISMS

Like a cliché, a **tired word** has been so overused that it has been drained of meaning. Take, for example, the word *awesome.* This word traditionally meant "inspiring a mixed emotion of reverence, respect, dread, and wonder inspired by authority, genius, great beauty, sublimity, or might." Now, through overuse, the word just means "good."

A **euphemism** is a vague word or phrase that substitutes for something considered blunt or offensive. Euphemisms are polite, inoffensive terms that are used to conceal an unpleasant fact. Following are common euphemisms you can find in your newspaper.

EUPHEMISM	TRANSLATION
peace-keeper	soldier
let go	fired
handyman special	run down house
preowned automobile	used car

Practice Your Skills

Tired Words and Euphemisms

Write the tired words and euphemisms in the following sentences. Then rewrite each sentence, using vivid, specific language.

1. Our trip to the city was really neat, and we had a great time.
2. The custodial engineer will mop the cafeteria floor after the meal is finished.
3. Tina's new video game has some awesome graphics.
4. Harold was walking on eggshells when he entered the class late.
5. The football game was an emotional roller coaster.

> **Writing Tip**
>
> Avoid **clichés** and **tired words** to keep your writing fresh and precise.

Use the following rubric to evaluate your word choice.

Word Choice Rubric			
4 Words are specific and powerful, rich in sensory images.	**3 Words are specific and some words appeal to the senses.**	**2 Some words are overly general and/or tired.**	**1 Most words are overly general and tired.**
• I used Standard English if required.	• I was aware of differences between Standard and Nonstandard English and made reasonable choices.	• I was not always aware of differences between Standard and Nonstandard English.	• I was not aware of differences between Standard and Nonstandard English.
• I used Nonstandard English if appropriate.			
• I used words with connotations that match my intended meaning.	• My word choice conveyed my meaning.	• I still need to work on finding the best, most specific word.	• Few of my words were as specific and vivid as they need to be.
• I used fresh, not tired words.	• I used fresh words often.	• I used a few tired expressions.	• I used many tired expressions.
• I used words that appeal to the senses.	• I made an effort to appeal to the senses but might have done more.	• I appealed to only one or two senses.	• I didn't really appeal to the senses.

PROJECT PREP *Figurative Language*

In your writing group, make suggestions to each writer for adding figurative language and eliminating worn out phrases or euphemisms. Using the rubric above, look for other ways to strengthen your word choice and make revisions accordingly.

In the Media

Newspapers

How do writers find ways to keep their stories lively and fresh? One way is to search for fresh synonyms for tired words. Another is to add powerful descriptive words. Here is an example from sports journalism.

The Chicago Bears were leading the Green Bay Packers in the first game since Bears legend Walter "Sweetness" Payton passed away. Green Bay was poised for a game-winning field goal. Here's how two *Chicago Tribune* writers described what happened.

> With a nod to Payton for the assist, [Bryan] Robinson capitalized on a low snap by the Packers and blocked what would have been a game-winning field goal by Ryan Longwell as time expired to preserve a 14–13 victory. . . .
>
> "I have just one word," said running back James Allen. "It's sweet. Sweetness."

> It will be Walter's Game forever now that the Bears have won it, the 159th rendering of pro football's most storied border war. This is, of course, absurd in any real, touchable sense. It was Bryan Robinson's and not Walter Payton's hand that blocked the dead-certain Packer field goal at the end. . . .
>
> Was it Payton who raised Robinson up to block that kick, the first blocked kick of Robinson's career?
>
> "Walter Payton picked me up in the air," insisted Robinson. "I can't jump that high."

There is some language that is the same in both pieces. *Field goal* and *blocked kick* mean something specific and cannot easily be replaced by synonyms. But there is plenty of variety for the many other actions and reactions that happen on the field.

Media Activity

Imagine you work at the rewrite desk of a newspaper. Rewrite the opening sentence of each story above. Keep the meaning the same, but rewrite using synonyms and fresh descriptions.

Creating Sentence Fluency and Variety

Good writing flows with the natural, varied rhythms of speech. As you read the passage below by Ernest Hemingway, notice how the varied rhythm of his sentences contributes to the pleasure of reading the paragraph.

MODEL: Sentence Variety

Before it was really light he had his baits out and was drifting with the current. One bait was down forty fathoms. The second was at seventy-five and the third and fourth were down in the blue water at one hundred and one hundred and twenty-five fathoms.

—Ernest Hemingway, *The Old Man and the Sea*

To appreciate how important rhythm is in writing, try reading a paragraph that consists only of a string of short sentences. Too many short sentences in a row make the writing choppy and difficult to read. When you revise your writing, you can improve the flow of short sentences by combining them to make longer, varied ones.

1 Combining Sentences with Phrases

One way to combine short sentences is to express some of the information in a phrase. The following examples show how to combine sentences using three kinds of phrases.

A. Handlers can usually train dogs. Training is in basic obedience. Training takes about eight weeks.

Handlers can usually train dogs **in basic obedience in about eight weeks.** (prepositional phrases)

B. Handlers and dogs work together. This strengthens the bond between pet and master.

Handlers and dogs work together, **strengthening the bond between pet and master.** (participial phrase)

C. A training collar helps the handler correct the dog. It is the handler's most important tool.

A training collar, **the handler's most important tool,** helps the handler correct the dog. (appositive phrase)

Combining Sentences with Phrases

Using the examples on page 55, combine each pair of sentences. The letter in parentheses indicates which example to use. Remember to insert commas where needed.

1. W. Timothy Gallwey wrote a classic book. He wrote about becoming a winner. (A: prepositional phrase)

2. His book captured great attention. His book is *The Inner Game of Tennis*. (C: appositive phrase)

3. Gallwey identifies an "inner game." This is a game between the player's actions and his or her thoughts and feelings. (B: participial phrase)

4. The inner game influences the play between opponents. The inner game tests a player's confidence and powers of concentration. (B: participial phrase)

5. Playing the inner game well brings rewards. The rewards are in concentration. The rewards are in relaxation. The rewards are in success in the game. (A: prepositional phrase)

6. Each player plays two roles that determine his or her skill. These are the director and the doer. (C: appositive phrase)

7. The director is the inner player. The director gives the doer such instructions as, "OK, hit the next volley high." (B: participial phrase)

8. In good players the director and the doer interact. They interact in harmony. (A: prepositional phrase)

9. In weaker players, the doer can become frustrated. The doer tries too hard and fails. (B: participial phrase)

10. Mastering the inner game has value. The value is in life as well as in tennis. (A: prepositional phrase)

PROJECT PREP *Drafting* **Style and Voice**

Using the feedback from your writing group, write a whole new draft of your composition. Make an effort to apply each lesson to each section so that your style and voice have continuity throughout the text.

The Power of Language ⚡

Participial Phrases: Getting into the Action

Adding *–ing* modifiers to sentences can make your writing come alive. Try using them to describe a person, thing, or action. (See pages 526 and 621–622.) Look, for instance, at how Maya Angelou used *–ing* phrases.

> **At the Beginning of a Sentence**
>
> **Remembering my manners,** I took nice little lady-like bites off the edges.
>
> **At the End of a Sentence**
>
> She had the grace of control to appear warm in the coldest weather, and on the Arkansas summer days it seemed she had a private breeze which swirled around, **cooling her.**

You can pack even more action into a sentence by using an absolute phrase. One way to create an absolute phrase is to add a noun before an *-ing* phrase. Consider these two sentences.

> We passed the triangular farm on our left. The path widened to allow us to walk together.

You can smooth out these sentences by combining them with an absolute phrase.

> We passed the triangular farm on our left, **the path widening to allow us to walk together.**

Try It Yourself

Write one sentence with an *–ing* phrase at the beginning and another with the *–ing* phrase at the end. You may imitate the sentences above if you wish. Try to write sentences on the topic you have chosen for your project and incorporate them into your draft if you can. During revision, check to see where adding other *–ing* modifiers might be good.

Punctuation Tip

When you add "extra" details like this, making the writing more interesting, separate the *–ing* phrase from the main part of the sentence with a comma.

② Combining Sentences by Coordinating

Another way to smooth out short, choppy sentences is to link ideas of equal importance with a coordinating conjunction.

COORDINATING CONJUNCTIONS						
and	but	for	nor	or	so	yet

The following sentences about dog training show how to combine sentences with coordinating conjunctions.

> **A.**   Kindness is important. Praise is important, too.
>
> **Kindness** <u>and</u> **praise** are also important. (compound subject)
>
> **B.**   Soon your dog will heel on command. Soon your dog will sit on command.
>
> Soon your dog **will heel** <u>and</u> **sit** on command. (compound verb)
>
> **C.**   The dog should be confined before each session. The place of confinement should be comfortable.
>
> **The dog should be confined before each session,** <u>but</u> **the place of confinement should be comfortable.** (compound sentence)

● **Practice Your Skills**

Combining Sentences by Coordinating

Combine each pair of sentences, using the model identified in parentheses following each pair. Add punctuation as needed.

1. F. M. Alexander, who lived in the 1800s, acted. He also gave speeches.
(B: compound verb)

2. In the 1880s he suddenly lost his voice. His career ground to a halt.
(C: compound sentence)

3. He visited doctors. None of them could help him. (C: compound sentence)

4. He had little choice but to help himself. He had no medical training.
(C: compound sentence)

5. His head moved when he talked. His neck also moved. (A: compound subject)

PROJECT PREP *Revising*   *Peer Response*

Bring your new draft to your writing group. As you read one another's papers, focus on the degree to which you find a consistent style and voice and on the ways in which the author has constructed sentences. Make suggestions that you think would improve each writer's draft.

③ Combining Sentences by Subordinating

If the ideas in two short sentences are of unequal importance, you can combine them by subordinating. To subordinate, express the less important idea in an adjective clause that begins with a relative pronoun or in an adverb clause that begins with a subordinating conjunction. The pronouns and conjunctions below are often used to begin clauses.

CHAPTER 2

FOR ADJECTIVE CLAUSES Relative Pronouns			FOR ADVERB CLAUSES Subordinating Conjunctions		
who	which	whose	after	because	unless
whom	that		although	whenever	until

The following sentences show how to combine sentences by subordinating.

A. Mother dogs use a barking sound to get their pups to obey. The barking sound resembles the word *out*.

Mother dogs use a barking sound, **which resembles the word *out*,** to get their pups to obey. (adjective clause)

B. Handlers can also use this sound. Dogs have a long memory of their mothers' stern corrections.

Handlers can also use this sound **because dogs have a long memory of their mothers' stern corrections.** (adverb clause)

● **Practice Your Skills**

Combining Sentences by Coordinating and Subordinating

Use the method in brackets to combine the sentences. Add needed punctuation.

(1) We wanted to do something different on our vacation. We chose backpacking in the wilderness. (compound sentence) (2) We walked the entire distance. We had packs on our backs. (prepositional phrases) (3) At one point we came to a lookout tower. It was in good condition. (adjective clause) (4) I climbed the tower. I strapped my camera around my neck. (participial phrase) (5) Fog had covered the valley. I could barely see the river below. (compound sentence) (6) A footpath followed the river. An old railroad track followed the river. (compound subject) (7) That foggy view has stayed in my memory to this day. It was a highlight of the vacation. (appositive phrase)

PROJECT PREP *Revising* *Using Feedback*

Use feedback from your writing group as you write a new draft of your text.

④ Varying Sentence Beginnings

The most natural way to begin a sentence is with the subject. If too many sentences begin in the same way, however, even a gripping story will sound dull. Look at how Hal Borland varied the beginnings of sentences in his novel *When the Legends Die:*

Subject	**The boy** caught trout in the pool and watched for his friend, the bear.
Adverb	**Reluctantly** the boy fastened the collar on the bear cub.
Phrase	**For days** he watched them. (prepositional phrase) **Driving with one hand,** he headed for home. (participial phrase)
Clause	**If he rode the horse with its own rhythm,** he could ride every horse in the herd. (adverb clause)

As you revise, vary the rhythm of your writing by starting sentences in different ways.

● **Practice Your Skills**

Varying Sentence Beginnings

Vary the beginning of each of the following sentences by using the openers suggested in parentheses.

1. The universe, stretching endlessly beyond the reaches of our imagination, holds many mysteries. (participial phrase)
2. There are 100 billion stars in just our own galaxy, the Milky Way. (prepositional phrase and appositive phrase)
3. However, only the nearest and brightest stars are visible when we gaze into the vast sea of stars. (adverb clause)
4. We can see fewer than 3,000 stars on a clear night. (prepositional phrase)
5. The Milky Way would look like a giant fried egg if we could look down on it. (adverb clause)
6. Our galaxy, bulging in the middle, spans 10,000 light-years at the center. (participial phrase)

PROJECT PREP *Revising* *Fluency*

Reread your draft, looking for opportunities to combine short sentences into longer ones to improve the flow. Make revisions accordingly.

⑤ Varying Sentence Structure

Another way to achieve a natural rhythm in your writing is to vary the sentence structure. In the following example, Marjorie Kinnan Rawlings describes a stay near an orphanage using a variety of sentence structures to create a flowing rhythm.

Complex →

Complex →

At daylight I was half wakened by the sound of chopping. Again it was so even in texture that I went back to sleep. When I left my bed in the cool morning, the boy had come and gone, and a stack of kindling was neat against the cabin wall. He came again after school in the afternoon and worked until it was time to return to the orphanage. His name was Jerry; he was twelve years old, and he had been at the orphanage since he was four.

← **Simple**

← **Compound-Complex**

← **Compound-Complex**

—Marjorie Kinnan Rawlings, "A Mother in Manville"

● Practice Your Skills

Revising for Sentence Variety

Revise the following paragraph, combining the sentences according to the structure indicated in parentheses. Use commas where needed.

Handwriting Analysis

(1) Handwriting analysis is not an exact science. Police often seek the opinion of a handwriting expert in cases of forgery. (complex) (2) The handwriting in question is placed under a microscope. A known piece of handwriting is placed beside it. (compound) (3) The handwriting expert analyzes the two samples. The expert does this by comparing significant details. These details include the dots above *i*'s, the crosses through *t*'s, the angle of the pen, and the beginnings and ends of pen strokes. (simple) (4) Experts sometimes contradict each other's analyses. Many people doubt the reliability of handwriting analysis. (complex) (5) Doubts persist. Courts allow handwriting experts to testify. Juries are often persuaded by the testimony of these experts. (compound-complex)

Writing Tip

Create sentence rhythm by varying **the beginning, length, and structure** of your sentences.

The Language of Power · Fragments

Power Rule: Use sentence fragments only the way professional writers do, after the sentence they refer to and usually to emphasize a point. Fix all sentence fragments that occur before the sentence they refer to and ones that occur in the middle of a sentence. (See pages 666–671.)

See It in Action In the passage below from *I Know Why the Caged Bird Sings,* Angelou begins with a compound sentence. What follows that is a sentence fragment, since it has no verb.

> I don't think I ever saw Mrs. Flowers laugh, but she smiled often. A slow widening of her thin black lips to show even, small white teeth, then the slow effortless closing.

To avoid a sentence fragment, Angelou could have used a comma instead of a period after the first sentence. A period, though, forces the reader to slow down, and that slowing down emphasizes the "slow widening" and "slow effortless closing."

In writing for school or the workplace, avoid sentence fragments. If you do use them in creative or expressive writing, be sure you use them effectively and for a reason.

Remember It Record this rule and example in the Power Rule section of your Personalized Editing Checklist.

Use It Read your text aloud, noting where your voice pauses and stops. When it stops, is it always after a complete sentence? If not, revise to eliminate the fragment.

PROJECT PREP *Revising* *Peer Revising*

Exchange papers with another student and help each other recognize opportunities to combine adjacent short sentences into longer ones. Also watch for places to correct sentence fragments by combining them with adjacent complete sentences.

Writing Concise Sentences

① Rambling Sentences

A sentence that rambles on too long is dull and hard to understand. In the following description, too many ideas are strung together in one sentence.

Rambling   The buzz saw screams as you watch the tree come up the conveyor belt, and as the tree hits the saw, chips fly left and right, and when it reaches the end of the saw, the log folds over into two slabs.

When you revise, eliminate rambling sentences by separating the ideas into a variety of short and long sentences.

Revised   The buzz saw screams as you watch the tree come up the conveyor belt. As the tree hits the saw, chips fly left and right. When it reaches the end of the saw, the log folds over into two slabs.

● **Practice Your Skills**

Revising Rambling Sentences

Revise the following paragraph by breaking up the rambling sentence. Use capital letters and punctuation where needed.

Winchester House

Winchester House is the name of a huge, rambling mansion in San José, California, that was built by Sarah Winchester, who was heir to the Winchester fortune and who believed that she would go on living as long as she was adding to the house, which has 160 rooms, 200 doors, and 47 fireplaces.

PROJECT PREP *Rambling Sentences*

Exchange papers with a partner. Look over each other's writing for rambling sentences. If you find any, make suggestions for how your partner can break up the rambling sentence into separate sentences that flow smoothly.

② Unnecessary Words

REDUNDANCY

Unnecessary repetition is called **redundancy.** In a redundant sentence, the same idea is expressed more than once with no new or different shades of meaning.

Redundant	The **hungry** wolf ate **ravenously.**
Concise	The wolf ate **ravenously.**
Redundant	The **hot, steamy** asphalt shimmered.
Concise	The **steamy** asphalt shimmered.

● Practice Your Skills

Revising to Eliminate Redundancy

Revise each of the following sentences by eliminating the redundancy:

1. Do you have a spare pencil that you are not using?

2. Friday is the final deadline for the report.

3. Each and every member of the class must help.

4. Can you keep this secret confidential?

WORDINESS

The use of words and expressions that add nothing to the meaning of a sentence is called **wordiness.** Like redundancy, wordiness is tiresome and distracting to a reader.

Empty Expressions One way to avoid wordiness is to rid your sentences of empty expressions. Notice how the revisions for conciseness improve the following sentences.

Wordy	I can't go out **due to the fact that** I have my guitar lesson tonight.
Concise	I can't go out **because** I have my guitar lesson tonight.
Wordy	**There are** dozens of games **that** resemble checkers.
Concise	Dozens of games resemble checkers.

EMPTY EXPRESSIONS			
what I want is	in my opinion	the thing that	due to the fact that
the thing/fact is	the reason that	on account of	there is/are/was/were
It is/was	it seems as if	what I mean is	I believe/feel/think that

Eliminating Empty Expressions

Revise each sentence by eliminating or replacing the empty expressions.

1. We canceled the game due to the fact that it rained.

2. The reason that I called is to ask if you need help.

3. Because of the fact that he was sick, his report is late.

4. The thing that I really hate is getting up early.

5. There are some places in the river that are dangerous.

Wordy Phrases and Clauses Another way to avoid wordiness is to shorten wordy phrases and clauses. In many cases a phrase can be reduced to a single word.

Wordy	Archaeologists found ancient tools **made of stone.** (participial phrase)
Concise	Archaeologists found ancient **stone** tools. (adjective)
Wordy	Elana spoke to the shy horse **in a gentle tone.** (prepositional phrase)
Concise	Elana spoke **gently** to the shy horse. (adverb)
Wordy	**To be tardy** is often a sign of laziness. (infinitive phrase)
Concise	**Tardiness** is often a sign of laziness. (noun)

Similarly, a clause can be reduced to a phrase or even to a single word.

Wordy	People **who are in show business** lead a hectic life of rehearsals and performances. (clause)
Concise	People **in show business** lead a hectic life of rehearsals and performances. (prepositional phrase)
Wordy	In Yosemite, **which is a national park in California,** cars are forbidden past a certain point. (clause)
Concise	In Yosemite, **a national park in California,** cars are forbidden past a certain point. (appositive phrase)
Wordy	Climates **that are dry** are good for people with allergy problems. (clause)
Concise	**Dry** climates are good for people with allergy problems. (adjective)

● **Practice Your Skills**

Revising Wordy Phrases and Clauses

Revise each of the following sentences by shortening the underlined wordy phrase or clause.

1. Misha likes chicken <u>cooked with barbecue sauce</u>.

2. Students <u>who are trying out for band</u> should come to school on Saturday morning.

3. An exchange student <u>who came to our neighborhood from France</u> lives with our neighbors.

4. Tamara, <u>who is an accident victim</u>, competed in the marathon in a wheelchair.

5. Games <u>that are in good condition</u> will be accepted for the charity drive.

> **Writing Tip**
>
> Create **concise** sentences by expressing your meaning in as few words as possible.

● **Practice Your Skills**

Applying Revision Techniques

Revise the following paragraph to eliminate the problems indicated in parentheses.

(1) Some people do not like going into skyscrapers. Being so high up makes them feel sick as a dog. (cliché, short and choppy sentences) (2) The fact is that acrophobiacs, who are people with a fear of heights, may even suddenly lose their balance and fall. (empty expression, wordy clause) (3) The tallest skyscrapers are the most frightening, since the top of one of these buildings can sway as much as three feet in the wind, and on a windy day, people who are riding in the elevator can hear it hitting the sides of the shaft. (rambling sentence, wordy clause) (4) Because of the fact that skyscrapers sway and move, some people feel airsick when they are on the upper floors. (empty expression, redundancy)

PROJECT PREP *Revising* *Concise Sentences*

In your writing group, point out any unnecessary words, phrases, and clauses in your partners' work. Then revise your composition to eliminate extraneous words, phrases, clauses, and ideas.

Using a Sentence Fluency Rubric

Evaluate your sentence fluency with the following rubric.

4 Sentences are varied in length and structure. Every sentence matters.	**3** Sentences are mostly varied in length and structure. A few words and sentences seem unnecessary.	**2** Many sentences are the same in length and structure. A number of words and sentences seem unnecessary.	**1** Most sentences are the same in length and structure. A number of words and sentences seem unnecessary.
• I combined short, choppy sentences into varied, longer ones. • I used coordinating and subordinating conjunctions to improve the flow and show the relationship of ideas. • I started my sentences in a variety of ways, not always with the subject first. • I avoided rambling sentences.	• I combined some short, choppy sentences into varied, longer ones, but in a few places there is still some choppiness. • I sometimes used coordinating and subordinating conjunctions to improve the flow and show the relationship of ideas. • I started most of my sentences in a variety of ways, not always with the subject first. • I avoided rambling sentences.	• A few parts of my work flow, but there is still choppiness. • I used a few conjunctions to improve the flow and show relationships, but I see now that I could have used more. • Many of my sentences start the same way, with the subject. • Several of my sentences ramble or contain unnecessary information.	• I didn't quite achieve a flow. My writing seems to start and stop. • I didn't often combine ideas into one sentence to improve the flow and show relationships. • Most of my sentences start the same way, with the subject. • Many of my sentences ramble or contain unnecessary information.

CHAPTER 2

PROJECT PREP Publishing *Final Version*

Using the rubric above, evaluate your composition with a focus on sentence fluency and make any changes that would improve the flow. Make sure that in your final polishing you do not lose your unique style and an appropriate voice.

TIME OUT TO REFLECT

As you learn more ways to improve your writing style, consider the impact of this improvement on your work in other classes. Is your writing for other subjects getting a better response?

Using a Sentence Fluency Rubric **67**

Project Corner

Speak and Listen Debate Pros and Cons: Lifelines

Some people feel that lifelines give people advantages that only make them lazy; these people believe that everyone is better off struggling on his or her own to achieve success. "If it doesn't kill you," they say, "it makes you stronger." **Debate this issue** as a class, using either formal or informal debating techniques. (You can find information on group discussions and oral presentations on pages 457–464 and 468–470.)

Get Dramatic Act It Out

In your writing group, select one person's memoir and **prepare a short play** that you either perform for the class or record and show to the class. Be sure to capture the mood of the story in your script and express the overall theme or underlying meaning the story conveys. (You can find information on writing scripts on pages 192–200 and on making videos on pages 480–485.)

Communicate with Technology
Twitter or Blog

Send a tweet in which you answer the question "What's happening?" with a pointer to a story in the local or national news about how someone has helped someone else by throwing a lifeline. What kinds of responses do you get? Or **write in your blog** about the role of lifelines in a healthy society. Who in society should receive lifelines? Who should provide the lifelines?

In Everyday Life
Oral Announcement

1. During National Fire Prevention Week, your school is inviting one student each day to deliver a fire safety message over the intercom. ***Prepare and deliver an oral announcement*** explaining a potentially life-saving strategy students can use. Remember that your audience is made up of listeners, not readers. Be sure to make your style and voice appropriate for the situation, purpose, and audience. (You can find information on oral presentations on pages 457–464.)

In the Workplace Memo

2. You have recently been promoted in your job at WZAP, a local television station. Your new task is to recommend four classic programs for the station's Saturday morning cartoon line-up. ***Write a memo to your boss*** listing your four favorite Saturday morning shows. Explain in concise terms what you like about each program. Vary your sentence beginnings and avoid redundancy. Try to make your writing style vivid and clear so your boss can see an image of each show in his mind. (You can find information on writing business memos on pages 451–453.)

Timed Writing ⏱ Album Review Rewrite

3. You run *The Groove Gazette,* an online music newsletter. You want to run a review of a new album, *Head 2 Paradise* by the Blister Sisters, but the writer's submission needs work. Revise the following review using specific words, varied sentences, and fresh language rather than clichés. Trim away wordiness, the passive voice, and redundancy. Use transitions to combine sentences and create flow. Also use rhetorical devices to convey subtle meaning. You have 15 minutes to complete your work.

> The Blister Sisters' *Head 2 Paradise* is like the pot of gold at the end of the rainbow. In collaborating on this album, the Sisters really worked together. Due to the fact that a record was not made by them since *Porcupine Love,* I feared that the Sisters might sound rusty, but I was relieved to hear an album tailor-made for all the fans who follow their music. *Head 2 Paradise* has a slow song. It is called "Chalkboard Blues." It is a sad song that made me feel pensive. The mellow new sound is a breath of fresh air.

After You Write Evaluate your review with the rubrics on pages 25, 53, and 67.

Structuring Writing

The **structure** of a written text is the arrangement of its parts.

Structures for texts take a variety of forms, as the following examples show.

- **A letter from an employer** begins with "Dear Applicant," continues with the news that the recipient has gotten the job, and ends with "Sincerely yours."

- **A fairy tale begins with "Once upon a time,"** moves on to tell a story with a conflict and a resolution, and ends with "And they all lived happily ever after."

- **A restaurant menu begins with appetizers,** moves on to main courses, and finally ends with desserts.

- **A biologist writes a hypothesis** about predators and their prey and then gathers evidence to test the hypothesis.

Writing Project

***Survival!* Write a carefully structured essay about someone or something that survives a threat.**

Think Through Writing The worlds of nature and society reward those who survive: animals or plants that withstand threats while preying on other life forms, people who endure through challenges and threats, even yourself if you have lived through dangerous circumstances. Choose a living subject you regard as a survivor. What is this person, creature, or plant? What threatens its life or well-being? What does it rely on to survive or defeat these threats? Write informally on this subject and explain in detail how it copes with threatening situations and grows into a stronger being.

Talk About It In a group of three to five students, discuss the subjects you have chosen. What characterizes the qualities, abilities, and natural defenses each subject calls on to survive? What characterizes the threats to its survival and health? What is common to the subjects and situations that each writer has focused on?

Read About It In the following account, Charles G. Finney describes a baby rattlesnake and its survival skills that enable it to compete and thrive in a dangerous world. Think about how the rattlesnake's condition compares to the ones you have written about and discussed in your writing group.

> MODEL: Structured Writing

From

The Life and Death of a Western Gladiator

Charles G. Finney

He was born on a summer morning in the shady mouth of a cave. Three others were born with him, another male and two females. Each was about five inches long and slimmer than a lead pencil.

Their mother left them a few hours after they were born. A day after that his brother and sisters left him also. He was all alone. Nobody cared whether he lived or died. His tiny brain was very dull. He had no arms or legs. His skin was delicate. Nearly everything that walked on the ground or burrowed in it, that flew in the air or swam in the water or climbed trees was his enemy. But he didn't know that. He knew nothing at all. He was aware of his own existence, and that was the sum of his knowledge.

The direct rays of the sun could, in a short time, kill him. If the temperature dropped too low he would freeze. Without food he would starve. Without moisture he would die of dehydration. If a man or a horse stepped on him he would be crushed. If anything chased him he could run neither very far nor very fast.

Thus it was at the hour of his birth. Thus it would be, with modifications, all his life.

But against these drawbacks he had certain qualifications that fitted him to be a competitive creature of this world and equipped him for its warfare. He could exist a long time without food or water. His very smallness at birth protected him when he most needed protection. Instinct provided him with what he lacked in experience. In order to eat he first had to kill, and he was eminently adapted for killing. In sacs

The first sentence in this paragraph states the topic for the paragraph: the snake's traits that would help it survive.

in his jaws he secreted a virulent[1] poison. To inject that poison he had two fangs, hollow and pointed. Without that poison and those fangs he would have been among the most helpless creatures on earth. With them he was among the deadliest.

He was, of course, a baby rattlesnake, a desert diamondback, named *Crotalus atrox* by the herpetologists[2] Baird and Girard and so listed in the *Catalogue of North American Reptiles* in its issue of 1853. He was grayish brown in color, with a series of large, dark, diamond-shaped blotches on his back. His tail was white with five black crossbands. It had a button on the end of it.

Little Crotalus lay in the dust in the mouth of his cave. Some of his kinfolk lay there too. It was their home. That particular tribe of rattlers had lived there for scores of years.

The cave had never been seen by a white man.

Sometimes as many as two hundred rattlers occupied the den. Sometimes the numbers shrunk to as few as forty or fifty.

The tribe members did nothing at all for each other except breed. They hunted singly; they never shared food. They derived some automatic degree of safety from their numbers, but their actions were never concerted toward using their numbers to any end. If any enemy attacked one of them, the others did nothing about it.

Young Crotalus's brother was the first of the litter to go out into the world and the first to die. He achieved a distance of fifty feet from the den when a Sonoran racer, four feet long and hungry, came upon him. The little rattler, despite his poison fangs, was a tidbit. The racer, long skilled in such arts, snatched him up by the head and swallowed him down. Powerful digestive juices in the racer's stomach did the rest. Then the racer, appetite whetted, prowled around until it found one of Crotalus's little sisters. She went the way of the brother.

Nemesis[3] of the second sister was a chaparral cock. This cuckoo, or road runner as it is called, found the baby amid some rocks, uttered a cry of delight, scissored

---

1 **virulent:** Extremely malignant.
2 **herpetologists:** Researchers who study reptiles.
3 **nemesis:** A victorious rival, from the name of a Greek goddess.

it by the neck, shook it until it was almost lifeless, banged and pounded it upon a rock until life had indeed left it, and then gulped it down.

Crotalus, somnolent[4] in a cranny of the cave's mouth, neither knew nor cared. Even if he had, there was nothing he could have done about it.

On the fourth day of his life he decided to go out into the world himself. He rippled forth uncertainly, the transverse[5] plates on his belly serving him as legs.

He could see things well enough within his limited range, but a five-inch-long snake can command no great field of vision. He had an excellent sense of smell. But, having no ears, he was stone deaf. On the other hand, he had a pit, a deep pock mark between eye and nostril. Unique, this organ was sensitive to animal heat. In pitch blackness, Crotalus, by means of the heat messages recorded in his pit, could tell whether another animal was near and could also judge its size. . . .

> Each sentence in this paragraph tells something about the snake's senses. Most of the paragraph focuses on the snake's most distinctive sense, its ability to sense heat.

The single button on his tail could not, of course, yet rattle. Crotalus wouldn't be able to rattle until that button had grown into three segments. Then he would be able to buzz.

He had a wonderful tongue. It looked like an exposed nerve and was probably exactly that. It was weird, and Crotalus thrust it in and out as he traveled. It told him things that neither his eyes nor his nose nor his pit told him.

Snake fashion, Crotalus went forth, not knowing where he was going, for he had never been anywhere before. Hunger was probably his prime mover.[6] In order to satisfy that hunger, he had to find something smaller than himself and kill it.

He came upon a baby lizard sitting in the sand. Eyes, nose, pit, and tongue told Crotalus it was there. Instinct told him what it was and what to do. Crotalus gave a tiny one-inch strike and bit the lizard. His poison killed it. He took it by the head and swallowed it. Thus was his first meal.

> The last sentence in this paragraph provides a conclusion to the events described in the paragraph.

---

4 **somnolent**: Drowsy.
5 **transverse**: Crosswise.
6 **prime mover**: The source of motion.

During his first two years, Crotalus grew rapidly. He attained a length of two feet; his tail had five rattles on it and its button. He rarely bothered with lizards any more, preferring baby rabbits, chipmunks, and roundtailed ground squirrels. Because of his slow locomotion,[7] he could not run down these agile little things. He had to contrive[8] instead to be where they were when they would pass. Then he struck swiftly, injected his poison, and ate them after they died.

At two he was formidable.[9] He had grown past the stage where a racer or a road runner could safely tackle him. He had grown to the size where other desert dwellers—coyotes, foxes, coatis, wildcats—knew it was better to leave him alone. . . .

---

7 **locomotion**: Way of moving from place to place.
8 **contrive**: To plan with cleverness; scheme.
9 **formidable**: Arousing fear; inspiring awe.

Respond in Writing Write about how the rattlesnakes survive. How are they like and unlike the survivors your group members have chosen as subjects?

Develop Your Own Traits Chart Work with your classmates to come up with your own ideas on qualities needed for survival.

Small Groups: In your writing group, create a chart that describes the characteristics of the survivors from your own writing and from Finney's.

Whole Class: Share your chart with the class while a student records each survival trait on a large sheet of paper or on the board. You can refer to this master chart as you write your essay.

Write About It You will write an informative text on your subject's survival. Use the following possibilities or others of your choice.

Possible Topics	Possible Audiences	Possible Forms
• a first-year student in a high school	• other students	• a guide to incoming students about high school
• a migrating goose	• the school's science club	• a formal report
• a palm tree in a hurricane-prone environment	• the television weather station	• a script for a special report
• a young teenager in a dangerous neighborhood	• the police	• a letter to the police commissioner

You will be creating most of the texts you write by forming a series of paragraphs. Each paragraph is made up of sentences. While each sentence *expresses* a complete thought, a paragraph *develops* a thought.

A **paragraph** is a group of related sentences that present and develop one main idea.

1 Paragraph Structure

In a good paragraph, every sentence plays a role. Notice the role of each sentence in the paragraph that follows, also from "The Life and Death of a Western Gladiator."

His venom was his only weapon, for he had no power of constriction. Yellowish in color, his poison was odorless and tasteless. It was a highly complex mixture of proteins, each in itself direly toxic. His venom worked on the blood. The more poison he injected with a bite, the more dangerous the wound. The pain rendered by his bite was instantaneous, and the shock accompanying it was profound. Swelling began immediately, to be followed by a ghastly oozing. Injected directly into a large vein, his poison brought death quickly, for the victim died when it reached his heart.

Topic Sentence: States the main idea

Supporting Sentences: Develop the main idea

Concluding Sentence: Adds a strong ending

Paragraph structure varies. While the model paragraph begins with a topic sentence and ends with a concluding sentence, you might construct a paragraph differently. You might express the main idea in two sentences rather than one. You might put the topic sentence in the middle or end of the paragraph. You might not end with a concluding sentence, particularly if the paragraph is part of a longer composition. Whatever structure you choose, the most important goal is to make sure the main idea is clear.

Guidelines for a One-Paragraph Composition

- Make your main idea clear.
- Develop your main idea fully.
- Provide a strong ending.

You may accomplish these three goals by including a clear topic sentence, a body of supporting sentences, and an effective concluding sentence in your paragraph.

TOPIC SENTENCE

Wherever your topic sentence appears—as the first sentence in the paragraph, the last sentence, or any one of the middle sentences—it serves the same purpose.

A **topic sentence** states the main idea of the paragraph.

Because it states the main idea, a topic sentence is usually more general than the sentences that develop that idea. At the same time, the topic sentence is specific enough to be developed adequately in one paragraph.

FEATURES OF A TOPIC SENTENCE

A topic sentence:

- states the main idea.
- focuses the limited subject to one main point that can be adequately covered in the paragraph.

MODEL: Topic Sentence

The Heavy Task of Fighting Fires

Fighting a major fire takes tremendous strength and endurance. The protective clothing that a fire fighter wears into a burning building will weigh more than 20 pounds. To protect himself from the smoke, the fire fighter will usually wear an oxygen tank and mask. These self-contained breathing units may weigh as much as 50 pounds. The weight of the hose and other tools that the fire fighter carries will raise the total weight to more than 100 pounds.

Topic Sentence

—Walter Brown and
Norman Anderson, *Fires*

As the following example shows, the topic sentence in the model is general enough to cover all the details yet specific enough to develop adequately in one paragraph.

Too General   Fire fighting is hard work.

Specific Enough   Fighting a major fire takes tremendous strength and endurance.

● **Practice Your Skills**

Evaluating Topic Sentences

Write the letter of the topic sentence that is specific enough to be covered adequately in a single paragraph.

1. a. Bats use sonar to locate prey.

    b. Bats are complex animals.

2. a. Many people like camping.

    b. Pitching a tent is easy if you follow directions.

● **Practice Your Skills**

Writing Topic Sentences

For each general statement below, write a topic sentence that is specific enough to be developed adequately in a single paragraph.

1. Life can be difficult at times.

2. Good health is important.

3. Holidays are nice.

SUPPORTING SENTENCES

A topic sentence on an interesting subject will usually prompt readers to ask questions as they read. Supporting sentences answer those questions and form the body of the paragraph.

Supporting sentences explain the topic sentence by giving specific details, facts, examples, or reasons.

The following topic sentence begins a paragraph about Robert Peary's successful return from the North Pole.

> ### MODEL: Topic Sentence
>
> On the sixth of September, 1909, the gallant little *Roosevelt* steamed into Indian Harbor, Labrador, and from the wireless tower on top of a cliff two messages flashed out.

Readers will naturally wonder, What were the two messages? The supporting sentences answer that question.

> ### MODEL: Supporting Sentences
>
> The first was to Peary's anxiously waiting wife, more eager, if the truth be known, to hear of her husband's safety than of the discovery of the Pole. This message read: "Have made good at last. I have the Pole. Am well. Love." The second one was to his country, for which he had sacrificed so much. It read: "Stars and Stripes nailed to the North Pole. Peary."
>
> —Marie Peary Stafford, *Discoverer of the North Pole*

When you write supporting sentences, think of the questions readers might ask and then answer those questions.

● **Practice Your Skills**

Writing Supporting Sentences

Write three sentences that would support each item.

1. Styles of dress may reveal people's personalities.

2. Life without a computer seems impossible.

3. Old photographs can help you understand history.

CONCLUDING SENTENCE

A paragraph often needs a concluding sentence to summarize the ideas.

A **concluding sentence** recalls the main idea and adds a strong ending to a paragraph.

Strategies for Ending a Paragraph

- Restate the main idea using different words.
- Summarize the paragraph.
- Add an insight about the main idea.
- Express how you feel about the subject.

An All-Around Player

Although Babe Ruth is best remembered for his home runs, he was also a great pitcher. In 1916, he led the American League in lowest earned-run percentage. He won 23 games that year, including 9 shutouts. The next year he won 24. Until 1961, Ruth held the record for pitching scoreless innings in the World Series. Ruth's impressive pitching statistics show that he was more than a great hitter.

Concluding Sentence

● **Practice Your Skills**

Writing Concluding Sentences

Write three more sentences that could each provide a strong conclusion to the paragraph about Babe Ruth.

PROJECT PREP *Prewriting* *Developing a General Plan*

In your writing group, discuss the possible points you wish to make about your topic and how you would present your explanation. Following is one possible way to organize your thoughts on the subject of surviving threats.

Beginning: Introduce your subject and how it is threatened in general.
Point 1: Discuss one specific threat and how the subject survives it.
Point 2: Discuss a second specific threat and how the subject survives it.
Point 3: Discuss a third specific threat and how the subject survives it.
Point 4: Discuss a fourth specific threat and how the subject survives it.
Additional points: Discuss additional threats and how the subject survives them.
Conclusion: Draw a conclusion about how your subject survives in a threatening world.

After the discussion, make a rough sketch of your composition. You might want to use a simple graphic organizer like the one below.

Beginning: How should I start?

Middle: What points do I want to make?

Ending: How shall I end it?

② Paragraph Development

A topic sentence is like a baseball score. It gives the general idea without the specifics of how the game developed. Readers, like sports fans, want to know the details. They want to see the idea developed play by play.

METHODS OF DEVELOPMENT

You can use a variety of methods to develop a topic sentence.

HERE'S HOW

Strategies for Developing Your Main Idea

- Give descriptive details.
- Give facts, examples, or reasons.
- Relate an incident.
- Make a comparison or draw a contrast.
- Give directions or explain the steps in a process.

> **Writing Tip**
>
> List **details** that suit the main idea of your paragraph and that explain the subject clearly.

ADEQUATE DEVELOPMENT

Insufficiently developed writing makes readers quickly lose interest. Even an interesting idea loses merit if not backed up with sufficient information. The supporting sentences in a paragraph develop the main idea with specific details. These specific details can take the form of facts or examples, reasons, incidents, or descriptive images. Regardless of the form, supporting details must be numerous and specific enough to make the main idea clear, convincing, and interesting. This is called **adequate development.**

The paragraph on the next page provides such ample specific details that readers can clearly picture the subject.

> **Writing Tip**
>
> Use specific details and information to achieve **adequate development** of your main idea.

Childhood Treasures

Aunt Sally's cabinet of art supplies was like a toy chest to me. The top shelf, beyond my reach, had an endless supply of paper. There was stiff, brilliant-white paper for watercolors, blank newsprint for charcoals, glossy paper, dull paper, tracing paper. On the second shelf sat oozing tubes of bright-colored oils, bottles of the blackest ink, and cartons of chalk in sunrise shades of pastels. The third shelf—my favorite—held the damp lumps of gray clay, waiting to be shaped into creatures only my aunt and I would recognize. On the bottom shelves were brushes and rags for cleaning up. Despite the thorough cleanups Aunt Sally insisted on, that cabinet was a paradise of play for me on countless Sunday afternoons.

USING A RUBRIC TO EVALUATE IDEA DEVELOPMENT

Refer to the following rubric to gauge how well you have developed your ideas.

4 Ideas are presented and developed in depth.	3 Most ideas are presented and developed with insight.	2 Many ideas are not well developed.	1 Most ideas are not well developed.
• I developed each idea thoroughly with specific details.	• I developed most ideas thoroughly with specific details.	• I tried to develop ideas but was more general than specific.	• I was more general than specific.
• My presentation of ideas is original.	• My presentation of some ideas is thoughtul.	• I listed rather than developed ideas.	• I listed rather than developed ideas.
• I made meaningful connections among ideas.	• I made some connections among ideas.	• I made few connections among ideas.	• I did not make connections among ideas.
• I took some risks to make my writing come alive.	• I played it safe and did not really put much of myself into the composition.	• I left a few things out but I think my meaning comes across.	• I left some important things out so my meaning isn't really clear.

PROJECT PREP *Evaluating* *Developing Ideas*

In your writing group, discuss each person's main idea, ways to develop it adequately, and where additional information about each subject can be located. Take notes. You can use them when you create a second draft.

③ Unity

In developing a paragraph fully, avoid straying from the main idea, which can confuse the reader. In a well-developed paragraph, all the supporting sentences relate directly to the main idea expressed in the topic sentence. This quality of a well-written paragraph is called **unity.** It is also called **focus.**

> ### Writing Tip
>
> Achieve **unity** by deleting sentences that do not relate directly to the paragraph's main idea.

In the following example, sentences that detract from the focus of the paragraph are underlined.

MODEL: A Paragraph Lacking Unity

Candlelight

Candles, which go back to prehistoric times, were a chief source of light for 2,000 years. The first candle may have been discovered by accident when a piece of wood or cord fell into a pool of lighted fat. In ancient times crude candles were made from fats wrapped in husks or moss. <u>Early people also used torches.</u> Later a wick was placed inside a candle mold, and melted wax was poured into the mold. Candles could be used to carry light from place to place and could be stored indefinitely. <u>The first lamps used a dish of oil and a wick.</u>

Although the underlined sentences relate to the general subject, they do not relate directly to the specific main idea expressed in the topic sentence.

● **Practice Your Skills**

Checking for Unity

Write the two sentences that destroy the paragraph's unity.

The First Cheap Car

Henry Ford was not the first person to build a car, but he was the first to figure out how to make cars cheaply. His assembly-line methods resulted in huge savings and changed the car from a luxury to a necessity. The mass-produced Model T sold for about $400, a price the average wage earner could afford. Ford sold over 15 million cars from 1908 to 1927. Ford reduced the workday for his employees from nine to eight hours. He set the minimum wage at $5 a day. By building a cheap, easy-to-operate car, Ford changed the nation.

PROJECT PREP *Drafting* *First Quick Draft*

1. Using all your work so far, write a quick draft including everything you know or have learned about your subject. You can use the plan you developed in the graphic organizer (see page 79), but write quickly just to get your thoughts down on paper.

2. Exchange papers with a partner. Read each other's drafts. Is there anything that does not belong? If so, point it out. Delete unnecessary points in your own draft.

4 Coherence

In a **coherent** paragraph, each idea leads logically and smoothly to the next.

HERE'S HOW

Strategies for Achieving Coherence

- Organize your ideas logically.
- Use transitional words and phrases.
- Occasionally repeat key words.
- Use synonyms or alternative expressions in place of key words.
- Use pronouns in place of key words.

Writing Tip

Achieve **coherence** by presenting ideas in logical order and by using transitions.

CHRONOLOGICAL ORDER

This kind of order, also called time order, is used in stories to tell what happened first, second, third, and so on. It is also used to explain a sequence of steps in a process.

MODEL: Chronological Order

Cracking an Ancient Code

The Rosetta Stone was discovered in 1799, but the ancient Egyptian hieroglyphics on it were a mystery. The first person to try cracking the code was Silvestre de Sacy. He figured out that some signs referred to proper names, but the rest stumped him. Then a Swedish expert, David Akerblad, made a little more progress. Next, Sir Thomas Young discovered that some of the signs stood for sounds as well as ideas. Finally, Jean François Champollion tackled the code. He had his first breakthrough in 1821. The puzzle pieces then began to fall swiftly into place. Others paved the way, but Champollion deserves the credit for discovering a 1,500-year-old secret.

SPATIAL ORDER

Spatial order is used in descriptions to show how objects are related in location.

A Formidable Mountain Barrier

The Sierra Nevada is a chain of peaks 400 miles long, longer than any one range of the American Rockies. The range stretches from Tehachapi Pass in the south nearly to Lassen Peak in the north where the Sierra block disappears beneath sheets of younger volcanic rocks. The Sierra's western flank rises gradually from one of the world's richest agricultural areas, the great Central Valley, while to the east the mountains rise in a magnificent abrupt escarpment to soar 7,000 to 10,000 feet above the arid basin of the Owens Valley. With not a single river passing through the range, the Sierra forms a formidable mountain barrier.

—Fred Beckey, *Mountains of North America*

ORDER OF IMPORTANCE, INTEREST, OR DEGREE

This method is often used in paragraphs that describe, persuade, or explain. It presents ideas in order of importance, interest, or size.

Training a Seeing-Eye Dog

Dogs who will aid the blind must be trained to overcome some basic fears. To learn how to keep calm in a crowd, the dogs are taken to playgrounds when students are leaving school. The dogs are sharply corrected if they get excited in all the bustle. To overcome any fear of loud noises, they must hold still while blanks are fired above their heads. Sometimes they are even trained on an airport runway. Especially important is overcoming a fear of heights, for the day may come when a dog will have to lead its master down a fire escape. A well-trained dog is more than a pair of eyes; it can also be a lifesaver.

SEQUENTIAL ORDER

This method is used in paragraphs that explain how to do something or how something works. It can also be used in paragraphs that explain a cause and effect.

MODEL: Sequential Order

Rope Jumping for Tennis Players

There are very few exercises that really help a tennis player get in shape and stay there. One form of exercise that I strongly urge on a player is to skip rope. It is wonderful for the wind and legs. If it is to do you any good at all, it must be done systematically, and not just now and again. Start slowly for your first week or so. Jump a normal "two-foot" skip, not over ten times without resting, but repeat five separate tens and, if possible, do it morning and evening. Take the ten up to twenty after two days, then in a week to fifty. Once you can do that, begin to vary the type of skipping. Skip ten times on one foot, then ten times on the other. Add a fifty at just double your normal speed. Once that is all mastered, simply take ten minutes in the evening and skip hard, any way you want and at any speed. Let your own intelligence direct you to what gives you the best results. Remember always that stamina is one of the deciding factors in all long, closely contested tennis matches, so work to attain the peak of physical conditioning when you need it most.

—Bill Tilden, *How to Play Better Tennis*

TRANSITIONS

Transitional words and phrases connect your ideas. The chart below lists commonly used transitions used with various forms of order.

You can learn more about ordering information on pages 20–21 and 84–88.

COMMONLY USED TRANSITIONS

Order of Importance	Chronological/ Sequential Order	Spatial Order	General Transitions
even more	after	above	also
finally	as soon as	ahead	besides
first	at first	behind	despite
more important	at last	below	for example
most	first, second	beneath	however
one reason	later	inside	in addition
to begin with	meanwhile	outside	while

Revising for Coherence

Revise the following paragraph, adding needed transitional words and phrases.

Days of Our Lives

Although the calendar we use today is the most accurate one yet devised, it has many irregularities. We have two different types of years: common years and leap years. The number of days in each month varies. April and June have 30 days. May and July have 31 and February 28 or 29. Many holidays fall on a different day each year, which causes considerable confusion. The calendar we use today has been keeping time successfully for more than 400 years.

● Practice Your Skills

Identifying Method of Organization

Write *chronological, spatial, sequential,* or *order of importance, interest, or degree* to identify the method of organization used in "Childhood Treasures" on page 81.

PROJECT PREP *Drafting* **Ordering**

Look back over your general plan (page 79) and first quick draft. Decide which organizational strategy to use to present your information. In your writing group, describe your strategy and listen for feedback. Offer suggestions to other members of your group on their plans.

CHAPTER 3

Using an Organization Rubric

Use the following rubric to determine how effectively you have organized a composition.

4 Ideas progress smoothly and the organizational strategies clarify meaning.	3 Most ideas progress smoothly and the organizational strategies are clear.	2 Some ideas progress smoothly but the organizational pattern is not consistent.	1 Few ideas progress smoothly and there is no clear organization.
• I stated the main idea creatively in the introduction and captured attention. • I used the best organization pattern to present the supporting paragraphs. • My conclusion helped make the composition feel complete. • My paragraphs and sentences flowed smoothly from one into another. • I used transitions to keep the order clear.	• I stated the main idea in the introduction and captured attention. • I used an appropriate organization pattern to present the supporting paragraphs. • My conclusion helped make the composition feel complete. • Most but not all of my paragraphs and sentences flowed smoothly from one into another. • I used some transitions to keep the order clear.	• I stated the main idea in the introduction but did not capture attention. • I used an appropriate organization pattern to present the supporting paragraphs but had some things out of order. • My conclusion provided an ending but it did not feel strong. • I repeated some ideas unnecessarily. • I could have used more transitions to keep the order clear.	• I did not state my main idea clearly. • I did not really use an organizational pattern. • I forgot about writing a conclusion. • I repeated some things and also had some things out of order or not related to the topic. • I did not use many transitions so the order was hard to follow.

TIME OUT TO REFLECT

As you work to improve your skills for developing topic, supporting, and concluding sentences, what have you learned about your writing? What are your strengths and weaknesses? On what areas do you spend the most time? In what areas do you feel confident? Do you have a talent for writing strong conclusions but find that your supporting sentences lack some necessary details? Take some time to note any weaknesses in your writing and jot down strategies for correcting them in the future. Record your thoughts in the Learning Log section of your journal.

The Power of Language ⚡

Parallelism: The Power of 3s

Informational writing does not have to plod along, one sentence after another, but can be enlivened with a variety of grammatical options, as Charles Finney amply demonstrates in his descriptive piece about the rattlesnake. One device he uses is **parallelism:** the same kind of word or group of words, grammatically speaking, in a series of three or more. Read the following sentence aloud, noticing the impact of the series of verbs:

> This cuckoo, or road runner as it is called, found the baby [snake] amid some rocks, uttered a cry of delight, scissored it by the neck, shook it until it was almost lifeless, banged and pounded it upon a rock until life had indeed left it, and then gulped it down.

Why do you think Finney chose to describe all these actions in one sentence? What effect does that have on you as a reader?

Now look at another way to express action in a series of parallel elements, from Annie Dillard's "Living Like Weasels" (pages 141–144):

> Or did the eagle eat what he could, gutting the living weasel with his talons before his breast, bending his beak, cleaning the beautiful airborne bones?

Compare the effect of this series of participial phrases with the effect of the parallel verbs in the first example.

Try It Yourself

Think about some person or animal whose actions you might describe in an informative piece. Brainstorm for possibilities, choose one, and write a sentence with at least three parallel verb phrases, as in the sentence from Finney's piece. Then follow the same steps again, this time using three participial phrases to convey the action.

Punctuation Tip

Use commas to separate items in a series. Use a comma before the final item and the word *and*.

Paragraph Writing Workshops

1 Narrative Paragraphs

Any time your purpose in writing is to tell what happened, you will be writing a narrative. Learning how to write a narrative paragraph will help you develop the skills for any kind of narrative writing.

A **narrative paragraph** tells a real or imaginary story.

Structuring a Narrative Paragraph

- In the **topic sentence,** capture the reader's attention and make a general statement that sets the scene.
- In the **supporting sentences,** tell the story event by event, often building suspense.
- In the **concluding sentence,** show the outcome, summarize the story, or add an insight.

MODEL: Narrative Paragraph

Rescue!

For thirteen-year-old Karen Edwards, July 17, 1972, became a day to remember. She was resting on the side of a motel pool in Duncansville, Pennsylvania, when she saw a young boy struggling in the deep end. Then she saw the boy's father dive in after him and not come up. While others stood by, Karen jumped in and towed the drowning boy to the side. Tired but not waiting to rest, she went back for the father, who was floating face down. As she dragged him to the side, he began struggling, his waving arms splashing water in Karen's eyes. Her chest heaving, she finally made it to the side of the pool, and in a few minutes father, son, and Karen were all well. Karen's quick thinking and heroic effort had saved two lives.

— L. B. Taylor, Jr., *Rescue!*

Topic Sentence

Supporting Sentences

Concluding Sentence

You can make a storyboard like the one below to help you plan a narrative paragraph. Include as many events as necessary to tell the story fully.

| Triggering Event | Next Event | Next Event | Climax | Outcome |

QuickGuide for Writing Narrative Paragraphs

→ Brainstorm, write freely, tell your story out loud, or create a storyboard to think of all the events in the story you want to tell. When you have them all, arrange them in chronological order.

→ Include the event that started the story in motion, the conflict and how it was approached, and the resolution.

→ Use transitions such as *first, the next day, at last* to keep the order clear.

→ Include a clear introduction and conclusion.

→ Collaborate with a partner, sharing drafts and making suggestions for improvements.

● Create Real-World Texts

1. Write a paragraph telling the story of a "first" in your life.

2. Write a story about a relative or ancestor who has become part of your family lore. Make an audio recording of your story and play it for family members.

3. Write a plot summary of a movie you have recently seen or know well.

4. Write about a decisive battle for your social studies class.

5. Relate to your brother the story of how you broke the mp3 player he let you borrow.

② Descriptive Paragraphs

Any time your writing purpose is to give someone a picture they can "see" in their minds, you will be writing a description. Learning how to write a descriptive paragraph will help you develop the skills for any kind of descriptive writing.

Descriptive writing creates a vivid picture in words of a person, an object, or a scene.

 Structuring a Descriptive Paragraph

- In the **topic sentence,** make a general statement about the subject and suggest an overall impression.
- In the **supporting sentences,** supply specific details that help readers use their five senses to bring the picture to life.
- In the **concluding sentence,** summarize the overall impression of the subject.

MODEL: Descriptive Paragraph

The Big Day

 The most important game of the year was almost under way. José Magarolas of our team crouched at center court, waiting to jump against Tech's big man. Positioned so that the tips of their sneakers nearly touched the white arc of the jump circle, our forwards, Jimmy Jones and Don Fox, stood against Tech's forwards. All four pairs of eyes already looked up into the space where the ball would soon be tossed. Outside the jump circle, behind one pair of forwards, Blake Roberts and a Tech guard of equal height readied themselves. Ken Wan, our captain, and Tech's other guard jogged to their positions at opposite ends of the court, still farther outside the center circle. The lights of the scoreboard showed only "Home 00, Visitor 00." Leaping and shouting along the edges of the court, cheerleaders for both teams stirred the crowd. From every seat around the court, in a multitude of red and green hues, Central and Tech fans screamed their delight that the championship game was about to begin.

Topic Sentence

Supporting Sentences

Concluding Sentence

You can make a wheel-spoke diagram like the one on the following page to help you plan a descriptive paragraph. Your overall impression goes in the center.

QuickGuide for Writing Descriptive Paragraphs

→ Brainstorm, write freely, or draw a picture to help you think of vivid sensory details that would bring your subject to life.

→ Choose details to create an overall impression, and organize them in spatial order or another logical order.

→ Use transitions such as *beyond, on the other side,* and *to the right* to keep the order clear.

→ Include a clear introduction and conclusion.

→ Collaborate with a partner, sharing drafts and making suggestions for improvements.

● **Create Real-World Texts**

1. Write a paragraph for an ad in the newspaper describing an item you want to sell.

2. Think of a TV show you like and know well. For a game, describe the setting without naming it and ask a friend to guess which show you are describing.

3. Describe a parade for a newspaper story.

3 Expository Paragraphs

Expository writing is the most common and practical of the four types of writing. In writing an expository paragraph, your goal is always to help your readers understand something. Any time your purpose is to explain or to inform, you will be using expository writing. Expository writing is also known as **informative** or **explanatory writing.**

Expository writing explains or informs.

Structuring an Expository Paragraph

- In the **topic sentence,** introduce the subject and state the main idea.
- In the **supporting sentences,** supply specific details such as facts and examples that support the main idea.
- In the **concluding sentence,** draw a conclusion about the subject or in other ways bring the paragraph to a strong ending.

MODEL: Expository How-To Paragraph

Orphans from the Wild

A small baby [mammal] that has no hair or whose eyes are not yet open may be picked up in your bare hands. Gently slide your fingers under the baby, scoop it up, and cradle it in your palms. Most babies, particularly very small ones, will enjoy the warmth of your hands. Adjust your fingers to fit snugly around the baby, so it can absorb the maximum warmth from your fingers, but not so snugly that it can't shift its position. The tiny, hairless baby will become quiet almost at once and will soon drop off to sleep.

—William J. Weber, *Wild Orphan Babies*

Topic Sentence

Supporting Sentences

Concluding Sentence

You might want to use one of the graphic organizers on pages 241–253 to help you organize your paragraph.

QuickGuide for Writing Expository Paragraphs

→ Brainstorm, write freely, or talk with others to help you think of facts, examples, reasons, or steps in a process that would help you explain your subject.

→ Arrange the details in a logical order. (See pages 84–86.)

→ Use transitions such as *for example, in contrast*, and *however* to keep the order clear.

→ Include a clear introduction and conclusion.

→ Collaborate with a partner, sharing drafts and making suggestions for improvements.

● **Create Real-World Texts**

1. Send an e-mail to an older relative explaining what a typical day at school is like.

2. For health class, explain how to read the nutritional label on packaged food.

3. Write a paragraph to yourself planning the week ahead.

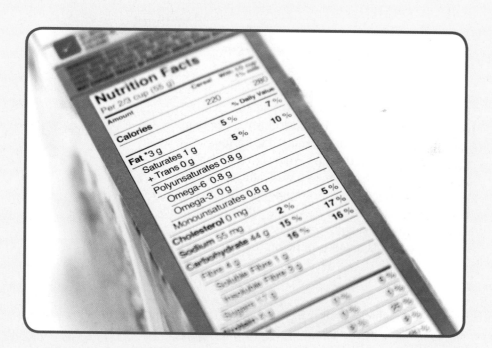

4 Persuasive Paragraphs

Whenever you are defending or disagreeing with a viewpoint or an action, you are using your skills of persuasion. Learning how to write a persuasive paragraph will help you develop the skills for any kind of persuasive writing. The kind of persuasive writing you will most commonly do in school is called **argumentative writing.**

Persuasive writing states an opinion or claim and uses facts, examples, and reasons to convince readers. See pages 254-283 for more on argument.

Structuring a Persuasive Paragraph

- In the **topic sentence,** assert an opinion or claim.
- In the **supporting sentences,** back up your assertion with facts, examples, reasons, and, if necessary, citations from experts. Appeal to the reader's reason but also engage the reader by appealing to emotion as well.
- In the **concluding sentence,** restate the assertion and draw a conclusion that follows from the supporting details.

MODEL: Persuasive Paragraph

UFOs?

Although the United States Air Force has dismissed reports of UFOs, there is so much evidence that UFOs exist that we should take them seriously. More than 12,000 sightings have been reported to various organizations and authorities. Many of these reports were made by pilots, engineers, air-traffic controllers, and other reliable people. According to a Gallup poll, five million Americans believe they have sighted UFOs, and some have even taken photographs. The great number of sightings warrants an open mind on the subject of UFOs.

Topic Sentence

Supporting Sentences

Concluding Sentence

You can make a graphic organizer like the one on the following page to help you plan a persuasive paragraph. The arrows represent transitional words and phrases.

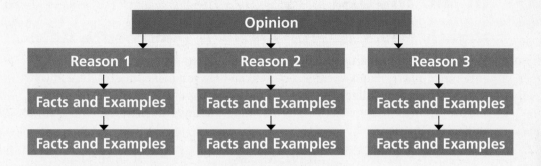

QuickGuide for Writing Persuasive Paragraphs

→ In discussions or through reading or watching television, identify subjects about which you have a strong opinion.

→ Brainstorm, write freely, or talk with others to help you think of facts, examples, reasons, or steps in a process that would help you back up your opinion.

→ Arrange the details in a logical order. (See pages 84–86.)

→ Use transitions such as *for example, in contrast,* and *most important* to keep the order clear.

→ Include a clear introduction and conclusion.

→ Collaborate with a partner, sharing drafts and making suggestions for improvements.

● **Create Real-World Texts**

1. Send a letter to the editor of your local newspaper expressing an opinion on a current civic event.

2. Your family is trying to decide where to go on vacation. Write a paragraph suggesting a place and giving reasons for your choice.

3. You want your class to lead the way on a school-wide canned food drive. Write an announcement to read to your class convincing them that the food drive is a good idea.

In the Media

Nightly News, Newsmagazines, Documentaries

Though they are primarily visual media, TV broadcasts also pay attention to structure. Understanding these structures can help you make the structure of your texts as strong as possible. The chart below shows the characteristics, elements, and arrangement that make three forms unique: the nightly news, newsmagazines, and documentaries.

NIGHTLY NEWS	NEWSMAGAZINES	DOCUMENTARIES
very brief (two to three minutes)	usually twenty-minute segments	fifty minutes or longer
introduction by anchor	introduction by anchor	dramatic visual before introduction
brief videotape shots	lengthy videos	carefully crafted
brief interview or quote from person involved	lengthy interviews/ multiple quotes and sources	multiple quotes and sources, real-life conversations
editing to stay within time limit, balanced presentation	editing with much concern for effect and balance	editing to enhance overall effect— music and voiceover added
closing by anchor	closing by anchor	conclusion strong
can be made on day news happens	requires preparation time (weeks at least)	requires longest preparation time

Media Activity

For practice, view an example of each of these visual media. Then describe how each type might present a major news event. Write a paragraph for each medium telling what the story might be like, giving special attention to how the length of each type might affect the quality and balance of the coverage. Then write another paragraph explaining how you might improve your writing by using some of the techniques used in these media.

Compositions

Effective communication in writing usually involves more than a single paragraph. On many subjects, you need to write several paragraphs to fully develop your main idea and communicate what you want to say. In short, you need to write a composition. Paragraphs within a composition can have a number of purposes. They can introduce the topic, provide supporting material, serve as a transition, and provide a conclusion.

The composition is one of the most flexible and familiar pieces of writing. You can use the composition form for a variety of purposes: to explain or inform, to create, to persuade, and to express your thoughts and feelings.

1 Structure of a Composition

A composition has three main parts—an introduction, a body, and a conclusion. As the following chart shows, these three parts of a composition parallel the three-part structure of a paragraph.

Paragraph Structure		Composition Structure
	Introduction	
topic sentence that introduces the subject and expresses the main idea	←⌣⌣→	introductory paragraph that introduces the subject and expresses the main idea in a **thesis statement** (See pages 101–102.)
	Body	
supporting sentences	←⌣⌣→	supporting paragraphs
	Conclusion	
concluding sentence	←⌣⌣→	concluding paragraph

As you read the following composition, notice how the three-part structure introduces the thesis statement and works to present the subject.

Cat Lovers, Dog Lovers

One controversy in this highly controversial era is that between those who love only cats and those who love only dogs. "I love dogs, but I can't stand cats" is a statement I often hear; or "I hate dogs, but I adore cats." I stand firmly on my belief that both dogs and cats give richness to life, and both have been invaluable to humankind down the ages.

Introduction

Thesis Statement

Historians agree that dogs moved into humans' orbit in primitive days when they helped hunt, warned of the approach of enemies, and fought off marauding wildlife. In return, bones and scraps were tossed to them, and they shared the warmth of the first fires. Gradually they became part of the family clan.

Body Paragraphs

As for cats, it was cats who saved Egypt from starvation during a period when rats demolished the grain supplies. . . . When the cats died, they were embalmed and were put in the tombs of the Pharaohs along with jewels, garments, and stores of food to help masters in their journey to the land of the gods. There was even a cat goddess, and a good many bas-reliefs picture her.

So far as service to humankind goes, I do not see why we should discriminate between dogs and cats. Both have walked the long roads of history with humankind. As for me, I do not feel a house is well-furnished without both dogs and cats, preferably at least two of each. I am sorry for people who limit their lives by excluding either. I was fortunate to grow up with kittens and puppies and wish every child could have that experience.

Conclusion

—Gladys Taber, *Country Chronicle*

● **Practice Your Skills**

Analyzing a Composition

Write answers to the following questions about "Cat Lovers, Dog Lovers."

1. What is the main idea that the author expresses in the introduction?
2. How does each paragraph of the body relate to the thesis statement?
3. What is the conclusion? How does it relate to the main idea?

PROJECT PREP *Prewriting* *Review and Evaluate*

Look back over the prewriting work you have done so far. Evaluate your plan. Does it still seem like the best way to proceed with your composition? If not, revise it.

② Introduction of a Composition

Like the topic sentence of a paragraph, the introduction of a composition prepares the reader for what will follow. When you write a short composition, you can usually complete the introduction in one paragraph.

FUNCTIONS OF THE INTRODUCTION

- It introduces the subject of your composition.

- It states or implies your purpose for writing.

- It presents the main idea of your composition in a thesis statement.

- It establishes your tone.

- It captures your readers' interest.

THESIS STATEMENT

The thesis statement is usually a single sentence. It may appear anywhere in the first paragraph, although it often has the strongest impact when it is first or last.

The **thesis statement** states the main or controlling idea and makes the purpose of the composition clear.

In the following example, the thesis statement is highlighted.

> **MODEL: Thesis Statement**
>
> My coming to America in 1979 was not very pleasant. When I was twelve, my parents had to leave my homeland, Vietnam. We lived near My Tho all my years and I did not want to leave, but they said we must. My two sisters were younger, four and seven, and they did not know what it meant to leave. My mother said that we must not tell any of our friends, that our going was a secret. It was hard for me to think I would never see my home or some of my family again. Some of my story I tell here I remember well, but some is not clear and is from stories my family tells.
>
> —Hieu Huynh, "Coming to America"

● Practice Your Skills

Identifying Thesis Statements

Read the following introductory paragraph and write the thesis statement. Then below the thesis statement, identify the purpose for writing: *to express thoughts and feelings, to explain or inform,* or *to persuade.*

> Running is the sport of the people. If it is not the largest participant sport already in terms of numbers, it no doubt is in terms of time devoted to it. It requires little in the way of skills or money, and no particular body type or age or location. It doesn't discriminate. Even at competitive levels it thrives on friendship. Where has it been all this time?
>
> —Robert E. Burger, *Jogger's Catalogue*

● Practice Your Skills

Writing a Thesis Statement

Write a thesis statement for each of the following subjects based on the ideas and information provided.

1. Subject	Savings accounts
Ideas and Information	Anyone can open one by making a deposit. Each deposit is added to the balance. Deposits and withdrawals are recorded. Banks pay interest on the balance. When interest is compounded daily, interest is paid on the interest and added to the balance. Banks may pay higher interest rates on an account that keeps a high minimum balance.
2. Subject	Brasília
Ideas and Information	Became capital of Brazil in 1960 Was built from scratch in Brazil's interior to open up the frontier to settlers Has buildings with unique, modern design Is a source of national pride Is isolated from older cities on coast Has problems: overpopulation, poverty

Think Critically

Drawing Conclusions

Before you can write a thesis statement, you will need to draw conclusions about your subject. When you **draw a conclusion,** you make a reasoned judgment based on all the information you have. The following list shows how Finney looked at the details of rattlesnake tribes and drew a conclusion about them.

Information	They hunted singly.
	They never shared food.
	They never worked together or defended one another.
Conclusion	"The tribe members did nothing at all for each other except breed."

Thinking Practice

Analyze the information given below and write three possible conclusions you could draw from it.

Subject	the Louisiana Purchase of 1803
Ideas and Information	Napoleon unexpectedly offered French territory in North America for sale
	purchase price only $15 million
	Jefferson almost passed up the opportunity because he thought the Constitution did not give a president the right to buy land.
	purchase doubled the size of the U.S.
	provided valuable waterways and natural resources

CAPTURING THE READER'S INTEREST

In her introduction to "Cat Lovers, Dog Lovers," Gladys Taber uses two eye-catching quotations. In "Life and Death of a Western Gladiator," Charles Finney provides a dramatic description of the first hours of a rattlesnake's life and the threatening dangers all around. He draws readers in by personalizing the young snake and making readers care for him. Below are several strategies for starting an introduction.

Strategies for Capturing the Reader's Interest

- Start with an interesting quotation.
- Start with a question.
- Present an unusual or little-known fact.
- Present an idea or image that is unexpected.
- Cite a statistic that is alarming or amusing.
- Lead in with a line of dialogue from a conversation.
- Give an example or illustration of the main idea.
- Relate an incident or personal experience.

The following introduction is from an essay by Elise Miller of Canton High School in Ohio. What strategy does she use to capture attention?

STUDENT MODEL: *Essay Introduction*

My Grandma Is My Hero

My grandma has taught me too many things to put down on this one sheet of paper. She has demonstrated a plethora of admirable characteristics that anyone striving to be a better person would desire to have. My grandmother has an incredible amount of wisdom, strength, patience, love, and courage. The person I am today and want to become is a direct result of how my grandma has affected my family life, faith, and my academics.

PROJECT PREP Drafting *The First Paragraph*

Using the information you have just learned about writing thesis statements, draft the introductory paragraph to your essay. For Charles Finney's article on a baby rattlesnake, a thesis statement might be, "Baby rattlesnakes are threatened by predators from the moment they are born and must rely on a combination of quickness, awareness, instinct, and their poisonous fangs in order to survive." Draft an introductory paragraph in which you state and develop the thesis that will guide the rest of your writing. Share this introduction with your writing group and use any feedback as the basis for a revision.

Body of a Composition

Following the introduction, the body of a composition explains the thesis statement by developing the main idea in supporting paragraphs. A composition body, therefore, is much like the body of a paragraph.

PARAGRAPH BODY	COMPOSITION BODY
The body consists of **sentences** that support **the topic sentence.**	The body consists of **paragraphs** that support the **thesis statement.**
All the sentences relate to the **main idea** expressed in the topic sentence.	All the paragraphs relate to the **main idea** expressed in the thesis statement. At the same time, each paragraph has a topic sentence, a body, and a conclusion of its own.
Each sentence develops a **supporting detail** that supports the main idea.	Each paragraph develops a **supporting idea** that supports the main idea. At the same time, each supporting idea contains **supporting details.**

SUPPORTING PARAGRAPHS

The information in the body of your composition may come from your own experience and observations or from research. Wherever it comes from, the information proves or supports your thesis by serving as the supporting paragraphs in the body of your composition.

The **supporting paragraphs** of a composition develop the thesis statement with specific details.

The topic sentence of each supporting paragraph supports the thesis statement of the composition. The sentences in each paragraph then develop that paragraph's topic sentence by giving supporting details. As you continue to read the student model, notice how each paragraph of the body develops the main idea that is expressed in the thesis statement. Also notice how each paragraph has its own structure, with a topic sentence and a body of supporting sentences.

First, my grandma amazes me with the amount of unconditional love she provides for my family. No matter whom she talks to, my grandma is open to everyone's opinions and thoughts on any topic. Everyone's feelings are important to her, and she loves hearing any ideas people might want to share. I applaud my grandma because she never has to get something to give something. She never wants anything but love in return for her gracious gifts to the family. Whether it is food, presents, or money that she distributes on holidays and birthdays, she never ever expects anything back for it. Overall, she loves to give people what makes them happy, and for that I praise her. Without my grandma, my family would not gather as often as we do. She assembles everyone into the wonderful environment she calls her home. When we walk in the door, we can smell the cinnamon bun scent sweeping through the air, and it makes everyone feel welcome. I feel just like I am at home. After all, togetherness with the people you love is the best gift you could give, isn't it? I definitely think so.

Secondly, my faith has been impacted immensely by my grandmother. My entire family attends church, but my grandma has been accompanying generation after generation of people to our house of God. Her firm religious beliefs have been helpful in keeping the church alive through tough times. She has lost so many people that were close to her in the past few years that I wonder how she does not break down and give up. She replies, "I know they're in a better place now with God. Heaven will keep them safe." From my grandma I receive the hope that I will be able to continue the tradition of faithfulness that she has begun. I will always aim to be as dependable and devoted to my church someday as she is.

Third and finally, my approach to academics has been inspired by my grandma beyond compare. After she graduated from high school, she went to medical school to become a nurse. Not only did she have to pay her own way through college, she had to finance herself completely on her car, gas, housing, food, and anything else that she needed because she had seven other siblings at home that her parents had to attend to also. When she was twelve years old, her father died leaving my great-grandmother with eight children to raise. Much was required of my grandma at a young age. I respect how hard working and driven my grandma is and was when she went to school. I would not have the motivation to pull the honorable grades that I do without the inspiration of her accomplishments despite the challenges she faced.

The body of this model can be presented in a simple outline.

| Thesis
Statement | The person I am today and want to become is a direct result of how my grandma has affected my family life, faith, and academics. |

I. First, my grandma amazes me with the amount of unconditional love she provides for my family.

II. Secondly, my faith has been impacted immensely by my grandmother.

III. Third and finally, my approach to academics has been inspired by my grandma beyond compare.

● **Practice Your Skills**

Listing Supporting Ideas

For the following thesis statement, list at least two supporting ideas that could be developed into two supporting paragraphs for the body of a composition. After you write each supporting idea, add at least two details you could use to develop that paragraph.

| Thesis
Statement | Holidays have important meanings in American life. |

The Language of Power   *Pronouns*

Power Rule: Use subject forms of pronouns in subject position. Use object forms of pronouns in object position. (See pages 716–725.)

See It in Action Sometimes usage that may sound natural in informal speech does not transfer well to formal writing. In speech you would be likely to say, for example: "No matter who you talk to, you get the same answer." In formal writing, though, you need to replace the subject form of the pronoun *who* with the object form, since in that construction the word serves as direct object. (See pages 716–725.) Elise Miller used the right choice in her essay on her grandmother.

> No matter whom she talks to, my grandma is open to everyone's opinions and thoughts on any topic.

Remember It Record this rule and example in the Power Rule section of your Personalized Editing Checklist.

Use It Read over your project text looking for the pronouns *who* and *whom*. Be sure that the subject forms of these pronouns are used in subject position and object forms in object position.

PROJECT PREP   *Drafting*   *The Body Paragraphs*

Draft the remainder of your composition, making sure that each paragraph is aligned with the thesis statement. Develop your ideas as fully as possible.

Unity, Coherence, and Clarity

Like a paragraph, a composition should keep to the subject, move smoothly from one idea to the next in a logical order, and make sense to the reader.

UNITY

A composition has **unity** if none of the ideas wanders off the subject. Every sentence in each paragraph of the body should develop the main idea expressed in the paragraph's topic sentence. At the same time, every paragraph in the composition should develop the thesis statement.

You can find more information on unity on pages 82–83 and 134.

COHERENCE

A composition has **coherence** if the ideas follow in logical order and if transitions are used to connect those ideas.

You can find more information on coherence on pages 84–87 and 134.

CLARITY

A composition has **clarity** if the meaning of the paragraphs, sentences, and words is clear. One way you can achieve clarity is by writing sentences that are not wordy or rambling. You can also add clarity to your paragraphs by making sure they are adequately developed. Using specific words and precise images also helps you make your writing clear.

You can find more information on clarity and adequate development on pages 80–81 and 133–134.

PROJECT PREP *Revising* **Using Feedback**

Bring your completed draft to your writing group. For each writer, provide feedback that enables the writer to present the subject's survival of threats as clearly as possible.

editing

Make the following wordy passage more "fuel efficient" by cutting out needless words and phrases.

> Ash trees, which grow straight and tall, face a new threat from a type of bug called the emerald ash borer.

⑤ Conclusion of a Composition

In the conclusion of a composition, you might summarize your supporting ideas and recall the main idea expressed in your thesis statement. As in the conclusion of a paragraph, you may also want to add an insight in the concluding paragraph of a composition. This concluding paragraph may be long or short, but it should end with a memorable sentence—the clincher. As the last sentence in your composition, the clincher sentence should leave as strong an impression as does the opening line of your introduction.

The paragraph below is the conclusion to the model composition about the heroic grandmother. Notice how it reinforces the main idea stated in the introduction: "The person I am today and want to become is a direct result of how my grandma has affected my family life, faith, and my academics."

Writing Tip

The **concluding paragraph** completes the composition and reinforces the main idea.

STUDENT MODEL: *Conclusion*

Regardless of the struggles that my grandma has been through, she is still as courageous and restless as a fearless child. Sometimes I ponder how someone who is significantly older than me can be packed with so much energy. I hope that eventually I will develop the wisdom, strength, patience, love, and courage that my grandma possesses. After contemplating for almost sixteen years how she completes all the miraculous acts of generosity and grace that she does, I still am boggled by her surplus of amazing attributes. I am not sure that I will ever be able to live up to the gift from God that I call my grandmother, but someday I hope in every way to be just like her. For others, heroes can resemble anything from cartoon characters to celebrities, and may change over time, but for me my grandma is and always will be my hero.

PROJECT PREP *Drafting* *Conclusion*

Add a strong ending to your composition. Try to leave a lasting impression in the mind of your readers through the force of your final sentence. (See pages 78–79.)

Ideas	4 The text conveys an interesting idea with abundant supporting details and is well chosen for the purpose and audience.	3 The text conveys a clear idea with ample details and suits the purpose and audience.	2 The text conveys a main idea with some supporting details and suits the purpose and audience.	1 The text does not convey a main idea and fails to suit the purpose and audience.
Organization	4 The organization is clear with abundant transitions.	3 A few ideas seem out of place or transitions are missing.	2 Many ideas seem out of place and transitions are missing.	1 The organization is unclear and hard to follow.
Voice	4 The voice sounds natural, engaging, and personal.	3 The voice sounds natural and personal.	2 The voice sounds mostly unnatural with a few exceptions.	1 The voice sounds mostly unnatural.
Word Choice	4 Words are specific, powerful, and precise.	3 Words are specific and some words are powerful and precise.	2 Some words are overly general.	1 Most words are overly general.
Sentence Fluency	4 Varied sentences flow smoothly.	3 Most sentences are varied and flow smoothly.	2 Some sentences are varied but some are choppy.	1 Sentences are not varied and are choppy.
Conventions	4 Punctuation, usage, and spelling are correct. The Power Rules are all followed.	3 Punctuation, usage, and spelling are mainly correct and Power Rules are all followed.	2 Some punctuation, usage, and spelling are incorrect but all Power Rules are followed.	1 There are many errors and at least one failure to follow a Power Rule.

CHAPTER 3

PROJECT PREP Revising and Editing Final Draft

Based on the feedback from your writing group, prepare a final, polished version of your essay. You might exchange papers with a writing partner for one final critique before you consider it done. When you are satisfied with your essay, publish it to the audience you targeted or in another appropriate way.

Writing Lab

Project Corner

Write Smart
Target Your Audience

Some of the possible audiences you could have chosen for your project are:

- other students
- the school's Science Club
- the television weather station
- the police

Find a partner who chose to write for the same audience you chose. Together, choose a different audience and discuss how your writing would need to change for that audience. Choose one paragraph each from each of your original essays and **rewrite that paragraph for your new audience**. Be prepared to read the original and the revision to the class and explain the changes you made and why you made them.

Speak and Listen Teach Street Smarts

In a small group, **develop a brief presentation** on how to stay safe on the streets. You could focus on keeping safe from criminals, or you could focus on safety issues related to transportation—biking, driving, crossing the streets. As you work on your presentation, make sure it contains solid information. However, think creatively about how to present it so that it will leave a lasting impression. After all the presentations, discuss with your classmates which were presented in the most creative way and what qualities made them stand out from the others.

Get Technical Produce a Public Service Announcement

With the group with whom you created your street smart presentation, use technology to **produce a public service announcement** that conveys the essence of your presentation. You can make a short video (see pages 480–485) or a Power presentation. Share your completed work with the class and ask for feedback.

In Everyday Life
Persuasive Letter

1. Your community is considering whether to build a new commuter railroad to a large office park where many people work. The train will go right through a residential neighborhood with homes, parks, and schools. *Write a persuasive one-paragraph letter* to a newspaper or blog, arguing either that the new railroad is a threat or that the failure to build the railroad is a threat to the community. Write a well-crafted paragraph that has a topic sentence, supporting ideas, and a conclusion.

In the Workplace Note to the Boss

2. You work at a company that designs roller coasters. Your boss has asked everyone on the staff to submit a detailed note for a brand-new kind of coaster. Right now Ms. Drudge just wants rough ideas, so you are free to let you imagination run wild. You can use tunnels and loops, laser lights, or any other features. *Write a note to your boss* explaining why the company should build your fantasy coaster. Be sure to include specific details and effective transitions. Check your paragraphs for unity, coherence, and clarity.

Timed Writing 🕐 Proposal for After-School Program

3. Using the line graph below, write a brief proposal to the director of the Modern Art Museum for an after-school art program and explain why it is a good idea. You have 15 minutes to complete your work.

Before You Write Consider the following questions: What is the subject? What is the occasion? Who is the audience? What is the purpose?

After You Write Evaluate your proposal using the rubrics on pages 81, 88, and 111.

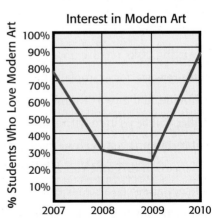

Interest in Modern Art

% Students Who Love Modern Art

Unit 2

Purposes of Writing

All writing tasks require a well-defined goal and a specific audience. Good movie reviews, for example, aim to summarize plot, analyze filmmaking technique, and give a "thumbs up" or "thumbs down." A review of the latest thriller will be written with teens and adults in mind, not young children. Writers tailor the style, tone, and content of each piece to specific goals and audiences. In this unit you will learn how to identify your purpose and your audience and keep a steady eye on both. Be sure, though, to find a seat in your own audience. If you aim to please yourself, good writing will follow.

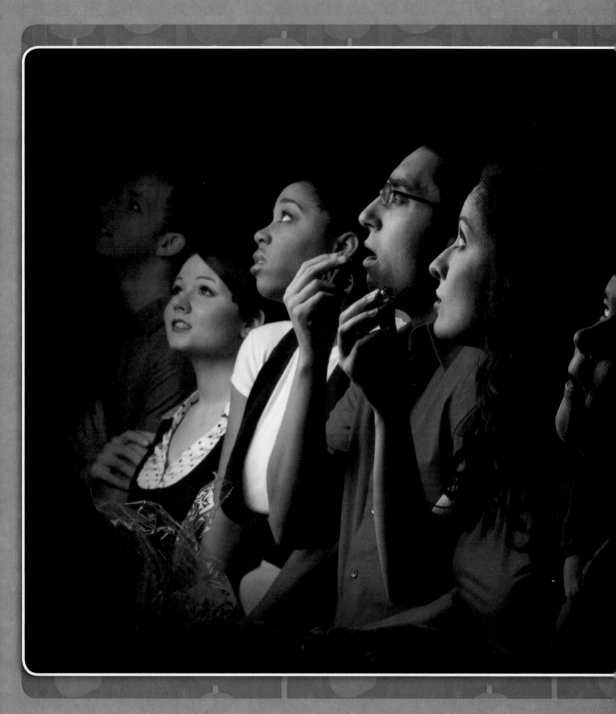

Keep in mind that the person to write for is yourself. Tell the story that you most desperately want to read. —Susan Isaacs

Personal Writing

A personal narrative expresses the writer's personal point of view on a subject drawn from the writer's own experience.

You encounter many examples of personal narratives, and you use personal narratives in different ways. Here are just a few examples.

- **A sports star writes an autobiography,** telling about the opportunities her career in soccer has given her.
- **Musicians reflect on the music they listened to while growing up** and the singers who influenced their own work for a magazine article.
- **An archaeology student working in Nepal writes letters to friends,** including stories about the foods she has tasted and the people she has met.
- **Teenagers share stories about their experiences volunteering in the community** and reveal the lessons they have learned from helping others.
- **A student writes a reflection** on what he learned by moving to a new neighborhood and entering a new school.

Writing Project *Personal Narrative*

Rebooting Your Life *Tell a story of when you started over, either by your own choice or because you had to.*

Think Through Writing Many people have an experience of starting over. You might have started over when you moved to a new neighborhood, started in a new school, left old friends for new, or got yourself a fresh start in some other way. Think of a time when you started over. What did you leave behind? Did you do so voluntarily or not? What was the experience of starting over like? What was exciting, frightening, different, unusual, or welcome about the change? Write informally, focusing on recording your experience and emotions more than on correctness at this point in the process.

Talk About It Share your writing with your writing group. What is common to each experience? What is unique about each writer's story?

Read About It In the following narrative Ernesto Galarza describes moving from the *barrio*—that is, a Latino neighborhood—to a neighborhood with few Latinos. Think about his experience of starting over in light of your writing. Prepare to talk about it as if Galarza were a member of your writing group.

> **MODEL: Personal Narrative**

From *Barrio Boy*

The New House

Ernesto Galarza

To make room for a growing family it was decided that we should move, and a house was found in Oak Park, on the far side of town where the open country began. The men raised the first installment for the bungalow on Seventh Avenue even after Mrs. Dodson explained that if we did not keep up the monthly payments we would lose the deposit as well as the house.

The real estate broker brought the sale contract to the apartment one evening. Myself included, we sat around the table in the living room, the gringo[1] explaining at great length the small print of the document in a torrent of words none of us could make out. Now and then he would pause and throw in the only word he knew in Spanish: "Sabe?"[2] The men nodded slightly as if they had understood. Doña[3] Henriqueta was holding firmly to the purse which contained the down payment, watching the broker's face, not listening to his words. She had only one question. Turning to me she said: "Ask him how long it will take to pay all of it." I translated, shocked by the answer: "Twenty years." There was a long pause around the table, broken by my stepfather: "What do you say?" Around the table the heads nodded agreement. The broker passed his fountain pen to him. He signed the contract and after him Gustavo and José. Doña Henriqueta opened the purse and counted out the greenbacks. The broker pocketed the money, gave us a copy of the document, and left.

> The first sentence states the setting for the rest of the story. Galarza's family is moving to a new home. Noting that it is on the "far side" of town suggests that it is going to be significantly different from his family's current home.

---

1 **gringo:** An English-speaking foreigner, especially from North America.
2 **Sabe?:** You know?
3 **Doña:** Respectful term of address, used before women's first names.

The last thing I did when we moved out of 418L was to dig a hole in the corner of the backyard for a tall carton of Quaker Oats cereal, full to the brim with the marbles I had won playing for keeps around the *barrio*.[4] I tamped the earth over my buried treasure and laid a curse on whoever removed it without my permission.

Adding this story shows how attached Galarza felt to his old home. He apparently thought he might come back to it someday.

Our new bungalow had five rooms, and porches front and back. In the way of furniture, what friends did not lend or Mrs. Dodson gave us we bought in the secondhand shops. The only new item was an elegant gas range, with a high oven and long, slender legs finished in enamel. Like the house, we would be paying for it in installments.

It was a sunny, airy spot, with a family orchard to one side and a vacant lot on the other. Back of us there was a pasture. . . . On every side our windows looked out on family orchards, platinum stretches of wild oats and quiet lanes, shady and unpaved.

We could not have moved to a neighborhood less like the *barrio*. All the families around us were Americans. The grumpy retired farmer next door viewed us with alarm and never gave us the time of day, but the Harrisons across the street were cordial. Mr. Harrison loaned us his tools, and Roy, just my age but twice my weight, teamed up with me at once for an exchange of visits to his mother's kitchen and ours. I astounded him with my Mexican rice, and Mrs. Harrison baked my first waffle. Roy and I also found a common bond in the matter of sisters. He had an older one and by now I had two younger ones. It was a question between us whether they were worse as little nuisances or as big bosses. The answer didn't make much difference but it was a relief to have another man to talk with. . . .

In this paragraph, Galarza starts by emphasizing the differences between his old and new neighborhoods. He ends, though, by showing what he and Roy had in common.

I transferred to the Bret Harte School, a gingerbread two-story building in which there was a notable absence of Japanese, Filipinos, Koreans, Italians, and the other nationalities of the Lincoln School. It was at Bret Harte that I learned how an English sentence could be cut up on the blackboard and the pieces placed on different lines connected by what the teacher called a diagram.

---

4 *barrio:* neighborhood of Spanish-speaking residents

The idea of operating on a sentence and rearranging its members as a skeleton of verbs, modifiers, subject, and prepositions set me off diagramming whatever I read, in Spanish and English. Spiderwebs, my mother called them, when I tried to teach her the art.

My bilingual library had grown with some copies of old magazines from Mexico, a used speller Gustavo had bought for me in Stockton, and the novels my mother discarded when she had read them. Blackstone was still the anchor of my collection and I now had a paperback dictionary called *El inglés sin maestro.*[5] By this time there was no problem of translating or interpreting for the family I could not tackle with confidence.

It was Gustavo, in fact, who began to give my books a vague significance. He pointed out to me that with diagrams and dictionaries I could have a choice of becoming a lawyer or a doctor or an engineer or a professor. These, he said, were far better careers than growing up to be a *camello,*[6] as he and José always would be. *Camellos,* I knew well enough, was what the *chicanos*[7] called themselves as the worker on every job who did the dirtiest work. And to give our home the professional touch he felt I should be acquiring, he had a telephone installed.

It came to the rest of us as a surprise. The company man arrived one day with our name and address on a card, a metal tool box and a stand-up telephone wound with a cord. It was connected and set on the counter between the dining room and the parlor. There the black marvel sat until we were gathered for dinner that evening. It was clearly explained by Gustavo that the instrument was to provide me a quick means of reaching the important people I knew at the Y.M.C.A., the boy's band, or the various public offices where I interpreted for *chicanos* in distress. Sooner or later some of our friends in the *barrio* would also have telephones and we could talk with them.

"Call somebody," my mother urged me.

With the whole family watching I tried to think of some important person I could ring for a professional conversation. A name wouldn't come. I felt miserable

Like many personal narratives, Galarza's includes remembered feelings as well as events.

5 *El inglés sin maestro:* English without a Teacher.
6 *camello:* Camel.
7 *chicanos:* Mexican Americans.

and hardly like a budding engineer or lawyer or doctor or professor.

Gustavo understood my predicament and let me stew in it a moment. Then he said: "Mrs. Dodson." My pride saved by this ingenious suggestion, I thumbed through the directory, lifted the earpiece from the hook, and calmly asked central for the number. My sisters, one sitting on the floor and the other in my mother's arms, never looked less significant, but they, too, had their turn saying hello to the patient Señora[8] Dodson on the other end of the line.

---

8 *Señora:* Mrs.

Respond in Writing In your journal, write about Galarza's experiences. If you were he, how might you have coped with this new situation? How might the move change your life?

Develop Your Own Ideas Work with your classmates to gather information on starting over.

Small Groups: In your writing group, discuss the following questions: Why do people start over? How much choice do they have in the matter? What do they leave behind? What does the change accomplish for them? On the whole, is starting over a positive experience for someone?

Whole Class: Share your answers with the class while a student tabulates the small group contributions on the board. Discuss what both Galarza and your classmates think about what it means to start over, especially for a teenager.

Write About It You will next write a personal narrative about an experience in which you started over. You can choose from any of the possibilities below or others of your own devising.

Possible Topics	Possible Audiences	Possible Forms
• moving to a new neighborhood • starting in a new school • living in a new home following a parent's divorce or remarriage • starting new friendships after old ones have ended	• other teenagers whose parents decide to move or are forced to move • teenagers in your school • parents of such children • either your new or old group of friends	• an article in a teen magazine • a guide to your school's incoming students • an article in a parenting magazine • a letter to a friend or relative

CHAPTER 4

① Getting the Subject Right

During prewriting, your mind should be free to roam through your memories and reflect on your experiences. As you think freely, you will discover ideas that you might develop into subjects of personal narratives. For example, you may recall an important conversation, a surprise, a disappointment, or a decision that had fateful consequences. In the following excerpt from a novel, the narrator recalls how she learned her personal history as a child.

> **MODEL: Subject of a Personal Narrative**
>
> From time to time, my mother would fix on a certain place in our house and give it a good cleaning. If I was at home when she happened to do this, I was at her side, as usual. When she did this with the trunk, it was a tremendous pleasure, for after she had removed all the things from the trunk, and aired them out, and changed the camphor balls, and then refolded the things and put them back in their places in the trunk, as she held each thing in her hand she would tell me a story about myself. Sometimes I knew the story first hand, for I could remember the incident quite well; sometimes what she told me had happened when I was too young to know anything; and sometimes it happened before I was even born. Whichever way, I knew exactly what she would say, for I had heard it so many times before, but I never got tired of it.
>
> — Jamaica Kincaid, *Annie John*

DRAWING ON PERSONAL EXPERIENCE

To think of subjects for a personal narrative, look through your **journal** entries and use freewriting, inquiring, or brainstorming to stimulate your thinking. You may also find the following sources helpful in jogging your memory.

IDEA SOURCES FOR SUBJECTS OF PERSONAL NARRATIVES

letters	family stories
photographs	favorite things
souvenirs or mementos	albums, scrapbooks, or old journals

EXPLORING THE MEANING OF AN EXPERIENCE

American novelist John Irving wrote, "Every writer uses what experience he or she has. It's the translating, though, that makes the difference." In this context, *translating* means "finding meaning in an experience." That insight could be the main idea of a personal narrative. The expression of your main idea then serves the same function as the thesis statement in other kinds of writing.

MODEL: Expressing the Meaning of an Experience

As she told me the stories, I sometimes sat at her side, leaning against her, or I would crouch on my knees behind her back and lean over her shoulder. As I did this, I would occasionally sniff at her neck, or behind her ears, or at her hair. She smelled sometimes of onions, sometimes of sage, sometimes of roses, sometimes of bay leaf. At times I would no longer hear what it was she was saying; I just liked to look at her mouth as it opened and closed over words, or as she laughed. How terrible it must be for all the people who had no one to love them so and no one whom they loved so, I thought.

—Jamaica Kincaid, *Annie John*

As Kincaid makes clear, the narrator's experience taught her the importance of loving and being loved. This insight is the main idea of her narrative.

PROJECT PREP *Prewriting* *Choosing a Subject*

Review what you have already written. Is the subject one you want to pursue in a fully developed narrative? If not, brainstorm, talk with others, or try another strategy that usually works to help you think of a better subject.

Think Critically

Interpreting Experience

Think about an event in your life that seems important to you now. Why is it important? What is the meaning of this event for you? Such questions may be hard to answer because when you are experiencing events, it is often difficult to stand back from them to see their significance. Only after some time has passed can you gauge their meaning. When you reexamine an experience to interpret its meaning, you might begin by completing a checklist like the one below.

 Checklist for Interpreting Experience

Experience: I unexpectedly received an award in sixth grade for showing the greatest improvement.

This experience is important to me now because it
    helped me see something in a new way.
    changed the way I felt about someone.
  ✓ changed the way I felt about myself.

I will always remember this experience because it
    strongly affected my emotions.
  ✓ gave me new knowledge or understanding.
    had important consequences.

This experience is worth writing about because
  ✓ it will be familiar to many readers.
    it is unique or extraordinary.
    writing will help me to understand it better.

Interpretation: This event boosted my self-confidence. It was the first time I realized I might amount to something. I became a better student because of it.

Thinking Practice

Think of any memorable experience and interpret it by developing a checklist like the preceding one.

② Refining Your Subject

When you have decided on a subject and its meaning for your personal narrative, you need to think about your writing purpose and your audience.

CONSIDERING PURPOSE

The overall purpose of personal narratives is to express thoughts and feelings in a way that will interest readers and win their appreciation. However, you may include paragraphs with various purposes to achieve specific aims within the broader purpose.

You can learn more about other kinds of paragraphs on pages 90–97.

PURPOSE IN PERSONAL WRITING	
Overall Purpose: to express thoughts and feelings about participating in an outdoor survival program	
Specific Aims	**Kinds of Paragraphs**
to explain why I felt ashamed	informative
to tell a funny story	narrative
to help readers see a mountain I climbed	descriptive

Writing Tip

Determine your purpose and audience when writing a personal narrative to help ensure that you capture and hold your readers' interest.

CONSIDERING YOUR AUDIENCE

Also take into account the interests and knowledge of your readers so you can make sure they will understand your purpose and meaning. Whether you write for friends, classmates, or wider audiences, your audience will partly determine the kinds of details you select to include in your narrative.

PROJECT PREP *Prewriting* **Reflecting on Your Experience**

In your writing group, discuss the following questions about your subject:
- Did the experience you are writing about help you see something in a new way, change the way you felt about others, or change how you understood yourself? Explain.
- Is this experience memorable because it strongly affected your emotions, gave you new knowledge or understanding, or had important consequences? Explain.
- Will this experience, when written about, hold the interest of a reader? Explain.

③ Developing and Organizing Details

SELECTING DETAILS

When you write a personal narrative, you want your readers to understand the event, experience it with you, and share your feelings about it. For this sharing to occur, you must give your readers ample details *showing* the event rather than just *telling* about it (for clarity) to bring your experience to life. **Descriptive details** help readers visualize the experience you describe. **Sensory details** engage all the senses of your readers and vividly convey your ideas, making your audience see, hear, smell, and feel the impression that you are trying to create. **Background details** provide a context so your readers can understand what is happening.

The following guidelines will help you choose the details to include in your personal narrative.

Guidelines for Selecting Details

- Choose details that develop your main idea.
- Choose details that are appropriate for your purpose.
- Choose details that are appropriate for your audience.
- Use factual details to provide background information.
- Use vivid descriptive and sensory details to bring your experience to life.

 Practice Your Skills

Identifying Different Types of Details

Reread parts of *Barrio Boy* on pages 117–120 and find details the author uses to make his experience real to you. List five examples under each category of details identified in the above guidelines.

ORGANIZING DETAILS

After you select your details, group them into categories and decide on an appropriate order. Each category becomes the basis of a supporting paragraph. The examples on the next page show common ways of organizing details in personal narratives.

You can find more information on types of order on pages 221–222.

CHAPTER 4

ORGANIZING DETAILS

Kind of Details	Type of Order
events in a story, narrated beginning to end	chronological order
descriptive details to help readers visualize a person, object, or scene	spatial order
background details and details explaining the meaning of an experience	order of importance or interest
sensory details and details leading up to an impression or interpretation of an experience	developmental order

● **Practice Your Skills**

Identifying Types of Order

Study paragraphs 4, 5, and 9 in *Barrio Boy* on pages 118–119. Identify the type of order used in each paragraph by writing *spatial, order of importance,* or *developmental*.

PROJECT PREP *Prewriting* **Noting Details**

In your writing group, discuss the details of your chosen experience that stand out to you in retrospect. Were there distinctive smells, tastes, sounds, views, and physical feelings? Did certain emotions arise in you? What differences were there In how people looked and acted around you? Based on your discussion, take notes that you could use in the next draft of your narrative.

The Power of Language ⚡

Appositives: Who or What?

Details that elaborate on a person, place, or thing that may be unknown to your reader will strengthen your personal narrative. You can add such details in the form of appositive phrases. An **appositive** is a noun or pronoun phrase that identifies or adds identifying information to a preceding noun. (See pages 860–861.) In the following sentence from *Barrio Boy*, for example, readers would not know who the Harrisons are without the appositive phrase, which comes in the middle of the sentence. Notice that the appositive phrase is set off by commas.

> **Appositive Phrase**   The Harrisons, the people across the street, were cordial to us.

In a similar way, Galarza uses an appositive to elaborate on his school with descriptive details. This time it comes at the end of the sentence. Notice that a comma separates the appositive phrase from the rest of the sentence.

> **Appositive Phrase**   I transferred to Bret Harte School, a gingerbread two-story building.

Try It Yourself

1. Write a sentence about your neighbors that imitates the structure and punctuation of the first example sentence above. Elaborate on the subject of your sentence with an appositive phrase.
2. Write a sentence about your school that imitates the structure and punctuation of the second sentence, with elaboration at the sentence end.
3. Write one sentence with each of the above structures on your project topic. Use the sentences in your draft if you can, and try creating other similar sentences. You can always add more details with appositives when you revise.

Punctuation Tip

Use **two commas** to enclose an appositive **in the middle** of a sentence. Use **one comma** to separate an appositive from the rest of the sentence when it appears **at the end**.

When you draft your personal narrative, you transform your groupings of details into sentences and paragraphs. Personal writing is less formal than other kinds of writing. Unlike informative writing, for example, a personal narrative is written from the first-person point of view and does not have a formal thesis statement. Like all compositions, however, a personal narrative should have a clear main or controlling idea, an attention-getting introduction, a well-organized body, and a strong conclusion.

① Drafting the Introduction

In a personal narrative, the introduction lets readers know what they are about to hear, who you are, and how you feel about your subject. The introduction should also interest readers enough so that they want to continue reading.

Strategies for the Introduction of a Personal Narrative

- Make clear the subject, purpose, and main idea of your personal narrative.

- Set the tone to reveal the writer's point of view.

- Capture the readers' interest.

You can find more information on writing introductions on pages 101–102 and 224–226.

CREATING A TONE

The **tone** of a personal narrative reveals the writer's attitudes toward the subject and the audience. The words and expressions you use give readers clues to your intentions. When you set the tone of your personal narrative, decide how you want readers to feel. Do you want them to laugh or cry, to feel nostalgic or reflective? Do you want them to feel sympathetic toward you and the insight you gained through your experience? The models on the next page show two different tones, each suited for its subject.

It was four o'clock on a humid afternoon and the household was in an uproar. J.C. was riling up the dog, which had reached a fever pitch of hysterical barking. My sisters in the next room were each listening to a different rock station on their radios, and Gramps had raised the volume on the television set to compensate for all the noise. Amidst the nerve-racking roar of sports fans, the brain-numbing basses of the two rock numbers, and the dog's pandemonium, I grabbed my guitar and headed for the roof. Peace at last, peace at last, peace at last!

STUDENT MODEL: *Edgy Tone*

"My name is Gretchen, and I am anorexic." Never in a million years could I have imagined I would be standing in group therapy saying this bold statement to a bunch of ignorant strangers. I was better than this; I am a model. I always told myself that the skinnier you are, the more beautiful you appear. Models aren't fat; models aren't even a size two! Where did it all begin? Eighth grade, when I decided my future career.

—Lindsay Kerr, Canton South High School, Canton, Ohio

● Practice Your Skills

Analyzing Tone

Reread each of the models of tone. Give examples of words and phrases that create the tone and explain how each captures the readers' interest.

● Practice Your Skills

Determining Tone

In *Barrio Boy,* the writer's tone is one of optimism toward his family and his own growing confidence and accomplishments. Work with a partner to make a list of the words, phrases, and sentences from *Barrio Boy* that best communicate this optimistic tone.

PROJECT PREP Drafting *Writing the Introduction*

Produce a draft of the beginning of your narrative. If a consistent tone is appropriate, think about what tone you wish to adopt and make sure that you stick with it throughout the composition. Set the stage for the details you have Identified in your writing group discussions that will help you tell your story.

❷ Drafting the Body

Use the groupings that you arranged to convert the details of your experience into paragraphs. As you write, make your interpretation of your experience clear and use vivid, well-organized details to hold your readers' attention.

Guidelines for Drafting the Body

- Make sure that each supporting paragraph has a topic sentence that supports the main idea.
- Write your ideas and details in logical order.
- Use transitions between sentences and paragraphs to give your personal narrative coherence.
- Include vivid details and sensory words to bring your experience to life.
- Add new details you discover if they will help you develop your main idea.

The writer who used the lighthearted tone in the introduction (page 129) drafted the following body for a short personal narrative.

MODEL: Body of a Personal Narrative

My escape to the rooftop started to work right away because I was listening only to my sounds for a change. As I sang along with my guitar, I could hear my own voice—however weak it may be. If I fingered the wrong strings or frets, then at least they were my mistakes. Whatever mistakes I make, my music always sounds good to me, because when I concentrate on playing the right notes and chords, the rest of the world seems far away.

The greatest value of escaping with my guitar, however, was the chance it gave me to express my feelings. The tunes I play depend on my mood. Sometimes I play simple, quiet ballads or sad, bluesy refrains. Other times I strum loud sets, joyous or angry, until my fingertips sting. On the rooftop that humid afternoon with my guitar, I felt as if I had had a good long talk with an understanding friend.

PROJECT PREP *Drafting* *Writing the Body*

Meet with your writing group to review your introductions. As you read one another's drafts, ask whether the text is appropriate for the audience and the form that the writer has selected. After the discussion, draft the body of your narrative.

③ Drafting the Conclusion

The conclusion of your personal narrative should emphasize the meaning of your experience. You might give your readers a sense of completion and make your last sentence as memorable as your first. You might also end your personal narrative in any of the following ways or a combination of them.

Ways to End a Personal Narrative

- Summarize the body.
- Restate the main idea in new words.
- Add an insight that shows a new or deeper understanding of the experience.
- Add a striking new detail or memorable image.
- Refer back to ideas in the introduction to bring your personal narrative full circle.
- Appeal to the readers' emotions.

The following conclusion ends the personal narrative about the rooftop escape. This conclusion refers back to the introduction on page 129 and restates the main idea.

MODEL: Conclusion of a Personal Narrative

By the time I came down from the roof, the television did not seem so loud anymore, and the dog seemed like his old self again. I even smiled when I heard my sisters' noisy radios. Although I came back to reality, I was glad to know that my guitar would be there for me the next time I needed to escape.

● Practice Your Skills

Analyzing a Conclusion

Reread the concluding paragraphs of *Barrio Boy* on pages 119–120. Using the suggestions on page 131, identify the techniques Galarza uses to end his personal narrative. Then write responses to these questions, using examples from the narrative: What makes this an effective conclusion? How does the author reinforce the significance of his family's leaving the *barrio*?

PROJECT PREP *Writing the Conclusion*

Review the ways to end a personal narrative above. Then write a conclusion to your narrative and share it with your writing group. Listen and take notes on feedback.

CHAPTER 4

In the Media

Newsmagazines

A 19-year-old wins a multimillion dollar lottery. Despite his winnings, however, his life begins to fall apart. He no longer seeks a career. His friends treat him differently. This story is reported on a television newsmagazine, featuring interviews with the winner, his friends, and his family. There is a dramatic reenactment of an emotional scene with his destitute grandmother.

In another newsmagazine, a story appears about a report showing that a high percentage of lottery-ticket buyers are from the low-income group and that some in this group spend as much money on tickets as they do on groceries. Critics of the report say that in many states the money raised by lotteries goes back into low-income areas, often to help support schools. The story contains interviews with lottery-ticket purchasers, authors of the study, lottery officials, and elected representatives.

Where is the line between news and entertainment? When is a personal story the appropriate subject of a respectable newsmagazine? How each story is handled will answer those questions. Some people feel, however, that a personal story is only news if it is one example of many others like it and it touches on a matter that can be acted upon in the public arena (changing the law, for example).

Media Activity

Few stories are completely news or completely entertainment. To learn to see the distinctions, watch a story as it is covered on a television newsmagazine this week. Are the camera angles noteworthy? Is there any music? How does the way the shots are edited convey meaning? Then rate the story on a scale of 1 to 10, 1 being pure entertainment and 10 being a pure news story. Write a paragraph explaining your rating.

Revising a personal narrative involves attention to three important points:

- Have you developed your personal narrative in sufficient detail?
- Have you made your ideas and feelings clear?
- Have you maintained a consistent tone?

1 Checking for Development of Ideas

In a strong personal narrative, the reader can clearly see and hear what you want to share. Be sure to include enough specific supporting details to give substance to your ideas. The following strategies will help.

Strategies for Revising for Adequate Development	
Events	Close your eyes and slowly visualize the experience you are writing about. Write down the details as you "see" them in your mind's eye.
People	Visualize each person you are writing about. Start by visualizing the head and face of each person and slowly move down to the feet. Write down details as you "see" them.
Place	Visualize the setting for your narrative. Start at the left and visualize to the right, then from the foreground to the background.
Feelings	Imagine yourself repeating the experience you are writing about. Focus on your thoughts and feelings as you relive the experience.

PROJECT PREP **Revising** *Using Feedback*

Based on feedback from your writing group, revise your draft to include more details that help develop your ideas. Use the strategies in the chart above to elaborate on your experience and bring into sharp focus details that you remember.

editing

Make the following wordy passage more "fuel efficient" by combining the sentences and cutting out needless words.

Only one time did I feel comfortable that first day. The time I felt comfortable was the time I entered the bandroom.

② Checking for Unity, Coherence, and Clarity

Use the checklist below to help you evaluate your personal narrative for unity, coherence, and clarity.

CHAPTER 4

✓ Evaluation Checklist for Revising

Checking Your Narrative

- ✓ Does your narrative fulfill its purpose? (page 124)
- ✓ Is your narrative appropriate for your audience and occasion? (pages 15–16 and 124)
- ✓ Does your story have all the features of the narrative genre? (pages 121–127)
- ✓ Does the beginning introduce the story by making a general statement, setting the scene, or capturing attention? (pages 128–129)
- ✓ Does the body tell the story event by event and answer the questions *Who? What? Where? Why? When?* and *How?* (page 130)
- ✓ Does each paragraph support the main idea in some way, giving it unity? (pages 82–83 and 134)
- ✓ Do the words you've used reflect your distinctive writing style and connect with the reader?
- ✓ Does your narrative have an organizational strategy with appropriate transitions to give it clarity? (pages 125–126 and 130)
- ✓ Did you use first person if you are a character in the story? Did you use third person if your story is about something that happened to someone else? (pages 173 and 181–182)
- ✓ Does your conclusion end the story by summarizing the events or making a strong point about the story? (page 131)

Checking Your Sentences

- ✓ Did you combine related sentences to avoid choppy sentences? (pages 55–59)
- ✓ Did you vary the length and beginnings of your sentences? (pages 60–62)
- ✓ Did you write concise sentences? (pages 63–66)

Checking Your Words

- ✓ Did you use precise, specific words? (pages 46–54)
- ✓ Did you use words that appeal to the senses? (pages 146–148)

PROJECT PREP Revising *Peer Evaluation*

Meet with a partner to read one another's narratives. Each should check for unity, coherence, and clarity in the other student's writing. Make suggestions for the final copy.

Now you are ready to edit, or polish, your writing.

The Language of **Power** *Run-ons*

Power Rule: Use the best conjunction and/or use punctuation for the meaning when connecting two sentences. Revise run-on sentences. (See pages 672–674.)

See It in Action The following passage is by Jamaica Kincaid. The incorrect version is a fused, or run-on, sentence. The correct version is the way she wrote it.

Incorrect	At times I would no longer hear what it was she was **saying I** just liked to look at her mouth as it opened and closed over words, or as she laughed.
Correct	At times I would no longer hear what it was she was **saying; I** just liked to look at her mouth as it opened and closed over words, or as she laughed.

Without the semicolon, the sentence rambles and is hard to follow. Kincaid used a semicolon to show how two sentences are clearly separate, but linked. You can think of the period part of the semicolon as separating the sentences, but the comma part as linking them.

Remember It Record this rule and example in the Power Rule section of your personalized checklist.

Use It Read through your personal narrative and look for run-on sentences. Use semicolons and conjunctions to fix any that you find.

 PROJECT PREP *Editing* *Final Copy*

Based on your writing partner's suggestions, prepare a final copy of your narrative.

TIME OUT TO REFLECT

How have your editing skills progressed? Compare the edited version of your personal narrative with an edited piece of writing you did earlier in the year. Can you see new ways to strengthen your writing? In your Personalized Editing Checklist, summarize your plan for continuing to develop your editing capabilities.

Evaluate your personal narrative with the following rubric.

	4	3	2	1
Ideas	**4** The text conveys a creative main idea which is well supported through the details of the narrative.	**3** The text conveys a main idea which is supported through the details of the narrative.	**2** The text relates a personal experience but does not draw meaning from it.	**1** The text does not relate a personal experience.
Organization	**4** The organization is clear with abundant transitions.	**3** A few ideas seem out of place or transitions are missing.	**2** Many ideas seem out of place and transitions are missing.	**1** The organization is unclear and hard to follow.
Voice	**4** The voice sounds natural, engaging, and personal.	**3** The voice sounds natural and personal.	**2** The voice sounds mostly unnatural with a few exceptions.	**1** The voice sounds mostly unnatural.
Word Choice	**4** Words are specific and powerful, rich in sensory images.	**3** Words are specific and some words appeal to the senses.	**2** Some words are overly general.	**1** Most words are overly general.
Sentence Fluency	**4** Varied sentences flow smoothly.	**3** Most sentences are varied and flow smoothly.	**2** Some sentences are varied but some are choppy.	**1** Sentences are not varied and are choppy.
Conventions	**4** Punctuation, usage, and spelling are correct. All Power Rules are followed.	**3** Punctuation, usage, and spelling are mainly correct, and all Power Rules are followed.	**2** Some punctuation, usage, and spelling are incorrect, but all Power Rules are followed.	**1** There are many errors and at least one failure to follow a Power Rule.

Personal Narrative Writing  Publishing

Complete the writing process by sharing your writing with your intended audience or with someone who was part of your experience or may have an interest in it.

On page 120, you were presented with a number of possibilities for the format of a personal narrative:

- an article in a teen magazine
- a guide to your school's incoming students
- an article in a parenting magazine
- a letter to a friend or relative

As you have read, the format of your personal narrative, or any writing you do, is a factor in how you craft your writing.

For example, if you were writing your personal narrative for a teen magazine, such as *Teen Ink* (either the print version or the Web site, www.teenink.com), you would take some time to understand the format of the articles published in that magazine and read a number of the published pieces to get an idea of what Teen Ink editors and readers might expect. If instead you were

writing your personal narrative as part of a guide for incoming students, you would probably be more informational and less literary about how you tell your story. You might emphasize the lesson learned from it more than the details of the story itself as a way to help others benefit from your experience.

PROJECT PREP Publishing / Final Copy

Publish your narrative in an appropriate form.

Writing Lab

Project Corner

Get Visual
Make a Storyboard

Imagine that you have an opportunity to create a television show, film, or video game based on your narrative. In your writing group, select one narrative from which to **develop a storyboard** that could serve as the basis for one of these productions. Then work with your group members to create the storyboard. Show your proposed idea scene by scene.

Make History Narratives as Primary Sources

The narratives of former slaves are essential documents for learning not only about the lives of slaves but also about the race relations in the United States and about American social and political history. When the Civil War ended and slavery was abolished, many former slaves faced the challenge of starting over in a society from which they had in many important ways been excluded. **Research some of these narratives**, which you can find at the Web site of the Library of Congress and the University of Virginia. **Report to the class on your research,** focusing on how the narrative or narratives you read address the theme of starting over.

Experiment
Change Contexts

Assume you work in a place where someone Is hired as a new employee or transferred to a new job or project within the company. **Write a one-page summary** of advice you would give this person about starting over.

In Everyday Life
Narrative Friendly Letter

1. Your cousin lives on a llama farm in a town with one stoplight. You are a city-dweller who rarely sets foot on grass. Your mother has invited your cousin to spend the summer with your family. In every picture you've ever seen of her, your cousin has been wearing rubber boots and a straw hat. You are worried that she might not fit into life in the big city. *Write a friendly letter* to your cousin preparing her for city life. Describe your daily routine and facts about city life of which she might be unaware. Use as much detail as possible to give your cousin an idea of what to expect. (You can find information on writing friendly letters on pages 440–442.)

In the Workplace Journal Entry

2. You have recently been promoted to head of the design department at the video game company where you work. You are so excited that you can barely restrain yourself from jumping up and down on your desk and shouting out all of your ideas for new educational video games. *Write a journal entry* that describes your feelings about receiving your big promotion. Also describe your plans for the new award-winning educational video games you want to design. Use vivid details and be sure to arrange them in a logical and coherent order. (You can find information on writing journal entries on pages 12–15 and 121.)

Timed Writing ⏱ Personal Narrative

3. Write a short essay addressed to your classmates describing a time when you were excited at a gathering of family, classmates, or friends, at a sporting competition, or at a public event. What happened? What did you see, hear, or feel? What did you do? In trying to explain the situation, be sure that your details convey the tone you want. Use chronological order, spatial order, or order of importance to organize your details. You have 20 minutes to complete your work. (For help budgeting time, see pages 420–421.)

Before You Write Consider the following questions: What is the situation? What is the occasion? Who is the audience? What is the purpose?

After You Write Evaluate your work using the six-trait evaluation form on page 136.

Descriptive Writing

Descriptive writing creates a vivid picture in words of a person, an object, or a scene by stimulating the reader's senses.

A clear description can be a gift. Think of how important accurate, vivid descriptions are in each of the cases listed below.

- **A research scientist documents the appearance** of a cell as part of an experiment to find a cure for a serious illness.
- **A student traveling abroad describes the sights and sounds** of a foreign city in e-mails sent home.
- **A fiction writer sets the scene** and creates lifelike characters.
- **A nature writer records the activities** of animals in the wild.

Writing Project

Awestruck Follow the directions below to write a description of an unforgettable experience.

Think Through Writing Have you ever had an experience so vivid, so gripping, and so life-changing that every second stands out to you in great detail? Write freely for five minutes as a way to recall such an event, trying to include important details that stand out to you even in retrospect.

Talk About It In a group of three to five students, discuss what you have written. Focus on what made this experience so powerful to you and describe the details that stand out to you the most.

Read About It In the following essay, author Annie Dillard describes an encounter with a weasel. She describes this event in extraordinary detail, even writing as though she had *become* the weasel in order to understand how it experiences the world. Based on her imaginative encounter, she concludes that humans can also seize their purpose in life tenaciously and with conviction.

From

Living Like Weasels

Annie Dillard

A weasel is wild. Who knows what he thinks? He sleeps in his underground den, his tail draped over his nose. Sometimes he lives in his den for two days without leaving. Outside, he stalks rabbits, mice, muskrats, and birds, killing more bodies than he can eat warm, and often dragging the carcasses home. Obedient to instinct, he bites his prey at the neck, either splitting the jugular vein at the throat or crunching the brain at the base of the skull, and he does not let go. One naturalist refused to kill a weasel who was socketed into his hand deeply as a rattlesnake. The man could in no way pry the tiny weasel off, and he had to walk half a mile to water, the weasel dangling from his palm, and soak him off like a stubborn label.

> Dillard uses a specific example to demonstrate her general point of how weasels refuse to let go when they bite. This rhetorical strategy foreshadows the main point of the essay.

And once, says Ernest Thompson Seton—once, a man shot an eagle out of the sky. He examined the eagle and found the dry skull of a weasel fixed by the jaws to his throat. The supposition is that the eagle had pounced on the weasel and the weasel swiveled and bit as instinct taught him, tooth to neck, and nearly won. I would like to have seen that eagle from the air a few weeks or months before he was shot: was the whole weasel still attached to his feathered throat, a fur pendant? Or did the eagle eat what he could reach, gutting the living weasel with his talons before his breast, bending his beak, cleaning the beautiful airborne bones?

> Comparing the weasel to a stubborn label is a *simile*, a type of figurative language that Dillard uses often.

I have been reading about weasels because I saw one last week. I startled a weasel who startled me, and we exchanged a long glance.

> Through visual details, Dillard creates a clear picture of the eagle in the mind of the reader.

Near my house in Virginia is a pond—Hollins Pond. It covers two acres of bottomland near Tinker Creek with six inches of water and six thousand lily pads. There is a fifty–five mph highway at one end of the pond, and a nesting pair of wood ducks at the other. Under every bush is a muskrat hole or a beer can. The far end is an alternating series of fields and woods, fields and woods, threaded everywhere with motorcycle tracks—in whose bare clay wild turtles lay eggs.

One evening last week at sunset, I walked to the pond and sat on a downed log near the shore. I was watching the lily pads at my feet tremble and part over the thrusting path of a carp. A yellow warbler appeared to my right and flew behind me. It caught my eye; I swiveled around—and the next instant, inexplicably, I was looking down at a weasel, who was looking up at me.

Weasel! I'd never seen one wild before. He was ten inches long, thin as a curve, a muscled ribbon, brown as fruitwood, soft—furred, alert. His face was fierce, small and pointed as a lizard's; he would have made a good arrowhead. There was just a dot of chin, maybe two brown hairs' worth, and then the pure white fur began that spread down his underside. He had two black eyes I did not see, any more than you see a window.

The weasel was stunned into stillness as he was emerging from beneath an enormous shaggy wild rose bush four feet away. I was stunned into stillness, twisted backward on the tree trunk. Our eyes locked, and someone threw away the key.

Our look was as if two lovers, or deadly enemies, met unexpectedly on an overgrown path when each had been thinking of something else: a clearing blow to the gut. It was also a bright blow to the brain, or a sudden beating of brains, with all the charge and intimate grate of rubbed balloons. It emptied our lungs. It felled the forest, moved the fields, and drained the pond; the world dismantled and tumbled into that black hole of eyes. If you and I looked at each other that way, our skulls would split and drop to our shoulders. But we don't. We keep our skulls.

He disappeared. This was only last week, and already I don't remember what shattered the enchantment. I think I blinked, I think I retrieved my brain from the weasel's brain, and tried to

This paragraph and the one before help set the scene for the encounter.

Dillard describes the weasel in detail. What are some of the words she uses to convey precise images?

Dillard examines the moment when she and the weasel looked at each other, not only observing but also recalling feelings.

memorize what I was seeing, and the weasel felt the yank of separation, the careening splashdown into real life and the urgent current of instinct. He vanished under the wild rose. I waited motionless, my mind suddenly full of data and my spirit with pleadings, but he didn't return.

Please do not tell me about "approach–avoidance conflicts." I tell you I've been in that weasel's brain for sixty seconds, and he was in mine. Brains are private places, muttering through unique and secret tapes—but the weasel and I both plugged into another tape simultaneously, for a sweet and shocking time. Can I help it if it was a blank?

What goes on in his brain the rest of the time? What does a weasel think about? He won't say. His journal is tracks in clay, a spray of feathers, mouse blood and bone: uncollected, unconnected, loose-leaf, and blown.

I would like to learn, or remember, how to live. I come to Hollins Pond not so much to learn how to live as, frankly, to forget about it. That is, I don't think I can learn from a wild animal how to live in particular—shall I suck warm blood, hold my tail high, walk with my footprints precisely over the prints of my hands?—but I might learn something of mindlessness, something of the purity of living in the physical senses and the dignity of living without bias or motive. The weasel lives in necessity and we live in choice, hating necessity and dying at the last ignobly in its talons. I would like to live as I should, as the weasel lives as he should. And I suspect that for me the way is like the weasel's: open to time and death painlessly, noticing everything, remembering nothing, choosing the given with a fierce and pointed will.

I missed my chance. I should have gone for the throat. I should have lunged for that streak of white under the weasel's chin and held on, held on through mud and into the wild rose, held on for a dearer life. We could live under the wild rose wild as weasels, mute and uncomprehending. I could very calmly go wild. I could live two days in the den,

In this paragraph, Dillard states the purpose of her essay: to explore what she might learn about living from reflecting on the weasel she saw.

As she did in the first paragraph, Dillard uses a short, punchy sentence to start the paragraph with a strong, clear point.

curled, leaning on mouse fur, sniffing bird bones, blinking, licking, breathing musk, my hair tangled in the roots of grasses. Down is a good place to go, where the mind is single. Down is out, out of your ever-loving mind and back to your careless senses. I remember muteness as a prolonged and giddy fast, where every moment is a feast of utterance received. Time and events are merely poured, unremarked, and ingested directly, like blood pulsed into my gut through a jugular vein. Could two live that way? Could two live under the wild rose, and explore by the pond, so that the smooth mind of each is as everywhere present to the other, and as received and as unchallenged, as falling snow?

> Here is another example of a vivid simile. This one compares time and blood.

We could, you know. We can live any way we want. People take vows of poverty, chastity, and obedience—even of silence—by choice. The thing is to stalk your calling in a certain skilled and supple way, to locate the most tender and live spot and plug into that pulse. This is yielding, not fighting. A weasel doesn't "attack" anything; a weasel lives as he's meant to, yielding at every moment to the perfect freedom of single necessity.

> The last two paragraphs provide a conclusion to this essay. What did Dillard learn from reflecting on the weasel?

I think it would be well, and proper, and obedient, and pure, to grasp your one necessity and not let it go, to dangle from it limp wherever it takes you. Then even death, where you're going no matter how you live, cannot you part. Seize it and let it seize you up aloft even, till your eyes burn out and drop; let your musky flesh fall off in shreds, and let your very bones unhinge and scatter, loosened over fields, over fields and woods, lightly, thoughtless, from any height at all, from as high as eagles.

Respond in Writing In your journal, write about what makes Dillard's story effective. What sorts of details does she use that help you to experience this encounter along with her?

Develop Your Own Descriptive Details Work with your classmates to identify the types of details that characterize Dillard's description.

Small Groups: Break into small groups of four or five students. Based on your journal writing, identify the details she uses and characterize them according to the senses of touch, smell, sight, sound, and taste.

Whole Class: Share your answers with the class while a student writes each one on a large sheet of paper or on the board. At the end of the discussion, you will have a list of answers from your entire class to the question: What sorts of details make Dillard's writing so memorable and gripping?

Write About It You will next write a description of your own that provides details that bring your subject to life for your readers. The following table provides possible ways in which you may write about this topic.

Possible Topics	Possible Audiences	Possible Forms
• an encounter with an animal • your first date • an experience that frightened you • something that happened at work	• teenagers sitting around a campfire • close friends • the general public • other teenagers	• an oral telling • a feature story for a local newspaper • a blog entry • an article in a teen magazine

Like a descriptive paragraph (see pages 92–93) a descriptive essay or other type of text consists of three main parts.

> ### Structure of a Descriptive Text
>
> - The **introduction** captures attention, introduces the subject, and often suggests an overall impression of the subject, or **tone**.
> - The **body of supporting paragraphs** presents details, especially sensory details, that bring the subject to life.
> - The **conclusion** reinforces the overall impression and gives a feeling of closure.

Vivid language plays an important role in each part of a descriptive text.

❶ Specific Details and Sensory Words

A main impression or **tone** is at the core of good descriptive writing. This tone—no matter what it is—comes to life when you use your supporting details to *show* the subject rather than simply *tell* about it. When you *show* readers, chances are you are using strong specific details and words that appeal to the senses. You are making your readers see, hear, smell, and feel the impression you are creating. These are the flesh and blood of descriptive writing.

Writing Tip

Use **specific details** and **sensory words** to bring your description to life.

Writer Barry Lopez is especially good at painting word pictures. In the following selection, he describes a wolf moving through the northern woods.

He moves along now at the edge of a clearing. The wind coming down-valley surrounds him with a river of odors, as if he were a migrating salmon. He can smell ptarmigan and deer droppings. He can smell willow and spruce and the fading sweetness of fireweed. Above, he sees a hawk circling, and farther south, lower on the horizon, a flock of sharp-tailed sparrows going east. He senses through his pads with each step the dryness of the moss beneath his feet, and the ridges of old tracks, some his own. He hears the sound his feet make. He hears the occasional movement of deer mice and voles. Summer food.

Toward dusk he is standing by a creek, lapping the cool water, when a wolf howls—a long wail that quickly reaches pitch and then tapers, with several harmonies, long moments to a tremolo. He recognizes his sister. He waits a few moments, then, throwing his head back and closing his eyes, he howls. The howl is shorter and it changes pitch twice in the beginning, very quickly. There is no answer.

—Barry Lopez, *Of Wolves and Men*

One reason this passage is so richly descriptive is that Lopez is really painting two pictures. First he recreates the wolf's experience from the wolf's point of view. Then Lopez presents the wolf from the perspective of an imaginary human observer. The most important reason this description succeeds so well, however, is the writer's generous use of specific details and sensory words.

SPECIFIC SENSORY DETAILS	
Sights	edge of a clearing, hawk circling, flock of sharp-tailed sparrows
Sounds	his own footsteps, occasional movement of deer mice and voles, howl of other wolf with its distinctive sound, his own shorter howl with its own distinctive changes of pitch
Smells	ptarmigan and deer droppings; willow, spruce, and fireweed
Taste	cool water
Feelings	wind, dryness of moss and ridges of old tracks through pads of his feet, throwing head back, closing eyes

CHAPTER 5

● **Practice Your Skills**

Identifying Specific Details

The next two paragraphs continue Lopez's description of the wolf. Read them carefully, and then answer the questions.

> The female is a mile away and she trots off obliquely through the trees. The other wolf stands listening, laps water again, then he too departs, moving quickly, quietly through the trees, away from the trail he had been on. In a few minutes the two wolves meet. They approach each other briskly, almost formally, tails erect and moving somewhat as deer move. When they come together they make high squeaking noises and encircle each other, rubbing and pushing, poking their noses into each other's neck fur, backing away to stretch, chasing each other for a few steps, then standing quietly together, one putting a head over the other's back. And then they are gone, down a vague trail, the female first. After a few hundred yards they begin, simultaneously, to wag their tails.
>
> In the days to follow, they will meet another wolf from the pack, a second female, younger by a year, and the three of them will kill a caribou. They will travel together ten or twenty miles a day, through the country where they live, eating and sleeping, birthing, playing with sticks, chasing ravens, growing old, barking at bears, scent-marking trails, killing moose, and staring at the way water in a creek breaks around their legs and flows on.

1. Compare the use of specific details and sensory details in this passage and in the previous passage. Which is richer in detail? Explain your answer.

2. Why do you think Lopez wrote such a long sentence (sentence 5) about the wolves' first meeting? What effect does it have?

3. The final sentence contains a long list of things the wolves do. Which of these activities is the most specific? Why do you think Lopez places that detail where it is?

PROJECT PREP _Prewriting_ _Sensory Details_

To help you develop specific details, make a sensory diagram of a general idea related to your subject. Here's how a **sensory diagram** might look on the general idea of a crowded swimming pool:

refreshing · cool temperature · welcoming · shimmering · clean smelling · chlorine · wall-to-wall heads · goggles · steady din of crowd · lifeguard's whistle

The pool was crowded.

Olympic-sized · community · rectangular · roped-off in thirds · swimmers of all ages · flutter of kicking feet

② Figurative Language

Many writers rely on imaginative comparisons to help pump life into their descriptions. These can be either similes or metaphors, or just general comparisons. Here are a few examples from selections about animals.

Metaphor	The wind coming down-valley surrounds him with **a river of odors**. . . . (The wind is compared to a river.)
Simile and Metaphor	He was ten inches long, **thin as a curve, a muscled ribbon,** brown as fruitwood, soft-furred, alert. (The weasel's thinness is compared to a curve with the word *as* signaling the simile; the weasel is also said metaphorically to be a ribbon.)
General Comparison	Hyenas eat the prey whole and cough back, like owls, the indigestible parts, such as hair and hooves. (The hyenas' eating habits are compared to those of owls.)

● Practice Your Skills

Understanding Figurative Language

Read the following passage from a description of an eclipse of the sun. Write a few sentences explaining the comparison John Updike, the author, is making. Try "translating" the imaginative language into everyday descriptive language.

> The eclipse was to be over 90 percent in our latitude and the newspapers and television had been warning us not to look at it. I looked up, a split second Prometheus, and looked away. The bitten silhouette of the sun lingered redly on my retinas. The day was half-cloudy, and my impression had been of the sun struggling, amid a furious huddle of black and silver clouds, with an enemy too dreadful to be seen, with an eater as ghostly and hungry as time.

PROJECT PREP *Prewriting* *Figurative Language*

Further develop the details that you charted in the previous project prep activity. Make a T-chart with the most important details in the left-hand column. In the right-hand column, brainstorm possible comparisons you might make to each detail using figurative language. Then share your T-charts with your writing group and provide feedback and constructive criticism to each author about the effectiveness of the figurative language. Use that feedback to improve your figures of speech and consider where and how you might use them in your description.

Some people think of writing as a product: a sentence, a paragraph, an essay. Yet writing is a process, a tool. Even though the term *prewriting* suggests an activity that takes place *before* writing starts, you should do your prewriting work *in writing*. Often you cannot really focus your thoughts until you put your ideas on paper.

Purpose, Subject, Audience, and Genre

PURPOSE

There *are* some purely descriptive texts—those whose purpose is to describe a subject as completely as possible. More often, though, writers use description in the service of some other writing purpose: to enrich a story they are narrating, to add interest and life to an explanation, to give heart and soul to an argument. Writing a description will give you the skills you need for enriching any essay you write.

SUBJECT

To Dillard in "Living Like Weasels," locking eyes with a weasel taught a profound life lesson. A good subject for a description does not have to be about one of life's profound meanings, but it does have to have real meaning to *you* if it is to be any good.

The following guidelines can help you choose the best subject for your description.

Guidelines for Choosing a Subject

- Choose a subject that matters to *you*. Your interest will carry over to the reader.
- Choose a subject that you can develop with descriptive details such as sensory words and figurative language.
- Choose a subject you know well enough to describe better than anyone else.

AUDIENCE

A naturalist writing for other naturalists would use scientific language and concepts that might not be familiar to the general reading public. A reader who does not know your school would need more background for a description of your campus than would a fellow student. Readers who do not know much about hyenas or weasels need some factual information to get a clear understanding. The following questions can help you shape your ideas for a specific audience.

Questions for Analyzing an Audience

- What does my audience already know about my subject?
- What background information, if any, do I need to provide to make the description more meaningful?
- What attitude does my audience have toward my subject?
- Do I want to reinforce that attitude or try to change it?

GENRE

What genre will you be using to express your thoughts? How you craft your writing depends in part on the answer to that question. For example, if you are writing a feature story for a local newspaper, you would probably use somewhat formal language and have a clear, traditional structure. If you are writing for your blog, your language might be more casual, your structure might be looser, and you may include links to Web sites with additional information and with images. Understanding your chosen genre will help you develop a crystal-clear subject.

PROJECT PREP *Prewriting* *Refining Your Subject*

So far you have written freely, charted details, and explored ways to use figurative language to help your reader experience what you experienced. Use all your previous work to home in now on a very focused subject that will be suitable for your purpose, audience, and genre. If you are writing about an unforgettable experience, for example, choose the exact experience you will write about, your purpose (will you be persuading someone to be more careful than you were, perhaps, or will you simply be relating an incident?), and your genre. Write a paragraph outlining your writing goals.

② Creating an Overall Impression

If you tried to record every detail about your subject, the resulting writing would be a meaningless overload. Readers depend on writers to filter out the details they do not need to know so they can focus on what is important. To know what is important, you need to develop the overall impression you want to convey. What is the general feeling you have about your subject?

The overall impression Dillard wants to convey about the weasel is a fierce but positive one that it lived according to its nature, and that it pursued its nature and its living single-mindedly. Although she does not state this position in a thesis statement at the beginning of the essay, she does provide factual examples that make this point by way of introducing her subject.

Writing Tip

Filter your **details** and develop your **overall impression** to make your writing meaningful for a reader.

● Practice Your Skills

Determining Overall Impressions

1. What overall impression does Barry Lopez create in his description of the wolves? (See page 147.)
2. Explain your answer to question 1 with examples from Lopez's writing.

PROJECT PREP *Prewriting* Creating an Overall Impression

1. In your writing group, share your prewriting work. Then discuss the dominant, overall impression you want to leave in the reader's imagination. In light of that overall impression, are you considering any details for the essay that may need to be filtered out because they suggest a different feeling?

2. Using the feedback, write a paragraph identifying the overall impression you want to create, the details that will help you create it, and the emotions you want to arouse in your readers.

In the Media

Product Packaging

The jolly faces of elves, a sports hero making a slam dunk, a fresh, ripe strawberry—all of these appear or have appeared on cereal boxes to help create a quick overall impression. Designers of product packaging work hard to choose an image that will appeal to potential buyers—an image that conveys a message. What message does this product convey?

Even if a busy shopper does not take the time to note the words about a free surprise, the colorful pieces of cereal suggest a kid-friendly cereal. Also, the smiling clown says, as if shouting from the shelf, "Children love this cereal!"

Media Activity

Try designing a package for a cereal product you know well. What is the main message you want to convey? What specific images and designs can you use to convey that message quickly? Describe the front of your box. Also draw a sketch and share it with your class.

③ Developing a Description

With your overall impression in mind, you can begin to flesh out the details you will use to develop your description. Consider your audience as well. With both of these in mind, use the strategies below for developing descriptive details.

Strategies for Developing a Description

- Use your memory and direct observation, if appropriate, to list the sights, sounds, smells, tastes, and feelings you associate with your subject. Making a chart like the one on page 148 may help.

- Brainstorm for a list of imaginative comparisons you might make to help readers understand your description. These could be metaphors, similes, or other types of comparisons.

- Gather any factual details and information you might need in order to provide background for your readers or to help set the stage for your overall impression.

- If you are describing a scene, draw a picture or a map so you can clearly see the relationship of one part of the subject to another.

- Apply your filter: Remember to test each detail against your desired overall impression to make sure it adds rather than detracts.

PROJECT PREP *Prewriting* *Developing Descriptive Skills*

For practice in harnessing descriptive details, try this classroom game:

1. Take a common object that several people in the class have with them and describe it so that a different student may identify it from the whole group of similar objects, based on the details of the description. Several students, for instance, might have watches, bracelets, earrings, pens, wallets, and scarves. Students should be grouped according to the common objects they will describe (all the scarf describers in one group, for example).

2. Individually, write the clearest, most meticulous description of your object as possible, without using overt descriptors such as brand names.

3. Place all of the objects that the group members have described on a desk along with your compositions. Each composition will then be given to a member of a different group who will try to find the corresponding object.

4. Students who could not find the correct object should provide feedback on what was lacking in the description.

Think Critically

Observing

A movie camera simply takes in images and places them on the film. This is an example of **objective observation:** observing facts, without opinion or perspective.

Most of the time, however, our observations are colored by our feelings and beliefs. In a hot, crowded lobby, the only details we notice are those that reinforce our discomfort. This is **subjective observation.**

Henry David Thoreau, an American author and philosopher, pointed out that there is no such thing as purely objective observation. We are always filtering what we see through our human prejudices and opinions. He writes, ". . . what the writer . . . has to report is simply some human experience."

Nonetheless, there may be some things about your subject that you can observe objectively. The following chart shows both objective and subjective observations Annie Dillard made about her weasel soulmate.

OBJECTIVE DETAILS	SUBJECTIVE DETAILS
size	quality of eyes
shape	alertness
colors	fierceness

If you compare the details, you can see that the objective ones can be verified by some tangible measure. The subjective details have no proof, but they are the details that make Dillard's essay as descriptive as it is.

Thinking Practice

Make a chart like the one above to record objective and subjective observations of an object in nature. Compare your work to that of other students.

Organizing a Description

How you organize your description depends on the goal or aim of your writing and the nature of your details. The chart below shows some good possibilities.

WRITING AIM	KINDS OF DETAILS	TYPE OF ORDER
to **describe** a person, place, object, or scene	sensory details	spatial (pages 20 and 85)
to **recreate** an event	sensory details, events	chronological (pages 20 and 221)
to **explain** a process or how something works	sensory and factual details, steps in a process, how parts work together	sequential (page 86)
to **persuade**	sensory and factual details, examples, reasons	order of importance (pages 20 and 221)
to **reflect**	sensory and factual details, interpretations	order of importance (pages 20 and 221)

● **Practice Your Skills**

Analyzing Organization

Reread the paragraphs by Barry Lopez on page 148 about the wolves that meet. What type of organization does he use? Identify some of the transitions he uses to make the order clear.

PROJECT PREP *Prewriting* / *Organizing Details*

Review your writing purpose. In light of that, and considering the details you have chosen, what is the best way to organize your essay? Share your decision with your writing group and invite feedback. Then sketch out an outline or graphic organizer showing the main parts of your essay and roughly what each part will contain.

The Power of Language

Adjectival Phrases: Adjectives Come Lately

Adjectives can come after the word they modify (see pages 538–541), and so can phrases—groups of words (see pages 610–630). Here are some examples from "Living Like Weasels" by Annie Dillard (pages 141–144):

> Brains are private places, muttering through unique and secret tapes.

> He was ten inches long, thin as a curve, a muscled ribbon, brown as fruitwood, soft-furred, alert.

> I was stunned into stillness, twisted backward on the tree trunk.

> There was just a dot of chin, maybe two hairs' worth, and then the pure white fur began that spread down his underside.

> He sleeps in his underground den, his tail draped over his nose.

> I waited motionless, my mind suddenly full of data and my spirit with pleadings, but he didn't return.

Try It Yourself

Write sentences imitating the structure of each of these sentences. If you can, add various kinds of descriptive phrases as you draft your own descriptive piece. Then later, see if there are other places where you might add details in phrases like these.

Punctuation Tip

These "extra detail" phrases are always set off from the rest of the sentence by a comma—or by two commas if they occur somewhere within the sentence. In that case, the interrupting modifier is enclosed by the two commas.

Descriptive Writing  Drafting

If you have taken your prewriting work seriously, by now most of the hard work of writing your description is over. During the drafting stage, concentrate on the flow of your ideas, always thinking about your reader. Keep the following points in mind as you draft your description.

HERE'S HOW **Tips for Drafting a Description**

- Experiment with interest-catching introductions. (Review the selections in this chapter for ideas.)
- Suggest your overall impression early in your writing to frame your description for readers.
- Follow your outline when drafting the body of your description, but feel free to make improvements as they occur to you.
- Use fresh, vivid, descriptive words that appeal to the senses as you write.
- Use transitions appropriate to the type of order you have chosen (pages 5 and 86) to help your reader get smoothly from one point to the next.
- Look for a strong way to end your description and consider referring back to an idea in your introduction to tie together the writing.

PROJECT PREP Drafting **Pulling It Together**

Draft your description, using the preceding tips along with what you have learned from the writing you have already. Write your description so that it is vivid for your readers and so that they can see, taste, feel, hear, and smell the situation just as you did. Be sure to use transitions to guide the reader along the way.

Use the checklist below as a tool for revising your description.

 Evaluation Checklist for Revising

Checking Your Introduction

✓ Does your introduction capture the reader's attention? (page 146)
✓ Does your introduction suggest an overall impression of your subject? (page 146)
  Does your introduction set the right tone for your subject and audience? (pages 146 and 150–151)
✓ Does your introduction provide enough background information for your audience? (pages 150–151)

Checking Your Body Paragraphs

✓ Have you supported your overall impression with appropriate details? (pages 152–153)
✓ Did you include well-chosen sensory words and details and avoid generalities? (pages 146–148)
✓ Is each paragraph within the body well developed, with a clear main idea and supporting details? (pages 146–149)
✓ Did you use comparisons and figurative language effectively? (page 149)
✓ Did you move logically from one paragraph to the next in a clear organization and with helpful transitions? (page 158)

Checking Your Conclusion

✓ Does your conclusion reinforce the overall impression you are trying to make? (pages 152 and 158)
✓ Do you refer back to your introduction to give a sense of completion? (page 158)
✓ Did you end with a memorable phrase or image that might linger in the reader's mind? (pages 110 and 158)

Checking Your Words and Sentences

✓ Are your words specific and lively, stimulating all the senses? (pages 46–54 and 146–149)
✓ Are your sentences varied? (pages 55–61)
✓ Have you used adjectives to bring your description alive for readers? (page 157)
✓ Have you varied the placement of adjectives for variety? (page 157)

PROJECT PREP   Revising   *Peer Response*

Revise your draft using the checklist above. Then share your draft with your writing group. Take notes on the suggestions they offer, and then revise further based on their feedback.

When you are happy with your latest revision, spend some time polishing it. During the editing stage, carefully go over your essay, looking for any errors. Consult your Personalized Editing Checklist to avoid repeating errors you are prone to make.

The Language of **Power** *Of v. Have*

Power Rule: Use the contraction *'ve* (not *of*) when the correct word is *have,* or use the full word *have.*

See It in Action In speech, *have* is often contracted to *'ve*, which sounds like *of*, as in phrases like *would've* or *should've*. Instead of writing the incorrect *would of* or *should of*, write these phrases as contractions, or write out the full word *have*.

> His face was fierce, small and pointed as a lizard's; he would have made a good arrowhead.

Remember It Record this rule and example in the Power Rule section of your Personalized Editing Checklist.

Use It Look for every instance of *would, should, could, may, might*, or *must* and see if it is followed by *of* instead of *'ve* or *have*. Fix that incorrect form whenever it occurs.

As you check for correct grammar, usage, and mechanics, also edit your work to eliminate needless words and phrases.

editing ☆

Make the following wordy passage more "fuel efficient" by cutting out needless words and phrases.

> Rapidly moving toward me was a wolf that was gaining on me with every step as it chased me down the road.

Using a Six-Trait Rubric — Descriptive Writing

You can use the following rubric to do a final evaluation of your descriptive writing. Strive for a score of "4" for each trait.

Ideas	**4** The text conveys an overall impression with abundant vivid details and is well chosen for the purpose and audience.	**3** The text conveys an overall impression with ample details and suits the purpose and audience.	**2** The text conveys an overall impression with some vivid details and suits the purpose and audience.	**1** The text does not convey an overall impression and fails to suit the purpose and audience.
Organization	**4** The organization is clear with abundant transitions.	**3** A few ideas seem out of place or transitions are missing.	**2** Many ideas seem out of place and transitions are missing.	**1** The organization is unclear and hard to follow.
Voice	**4** The voice sounds natural, engaging, and personal.	**3** The voice sounds natural and personal.	**2** The voice sounds mostly unnatural with a few exceptions.	**1** The voice sounds mostly unnatural.
Word Choice	**4** Words are specific and powerful, rich in sensory images.	**3** Words are specific and some words appeal to the senses.	**2** Some words are overly general.	**1** Most words are overly general.
Sentence Fluency	**4** Varied sentences flow smoothly.	**3** Most sentences are varied and flow smoothly.	**2** Some sentences are varied but some are choppy.	**1** Sentences are not varied and are choppy.
Conventions	**4** Punctuation, usage, and spelling are correct. The Power Rules are all followed.	**3** Punctuation, usage, and spelling are mainly correct and Power Rules are all followed.	**2** Some punctuation, usage, and spelling are incorrect but all Power Rules are followed.	**1** There are many errors and at least one failure to follow a Power Rule.

CHAPTER 5

ONLINE COLLABORATION

In addition to face-to-face collaboration during revising and editing, you can also collaborate online with a variety of tools. One of the most popular is Google Docs. With a (free) Gmail or Google account, anyone can create and share documents online. The chart below shows the basic procedure for using Google Docs for collaborative writing, revising, and editing.

Using Google Docs for Collaborative Writing

- Navigate to http://docs.google.com and create an account if you don't already have one.
- Sign into Google Docs and select the Create New menu. From there choose the type of file you want to create (document, presentation, spreadsheet, form, or folder).
- If you choose Document, a blank page will appear that looks—and acts—like any other word processing program. Start typing.
- You can use the word processing features to format your text as you wish, and to delete and rearrange just as you would in a regular word processing program.
- When you save your work, you can name it whatever you want. You can also invite other people to share the file. Select Share and enter the e-mail addresses of the people you want to invite. They will receive an e-mail message from Google giving them instructions on how to access the file.
- You can decide when you are sharing your documents if your collaborators will be able to edit the text or just read it.
- More than one person can work at the same time on the same document, even if they are on opposite sides of the world.
- Google Docs keeps track of who works on each document so you can see who made which changes.
- You can use a built in spell checker to help you edit your text.
- You can publish your finished work with a simple click and share it with readers.

PROJECT PREP Editing *Polishing*

Using all the tools at your disposal, edit your descriptive essay. Make full use of the features on your word processor, such as the spell checker or the grammar checker. Also use the help of your writing group members. Read over one another's essays looking for any mistakes in grammar, usage, mechanics, or spelling.

You have been considering your purpose, audience, and occasion throughout the process of writing your descriptive essay and have been making revisions accordingly. The medium in which you publish writing also has a bearing on the style and format of your work. Consider the requirements of each of the following types of publications.

CHARACTERISTICS OF ASSORTED PUBLISHING FORMATS

Blog	• style is often more casual than printed text • may be written to invite interaction from readers in the form of comments to the blog • reader-friendly formatting techniques, such as bullet lists and a clear heading structure, assist in reading from the computer screen • graphics may be added to enhance the message • hyperlinks lead to related stories
Magazine or newspaper feature article	• article's style and tone need to fit with the style and tone of the publication. For example, an article in a history magazine would likely need to be somewhat formal. • in some two-column magazines paragraphs tend to be short • graphics often accompany the article
Letter	• has standard parts: salutation, body, and closing • often uses a personal tone and style, addressing one reader
Diary	• generally has very personal tone and informal language • no set format

PROJECT PREP Publishing / Final Copy

Consider how your chosen publishing medium (see pages 145 and 163) might affect the format of your final copy. Make any necessary adjustments, and then publish your descriptive essay.

TIME OUT TO REFLECT

In your Learning Log, write an analysis of how you have improved in writing descriptions. Also note what you think you need to work on to make further progress.

Writing Lab

Project Corner

Speak and Listen
Make Sense

Do an oral interpretation of your composition and **present a dramatic reading** that amplifies the sensory description in your writing. (For more on speaking and listening skills, see pages 457–468.)

Get Technical
Multimedia Presentation

Create a multimedia presentation based on your descriptive essay. Use features of the application that allow the five senses to figure prominently in the description. Use audio, video, and any other media that will help convey your experience.

Think Critically
Draw Conclusions from Settings

Work with a partner. Remember or watch again the openings of five of your favorite movies. What do the first few minutes of each movie establish as the overall impression or tone? What details contribute to this tone?

Next think about the movie as a whole. What is the relationship between the overall impression established at the beginning of each movie and the theme of that movie? In other words, **draw conclusions about the meaning of the descriptive setting** that establishes the framework for the rest of the story.

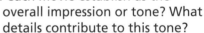

In Everyday Life
A Descriptive Letter

1. You are on vacation in Hawaii and are spending the day scuba diving. Unfortunately you knock your camera overboard while you are putting on your fins and goggles. Once underwater, you are amazed by the color of the water and the marine life that you see, and you regret not having your camera. *Write a letter* describing your experience to your friend Gina, who has never gone swimming in the ocean. Paint a written picture for her, including descriptions of what you saw, what it felt like to be underwater with the fish, and your excitement at being there. Try using similes and metaphors in your description. (You can find information on writing friendly letters on pages 440–442.)

In Spoken Communication
A Descriptive Phone Call

2. All of your friends have tickets to a rock concert tonight. You could not get a ticket. As you are walking home, a stretch limousine pulls up next to you. The back window rolls down and suddenly you are face to face with the artist who will be performing, giving him directions to the concert hall. *Improvise a telephone conversation* with your best friend describing the experience of meeting the artist. Use colorful words that will make your best friend see, hear, smell, and feel what you are describing. (You can find information on informal conversations on pages 43–45.)

Timed Writing ⏱
Descriptive Article

3. Your English class is creating a travel book with articles describing interesting places. The articles are to describe the terrain, weather, and architecture of places as vividly as possible. Write an article describing an amazing place you have visited. It does not have to be an exotic, far-away location—it can be a place in or near your hometown. Include specific details and vivid sensory words and figurative language to create an overall impression with your description. You have 20 minutes to complete your work. (For help budgeting time, see pages 420–421.)

Before You Write Consider the following questions: What is the situation? What is the occasion? Who is the audience? What is the purpose?

After You Write Evaluate your work using the six-trait evaluation rubric on page 161.

CHAPTER **6**

Creative Writing

Stories, plays, and poems provide an opportunity for writers to express perceptions and points of view that they might not be able to express otherwise. They enable people to think about old issues in new ways. They give "voice" to new ideas and the unexplored.

Here are just some of the forms in which the creative power of stories, plays, and poems can be found in the real world.

- **People read stories for entertainment** in magazines, books and online and see stories performed in movies and on television.
- **People write poems** in journals to express their deepest feelings and to think about their problems and joys.
- **Parents and child-care workers read stories to children** to help them go to sleep.
- **Theater groups present plays** in community centers and senior centers.
- **Campers tell one another scary stories.**
- **Older people tell young people stories about the histories of their families** or communities.

Writing Project *Story, Scene, and Poem*

Point of View *Write a story about a conflict between people who view an event differently. When you are done, write the same story as a play or poem.*

Think Through Writing Think of a situation, either real or imagined, in which two or more people view the same situation from very different perspectives. It's often said, for instance, that a car accident is viewed differently by everyone who observes it. Your situation need not be as dramatic as a car accident. It may be a difference in how you and your parents view something you've done, how a student and teacher interpret the student's behavior, or a similar sort of conflict you have experienced yourself or seen your friends go through. Write informally about such a situation and how the two different parties' points of view affect their interpretation and their interactions with one another.

Talk About It In a group of three to five students, discuss the situations you have each written about. Undoubtedly, you have sympathies more with one side than the other. With your classmates, do your best to elaborate each perspective so that it is understood. That is, try to sketch in greater detail who the two people might be, what their positions and perspectives are, and how they might express their point of view in words or actions to each other.

Read About It In the following model, writer Ernest Hemingway tells a story from the perspective of a father trying to comfort his son. The father and son view the son's condition from very different points of view and project very different outcomes. Read this story and consider the ways in which a single condition or event may be viewed from different perspectives.

MODEL: Short Story

A Day's Wait

Ernest Hemingway

He came into the room to shut the windows while we were still in bed and I saw he looked ill. He was shivering, his face was white, and he walked slowly as though it ached to move.

"What's the matter, Schatz?"

"I've got a headache."

"You better go back to bed."

"No. I'm all right."

"You go to bed. I'll see you when I'm dressed."

But when I came downstairs he was dressed, sitting by the fire, looking a very sick and miserable boy of nine years. When I put my hand on his forehead I knew he had a fever.

"You go up to bed," I said, "you're sick."

"I'm all right," he said.

When the doctor came he took the boy's temperature.

"What is it?" I asked him.

In the first paragraph, Hemingway begins to establish the main conflict in the story. The boy, Schatz, is ill and struggling to get healthy.

What do you think the father's short, direct sentences say about his personality?

"One hundred and two."

Downstairs, the doctor left three different medicines in different colored capsules with instructions for giving them. One was to bring down the fever, another a purgative, the third to overcome an acid condition. The germs of influenza can only exist in an acid condition, he explained. He seemed to know all about influenza and said there was nothing to worry about if the fever did not go above one hundred and four degrees. This was a light epidemic of flu and there was no danger if you avoided pneumonia.

Back in the room I wrote the boy's temperature down and made a note of the time to give the various capsules.

"Do you want me to read to you?"

"All right. If you want to," said the boy. His face was very white and there were dark areas under his eyes. He lay very still in the bed and seemed very detached from what was going on.

I read aloud from Howard Pyle's Book of Pirates; but I could see he was not following what I was reading.

"How do you feel, Schatz?" I asked him.

"Just the same, so far," he said.

I sat at the foot of the bed and read to myself while I waited for it to be time to give another capsule. It would have been natural for him to go to sleep, but when I looked up he was looking at the foot of the bed, looking very strangely.

"Why don't you try to go to sleep? I'll wake you up for the medicine."

"I'd rather stay awake."

After a while he said to me, "You don't have to stay in here with me, Papa, if it bothers you."

"It doesn't bother me."

"No, I mean you don't have to stay if it's going to bother you."

I thought perhaps he was a little light-headed and giving him prescribed capsules at eleven o'clock I went out for a while.

The entrance of the doctor into the story moves the plot forward. It establishes the boy's temperature and that his illness is not dangerous.

By going out, the father shows that he thinks the illness is not dangerous without having to say this directly.

It was a bright, cold day, the ground covered with a sleet that had frozen so that it seemed as if all the bare trees, the bushes, the cut brush and all the grass and the bare ground had been varnished with ice. I took the young Irish setter for a little walk up the road and along a frozen creek, but it was difficult to stand or walk on the glassy surface and the red dog slipped and slithered and I fell twice, hard, once dropping my gun and having it slide away over the ice.

We flushed a covey of quail under a high clay bank with overhanging brush and I killed two as they went out of sight over the top of the bank. Some of the covey lit in trees, but most of them scattered into brush piles and it was necessary to jump on the ice-coated mounds of brush several times before they would flush. Coming out while you were poised unsteadily on the icy, spongy brush they made difficult shooting and I killed two, missed five, and started back pleased to have found a covey close to the house and happy there were so many left to find on another day.

At the house they said the boy had refused to let anyone come into the room.

"You can't come in," he said. "You mustn't get what I have."

I went up to him and found him in exactly the position I had left him, white-faced, but with the tops of his cheeks flushed by fever, staring still, as he had stared, at the foot of the bed.

I took his temperature.

"What is it?"

"Something like a hundred," I said. It was one hundred and two and four tenths.

"It was a hundred and two," he said.

"Who said so?"

"The doctor."

"Your temperature is all right," I said. "It's nothing to worry about."

"I don't worry," he said, "but I can't keep from thinking."

"Don't think," I said. "Just take it easy."

"I'm taking it easy," he said and looked straight ahead. He was evidently holding tight onto himself about something.

"Take this with water."

"Do you think it will do any good?"

"Of course it will."

I sat down and opened the Pirate book and commenced to read, but I could see he was not following, so I stopped.

"About what time do you think I'm going to die?" he asked.

"What?"

"About how long will it be before I die?"

"You aren't going to die. What's the matter with you?"

"Oh, yes, I am. I heard him say a hundred and two."

"People don't die with a fever of one hundred and two. That's a silly way to talk."

"I know they do. At school in France the boys told me you can't live with forty-four degrees. I've got a hundred and two."

He had been waiting to die all day, ever since nine o'clock in the morning.

"You poor Schatz," I said. "Poor old Schatz. It's like miles and kilometers. You aren't going to die. That's a different thermometer. On that thermometer thirty-seven is normal. On this kind it's ninety-eight."

"Are you sure?"

"Absolutely," I said. "It's like miles and kilometers. You know, like how many kilometers we make when we do seventy miles in the car?"

"Oh," he said.

But his gaze at the foot of the bed relaxed slowly. The hold over himself relaxed too, finally, and the next day it was very slack and he cried very easily at little things that were of no importance.

> At this point, Schatz expresses the central issue in the story. Because of a misunderstanding, he thinks he is going to die.

> In the conclusion to the story, the boy is getting well, but the aftermath of the fear he felt continues.

Respond in Writing Write freely about how the two characters view the same situation. What is different in their perspectives?

Develop Your Own Story Ideas Work with your classmates to develop ideas that you might use in writing a story about two characters who see the same situation in very different ways.

Small Group: Discuss the writing you have done. Answer the following questions to help think of details for each author's story.

Questions for Thinking of Details

- What is the setting of the story? In what ways does the setting affect what happens in the story?
- What is the nature of the problem that is viewed differently by the two main characters?
- How is the situation viewed by one of the two characters?
- How is the situation viewed by the other main character?
- How, if at all, are the different perceptions resolved in the story?

Whole Group: Take part in a class discussion to see how different members of the class constructed characters who see the same situation in different ways.

Write About It You will next write a short story about two people who view the same situation in different ways. You can choose from any of the following possible topics, audiences, and forms.

Possible Topics	Possible Audiences	Possible Forms
• a parent and teenage son or daughter view the teenager's behavior in different ways • two friends view the same situation in different ways • two enemies see the same situation in different ways • a police officer and citizen view the same situation in different ways	• parents • teenagers • a teacher • a judge	• a short story • a narrative poem • a television or movie script • a graphic novel

Analyzing a Story

A **short story** is a fictional account of characters resolving a conflict or situation.

Your purpose in writing a short story is to create a piece of fiction that will entertain your reader. In the process you will be using both your narrative skills and your descriptive skills to express yourself. In a short story, you tell what happens to a character or characters who try to resolve a conflict or problem. As the narrative unfolds, you describe the characters, places, events, and objects in order to give the reader a clear picture of what happens.

You can learn more about narrative and descriptive writing on pages 90–93, 116–165.

ELEMENTS OF A SHORT STORY

All short stories have three main sections: a beginning, a middle, and an end. Usually in the beginning of a story, the writer provides all the necessary background information that readers will need to understand and to enjoy the story. For example, readers will find out where the story takes place, who the main characters are, and what problem, or **conflict,** the main character has to solve or overcome. The middle of the story then develops the plot; that is, the writer relates—usually chronologically—what happens to the characters as a result of the conflict and how the characters react to those events. The ending of the story tells the outcome or shows how the **resolution** of the central conflict is resolved.

For information about how the elements of a short story contribute to its meaning, turn to pages 297–298.

Engaging Plot and Central Conflict

The **plot**—the sequence of events leading to the outcome or point of the story—is the story's core. The plot tells what happens as the characters meet and struggle to resolve a central conflict. This conflict can come from within a character, such as a conflict of conscience; between characters, such as a conflict between friends; or between characters and the outside world, such as a struggle against the forces of nature. The plot usually begins with an event that triggers the central conflict. Once the central conflict is revealed, the plot develops more quickly, bringing the story to a **climax,** or high point. After resolving the conflict (or explaining why it remains unresolved), the story ends. If a story ends too abruptly, the resolution does not seem complete. In a well-developed resolution, the various strands of the plot are woven together and the future of the characters can be imagined.

Believable Characters

Most short stories focus on one main character who has or faces the conflict or on two main characters whose relationship is often the source of the conflict. The other characters in the story—the minor, or supporting, characters—either help or hinder the main character in resolving the crisis. In the best short stories, characters are colorful, believable, and memorable to readers in some way. Authors develop characters through the actions the characters take, the words they speak, and the words the narrator and others speak about them in the story.

Setting

The setting of a story is the environment in which the action takes place. It is like the backdrop of scenery and the props on a stage set. The setting also includes the time during which the story occurs. One of the functions of a setting is to create a **mood**—the overall feeling that the story conveys. The mood of the setting might reflect the story's theme. A neglected park at dusk, for instance, might make a tale of suspense more suspenseful. An author might also plan settings that either match or contrast with the main character's mood. For example, a confused character might be lost at sea in a dense fog or might wander around in a perfectly ordered formal garden.

Narrator

The person who tells a story is the narrator. Readers see the events of a story through the eyes of the narrator, or from the narrator's **point of view.** The following chart describes the different points of view from which a story can be told.

POINT OF VIEW	NARRATOR'S ROLE IN THE STORY
First-Person	Participant in the action; relates the events as he or she sees them; uses pronouns such as *I, me, we, us,* and *our*
Third-Person Objective	Does not participate in the action; relates the words and actions of characters but not thoughts or feelings; uses pronouns such as *he, she, they, him, her,* and *them*
Third-Person Omniscient ("All-Knowing")	Does not participate in the action; relates the thoughts and feelings of all the characters as well as their words and actions

Each point of view has certain advantages. For example, the third-person objective narrator can relate two events happening simultaneously in different places. The omniscient narrator can relate not only simultaneous events but also all of the characters' thoughts and feelings; that is, the inner life of the characters as well as the outer action. In the following excerpt, the narrator reports the characters' thoughts and feelings.

> ## MODEL: Third-Person Omniscient Point of View
>
> Neither [Mr. nor Mrs. Delahanty] wanted, in the midst of their sorrow for the good man whose life was ending, to enter into any discussion of Cress [their daughter]. What was the matter with Cress? What happened to her since she went away to college? She, who had been open and loving? And who now lived inside a world so absolutely fitted to her own size and shape that she felt any intrusion, even that of the death of her own grandfather, to be an unmerited invasion of her privacy . . . .
>
> —Jessamyn West, "Sixteen"

Theme

Most short stories have a **theme,** or main idea, of some kind, such as the healing power of love, the rewards of showing courage, or the wastefulness of despair. The outcome of the story may then imply some lesson or moral about the theme, or it may affirm some meaningful observation or conclusion about life. However, some short stories aim chiefly to surprise or entertain readers rather than to give a message.

> ## PROJECT PREP   *Short Story Elements*
>
> Write answers to the following questions about "A Day's Wait" on pages 167–170.
>
> 1. What is the plot of the story? Briefly outline the main events.
> 2. What is the central conflict? Briefly describe it.
> 3. Who are all the characters in the story? Which one is the main character and how do you know that?
> 4. What is the setting? Describe it in a few sentences.
> 5. From what point of view is the story told? How do you think that point of view affects the story?
> 6. What do you think the theme of the story is? Express the theme in a few sentences in your own words.

Author Kurt Vonnegut once compared writing fiction to making a movie, saying, "All sorts of accidental things will happen after you've set up the cameras. . . . You set the story in motion, and as you're watching this thing begin, all these opportunities will show up. Keeping your mind open to opportunities will help you imagine your story." Unless you think through the basic elements of your story, however, it may remain only as bits of "footage." For this reason your prewriting work should include building a plot.

1 Building an Engaging Plot

Many of your best ideas for a plot will come from your own experiences and observations, while others will come from your imagination. The following strategies may stimulate your thinking about plot ideas.

Strategies for Thinking of a Plot

- Brainstorm for a list of story ideas based on conflicts you have experienced or observed firsthand. Then use clustering or inquiring to develop plot details. For each conflict you think of, identify the triggering event and describe the resolution or outcome.

- Scan newspaper headlines and news items for an event you could build into a fictional story. Some items might suggest a comic or a tragic tale, for example, or might report a discovery or a mystery that you could explore in fiction.

- Think of conflicts or events in history—including your family history and local history—that might be interesting to develop in fiction writing.

- Observe people and events in your life. Sometimes even small events or snatches of conversation will suggest a conflict on which to build a plot. An incident that you noticed in a mall, for example, could become the basis of a story.

Once you have a story idea and a conflict, you can build the plot around it. A plot usually unfolds from the event that triggers the conflict to the event that resolves it. You will probably arrange the details of your plot so that they naturally unfold as the story progresses. The chart on the next page shows some steps for developing a plot, along with examples.

Strategies for Developing a Plot

1. Introduce the event or circumstance that triggers the action. Include descriptive details about the triggering event, making the source of the conflict clear.

   From Within a Character   the desire to change one's circumstances

   From the Outside World   the receipt of a letter or phone call
                                  an accident

2. Develop details describing the nature of the conflict.

   Conflict with Self   one's conscience

   Conflict with Others   friend or family members
                                enemies or strangers

   Conflict with Nature   severe weather conditions
                                disease or disability

3. Develop details about the obstacles the characters will struggle against or overcome to resolve the central conflict.

   Within a Character   fears or other emotions

   In the Outside World   other characters
                                trials of nature

4. Develop details about how the main character might overcome the obstacles.

   By the Character   strength of character
                            perseverance

   Through Outside Events   luck or chance
                                  new knowledge or understanding

5. Develop details about how the conflict will be resolved and how the story will end.

   Obstacles Overcome   new wisdom
                              success or satisfaction

   Obstacles Not Overcome   acceptance of shortcomings
                                  decision to try again

The diagram on the next page shows the general shape of a storyline.

CLIMAX

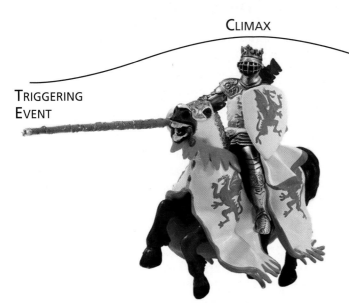

TRIGGERING
EVENT

RESOLUTION OR
OUTCOME

PROJECT PREP *Prewriting* *Plot, Central Conflict, and Characters*

In your small group, return to your own story sketch. Keeping in mind the elements of the story just reviewed, continue to plot a possible story line. For each member of your group, discuss and refine possibilities for:

Plot and Central Conflict What is the central conflict in the story, and how will the story unfold?

Characters Who are the characters who come into conflict, and what about their differences of perspective put them into conflict?

Setting Where does the story take place, and why is this a good setting for this conflict to come to the surface?

Narrator Who will tell the story? Will it be one of the main characters? Will it have more than one narrative perspective? Will someone other than the main characters tell the story? What advantages and disadvantages follow from this choice of narrator? How reliable is your choice of narrator in telling the story with some semblance of credibility? Is it possible to build in flaws so readers may doubt the narrator's perspective and appreciate other perspectives better?

② Sketching Believable Characters

Readers usually enjoy and remember stories that have interesting, believable characters. As you plan your story, you should visualize the characters that will appear in it. You could, for example, write a brief sketch of each one by brainstorming for details such as the character's name, age, physical appearance, voice, mannerisms, background, and personality traits.

The more completely you visualize your characters, the more independent they can become in your imagination. Many fiction writers report that the characters themselves seem to come alive during writing, directing the plot and dictating the dialogue. In a sense, therefore, visualizing your characters gives them life. Notice how the following writer uses details that allow you to visualize the character.

MODEL: Characterization

In the smallest of these huts lived old Berl, a man in his eighties . . . Old Berl was one of the Jews who had been driven from their villages in Russia and had settled in Poland. In Lentshin, they mocked the mistakes he made while praying aloud. He spoke with a sharp "r." He was short, broad-shouldered, and had a small white beard, and summer and winter he wore a sheepskin hat, a padded cotton jacket, and stout boots. He walked slowly, shuffling his feet. He had a half acre of field, a cow, a goat, and chickens.

—Isaac Bashevis Singer,
"The Son from America"

To help you develop characters, learn to be a careful observer. Focus on details of how people move and stand, how they sound, and how they look and dress. Make notes in your journal for use later. You can also create a cluster of details to help you. Your objective is to use such details to develop characters.

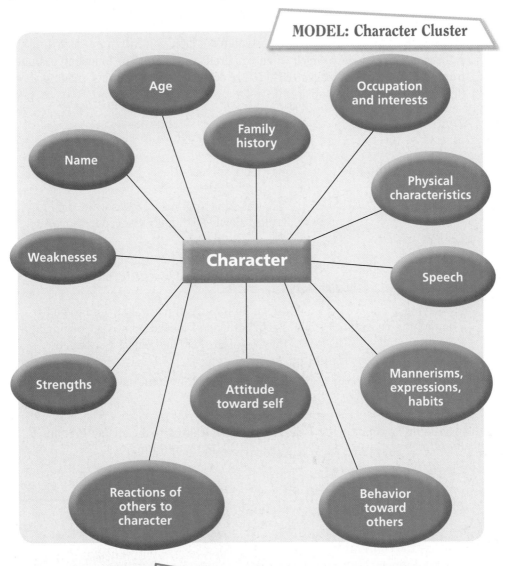

MODEL: Character Cluster

Age

Occupation and interests

Name

Family history

Physical characteristics

Weaknesses

Character

Speech

Strengths

Attitude toward self

Mannerisms, expressions, habits

Reactions of others to character

Behavior toward others

PROJECT PREP *Prewriting Character Sketch*

After visualizing the characters that will appear in your story, write a character sketch of each one. Make a character cluster if you wish, or draw a picture. Then review your sketches with the members of your group, using their feedback to expand on and elaborate the appearance, traits, and behavior of your characters.

Think Critically

Imaging

To create characters and events, fiction writers often use imaging—visualizing and feeling what it would be like to be a character and to experience an imaginary event. If you take time for imaging as you plan, later you will more easily find the right words to express yourself when you draft your story. The following passages from "A Day's Wait" on pages 167–170 are evidence of the author's imaging about Schatz's experience of his pain.

IMAGING CHART	
Imaging of the Boy	**Written Expression**
in pain	"He was shivering, his face was white, and he walked slowly as though it ached to move."
	"He lay very still in the bed and seemed very detached from what was going on."
worrying about something he cannot discuss	"It would have been natural for him to go to sleep, but when I looked up he was looking at the foot of the bed, looking very strangely."
	"He was evidently holding tight onto himself about something."
realizing he is not dying	"He had been waiting to die all day, ever since nine o'clock in the morning."

Thinking Practice

For ten minutes, use imaging to visualize the conversation in which Schatz's French classmates tell him that people die when their body temperature reaches forty-four degrees. Describe to your classmates what you "saw" and "heard" during your imaging.

3 Framing Your Story

When you have your plot and characters in mind, you can frame your story by creating a meaningful setting and deciding on what point of view to use.

CREATING A SETTING

The setting of a story often mirrors the feelings of the main character. An early spring day, for example, might be a good setting for a story about a character on the verge of shedding a dark burden and starting a new life. By relating the setting to the central conflict and to the characters' feelings, you can create the mood you want for your story. In a sketch of your setting, you might note details you could use to describe the indoor or outdoor location where the action of the story takes place. For example, you might visualize objects, dimensions, terrain, the time of day, the weather, or the season of the year. Notice how the following description of a setting creates a suspenseful mood.

For more information about descriptive writing, turn to pages 92–93 and 140–165.

> **MODEL: Details of a Setting**
>
> At the most remote end of the crypt there appeared another . . . Its walls had been lined with human remains, piled to the vault overhead, in the fashion of the great catacombs of Paris. . . . From the fourth side the bones had been thrown down . . . forming at one point a mound of some size. Within the wall thus exposed by the displacing of the bones, we perceived a still interior crypt or recess, in depth about four feet, in width three, in height six or seven.
>
> —Edgar Allan Poe, "The Cask of Amontillado"

CHOOSING A POINT OF VIEW

As you read on page 173, you can choose among three different points of view for telling your stories: first-person, third-person objective, and third-person omniscient. If you are writing a story with a narrator who is a participant, the first-person point of view is probably the most natural. If the narrator is writing about other characters and is not a participant in the story, use third-person objective or omniscient. Use the same point of view throughout your story unless you have intentionally introduced another point of view to add interest and subtlety.

> **Writing Tip**
>
> Plot, characters, setting, point of view, and other story elements should all fit together so that the reader believes in the story and finds meaning in it.

PROJECT PREP *Prewriting* *Setting and Point of View*

1. Focus next on the setting of your story. Where would the characters you have created come into contact? What characterizes the physical setting of their meeting? What sensory details can you come up with that contribute to the construction of a suitable mood for their encounter? Write a description of the setting in which you help readers see, feel, hear, smell, and/or taste the environment.

2. When you have completed this description, share it with your small group. Help each other decide which of the elements you have included are effective and worth keeping and perhaps elaborating, and which do not belong in your story.

3. Next, imagine how your story would read if it were told from the point of view of your main character and from that of each of the other characters. (You might even want to write a draft from each character's point of view.) Also imagine how your story would sound if it were told from the first-person, the third-person objective, and the third-person omniscient points of view. Finally, choose the best point of view for your story and decide how you will tell the story from that character's perspective.

4 Ordering Events

After getting the basic story elements in mind, visualize all the events you want to include and arrange them in chronological order. You may later decide to deviate from this order. For instance, you could start your story at the end and then go back to the beginning, or you could start in the middle and remember back to the beginning in a flashback before ending your story (see page 187). Whatever order you decide to use when you draft, you will find it helpful to have a chronological list of all the events you plan to include.

USING A STORY MAP

A story map is a useful tool in helping you track the order of events in the story and in understanding their relation to the entire story. The following story map shows the shape of the plot in "A Day's Wait." The triggering event is written on the first line of the diagram.

❷ Doctor comes, takes his temperature, and leaves medications.

❸ Papa sits with him and reads.

❹ Papa goes out hunting with a young Irish setter.

❺ Papa returns home and finds Schatz does not want anyone in the room.

❻ Papa takes Schatz's temperature again and tries to read to him some more.

❼ Schatz reveals that he thinks he is going to die.

❽ Papa explains the confusion.

❾ Schatz relaxes.

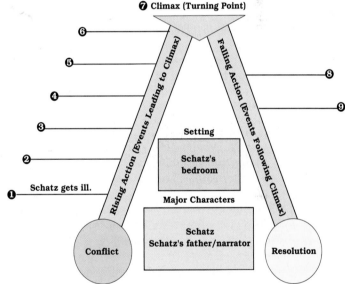

PROJECT PREP *Prewriting* *Order of Events*

After you list all the events you plan to include in your story, arrange them in chronological order. As you study your list, think of other possible ways to order the events that would make sense to readers and would capture their interest. Create a story map that outlines the way in which the story will unfold. Then consult with the members of your writing group to get their feedback on the sequence you have drafted and revise it if necessary.

The Power of Language ⚡

Fluency: Let It Flow

To make your writing flow invitingly, vary the length and beginnings of your sentences. In the following passage from Hemingway's "The Big Two-Hearted River," the second sentence is a very short one amidst medium and long sentences. The varied beginnings of the sentences are highlighted: yellow for subjects first, blue for introductory phrases.

> The road ran on, dipping occasionally, but always climbing. He went on up. Finally after going parallel to the burnt hill, he reached the top. Nick leaned back against a stump and slipped out of the pack harness. Ahead of him, as far as he could see, was the pine plain. The burned country stopped off at the left of a range of hills. On ahead islands of dark pine trees rose out of the plain. Far off to the left was the line of the river. Nick followed it with his eye and caught glints of the water in the sun.

In "A Day's Wait," Hemingway varies the somewhat stark dialogue between the father and son with longer sentences describing the hunting expedition.

> After a while he said to me, "You don't have to stay in here with me, Papa, if it bothers you."
>
> "It doesn't bother me."
>
> "No, I mean you don't have to stay if it's going to bother you."
>
> I thought perhaps he was a little light-headed and giving him prescribed capsules at eleven o'clock I went out for a while.
>
> It was a bright, cold day, the ground covered with a sleet that had frozen so that it seemed as if . . . the bare ground had been varnished with ice. I took the young Irish setter for a little walk up the road and along a frozen creek, but it was difficult to stand or walk on the glassy surface and the red dog slipped and slithered and I fell twice, hard, once dropping my gun and having it slide away over the ice.

Punctuation Tip

Use a comma after certain introductory elements in a sentence. (See pages 852–853.)

Try It Yourself

Write a passage of about five sentences on your project topic. Use different colored highlighters to see how you started your sentences. If you have only one color, revise until you have variety. Also count the number of words in each sentence. If they are all about the same, look for ways to vary their length to achieve a smoother flow.

As you write your story, keep in mind your reasons for writing and your audience. While the purpose of all creative writing is to create, you may have other writing goals as well. For example, you may want your readers to laugh or cry, or you may want them to identify with your main character. To achieve these purposes, you have available a variety of types of writing. For instance, you can use narrative writing to advance the plot. You can use descriptive writing to create the settings and characters' appearances (pages 146–149 and 178–179). Informative writing allows you to explain background information about the plot or characters (pages 210–253). In addition to these basic types of writing, you can use the following strategies, which are specific to fiction writing.

Strategies for Drafting a Short Story

- Use vivid language and interesting details to introduce the characters and the central conflict.

- Use sensory details to create a mood.

- Use background details to set the time and place of the story and to capture your readers' interest.

- Aim for originality in your writing by avoiding stereotypes and by using vivid words to bring the story to life.

- Start the plot early in the story by introducing the triggering event.

- Reveal the characters and unfold the plot through a combination of description, narration or action, dialogue, and reflection.

- Maintain a clear and consistent point of view. If you intentionally introduce another point of view, keep it clearly distinctive.

- Pace the plot so that the action moves along in an engaging way.

- Include only those events that have a direct bearing on the plot and the central conflict. Connect the events in your story by showing how each event in the plot relates naturally and logically to the central conflict.

- Use chronological order and transitions to show the passing of time and to build up tension.

- End your story in a way that makes the outcome clear and that leaves a strong emotional impression on your readers.

USING DIALOGUE

In many cases you can use dialogue to develop your characters and to advance your plot. The following examples from "A Day's Wait" show how Hemingway used dialogue for a variety of purposes.

EXAMPLES: Using Dialogue

To Present the Central Conflict	When the doctor came he took the boy's temperature. "What is it?" I asked him. "One hundred and two."
To Reveal Thoughts	After a while he said to me, "You don't have to stay in here with me, Papa, if it bothers you." "It doesn't bother me." "No, I mean you don't have to stay if it's going to bother you." I thought perhaps he was a little light-headed and giving him prescribed capsules at eleven o'clock I went out for a while.
To Advance the Plot	"You can't come in," he said. "You mustn't get what I have." I went up to him and found him in exactly the position I had left him, white–faced, but with the tops of his cheeks flushed by fever, staring still, as he had stared, at the foot of the bed. I took his temperature. "What is it?" "Something like a hundred," I said. It was one hundred and two and four tenths. "It was a hundred and two," he said. "Who said so?" "The doctor." "Your temperature is all right," I said. "It's nothing to worry about." "I don't worry," he said, "but I can't keep from thinking." "Don't think," I said. "Just take it easy."
To Express the Climax	"About what time do you think I'm going to die?" he asked. "What?" "About how long will it be before I die?" "You aren't going to die. What's the matter with you?" "Oh, yes, I am. I heard him say a hundred and two." "People don't die with a fever of one hundred and two. That's a silly way to talk." "I know they do. At school in France the boys told me you can't live with forty–four degrees. I've got a hundred and two."
To Express the Resolution	"You poor Schatz," I said. "Poor old Schatz. It's like miles and kilometers. You aren't going to die. That's a different thermometer. On that thermometer thirty–seven is normal. On this kind it's ninety–eight." "Are you sure?" "Absolutely," I said. "It's like miles and kilometers . . ."

Writing Dialogue

Imagine each of the following situations. Then select one of the situations or another of your choice and write a dialogue about 12 lines long between the characters. You may want to review the correct form for writing dialogue on the preceding pages and page 882.

1. A stranger asks for directions to the police station.

2. A hurried shopper seeks help from a salesclerk.

3. A student has a conference with his or her advisor.

4. Two teenagers discuss someone else's problem.

5. Two friends argue over what movie to see.

ENHANCING THE PLOT

One of the great pleasures of reading is the sense of being swept up in a story. You may feel anxious as you read, fearing trouble ahead for the main character. You may be intrigued by missing pieces in the story that are only revealed in unexpected places or unexpected order. These feelings are the result of the writer's skill in using devices to enhance the plot. Try using these devices to add excitement and flavor to your plot.

DEVICES FOR ENHANCING THE PLOT	
Flashback	an event from the past that is presented out of sequence and interrupts the chronological order
Foreshadowing	clues that help the reader anticipate what is to come
Story within a Story	a story that is told during the telling of another story
Subplot	a secondary plot line that reinforces the main plot line
Juxtaposition	placing two normally unrelated events, characters, or words next to one another to create a surprise effect

Hemingway uses juxtaposition in "A Day's Wait" when the narrator leaves the fevered boy's sick room and heads into the "bright, cold day."

PROJECT PREP *Drafting* Dialogue and Plot Techniques

Review all your prewriting about conflct, character, setting, plot, and narrator. Then write the first draft of the short story you have been developing. Work in dialogue that sounds realistic and that advances the plot. Try using some devices from the chart above to enhance your plot and make it more gripping. Use peer conferencing to test your ideas or to get help with trouble spots. Keep writing until you have a workable first draft.

Writing a Short Story  Revising

Many fiction writers report that they often keep only the few best parts of a first draft and drop all the rest. When you revise, therefore, be ready to give up ideas or details that weaken your short story or that rob it of life. Look especially for ways of strengthening your plot, enhancing your descriptions, and sharpening your characterizations.

HERE'S HOW

Revising Strategies for Short Stories

Strengthening the Plot
- Add background details and transitions to ensure adequate development and coherence.
- Delete any plot details that do not relate to the central conflict and its resolution or to subplots.
- Check for clarity to ensure that readers will understand the story's meaning, point, or theme.
- Use such devices as flashbacks and foreshadowing to enhance the plot.

Enhancing Descriptions
- Add or substitute sensory details to enliven descriptions of characters, settings, and actions.
- Use imaging to visualize your descriptions again so you can improve them.
- Enrich your descriptions by using figurative language.

Sharpening Characterizations
- Add or eliminate details to sharpen the characterization of your main character.
- Look for ways to reveal characters and their motivations through dialogue, action, and reflection.
- Rewrite dialogue until it sounds as natural as real-life conversations.

After you have applied the revising strategies above, review the structure and content of your story. The checklist on the next page will help you remember the basic points to look for as you revise your short story.

Evaluation Checklist for Revising

✓ Does the beginning of your story describe the setting, capture the readers' attention, introduce characters, and include the triggering event? (pages 172–182)

✓ Does the middle develop the plot by making the central conflict clear and by including events that are directly related to that conflict? (pages 175–177)

✓ Are events in the plot arranged in chronological order or in an order that makes the chronology of events clear? (pages 183 and 185)

✓ Does the story build until the action reaches a climax? (pages 172 and 185-186))

✓ Does the pacing of the events keep the story moving along in an engaging way? (page 185)

✓ Did you use dialogue and description to show subtleties of your characters' personalities? (pages 173, 178–179, and 185–187)

✓ Does the ending show how the conflict was resolved and bring the story to a close? (pages 172 and 185)

✓ Did you choose an appropriate point of view and stick to it throughout the story? (pages 173–174 and 181–182)

✓ Does the story have a theme or express your reasons for writing it? Does it accomplish your specific purpose for creative writing, and is it appropriate for your audience? (pages 171–174 and 185)

PROJECT PREP *Revising* *Using Strategies and a Checklist*

Use the **Revising Strategies for Short Stories** on page 188 to review and revise your story. Then, with your writing group members, exchange papers and use the checklist above for evaluating your partner's story. Revise your work based on your partner's feedback.

Once you have drafted your short story and revised it to your satisfaction, you are ready to edit it. In the editing stage, you correct your writing so that it shows accurate spelling, punctuation, and capitalization, as well as control over grammatical elements such as subject-verb agreement, pronoun-antecedent agreement, verb forms, and parallelism.

The Language of Power *Past Tense*

Power Rule: Use mainstream past tense forms of regular and irregular verbs. (See pages 684–703.)

See It in Action Some verb forms are especially tricky to keep straight. In the following passage from "A Day's Wait," Hemingway uses the correct form of the past tense of *lie*.

> His face was very white and there were dark areas under his eyes. He **lay** very still in the bed and seemed very detached from what was going on.

The verbs *lie* and *lay, sit* and *set,* and *rise* and *raise* are often confused, so it's a good idea to just memorize the correct forms of each. (See pages 691–692.)

Remember It Record this rule and example in the Power Rule section of your Personalized Editing Checklist.

Use It Read through your short story and check for places where you used the words *lie* and *lay, sit* and *set,* or *rise* and *raise* and make sure you have used the correct form.

PROJECT PREP *Evaluating* **Editing and Publishing**

Use the six-trait rubric to evaluate your story. Submit it to your teacher and make changes in response to his or her feedback. Create a class anthology of your finished stories.

Ideas	4 The plot, setting, characters, and dialogue are original and creative.	3 The plot, setting, characters, and dialogue are effective.	2 Most aspects of the plot, setting, characters, and dialogue are effective.	1 Most aspects of the plot, setting, characters, and dialogue are ineffective.
Organization	4 The organization is clear with abundant transitions.	3 A few events or ideas seem out of place or transitions are missing.	2 Many events seem out of place and transitions are missing.	1 The order of events is unclear and hard to follow.
Voice	4 The story has an appropriate point of view. The storyteller's voice sounds natural.	3 The story has an appropriate point of view. The storyteller's voice sounds mostly natural.	2 The point of view is inconsistent. The storyteller's voice sounds unnatural at times.	1 The story does not have an appropriate point of view. The storyteller's voice sounds unnatural.
Word Choice	4 Specific words help readers picture characters and setting.	3 Some words are specific and help readers picture characters and setting.	2 Some words are overly general and do not bring characters or setting into focus.	1 Most words are overly general and do not bring characters or setting into focus.
Sentence Fluency	4 Varied sentences flow smoothly and dialogue reflects characters.	3 Most sentences are varied and flow smoothly, and dialogue reflects characters.	2 Some sentences are choppy and dialogue seems forced.	1 Sentences are choppy and not varied, and dialogue seems forced or is missing.
Conventions	4 Conventions, including dialogue and punctuation are correct and Power Rules are followed.	3 Conventions including dialogue and punctuation are mainly correct. Power Rules are followed.	2 Some conventions are incorrect but Power Rules are followed.	1 There are many errors and at least one failure to follow a Power Rule.

CHAPTER 6

Writing a Play

The main difference between plays and other kinds of writing is that plays are written to be performed, not just read. In a play, the story is told through the use of dialogue and the actions of the characters.

A **play** is a piece of writing intended to be performed on a stage by actors.

In the following scene from Arthur Miller's *The Price*, a husband and wife discuss the idea of asking his brother for help. The men's father has just died, and they are in his house trying to figure out what to do with his possessions. As you read the scene, think about your responses to the following questions: Why should the content in this play be performed and not just read? What makes this play a success or failure and why?

The Price

Esther: I don't want to be a pest—but I think there could be some money here, Vic.

He is silent.

You're going to raise that with him, aren't you?

Victor: *with a formed decision*: I've been thinking about it. He's got a right to his half, why should he give up anything?

> This stage direction makes it clear how Victor is feeling.

Esther: I thought you'd decided to put it to him?

Victor: I've changed my mind. I don't really feel he owes me anything, I can't put on an act.

Esther: But how many Cadillacs can he drive?

Victor: That's why he's got Cadillacs. People who love money don't give it away.

Esther: I don't know why you keep putting it like charity. There's such a thing as a moral debt. Vic, you made his whole career possible. What law said that only he could study medicine—?

> What do you learn about Esther from her words?

Victor: Esther, please—let's not get back on that, will you?

Esther: I'm not back on anything—you were even the better student. That's a real debt, and he ought to be made to face it. He could never have finished medical school if you hadn't taken care of Pop. I mean we ought to start talking the way people talk! There could be some real money here.

Victor: I doubt that. There are no antiques or—

Esther: Just because it's ours why must it be worthless?

Victor: Now what's that for?

Esther: Because that's the way we think! We do!

Victor, *sharply*: The man won't even come to the phone, how am I going to—?

Esther: Then you write him a letter, bang on his door. This belongs to you!

Without ever being told directly, the audience gets a clear sense of what the relationship between Victor and his brother is like.

Victor, *surprised, seeing how deadly earnest she is*: What are you so excited about?

Esther: Well, for one thing it might help you make up your mind to take your retirement.

A slight pause.

Victor: *rather secretively, unwillingly*: It's not the money been stopping me.

Esther: Then what is it?

He is silent.

I just thought that with a little cushion you could take a month or two until something occurs to you that you want to do.

Victor: It's all I think about right now, I don't have to quit to think.

Esther: But nothing seems to come of it.

Victor: Is it that easy? I'm going to be fifty. You don't just start a whole new career. I don't understand why it's so urgent all of a sudden.

Esther—*laughs*: All of a sudden! It's all I've been talking about since you became eligible—I've been saying the same thing for three years!

Victor: Well, it's not three years—

Esther: It'll be three years in March! It's *three years*. If you'd gone back to school then you'd almost have your Master's by now; you might have had a chance to get into something you'd love to do. Isn't that true? Why can't you make a move?

Victor—*pause. He is almost ashamed*: I'll tell you the truth. I'm not sure the whole thing wasn't a little unreal. I'd be fifty-three, fifty-four by the time I could start doing anything.

Esther: But you always knew that.

Victor: It's different when you're right on top of it. I'm not sure it makes any sense now.

Esther, *moving away, the despair in her voice*: Well . . . this is exactly what I tried to tell you a thousand times. It makes the same sense it ever made. But you might have twenty more years, and that's still a long time. Could do a lot of interesting things in that time. *Slight pause.* You're so young, Vic.

Victor: I am?

Esther: Sure! I'm not, but you are. God, all the girls goggle at you, what do you want?

Victor—*laughs emptily*: It's hard to discuss it, Es, because I don't understand it.

Esther: Well, why not talk about what you don't understand? Why do you expect yourself to be an authority?

> What does the dialogue reveal about the relationship between Esther and Victor?

Victor: Well, one of us has got to stay afloat, kid.

Esther: You want me to pretend everything is great? I'm bewildered and I'm going to act bewildered! *It flies out as though long suppressed*: I've asked you fifty times to write a letter to Walter—

Victor, *like a repeated story*: What's this with Walter again? What's Walter going to—?

Esther: He is an important scientist, and that hospital's building a whole new research division. I saw it in the paper, it's his hospital.

Victor: Esther, the man hasn't called me in sixteen years.

Esther: But neither have you called him!

He looks at her in surprise.

Well, you haven't. That's also a fact.

Victor, *as though the idea were new and incredible*: What would I call him for?

Esther: Because, he's your brother, he's influential, and he could help—Yes, that's how people do, Vic! Those articles he wrote had a real idealism, there was a genuine human quality. I mean people do change, you know.

Victor, *turning away*: I'm sorry, I don't need Walter.

● **Practice Your Skills**

Analyzing Dramatic Elements

Write answers to the following questions about the scene from *The Price*.

1. What is the central conflict? Briefly describe it.
2. Who are all the characters in the story? Which one is the main character and how do you know that?
3. What is the setting? Describe it in a few sentences.

THEME AND MOOD

Like stories and other works of literature, plays express themes. Some themes of Arthur Miller's *The Price,* for example, are materialism and family relationships. Themes can be explicit or implicit. An **explicit theme** is one that is stated clearly in the play. If a character in *The Price*, for example, says, "Money is the root of family evil," he would be expressing an explicit theme of the play. An **implicit theme,** in contrast, is not stated directly. Instead it is a message derived from the characters' actions and dialogue—a judgment the viewer makes by interpreting the characters' words and interactions. An implicit theme of *The Price* might be, "Issues of family justice are often played out through conflicts over money and material possessions."

Plays also convey moods. **Mood** is the atmosphere created by the setting and other details. The mood of *The Price* might be described as oppressive. The setting is the home of the recently deceased father of Victor and Walter, so a sense of heaviness accompanies that. The clearly unresolved issues between Esther and Victor hang heavy above them. The stage directions heighten this mood: Victor responds "secretly, unwillingly"; Esther speaks, "moving away, the despair in her voice."

Closely related to mood is tone. In drama, **tone** is the speaker's attitude toward his or her listener. The tone in the scene between Victor and Esther is frustrated, since both feel they can't get through to one another. Esther's tone might be further described as nagging, and Victor's might be described as defensive.

Tone might also refer to the writer's attitude toward his or her characters. Such tone might be sympathetic or judgmental, straightfoward or ironic.

● **Practice Your Skills**

Experimenting with Tone

Choose a portion of the scene from *The Price* that you find especially tense. Rewrite the conversation between Victor and Esther so that it has a different tone.

FINDING IDEAS FOR A PLAY

Like stories and novels, plays are based upon conflict. A conflict can occur between two or more people. To find possible subjects for a play scene, think about conflicts you have seen and heard—or just heard of. They may come from your own life, the lives of people you know, or your imagination. Freewrite about some of them in your journal. Visualize them in all their drama. Use other prewriting techniques that you like, too, such as clustering or self-questioning.

● **Practice Your Skills**

Finding Ideas for a Scene in a Play

Freewrite a response to each question below. Elaborate with details. Save your work.

1. What is the most dramatic conflict that you have lived through, witnessed, or heard about?
2. What events in the news or in history have made you feel most strongly?
3. Who are the most interesting two or three people you know, and why? What might happen if they clashed?
4. How would you change if, in a few years, you lived through a major event such as war, serious illness, or falling in love?
5. What might you be like if you had grown up in a different family or a different place?
6. What would be the most surprising thing that could happen to you today? How would you respond? How would it change you?

DEVELOPING CHARACTERS

As in stories and novels, characters are the basis of plays. In plays, the characters are brought to life by actors, real people who move and talk and have individual gestures and tones of voice. Each actor shapes a role in his or her own special way, but the character must be vividly brought out by the playwright's words.

● Practice Your Skills

Sketching Characters

Return to your answer to Question 3 in the previous activity. For each of the people you named, write a character sketch. Each sketch should be a paragraph describing the important facts and details about the person. An actor preparing to play the role of the character should be able to learn a lot from the sketch.

CREATING SETTING

Novels, stories, and movies can wander from setting to setting: the action might be on Earth one minute and on Mars the next. In contrast, most plays remain within a very limited setting. It may be one room. That is the simplest of settings, for it requires no changes of scenery. If a play contains more than one setting—such as several rooms within a house, or the apartments of two different characters—the scenery must be changed, usually between acts. One of the playwright's first jobs is to visualize an interesting, dramatic setting that can be shown physically on a stage.

● Practice Your Skills

Visualizing Settings

Make a list of five or six places in your community that might make good settings for stage plays. For each location, state briefly your reason for thinking it would make a good stage setting. Be sure your settings are specific enough to be physically shown on a stage. For example, "school" is not a specific setting, because an entire school cannot be shown onstage at one time. "The gym" is specific enough to be shown in that way.

WRITING DIALOGUE

Because plays consist of live action, and because one of the things that makes human life interesting is talk, most plays contain a lot of dialogue—that is, the words spoken by the characters. Dialogue is the medium through which the action in most plays transpires; it expresses emotion and conveys meaning. It is through dialogue, in fact, that the audience is informed of the dramatic situation and its background.

As in a story, the dialogue in a play should seem real. Each character should have his or her own personal way of speaking. In addition, the dialogue in plays needs to deliver information to the audience. The audience watching a play is not reading any descriptions or any background information. Everything that the audience learns about the characters must be conveyed through action and dialogue. For example, if a character returned home injured from a war five years before the play began, some character at some point is probably going to say something like, "Well, it's been five years since Jill came home from that war with her arm in a cast." The need to express information and characterization at the same time makes the dialogue in plays particularly rich in content.

Writing Dialogue

Write a conversation between a teenager and his or her parent in which the two characters disagree about the teen's goals. Set the conversation in a community like your own, and have the characters be people from a background similar to yours. Write at least two separate speeches for each character. Write only the dialogue; do not include descriptions. Save your work.

WRITING STAGE DIRECTIONS

Playwrights usually supply some directions for the reader (and the actor and director) about how the characters speak and move. These are called **stage directions.** They are usually found in italic print. Most modern playwrights like to keep their stage directions short. They feel that the dialogue itself should convey most of what the audience learns about the characters. For example, if the character's words are angry, it should not be necessary to add a stage direction, *Angrily*. Stage directions are necessary at times, however. For instance, they state which characters are entering or exiting. They also express meaningful actions, such as *He stands slouched over, and Troy shoves him on his shoulder*. At the beginning of a play, there is usually a brief description of the set; when a new character appears, there is usually a brief physical description of the character, perhaps including how the character is dressed. **Props**—short for *properties,* or physical objects that appear on stage—are also mentioned in stage directions.

● **Practice Your Skills**

Writing Stage Directions

Return to the parent-teen dialogue you wrote and add at least two stage directions. Make sure that they express aspects of the characters' speech or actions that the dialogue does not already express.

Using a Rubric for Dramatic Scenes

Use the rubric below as a guide to revising your dramatic scene.

Dramatic Elements	**4** The plot, setting, characters, and dialogue are original and creative. The theme is meaningful.	**3** The plot, setting, characters, and dialogue are effective. The theme is clear.	**2** Most aspects of the plot, setting, characters, and dialogue are effective, but the theme is unclear.	**1** Most aspects of the plot, setting, characters, and dialogue are ineffective. The theme is unclear.
Stage Directions	**4** The stage directions clearly indicate actions and states of mind and add depth and subtlety.	**3** The stage directions indicate actions and states of mind.	**2** The stage directions indicate actions but do not go deeper.	**1** There are few if any stage directions.
Mood and Tone	**4** The scene establishes a mood effectively and the mood is appropriate to the theme. The tone enhances the mood and theme.	**3** The scene establishes a mood effectively and the mood is appropriate to the theme. The tone reflects the mood and theme.	**2** The scene establishes a mood but some of the details included don't seem related to that mood. The tone is not clearly tied to the mood and theme.	**1** The mood and tone are hard to identify.

PROJECT PREP Changing Genres *From Story to Scene*

Return to the story you wrote (or another text from your portfolio). Choose a portion of it that you think would lend itself well to being enacted and write a script for it. Have members of your writing group read it aloud to make sure the dialogue sounds real. Then revise, thinking about how to strengthen your dialogue and how to make the action more vivid and believable. Also consider how effectively you conveyed mood, tone, and theme. Did you use details that help create the mood you want? What tone do your characters have with one another? Does a theme come through, whether it is explicit or implicit? Have you used language and stage directions to express subtle shades of meaning? Using feedback, revise again. Then make a final copy following the play-script format as in the scene from *The Price*. You might want to gather a group of friends and give a live or recorded performance of your scene.

In the Media

Across the Media: Evaluating Artistic Performances

Some literary works—even nondramatic ones—cannot be fully appreciated until they are performed. This process can in fact help both the performer and the audience understand the work more fully. Books on tape, poetry and short-story readings on the radio, and literary television shows attract faithful listeners and viewers.

How can you tell if such an artistic performance is effective? Here are some of the criteria that may help you evaluate artistic performances.

 Criteria for Evaluating Artistic Performances

✓ Does the performance move you?

✓ Does the performance make confusing parts clearer?

✓ Are the performers confident and well prepared?

✓ Did the performers establish eye contact and use effective body language?

✓ Do the performers use vocal variety to express the work's underlying meanings?

✓ Does the performance use the stage effectively, with variety of pacing and use of space?

✓ For example, are camera angles, lighting, editing, and music used effectively? How do they contribute to the overall effect?

Media Activity

Use the criteria above to evaluate the poem "On the Pulse of the Morning" by Maya Angelou, read at President Clinton's first-term inauguration in 1993. Practice reading it aloud and take turns performing it for the class.

You can find a clip online of Maya Angelou reading her poem "On the Pulse of the Morning."

Writing a Poem

"Poetry is the art of understanding what it is to be alive," wrote Archibald MacLeish. Even before writing was invented, poets sang or chanted the deepest feelings of humanity, and people listened. Poetry is a way of using language that gets the most out of each word and syllable.

Poetry is a writing form that expresses powerful feelings through sound, images, and other imaginative uses of language.

Feel how much is expressed in so few words as you read this poem written by Walt Whitman. Think about how these feelings would be expressed in a play or a short story.

When I Heard The Learn'd Astronomer

When I heard the learn'd astronomer,

When the proofs, the figures, were ranged in columns
    before me,

When I was shown the charts and diagrams, to add,
    divide, and measure them,

When I sitting heard the astronomer where he lectured
    with much applause in the lecture-room,

How soon unaccountable I became tired and sick,

Till rising and gliding out I wander'd off by myself,

In the mystical moist night-air, and from time to time,

Look'd up in perfect silence at the stars.

❶ Finding Ideas for Poems

Poetry is the form of writing that depends most upon the emotions of the writer. In choosing a subject for a poem, find something that moves you. It may move you to joy, to sadness, to anger, to laughter, or to any other emotional response. One good way to discover the emotionally powerful ideas that are already within you is to make an **Idea Chart** like the one below. List general subject areas on the left side of the chart. Write down some specific examples on the right-hand side. You can explore those examples further by additional brainstorming, freewriting, clustering, or questioning.

IDEA CHART	
Events	getting an A; buying shoes; playing trumpet
Scenes	an empty schoolyard at night; a crowded beach; a sailboat skimming the waves
Sensations	the sound of a subway train; the taste of hot peppers; the sight of sunset

● **Practice Your Skills**

Charting to Find Ideas for a Poem

Create an idea chart using the following general topics as the left–hand entries. Think of at least five examples for each topic. Save your work.

1. growing up

2. emotions

3. places

4. hopes and dreams

5. imaginary worlds

● **Practice Your Skills**

Freewriting to Find Ideas for a Poem

Select one of the specific examples you wrote in your Idea Chart and freewrite about it for two to five minutes. Save your work.

PROJECT PREP *Changing Genres* **From Story to Poem**

Return to the story you wrote (or another you have in your portfolio) and hold a magnifying glass to it, looking for moments in it—or feelings it evokes—that could be the substance of a poem. Choose a few and freewrite about those in your journal. Let your mind and pen run freely, exploring comparisons and imaginative ways of looking at the ideas.

② Poetic Techniques

Not only can the sounds, rhythms, and meter of the words be beautiful in themselves, but they can make beautiful connections among ideas in a poem, highlight the poem's meaning, and affect how the reader feels.

SOUND DEVICES

Poets use certain sound devices to please the ear and to stir the emotions. Use some of these devices when you write a poem.

SOUND DEVICES	
Onomatopoeia	Use of words whose sounds suggest their meanings: *hum, splash, whistle, hoot, murmur, fizz*
Alliteration	Repetition of a consonant sound or sounds at the beginning of a series of words: **B**aa, **b**aa, **b**lack sheep
Consonance	Repetition of a consonant sound or sounds, used with different vowel sounds, usually in the middle or at the end of words: the pa**tt**er of li**tt**le feet
Assonance	Repetition of a vowel sound within words: the b**o**wling ball r**o**lled **o**ver and **o**ver
Repetition	Repetition of an entire word or phrase: O **Captain**! my **captain**! rise up and hear the bells; Rise up—**for you** the flag is flung—**for you** the bugle trills. —Walt Whitman, "Oh Captain! My Captain!"
Rhyme	Repetition of accented syllables with the same vowel and consonant sounds: The woods are lovely, dark, and **deep,** But I have promises to **keep,** And miles to go before I **sleep.** —Robert Frost, "Stopping by Woods on a Snowy Evening"

RHYTHM AND METER

Almost all poems have rhythm—a sense of flow produced by the rise and fall of accented and unaccented syllables. In many poems, the rhythm is a specific beat called a meter. The accented and unaccented syllables of metered poetry follow a regular, countable pattern like the beats of a piece of music. In the lines on the next page, the accented syllables are marked with ′ and unaccented syllables are marked with ˘. Read the lines and notice the strong, regular rhythm.

Tyger, tyger, burning bright,

In the forests of the night:

What immortal hand or eye

Could frame thy fearful symmetry?

—William Blake, "The Tyger"

Poetry without meter is called **free verse.** Poems in free verse have rhythm, but not a regular, patterned beat. "When I Heard the Learn'd Astronomer" is free verse like most of Walt Whitman's poems. Its rhythm comes from repetition, variation, and the natural flow of speech. Notice the use of repetition in the following free-verse poem.

The Loon on Oak-Head Pond

cries for three days, in the gray mist.
cries for the north it hopes it can find.
plunges, and comes up with a slapping pickerel.
blinks its red eye.
cries again.
you come every afternoon, and wait to hear it.
you sit a long time, quiet, under the thick pines,
in the silence that follows.
as though it were your own twilight.
as though it were your own vanishing song.

—Mary Oliver

● **Practice Your Skills**

Developing Sound Devices

Write a series of statements on the subject Life at School, as follows. Your statements may be either in prose or in verse, but they must contain the listed sound devices.

1. a statement containing rhyme

2. a statement containing alliteration

3. a statement containing assonance

4. a statement using a strong rhythm

5. a statement using onomatopoeia

FIGURATIVE LANGUAGE

Good readers see mental pictures of the things they read about, and good poets help them by using figurative language that is vivid and imaginative. The following chart illustrates the major kinds of figurative language.

FIGURATIVE LANGUAGE	
Imagery	use of visual details or details that appeal to other senses Cold and raw the north wind blows/Bleak in the morning early. All the hills are covered with snow/And winter's now come fairly. —Nursery Rhyme
Simile	comparison using the words *like* or *as:* My love is like a red, red rose —Robert Burns, "My Love is Like a Red, Red Rose"
Metaphor	implied comparison that does not use *like* or *as:* Life is a broken-winged bird That cannot fly. —Langston Hughes, "Dreams"
Personification	use of human qualities to describe something non-human Because I could not stop for Death—He kindly stopped for me— —Emily Dickinson, "Because I Could Not Stop for Death"
Hyperbole	use of extreme exaggeration or overstatement And fired the shot heard 'round the world. —Ralph Waldo Emerson, "Concord Hymn"
Oxymoron	use of opposite or contradictory terms such as *living death, black snow, happy to be sad*
Symbol	use of an object or action to stand for another, as William Blake's tiger is a symbol of nature's untamed natural destructiveness Tyger, tyger, burning bright, In the forests of the night: What immortal hand or eye Could frame thy fearful symmetry? —William Blake, "The Tyger"

● Practice Your Skills

Developing Figurative Language for Poems

Return to the subject of Life at School, which you wrote about in the previous activity. Now write statements (in prose or verse) as follows.

1. a statement using imagery

2. a statement using a simile

3. a statement using a metaphor

4. a statement using personification

5. a statement using hyperbole

6. a statement that includes an oxymoron

7. an explanation of how some object in school is a symbol
for some idea or quality

PROJECT PREP *Drafting* *Poetic Techniques*

Using the freewriting from the previous Project Prep, work with your writing group to consider ways in which you could create a poem that distills the ideas and impressions from the writing. What would you need to do to convert prose to poetry? Based on this discussion, draft a poem that, in relatively few words, conveys important and provocative ideas.

Poetry depends on brevity—saying as much as possible in as few words as possible. Rewrite the following bloated lines of poetry to make the words sing.

> The shady tree, tall and high, blocking the sun from the grass-covered ground
>
> Seemed ancient and old as the hills, as it stood in silence not making a sound.

③ Choosing a Form

The form of a poem should fit its subject, mood, and tone. For example, if your subject is a snake slithering quickly through the grass, you might choose the form of free verse in short lines to create a lively, dashing rhythm. In contrast, if your subject is the tragedy of world hunger, you might choose to write longer lines in a strong, solemn meter. If you are writing a comic poem, you might use bouncy, simple rhymes; if you are expressing deep, sincere feeling, you might omit rhyme. At times, you might find yourself writing a poem in a certain form simply because it feels right, without being able to explain exactly why.

If you choose to write in rhyme, you will need to use a **rhyme scheme**—a regular pattern of rhyming. A poem's rhyme scheme can be shown by letters of the alphabet. Each rhyming sound gets its own letter.

a	It was many and many a year ago,
b	In a kingdom by the sea,
a	That a maiden there lived whom you may know
b	By the name of Annabel Lee;
c	And this maiden she lived with no other thought
b	Than to love and be loved by me.

—Edgar Allan Poe, "Annabel Lee"

The six lines from "Annabel Lee," above, make up one stanza of that long poem. A **stanza** is a group of lines that the poet decides to set together, separated from other stanzas by a space. There are some specific kinds of stanzas in English, such as the quatrain (four lines). You do not need to choose stanzas of a specific length, but if you do, you should be consistent.

PROJECT PREP *Drafting* Choosing a Form

Using your latest draft as a base, write a poem consisting of two stanzas. For a poem based on the story of conflicting perspectives, provide one character's point of view in the first stanza and the other character's perspective in the second. After completing the stanzas, obtain feedback from your peers, and reread the poem yourself. Make any changes you feel would improve it, including changes of form. Read the final draft aloud to interested classmates or friends. Gather your poem with others by your classmates into a class anthology.

TIME OUT TO REFLECT You have had opportunities to write a story, play scene, and poem in this chapter. Which form do you prefer working in and why? How has your experience in writing a story, a play, and a poem changed since you read this chapter? Which skills do want to practice more? Discuss your reflections or record them in your Learning Log.

Writing Lab

Project Corner

Speak and Listen Poetry Slam

Hold a poetry slam, a contest among people performing their poems. At a slam, poets do more than simply read their poems: they find imaginative ways to perform them that might include rap, broad gestures, and/or great vocal variety. Listeners don't just applaud politely afterwards—they get (appropriately) rowdy and hoot their pleasure. They also get a chance to judge the poets, and a winner is declared. You may wish to use the rubric below to help you choose a winner. At most poetry slams, contestants are rated on a scale of 1–10.

Poetry Slam Rubric
Poem
The poem moved me in some way.
The poem used poetic techniques (sound devices, rhythm, and meter) effectively.
The poem had a form, even if it was loose.
The poet's words were well chosen, and figurative language created vivid images.
Performance
The poet projected clearly and took the performance seriously, even if it was fun.
The poet knew the poem by heart.
The poet used gestures, movements, and vocal changes to express a range of feelings.

Collaborate and Create Collaborative Fiction

With your writing group members, **collaborate on a literary work** by taking turns writing sections of it. For example, one student might start it off by introducing the characters; the next might introduce the conflict; and the next might show the rising tide of the action, at which point the work returns to the first writer to continue the action. As a first step, come up with a list of rules for the collaboration. These might include such items as sticking to the chosen genre or not being silly (or being silly). With your rules in place, create your work. Share it with your classmates when you have finished it. Ask if they can tell where one person's work stopped and another's began.

In the Workplace
Narrative E-mail

1. This morning you were ten minutes late for work. When you arrived, the boss's secretary was not happy, and he vowed he would report your lateness. You have a good reason for being late, but you admit it is very hard to believe. You decide to **write an e-mail** to your boss explaining why you were late for work. Use the narrative form, with first-person point of view. Keep the events of your story ordered in a concise and chronological manner. Try to include strong and vivid physical and sensory details that will make your boss believe your story. (You can find information on writing e-mails in the *Guide to 21st Century School and Workplace Skills on* pages 445, 453, and 493–497.)

For Oral Communication Dramatic Scene

2. You work for a public radio station devoted to producing radio dramas. Your boss has finally given you a chance to write a short dramatic scene to be performed during the ten minutes of free airtime before the 3 a.m. news. Your boss gives you only one requirement for the scene—it has to be exciting enough to keep the late-night audience awake! **Write a lively scene for a radio drama** that will be performed by two or three actors. During the prewriting stage, consider the setting and make character sketches. Then perform the scene with other members of your class. (You can find information on writing plays on pages 192–199.)

Timed Writing ⏱ Short Story

3. You have been chosen to submit an entry for a book of short stories about the experiences of contemporary American high school students. Although all the entries will be very short pieces of fiction—no more than 600 words long (about one paged typed)—the editors want you to base the stories on your own experience. Write a short story about an extremely important moment in your life. Use the third-person point of view. You have 30 minutes to complete your work.

Before You Write Consider your purpose and audience, and spend time prewriting. Include important and vivid details, but stay within the length limits. Use background details to set the time and place of the story and to capture your reader's interest. Be sure the story has a beginning, middle, and end. Decide what conflict was at the center of your important moment, and resolve it by the end of the story. Use rhetorical devices to deepen meaning.

After You Write Evaluate your story using the six-trait rubric on page 191.

Expository Writing

Expository writing presents information or offers an explanation. One type of expository writing is **analytical**, writing that analyzes or takes apart a subject.

You rely on expository writing in your everyday life: to obtain information you need, to obtain information that interests you, and to communicate information that you want to share. Consider all these examples:

- **A high school student gives an oral report** on the history of the National Aeronautics and Space Administration (NASA).

- **A newspaper sportswriter reviews the highlights** of a local team's championship season.

- **A club secretary uses notes** from the last meeting to write the minutes, a record of what happened and what was decided.

- **A health and beauty magazine publishes a feature** on the 20 best foods and the 20 worst foods for your body.

- **A television writer creates a script** for a documentary on the behavior of gorillas in the wild.

- **A healthcare worker updates the hospital's Web site** with text, photographs, and video clips that summarize new research on happiness and how to achieve it.

Writing Project *Analytical*

What Makes Teens Happy? *Create your own analytical expository text on the subject of teenagers and happiness by completing the following project.*

Think Through Writing Do you think teenagers today are generally happy? How do you define happiness? What can people do to be happier? Write freely in your journal for five minutes trying to answer these questions.

Talk About It At the end of five minutes, share your ideas with your classmates. Also discuss what questions you would need to ask if you were to take a survey to determine the happiness level of teenagers in the United States.

Read About It The following text is from the Web site of Social Technologies, a research group. It presents information on a study of what makes teenagers and young adults happy. What do you think the study found?

The Future of Happiness

What makes 12–24 year olds happy? That was the topic of a study that MTV commissioned Social Technologies to conduct [in 2008]. The findings surprised many. "We knew friends and technology would be important to this demographic, but going in we also had the preconceived notion that 12 to 24 year olds were slightly indifferent, self-serving, and perhaps even a bit apathetic," explains Andy Hines, Social Technologies' director of custom projects, who led the study. "The biggest thing we learned was never to judge a book by its cover."

— Introduction captures attention with a question.

— Quotes by the leader of the study are worked into the article.

Key findings from the happiness study included:

BFF. Friends are and will continue to be the most important relationships contributing to youth happiness. 80% of the youth polled said that having lots of close friends is very or somewhat important; 23% said that when they go out with friends, they stop feeling unhappy.

— Boldface headings present information in easy-to-grasp chunks.

No Body's Perfect. Body image and traditional routes to good health will be important aspects of happiness for many youth. "At my school, skinny is what everyone's trying to be," said Vanessa A., 13, of Philadelphia. "People make fun of fat [but] also of the skin-and-bones look."

My Life, My Time, My Way. Youth will take control of their own happiness. 91% said they have goals for the future (81% have career/work goals, 64% education, 62% family, 63% money, 48% travel, 17% sports, while 12% hope for fame).

— Statistics back up the main ideas.

Virtual Community. Technology will be important for staying in touch as well as for the pleasure of the moment. 37% of the youths polled said they play videogames to stop unhappiness. 61% said technology helps them make new friends. In the 24 hours before the survey, half of the respondents said, they sent a text message; 71% said they received one.

So what does make American youth happy?

The bottom line is that today's 12–24 year olds define happiness differently than previous generations did, the Social Technologies team determined.

Results are interpreted to formulate general conclusions.

"The characteristic that will most shape their current and future pursuit of happiness may be a deep-seated pragmatism," explains project manager Traci Stafford Croft, who traveled to three cities (Philadelphia, Phoenix, and Atlanta) with MTV's staff to interview about five dozen 12-24 year olds. In the study's next phase, the Associated Press surveyed another 1,200 youths to further flesh out the findings.

In the end, the research showed that it is a popular misconception that today's youths are self-absorbed or indifferent to social issues. Instead, any apparent indifference "might reflect the fact that they have a good grasp on reality and are simply being practical about what they get upset about or involved in," Croft explains.

Hines adds: "No, this generation is not likely to march in DC to protest the war in Iraq. But they do care about the country, the environment, and the planet. They are just showing it in a way that is different from their parents and grandparents."

As for today's so-called helicopter parents, notorious for hovering protectively around their offspring in this generation, well, the respondents' views of this parental behavior were the finding that most amazed the Social Technologies team.

Article saves most surprising finding for the end.

"We thought the kids would really resent having their parents come in and make a fuss at school or on the playing field, but the youths didn't feel as if that was an obstacle to their happiness," Croft concludes. "Sure, it was a little embarrassing for them, but ultimately they said they appreciated that their parents are looking out for them."

Respond in Writing In your journal, write responses to the following questions. Do the findings reported in this article ring true? What do you think made your parents happy when they were teenagers? Do you agree that your generation finds happiness in a different way from that of your parents' generation? Is any element of teenage happiness missing in this report, in your opinion?

Develop Your Own Supporting Ideas Work with your classmates to come up with your own statistics on teenage happiness.

Small Groups: Break into small groups of four or five students. Ask one another what makes you happy and try to come up with at least four answers each, keeping track of all the answers mentioned.

Whole Class: Share your answers with the class while a student writes each one on a large sheet of paper or on the board. At the end of the discussion, you will have a list of answers from your entire class to the question: What makes you happy? You can use that information to complete the following activity.

Write About It You will write an analytical essay on the subject of happiness and teenagers. You will choose your topic, audience, and form from the options below. With your teacher's approval you may also develop your own topic, audience, and form.

Possible Topics	Possible Audiences	Possible Forms
• what the survey of your classmates tells you about what makes them happy • how the results of your survey are like and unlike the results reported in the article • how to make every day happier • the relationship between happiness and health • the effects of happy teenagers in families, in schools, in the community, and in the workplace	• your parents or guardian • a good friend • school officials in charge of extra-curricular activities • a younger sibling • advertising executives for companies that market their products to teenagers • a local elected official	• a letter • an essay • a powerpoint presentation • a video • an article for a Web site

The prewriting stage of the writing process helps you discover possible subjects for an expository text, develop your ideas, and shape those ideas into an organized plan.

① Getting the Subject Right

If you get your subject just right, you will be off to a strong start. Choose a subject you care about, make sure it is appropriate for your audience, and limit it to a manageable scope.

DISCOVERING AND CHOOSING A SUBJECT

In school you may often be given a subject to write about. For those times when you need to choose your own, use the following strategies to help you settle on a topic that is genuinely interesting to you.

Strategies for Finding Subjects for Expository Essays

- Brainstorm or freewrite to list subjects that you know well enough to explain.

- Ask yourself questions about your interests and skills.

- Review your journal entries to find possible subjects that are suitable for explaining or informing.

- Skim books, newspapers, and magazines for subjects that interest you.

- Read your notes from courses in other subject areas to find possible subjects.

- View television documentaries or educational television programs to discover subjects that you would like to explore in writing.

- Search for interesting contemporary topics on the Internet.

DETERMINING YOUR AUDIENCE

Sometimes your choice of a subject will depend in part on who will be reading your essay. You might choose one subject if you were writing for a classmate, a very different one if you were writing for a teacher, and still another if you were writing to the editor of the school newspaper. At other times you will be able to choose both your subject and the audience you wish to write for. For example, you may decide to write an essay about synthesizers for an audience of musicians and others who are interested in electronic keyboards.

Whether you choose a subject to suit your audience or choose an audience for the subject you want to write about, you will need to take into account the interests, knowledge, opinions, and needs of your audience.

You can learn more about analyzing an audience on pages 15–16, 151, and 266.

LIMITING AND FOCUSING A SUBJECT

Many expository subjects—such as happiness—may be too broad to be developed adequately in a short essay. To limit a subject, think of specific aspects or examples of it. If your new subjects are still too broad, continue the process. The following example shows how a writer might limit the subject of happiness to arrive at subjects suitable for a short expository text.

EXAMPLE: Limited Subjects

Limited Subjects	More Specific Subjects
in teens	surveys about teen happiness
happiness and health	the physical effects of mental states
changing standards of happiness	past generations' versus present generation's
happiness self-help	books on how to be happy

After you have limited a subject, your next step is to focus. Read about your subject, or brainstorm general questions you could ask about the subject based on what you know about it.

For example, if you chose books on how to be happy as your limited subject, you might decide to focus on one that is a current best-seller whose author is making the rounds of talk shows. Focusing from a different angle, you might zero in on comparing and contrasting one self-help approach with another.

Strategies for Focusing a Subject

- Focus on a specific event or incident.

- Focus on a specific time and place.

- Focus on one example that best represents your subject.

- Focus on one person or group that represents your subject.

The example below shows how the limited subject of books on how to be happy may have more than one possible focus.

Possible Focuses

- how one approach differs from another

- elements that several approaches have in common

- differences between books for females and books for males

- differences between books for young people and books for old people

- the most famous or popular book on achieving happiness

PROJECT PREP   *Prewriting*   *Subject/Audience*

1. Review the topic choices on page 213. Which one genuinely interests you the most? Write your topic and audience choice on a sheet of paper. Is the topic appropriately limited? Is it sufficiently focused? If not, use the strategies on pages 215–216 to limit and focus your subject.

2. Review the audience choices on page 213. Which audience seems best suited for an informational text on your topic? What considerations might you keep in mind to address your chosen audience in the most effective way? What would you tell this audience that you might not tell to others?

3. Review the choice of forms on page 213 and choose the one you want to use. What content, tone, style, and vocabulary are suitable for the form you chose? What content, tone, style, and vocabulary would you avoid?

4. Share your decisions with your writing group. Talk through how your decisions will affect the choices you make as you compose your expository text.

Exploring and Refining the Subject

GATHERING INFORMATION

Once you have a focused subject, gather information so you can explain it clearly to your reader. Use brainstorming, freewriting, clustering, inquiring, or researching to explore your subject and find details that will help you to inform others about it. The details may include any of the types shown in the box below, including such rhetorical devices as analogies and examples. Remember that the type of detail often indicates the best method of development for your paragraphs.

You can learn more about gathering information on pages 332–336 and 460 and about methods of development on page 221.

TYPES OF DETAILS USED IN EXPOSITORY WRITING

facts and examples	analogies	similarities
reasons	incidents	differences
steps in a process	definitions	causes and effects

The information in the following model shows examples of books on happiness discovered by checking titles at an online bookseller's site. Notice that the information is not yet arranged in any logical order.

DEVELOPING A WORKING THESIS

As you gather information, a main idea for your essay will begin to emerge. At this point you should express this emerging main idea as a **working thesis**—a preliminary statement of what you think the main idea will be. For example, as you look over the books on happiness, you might write the thesis on the next page.

MODEL: Gathering Information

Current books on happiness

- *Mary Lou Retton's Gateways to Happiness,* 2000—former Olympian on giving 110%, refers to Christian faith

- *The Art of Happiness: A Handbook for Living,* by Dalai Lama, 1998—based on Buddhist meditations

- *How to See Yourself as You Really Are,* by Dalai Lama, 2007—focuses on realistic self-knowledge

- *The How of Happiness,* Sonja Lyubomirsky, reprint edition 2008—takes scientific approach

- *Climb Your Stairway to Heaven: The 9 Habits of Maximum Happiness,* David Leonhardt, 2001—relies on psychology

- *Stumbling on Happiness,* by Daniel Gilbert, 2007—scientific look at how trying to predict the future steers us away from happiness

> **Working Thesis** Current books on happiness seem to approach the topic from many different angles.

This working thesis would guide you in selecting information to use in your essay. That is, you would select details from the list only about books on happiness and not about books on self-knowedge, even though the two topics might be related. If you wanted to include information about Dalai Lama's book on self-knowledge, you could broaden your working thesis.

> **Revised Working Thesis** Current books on happiness seem to approach the topic from many different angles, including the importance of really knowing who you are.

As you can see, a list of details can lead to several different theses. As you gather and think about information, you may wish to modify your working thesis. You may find the following steps helpful in developing a working thesis.

HERE'S HOW **Steps for Developing a Working Thesis**

- Look over the information you have gathered.

- Express the main idea you plan to convey.

- Select the details you will use to support your main idea.

- Check that the working thesis takes into account all of the information you selected to include in your essay.

Writing Tip

Think of a working thesis as a place to start in identifying the main idea of your informative essay. You can revise a working thesis as many times as needed to include new details that will make your essay more interesting and informative.

PROJECT PREP *Prewriting* *Working Thesis*

1. Review your focused topic. Do you have enough information to develop your idea fully? If so, make a list of all the relevant details. If not, develop a plan for gathering that information and carry it out.

2. As you gather information, keep track of the details that will help you develop your topic. Then look for patterns and draw conclusions. For example, on the subject of the class survey, you might draw these two conclusions from the many different responses:

   - kids enjoy doing things more than they enjoy being passive;
   - kids are happy when they are with other kids, either in person or online.

3. Develop a working thesis that reflects your conclusions. Meet with your writing group to discuss your working thesis and how you arrived at it. Be open to suggestions.

Think Critically

Evaluating Information for Relevance

To decide which ideas and details to include in an essay, evaluate the information for **relevance** by asking yourself the following questions: Is it appropriate for my purpose in writing? Does it relate directly to my working thesis? Will it help me support or prove my thesis? Study the following prewriting notes. Which ideas and information do you think lack relevance to the given thesis?

THESIS STATEMENT	The chambered shell of the nautilus has long fascinated marine biologists.
1. Supporting Idea Details	The nautilus is a marine mollusk. • soft-shelled sea animal • lives in warm waters of South Pacific
2. Supporting Idea Details	The nautilus grows a unique shell with many chambers. • adds chambers as it grows • moves into new chamber and closes old one
3. Supporting Idea	Oliver Wendell Holmes was inspired to write a poem about the nautilus. • calls it a "ship of pearls" • nautilus is a metaphor for the human soul

The first idea and its details are relevant because they describe the subject. The second idea and details are also clearly relevant because they are about the shell of the nautilus. The third idea, however, is not directly relevant.

Thinking Practice

Explain why item 3 above is not directly relevant. Then refine the thesis statement to make this item relevant to an essay about the nautilus.

③ Organizing Your Essay

Clear organization lets a reader follow your ideas without confusing distractions. There are several steps involved in discovering an effective organization. First you need to group your details into meaningful categories by examining connections and distinctions among ideas. Then you need to arrange those categories in a logical order.

GROUPING INFORMATION INTO CATEGORIES

A **category** is a group, or class, of related pieces of information. When you examine the information you gather, look for ways that the separate pieces relate to one another. For example, if you have collected a lot of information on happiness books, you might notice that some of them draw on religious teachings while others seem to rely on science. The following example shows how the books might be arranged in categories.

MODEL: Classifying Details

Category 1

Religion

- *Dali Lama's The Art of Happiness* (Buddhism)
- *Mary Lou Retton's Gateway to Happiness* (Christianity)

Category 2

Science

- *Climb Your Stairway to Heaven*
- *The How of Happiness*
- *Stumbling on Happiness*

ARRANGING CATEGORIES IN LOGICAL ORDER

Next arrange your categories in the order in which you want to present them in your text. The type you choose will depend partly on your subject and partly on your thesis. For example, the thesis that radioactivity is more common in nature than most people think lends itself to an organization based on order of importance or developmental order. The thesis that radioactivity was an important discovery in the history of science, on the other hand, suggests chronological order. Keep your audience and purpose in mind as you think about your organizing structure. The following chart shows some commonly used types of logical order.

TYPES OF ORDER

Chronological Order	Information is presented in the order in which it occurred.
	Example books on happiness presented in the order of the oldest to the newest
Spatial Order	Information is given according to location.
	Example books on happiness presented according to the parts of the world where they are from
Order of Importance	Information is given in order of importance, interest, size, or degree.
	Example books presented in the order of least to most interesting, influential, or popular
Developmental Order	Information of equal importance is arranged to lead up to a conclusion.
	Example books on happiness presented in the order of the different sources they come from, such as religion and science
Comparison/Contrast	Information is arranged to point out similarities and differences (see pages 244–249 for more on comparison/contrast).
	Example books from different regions, or from different sources, or aimed at different ages, examined in terms of likenesses and differences

When you select and group details, you probably write simple outlines to keep track of your decisions. You might number the points you want to make, for example. By developing an even more detailed outline, you can plan the whole body of your text.

When you write a formal outline for the body of your text, you use Roman numerals for each idea that supports your thesis. Each idea becomes the **main topic** of a supporting paragraph. You then use capital letters for each category of information that comes under a topic. Then, under each subtopic, you use Arabic numerals to list the **supporting points** or details. The information below each Roman numeral in the outline will correspond with a separate paragraph when you draft the body of your work.

 Guidelines for Making an Outline

- Use Roman numerals for topics.

- Use capital letters for subtopics and indent them under the topic. If you use subtopics, always include at least two of them.

- Use Arabic numerals for supporting points and indent them under the subtopic. If you use supporting points, include at least two of them.

- Use lowercase letters for any other details and indent them under the supporting point to which they refer. If you use supporting details, include at least two of them.

MODEL: Outline Form

I. (Main topic)
  A. (Subtopic)
    1. (Supporting point)
    2. (Supporting point)
      a. (Detail)
      b. (Detail)
  B. (Subtopic)
    1. (Supporting point)
      a. (Detail)
      b. (Detail)
    2. (Supporting point)

II. (Main topic) Etc.

PROJECT PREP *Prewriting* Outline

1. Review the conclusions you drew for your expository text. Each of them could serve as the topic sentence of a paragraph in your text. In what order should you present them? Decide on an ordering scheme from the Types of Order chart on page 221. You may also wish to review the **Writing Workshops** on pages 240–253 for ideas about organizing your text. Then arrange your conclusions and the details that support them accordingly. Sketch out the structure.

2. Refine your rough structure. Determine what your topics, subtopics, and supporting points will be. Follow the guidelines above to write an outline of the body of your article. Rework your outline until you are satisfied with the content, order of information, and form.

The Power of Language ⚡

Semicolons: Catch and Release

You can think of a semicolon as a hybrid of comma and period. The comma part joins two sentences closely related in meaning; the period part separates them grammatically. Look at the following examples from "The Future of Happiness" and think about why the semicolon is appropriate:

> 80% of the youth polled said that having lots of close friends is very or somewhat important; 23% said that when they go out with friends, they stop feeling unhappy.

The writer could have used two separate sentences, or used a word between them that spelled out their relationship. In the first example, the writer could have written:

> 80% of the youth polled said that having lots of close friends is very or somewhat important. For example, 23% said that when they go out with friends, they stop feeling unhappy.

By using only the semicolon, however, the writer lets the reader supply the connecting idea. In this way, the semicolon helps create an engaging style.

Try It Yourself

Write two complete sentences closely related in meaning and join them with a semicolon. Try this twice more, creating sentences on the topic of your project. Use these sentences in your draft if appropriate, and return during revision to see if there are other places where the semicolon seems to be the best stylistic choice.

Punctuation Tip

To simply connect and/or separate two complete sentences, there are usually three punctuation options. Which you choose is a stylistic decision.

Separate with a period: The comma part joins. The period part separates.

Join with a comma plus *and*: The comma part joins, and the period part separates.

Join/separate with a semicolon: The comma part joins; the period part separates.

During the drafting stage of the writing process, you will use your prewriting notes and outline to write an introduction, a body, and a conclusion.

Drafting the Introduction

WRITING A THESIS STATEMENT

Before you begin drafting your whole essay, take time out to refine your working thesis into a thesis statement. The thesis statement, which expresses your main idea, should appear somewhere in the introduction of the essay. Thesis statements are often most effective when they appear at the beginning or at the end of the introduction.

> The **thesis statement** makes the main idea of the essay clear to readers.

In an expository essay, the key feature of a thesis statement is that it accurately covers all of the information you include. You can follow the steps on the next page to refine your working thesis into an effective thesis statement.

Drafting a Thesis Statement

- Look over your outline and revise your working thesis so that it covers all of your main topics.
- Express your working thesis in a complete sentence.
- Check your thesis statement for clarity and voice; use peer conferencing for feedback on both.
- Look over all your information again to make sure it is relevant to the thesis statement.
- Continue to refine your thesis statement as you take into account any changes you make in the main idea or in the information you include.

CAPTURING ATTENTION

Besides stating the thesis, the introduction sets the tone of an essay and captures the reader's interest. Because the purpose of writing an expository essay is to inform, analyze, or explain, a formal style and objective tone are usually appropriate. The following are common ways to draw readers into an expository essay.

Writing Introductions for Expository Essays

- Tell about an incident that shows how you became interested in your subject.
- Give some background information.
- Cite an example that illustrates your thesis.
- Cite a startling statistic about the subject.
- Define or describe the subject.
- Quote an expert on the subject.

The model on the next page presents an introduction for an essay about books on happiness. Notice how this introduction introduces the subject, captures interest, and sets the tone. Also the main idea is clearly expressed in a refined thesis statement.

MODEL: Introduction of an Expository Essay

Self-help books on happiness line shelf after shelf of bookstores and libraries. Their covers promise 10 easy steps or 5 golden rules or whatever magic number or formula might be the latest key to happiness. Despite their great numbers, though, these guides to happiness tend to come in two main types: books that help people draw on their religious faith or spiritual beliefs, and books that explain the scientific side of happiness and how to achieve it.

Refined Thesis Statement

PROJECT PREP Drafting *Introduction*

1. Review all your previous project work. Then refine your working thesis statement using the drafting strategies on page 225. Next, draft a whole introductory paragraph that captures attention and focuses your reader on your topic. As you draft, pay special attention to the needs of your audience. What approach will make your subject as clear as possible to your readers?

2. After drafting your opening paragraph, share your writing with your group and evaluate one another's drafts for:

   • The clarity and focus of the thesis statement.
   • The clarity of the introductory paragraph as it outlines the purpose of the text.
   • The effectiveness of the attention getting.
   • The appropriateness of the writing to the expectations of the reader(s).
   • The suitability of the writing to the form in which you are presenting your report.

3. Based on your group's feedback, revise your introductory paragraph.

In the Media

Grabbing Attention

Understanding how other media present information can help you improve your expository writing. Techniques for grabbing a reader's attention are especially useful to study. A newspaper story usually begins with the whole story summarized in the first sentence, for example. The rest of the story supplies the details, but the reader is drawn in by knowing the outcome. A newsmagazine, in contrast, might begin with a paragraph setting the scene, and then take time leading up to the outcome.

Media Activity

Skim through a newspaper until you find a headline that interests you. Read the first few paragraphs. Then scan the table of contents of a newsmagazine until you find an article in which you are interested. Read only the first few paragraphs. Finally, surf the Internet until you find a Web site that interests you. Read only the first screenful of text.

For each introduction, ask yourself the following questions:

- Does the introduction grab my attention? Why or why not?
- What method did the writer use to get my attention?
- What is the implied or stated thesis statement? If it is stated, where is it placed in the introduction?

In a paragraph, sum up what you have learned about writing introductions to expository essays from the three pieces you examined from other media.

② Drafting the Body

Follow your outline when you draft the body of your expository essay. Each main topic, with some or all of the subtopics and supporting points, will become at least one paragraph. If you have a number of supporting details, you may need two or more paragraphs to cover each topic adequately. Make sure to include enough detail to help support your ideas.

Guidelines for Adequately Developing an Essay

- Include enough supporting ideas to develop your thesis statement fully.
- Leave no question unanswered that you would expect readers to ask.
- Include enough information to present each topic and subtopic fully.
- Use specific details and precise language to present each piece of information fully.

As you draft the body of your expository essay from your outline, connect your words, sentences, and paragraphs with transitions to make the essay read smoothly and to give it unity, coherence, and clarity.

LOGICAL DEVELOPMENT

The ideas you develop to support your thesis statement are claims.

Claims are statements asserted to be true.

In the opening reading "The Future of Happiness," some of the claims are:

- Friends are the most important relationships contributing to youth happiness.

- Body image will be related to youth happiness.

- Technology provides connections and enjoyment.

The study develops these claims with supporting information and examples.

CLAIMS	SUPPORTING INFORMATION
Friends are the most important relationships contributing to youth happiness.	80% of youth polled felt friendship was important.
Body image will be related to youth happiness.	Vanessa A. reports that skinny and fat kids are teased but that kids want to be skinny.
Technology provides connections and enjoyment.	37% of youth polled said they play games to avoid unhappiness; 61% credit technology with helping them make friends.

Simply providing examples for claims, however, does not support your assertion that they are true. You need to go further and provide a warrant for each claim.

> A **warrant** is a statement that explains how an example serves as evidence for a claim.

Warrants often use the word *because* as in the following example.

Claim	Friends are the most important relationships contributing to youth happiness.
Information	80% of youth polled felt friendship was important.
Warrant	Because four out of five youth polled in a study reported that friends were important to their happiness, friendship must be a key factor contributing to youth happiness.

VALID INFERENCES

In addition to providing warrants for your claims, you also need to make sure that your conclusions or inferences are valid. A **valid inference** is one that follows logically from the claims. For example, suppose you make these claims:

Claim	All teenagers like and use technology.
Claim	Amit is a teenager.
Valid Inference	Amit likes and uses technology.

That inference is valid because the first claim asserts that all teenagers like and use technology; in that case, if someone is a teenager, that person will like and use technology. Even though the first claim is false (of course, not *all* teenagers like and use technology), the inference still follows logically from the claim.

Suppose, though, you make these claims:

Claim	All teenagers like and use technology.
Claim	Amit likes and uses technology.
Invalid Inference	Amit is a teenager.

The inference is invalid because it does not follow logically from the claims. The original claim is that all teenagers like and use technology, not that *only* teenagers like and use technology. Just because Amit likes and uses technology does not logically lead to the inference that he is a teenager.

COHERENCE

As you draft the body of your expository essay, connect your words, sentences, and paragraphs with transitions to make the essay read smoothly and to give it unity, coherence, and clarity.

You can learn more about making transitions on pages 86–87. Check pages 80–88, 109, and 133–134 for guidance on achieving unity, coherence, clarity, and adequate development.

Strategies for Achieving Coherence

- Use transitional words and phrases.
- Repeat a key word from an earlier sentence.
- Use synonyms for key words from earlier sentences.
- Use a pronoun in place of a word used earlier.

PROJECT PREP *Body Paragraphs*

Following your plan, draft the body of your composition. Provide adequate development and support each claim with a warrant. You might want to make a chart like the one below to help you keep track of your claims and warrants.

Body Paragraphs	Topic sentence (claim)	Example/ Information	Warrant
First			
Second			
Third			

As you draft, provide smooth transitions from your introduction to the body and between body paragraphs. Ask yourself: are my voice, tone, and style appropriate?

③ Drafting the Conclusion

The conclusion sums up your information and reinforces your thesis. You might also add an interesting detail from your notes that you did not previously include.

You can learn more about the conclusion of an essay on page 110.

Strategies for Writing a Conclusion

- Summarize the body of the essay.
- Restate the thesis in new words.
- Draw a conclusion based on the body of the essay.
- Add an insight about the thesis.
- Explain the implications or significance of your topic.

The following paragraph is a draft of a concluding paragraph for the essay on books for happiness. Notice that the conclusion adds some specific, interesting details about a very popular exception to the pattern and also restates the thesis in a memorable sentence.

MODEL: Conclusion of an Expository Essay

Of course, not all books fall into these two categories. A book called *14,000 Things to Be Happy About* presented, yes, 14,000 random things to be happy about and now has more than a million copies in print. That book celebrates such happiness-givers as "pitching a tent" and "running to a hug." Far more frequently, though, happiness-seekers will end up turning to the two realms most endeavors end up leading to: belief and reason.

Drafting a Title

To complete your first draft, think of an appropriate title. A good title suggests the main idea of your essay and captures the attention of your audience.

PROJECT PREP *Drafting* Conclusion

Reread the introduction and body of your text. Then draft a strong concluding paragraph with a final clincher sentence. Try to make the conclusion flow smoothly from the body. Write two or three possible titles. Choose the best one and save your draft for use later.

If time allows, put away your draft for a day or two so you can revise it with a fresh eye. Also read your draft aloud to notice parts that need improvement. A peer reader can also tell you whether your explanations are clear. During revising, also check the six traits: ideas, organization, voice, word choice, sentence fluency (see pages 5–6), and conventions.

① Checking for Unity, Coherence, and Clarity

In revising, as in drafting, you should be alert for ways to improve the unity, coherence, and clarity of your essay. The following questions will help you to check for these qualities. Refer back to the pages mentioned for help with any of these.

 Checklist for Unity, Coherence, and Clarity

Checking for Unity
- ✓ Does each idea and each piece of information relate to the subject? (pages 217–219 and 228–230)
- ✓ Does every paragraph support the thesis statement? (pages 228–230)
- ✓ Does every sentence in each paragraph support its topic sentence? (pages 228–231)

Checking for Coherence
- ✓ Did you follow a logical order of ideas or topics? (pages 220–222)
- ✓ Did you follow a logical order of supporting points or details? (pages 220–222)
- ✓ Did you use transitions to connect the introduction, body, and conclusion and clarify the relationships among ideas? (pages 228 and 230)
- ✓ Did you use transitions between paragraphs? (pages 228 and 230)
- ✓ Did you use transitions between sentences within each paragraph? (pages 228 and 230)

Checking for Clarity
- ✓ Does each word express clearly and precisely what you want to say?
- ✓ Does the introduction make your subject, purpose, tone, and thesis clear to readers? (pages 224–227)
- ✓ Does the body clearly support the thesis and lead to the conclusion? (pages 228–230)
- ✓ Does the conclusion make clear how the body supports the thesis? (page 231)

PROJECT PREP Revising *Unity, Coherence, Clarity*

Work with your group. Review one another's writing to point out places where unity, coherence, and emphasis could be improved. Revise until your text is the best it can be.

② Strategies for Revising

As you see need for revisions, you can use four basic strategies for improving your draft. The following chart shows how you can use these strategies with expository writing.

HERE'S HOW

Revision Strategies	
Elaborating	• Add supporting details such as facts, examples, extended definitions, concrete details, and quotations to boost the development of your ideas.
Deleting	• Cut out needless words and phrases and ideas that do not relate to your thesis statement.
Substituting	• If a word is overused or overly general, substitute a fresher, more specific and vivid word. If a supporting detail is weak, substitute a stronger one. If literal language seems too plodding, substitute a rhetorical device, such as a metaphor, simile, or analogy.
Rearranging	• If a better organizational structure occurs to you, rearrange the parts of your composition, redoing transitions as needed. If you need more sentence variety, rearrange the parts of the sentence so your sentences have a variety of beginnings.

The following excerpt from an essay titled "Fifties Fashions" shows these strategies in action.

MODEL: Elaborating, Deleting, Substituting, and Rearranging

Fifties Fashions

As every era, the 1950s had its own distinctive fashion code for teenagers. The uniform was ~~unmistakable and~~¹ easy to spot. (Matching sweater)²

sets were very popular. The fashionable teenage ³*often with a scarf around the rubber band* girl of the fifties wore her hair in a ponytail.

The fifties girl also usually wore her hair with bangs. It was considered very ~~awesome~~ to wear ⁴ ^*cool* a sweater clip connecting the two sides of the cardigan, rather than buttoning the sweater.

1 deleted: redundant

2 rearranged: moved closer to other details about sweaters

3 elaborated: good detail added

4 substituted: "awesome" is overused and current; "cool" is the term from the 50s

---

PROJECT PREP *Revising* Strategies

Work with your group. Review one another's writing to point out places where adding, deleting, substituting, or rearranging will strengthen the text to make your work the best it can be.

TIME OUT TO REFLECT

Compare your process of revising this piece of informative writing with the way you revised your writing earlier in the year. In what ways have you improved your writing? What strategies have helped you do a better job of revising, such as setting a draft aside for a few days? Record your responses in your Learning Log.

As you revised your expository essay, you looked for ways to be sure it is clear, unified, and coherent. Now you are ready to edit your essay by checking for errors in usage, spelling, capitalization, and punctuation. Use the Spelling and Grammar Check features on your word processing software to help you.

The Language of Power ⚡ Verb Tense

Power Rule: Use a consistent verb tense except when a change is clearly necessary. (See pages 693–703.)

See It in Action The conclusions from the study on teenage happiness are easy to follow in part because the verb tenses are consistent. The words in bold type are all future-tense verbs.

> Friends are and **will continue to be** the most important relationships contributing to youth happiness. Body image and traditional routes to good health **will be** important aspects of happiness for many youth. Youth **will take control** of their own happiness.

Remember It Record this rule and example in the Power Rule section of your Personalized Editing Checklist.

Use It Read through your personal narrative to make sure you have used consistent verb tenses. Highlight or underline verbs to help you keep track of tenses as you edit.

PROJECT PREP Editing

Read through your paper several times, looking for different kinds of errors each time. Use the checklist on page 29 to be sure you have caught any mistakes. Check that you have followed the Power Rules. When you have finished, use the rubric on the following page to evaluate the six traits of writing in your work.

Ideas	**4** The topic, focus, and details convey information powerfully with valid inferences.	**3** The text conveys information, using valid inferences.	**2** Some aspects of the topic are not clear and/or well developed.	**1** Most aspects are not clear and/or well developed.
Organization	**4** The organization is clear and easy to follow. Transitions provide coherence.	**3** The organization is clear, but a few ideas seem out of place or disconnected.	**2** Many ideas seem out of place and transitions are missing.	**1** The organization is unclear and hard to follow.
Voice	**4** The voice sounds natural and knowledgeable and is appropriate for the audience.	**3** The voice sounds mostly natural and knowledgable and is right for the audience.	**2** The voice sounds a bit unnatural and does not seem right for the audience.	**1** The voice sounds mostly unnatural or is inappropriate for the audience.
Word Choice	**4** Words are specific and figures of speech are used.	**3** Words are vivid and specific.	**2** Some words are overly general.	**1** Most words are overly general.
Sentence Fluency	**4** Varied sentences flow smoothly. Sentences vary in structure and length.	**3** Most of the sentences are varied and smoothly flowing.	**2** Some sentence patterns are not varied and some sentences are choppy.	**1** Sentences are not varied and are choppy.
Conventions	**4** Punctuation, usage, and spelling are correct and all Power Rules are followed.	**3** There are only a few errors in punctuation, usage, and spelling and no Power Rule errors.	**2** There are several errors in punctuation, usage, and spelling but no Power Rule errors.	**1** There are many errors and at least one Power Rule error.

PROJECT PREP *Evaluating* *Peer Evaluation*

Meet in small groups with other students who chose the same topic you did. Compare your treatment of the subject. Exchange papers with a group member. Use the evaluation form above to assign a number to each trait of that student's writing, and write a brief paragraph explaining your rating. Revise your own work as appropriate.

Expository Writing  Publishing

As you consider options for publishing your work, think about your audience and your purpose and choose the publishing format that suits those best. Your presentation should convey a distinctive point of view no matter what format you choose.

Publishing Options for Expository Writing

- a formal essay (see pages 32–33 for proper manuscript form)
- an article (see pages 163 and 281 for reader-friendly formatting techniques)
- a speech (see pages 457–464 for a guide for presenting speeches)
- a multimedia presentation (see pages 471–485 for using presentation software effectively)
- a video (see pages 480–485 for a guide to creating video presentations)

PROJECT PREP Publishing

Meet in small groups with others who chose to present their expository text in the same format you chose (letter, essay, power presentation, video, article for a Web site). Discuss the characteristics of the format you chose that make it a good way to present your information. Come up with a description of the features you need to include to make your published text as effective as possible.

Writing Lab

Project Corner

Speak and Listen
Discuss Happiness

In groups of five, **plan and present a panel discussion** on the subject of teen happiness. (See pages 468–470 on Group Discussions and pages 467–468 on Listening for Information.) Develop a set of questions based on your happiness project. Include a question-and-answer period. When your group is not presenting, be ready to contribute a comment or question.

Collaborate and Create Write a Summary

Work with two other students who wrote on the same topic as you did to **create a summary** of your projects. (See pages 337 and 397 for help with summarizing.) Figure out the process you will follow to complete the summary, and assign each group member a task. In the summary, use transitions to connect the various parts, and include direct quotes from each paper.

Experiment
Try a Different Form

Review the suggested project forms on page 213. Think about how your project would be different if it were in one of those forms you didn't use or another that you can think of. Choose a part of your project and **recast it in that new form**. What changes would you need to make? Write a brief paragraph explaining those changes.

In Everyday Life
An Informative E-Mail

1. You are trying to make plans to go to Chilly Thrills Amusement Park. A couple of your friends think the rides are dangerous. They say they are especially afraid of riding the new Icy Road Roller Coaster. **Write an e-mail** to your friends informing them about the safety precautions amusement parks take to make roller coasters safe. Gather the necessary information. Outline your ideas first so your friends get an organized, well-developed explanation.

In the Workplace An Informative Note

2. You have just been hired by Virtually Fun, an educational video-game company. Your boss wants you to help develop a new game that will appeal to fans of both rock music and skateboarding (or the sport of your choice). **Write a note** to your boss informing her of the features that make video games fun. Suggest ways to apply the features to the video game that incorporate both the sport and rock music. Arrange the information in your note in developmental order.

Timed Writing ⏱ A Newspaper Article

3. Your principal plans to renovate the cafeteria. Your assignment as a reporter for the school newspaper is to write an article informing the faculty of how the students would like the new cafeteria to be designed. Write about what kind of furniture and what type of food you think the student body would prefer. You have 20 minutes to complete your work. (For help budgeting time, see pages 420–421.)

Before You Write Consider the following questions: What is the subject? What is the occasion? Who is the audience? What is the purpose?

Prewrite to develop ideas and create an outline. Draft a strong thesis statement and an introduction with background information. Organize the body of your article in spatial order. Use specific details and precise language to present each piece of information fully.

After You Write Evaluate your work using the six-trait evaluation form on page 236.

Expository Writing Workshops

Information can be "packaged" in many different ways depending on its purpose and audience. These workshops will give you practice in gathering and presenting information in a variety of ways.

How-To, or Procedural, Texts

A **procedural text** gives step-by-step instructions for doing or making something.

You will find procedural texts in directions, user manuals, school handbooks, and workplace memos.

MODEL: Procedural Text from Journalism Handbook

Interviewing an Expert

To conduct a successful interview with an expert, follow these steps.

- First, contact the person. Explain who you are and what your purpose is in seeking an interview. Then arrange a date and time to meet or speak by phone. Find out how much time the expert will have to talk so you know how many questions you can ask.

- Next, learn as much as you can about both the expert's background and the topic you want to discuss. Make a list of questions, and arrange them in a logical order. If you will be recording the interview, test your equipment in advance, and be sure to ask your subject's permission to record.

- On the day of the interview, be on time. Follow your list of questions and stick to the agreed-on schedule. End the interview by thanking the person for talking with you.

Following these steps will help make the interview pleasant and productive.

You can use a graphic organizer like the one below to help organize a how-to text. The chain links between steps represent transitions.

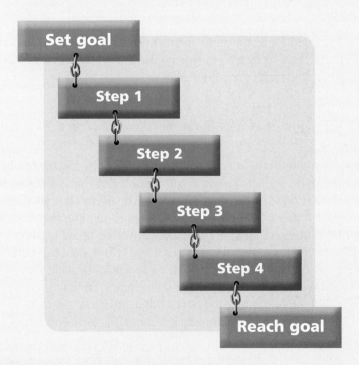

QuickGuide for Writing Procedural Texts

→ List the steps involved and arrange them in the order in which they need to be completed.

→ Use transitions such as *first, next,* and *finally* to emphasize the order.

→ Use reader-friendly formatting techniques, such as bullet points, boldface heads, and illustrations if they would be helpful.

→ Include a clear introduction and conclusion.

● Create Real-World Texts

1. Write a paragraph providing instructions for a child on how to use a combination lock.

2. Compose an e-mail to someone you know well who has never been to your home giving directions on how to get to your house from school.

3. Write out your favorite recipe and give it as a gift to someone you like.

② How-It-Works Texts

A **how-it-works text** describes how something happens, forms, or is put together.

This type of writing explains a technical or abstract process rather than something readers could do themselves, as in how-to writing. How-it-works writing follows chronological order and resembles narrative writing.

MODEL: How-It-Works Paragraph from Science Magazine

The perfect condition for a tornado to form is when cold air meets hot air near Earth's surface. Here's what happens. Cold air is heavier than hot air, so it flows under the warmer air. The lighter hot air rises quickly and, as it does, it spins around and spreads out, creating a twisting funnel of air. (That's why tornadoes are often called twisters.) The small part of the funnel touches the ground, while the large part reaches into storm clouds in the sky. The air around a tornado all moves toward the funnel, feeding a roaring, spinning wind that can reach up to 300 miles an hour, the fastest wind on Earth. Meanwhile, storm winds push the funnel along the ground. Most tornadoes occur during April, May, and June, when Earth's surface is warming but cold air can still sweep in to disturb it. And what a disturbance a powerful tornado can be!

You can use a graphic organizer like the one below to help organize a how-it-works text. The arrows between steps represent transitions.

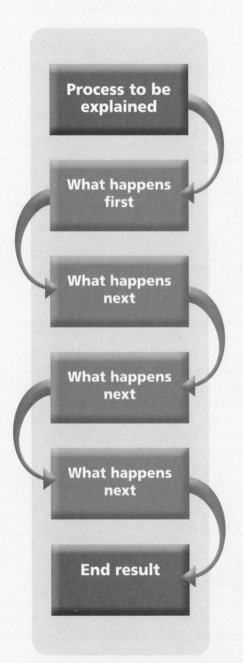

Process to be explained

What happens first

What happens next

What happens next

What happens next

End result

QuickGuide for Writing How-It-Works Texts

→ List the steps or stages involved and arrange them in the order in which they happen.

→ Use transitions such as *first, next,* and *finally* to emphasize the order.

→ Use reader-friendly formatting techniques, such as bullet points, boldface heads, and illustrations or diagrams if they would be helpful.

→ Include a clear introduction with a main idea, plenty of supporting details to make the process clear, and a strong conclusion.

● **Create Real-World Texts**

1. For the school handbook, write out the process by which a student can try out for a sports team.

2. Your younger brother wants to know how an elevator works. Explain the process with a diagram.

3. On an invitation to your party, explain how laser tag works.

4. For science class, explain the process of mitosis.

③ Compare-and-Contrast Texts

A **compare-and-contrast text** examines the similarities and differences between two subjects.

This type of text will help you interpret, understand, and explain two related subjects or events (such as a film and a book on the same topic).

> **MODEL: Compare-and-Contrast Text from a Veterinarian's Newsletter**
>
> ### Pet Personalities
>
> If cats and dogs are different, so are cat owners and dog owners. Granted, both types of owners are alike in their willingness to share their homes with a furry creature they love. But they are different in some ways, too. For example, some cat owners are independent people. They admire their feline companions for their solitary ways and seem to secretly long to be as indifferent to the world as their "purrfect" pets. Many dog owners, on the other hand, are open, friendly, and as comfortable being part of a pack as their canine pals. They value the loyalty, trust, and eagerness to please that their good-natured hounds display. Of course, just as there are sociable cats and unfriendly dogs, there are exceptions among cat people and dog people, too. For the most part, however, if you want to get a snapshot of someone's personality, ask whether the person has or prefers a cat or a dog.

Venn diagrams can help you clearly see the similarities and differences between two subjects. In the Venn diagram below, you would note the things that cat owners and dog owners have in common in the middle (green) area. In the outer areas you would note the features that are specific to either cat owners or dog owners.

dog owners   cat owners

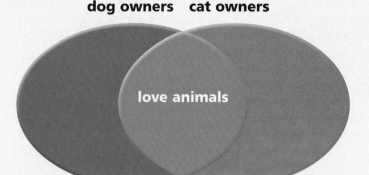

love animals

Organizing Comparison and Contrast

You have two ways to organize your information in a compare-and-contrast text. One way is to write first about one subject and then about the other subject. For example, if you were writing about cat owners (subject A) and dog owners (subject B), you would first write all your information about subject A (cat owners). Then you would write all your information about subject B (dog owners). For convenience this is called the **AABB pattern** of comparison and contrast.

You could use the AABB pattern within a paragraph by discussing subject A in the first half of the paragraph and subject B in the second half. As an alternative, you could use the AABB pattern in two paragraphs by discussing subject A in the first paragraph and subject B in the second one. The following portion of an essay for an American history class shows how the AABB pattern works.

> **MODEL: AABB Pattern of Organization**
>
> ## Conflict Between the North and the South
>
> As Americans pushed westward during the early 1800s, conflict grew between the North (subject A) and the South (subject B). Since the nation's early days, the northern and southern parts of the United States had followed different ways of life. Each section wanted to extend its own way of life to the western lands.
>
> **(A)The North** had a diversified economy with both farms and industry. **(A)Northern farmers** raised a variety of crops that fed the thriving northern cities. **(A)Mills and factories in the North** competed with Great Britain in making cloth, shoes, iron, and machinery. For both its farms and factories, **(A)the North** depended on free workers. Such workers could move from place to place to meet the needs of industry. They could also be laid off when business slumped.
>
> **(B)The South** depended on just a few cash crops, mainly cotton. To raise cotton, **(B)planters in the South** needed a large labor force year-round. They relied on slave labor. **(B)Southerners** traded their cotton for manufactured goods from Europe, especially from Great Britain. **(B)The South** had little industry of its own.

In the second paragraph on the previous page, the writer makes several points about the economy of subject A—the North. In the third paragraph, the writer turns to subject B—the South—and presents several ways in which the economy of the South was different from that of the North.

The second way to organize comparison and contrast is called the ABAB pattern. As you might expect, in the **ABAB pattern**, first you compare both subject A and subject B in terms of one similarity or difference. Then, you compare both of them in terms of another similarity or difference. The following continuation of the essay on the conflict that led to the Civil War switches to the ABAB pattern.

CHAPTER 7

MODEL: ABAB Pattern of Organization

The economic differences between the two sections soon led to political conflicts. The worst conflicts arose over slavery. **(A)Many people in the North** considered slavery morally wrong. They wanted laws that would outlaw slavery in the new western territories. Some wanted to abolish slavery altogether. **(B)Most white Southerners, on the other hand,** believed slavery was necessary for their economy. They wanted laws to protect slavery in the West so that they could raise cotton on the fertile soil there.

(A)Northerners had great political power in the national government. **(B)Southerners** feared the North's rising industrial power and growing population. Soon, they reasoned, the North would completely dominate the federal government. The election of 1860 seemed to confirm their worst fears. Abraham Lincoln, a Northern candidate who opposed the spread of slavery, was elected president.

In this passage the writer discusses the differences between the North and the South regarding attitudes toward slavery. Then the writer discusses differences between the North and the South regarding political power at the federal level.

Making an Outline

Before you draft your compare-and-contrast text, you may want to outline it, following the organzational pattern you chose. The following outline served as the basis for the first half of the American history essay on the North and the South.

MODEL: Compare-and-Contrast Outline

I. The way of life in the North
  A. Had a diversified economy
    1. Had farms and industry
    2. Had a variety of crops
    3. Fed thriving cities
  B. Had industry
    1. Had mills and factories
    2. Competed with Great Britain in making goods such as cloth, shoes, iron, and machinery
  C. Depended on free workers
    1. Could move from place to place to meet the needs of industry
    2. Could be laid off when business slumped

II. The way of life in the South
  A. Depended on a few cash crops
    1. Grew mainly cotton
    2. Needed a large labor force year-round
    3. Depended on slave labor
  B. Depended on trade with Europe
    1. Traded cotton for manufactured goods
    2. Traded mainly with Great Britain
    3. Had little industry of its own

You can use the following graphic organizers for arranging your compare-and-contrast text.

AABB Organizer

Subject for Compare/Contrast

Topic 1 about subject A
Topic 2 about subject A
Topic 3 about subject A

Transition

Topic 1 about subject B
Topic 2 about subject B
Topic 3 about subject B

ABAB Organizer

Subject for Compare/Contrast

Topic 1 about subject A
Topic 1 about subject B

Transition

Topic 2 about subject A
Topic 2 about subject B

Transition

Topic 3 about subject A
Topic 3 about subject B

QuickGuide for Writing Compare-and-Contrast Texts

→ List the similarities and differences. Use a Venn diagram to help.

→ Decide how to organize your information.

→ Use transitions such as *in contrast, on the other hand,* and *similarly* to emphasize the order.

→ Include a clear introduction and conclusion.

● Create Real-World Texts

1. Write a tribute to your best friend. Tell what traits you have in common and what traits are unique to each of you. Illustrate your tribute and give it to your friend.

2. For one of your classes, think of two subjects you could compare and contrast to understand them better. For example: atoms and molecules; Asia and Africa; Christianity and Judaism; octagons and triangles. Create a bifold to show your understanding.

3. Create a post on an electronic social network comparing yourself to your avatar.

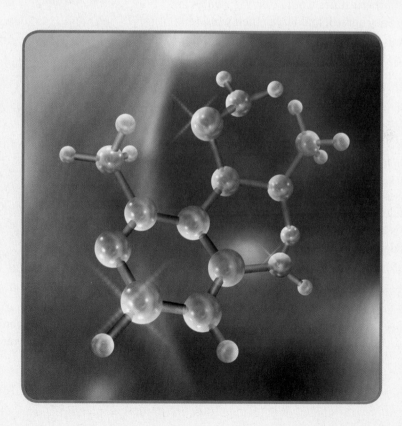

④ Cause-and-Effect Analysis Texts

A **cause-and-effect text** explains why actions or situations (causes) produce certain results (effects).

A simple cause-and-effect explanation deals with a single cause, such as an icy sidewalk, and a single effect, such as a fall. A more complex analysis describes a series of causes and effects–a chain of events–each one dependent on the one before.

> **MODEL: Cause-and-Effect Text from a Web Site About Presidents**

The Secret Oath

Rutherford B. Hayes is the only U.S. president ever to be secretly sworn into office before his public inauguration. In the election of 1876, Hayes lost the popular vote to his opponent, Samuel Tilden. But neither candidate won a majority of the electoral votes because there were votes, mainly from southern states, that were in dispute. Hayes promised to end Reconstruction and remove all federal troops from the South if the southern states would cast their votes for him. They agreed, and Hayes then won the electoral vote. However, Tilden's supporters were so angry at what they thought was a stolen election that there was fear they would riot to prevent Hayes's inauguration. So three days before the ceremony at the Capitol, Hayes took the oath of office in the Red Room of the White House, with the outgoing president, Ulysses S. Grant, as witness. Today, President Hayes's official portrait hangs in the Red Room, where his presidency secretly began.

You can use graphic organizers like the following one to help develop and organize a cause-and-effect text. You can start with the cause and explain the effects or you can start with the effect and explain the causes.

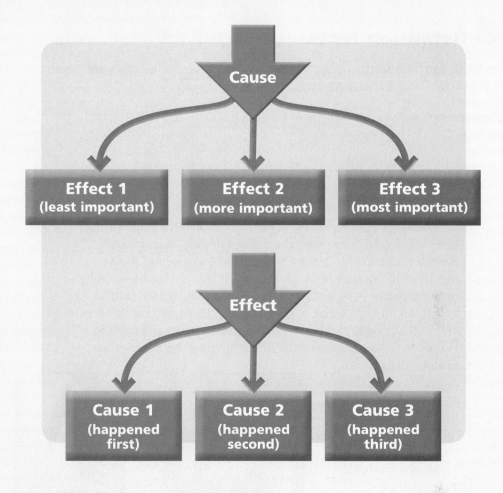

QuickGuide for Cause-and-Effect Texts

→ Identify the effect(s) you want to analyze and list the causes you know.

→ Gather information to check for accuracy and add details.

→ Use logical order. Explain multiple causes in the order they occurred, or list them by order of importance. Start with the effect and explain what caused it, or start with the cause(s) and build up to the effect.

→ Include a clear introduction and conclusion.

● Create Real-World Texts

1. With a team, create a Go Green campaign for your school. Make posters showing the effects on the environment of energy-saving practices.

2. Write a paragraph explaining and interpreting the results of an experiment you recently completed in science.

⑤ Definition Texts

A **definition text** analyzes the nature and characteristics of a word, object, concept, or phenomenon.

The paragraph below is an example of a definition for an abstract concept.

MODEL: Definition Text from an Encyclopedia

Democracy

Democracy is a form of government in which the people being governed play an active role. The concept originated in ancient Greece, where an elite group of educated citizens helped make laws. Roman imperial rule ended this early attempt, and it was not until the Middle Ages that kings began to appoint representatives to petition them on behalf of their subjects. Later political thinkers argued that a natural contract existed between ruler and ruled. If the contract were broken by the ruler, the ruled could take power. In Great Britain and especially in the United States, the idea of democracy was more fully developed to expand the freedoms to which people are entitled. Today, participation by representation, individual rights, and limits on governmental power are the hallmarks of Western democracy.

You can use a graphic organizer like the one on the following page to help develop a definition text.

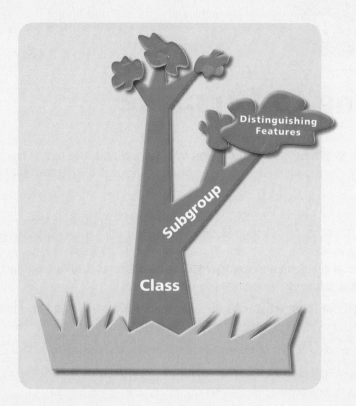

QuickGuide for Writing Definition Texts

→ Brainstorm for what you know about the nature and characteristics of your subject. Gather information as needed and decide which order to present the characteristics of your subject.

→ Include three basic parts: the subject you are defining, the class it belongs in, and the characteristics that make it different from other members of that class.

→ Include a clear introduction and conclusion.

→ Use clear, everyday language and avoid phrases like "a democracy is when…" or "a democracy is where…."

● Create Real-World Texts

1. Define *vertebrate* for your science class and create a chart to help explain it.

2. Make a valentine card. Inside it, write a definition of a true friend. When Valentine's Day comes, give the card to a true friend of yours.

3. Write a definition of the job you would love to have when you are finished with your education.

Writing to Persuade

Persuasive writing states an opinion on a subject and uses facts, reasons, and examples to convince readers. Persuasive writing is also called **argumentative writing**.

All of the following examples show ways people in different positions and professions use persuasive writing to influence others' views and, ultimately, their actions and opinions.

- **The editor of the school newspaper writes an editorial** speaking out against a proposal that students be required to wear uniforms.

- **A candidate for state senator hands out a pamphlet** explaining her qualifications for office and why she is a better choice than her opponent.

- **A charity sends a letter** detailing a crisis overseas and asking for donations to help.

- **An outraged sports writer pens a column** calling for the dismissal of a coach whose team loses consistently.

- **The president gives a speech** asking people to work harder and save more money to create "a stronger America."

Writing Project *Argumentative*

Expose a Stereotype Write an argumentative essay that focuses on the ways stereotyping is unfair.

Think Through Writing Social, cultural, ethnic, and gender groups all seem to be subject to some kind of stereotyping—often in negative ways. Assumptions are made on the basis of gender, race, nationality, and even hair color. Think of ways in which group members you know or have read about have been the subject of stereotyping, for better or worse. Write freely about this situation: who is stereotyped, who does the stereotyping, what form the stereotype takes, what the consequences might be for the perpetuation of the stereotype. At this point, don't worry about using formal writing conventions. Rather, just express your ideas freely and worry about correctness later.

Talk About It Share your writing with your writing group. Were the same groups selected to write about, or different ones? Are there common observations made by the different writers, even if the topics are different? Think about what is common to all stereotyping and whether or not you yourself contribute to the stereotyping of other groups.

Read About It In the following two articles, Gary Kimble and Bob DiBiasio give two different perspectives on the stereotyping of Native Americans through the ways in which sports team nicknames featuring Native American groups are depicted. As you read, consider the ways in which the writers state and defend their positions on whether or not using a Native American nickname for a sports team involves stereotyping, and if so, what sorts of images and impressions are perpetuated by those who create and use the nickname.

> **MODEL: Persuasive Writing**

Are Native American Team Nicknames Offensive?

YES

At the Association on American Indian Affairs, we support any Native American community that finds certain nicknames, logos, or portrayals of Native American people to be offensive. We support its right to express its pain, to go out and protest, and to work to try to get a nickname changed.

The writer's position is stated clearly and strongly.

A lot of the sentiment among Native Americans today has to do with their concern over other people's appropriation of Indian spiritual activities. Some non-Indian people are trying to create the idea that they have secret knowledge of the Indians. They disguise their own beliefs and theories as Indian beliefs. New Age gurus, for instance, pass themselves off as Indian medicine men. Native Americans' dissatisfaction with such practices is the foundation for the protest against names and logos in sports. One controversy energizes the other.

This is the most important reason. At the end of the paragraph, Kimble identifies it as the foundation for the protest against the use of Native American names in sports.

Any kind of portrayal of Native Americans that isn't respectful bothers me. Too many times, we're portrayed as hostile and criminal, as some kind of blood-thirsty savages. Or we're *noble* savages, nobler than other people because supposedly we're closer to nature. Both portrayals are stereotypes. Anytime you turn people into symbols and move away from reality, that's bad.

This paragraph puts forward another reason: disrespectful stereotypes.

A lot of people are offended by caricatures such as the one the Cleveland Indians use for their logo. When you do a caricature, you're dealing with someone's identity, and that puts you on thin ice. Even the name makes you wonder. They wouldn't call themselves the "Cleveland White People" or the "Cleveland Black People." What would happen if a soccer team in South Africa wanted to name itself the "Johannesburg White People"?

A name such as "Redskins"[1] causes concern because certain tribes feel the term is a holdover from the days when there was a bounty on American Indians. Suzanne Harjo, a Cheyenne, has written that "redskin" was a designation used by bounty hunters: Instead of bringing in the whole Indian, the hunters would just bring in the hide. They'd get paid the same for it, and it was less cumbersome than carrying around the whole body.

Not all the relationships between sports and Native Americans are bad. When Joe Robbie was the owner of the Miami Dolphins, for example, his major philanthropy work involved American Indians. Few people know he was one of the best friends our people ever had. I also recognize the danger in becoming too politically correct. I wouldn't want to see things get to the point where we can't ever enjoy ourselves or create a fun atmosphere. The tomahawk chop[2] doesn't bother me that much, and a name such as "Braves"[3] is fairly neutral.

However, there has to be some kind of balance struck, to make sure that no particular group is demeaned or damaged. And many Native Americans today believe that some of the teams they see in sports haven't found that balance.

Gary N. Kimble, a Native American, was formerly executive director of the Association on American Indian Affairs in Sisseton, South Dakota. In 1994, President Clinton appointed him commissioner for the Administration for Native Americans in the Department of Health and Human Services, Washington, D.C.

Often, showing a counter-example can reveal the weaknesses of a position or practice.

This paragraph focuses on one specific example and explains the very understandable reason—probably unknown to many—that the term is offensive.

Here Kimble shows his respect for people in the sports world and his moderate views on less emotionally charged terms as "Braves" and the tomahawk chop.

Kimble returns to his main point but acknowledges a balance should be struck.

---

1 **"Redskins":** Name of a football team based in Washington, D.C., the Washington Redskins.
2 **tomahawk chop:** Popular way for fans to root for the baseball team the Atlanta Braves.
3 **"Braves":** Name of a baseball team based in Atlanta, the Atlanta Braves.

NO

Our organization is very aware of the sensitivities involved in this issue, and we have gone to great lengths to respect those sensitivities. In no way do we intend to demean any group, especially one as proud as Native Americans.

Any discussion of the Cleveland Indians' name and the team logo, Chief Wahoo, must begin with a history lesson. Not many people realize the origin of "Indians," but there is a historical significance to how the Cleveland franchise got its name.

From 1901 to 1914, Cleveland's entry in the American League utilized three different names: Blues, Bronchos, and Nap—the last of which honored the legendary Nap Lajoie. Upon Lajoie's retirement in 1914, the officials of the Cleveland team determined a new name was in order for the following season. They turned to a local newspaper and ran a contest. The winning entry, Indians, was selected in honor of Louis Francis Sockalexis, a Penobscot Indian who was the first Native American to play professional baseball. *(Sockalexis played from 1897 to 1899 for the Cleveland Spiders of the National League.)*

Newspaper accounts at the time reported that the name Indians was chosen as "a testament to the game's first American Indian." Today, 79 years later, we're proud to acknowledge and foster the legacy of Sockalexis. That's why you don't see us animating or humanizing our logo in any way; it's simply a caricature that has enjoyed decades of fan appeal in the Northeast Ohio area. The name and logo received public support in the form of a recent "Save the Chief" campaign. We also go to great lengths to avoid any use of tomahawks, tepees, or warriors on horseback—Indian motifs that are questionable, at best.

There is an inconsistency among Native American groups as to what they think on this matter. The team name is one issue, the logo is a separate issue, and the combination of the name and the logo is yet another issue. All three elements elicit different reactions, but many Native Americans in the Northeast Ohio area have an appreciation for our understanding of their sensitivity.

DiBiasio is responding directly to Kimble's article, and he begins by stressing respect for cultural sensitivities.

Much of DiBiasio's response depends on the reason the name was given in the first place. As it turns out, it was to honor professional baseball's first Native American player.

Here DiBiasio indicates there is widespread "public support" for the name. In what way does that information contribute to his argument?

DiBiasio is saying here that even Native Americans don't agree on whether certain names and logos are offensive.

They consider our name to be an honoring of both their culture and the memory of Sockalexis.

Our view of this issue doesn't get a lot of publicity in the media, but we don't belabor it because we're comfortable with our position. Once you have an understanding of the historical significance of why we are named the Indians and understand the organization's conscious efforts to present that issue, we believe it becomes a matter of individual perception.

> The main point is reinforced here—that if you know the history of the name, you wouldn't find it offensive.

When someone looks at our name and logo, he or she thinks of Cleveland Indians baseball, and the great moments in the team's history. They don't think of Native American people; they just think of Bob Feller,[4] Al Rosen,[5] Larry Doby,[6] and Sam McDowell.[7]

Bob DiBiasio is Vice President of Public Relations for the Cleveland Indians.

---

4 **Bob Feller:** Cleveland Indians pitcher elected to the Baseball Hall of Fame in 1962; pitched no-hit games during the 1940, 1946, and 1951 seasons.
5 **Al Rosen:** Cleveland Indians player who received the Most Valuable Player Award in 1953.
6 **Larry Doby:** Cleveland Indians player elected to the Baseball Hall of Fame in 1998; first African American player in the American League.
7 **Sam McDowell:** Star Cleveland Indians pitcher in the 1960s.

Respond in Writing In your journal, write responses to the following questions. What was Kimble's main argument? What was DiBiasio's counter-argument? Which side of the argument did you find more persuasive? Why? Are there any additional points you would add on either side?

Develop Your Own Ideas Work with your classmates to come up with your own ideas on stereotyping that you might be able to use in your argumentative essay.

Small Groups: Discuss the writing you have done. Consider the two articles on Native American team mascots and:

- what it means to engage in stereotyping
- whether a stereotype contains any truth
- whether a stereotype can ever present a whole group of people fairly
- how stereotyping affects those people being stereotyped
- how stereotyping affects the people doing the stereotyping

Whole Class: Share your answers with the class while a student writes each idea on a large sheet of paper or on the board. At the end of the discussion, you will have a list of answers from your entire class that help to characterize stereotyping broadly speaking and how it affects people.

Write About It You will write an argumentative essay in which you explain why a particular stereotype is or is not fair to both the people being stereotyped and those who perpetuate and encounter the stereotype. You may choose from the options in the project possibilities chart below.

Possible Topics	Possible Audiences	Possible Forms
• lawyers who are stereotyped as people who care about winning but not about what is right • rappers who are stereotyped as illiterate social outcasts who have no formal musical training • computer experts who are stereotyped as geeks and nerds who have no social skills and don't like to have fun • overweight people who are stereotyped on television as "kooky" or gluttonous and are present mainly for comic relief	• the Screen Actors Guild • students on Career Day • newspaper readers • other teenagers	• a letter of protest • a speech to the school assembly • a letter to the newspaper editor following a story that perpetuates this stereotype • readers of a teen magazine

Good persuasive writing is a response to real life—to events, problems, and questions in the here and now that people care about. It requires thought, reflection, and often research to develop an argument supported by solid evidence that will convince your readers.

 1 Structure

Like all essays, the argumentative essay has three main parts: an introduction, a body, and a conclusion. The following chart shows how each part helps develop an argument.

HERE'S HOW   **Structuring a Persuasive Essay**

- In the **introduction,** capture the audience's attention, present the issue, and introduce your precise claim in a clear thesis statement. (See page 228 for more on claims.)
- In the **body of supporting paragraphs,** present reasons, data, facts, examples, and expert opinions to support your claims. Clearly distinguish your claims from others.
- In the **conclusion,** present a summary or strong conclusive evidence—logically drawn from the arguments—that drives home the writer's opinion.

Within these basic parts, a strong argumentative text also:

- considers a **whole range of information and views** on the topic and represents them honestly and accurately
- develops **claims and counterclaims** fairly, anticipating audience concerns and knowledge
- uses **language to link sections and clarify relationships** among claims, counterclaims, evidence, and reasons

PROJECT PREP  Analyzing **Development**

With your writing group, discuss how your rough, first writing can be developed into an argumentative essay that will convince other people about your perspective on your topic. For example, have you provided solid reasons for your positions or mainly just stated your opinions? Did your writing take any form, or will you need to shape it into a well-structured composition? Help each writer focus on the task ahead.

CHAPTER 8

❷ Facts and Opinions

Stories in the front section of a newspaper report the news as it happened—simply presenting the facts. Facts are statements that can be proved. The editorial page presents opinions based on facts. Opinions are beliefs or judgments that can be supported but not proved.

A **fact** is a statement that can be proved.

An **opinion** is a belief or judgment that cannot be proved.

Facts and opinions work together in argumentative writing. The thesis statement is a claim—the author's reasoned judgment on a subject of controversy. The body of the essay backs up the thesis statement with facts and supporting examples.

There are several ways to test whether a statement is a fact or an opinion. First, ask yourself, "Can I prove this statement through my own experience and observation?"

> **Fact** Some physical education programs stress competitive sports. (Your own school may do this.)

Another test of a fact is to ask, "Can I prove this statement by referring to accepted authorities and experts?"

> **Fact** Muscle tension increases the risk of injury during sports. (You might suspect this yourself, but to know for sure you could ask a sports doctor.)

Some opinions, unlike facts, can never be proved. They are judgment calls, personal likes or dislikes, and interpretations that vary from person to person. Consider these opinions.

Movies are **more satisfying** on a big screen than on TV.

Competition **should be** downplayed in school sports.

> **Writing Tip**
>
> Use your own experiences and observations as well as reliable authorities to verify **facts**.

The following words often signal opinions.

OPINION WORDS		
should	good, better, best	probably
ought	bad, worse, worst	might
can	beautiful	perhaps
may	terrible	usually

Opinions gain strength when they are supported by factual evidence, logical arguments, or both.

Unsupported Opinion   Volleyball is more fun than soccer. (There are no supporting facts available.)

Supported Opinion   Noncompetitive volleyball may teach positive social skills. (Experts in sports and society can offer supporting facts.)

Writing Tip

Support your **opinions** with convincing **facts** and with evidence from real life as well as from knowledgeable experts and authorities.

PROJECT PREP *Analyzing* **Facts and Opinions**

With a partner, identify where you will need facts to support your assertions. Make a list of facts, examples, and data you might find useful. Next to each item, indicate where you might find the information you need. (Refer to pages 332–334 for help in locating research sources.) Consider the full range of information on the topic and then gather the most relevant and precise evidence you can find.

● **Practice Your Skills**

Identifying Facts and Opinions

Write fact or opinion for each of the following statements.

1. Games are an age-old way of passing time.
2. Michael Jordan is the greatest basketball player ever.
3. Chess clubs are popular activities in school.
4. Made-for-TV movies are inferior to theatrical releases.
5. Video games are engaging and educational.

● **Practice Your Skills**

Supporting Opinions

Write one fact that could be used as evidence to support each of the following opinions. Use the library or media center as needed.

1. Only touch football should be allowed in schools.
2. Watching too much TV is bad for the mind and body.
3. Playing games is a good way to develop thinking skills.

PROJECT PREP *Prewriting* **Claims and Warrants**

Based on the discussions you have had with your classmates, sketch out a persuasive text. On the subject of stereotyping, for example, ask yourself what argument might you make based on what you know about the stereotyping. Who is your audience, and what belief or action would you be persuading those readers to embrace? Organize the plan for your argument into a three-column chart like the one below in which you make a series of claims about the problem, give examples that Illustrate each claim, and assert a warrant that explains how the example illustrates the claim. (See pages 228–230 and 309 for more information on claims, examples, and warrants.)

Claims	Examples	Warrants
A stereotype takes a few instances and expands them into a generality.	A few computer experts might wear glasses and use a pocket protector for their pens.	Because this image appears in the media, people begin to associate computer users with people who wear glasses and use pocket protectors and stereotype them as nerds.

Think Critically

Developing Counter-Arguments

In order to form a strong argument to back your opinion, anticipate all the possible objections, or counterclaims, to your argument. Then think of a **counter-argument**—an answer—to address each objection.

Thinking Practice

Ask a partner to play the role of a person who disagrees with you. Use your conversation to create a list of objections and counter-arguments. You can then create a chart similar to the one below to help you develop your argumentative essay. When you write such an essay, your counter-arguments should be based on evidence.

Opinion: Volunteer work should be a requirement for entry into any government-funded college.

Me: Students should have to do volunteer work to get into any college that receives government money.

Alice: Students are too busy with school work to do volunteer work.

Me: Sure, but it's hard for students to get jobs without experience; volunteer work looks good on a résumé.

Alice: I'd still rather concentrate on getting good grades so I can get into a good college.

Me: Most colleges look at more than grades. They want to see that students are well rounded.

OBJECTION	COUNTER-ARGUMENTS
1. students have a lot of school work to do and don't have time for extra activities	1. students will gain hands-on experience and education, which is the most valuable way to learn
2. students should get paid for work that they do	2. volunteer experience can help students get good jobs later
3. students need to focus on grades to get into college	3. most colleges look for extra activities such as volunteer work as well as grades when considering student applications

1 Purpose, Subject, and Audience

In a persuasive essay, your purpose is to win your readers over to your point of view—and sometimes to convince them to take an action that you recommend. To achieve this purpose, you need to build a convincing, logical argument and present it in a convincing and powerful way. The strategies that follow will help you accomplish your purpose effectively.

Thinking your subject through carefully and marshaling the best possible evidence are the surest ways to develop a good argument. If you take your time during prewriting, you will be able to anticipate your opponents' reactions and be ready for them.

CHOOSING A SUBJECT

The two most important aspects of a good argumentative subject are (1) that the subject is genuinely controversial and (2) that you feel strongly about it. Brainstorm a list of possible subjects about which you can say, "I believe," while some other people would say, "I don't believe." Use brainstorming, freewriting, clustering, or other strategies to narrow your list of possible subjects. Then use the following guidelines to choose one.

Guidelines for Choosing a Subject

- Choose a subject about an issue that is important to you.
- Choose a subject about an issue on which people hold very different opinions.
- Choose a subject that you can support with examples, reasons, and facts from your own experiences or from other reliable sources.
- Choose a subject for which there is an audience whose beliefs or behavior you would like to influence.

IDENTIFYING AN APPROPRIATE AUDIENCE

Identify your target audience when writing a persuasive essay. Readers who initially disagree with your viewpoint will mentally try to block your ideas. Be sure to consider the whole range of views your audience might have and represent them fairly and accurately in your essay. The questions on the following page will help you understand your readers so you can learn how to convince them to agree with your point of view.

Questions for Analyzing an Audience

- What does my audience already know about my subject?
- What is my audience's point of view about my subject?
- Do they already agree or disagree with my position?
- What are the chances of changing the opinions and behavior of my audience?
- Are there any sensitive issues I should be aware of?

Writing Tip

If your audience disagrees with your position, make sure you know exactly why they disagree. That way you will be better able to develop a strong argument that directly or cleverly counters their specific point or points of opposition.

● **Practice Your Skills**

Identifying Your Audience

Suppose you wanted to start a chess club at school. Decide whether each of the following statements would be more persuasive to students or to the principal. If you think they hold equal importance to both audiences, write both.

1. A parent has offered to organize and supervise the club.
2. Small dues would pay for all the expenses of the club.
3. Chess is lots of fun. Speed chess is even thrilling.
4. The school's prestige would rise with a winning team.
5. The club would provide a chance to make new friends.
6. There are plenty of rooms available after school.
7. Players would be grouped according to ability, so even beginners could compete at their own level.
8. The cost of running the club would be low because sets are not expensive.
9. Playing chess is a good way to develop strategic skills.
10. Students who win national chess championships can win cash prizes.

PROJECT PREP *Prewriting* **Subject and Audience**

In your writing group, discuss and then choose your topic, audience, and form for your argumentative essay (see page 259). Then use the questions on this page to help each author profile his or her audience and anticipate their views on the subject.

In the Media
Presentations in Public Forums

How does a newspaper decide to write an editorial? In many cases, the idea comes from an interested citizen or group. For example, suppose a citizens' group wants affordable health care. The group will present its arguments to the editors of a local newspaper. The editors, however, could decide to do an editorial supporting the opposing point of view.

Virtually all of the persuading that leads up to a newspaper editorial is oral. For practice in making strong oral presentations of your arguments, complete the following activities. Work in three groups of eight to ten.

First decide on an issue to address—anything students in your school are talking about. Have one of the three groups be the editorial board, another present the issue, and the third present the opposing side.

Carefully think through the best way to divide up your points and express them as effectively as possible. Decide who will be the best speaker to make each point. Be sure all group members understand and practice the plan.

The editorial board must evaluate the presentations, using the following questions.

Questions for Evaluating Public Presentations

- How impressive was each group?
- What really hit home in what they were saying? What fell flat?
- How strong was their evidence and other supporting information?
- Did the group use any fallacious reasoning? (See pages 274-276.)
- How effective was the group's rhetoric? (See page 217.)
- How effective were they in using eye contact, posture, and in varying the pitch and tone of their voices?

Put these evaluations in writing. Then collaborate on preparing a brief editorial. Choose one person to present that editorial to the class as effectively as possible.

The other groups should now evaluate the editorial using the questions above. Discuss what the class learned from the experience.

② Developing a Thesis Statement

Once you have chosen a subject and identified your audience, you are ready to develop a **thesis statement**—a statement that clearly and strongly expresses the viewpoint you will be arguing for in your essay. A strong thesis statement expresses a supportable opinion, or claim, not just a simple preference. Often a thesis statement will take the form of a recommendation for action.

Simple Preference	Horseback riding is a better pastime than watching television. (unsuitable)
Supportable Opinion, or Claim	Although horseback riding is a pleasurable pastime, it should not be enjoyed at the expense of the horses' well-being.
Call for Action	Until the care of the horses at Sunset Ridge Stables improves, riders should avoid doing business there.

The guidelines that follow will help you develop your thesis statement.

Guidelines for Developing a Thesis Statement

- Choose a debatable opinion—one that has two sides.
- State the thesis simply and directly in one sentence.
- Avoid hasty generalizations by limiting your statement.
- Give a supportable opinion or a recommendation for action.
- As you consider the whole range of information on the subject, continue to revise the thesis statement until it is clear-cut and defensible and covers all the evidence.

If your thesis does not meet all of these guidelines, rethink your position or look for a more appropriate issue.

PROJECT PREP   *Prewriting*   *Thesis Statement*

In your writing group, help each author develop an effective thesis statement. Help each author confirm that each of the claims is in line with the paper's overall thesis and that each makes a point that contributes to the essay's main purpose. Discuss the relative value of the data, facts, and ideas used as examples and warrants to support each claim. Consider whether additional precise and relevant information is needed to make other points that will help persuade readers.

③ Developing an Argument

After you have defined your thesis, build a sound case to convince your jury of readers. Use the following guidelines to develop your argument.

Guidelines for Developing an Argument

- List pros and cons in separate columns in your notes. Be prepared to address the opposing views point by point.
- Use facts and examples rather than more opinions to support your claims, but evaluate them to determine their relative value. Some data and "facts" are not as reliable as others. (For more information on evaluating sources, see pages 335–336.)
- If those with the opposing view have a good point, admit it. Then show why the point is not enough to sway your opinion. Such an admission is called *conceding a point*, and it will strengthen your credibility.
- Use reasonable language rather than words that show bias or overcharged emotions.
- Refer to respected authorities who agree with your position.

SUPPORTING OR CONTRADICTING AN ARGUMENT

A decision chart like the one below can help you identify the pros and cons of your argument and check to make sure you have enough information to support your position.

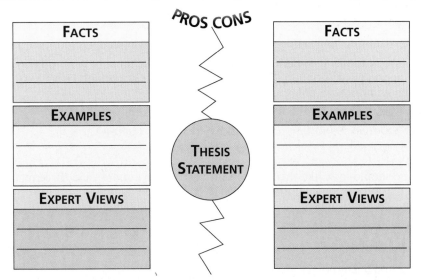

PROS CONS

| FACTS | | FACTS |

| EXAMPLES | | EXAMPLES |

THESIS STATEMENT

| EXPERT VIEWS | | EXPERT VIEWS |

PROJECT PREP *Prewriting* *Developing Your Argument*

In your writing group, help each author anticipate and address objections to the author's assertions. Discuss ways that the evidence the author has gathered can be used to develop counter-arguments. Take notes to help you when you draft.

4 Organizing an Argument

Presenting your evidence in a well-organized way will strengthen your position. The most common organization for persuasive essays is **order of importance**— beginning with the least important point and working up to the most important. Saving your best point for last will help your readers remember your most convincing evidence.

To help your readers follow your organizing structure, remember to use transitional words and phrases. The transitions that follow are very useful when you are conceding a point or showing contrasting viewpoints.

TRANSITIONS FOR PERSUASIVE WRITING		
although	instead	on the other hand
admittedly	nevertheless	still
however	nonetheless	while it is true that

USING AN OUTLINE

The following tips will help you organize and outline your ideas.

HERE'S HOW

Tips for Organizing and Outlining an Argumentative Text

- Revise the thesis statement, if necessary, to express your view.
- Review the supporting evidence you prepared. Then list three or more points that support your position in the order of least to most important. Leave two blank lines under each point.
- Assign each of your points a Roman numeral, as in an outline.
- Add at least two supporting points under each Roman numeral.

Your outline should look like this, though it may well have more than three main points.

I. (Least important point)
  A. (Supporting point)
  B. (Supporting point)

II. (More important point)
  A. (Supporting point)
  B. (Supporting point)

III. (Most important point)
  A. (Supporting point)
  B. (Supporting point)

Using a Reasoning Pillar

Another way to picture a solidly built argumentative text is to see it as a pillar, with each block strengthening the whole.

Thesis Statement	Without support, the claim expressed in the thesis statement would topple.
Least Important Point —supporting point —supporting point	You may want to include and address opposing views with your counter-arguments for each main point.
More Important Point —supporting point —supporting point	Supporting points are presented so that each one rests on an even stronger one.
Most Important Point —supporting point —supporting point	You may want to wait until the end of your own argument to address opposing views with your counter-arguments.
Strong restatement of thesis, now with evidence to support it	A thesis with compelling evidence is the foundation for an effective essay.

PROJECT PREP  *Prewriting* *Organizing Ideas*

In your writing group, discuss the best way to organize each writer's ideas. Talk through which are the most important ideas and what kind of supporting material each requires. Discuss where in the paper the counter-arguments will be presented. Help one another make an outline, reasoning pillar, or some other graphic organizer for the structure of the composition.

The Power of Language ⚡

Adverbial Phrases: Scene Setters

If you really want to be persuasive, you have to communicate well. This means using language to draw your readers in and keep them interested.

Examine the following sentences. Pay attention to the highlighted scene-setting adverbial phrases.

> We're portrayed too many times as hostile and criminal, as some kind of blood-thirsty savages.

> We're proud to acknowledge and foster the legacy of Sockalexis today, 79 years later.

Compare the versions above with what Kimble and DiBiasio actually wrote in "Are Native American Team Nicknames Offensive?"

> Too many times, we're portrayed as hostile and criminal, as some kind of blood-thirsty savages.

> Today, 79 years later, we're proud to acknowledge and foster the legacy of Sockalexis.

The authors put these scene setters at the beginning of their sentences. There the scene-setting information is the most helpful: before one reads the main part of the sentence. Putting the adverbial phrases at the beginning also avoids having an interruption of the main statement, and it avoids a distraction at the end, where the most important information is often placed.

Try It Yourself

Write three sentences with at least one adverbial scene setter each. When you draft your persuasive piece, try to put your scene setters first. You can always come back later, if needed, and rearrange your sentences even more.

Punctuation Tip

If your scene setter is **four words or more,** be sure to put a **comma after it,** though even shorter ones may also be followed by a comma. If you want your reader to pause, put a comma after your scene setter. (See pages 852–853 on introductory elements.)

1 Using Your Outline

Your outline will guide you as you draft your argumentative essay. You may notice that certain sections of your essay need additional supporting details to be convincing. Make notes in the margin to remember these locations. Rethink your thesis if your draft is not developing as you had hoped.

Pay special attention to the **introduction**. You may want to begin with an incident or example to show the importance of the issue. Many writers save their thesis statement for the end of the introduction.

When drafting the **body**, follow your outline ideas unless you see a better way to organize. Write one full paragraph for each of your main supporting points. At appropriate spots, address your opponents' possible differing viewpoints. To achieve a smooth flow, use transitional words and phrases. Transitions also help you clarify the relationships among claims, counterclaims, evidence, and reasons.

You may wish to review transitions on pages 5, 86, and 270.

In your **conclusion**, combine your ideas in a compelling and memorable summary. Restate your recommendations for action, if you are including any. Then add a title that will engage the interest of your audience.

USING PERSUASIVE LANGUAGE

Overly emotional language weakens your arguments. Establish and maintain a formal style and objective tone. Use strong but direct words. Be aware of the connotations of the words you use in order to convey meaning accurately and tactfully. (See pages 47–48.)

Emotional Language	The **slave-driving** owners of the **sickeningly run-down** stables **deserve the treatment** they give their animals.
Forceful Language	The **unsympathetic** owners of the **poorly kept** stables should begin to consider the animals' welfare.

PROJECT PREP *Drafting* *Following the Plan*

Use your outline to get the first draft of your argumentative essay down on paper. Provide transitions as you move from one point to another or when you introduce and respond to opposing views with counter-arguments. Read over your draft and change any overly emotional words to more reasonable terms.

② Avoiding Logical Fallacies

Well-chosen, powerful words often appeal to a reader's emotions and sometimes stir people to action. The best persuasive texts, however, couple the appeal to emotions with clear-headed logic and reasoning, appealing to a reader's rational side as well. As you draft, challenge your thinking at every stage. Watch especially for the following logical fallacies. You can see many of these in advertising.

Propaganda People who read or listen with care and discernment know that words can sometimes be misleading. This is especially true when writers and speakers use **propaganda** instead of facts and examples to get you to accept their point of view. Rather than provide facts and examples as evidence, speakers who use propaganda distort or misrepresent information or disguise opinions as facts. Propaganda techniques also appeal to people's emotions by using emotional language, stereotypes, and exaggerations. Be sure not to slip into propaganda as you draft your persuasive text, and watch for it in what you read and hear to judge its objectivity and accuracy.

Bandwagon Appeals A **bandwagon appeal** is an invitation to do or think the same thing as everyone else. Advertisements that use bandwagon appeals often try to make consumers feel inferior if they do not conform. A political campaign may use bandwagon appeals to make voters feel useless if they do not vote on the winning side. Common slogans associated with this type of propaganda include *Get on board! Join the crowd! Don't be left out!*

Testimonials A **testimonial** is a statement, usually given by a famous person, that supports a product, a candidate, or a policy. A testimonial can be misleading because it suggests that a famous person's opinions must be right or that a product must be excellent if a celebrity endorses it. You can use respected authorities to back up your points, but emphasize the strength of the ideas, not the fame of the person.

Hi! I'm Greg Husky, quarterback for the Longhorns. Since getting to each game on time is important, I depend on my Goldex watch to get me there on time!

Unproved Generalization A **generalization** is a conclusion that is based on many facts and examples. However, a generalization that is based on only one or two facts or examples is unsound. Unsound generalizations are misleading when they are used as if they were facts that apply to all cases. Unproved generalizations often contain words such as *always, never, all,* or *none.*

Unproved Generalizations	Television **always** makes children behave badly. Watching a movie is **never** as good as reading a book.
Accurate Generalizations	**Some** children behave badly after watching violent TV programs. Watching a movie is **often** not as satisfying as reading a book.

Glittering Generalities **Glittering generalities** are words and phrases most people associate with virtue and goodness that are used to trick people into feeling positively about a subject. The "virtue words" listed below stir powerful feelings in the minds of most people. Like flashbulbs, they make it difficult to focus on anything other than the light itself.

VIRTUE WORDS		
democracy	family	motherhood
values	moral	education

A politician who says, "This law will keep the country safe for democracy" assumes that you have strong feelings about democracy and would do anything to preserve it. The following guidelines, adapted from those recommended by the Institute for Propaganda Analysis, will help you recognize and avoid using glittering generalities.

Questions for Analyzing Propaganda

- What does the virtue word really mean?
- Does the idea in question have any legitimate connection with the real meaning of the virtue word?
- Is an idea being "sold" to me merely by its being given a name that I like?
- Leaving the virtue word out of consideration, what are the merits of the idea?

● **Practice Your Skills**

Dimming a Glittering Generality

Analyze the following glittering generality by writing answers to the four questions above.

Because nothing is more corrosive to the moral fiber of our democracy than rock and roll, you should vote to close down the House of Rock.

PROJECT PREP *Revising* *Checking for Propaganda Techniques*

Share your draft with your writing group. Review each writer's draft looking for any propaganda and other logical fallacies. Also comment on the overall flow of the draft, making suggestions when appropriate to strengthen the argument, the organization, or the style.

In the Media

Advertising

Unsound generalizations may occur most often in advertisements, which are often slanted toward emotion rather than reason. Ads can also contain misleading information. Look at the following example:

ARENT WE ALL IN THE PURSUIT OF

HAPPINESS?

Bandwagon: invites the viewer to do what everyone else is doing

Stereotype: attracts audiences who identify with the fantasy

Unsound generalization: based on only one or two details and contains the word *all*

Testimonial: an opinion associated with a celebrity, who is endorsing a product

Glittering generality: ties product to patriotic buzzword

Symbol: equates fresh, clean image of water with product

Media Activity

Work with a partner. Look for illustrated dramatic ads from a magazine or newspaper and take turns showing them and reading them aloud to the class. Listeners should identify facts/opinions, bandwagon appeals, unsound generalizations, and other propaganda techniques.

1 Checking for Unity, Coherence, and Clarity

You can revise your work on your own by studying it carefully for flaws in unity, coherence, and clarity. When considering unity, ask yourself, "Have I stuck faithfully to my intended subject? Do all of my supporting points relate directly to my thesis statement? Did I include any unnecessary and distracting information?"

When checking for coherence, carefully review your organizational structure. Is it appropriate to your purpose, audience, and context? Did it follow a logical order? Does one idea flow smoothly and logically to the next? Did you include clear and ample transitions?

When evaluating your essay for clarity, check to make sure there is no possibility that your points could be misunderstood. Replace vague language with forceful, specific words. Make sure all terms are clearly defined within the context of your subject. Fully explain any reasons or examples that fail to support your thesis clearly. Erase from your mind all that you already know about your subject and imagine that you are a reader who is completely unfamiliar with the issues of your argument. Will the pros and cons be clear to such a reader?

editing ⭐

The following sentence uses emotionally charged words. Write the sentence and circle the overly emotional words. Then revise the passage (you can use more than one sentence in the revision) in straightforward, forceful language.

Using a nasty stereotype is often the formidable cause of untold pain and suffering to the poor recipient.

PROJECT PREP Revising *Unity, Coherence, and Clarity*

Based on the feedback you've gotten from your writing group, write a new draft of your persuasive essay, with attention to unity, coherence, and clarity. Correct any spelling, grammar, and punctuation errors you may find.

2 Using a Revision Checklist

Use the following checklist to go over your persuasive text one more time.

✓ Evaluation Checklist for Revising

Checking Your Introduction

- ✓ Does the thesis statement express your claim effectively? (pages 260–261, 268, and 273)
- ✓ Will your introduction convince readers that your topic is important? (pages 260 and 273)
- ✓ Is the language you use both formal and objective? (pages 273–275)

Checking Your Body Paragraphs

- ✓ Does each paragraph have a topic sentence? (pages 76–78)
- ✓ Have you supported your main points with precise and relevant evidence by analyzing the relative value of specific data, facts, and ideas? (pages 261–263)
- ✓ Have you developed arguments and organized them as appropriate to the purpose, audience, and context? (pages 269–271)
- ✓ Have you considered the full range of views on the topic and represented them fairly and accurately? (pages 264, 269, and 274–275)
- ✓ Have you included counter-arguments based on evidence to anticipate and address objections? (pages 260, 264, and 269–271)
- ✓ Have you used transitions to help your reader follow your argument? (pages 270 and 273)

Checking Your Conclusion

- ✓ Does your conclusion summarize your main points? (pages 260 and 273)
- ✓ Did you restate your thesis?
- ✓ Is your conclusion logically drawn from your arguments? (pages 260 and 273)

Checking Your Words and Sentences

- ✓ Have you used constructions that allow you to present subtleties? (pages 47–49)
- ✓ Have you avoided biased, emotionally charged words? (pages 273–275 and 277)

PROJECT PREP *Revising* *Add, Delete, Substitute, and Rearrange*

Exchange drafts with a classmate. Ask your partner whether your points are clearly organized and whether your words are convincing. Consider your classmate's comments, your own evaluation, your teacher's suggestions, and the checklist above to guide you in strengthening your essay.

After you have revised your essay, edit it for errors in sentence structure, spelling, grammar, capitalization, and punctuation. Use the mini-lesson below and the checklist on page 29 as sources for guidance. You may want to share your work with classmates or family members for additional feedback.

The Language of Power *Possessive Nouns*

Power Rule: Use standard ways to make nouns possessive. (See pages 895–897.)

See It in Action The apostrophe is a handy little mark (') that helps show ownership. You might think of it as a link that connects a noun to the *s* that indicates possession. Notice how the authors of "Are Native American Team Nicknames Offensive?" use possessives in the sentences below.

> A lot of the sentiment among Native Americans today has to do with their concern over other people's appropriation of Indian spiritual activities.

As a collective noun, *people* is a single noun made possessive in the standard way—by adding *'s*. In the sentence above, *Native Americans* is a simple plural noun. Since Americans ends in an *s*, to make the phrase possessive, an apostrophe is added:

> Native Americans' dissatisfaction with such practices is the foundation for the protest against names and logos in sports.

The single noun *Indian* would become possessive with the addition of the *'s*: *Indian's*. The plural, however, would require only an apostrophe: *Indians'*.

> Any discussion of the Cleveland Indians' name and the team logo, Chief Wahoo, must begin with a history lesson.

Remember It Record this rule and example in the Power Rule section of your Personalized Editing Checklist.

Use It Read through your persuasive text and circle any possessive nouns in your sentences. Check that the apostrophes are in the right position.

Using a Six-Trait Rubric ·Persuasive Writing·

Ideas	**4** The thesis statement is clear. Evidence is solid and there are no logical fallacies. Rebuttals are effective.	**3** The thesis statement is clear. Most evidence is solid and there are no logical fallacies. Some rebuttals are effective.	**2** The thesis statement could be clearer. Some evidence is solid, but there is one logical fallacy. Rebuttals are weak.	**1** The thesis statement is missing or unclear. Some evidence is solid, but there are logical fallacies. No rebuttals are offered.
Organization	**4** The organization is clear with abundant transitions.	**3** A few ideas seem out of place or transitions are missing.	**2** Many ideas seem out of place and transitions are missing.	**1** The organization is unclear and hard to follow.
Voice	**4** The voice sounds natural, engaging, and forceful.	**3** The voice sounds natural and engaging.	**2** The voice sounds mostly natural but is weak.	**1** The voice sounds mostly unnatural and is weak.
Word Choice	**4** Words are specific and powerful. Language is respectful.	**3** Words are specific and language is respectful.	**2** Some words are too general and/or emotional.	**1** Most words are overly general and emotional.
Sentence Fluency	**4** Varied sentences flow smoothly.	**3** Most sentences are varied and flow smoothly.	**2** Some sentences are varied but some are choppy.	**1** Sentences are not varied and are choppy.
Conventions	**4** Punctuation, usage, and spelling are correct. The Power Rules are all followed.	**3** Punctuation, usage, and spelling are mainly correct, and Power Rules are all followed.	**2** Some punctuation, usage, and spelling are incorrect, but all Power Rules are followed.	**1** There are many errors and at least one failure to follow a Power Rule.

PROJECT PREP Editing *Final Review*

In your writing group, evaluate one another's persuasive text using the rubric above. Make any revisions that seem appropriate.

The medium in which you publish writing also has a bearing on the style and format of your work. Consider the different requirements of the following types of publications.

CHARACTERISTICS OF ASSORTED PUBLISHING FORMATS

Blog
- style is often more casual than printed text
- may be written to invite interaction from readers in the form of comments to the blog
- reader-friendly formatting techniques, such as bulleted lists and a clear heading structure, assist in reading from the computer screen
- graphics may be added to enhance the message
- hyperlinks lead to related stories

Magazine article
- article's style and tone need to fit with the style and tone of the publication. For example, an article in a financial magazine would likely need to be somewhat formal.
- in some two-column magazines, for clarity paragraphs tend to be short
- graphics often accompany the article

E-mail notice
- e-mails need to be concise and to the point
- the text is often "chunked" in manageable amounts for ease of reading
- hyperlinks are often provided

Public announcement
- generally has very neutral and formal language
- may include charts and other graphics

PROJECT PREP  Publishing Submissions

Complete the writing process by sharing your work with those who are interested in the subject of your persuasive essay. Think about using one of the formats above.

TIME OUT TO REFLECT

If you have written a persuasive essay earlier in the year, take it out and read it again. How does it differ from the work you just completed? What did you do better in your most recent work? Is there anything you did better before? What would you like to improve in writing your next persuasive essay? Record your responses in your Learning Log.

Writing Lab

Project Corner

Speak and Listen
Group Discussion

With your classmates, **discuss the ways in which people stereotype one another.** In addition to discussing the kinds of stereotypes that seem prominent, also consider the moral implications for society when assumptions are made about an individual's character based on preconceived notions about his or her ethnicity, gender, race, religion, or profession. Be sure to ask for clarification if your classmates say something you do not understand. (See pages 468–470 for more on group discussions.)

Collaborate and Create A Comedy Sketch

With your writing group, **write a comedy sketch** about a stereotype that backfires. In other words, take a common stereotype and make fun of it. Your goal is to expose the foolishness of stereotyping others.

Get Technical
A Web Site

Using the essays from your class, **create a Web site** designed to alert people to the dangers of judging others based on a stereotype. Divide the labor so that people with experience in designing Web sites are in charge of layout and the linking and uploading of the essays, while people who are good writers produce the home page's text, and people with graphic arts ability create graphics and take charge of the look and feel of the site. (See pages 473–497 for more on Web sites and electronic publishing.)

In the Workplace
Persuasive Presentation

1. You work in a small office where, to your dismay, a good deal of stereotyping takes place. You want to get together with co-workers who feel as you do and brainstorm a way to bring this upsetting situation to the attention of those practicing the stereotyping. You and your co-workers decide that a dramatic presentation might be the best way to go. *Produce a brief play* in which you depict the words and actions of people similar to your co-workers. After the play is presented, discuss its effectiveness with the audience.

For Oral Communication Persuasive Talk

2. You have a summer job working for the street division of Rockin' Robots Incorporated. Someone approaches who seems interested in the robots. *Prepare and deliver an oral presentation* persuading the person that buying a Rockin' Robot will improve the qualiy of his or her life. Offer a thesis and use examples to support it. Remember to use transitions for persuasive writing and a voice appropriate to your audience. Deliver your proposal to classmates or family members who will listen as the potential customer. (You can find more information on oral presentations on pages 457–464.)

Timed Writing 🕐 Persuasive Letter

3. You play in a rock-and-roll band called The Garbage Gurus. Some executives at the record company are unhappy with a song from your latest recording session called "My Record Company Stinks" and do not want it included on your next CD. This is your favorite song from the session, and you also really believe it will be a big seller. You have to persuade the executives to include this song on your album. Write a letter to Recycled Records explaining why "My Record Company Stinks" should be included on your next album. You have 25 minutes to complete your work.

Before You Write Consider the following questions: What is the subject? What is the occasion? Who is the audience? What is the purpose?

Be sure to present both sides of the issue, acknowledging opposing views. Use facts and examples to support your position. Make sure your letter has an introduction, supporting details, and a conclusion. Also make sure you are using a voice appropriate to your audience.

After You Write Evaluate your work using the six-trait rubric on page 280.

CHAPTER 9

Writing About Literature

A literary analysis presents an interpretation of a work of literature and supports that interpretation with appropriate responses, details, and quotations.

Written and oral responses to literature take many different forms. Here are some examples you may have read, heard, or experienced.

- **A television movie critic reviews a new film**, analyzing plot, character development, imagery, and dialogue.

- **A reporter discusses a poem that was recited at a presidential inauguration,** commenting on how it appropriately commemorates the event.

- **An Internet company encourages users to post online reviews of books and movies** to guide other shoppers and boost sales.

- **Members of a book group share** their personal responses to a new novel.

- **A student presents her first oral report** on a book she has read, explaining what the story was about and why she liked it.

Writing Project   *Interpretive Response*

Literary Analysis *Write a response to a literary work that uses evidence from the work to support a thoughtful interpretation.*

Think Through Writing Think about a play, a poem, or a short story that you like and write about why you like it. Is it because of the characters, the story, the theme, the style, or something else? Or you may want to explain what you didn't like about a play, a poem, or a short story.

Talk About It In your writing group, discuss the writing you have done. What kinds of stories or poems did people write about? What do you and your writing group members like when you read?

Read About It In the following passage from "Say It with Flowers," notice how the author, Toshio Mori, builds the character's internal conflict.

From *Yokahama, California*

Say It with Flowers

Toshio Mori

He was a queer one to come to the shop and ask Mr. Sasaki for a job, but at the time I kept my mouth shut. There was something about this young man's appearance which I could not altogether harmonize with a job as a clerk in a flower shop. I was a delivery boy for Mr. Sasaki then. I had seen clerks come and go, and although they were of various sorts of temperaments and conducts, all of them had the technique of waiting on the customers or acquired one eventually. You could never tell about a new one, however, and to be on the safe side I said nothing and watched our boss readily take on this young man. Anyhow we were glad to have an extra hand because the busy season was coming around.

Mr. Sasaki undoubtedly remembered last year's rush when Tommy, Mr. Sasaki and I had to do everything and had our hands tied behind our backs from having so many things to do at one time. He wanted to be ready this time. "Another clerk and we'll be all set for any kind of business," he used to tell us. When Teruo came around looking for a job, he got it, and Morning-Glory Flower Shop was all set for the year as far as our boss was concerned.

When Teruo reported for work the following morning Mr. Sasaki left him in Tommy's hands. Tommy had been our number one clerk for a long time.

"Tommy, teach him all you can," Mr. Sasaki said. "Teruo's going to be with us from now on."

"Sure," Tommy said.

"Tommy's a good florist. You watch and listen to him," the boss told the young man.

"All right, Mr. Sasaki," the young man said. He turned to us and said, "My name is Teruo." We shook hands.

We got to know one another pretty well after that. He was a quiet fellow with very little words for anybody, but his smile disarmed a person. We soon learned that he knew nothing about the florist business. He could identify a rose when he saw one, and gardenias and carnations too; but other flowers and materials were new to him.

"You fellows teach me something about this business and I'll be grateful. I want to start from the bottom," Teruo said.

Tommy and I nodded. We were pretty sure by then he was all right. Tommy eagerly went about showing Teruo the florist game. Every morning for several days Tommy repeated the prices of the flowers for him. He told Teruo what to do on telephone orders; how to keep the greens fresh; how to make bouquets, corsages, and sprays. "You need a little more time to learn how to make big funeral pieces," Tommy said. "That'll come later."

In a couple of weeks Teruo was just as good a clerk as we had had in a long time. He was curious almost to a fault, and was a glutton for work. It was about this time our boss decided to move ahead his yearly business trip to Seattle. Undoubtedly he was satisfied with Teruo, and he knew we could get along without him for a while. He went off and left Tommy in full charge.

During Mr. Sasaki's absence I was often in the shop helping Tommy and Teruo with the customers and the orders. One day Teruo learned that I once worked in the nursery and had experience in flower-growing.

"How do you tell when a flower is fresh or old?" he asked me. "I can't tell one from the other. All I do is follow your instructions and sell the ones you tell me to sell first, but I can't tell one from the other."

I laughed. "You don't need to know that, Teruo," I told him. "When the customers ask you whether the flowers are fresh, say yes firmly. 'Our flowers are always fresh, madam.'"

Teruo picked up a vase of carnations. "These flowers came in four or five days ago, didn't they?" he asked me.

"You're right. Five days ago," I said.

"How long will they keep if a customer bought them today?" Teruo asked.

"I guess in this weather they'll hold a day or two," I said.

"Then they're old," Teruo almost gasped. "Why, we have fresh ones that last a week or so in the shop."

"Sure, Teruo. And why should you worry about that?" Tommy said. "You talk right to the customers and they'll believe you. 'Our flowers are always fresh? You bet they are! Just came in a little while ago from the market.'"

Teruo looked at us calmly, "That's a hard thing to say when you know it isn't true."

"You've got to get it over with sooner or later," I told him. "Everybody has to do it. You too, unless you want to lose your job."

"I don't think I can say it convincingly again," Teruo said. "I must've said yes forty times already when I didn't know any better. It'll be harder next time."

"You've said it forty times already so why can't you say yes forty million times more? What's the difference? Remember, Teruo, it's your business to live," Tommy said.

"I don't like it," Teruo said.

"Do we like it? Do you think we're any different from you?" Tommy asked Teruo. "You're just a green kid. You don't know any better so I don't get sore, but you got to play the game when you're in it. You understand, don't you?"

Teruo nodded. For a moment he stood and looked curiously at us for the first time, and then went away to water the potted plants.

In the ensuing weeks we watched Teruo develop into a slick salesclerk but for one thing. If a customer forgot to ask about the condition of the flowers Teruo did splendidly. But if someone should mention about the freshness of the flowers he wilted right in front of the customers. Sometimes he would splutter. He would stand gaping speechless on other occasions without a comeback. Sometimes, looking embarrassedly at us, he would take the customers to the fresh flowers in the rear and complete the sales.

"Don't do that anymore, Teruo," Tommy warned him one afternoon after watching him repeatedly sell the fresh ones. "You know we got plenty of the old stuff in the front. We can't throw all that stuff away. First thing you know the boss'll start losing money and we'll all be thrown out."

"I wish I could sell like you," Teruo said. "Whenever they ask me, 'Is it fresh?' 'How long will it keep?' I lose all sense about selling the stuff, and begin to think of the difference between the fresh and the old stuff. Then the trouble begins."

"Remember, the boss has to run the shop so he can keep it going," Tommy told him. "When he returns next week you better not let him see you touch the fresh flowers in the rear."

On the day Mr. Sasaki came back to the shop we saw something unusual. For the first time I watched Teruo sell some old stuff to a customer. I heard the man plainly ask him if the flowers would keep good, and very clearly I heard Teruo reply, "Yes, sir. These flowers'll keep good." I looked at Tommy, and he winked back. When Teruo came back to make it into a bouquet he looked as if he had a snail in his mouth. Mr. Sasaki came back to the rear and watched him make the bouquet. When Teruo went up front to complete the sale Mr. Sasaki looked at Tommy and nodded approvingly.

When I went out to the truck to make my last delivery for the day Teruo followed me. "Gee, I feel rotten," he said to me. "Those flowers I sold to the people, they won't last longer than tomorrow. I feel lousy. I'm lousy. The people'll get to know my word pretty soon."

"Forget it," I said. "Quit worrying. What's the matter with you?"

"I'm lousy," he said, and went back to the store.

Then one early morning the inevitable happened. While Teruo was selling the fresh flowers in the back to a customer Mr. Sasaki came in quietly and watched the transaction. The boss didn't say anything at the time. All day Teruo looked sick. He didn't know whether to explain to the boss or shut up.

While Teruo was out to lunch Mr. Sasaki called us aside. "How long has this been going on?" he asked us. He was pretty sore.

"He's been doing it off and on. We told him to quit it," Tommy, said. "He says he feels rotten selling old flowers."

"Old flowers!" snorted Mr. Sasaki. "I'll tell him plenty when he comes back. Old flowers! Maybe you can call them old at the wholesale market but they're not old in a flower shop."

"He feels guilty fooling the customers," Tommy explained.

The boss laughed impatiently. "That's no reason for a businessman."

When Teruo came back he knew what was up. He looked at us for a moment and then went about cleaning the stems of the old flowers.

"Teruo," Mr. Sasaki called.

Teruo approached us as if steeled for an attack.

"You've been selling fresh flowers and leaving the old ones go to waste. I can't afford that, Teruo," Mr. Sasaki said. "Why don't you do as you're told? We all sell the flowers in the front. I tell you they're not old in a flower shop. Why can't you sell them?"

"I don't like it, Mr. Sasaki," Teruo said. "When the people ask me if they're fresh I hate to answer. I feel rotten after selling the old ones."

"Look here, Teruo," Mr. Sasaki said. "I don't want to fire you. You're a good boy, and I know you need a job, but you've got to be a good clerk here or you're going out. Do you get me?"

"I get you," Teruo said.

In the morning we were all at the shop early. I had an eight o'clock delivery, and the others had to rush with a big funeral order. Teruo was there early. "Hello," he greeted us cheerfully as we came in. He was unusually high-spirited, and I couldn't account for it. He was there before us and had already filled out the eight o'clock package for me. He was almost through with the funeral frame, padding it with wet moss and covering it all over with brake fern, when Tommy came in. When Mr. Sasaki arrived, Teruo waved his hand and cheerfully went about gathering the flowers for the funeral piece. As he flitted here and there he seemed as if he had forgotten our presence, even the boss. He looked at each vase, sized up the flowers, and then cocked his head at the next one. He did this with great deliberation, as if he were the boss and the last word in the shop. That was all right, but when a customer soon came in, he swiftly attended him as if he owned all the flowers in the world. When the man asked Teruo if he was getting fresh flowers Teruo without batting an eye escorted the customer into the rear and eventually showed and sold the fresh ones. He did it with so much grace, dignity and swiftness that we stood around like his stooges. However, Mr. Sasaki went on with his work as if nothing had happened.

Along toward noon Teruo attended his second customer. He fairly ran to greet an old lady who wanted a cheap bouquet around fifty cents for a dinner table. This time he not only went back to the rear for the fresh ones but added three or four extras. To make it more irritating for the boss, who was watching every move, Teruo used an extra lot of maidenhair because the old lady was appreciative of his art of making bouquets. Tommy and I watched the boss fuming inside of his office.

When the old lady went out of the shop Mr. Sasaki came out furious. "You're a blockhead. You have no business sense. What are you doing here?" he said to Teruo. "Are you crazy?"

Teruo looked cheerful. "I'm not crazy, Mr. Sasaki," he said. "And I'm not dumb. I just like to do it that way, that's all."

The boss turned to Tommy and me. "That boy's a sap," he said. "He's got no head."

Teruo laughed and walked off to the front with a broom. Mr. Sasaki shook his head. "What's the matter with him? I can't understand him," he said.

While the boss was out to lunch Teruo went on a mad spree. He waited on three customers at one time, ignoring our presence. It was amazing how he did it. He hurriedly took one customer's order and had him write a birthday greeting for it; jumped to the second customer's side and persuaded her to buy Columbia roses because they were the freshest of the lot. She wanted them delivered so he jotted it down on the sales book, and leaped to the third customer.

"I want to buy that orchid in the window," she stated without deliberation.

"Do you have to have orchid, madam?" Teruo asked the lady.

"No," she said. "But I want something nice for tonight's ball, and I think the orchid will match my dress. Why do you ask?"

"If I were you I wouldn't buy that orchid," he told her. "It won't keep. I could sell it to you and make a profit but I don't want to do that and spoil your evening. Come to the back, madam, and I'll show you some of the nicest gardenias in the market today. We call them Belmont and they're fresh today."

He came to the rear with the lady. We watched him pick out three of the biggest gardenias and make them into a corsage. When the lady went out with her package a little boy about eleven years old came in and wanted a twenty-five-cent bouquet for his mother's birthday. Teruo waited on the boy. He was out in the front, and we saw him pick out a dozen of the two-dollar-a-dozen roses and give them to the kid.

Tommy nudged me. "If he was the boss he couldn't do those things," he said.

"In the first place," I said, "I don't think he could be a boss."

"What do you think?" Tommy said. "Is he crazy? Is he trying to get himself fired?"

"I don't know," I said.

When Mr. Sasaki returned, Teruo was waiting on another customer, a young lady.

"Did Teruo eat yet?" Mr. Sasaki asked Tommy.

"No, he won't go. He says he's not hungry today," Tommy said.

We watched Teruo talking to the young lady. The boss shook his head. Then it came. Teruo came back to the rear and picked out a dozen of the very fresh white roses and took them out to the lady.

"Aren't they lovely?" we heard her exclaim.

We watched him come back, take down a box, place several maidenhairs and asparagus, place the roses neatly inside, sprinkle a few drops, and then give it to her. We watched him thank her, and we noticed her smile and thanks. The girl walked out.

Mr. Sasaki ran excitedly to the front. "Teruo! She forgot to pay!"

Teruo stopped the boss on the way out. "Wait, Mr. Sasaki," he said. "I gave it to her."

"What!" the boss cried indignantly.

"She came in just to look around and see the flowers. She likes pretty roses. Don't you think she's wonderful?"

"What's the matter with you?" the boss said. "Are you crazy? What did she buy?"

"Nothing, I tell you," Teruo said. "I gave it to her because she admired it, and she's pretty enough to deserve beautiful things, and I liked her."

"You're fired! Get out!" Mr. Sasaki spluttered. "Don't come back to the store again."

"And I gave her fresh ones too," Teruo said.

Mr. Sasaki rolled out several bills from his pocketbook. "Here's your wages for this week. Now, get out," he said.

"I don't want it," Teruo said. "You keep it and buy some more flowers."

"Here, take it. Get out," Mr. Sasaki said.

Teruo took the bills and rang up the cash register. "All right, I'll go now. I feel fine. I'm happy. Thanks to you." He waved his hand to Mr. Sasaki. "No hard feelings."

On the way out Teruo remembered our presence. He looked back. "Good-bye, Good luck," he said cheerfully to Tommy and me. He walked out of the shop with his shoulders straight, head high, and whistling. He did not come back to see us again.

Respond in Writing In your journal, answer these questions: What is Teruo's inner conflict? How does he resolve it? What does Mori seem to be saying about the individual and the marketplace?

Develop Your Own Ideas for Analysis Work with your classmates to come up with ideas that might help in writing a literary analysis of your own.

Small Groups: Break into small groups of four or five. Discuss the writing you have done. Make an organizer like the following to help you gather evidence to support your interpretation of "Say It with Flowers."

Overall Meaning (Theme): What is the major theme of this story?	
Literary Elements	**Evidence from Story**
What passage in the story offers the best clue to the theme? Why?	
How does the setting affect the characters in the story?	
What do you learn about the characters' histories, personalities, dreams, etc.?	
How does using a first-person narrator impact the story?	
How does the author's style draw the reader into the story?	
What motivates each character, and what consequences follow from his or her actions?	

Whole Class: Make a master chart of all of the ideas generated by the small groups to see how different members interpreted the story.

Write About It In this chapter you will write a literary analysis that considers important aspects of the story "Say It with Flowers." For your analysis you can choose from any of the following possible topics, audiences, and forms.

Whatever topic you choose, analyze how the author's style and use of rhetorical devices such as flashback, foreshadowing, and irony contribute to the aesthetics (artistic quality) of the story.

You can learn more about style in Chapter 2 and about literary rhetorical devices in Chapter 6.

Possible Topics	Possible Audiences	Possible Forms
• an interpretation of Teruo's character and motivation • an interpretation of the story's theme • an interpretation of the narrator's role in the story • an interpretation of how the setting affects the theme	• English teachers • classmates • others who have read the story • another fiction writer	• an essay • a blog • a post to a Web-based discussion board

Responding to Literature

Reading literature is a creative process in which the reader interacts with a literary work. Before writing formally about a work, experience this creative process by understanding your response to what you read. Read the chart below to further understand the variables that influence the ways a reader might respond to a given work.

 Factors in a Reader's Response to Literature

- age, gender, and personality
- cultural or ethnic origins, attitudes, and customs
- personal opinions, beliefs, and values
- life experiences and general knowledge
- knowledge of literature and literary genres
- knowledge of the historical and social climate in which the work was written
- reading and language skills

All of these factors combine to affect your response to what you read. Who you are, where you live, and what your life has been like so far may enable you to identify with a piece of writing. The more closely you can identify with a work of literature, the more you will enjoy it.

① Characteristics of Literary Genres

"Say It with Flowers" is a short story. Other literary forms, called **genres,** include novels, poems, and plays. These genres have the following characteristics.

CHARACTERISTICS OF LITERARY GENRES	
Short Story	A short work of narrative fiction. The story often occurs within a short period of time and involves few characters and settings. Description and dialogue reveal the plot (the central conflict and its outcome), the characters, setting, and theme.
Novel	A long work of narrative fiction. The story may span decades. Like short stories, a novel revolves around a plot, characters, setting, and theme.
Poem	A work that presents images using condensed, vivid language chosen for the way it sounds as well as for its meaning. Meter, rhyme, and figurative language are often employed in poems.
Play	A work written for dramatic performance on the stage. Like a short story, a play usually tells a story that revolves around the resolution of a central conflict. The audience relies on dialogue, stage sets, and action to understand the setting, plot, characters, and theme.

❷ Responding from Personal Experience

"Books let us into their souls and lay open to us the secrets of our own," wrote the critic William Hazlitt. Readers acquire not only insight into the world but a better understanding of their own place in it. An idea in a story, play, or poem will often trigger ideas in readers—and new questions and insights also.

In opening your heart and mind to the lives of the characters in books, you often discover things about yourself you didn't know. If you identify with Teruo in "Say It with Flowers," you may discover an understanding of the inner conflict one feels when forced to do something against one's principles. The story of Teruo becomes even deeper and richer then. Read the strategies below for help when responding to a literary work.

Personal Response Strategies

1. Freewrite answers to the following questions:

   a. When you approached this reading, did you have any expectations of the text? In other words, did you expect to be bored? to experience pleasure? to be stimulated? to have difficulty? Were your expectations met? How? Were you surprised? If so, explain why.

   b. Where in the poem, story, novel, or play do you see yourself? In other words, with what character or characters do you most closely identify? Why? Do your feelings about the character or characters stay the same? Do they change? If so, when and why do they change?

   c. What characters remind you of other people you know? In what ways are they like those real people? In what ways are they different? How has your experience with those real people influenced your reactions to the characters in the work?

   d. If you were a character in the work, would you have behaved any differently? Why or why not? What actions or behaviors puzzle you?

   e. What experiences from your own life come to mind as you read this work? How are they similar to the events portrayed? How are they different? What feelings do you associate with the experiences? Are those feelings represented in the work?

   f. What moved you in the work? How and why did it affect you?

2. Write a personal response statement explaining what the work means to you.

3. In small discussion groups, share your personal response statement and your various reactions to the questions above. Listen carefully to your classmates' reactions and, if appropriate, contrast them with your own. Be open to changing your responses if you find other points of view convincing. Afterward write freely about whether your ideas changed and why.

Practice Your Skills

Responding from Personal Experience

Review the short story "Say It with Flowers" on pages 285–291. Then answer the following questions.

1. Based on your first reading of "Say It with Flowers," write your answers to the questions in the **Personal Response Strategies** on the previous page.

2. Reread the story up to the last paragraph on page 286, and stop to write your reactions. What do you think of the characters? What do you think of Teruo's approach to learning his job? When you first read the story, what did you think was going to happen next?

3. Continue rereading, this time stopping before the last paragraph on page 287. Again write your reactions. Have your feelings about any of the characters changed? What does Teruo mean by saying, "I'm lousy"? What is he trying to do when he defies his boss? Did your predictions about the ending change at this point? Why or why not?

4. Finish rereading the story, and write whether your predictions were accurate. Then write freely about the impact this story had on your own way of looking at things. Conclude by writing a personal response statement that explains what this story means to you. Save your work for later reference.

Writing Tip

Literary works mean different things to different readers. Responding from **personal experience** will help you discover what a literary work means to you.

PROJECT PREP   Prewriting   Personal Responding

Reread the excerpt from "I Know Why the Caged Bird Sings" (pages 37–40) by Maya Angelou. With your classmates, talk about the feelings it evokes in you. Then write a personal response statement about her autobiography. Explain how you feel about the people Angelou writes about and what the story means to you.

③ Responding from Literary Knowledge

As a reader, you not only respond to what you read on the basis of your feelings, experiences, and background, but you also apply your knowledge of other stories, poems, or plays that you have read. This knowledge helps you interpret a work and appreciate a writer's skill. When you respond to literature on the basis of your literary knowledge, you analyze its elements through repeated, **close readings.**

The following chart describes the main elements of fiction, poetry, and drama.

ELEMENTS OF LITERATURE	
Fiction	
Plot	the events in a story that lead to a **climax** (high point) and to an outcome that resolves a central conflict
Setting	when and where the story takes place
Characters	the people in the story who advance the plot through their thoughts and actions
Dialogue	conversations among characters that reveal their personalities, actions, and **motivations,** or reasons for behaving as they do
Tone	the writer's attitude toward her or his characters
Point of View	the "voice" telling the story—first person *(I)* or third person *(he, she, or they)*
Theme	main idea or message of the story
Poetry	
Persona	the person whose "voice" is saying the poem, revealing the character the poet is assuming
Meter	the rhythm of stressed and unstressed syllables in each line of the poem
Rhyme Scheme	the pattern of rhymed sounds, usually at the ends of lines
Sound Devices	techniques for playing with sounds to create certain effects, such as **alliteration** and **onomatopoeia**
Figures of Speech	imaginative language, such as **similes** and **metaphors,** which creates images by making comparisons
Shape	the way a poem looks on the printed page, which may contribute to the underlying meaning of the poet's thoughts and feelings
Theme	the overall feeling or underlying meaning of the poem, which expresses the poet's thoughts and feelings

Because drama has many of the same elements as fiction and poetry, those listed below show only how reading a dramatic work differs from reading other kinds of fiction.

Drama	
Setting	the time and place of the action; lighting and the stage sets, as described in the stage directions
Characters	people who participate in the action of the play
Plot	the story of the play divided into acts and scenes and developed through the characters' words and actions
Theme	the meaning of a play, revealed through the setting and the characters' words and actions

How Literary Elements Contribute to Meaning

The elements of each genre contribute to the meaning of a work. The author's style and use of various literary or rhetorical devices are the means for developing these elements and creating the overall artistic quality of a work. The following list of questions can help you explore the meaning of a poem, a play, a short story, or a novel.

Questions for Finding Meaning in Fiction

Plot
- What is the impact of each main event in the development of the plot? How does each event affect the main characters?
- What details in the plot reveal the narrator's attitude toward the central conflict? What do the climax and the ending reveal about the theme?
- What parts of the work puzzle me? What would I like to understand better?
- What does the work "say" to me? What message does it convey? What insight or understanding have I gained?

Setting
- How does the setting contribute to the mood of the story and the characters' action?
- What details of the setting are most important in the development of the plot?
- How do details relate to the theme?

Theme
- What passages and details in the story best express the main theme? What other story elements contribute to the meaning?
- How does the author communicate the theme through the development of setting, characters, and plot?
- What else have you read that has a similar theme?

Questions for Finding Meaning in Poetry

- What is the poet's persona? How does the persona relate to the subject, mood, and theme of the poem?
- How does the meter affect the rhythm of the poem? How does that rhythm express the mood?
- How does the rhyme scheme affect the expression of thoughts and feelings?
- If the poet uses sound devices like alliteration and onomatopoeia, what sounds do you hear in the poem? What images do those sound devices create in your mind?
- What images do the figures of speech create? What feelings do those images suggest?
- How does the shape of the poem relate to the subject, mood, or theme?
- What effect does the poem have on you? How does the poem achieve its effect? What meaning does the poem have for you?
- What feeling, theme, or message does the poem express?
- What specific word choices are memorable and effective?

Questions for Finding Meaning in Drama

- What details of setting and character do the stage directions emphasize? How do those details contribute to the impact of the play?
- What are the key relationships among the characters? How do those relationships reveal the central conflict? What changes in the relationships help resolve the conflict?
- How does the dialogue advance the plot? What plot developments occur with each change of act and scene?
- What subject and theme does the play treat? What in the play has meaning for you?

EVALUATING A LITERARY WORK

You may find it helpful to know the criteria by which any great work of literature, or classic, is usually judged. **Classics** are literary works that withstand the test of time and appeal to readers from generation to generation and from century to century. You can set standards to judge how well standards are met as you evaluate the work as a whole—its meaning for you and for others. However, your personal judgment and the judgment of others may not agree. On the following page, you will find criteria by which great literature is judged.

SOME CHARACTERISTICS OF GREAT LITERATURE

- Explores great themes in human nature and the human experience that many people can identify with—such as growing up, family life, love, the courageous individual's struggle against oppression, and war

- Expresses universal meanings—such as truth or hope—that people from many different backgrounds and cultures can appreciate

- Conveys a timeless message that remains true for many generations of readers

- Creates vivid impressions of characters, situations, and settings that many generations of readers can treasure

You can also apply other standards of evaluation. When you are making judgments about a work, ask yourself the following questions.

Questions for Evaluating Literature

- How inventive and original are the style, plot, and characters?
- How vividly and believably are the characters, settings, dialogue, and actions portrayed?
- How well structured is the plot? Is there a satisfying resolution of the central conflict?
- How does the writer's use of stylistic devices (word choice, sentence structure, and figurative language, for example) and such rhetorical devices as flashback, foreshadowing, and irony affect the artistic quality of the work?
- How strongly did I react to the work? Did I identify with a character or situation?
- Did the work have meaning for me? What will I remember about it?

● Practice Your Skills

Responding from Literary Knowledge

Express your opinions about "Say It with Flowers" on pages 285–291 by answering the following questions.

1. Why does Teruo behave the way he does when he is working at the flower shop? Explain how and why his actions do or do not change.
2. How do the other characters react to Teruo's actions? Do their opinions of him change? Why do they decide that Teruo would not succeed in business?
3. What details in the setting bring the story to life?
4. What is the theme of the story? What message does the story convey?
5. How would the story have changed if it were told from Teruo's point of view?

PROJECT PREP *Prewriting* *Responding from Literary Knowledge*

Identify the literary elements in "Say It with Flowers." How do they affect your response?

1 Choosing a Subject

As you respond to a work by using both your personal experience and your literary knowledge, you will develop some definite ideas about the meaning of the work. Your teacher may assign a subject for writing about literature, or you may be expected to choose your own subject. The questions below will help you think of subjects of personal interest.

HERE'S HOW Questions for Choosing a Subject

- What elements of the work would you like to understand better? What parts of the work puzzle you?
- What parts of the work do you find especially moving? Why?
- What images and details made a strong impression on you? What do they contribute to the overall work?
- With which character do you identify the most? Why?
- How do the characters relate to one another? How do their relationships affect the plot?
- What feeling, meaning, or message does the work convey to you? What insight or understanding have you gained?

You will probably find the answers to some of these questions in the responses you have already made while working on this project. Review your written responses looking for aspects of the literary work that are most interesting to you. Reread the work to see if you have any fresh responses now that you know the work better. One of your answers to the questions above could become the subject for a composition about literature.

● Practice Your Skills

Choosing Subjects

Review "Say It with Flowers" on pages 285–291. For each of the following literary elements, think of a possible subject for analyzing the story.

Example   theme

Possible Answer   acting on what you believe in

1. character   **3.** tone

2. theme   **4.** plot

SYNTHESIZING PERSONAL AND LITERARY RESPONSES

Another strategy for choosing a subject is to **synthesize,** or combine, your personal responses with responses based on your literary knowledge. For example, in discussing or writing about "Say It with Flowers," you may have expressed disapproval of dishonest business practices. Perhaps you once had an unpleasant experience as a consumer in which you were not dealt with honestly. To synthesize that personal reaction with a literary response, you might discuss the central conflict in the story, which relates to the issue of dishonesty in business. By synthesizing your personal and literary responses in this way, you can best focus your thoughts for a literary analysis.

LIMITING A SUBJECT

Once you have focused on a subject, ideas may start to overwhelm you. Take the time to limit your subject by making sure you are focused on a specific aspect of the work. Ask yourself, "What do I want to say about my subject?" When you can clearly answer that question in a phrase or short sentence, you have suitably focused your subject.

EXAMPLE: Limiting a Subject

Too General	The character Teruo
Ask Yourself	What stands out about Teruo's character
Possible Answer	Teruo's refusal to compromise his high principles makes him a heroic character
Focused Subject	Qualities Teruo exhibits that make him heroic

● Practice Your Skills

Choosing and Limiting a Subject

For each of the following literary elements, think of a possible subject for a literary analysis of "Say It with Flowers." Then limit each subject by expressing it in a phrase or a sentence.

1. character   **5.** setting

2. point of view   **6.** tone

3. plot   **7.** dialogue

4. theme   **8.** conflict

PROJECT PREP *Prewriting* Subject

In your writing group, discuss possible subjects for your literary analysis. Be sure to limit your subject appropriately. After your discussion, write a phrase or sentence that expresses your focus. Save your work for later use.

Think Critically

Making Inferences

Making inferences, or **inferring,** means filling in the gaps in your knowledge on the basis of what you already know. The following chart shows you how to make inferences about a character from his or her appearance, behavior, and speech.

CHARACTER CHART

Question: In "Say It with Flowers," why does Teruo give away flowers?

Type of Clue	Clue
Descriptions of the Character	Teruo's appearance did not "harmonize with a job as a clerk in a flower shop"; he was "a quiet fellow with very little words for anybody, but his smile disarmed a person."
Statements About the Character's Actions	He added extra flowers "because the old lady was appreciative of his art of making bouquets"; gave roses to a child with 25 cents to spend for his mother's birthday; gave a dozen roses to a pretty girl.
The Character's Own Words	"I just like to do it that way, that's all." "I gave it to her because she admired it, and she's pretty enough to deserve beautiful things, and I liked her."

Logical valid inferences about Teruo's motives based on these clues:

In giving away flowers, Teruo bases his decisions on personal values of honesty and generosity. He gives away flowers to people he thinks deserve them. His actions represent his decision not to compromise his values, even if it means getting fired.

Thinking Practice

Make a chart like the one above to help you infer an answer to this question:

In "Say It with Flowers," how does the narrator feel about Teruo?

② Developing a Thesis

When you clearly focus your subject, you will discover the **thesis,** or main idea, for your literary analysis. By expressing your main idea in a complete sentence, you will have a working thesis statement on which to build. Your specific purpose in writing a literary analysis is to prove that your thesis, or interpretation, is true. Your thesis is a proposition that you must defend by presenting evidence that will convince the reader that your interpretation is valid.

In the following example, the working thesis statement makes a definite proposition that was only hinted at in the limited subject.

EXAMPLE: Thesis Statement

Focused, Limited Subject	Qualities Teruo exhibits that make him heroic.
Thesis Statement or Proposition	Although Teruo must work to earn a living, he realizes that he cannot compromise his principles to the demands of his employer.

To develop your thesis, cast your focused, limited subject into the form of a complete sentence. Pin your subject down by saying something definite and concrete about it. Once again, you can ask yourself, "What *about* my subject?" until you have a statement that is expressed in a complete sentence.

● Practice Your Skills

Writing a Working Thesis Statement

Write one working thesis statement for each of the following focused subjects from "Say It with Flowers."

1. the mood created by descriptions of the setting

2. how the characters in the story are affected by their jobs

3. how the other characters respond to Teruo

PROJECT PREP *Prewriting* *Thesis Statement*

With your writing group, review each person's focused, limited subject. When satisfied that each phrase or sentence fully captures the subject, help each author come up with an effective working thesis. Remember that you will be adjusting and improving your thesis statement as you draft and revise.

③ Gathering Evidence

To prove the truth of your thesis, you must supply the reader of your literary analysis with evidence. You automatically gather evidence when you read, whether you are aware of it or not. Each detail fits into a pattern of ideas that you develop as you read. This pattern of ideas leaves you with an overall impression of a work and leads you to your thesis.

After you have stated your thesis, however, you should reread the work and look for specific details that will help you prove it. The kinds of details you will use include specific examples of dialogue, action, imagery, and characters' thoughts.

EXAMPLES: Kinds of Evidence in Literature

Background Details	We were glad to have an extra hand [in the flower shop] because the busy season was coming around.
Descriptive Details	Teruo came back to the rear and picked out a dozen of the very fresh white roses.
Narrative Details	He told Teruo what to do on telephone orders; how to keep the greens fresh; how to make bouquets, corsages, and sprays.
Dialogue	Teruo looked at us calmly. "That's a hard thing to say when you know it isn't true." "You've got to get over it sooner or later," I told him.
Action	He hurriedly took one customer's order and . . . jumped to the second customer's side and persuaded her to buy Columbia roses. . . .

To develop a list of supporting details, skim the work from start to finish, looking for any elements that will directly contribute to proving your thesis. As you skim, jot down each supporting detail you find—either on a note card or on a separate sheet of paper.

> **Writing Tip**
>
> Even if you are not sure a story detail supports your **thesis**, note it on a card or a sheet of paper. You can always discard it later if you decide it is not relevant.

MAKING NOTES

The following models show how one writer gathered evidence on commentary cards to support her proposition that, while he could not accept the way the flower shop was run, Teruo did have qualities that could help him succeed in business. Notice that each card has a page reference for easily locating the passage used. In addition, each card includes a brief note reminding the writer of why that detail helps support the thesis.

MODEL: Gathering Evidence for "Say It with Flowers"

Text Portions

We soon learned that he knew nothing about the florist business. He could identify a rose when he saw one . . . but other flowers and materials were new to him. "You fellows teach me something about this business and I'll be grateful. I want to start from the bottom," Teruo said.

In a couple of weeks Teruo was just as good a clerk as we had had in a long time. He was curious almost to a fault, and was a glutton for work.

When I went out to the truck . . . Teruo followed me. "Gee, I feel rotten," he said to me. "Those flowers I sold to the people, they won't last longer than tomorrow. I feel lousy. I'm lousy. The people'll get to know my word pretty soon."

Commentary Cards

1.a "knew nothing about the florist business," "flowers and materials were new to him" (narrator) "You fellows teach me something about this business and I'll be grateful. I want to start from the bottom." (Teruo, p. 285)

1.b —shows that Teruo is willing to learn and to work his way up

2.a Became a good clerk in two weeks, "was curious almost to a fault, and was a glutton for work" (narrator, p. 286)

2.b —shows that Teruo is a fast learner and a hard worker

3.a "I feel rotten" [for selling old flowers], "I'm lousy. The people'll get to know my word pretty soon." (Teruo, p. 287)

3.b —shows that Teruo has integrity, cares about customers, and cares about his reputation

"You've been selling fresh flowers and leaving the old ones go to waste. . . ." Mr. Sasaki said. "Why don't you do as you're told? We all sell the flowers in the front. . . . Why can't you sell them?"

"I don't like it, Mr. Sasaki," Teruo said. "When the people ask me if they're fresh I hate to answer. I feel rotten after selling the old ones."

4.a "Why don't you do as you're told?" (Mr. Sasaki, p. C475) "I don't like it. . . . When the people ask me if they're fresh I hate to answer. I feel rotten after selling the old ones." (Teruo, p. 288)

4.b —shows that Teruo cares about customers, values honesty, and does not easily obey orders that go against his moral principles

Teruo was there early. "Hello," he greeted us cheerfully as we came in. . . . He was there before us and had already filled out the eight o'clock package. . . . When Mr. Sasaki arrived, Teruo waved his hand and cheerfully went about gathering the flowers. . . . As he flitted here and there he seemed as if he had forgotten our presence. . . .

5.a "Teruo was there early," "greeted us cheerfully," "had already filled out the eight o'clock package," "cheerfully went about gathering the flowers," "flitted here and there" (narrator, p. 288)

5.b —shows that Teruo is prompt, cheerful, and industrious

He looked at each vase, sized up the flowers, and then cocked his head at the next one. He did this with great deliberation, as if he were the boss and the last word in the shop
. . . . [W]hen a customer soon came in, he swiftly attended him as if he owned all the flowers in the world. . . .

6.a Worked "with great deliberation, as if he were the boss and the last word in the shop," "swiftly attended [a customer] as if he owned all the flowers in the world" (narrator, p. 288)

6.b —shows that Teruo can take charge and is self-confident and efficient

He [sold the fresh flowers] with so much grace, dignity and swiftness . . .

... Mr. Sasaki came out furious. "You're a blockhead. You have no business sense. . . ."

Tommy nudged me. "If he was the boss he couldn't do those things," he said.

"In the first place," I said, "I don't think he could be a boss."

7.a "You have no business sense." (Mr. Sasaki, p. 289) "If he was the boss he couldn't do those things [give away flowers]." (Tommy, p. 290) "I don't think he could be a boss." (narrator, p. 290)

7.b —shows that the others don't understand that Teruo has what it takes to succeed in business. As a boss, Teruo could give up some profits in exchange for customer goodwill and could insist on selling only quality products.

USING AN ARCH DIAGRAM

Another way to collect evidence is to make an arch diagram like the one below. The details in the columns all support the thesis, which is stated in the arch.

Teruo has qualities that will enable him to succeed in business.

Thesis Statement (Main Idea)

"You fellows teach me something about this and I'll be grateful"

Supporting Detail | Supporting Detail | Supporting Detail

PROJECT PREP *Prewriting* *Gathering Evidence*

Gather possible evidence, including stylistic and rhetorical devices, that would support your thesis. You may wish to use an arch diagram to collect and evaluate your evidence. Share your evidence with your writing group for their evaluation as well. Is it enough?

Organizing Details into an Outline

For your literary analysis, you should group your details into categories. Then you can arrange your ideas and information in a logical order. You might arrange your details in the order in which they appear in the work.

The following chart shows examples of how different types of order may be appropriate for proving different kinds of theses.

ORDERING EVIDENCE	
Kind of Thesis	**Type of Order**
To show how a character or elements of a plot change or develop over time	Chronological order (See pages 183 and 185.)
To show similarities and differences between characters or to compare two different works of literature	Comparison/contrast, using the AABB or the ABAB pattern of development (See pages 244–249.)
To analyze a character's motivation or to explain the significance of the setting	Order of importance or cause and effect (See pages 250–251.)
To draw conclusions about the theme	Developmental order (See pages 126 and 221.)

After you decide how to organize your ideas and evidence, you should make a list, chart, or outline to use as a guide for writing your literary analysis. When outlining, you may use either an informal outline—a simple listing, in order, of the points you wish to cover—or a formal outline like the one on page 222.

Writing Tip

As you order your **evidence,** check to be sure each detail directly supports your **thesis.** Set aside **commentary cards** with details that you decide are not relevant.

Following is a simple outline for a literary analysis about "Say It with Flowers." Notice that the writer included ideas for the introduction and the conclusion. Also, because the details have equal importance in proving the thesis, the writer placed them in developmental order. In developmental order, information is arranged to lead up to a conclusion.

MODEL: Outline

Background details about Teruo's experience — Introduction

Thesis statement: Despite his experience in Mr. Sasaki's shop, Teruo has qualities that would help him succeed in business without having to compromise his high principles.

Qualities Teruo has for success in business: — Body

I. Willingness to learn and to work hard (commentary cards 1, 2, and 5)

II. Positive attitude and the ability to take charge (commentary cards 5 and 6)

III. Honesty and integrity (commentary cards 3 and 4)

Why the other characters thought that Teruo could not succeed in business (commentary card 7) How my evidence shows that they were wrong — Conclusion

CHAPTER 9

PROJECT PREP *Prewriting* *Outline*

Review your notes and decide which supporting details you will use to persuade readers that your literary interpretation is sound. Use a graphic organizer to plan the analysis. For each body paragraph, focus on one point (a claim). Support the claim with evidence from the literature, and justify it with a warrant (a statement that explains how the evidence supports the claim). Share your completed chart with your group for feedback.

Point	Claim	Evidence	Warrant
Point 1			
Point 2			
Point 3			

In the Media

Imagery

In one of the most famous scenes in movie history, the camera moves in for a close-up of a dying man's lips as he pronounces the word "Rosebud" after a snowglobe has dropped from his hand. Much of the rest of the movie is a journey toward understanding what that word meant to the dying man. It turns out that *Rosebud* was the word written on a sled he had when he was a child, before he was torn from his parents. The sled is a symbol of that hopeful and innocent childhood. Its name stirs positive feelings of hope and promise through the imagery of a flower not yet opened, full of possibilities.

Imagery and symbolism are two of many **rhetorical devices** artists use to create emotional effects and add subtle meaning to their works. The story of the dying man could have been told without that last word, or without the image near the end of the movie of his old childhood sled being burned as trash. Without the image, however, the viewer would not have the same understanding of what the man had known—and lost. The well-constructed devices help give the movie artistry and raise it above the mere telling of a man's life.

The story "Say it with Flowers" also uses flower imagery. The whole story, of course, is set in a flower shop. However, the author also uses words related to flowers as he describes Teruo. "But if someone should mention about the freshness of the flowers he wilted right in front of the customers." The word *wilted* is one that is usually used to describe flowers. The imagery gives the reader an emotional understanding of Teruo—like the stale flowers in the front of the store, Teruo feels stale when he lies about the freshness of the flowers.

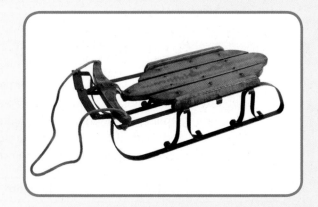

MEDIA ACTIVITY

With a partner, discuss some of your favorite movies. Choose one that you both found to be moving. Talk about the parts of the movie that made you feel the strongest response. Try to identify such rhetorical devices as imagery, symbolism, metaphor, simile, or irony that the screenwriter may have used to affect viewers' feelings. Report back to the class what you have identified and its effect on you.

Writing a Literary Analysis  Drafting

An outline and graphic organizers will be invaluable when you begin working on your literary analysis. The guidelines below will help you work through your first draft.

 Guidelines for Drafting a Literary Analysis

- Use present-tense verbs throughout your essay.

- In the introduction identify the author and the title of the work you are discussing.

- Include your thesis statement somewhere in the introduction. Refine it as needed and work it in as smoothly as possible.

- In the body of your literary analysis, include clearly organized supporting details, using transitions to show how one detail relates to another. Throughout your essay use direct quotations from the work if they strengthen the points you are tying to make. (Always enclose direct quotations in quotation marks.)

- In the conclusion draw together the details you have included to reinforce the main idea of your essay.

- Add an interesting, appropriate title that suggests the focus of your analysis.

USING QUOTATIONS

The best supporting evidence when writing about literature comes from the work itself. Your essay should contain plenty of quotations. To give strong support to your thesis statement, use quotations that make a strong point. The guidelines below will help you.

Guidelines for Writing Direct Quotations Follow the examples below when writing **quotations in different positions** in a sentence. Notice that quotations in the middle of a sentence are not usually capitalized.

Begins Sentence	"You have no business sense," Mr. Sasaki accuses. "If he was the boss he couldn't do those things," Tommy says.
Interrupts Sentence	His coworkers are awed by his "grace, dignity, and swiftness" as he works.
Ends Sentence	Like them, readers might conclude that Teruo would be a failure in business unless he learns to "play the game."

If you need to show that words have been left out of a quotation, use an **ellipsis**—a series of three dots—for the missing words.

Ellipsis   When Teruo is forced to go against his principles by lying and selling flowers that are not fresh, he says, "I feel rotten. . . . I'm lousy.

After each quotation, cite the page number of the source in parentheses. The citation should precede punctuation marks such as periods, commas, colons, and semicolons. For plays or long poems, also give the act and scene of the play or part of the poem, plus line numbers.

The following literary analysis will give you an idea of how to create a convincing presentation of your interpretation. It was written from the outline on page 309 and the commentary cards on pages 305–307. Notice how the model, which has already been revised and edited, follows the guidelines above.

MODEL: A Literary Analysis

Teruo in Business

Title: Identifies focus

In the story "Say It with Flowers," author Toshio Mori explores the potential conflict between succeeding in business and preserving one's integrity. For Teruo, the eager young clerk in the flower shop, preserving his integrity means selling only the freshest flowers. He even gives flowers away to customers. For his actions he earns the scorn of his co-workers and of his boss, Mr. Sasaki, who eventually fires him. Like them, readers might conclude that Teruo would be a failure in business unless he learns to "play the game." Despite his experience in Mr. Sasaki's shop, however, Teruo has many qualities that would help him succeed in business without having to compromise his high principles.

Introduction: Identifies author and purpose

Thesis Statement

When Teruo first comes to work at the shop, he asks his coworkers to teach him about the florist business. "You fellows teach me something about this business and I'll be grateful. I want to start from the bottom," he explains, implying that he might someday like to run his own flower shop. In only two weeks, Teruo becomes a good clerk who is "curious almost to a fault" and "a glutton for work." This behavior shows that Teruo is willing to learn and to work his way up. He is also a fast learner and a hard worker. These are all qualities that are needed for success in business.

Details in the first supporting paragraph

Teruo has positive attitudes that would contribute to any person's success in business. Descriptions of his work in the Morning-Glory Flower Shop, for example, show that he is prompt, conscientious, cheerful, and industrious. In addition, he works "with great deliberation, as if he were the boss and the last word in the shop." He swiftly attends to customers "as if he owned all the flowers in the world." His coworkers are awed by his "grace, dignity, and swiftness" as he works. These observations show that Teruo can take charge and can use his initiative. He is clearly self confident and efficient in his work.

Details in the second paragraph of the body

When Teruo is forced to go against his principles by lying and selling flowers that are not fresh, he says, "I feel rotten. . . . I'm lousy. The people'll get to know my word pretty soon." Even after Mr. Sasaki confronts him and tells him to do as he's told, Teruo insists, "When the people ask me if they're fresh I hate to answer. I feel rotten after selling the old ones." This quote shows that Teruo values his honesty and integrity—qualities that certainly contribute to success in business. He cares about his customers and about his reputation. He risks losing his job rather than going against his moral values.

Third supporting paragraph

The other characters in the story do not understand that Teruo has what it takes to succeed in business. "You have no business sense," Mr. Sasaki accuses. "If he was the boss he couldn't do those things," Tommy says. "I don't think he could be a boss," the narrator replies. As a boss, however, Teruo could choose to give up some of his profits in exchange for customer goodwill, more customers, and more business. He could insist on selling only the best quality products and still afford to be generous toward his customers. When viewed in this way, everything about Teruo's character suggests that he could become a successful businessman— without compromising his high principles.

Conclusion

PROJECT PREP Drafting *Literary Analysis*

With your writing group, discuss your plans for writing your analysis. Invite comments from the group and be open to using any of them that help support your thesis. Then write a first draft. When you have a rough draft you are happy with, submit it to your teacher for review, if appropriate.

The Power of Language ⚡

Dashes: Dash It All

The dash can be used, sparingly, to create a sharp break between most of a sentence and something the writer wants to emphasize. In writing about the character of Teruo, the person working on a research report might use these examples:

> This quote shows that Teruo values his honesty and integrity—qualities that could contribute to his success in life and perhaps in business endevaors.
>
> When viewed in this way, everything about Teruo's character suggests that he could become a successful businessman—without compromising his high principles.

In both of these cases, the dash presents a break between the statement and the explanation of its meaning. The dash offers more pertinent information about the statement.

For examples of a pair of dashes used to set off something in the middle of a sentence, see page 915.

Try It Yourself

On the topic chosen for your literary analysis, write three sentences similar to these, with a dash preceding and emphasizing the important material that ends the sentence.

Punctuation Tip

Notice that just one dash is used in the examples above. To create a dash on the computer, type two hyphens, with no space before and none after, or press the shift and option keys and the dash key to create a dash (—).

Writing a Literary Analysis  Revising

After completing your first draft, set it aside for a day or two so that you can return to it with a critical eye. You may want to share your literary analysis with a peer reader. Using your partner's comments and the following checklist, you should then revise your essay.

 Evaluation Checklist for Revising

Checking Your Essay

✓ Do you have a strong introduction that identifies the author and work you will discuss? (page 311)

✓ Does your introduction contain a clear thesis? (page 311)

✓ In the body of your essay, have you provided ample quotations from the work to use as evidence to support your thesis? (pages 311–312)

✓ Does your essay analyze the aesthetic effects of an author's use of stylistic or rhetorical devices? (pages 297–299)

✓ Does your conclusion summarize the details in the body of your essay and reinforce your thesis statement? (page 311)

✓ Does your whole essay have unity and coherence? (pages 82–83 and 134)

✓ Did you add a title showing the focus of your essay? (page 311)

✓ Does your essay meet the requirements for your purpose and audience? (pages 15–16 and 292)

Checking Your Paragraphs

✓ Does each paragraph have a topic sentence? (pages 76–78)

✓ Is each paragraph unified and coherent? (pages 82–83 and 134)

Checking Your Sentences and Words

✓ Are your sentences varied and concise? (pages 55–66)

✓ Did you use lively, specific language? (pages 146–149)

PROJECT PREP *Revising* *Using a Checklist*

Exchange the draft of your literary analysis with a partner. Comment on the strengths and weaknesses of your partner's paper. Consider your partner's comments as you use the **Evaluation Checklist for Revising** above to improve your draft. Also take into account any comments you have received from your teacher.

 TIME OUT TO **REFLECT**

With the comments from your peer fresh in your mind, think back to responses to other essays you have written. Are your reviewers and teachers making similar remarks each time? Record your findings, as well as strategies for improving, in the Learning Log section of your journal.

Using a Six-Trait Rubric Literary Analysis

Use the rubric below to evaluate a literary analysis.

Ideas	4 The thesis statement is clear. Evidence is solid. The analysis goes beyond mere summary.	3 The thesis statement is clear. Most evidence is solid. The analysis goes beyond mere summary.	2 The thesis statement could be clearer. Some evidence is solid, but there is too much simple summary.	1 The thesis statement is missing or unclear. There is little evidence, and the ideas rarely go beyond summary.
Organization	4 The organization is clear with abundant transitions.	3 A few ideas seem out of place or transitions are missing.	2 Many ideas seem out of place and transitions are missing.	1 The organization is unclear and hard to follow.
Voice	4 The voice sounds natural, engaging, and forceful.	3 The voice sounds natural and engaging.	2 The voice sounds mostly natural but is weak.	1 The voice sounds mostly unnatural and is weak.
Word Choice	4 Words are specific and powerful. Language is appropriate.	3 Words are specific and language is appropriate.	2 Some words are too general and/or inappropriate.	1 Most words are overly general and inappropriate for the purpose and audience.
Sentence Fluency	4 Varied sentences flow smoothly.	3 Most sentences are varied and flow smoothly.	2 Some sentences are varied but some are choppy.	1 Sentences are not varied and are choppy.
Conventions	4 Punctuation, usage, and spelling are correct. Quotes are handled correctly. The Power Rules are all followed.	3 Punctuation, usage, and spelling are mainly correct and Power Rules are all followed.	2 Some punctuation, usage, and spelling are incorrect but all Power Rules are followed.	1 There are many errors and at least one failure to follow a Power Rule.

PROJECT PREP Revising Using a Rubric

After evaluating your essay using this rubric, make any appropriate changes and revisions.

When you are satisfied that your composition clearly conveys your interpretation of the work you have chosen to write about, you can move on to polishing it and presenting it to readers. The following checklist will help you edit your work. In the process of editing, use the proofreading marks on page 11.

Editing Checklist

✓ Are your sentences free of errors in grammar and usage?

✓ Did you spell each word correctly?

✓ Did you capitalize and punctuate correctly?

✓ Did you use quotation marks around all direct quotations from the work?

✓ Did you check your Personalized Editing Checklist to make sure you have avoided errors you sometimes make?

editing ★

While editing, read aloud what you've written before going on to the next part. Writers often catch obvious problems by going through each sentence carefully, checking for verb agreement, correct word, and other conventions. How would you edit the following statement if you came across it in your draft?

> Teruo, with his mild-mannered and eager-to-please ways, may not seem to you to be a heroic fellow. However, when he gave the security of the flower shop job the heave-ho, he showed his courage. . . and he walks right into the pantheon of fictional heroes.

The Language of Power *Verb Tense*

Power Rule: Use a consistent verb tense except when a change is clearly necessary. (See pages 693–703.)

See It in Action When you write about literature and refer to events in the work, you use the present tense. If you are not familiar with this convention, you may find yourself slipping back into past tense. The writer who analyzed "Say It with Flowers" found some tense shifts as he was editing his paper, as shown below.

> For Teruo, the eager young clerk in the flower shop, preserving his integrity means selling only the freshest flowers. He even gave flowers away to customers. For his actions, he earns the scorn of his co-workers and his boss …

During revising, the writer corrected this error to read:

> For Teruo, the eager young clerk in the flower shop, preserving his integrity means selling only the freshest flowers. He even gives flowers away to customers. For his actions, he earns the scorn of his co-workers and his boss …

Remember It Record this rule and example in the Power Rule section of your Personalized Editing Checklist.

Use It As you edit your paper, check to make sure the verb tense stays consistent unless there is a genuine reason it must change.

PROJECT PREP *Editing Conventions*

Edit your revised draft for grammar errors. Try reading your draft aloud to hear sentences that sound incorrect. Listen especially for verbs. Note any that switch tenses unnecessarily and fix those. Also refer to your Personalized Editing Checklist for mistakes you are prone to making and be sure you have avoided them—and violations of the Power Rules. When you are satisfied with your changes and corrections, save your work, but do not yet prepare a final copy.

Complete the writing process by connecting your literary analysis with a reader who would have an interest in it. You might want to submit your essay to the school literary magazine. If your school has an Intranet, you might consider publishing your essay as a Web page.

PROJECT PREP Publishing *Connecting with Readers*

For the chapter project, you were free to choose among three types of publications for your literary analysis: an essay (the most common medium for writing of this type); a blog or a Web-based discussion board (increasingly popular ways to share ideas about literature); and a letter (some people exchange letters or e-mails to share their understanding of literary works, much as people discuss works in a book group). In your writing group, discuss ways in which a blog and a letter would require different treatment from a writer. After the discussion with your writing group, make any changes that would be fitting for the medium you chose and make an effort to connect your literary analysis with one or more readers.

Entering your literary analysis in a competition is a good way to share your work with others. For information on literary contests, write to the National Council of Teachers of English, 1111 Kenyon Road, Urbana, IL 61801. Be sure to follow standard manuscript form and follow any specific entry rules for the competition.

It's always a good idea to try to publish a class anthology, or collection, of student compositions on literary works. Decide how to organize, illustrate, bind, and circulate your anthology.

Writing Lab

Project Corner

Speak and Listen
Class Discussion

With your classmates, **discuss what you enjoy about reading fiction**. Also discuss answers to these questions: How does literary analysis fit in with the reasons you read fiction? What do you learn from conducting a literary analysis? (See pages 468–470 for help with group discussions.)

Think Critically Sequel

What do you think happens to Teruo after he leaves Morning-Glory Flower Shop? Write a short story, poem, or play that investigates his life after he says his last good-bye. Be sure to base your sequel on the events of the original so that the characters are true to their original creation.

Get Technical
Twitterature

Twitterature is the name of a book written by two college students in which they provide tweets that try to convey the essence of 80 great books (and also make jokes). With your class, develop a list of 10 of the greatest books and/or stories you have read. Then choose one and, sticking to the 140-character count limit, **Twitter a series of 10 tweets** on the work you chose. Feel free to have fun. Making good jokes about a work is one way to show you understand it.

In the Workplace
Analytical Oral Presentation

Apply and Assess

1. You are applying for a job at a detective agency. They need somebody disguised as a poet to stake out a coffee shop. To get the job you have to analyze a poem. *Prepare an oral presentation* analyzing the meaning of your favorite poem. What images do the figures of speech in the poem create? What feelings do those images elicit? What meaning does the poem have for you? Be sure that you support your analysis with quotes from the poem. (You can find information on oral presentations on pages 457–464.)

For Oral Communication Analytical Phone Message

2. Every Friday night you and your friend go to the Megaplex 50 to see the latest movie. This Friday, however, you go alone because your friend can't make it. The movie is the greatest comedy you have ever seen. You call your friend to tell her, but she doesn't pick up. *Prepare a phone message* for your friend analyzing a favorite comic film. Describe how the setting of the comedy contributes to the tone or mood of the story. Practice delivering your phone message to classmates or family members.

Timed Writing ⏱ Literary Review

3. AwesomeArtReview.com is inviting readers to submit reviews of books, plays, and films for a writing competition. Reviews must focus on works that teach people something worth learning. Choose a novel, play, or short story that you think can inspire people to learn something valuable about life. Write a review in which you analyze the work in terms of its value to the reader/viewer. You have 25 minutes to complete your work. (For help budgeting time, see pages 420–421.)

Before You Write Consider the following questions: What is the subject? What is the occasion? Who is the audience? What is the purpose?

Use quotes, scenes, and specific lines from the work to support your thesis of the work's importance. Organize your content logically. Proofread your review for appropriateness of organization, content, style, and conventions.

After You Write Evaluate your work using the six-trait rubric on page 316.

Unit 3

Research and
Report Writing

Research begins with exploration. The best researchers start by hiking through their subject, crossing its plains, climbing its mountains. This unit will help you navigate through the wilderness of facts about your own subject until you find something astonishing. You will then learn to devise and follow an effective plan of attack: mine the most relevant facts, synthesize them, organize them, and draw conclusions about them. If your plan is solid, and you follow it with zeal and care, your subject is sure to astonish others.

The way to do research is to attack the facts at the point of greatest astonishment. — *Celia Green*

CHAPTER 10

Research: Planning and Gathering Information

Research reports are essays based on information drawn from sources such as books, periodicals, the media, and interviews with experts.

Writing that is the product of well-documented research is one of the most effective means of presenting information. A strong report—with the potential to influence the viewpoints, decisions, and actions of those who read it—is always made up of accurate and compelling facts and opinions from reliable experts and other sources. People in many professions and occupations use research reports to communicate and acquire information or to recommend and justify a particular course of action. Here are just a few examples.

- **A report by the U.S. Surgeon General on the dangers of secondhand smoke** is used to create laws regulating smoking in public places.

- **An educator advocating year-round schooling presents a report on the educational benefits of shorter vacation periods** to justify his argument.

- **A NASA report on the challenges and opportunities for future space exploration** is released on the Internet to build grassroots support for new space initiatives.

- **A presidential commission studying environmental concerns issues a report** identifying key problems and proposals for the next decade.

- **A business executive prepares a marketing report** that includes information on the buying patterns of 14- to 19-year-olds.

Writing Project Research Report

Digging into My Culture *Begin a research report that focuses on one element of your culture. Start by choosing an appropriate topic and doing research.*

Think Through Writing Each of us comes from a particular culture. That culture is complex and multi-faceted and may be defined by our ethnicity, our region of the country, our gender, our religion, our musical tastes, our interests, or any other factor that leads us to become part of an ongoing social group and to take part in its social practices. Brainstorm about the cultures to which you belong by writing down everything that comes to mind about them. Then focus on something that you would like to learn more about through research. Write about your culture, the specific cultural practices you find interesting, and how you might conduct research to learn more about them. At this point, don't worry about using formal academic language; just write freely in order to explore your ideas.

Talk About It In your writing group, share your writing. Discuss the different cultures identified by the various writers, the cultural practices considered, and where the writers can locate information to help them understand those practices better.

Read About It In the following passage, Le Ly Hayslip writes about her experiences as a young girl from a peasant family farming rice in her home village of Ky La, near Da Nang, Vietnam. She describes the rituals and routines surrounding the planting, growing, and eating of rice, the mainstay of the Vietnamese diet. Think about how she describes this important cultural practice and how you might describe something from your own culture, both from experience and from research that gives you additional knowledge.

> MODEL: Informative Essay

From

When Heaven and Earth Changed Places

Le Ly Hayslip

Although we grew many crops around Ky La—sweet potatoes, peanuts, cinnamon, and taro—the most important by far was rice. Yet for all its long history as the staff of life in our country, rice was a fickle provider. First, the spot of ground on which the rice was thrown had to be just right for the seed to sprout. Then, it had to be protected from birds and animals who needed food as much as we did. As a child, I spent many hours with the other kids in Ky La acting like human scarecrows— making noise and waving our arms—just to keep the raven-like *se-se* birds away from our future supper. . . .

When the seeds had grown into stalks, we would pull them up—*nho ma*—and replant them in the

In the first sentence, Hayslip states the topic of her text, rice, and places it in the broader context of other foods grown in her area.

In the first paragraph, Hayslip narrows the focus to one aspect of rice: the steps involved in growing it.

paddies—the place where the rice matured and our crop eventually would be harvested.

After the hard crust had been turned and the clods broken up with mallets to the size of gravel, we had to wet it down with water conveyed from nearby ponds or rivers. Once the field had been flooded, it was left to soak for several days, after which our buffalo-powered plow could finish the job. In order to accept the seedling rice, however, the ground had to be *bua ruong*—even softer than the richest soil we used to grow vegetables. We knew the texture was right when a handful of watery mud would ooze through our fingers like soup.

> By using "I" and "we" repeatedly, Hayslip makes clear that she is discussing her family. Her source is her personal experience.

Transplanting the rice stalks from their "nursery" to the field was primarily women's work. Although we labored as fast as we could, this chore involved bending over for hours in knee-deep, muddy water. No matter how practiced we were, the constant search for a foothold in the sucking mud made the tedious work exhausting. Still, there was no other way to transplant the seedlings properly; and that sensual contact between our hands and feet, the baby rice, and the wet, receptive earth, is one of the things that preserved and heightened our connection with the land. . . .

> Highly descriptive details help Hayslip put the reader in her shoes as she conveys her experience.

Beginning in March, and again in August, we would bring the mature rice in from the fields and process it for use during the rest of the year. In March, when the ground was dry, we cut the rice very close to the soil— *cat lua*—to keep the plant alive.

> Hayslip uses chronological order as she relates the growing cycle for rice.

In August, when the ground was wet, we cut the plant halfway up—*ca gat*—which made the job much easier.

The separation of stalk and rice was done outside in a special smooth area beside our house. Because the rice was freshly cut, it had to dry in the sun for several days. At this stage, we called it *phoi lua*—not-yet rice. The actual separation was done by our water buffalo, which walked in lazy circles over a heap of cuttings until the rice fell easily from the stalks. We gathered the stalks, tied them in bundles, and used them to fix roofs or to kindle our fires. The good, light-colored rice, called *lua chet*, was separated from the bad, dark-colored rice—*lua lep*—and taken home for further processing.

> Here Hayslip uses sequential order to explain the process of separating stalk and rice.

Once the brown rice grains were out of their shells, we shook them in wide baskets, tossing them slightly into the air so that the wind could carry off the husks. When finished, the rice was now ready to go inside where it became "floor rice" and was pounded in a bowl to crack the layer of bran that contained the sweet white kernel. When we swirled the cracked rice in a woven colander, the bran fell through the holes and was collected to feed the pigs. The broken rice that remained with the good kernels was called *tam* rice, and although it was fit to eat, it was not very good and we used it as chicken feed (when the harvest was good) or collected it and shared it with beggars when the harvest was bad.

We always blamed crop failures on ourselves—we had not worked hard enough or, if there was no other explanation, we had failed to adequately honor our ancestors. Our solution was to pray more and sacrifice more and eventually things always got better. Crops ruined by soldiers were another matter. We knew prayer was useless because soldiers were human beings, too, and the god of nature meant for them to work out their own karma[1] just like us.

In any event, the journey from seedling to rice bowl was long and laborious and because each grain was a symbol of life, we never wasted any of it. Good rice was considered god's gemstone—*hot ngoc troi*—and was cared for accordingly on pain of divine punishment. Even today a peasant seeing lightning will crouch under the table and look for lost grains in order to escape the next bolt. And parents must never strike children, no matter how naughty they've been, while the child is eating rice, for that would interrupt the sacred communion between rice-eater and rice-maker. Like my brothers and sisters, I learned quickly the advantages of chewing my dinner slowly.

Hayslip concludes her account "from seedling to rice bowl" with a personal note explaining why she learned to eat rice slowly.

---

1 **karma:** in Buddhism, the force generated by a person's actions; fate.

Respond in Writing What do you remember most from this reading? What details stay clearly in your mind? After answering those questions, explain why you think you remembered what you did and what lessons you might learn from the experience to help you in your own writing about your culture.

Develop Ideas and Plans

Small Groups: In your writing group, discuss in greater detail the cultural traditions you have chosen to write about, along with Le Ly Hayslip's account of Vietnamese rice farming. As a group, consider the following questions.

1. What purposes do the traditions serve for members of the culture?
2. How do the traditions connect people in the present to their cultural past and future?
3. What is missing from the accounts of these traditions, and where might the writer find additional information?

Whole Class: Each group should report to the whole class its answers to each of these three questions. Be sure to take notes that will help you in the research you will next conduct. Ask questions to clarify your understanding of something a classmate reports.

Write About It You will next write a research report on some tradition, ritual, or recurring practice that occurs in your culture. You might choose from any of the following possibilities. You might instead generate your own question or problem to research.

Possible Topics	Possible Audiences	Possible Forms
• food production, preparation, and/or consumption • language and ways of interacting • holiday traditions • outdoor activities • sports • religious ceremonies	• your parents or guardian • a good friend • other members of your culture • people who know little about your culture	• a letter • an essay • a slide show using presentation software • a documentary film • an article for a Web site

One challenge in writing a research paper is keeping track of the information you collect from several different sources. The first step, therefore, is to gather the supplies you will need to organize your research. These supplies usually include a notebook, a folder with pockets, and index cards. If you are working electronically, create a bookmark folder for your report topic so you can keep track of all the Internet sources you consult. The next step is to choose a subject that is limited enough to allow you to cover it adequately.

 ## Choosing and Limiting a Research Subject

Sometimes teachers assign research subjects or list alternatives for you to choose among. Often, however, the choice of a research topic is left entirely to you. The most satisfying research topics have some depth and complexity, like an intriguing puzzle. They are also *multi-faceted*, meaning they have many sides to consider. The following suggestions may be helpful when you begin searching for a good topic.

 Finding Ideas for Research Reports

- Use brainstorming to complete this statement: I've always wondered how . . . (You can learn more about brainstorming on page 18.)
- Using the online library catalog, find a section in the library or media center that interests you. Then walk through the aisles, looking for book titles that catch your eye.
- Skim through magazines and other periodicals, in print or online.
- Skim through an encyclopedia volume or explore an online encyclopedia.
- Ask your potential readers what they would like to know more about.
- Check the assignments in your other courses to see if any require a research paper.
- Do a keyword search and browse Web sites that interest you for report subjects.
- Watch documentary television programs or videos that might contain report topics.

After you have listed five to ten possible major research topics, choose one for which the following statements hold true.

 Choosing a Suitable Research Subject

- I would like to know more about this subject.
- My audience would like to know more about this subject.
- This subject is appropriate for my purpose; that is, I can explain it well in a short research report of three to five pages.
- I can find enough information on this subject by using resources such as those in the library or media center and through other sources, such as interviewing or searching on the Internet.

Once you have chosen a broad topic, the next step is to limit it. One way to limit a subject is to break it down into its different aspects or elements. Suppose, for example, that you decided to write a report on the movie *The Wizard of Oz*. Realizing that this subject is too broad for a short research paper, you might then list the following aspects of the movie as possible limited subjects.

Subject	*The Wizard of Oz*	
Limited Subjects	the story	the cast
	the music	the special effects
	the sets	the costumes

Writing Tip

Limit a subject for a research paper by listing elements, or aspects, of the subject and by selecting one of them to research. Even a complex, multi-faceted topic should be focused enough for you to cover adequately in the length allotted to your report.

● Practice Your Skills

Limiting Research Subjects

With a partner, decide which of the following subjects are suitable for a research paper of three to five pages and which ones are too broad. Answer each item by writing *limited enough* or *too broad*. Then, using reference materials if necessary, limit each subject that is too broad by listing three aspects that could serve as limited subjects. Compare your answers to those of the rest of your class when you are finished.

1. types of helicopters
2. the movie *Star Wars*
3. the brain
4. World War II
5. the life cycle of a tarantula
6. basic moves in the merengue

PROJECT PREP Planning Choosing a Focus

In your writing group, brainstorm to discover the best possible focus for your research report. Your thinking might take the following course, for instance:

Food	Very broad; could lead in too many directions to be useful as a focus
Holiday meals	More specific, but covers too many topics for a research report
Thanksgiving dinner	Very specific; might be focused enough for a research report

② Developing Research Questions

After you have limited your subject, decide what you already know about it. Then pose questions about what more you would like to find out. These questions will serve as a research plan for gathering more information. By summarizing your questions into one **major research question**, you can focus your efforts and thoughts. The chart below shows how this questioning process works.

Limited Subject: special effects in *The Wizard of Oz*	
Focus Questions	**Possible Answers**
What Do I Already Know About These Special Effects?	I saw the movie. I remember the tornado, the flying monkeys, and the melting witch. I saw a program on how the special effects for another movie were made.
What More Do I Want to Find Out?	What other special effects are in *The Wizard of Oz?* How were the tornado, flying monkeys, melting witch, and other special effects created? Which effects were easiest to make? Which were the hardest and costliest? How do the special effects in *The Wizard of Oz* compare with those in that other movie?
Major Research Question	How were the special effects in *The Wizard of Oz* created?

You can organize your questions in a **KWL chart** like the one below. You would fill in the final column after you have gathered your information.

Subject and Research Question:		
What do I **know** about the subject?	What do I **want** to learn about the subject?	What have I **learned** about the subject?

PROJECT PREP *Planning* Identifying a Research Question

To develop your limited subject, use a KWL chart to generate a list of facts you already know and a list of questions you would like to answer through your research. Formulate a major research question that will guide your efforts in gathering information.

CHAPTER 10

With your research questions clearly in mind, you can begin planning your research on a complex, multi-faceted subject. Decide how to find the information you need to answer your questions. As you find answers, be alert for possible main ideas that you could use as the thesis of your research paper.

1 Finding Relevant Sources

Use the following guidelines to gather the information you need to answer your research questions.

Guidelines for Gathering Information

- Consult a general reference work, such as a digital or printed encyclopedia, to find an overview of your subject, some references to other resources on that subject, and cross-references to related topics.

- Use the online catalog to do a keyword search in the library or media center.

- Consult your library's online databases or a news index, such as *Facts on File,* in print or online, to find magazine and newspaper articles on your subject.

- Use an Internet search engine to find Web sites related to your limited subject. Remember, not all Web sites contain accurate and reliable information. (You can learn about evaluating online sources on pages 335–336.)

- Keep an eye out for graphics and illustrations that will help you explain the concepts in your report. You may be able to adapt them for your use or get permission from the copyright holder to use them in your report.

- Make a list of all your sources. For each book or video write the author, title, copyright year, publisher's name and location, and call number (if available). For each periodical, include the author and title of the article and name of the periodical, the date (month, day, and year), the volume, the issue number, and the pages. For each Web site, include the exact address, the site author, and the date accessed. If you find the source through an online database, include the name of the database along with the other information.

- Assign each source on your list a number that you can use to refer to that source in your notes.

A list of some sources for the report on the special effects in *The Wizard of Oz* appears on the next page.

Books

Down the Yellow Brick Road by Doug McClelland, 1989, Bonanza Books, New York, 791.437 W792M (1)

The Making of The Wizard of Oz by Aljean Harmetz, 1989, Delta, New York, 791.437 W792H (2)

Magazine

"The Fabulous Land of Oz: Dream World via Cyclonic Ride Recreated in Technicolor" *Newsweek*, August 21, 1939, pp. 23–24 (3)

Newspaper

Frank S. Nugent, "The Screen in Review: 'The Wizard of Oz,' Produced by the Wizards of Hollywood, Works Its Magic on the Capitol's Screen." *The New York Times*, Aug 18, 1939, page 16, *Historical NY Times* database (4)

Internet

"Baum, L. Frank," Columbia Encyclopedia online, 2007. <http://www.questia.com/library/encyclopedia/baum_l_frank.jsp> 15 Mar 2009. (5)

Review of *The Wizard of Oz* by James Berardinelli, 1998. <http://www.reelviews.net/movies/w/wizard_oz.html> 17 Mar 2009. (6)

When researching a subject from the past, such as the 1939 movie *The Wizard of Oz*, you may want to locate primary sources from that period, such as statements by the actors or director at the time of filming or comments by reviewers when the film was originally released. You might find such direct, firsthand information in magazines and newspapers of the time. Remember, you need to distinguish between direct statements and opinions or comments derived from those original statements. These resources, as well as books listed as out-of-print in an online resource, may be found in a library or media center collection on microfilm or in an online database that focuses on archived articles. (See pages 351–352 for more information on microfilm and other information sources.)

PROJECT PREP *Planning* *Writing an Informal Account*

What I Need to Know	Why I Need to Know It	Where I Can Find It	What I Will Learn from It	What I Learned

Taking into account your discussions and the KWL chart you have developed, write an informal account of your research subject, keeping your major research question in mind. You might start by writing about what you already know, as Le Ly Hayslip does in writing about rice farming in Vietnam. As you write, use an asterisk (*) to indicate where you need to look up information to make your account more complete. Then use the chart above to help you plan how to find that information and to organize it when you find it.

2 Evaluating Sources

As you begin the research process, keep in mind that not all sources of information you discover will be equally useful to you. Before using a source, you need to evaluate it critically. Regardless of your specific topic, all of your sources should be relevant, reliable, up to date, and objective. The author should be a respected, trusted expert. If your topic is controversial, your report should present different points of view and identify major issues and debates on the topic.

EVALUATING PRINT SOURCES

Just because a particular print source is in your library catalog or database doesn't mean that it's appropriate for your project. You still need to decide if it's relevant to your subject and whether the information is valid, accurate, up to date, and appropriate for your report. The following guidelines can help you evaluate print sources.

Guidelines for Evaluating Print Sources

- **Who's the authority?**
  Find out the author's background. A library catalog entry or online book reviews may give information about the education or experience that makes the author an expert. Magazine or newspaper articles often provide a brief summary of their author's credentials. Get recommendations from a teacher, librarian, or someone else who is knowledgeable about the topic.

- **Who's behind it?**
  See if the author is associated with a particular organization and whether that organization might be biased. Find out who published the book. If the publisher is unfamiliar, do an online search to find out more about it. A librarian can lead you to the best sources for particular types of information.

- **What's right for you?**
  Make sure the book or article is relevant to your limited subject. Some sources may be too general or too specific for what you are trying to accomplish. They may be written at a level that is either too simple or too complex for a student researcher.

- **Look inside.**
  Check the publication date to make sure the information is current. Read the book jacket or an inside page to find out about the author's background. Look at the table of contents and index to see whether your particular topic is covered in appropriate detail. Skim relevant sections to see if sources are given to back up the facts presented. Does the author support his or her opinions with solid evidence?

EVALUATING ONLINE SOURCES

When you check out a library book, a librarian has already evaluated the book to make sure it's a reliable source of information. However, no one regulates the Internet to keep out unreliable sources. Here are a few guidelines on how to evaluate an online source.

Guidelines for Evaluating Online Sources

- **Play the name game.**
  First, find out who publishes the site and consider their objectivity. Does the URL end in ".com" (which means it's a commercial company)? If so, is it a reputable company? Or is it one you've never heard of that might just be trying to sell you something? An educational site in which the URL ends in ".edu," such as a college or university, might be a more reliable choice. A site sponsored by a well-known organization with a URL that ends in ".org," such as the American Red Cross <http://www.redcross.org>, would also probably be a reliable source.

- **Scope it out.**
  Click around the site and get a feel for what it's like. Is the design clean and appealing? Is it easy to get around the site and find information? Are the sections clearly labeled? Does the site accept advertising? If you think the site seems disorganized, or you just have a negative opinion of it, listen to your instincts and move on to another one.

- **Says who?**
  Suppose you find an article on the Web that seems chock-full of great information. The next question you need to ask yourself is, "Who is the author? Is the person recognized as an expert on the subject?" If you don't recognize the author's name, you can do a search on the Web, using the author's name as the keyword to get more information about him or her. In some cases, an article won't list any author at all. If you don't find an author's name, be cautious. A reliable site clearly identifies its authors and usually lists their professional background.

- **Is this old news?**
  If you are doing research on the pyramids, it's probably all right if the information wasn't posted yesterday. But if you're looking for information in quickly changing fields, such as science and politics, be sure to check the publication date before you accept the information as valid and accurate.

- **Ask around.**
  Reliable Web sites frequently provide e-mail addresses or links to authors and organizations connected to the content on the site. Send off a quick e-mail to a few of these sources, tell them what you are writing, and ask them: "Is this material accurate?"

The best way to check the accuracy of any information on a Web site is to check it against another source—and the best source is your local library or media center.

You can learn more about using the Internet for research on pages 358–361.

PROJECT PREP Gathering Information **First Pass**

Go to the library with your writing group and begin consulting sources. Discuss the reliability of each source that you consult. Try to find roughly the same information in more than one source. Find at least five sources to help you with your project.

After you have developed a list of print and online sources, gather the books and periodicals together and bring them, along with printouts of any online source materials, to the place you plan to work. Then skim each source, looking for the information you need for your research report. With books, you will find the tables of contents and the indexes especially helpful in your search. Once you have located the relevant portion of a reliable source, take a note card and, in the upper right-hand corner of the card, write the identifying number you gave that source. This number should appear on each note card you use for that source. Keep the following goals in mind as you read the source and begin taking notes.

CHAPTER 10

SUMMARIZING

When you **summarize,** you write information in a condensed, concise form, touching only on the main ideas. To record direct quotations, you copy the words exactly and enclose them in quotation marks. Always write the name of the person who made the statement you are quoting and the page number where you found the statement in the source. The example below shows the form for quotations and summaries.

Quotation	"Beginning in March, and again in August, we would bring the mature rice in from the fields and process it for use during the rest of the year." (Hayslip, page 326)
Summary	We harvested and processed rice in March and August.

The excerpt on the following page is from page 244 of the book *The Making of the Wizard of Oz*. The note card that follows the excerpt shows how this information can be summarized.

MODEL: Taking Notes from a Source

Basically, what Gillespie [the special-effects director] knew about tornados in 1938 was that "we couldn't go to Kansas and wait for a tornado to come down and pick up a house." Everything beyond that was an experiment. . . . "I was a pilot for many years and had an airplane of my own. The wind sock they used in airports in the old days to show the direction of the wind has a shape a little bit like a tornado and the wind blows through it. I started from that. We cast a cone out of thin rubber. We were going to whirl the rubber cone and rotate it. But tornados are called twisters and the rubber cone didn't twist. So that was rather an expensive thing down the drain. We finally wound up by building a sort of giant wind sock out of muslin." The giant thirty-five-foot muslin tornado was—technically—a miniature.

—Aljean Harmetz, *The Making of the Wizard of Oz*

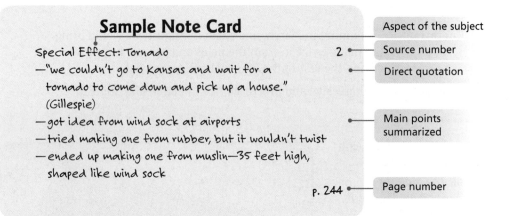

Sample Note Card

Aspect of the subject

Special Effect: Tornado   2   Source number

—"we couldn't go to Kansas and wait for a   Direct quotation
   tornado to come down and pick up a house."
   (Gillespie)

—got idea from wind sock at airports   Main points summarized
—tried making one from rubber, but it wouldn't twist
—ended up making one from muslin—35 feet high,
   shaped like wind sock

        p. 244   Page number

Writing Tip

You can use a variety of graphics to organize your information from multiple sources. For example, you could create a two-column chart that lists your sources in one column and the notes you take in the other. You could also make a three-column chart for each source, with the source name in the first column, your notes in the second, and your comments in the third.

● **Practice Your Skills**

Taking Notes

The excerpt below is from an article in *Time* magazine, August 25, 2008, page 57. Assume the article is your third source and make a note card for the following excerpt.

> Making a 3-D movie involves filming an image from two perspectives: one representing the left eye, the other the right. When synchronized and watched through glasses that allow each eye to see only its own movie, the two films create an illusion of depth. Until recently, perfect synchronization was nearly impossible, and production and exhibition were cumbersome. Digitization has eliminated many of the flaws of old 3-D movies—like nausea and headaches brought on by poor synching—and has motivated studios to push the format on exhibitors and filmmakers. "It's an important part of our business going forward," says Alan Bergman, president of Walt Disney Studios, which will release an animated canine-superhero movie, *Bolt,* in 3-D in November, as well as all its future Pixar films.
>
> —Rebecca Winters Keegan, "Don't Duck"

PROJECT PREP *Prewriting* / *Taking Notes*

Follow the model for note taking on page 338 to gather information from your sources for your report. Keep all your note cards together in a folder. If you are working on a computer, create a folder for your research paper so you do not lose track of your notes. If you are using graphics to organize your notes, keep track of them by placing them in a folder or saving them electronically.

Writing Lab

Project Corner

Speak and Listen Discuss Reliability

Have a panel discussion on the validity of Internet-based information resources. How do you know that a source is trustworthy? What is the value of different types of Web sites for particular purposes? In part of your discussion, focus on specific Web sites that you find either trustworthy or untrustworthy. (See pages 468–470 on group discussions and pages 467–468 on listening for information.)

Get Graphic Explain Concepts

Review the information you gathered. Look for information that might be easier to understand in graphic form than in print. For example, if you have a number of statistics, you may want to **create a table or chart** to present them. In addition, make a list of points you want to explain in your report that would be best conveyed through an illustration, such as a photograph or diagram. **Look for or develop your own illustrations** to explain concepts in your report.

Chart It Evaluate Sources

In your writing group, **make a chart** that depicts the sources you have consulted for your research. Where do you draw from to produce a valid inquiry? Organize the chart according to categories, such as encyclopedias, books, articles, Web sites, documentary films, informative programming, and any other information sources, including interviews. Further, construct your chart to indicate the degree of trustworthiness you have assigned to each type of source and each individual source. You can make the chart by hand or use a feature in a spreadsheet program such as Microsoft Excel® to create your chart.

In the Workplace
Business Memo

1. You work for a construction consulting company that is evaluating whether to build a highway through the Florida Everglades. Your boss has organized two teams to study the issue, one to focus on economic issues and the other to focus on environmental issues. Choose your team, find appropriate sources, and take notes from those sources. Then **write a memo** to your boss laying out your position and listing the sources you used to research facts and specific details that support your point of view. (See pages 254–283 for help with persuasive writing.)

For Spoken Communications
Questions for Informational Interview

2. You have been hired as a style consultant for an athletic shoe and clothing company. The company wants you to interview the trendsetters in your community about what kind of athletic clothing they think will become popular. **Prepare five interview questions** that you could ask to gather this information. Then conduct an oral interview with three members of your class. Select information that is relevant to your topic. (See pages 467–468 on listening for information.)

Timed Writing ⏱ List of Priority Topics

3. You work for a newly elected member of Congress. As part of her campaign, the congresswoman promised to "protect the environment," but she did not provide any specific details. Your job is to help her establish a list of priorities. Write a list of possible topics for a report about protecting the environment. You might consider the protection of a river, mountains, or park land in your area. When you have finished your list, choose the topic that interests you most and do some research about what kinds of environmental problems affect the place. Take notes and compare your sources of evidence. You have 30 minutes in the library media center to complete your work.

Before You Write Consider the following questions: What is the subject? What is the occasion? Who is the audience? What is the purpose?

After You Write Assess your work by evaluating your sources as outlined on pages 335–336.

Research Companion

Doing research and exploring a topic in depth is like solving a mystery. Reference materials provide the information you need to investigate your topic and answer your unsolved questions. Determining the right reference materials is the only way to find the information that will make your writing stand out. To gain knowledge, you need to do research, and to do good research you need to improve your reference skills. For all of your future research projects, solid reference skills will make your writing richer and broader.

Using the Library or Media Center

The library or media center is the best place to begin researching, whatever your topic may be. This storehouse of knowledge and information includes printed media, such as books, newspapers, magazines, encyclopedias, and other forms of writing, and an ever-increasing variety of electronic or online resources, such as downloadable electronic books, computer databases, and access to the World Wide Web. Whenever you start a new research project, however, the most valuable resource may be the librarian or media specialist—the trained professional who can help you find the references that you need most.

FICTION

The books you find in this section may be inspired by factual information, but the stories that fill them are creations of the authors' imaginations. In the fiction section of the library, the books are shelved alphabetically according to the authors' last names. Here are a few guidelines for locating these resources.

Guidelines for Finding Fiction

- Two-part names are alphabetized by the first part of the name.
  De Soto   **O'**Connor   **Van** Buren
- Names beginning with *Mc* or *St.* are alphabetized as if they began with *Mac* or *Saint*.
- Books by authors with the same last name are alphabetized first by last name, and then by first name.
- Books by the same author are alphabetized by the first important word in the title.

NONFICTION

Books in this section include factual information and document real events. These reference materials are perfect for finding information in different subject areas.

More than a hundred years ago, an American librarian, Melvil Dewey, came up with a numerical system to categorize nonfiction books. Today his system, known as the **Dewey decimal system,** is used in most school libraries around the country. If you want to find a specific book on boa constrictors, for example, the book would have the same **call number**—or number and letter code, identifying it by subject and category—throughout the country. Books are then arranged on the shelves in numerical order. The following categories are included in the Dewey decimal system.

DEWEY DECIMAL SYSTEM	
000–099	General Works (reference books)
100–199	Philosophy
200–299	Religion
300–399	Social Science (law, education, economics)
400–499	Language
500–599	Science (mathematics, biology, chemistry)
600–699	Technology (medicine, inventions)
700–799	Fine Arts (painting, music, theater)
800–899	Literature
900–999	History (biography, geography, travel)

Each general subject is then divided into smaller categories.

800–899 LITERATURE			
800–809	General	850–859	Italian
810–819	American	860–869	Spanish
820–829	English	870–879	Latin
830–839	German	880–889	Greek
840–849	French	890–899	Other

Because ten numbers and categories are not enough to cover the many books about American or French literature, one or more decimal numbers may also be used.

BIOGRAPHIES AND AUTOBIOGRAPHIES

Biographies and autobiographies are usually in a separate section and are shelved in alphabetical order by the subject's last name rather than by the author's last name. Each book is labeled B for biography or 92 (a shortened form of the Dewey decimal classification of 920), followed by the first letters of the subject's last name. A biography of George Washington, for example, is labeled on the spine of the book in one of the following ways.

Biography	B	92
Beginning of Subject's Last Name	WAS	WAS

● **Develop Research Skills**

Using the Dewey Decimal System

Using the chart on page 343, write the range of numbers and the general category for each of the following titles.

1. *The Joy of Music*

2. *All About Language*

3. *Basic Biology*

4. *The Making of a Surgeon*

5. *You and the Law*

6. *Chemistry Today*

7. *Trial by Jury*

8. *Shakespeare's Plays*

9. *To a Young Dancer*

10. *The European Middle Ages*

THE LIBRARY CATALOG

Most libraries and media centers store records of their holdings in an online catalog. Computer systems can vary from library to library, but generally the search methods are the same. The computer will present a list of items for each search request (by the author's last name, book title, or subject). Depending on how many references are provided, you may have to make more specific selections. If your book is available, the computer displays information about the book similar to that in the example on the next page.

A tale of two cities

Dickens, Charles, 1812–1870.

Personal Author:	Dickens, Charles, 1812–1870.
Title:	A tale of two cities/Charles Dickens.
Publication info:	Champaign, IL : Book Jungle, [2007].
Physical descrip:	370 p. ; 24 cm.
General Note:	Reprint : New York : Globe Book Co., 1921.
Held by:	EPLMAIN
Subject term:	French–England–London–Fiction.
Subject term:	Executions and executioners–Fiction.
Subject term:	Fathers and daughters–Fiction.
Subject term:	Lookalikes–Fiction
Geographic term:	France–History–Revolution, 1789–1799–Fiction.
Geographic term:	Paris (France)–History–1789–1799–Fiction.
Geographic term:	London (England)–History–18th century–Fiction.
Genre index term:	Historical fiction.
Genre index term:	War stories.
Control Number:	ocn183901268
ISBN:	9781604240719 (pbk.) : $9.45
ISBN:	1604240717 (pbk.) : $9.45

You may also find a simpler record of the book that may appear as follows. This type of catalog entry tells you where you can find the book in the library. It may also include a brief summary of the book.

A tale of two cities

Dickens, Charles, 1812–1870.

"It was the best of times, it was the worst of times" are the words that begin this classic by Charles Dickens. The story begins with the years preceding the French Revolution. Two very different men, a cynical Englishman and a romantic French man are in love with the **read more...**

Publisher:	Book Jungle,
Pub date:	[2007].
Pages:	370 p. ;
ISBN:	9781604240719
A Look Inside:	

Holdings

Evanston Public Library Main

	Material	**Location**
YA Fiction Dicke.C	Book	Young Adult Collection –3rd Floor Loft

To search the listings in an online catalog, you select a category—author, title, or subject—and enter the necessary commands. On some systems, you can also do a keyword search, just as you would on an Internet search engine. A keyword search can search the library's collections for both title and subject headings at the same time. If the book you are looking for is not listed or not available, the computer can tell you if it has been checked out and when it is due back. By using the Web to search other library databases, the media specialist can tell you if the book is available elsewhere.

Search Tip

You can use the **online catalog** in your library or media center to search for a book by subject, author, or title. In some databases, a keyword search can do this even more quickly by searching subject and title categories at the same time.

Strategies for Using an Online Catalog

Think about what you already know that can limit your search. A title or author search will always give you more focused results than a subject search. If you are doing a subject search, find a way to limit the category, either by year or by subcategory.

Searching by Author's Name

- If the last name is common, type the author's complete last name followed by a comma, a space, and the author's first initial or complete first name.
- Omit all accent marks and other punctuation in the author's name.
- For compound names, try variations in placement of the parts: **von neuwirth james** or **neuwirth james von**

Searching by Title

- If the title is long, type only the first few words. Omit capitalization, punctuation, accent marks, and the articles *a, an,* and *the.*
    - **red badge of cour** (you need not include the full title)
    - **sun also rises** (omit initial article words)
    - **red white and blue** (omit punctuation)
- If you are unsure of the correct form of a word, try variations such as spelling out or inserting spaces between initials and abbreviations; entering numbers as words; using an ampersand (&) for *and*; spelling hyphenated words as one or two words.

Searching by Subject

- Omit commas, parentheses, and capitalization.
- Broad categories can be divided into subcategories to make your search more specific.
- If you don't know the correct subject heading, find at least one source relevant to your topic by doing a title or keyword search. Use one or more of the subject headings listed there for additional searches.

Searching by Keyword

- Searching with a single word, such as *computers,* will look for that word anywhere in the entry: in the title, author, subject, or descriptive notes.
- A phrase, such as *solar energy,* finds entries containing the words *solar* and *energy.* To search for *solar energy* as a phrase, type *solar and energy,* or *solar adj energy* (*adj* = adjacent).
- An open search will look anywhere in the entry for your word. You can limit your keyword searches to specific search fields—author, title, or subject—by doing an advanced search and selecting the appropriate field.

Develop Research Skills

Searching Online Catalogs

Write the category you would select for a search on the following items. Then write the words that you would enter to find each item.

1. the life and times of Barbara Jordan

2. the books of C. S. Lewis

3. the skills of snowboarding

4. the work of Jane Goodall

5. the country's best roller coasters

6. ancient Egypt

7. expeditions to the Polar regions

8. how insects change and grow

Barbara Jordan

PARTS OF A BOOK

Once you find several sources that you think may be useful for your project, you need to spend some time looking through them to see if they have information that you need. Finding this information is easier if you know how to use the parts of a book. Each part of a book gives you different types of information.

INFORMATION IN PARTS OF A BOOK

Title Page	shows the full title, author's name, publisher, and place of publication
Copyright Page	gives the date of first publication and dates of any revised editions
Table of Contents	lists chapter or section titles in the book and their starting page numbers
Introduction	gives an overview of the author's ideas in each chapter and in relation to the work that other writers have done on the subject
Appendix	gives additional information on subjects in the book; charts, graphs, and maps are sometimes included
Glossary	lists, in alphabetical order, difficult or technical words found in the book and their definitions
Bibliography	lists sources that the author used in writing the book, including titles and publication information
Index	lists topics that are mentioned in the book and gives the page numbers where these topics can be found

● Develop Research Skills

Using Parts of a Books

Write the part of the book you would use to find each of the following items of information.

1. the year of publication

2. definition of a difficult or technical word

3. a specific topic or person mentioned in the book

4. the title and publication information for a source used by the author

5. the name and location of the publisher

6. a chart or graph with additional information

7. the title of a specific chapter

8. the author's explanation of the book's contents

Print and Nonprint Reference Materials

Along with fiction and nonfiction sections, most libraries or media centers have a separate area called a reference room. This room contains encyclopedias, dictionaries, atlases, almanacs, and reference books on specific subjects. Many libraries and media centers now have online versions of these print sources as well.

Most libraries today subscribe to **online databases** that can be accessed through computers in the library. Often, anyone with a library card may use a computer at home to search the databases through the library's Web site. These databases provide a wealth of information that is not usually available for free just by searching on the Internet. Some databases are especially designed for students.

The following chart indicates the kinds of reference works available in most libraries and media centers.

PRINT AND ELECTRONIC REFERENCES

- general and specialized encyclopedias
- general and specialized dictionaries
- atlases, almanacs, and yearbooks
- specialized biographical and literary references
- online databases and indexes of periodicals (including magazines, newspapers, and journals)
- microfilm and microfiche files of periodicals and government documents
- computers with access to the Internet and World Wide Web
- audio recordings and video documentaries

PERIODICALS—MAGAZINES AND NEWSPAPERS

Periodicals, including magazines and journals, are excellent sources for current information. The periodical reading room in the library or media center should have the most recent print issues of all the periodicals to which the library subscribes. You can usually search for periodical titles in the library's online catalog but you cannot search for individual articles. The entry will describe the extent of the library's holdings. For example, a library may keep two months of a daily newspaper and two years of weekly or monthly magazines.

By subscribing to online databases, libraries can now offer people access to a wider variety of periodicals than they would have space for in the library. Databases may cover general interest periodicals, scholarly journals, or periodicals covering specialized fields such as business or health. A librarian or media specialist can help you determine which databases are best for your particular research project. You can search in a database using keywords as you would with an Internet search engine. Database entries provide an abstract or short summary of the article so you can decide if it is useful to read the full text. Full text is available for many articles from the 1990s onward. These full-text articles can be downloaded or printed. Many databases allow you to save your search results in folders for future reference.

You can learn more about searching with keywords on pages 347 and 359–360.

Newspapers Newspapers are valuable sources of current and historical information. Some online databases contain only newspapers and others combine newspapers and magazines. Some even include radio and television news transcripts. Many databases allow you to limit your search to specific dates or even specific periodical titles. While most databases focus on articles from the 1990s to the present, some include references to articles from earlier periods. The *Historical New York Times* database offers full text articles back to the newspaper's first issue in 1851.

Most major newspapers now have Web sites and electronic databases where you can view current issues and search for archived articles. The following examples are only a few of the many available online.

The Chicago Tribune	http://www.chicago.tribune.com
The Dallas Morning News	http://www.dallasnews.com
The Los Angeles Times	http://www.latimes.com
The Miami Herald	http://www.herald.com
The New York Times	http://www.nytimes.com

By going directly to the Web, you can also search databases that locate and access the home pages of newspapers from every state in the United States and many countries around the world. Both of the following sites list hundreds of newspapers by location (country and state) and by subject (business, arts and entertainment, trade journals, or college papers).

ipl2 (The Internet Public Library)	http://www.ipl.org/div/news
Newspapers.com	http://www.newspapers.com

Remember: always read the guidelines at the home page for each newspaper. Recent articles are usually available free of charge, but you may have to pay a fee to download and print an archived article.

Older Periodicals To save space, many libraries store older issues of some magazines and newspapers as photographic reproductions of print pages on rolls and sheets of film. These **microform** holdings may be included in the library's online catalog or may have a separate catalog or list in the microform area of the library or media center. **Microfilm** (rolls) or **microfiche** (sheets) are stored in filing cabinets and can be viewed easily on special projectors. Newspapers, for example, are arranged in file drawers alphabetically by keywords in their titles. The holdings for each newspaper are then filed chronologically by date. For example, if you wanted to know what happened in Houston, Texas, on New Year's Eve in the year you were born, you could go to the file cabinets and get the roll of film for the *Houston Chronicle* on that day in that year. Check with a librarian to see if there are indexes for any of the newspapers to help you locate articles on specific topics.

Researchers looking for older magazine articles not covered in online databases may use *The Readers' Guide to Periodical Literature,* an index of articles, short stories, and poems published in a large number of magazines and journals. Articles are indexed by date, author, and subject. Libraries may subscribe to print or online versions of the *Readers' Guide*. A search of the library's catalog will tell you which issues of the guide are available in your library and whether they are in print or electronic form. Once you know the name of the magazine or journal you want, you will need to check the library's catalog to see if that specific periodical is available.

ENCYCLOPEDIAS

Encyclopedias are a good place to start gathering information. They contain general information on a wide variety of subjects. The information in most encyclopedias is arranged alphabetically by subject. Guide letters on the spine show which letter or letters are covered in each volume. Guide words at the top of each page help you find your subject. When looking for information in an encyclopedia, the index will tell you if your subject is discussed in more than one volume or if it is listed under another name.

Online encyclopedias are arranged in the same manner as printed encyclopedias—alphabetically, but there are no guide words or indexes. Instead, in order to find information on a particular subject, enter the subject in a search box. The best online encyclopedias are the ones available through your library's databases. Open source encyclopedias with unsigned articles are less reliable because they may be changed without being reviewed by an expert.

Print and Online	Through libraries and media centers:
	Compton's by Encyclopaedia Britannica
	World Book Encyclopedia
	Encyclopedia Americana
	Grolier Multimedia Encyclopedia
Online	Reliable free encyclopedias:
	Columbia Encyclopedia http://www.bartleby.com/65/
	Encyclopedia.com http://www.encyclopedia.com

SPECIALIZED ENCYCLOPEDIAS

Specialized encyclopedias focus on a variety of specific subjects from auto racing to weaving. Because they concentrate on a specific subject, these encyclopedias provide more in-depth information than general encyclopedias do. Specialized encyclopedias can also be found in the reference section of the library or media center. Specialized encyclopedias online let you search for information by subject and connect to other Web sites on your topic through hyperlinks.

Print	*World Sports Encyclopedia*
	International Wildlife Encyclopedia
	The International Encyclopedia of the Social Sciences
Online	*Encyclopedia Smithsonian*
	http://www.si.edu/Encyclopedia_SI/default.htm
	A collection of almost 50 different encyclopedias
	http://www.encyclopedia.com

BIOGRAPHICAL REFERENCES

Information about famous historical figures is usually found in encyclopedias; for information about contemporary personalities or people who are well known in specialized fields, you may need to turn to other biographical references. Some biographical references contain only a paragraph of facts about each person, such as date of birth, education, occupation, and the person's accomplishments. Others, such as *Current Biography* and *Who's Who in America*, contain long articles.

Many libraries subscribe to one or more biographical databases that contain information from published sources including books and magazine articles and have links to reliable Web sites with information on the person.

Print	*Current Biography*
	Who's Who and *Who's Who in America*
	Merriam-Webster's Biographical Dictionary
	Dictionary of American Biography
	American Men and Women of Science
Online	*Distinguished Women of Past and Present*
	http://www.distinguishedwomen.com
	Encyclopaedia Britannica Guide to Black History
	http://search.eb.com/blackhistory/

REFERENCES ABOUT LITERATURE

Quotations are wonderful devices to liven up reports and add weight to already factual information. Books of quotations are often arranged by topic or by author. If you have a specific quotation in mind but can't remember all the words, an index of first lines and keywords at the end of the book will lead you to the page where the full quotation can be found.

Other references about literature focus on actual stories or literary elements, including plot summaries, descriptions of characters, information about authors, or definitions of literary terms, such as *imagery* and *plot*. Indexes are useful for finding a particular poem, short story, or play. An index such as *Granger's Index to Poetry* lists the books that contain the particular selection you are looking for. The *Gale Literary Index* contains information about authors and their major works.

Comprehensive online databases combine many of these literary references into a convenient resource that you can search by author, title, subject, or keyword. You may find complete works along with biographical information and literary criticism. A database likely contains information from hundreds of sources on thousands of authors. Ask your librarian what your library provides.

Print	*Bartlett's Familiar Quotations*
	The Oxford Dictionary of Quotations
	Reader's Encyclopedia
	The Oxford Companion to American Literature
Online	*About.com: Classic Literature* http://classiclit.about.com/
	Gale Literary Index http://www.galenet.com/servlet/LitIndex
	Bartlett's Familiar Quotations http://www.bartleby.com/100
	The Quotations Page http://www.quotationspage.com/

ATLASES

An atlas is generally a book of maps, but you can often find much more information in one. An atlas usually contains information about the location of continents, countries, cities, mountains, lakes, and other geographical features and regions. Moreover, some atlases also have information about population, climate, natural resources, industries, and transportation. Historical atlases include maps of the world during different moments in history. Some online resources from the U.S. Geological Survey incorporate satellite imagery to let you examine the geography of the United States by state and by region.

Print	*Rand McNally International World Atlas*
	The Times Atlas of the World
	The National Geographic Atlas of the World
	Rand McNally Atlas of World History
Online	*National Atlas of the United States* http://www-atlas.usgs.gov/

ALMANACS

Almanacs, which are generally published each year, contain up-to-date facts and statistical information on topics related to population, weather, government, and business. If you want to know the batting averages of Hall of Fame baseball players, countries that suffered natural disasters last year, or the most popular films and television shows in any year, an almanac is a good place to look. Almanacs also provide historical facts and geographic information. Some, such as *The Old Farmer's Almanac*, focus on weather-related and seasonal information.

Print	*Information Please Almanac*
	World Almanac and Book of Facts
	Guinness Book of World Records
Online	*The Old Farmer's Almanac* http://www.almanac.com
	Infoplease http://www.infoplease.com/

SPECIALIZED DICTIONARIES

If you are doing research for a report on a specialized topic, you may come across an unusual word that you do not recognize. A specialized dictionary is a good resource for learning more about the word. These dictionaries provide information about specific fields of study, such as medicine, music, and computer science. Some online sites include dictionaries in several languages and excerpts from guidebooks on writing.

Print
- *Harvard Dictionary of Music*
- *Concise Dictionary of American History*
- *Merriam-Webster's Geographical Dictionary*

Online
- Medical, legal, and multilingual dictionaries and a style guide
  http://dictionary.reference.com/
- *Strunk's Elements of Style*
  http://www.bartleby.com/141/

BOOKS OF SYNONYMS

In all of the writing that you do, word choice and word usage are always important. Another type of dictionary, called a **thesaurus,** features synonyms (different words with the same meanings) and antonyms (words with opposite meanings). This resource is especially helpful if you are looking for a specific word or if you want to vary your word usage and build your vocabulary. Many Web browsers, online databases, and word processing software programs include dictionary and thesaurus features.

Print
- *Roget's 21st Century Thesaurus in Dictionary Form*
- *Merriam-Webster Dictionary of Synonyms and Antonyms*
- *Oxford American Writer's Thesaurus*

Online
- *Roget's Thesaurus*
  http://thesaurus.reference.com/
- *Merriam-Webster Dictionary and Thesaurus*
  http://www.merriam-webster.com/

Using Specialized Reference Materials

Write one kind of reference book, other than a general encyclopedia, that would contain information about each of the following subjects.

1. famous Americans   **6.** the source of a quotation

2. records in sports   **7.** the location of the Andes

3. countries of Asia   **8.** the life of Sonia Sotomayor

4. Spanish phrases   **9.** dates of past hurricanes

5. synonyms for *run*   **10.** polar bears

OTHER REFERENCE MATERIALS

Most libraries and media centers have a variety of printed resources that are not found in bound forms such as books and magazines. They also have other nonprint resources such as audio recordings and video documentaries that often provide information that cannot be conveyed in print form.

Vertical Files Most libraries keep a collection of printed materials, including pamphlets, pictures, art prints, unpublished letters and papers, and government publications and catalogs. These materials are usually arranged alphabetically by subject and kept in a filing cabinet in the library called the vertical file.

Government Documents and Historical Records Many libraries and media centers save storage space by storing some documents and back issues of periodicals on microfilm and microfiche—photographic reproductions of printed material that are stored on rolls or sheets of film. References stored on microforms may include government documents from state and federal agencies, and original, historic records and papers. These rolls and sheets of film are stored in filing cabinets in a separate part of the library or media center and can be viewed easily on special projectors. Libraries may also subscribe to databases that provide access to some government documents or historical records. Many government Web sites also provide access to such documents. Two useful sites for federal government documents are <http://usasearch.gov/> and <http://www.gpoaccess.gov/>.

Audiovisual Materials Audiovisual materials can be valuable sources of information and are often available through your library or media center. Audiovisual materials may include recordings of interviews and speeches, and DVDs of documentaries and educational programs. If you cannot check out these materials to view in the classroom, listening and viewing equipment is usually available in the library. CD-ROMs have largely been replaced by online databases and other online or electronic resources. Some libraries may still have specialized indexes, databases, encyclopedias, or dictionaries such as the complete *Oxford English Dictionary* on CD-ROM. Check with the media specialist to see which resources are available in these forms.

Using the Internet for Research

The Information Superhighway could be the best research partner you've ever had. It's fast, vast, and always available. But like any other highway, if you don't know your way around, it can also be confusing. It takes time to learn how to navigate the Net and zero in on the information you need. The best thing to do is practice early and often. Don't wait until the night before your paper is due to learn how to do research on the Internet!

GETTING STARTED

Just as there are several different ways to get to your home or school, there are many different ways to arrive at the information you're looking for on the Internet.

Internet Public Library Perhaps the best place to start your search for reliable information on the Web is to go to ipl2, the Internet Public Library site <http://www.ipl.org/>. This virtual reference library provides links to Web sites that have been reviewed and recommended by librarians. The home page is organized with links to sections much like those at your local library or media center. There is even a special section for teens. Clicking on the links that relate to your subject will take you to a list of suggested resources.

Search Bar Another good first step is your browser's search bar. You can usually customize your browser by adding the search tools you use most often to the drop down menu.

Search Tools There are several different free search services available that will help you find topics of interest by entering words and phrases that describe what you are searching for. Some of the most popular **search engines** include:

AltaVista—http://www.altavista.com/

Ask—http://www.ask.com/

Bing—http://www.bing.com/

Google—http://www.google.com/

Lycos—http://www.lycos.com/

Yahoo!—http://www.yahoo.com/

Metasearch engines search and organize results from several search engines at one time. Following are a few examples:

Clusty—http://clusty.com/

Dogpile—http://www.dogpile.com/

Ixquick Metasearch—http://ixquick.com/

Search services usually list broad categories of subjects, plus they may offer other features such as "Random Links" or "Top 25 Sites," and customization options. Each one also has a search field. Type in a **keyword,** a word or short phrase that describes your area of interest. Then click Search or press the Enter key on your keyboard. Seconds later a list of Web sites known as "hits" will be displayed containing the word you specified in the search field. Scroll through the list and click the page you wish to view.

So far this sounds simple, doesn't it? The tricky part about doing a search on the Internet is that a single keyword may yield a hundred or more sites. Plus, you may find many topics you don't need.

For example, suppose you are writing a science paper about the planet Saturn. If you type the word *Saturn* into the search field, you'll turn up some articles about the planet, but you'll also get articles about NASA's Saturn rockets and Saturn, the automobile company.

SEARCH SMART

Listed below are a few pointers on how to narrow your search, save time, and search *smart* on the Net. Not all search strategies, however, work with all search engines.

Guidelines for Smart Searching

- The keyword or words that you enter have a lot to do with the accuracy of your search. Focus your search by adding the word "and" or the + sign followed by another descriptive word. For example, try "Saturn" again, but this time, add "Saturn + space." Adding a third word, "Saturn + space + rings," will narrow the field even more.

- Specify geographical areas using the word "near" between keywords as in "islands near Florida." This lets you focus on specific regions.

- To broaden your search, add the word "or" between keywords. For example, "sailboats or catamarans."

- Help the search engine recognize familiar phrases by putting words that go together in quotes such as "Tom and Jerry" or "bacon and eggs."

- Sometimes the site you come up with is in the ballpark of what you are searching for, but it is not exactly what you need. Skim the text quickly anyway. It may give you ideas for more accurate keywords. There might also be links listed to other sites that are just the right resource you need.

- Try out different search engines. Each service uses slightly different methods of searching, so you may get different results using the same keywords.

- Check the spelling of the keywords you are using. A misspelled word can send a search engine in the wrong direction. Also, be careful how you use capital letters. By typing the word *Gold,* some search services will only bring up articles that include the word with a capital *G*.

You can learn more about evaluating online sources on pages 335–336.

INTERNET + MEDIA CENTER = INFORMATION POWERHOUSE

Although the Internet is a limitless treasure chest of information, remember that it's not catalogued. It can be tricky to locate the information you need, and sometimes that information is not reliable. The library is a well-organized storehouse of knowledge, but it has more limited resources. If you use the Internet *and* your local media center, you've got everything you need to create well-researched articles, reports, and papers.

 Using the Internet and Media Center

Use the Internet to

- get great ideas for topics to write about
- gather information about your topic from companies, colleges and universities, and professional organizations
- connect with recognized experts in your field of interest
- connect with other people who are interested in the same subject and who can put you in touch with other sources

Use the Media Center to

- find reliable sources of information either in print or online
- get background information on your topic
- cross-check the accuracy and credibility of online information and authors.

TIME OUT TO **REFLECT**

How does the Internet compare to some of the print resources you have used in terms of access, quality, and reliability? Why might one resource—print or online—be better than another? What strategies have you learned that will make researching easier in the future? What notes would you make to improve your reference skills for the future? Record your thoughts in your Learning Log.

Research: Synthesizing, Organizing, and Presenting

Like a cook, when you are putting together a research report you need to prepare your kitchen and gather your ingredients together before mixing. In the previous chapter you did just that. You

- chose and limited a subject
- posed a major research question
- developed a research plan
- used your library and media center to find sources
- evaluated those sources
- took notes

The activities in this chapter will take you through the rest of the process of preparing a research report.

Writing Project — Research Report

Digging Into My Culture *Complete a research report on your culture, focusing on what makes it unique and what it means to you.*

Review In the previous chapter you gathered and organized information for your research report, using your major research question as the focus for your inquiry and refining that question. You have taken notes from sources to record information to use when answering your research question, and have converted both graphic and written material from your sources to written notes for your report. You may have used a word processing program to take notes as you accumulated new information. In this chapter you will learn how to take the information you have gathered and use it to write the research report itself.

ELEMENTS OF A RESEARCH REPORT

Like most other compositions, a research report has three main parts: an introduction, a body, and a conclusion. In addition, a research report usually contains some form of references—such as parenthetical citations or footnotes—and a works-cited page that, like a bibliography, lists all the sources you used. The following chart shows the function of each part of a report.

STRUCTURE OF A RESEARCH REPORT

PART	PURPOSE
Title	Suggests the subject of the research report
Introduction	Captures the readers' attention Provides necessary background information related to the subject Contains the thesis statement
Body	Supports the thesis statement and related claims Has paragraphs that each cover one topic or subtopic Uses graphics and illustrations to explain concepts
Conclusion	Brings the research to a close, often by restating the thesis in different words
Citations	Give credit to other authors for their words and ideas
Works Cited	Lists all the sources that you have cited in the research report Appears at the end of the research report

1 Developing a Thesis

During your research you will likely discover what you want to say about your subject. After following your research plan to gather information and take notes from authoritative sources, your next step is to pull together your ideas and information to form a working thesis. A **working thesis** is a statement that expresses a possible main idea for your research paper. In a research paper, as in a critical essay, you may frame your thesis as a statement that you intend to prove is true. You then give the information you researched as evidence to support your thesis. In such a paper it is necessary to identify the major issues and debates related to your major research topic. Your analysis should reflect a clear point of view on the issue.

You may change your working thesis as you continue to develop your research report. When organizing your notes to write a first draft, you may even think of new ideas that lead you to change your thesis and do additional research. You may modify your working thesis at any stage in the process of planning, drafting, and revising your report.

To create your working thesis, think about what you have discovered about your subject. For instance, a student writing a research report on *The Wizard of Oz* gathered information about how the special effects in that film were made. One example was how the filmmakers used a 35-foot wind sock to create the impression of a tornado. From this and similar examples, the writer concluded that the special-effects creators had used great ingenuity. A working thesis based on this conclusion was easy to write.

EXAMPLE: Working Thesis

Limited Subject	special effects in *The Wizard of Oz*
Working Thesis Statement	Much wizardry went into creating the special effects in *The Wizard of Oz*.

PROJECT PREP *Prewriting* *Working Thesis*

Using all your notes for your research report, develop three or four possible theses. Select the one you like best as the working thesis of your report. Share them with your writing group for feedback and make adjustments as you see fit following the discussion.

② Organizing Your Notes

As you take notes, you will begin to notice closely related ideas that could be grouped together into a single category. Building a system of categories is the first step in organizing your notes into an outline.

To create meaningful categories, review the information in your note cards, looking for ideas that are closely related. Then think of a category that would cover each group of related ideas. Using a graphic organizer may help you focus your thinking and sort your ideas. Once you have determined your categories, you can easily sort through your notes and clip together all the cards that belong in each category.

If some of your notes do not fit into any of the categories, clip them together separately for possible use in your introduction or conclusion. After you have arranged your categories in a logical order, wrap the whole bundle of note cards together with a rubber band to prevent losses or mix-ups.

The writer of the research report on the special effects in *The Wizard of Oz* initially sorted the notes into the following categories.

MODEL: Classifying Details Part I

Category 1	General information: cost, year of release, quotations from reviews, name of special-effects director
Category 2	The tornado
Category 3	The melting witch
Category 4	Glinda's arrival in the glass bubble
Category 5	The flying monkeys
Category 6	The horse-of-a-different-color
Category 7	The crystal ball
Category 8	The lifting and dropping of the house

After reviewing all of the information in the eight categories, the writer decided to combine some categories to create a smaller number of them to serve as main topics in an outline. For example, the special effects in categories 3, 4, 7, and 8 had something in common: they were all simple tricks that were easy to achieve.

The following revised organization consists of only four categories, which are broad enough to cover all the information.

MODEL: Classifying Details Part II

Category 1	General information
Category 2	Hardest effect to achieve—tornado
Category 3	Simple tricks: house being picked up and dropped, crystal ball, glass bubble, melting witch
Category 4	Simple tricks that proved difficult: flying monkeys, horse-of-a-different-color

Based on these categories, the writer chose to arrange the information in order of importance. For a memorable effect, the writer decided to place the more interesting information at the beginning of the report to draw in readers and at the end of the report in order to finish up with a bang.

Always think back to your purpose, audience, and context or occasion as well. The organizing structure of your report must be appropriate for these.

Writing Tip

Group your notes into three to five main categories that are broad enough to include all your information.

PROJECT PREP *Prewriting* *Organization of Information*

Sort your notes for your research report into three to five broad categories that you will use later to organize an outline of your report. Organize your note cards and keep them banded together in categories in your writing folder. There are a number of software programs that you can download from the Internet that allow you to keep notes in user-defined categories and save the information securely on your computer. Do not destroy your notes until you are absolutely sure you won't need them again.

Think Critically

Synthesizing

Often in your research projects, you will need to **synthesize,** or merge together, information from different kinds of sources. The following diagram shows the steps you can take to synthesize information.

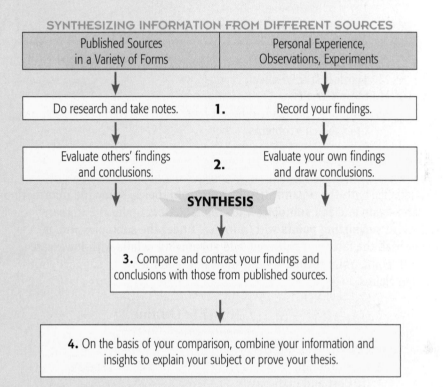

SYNTHESIZING INFORMATION FROM DIFFERENT SOURCES

Published Sources in a Variety of Forms	Personal Experience, Observations, Experiments

1. Do research and take notes. / Record your findings.

2. Evaluate others' findings and conclusions. / Evaluate your own findings and draw conclusions.

SYNTHESIS

3. Compare and contrast your findings and conclusions with those from published sources.

4. On the basis of your comparison, combine your information and insights to explain your subject or prove your thesis.

Thinking Practice

Choose one of the research questions below. Then write a short paper synthesizing information from both published sources and personal study.

1. What were the common forms of marriage ceremony and celebration in your grandparents' native land?

2. Who are the heroes that are popular in the culture into which you were born?

3. Are special privileges afforded people based on their age, economic status, or gender in this culture?

③ Outlining

The final step in the prewriting stage is to develop an **outline** as a guide to drafting. Your outline is the framework for your report and is based on the notes you took on your subject. In your outline, each main category becomes a main topic with a Roman numeral. The outline covers only the body of your report. See the model below for the body of the report on special effects in *The Wizard of Oz*.

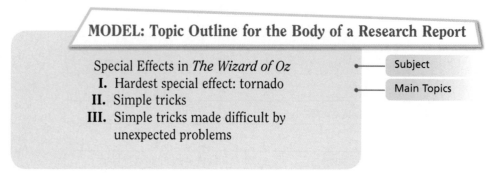

MODEL: Topic Outline for the Body of a Research Report

Special Effects in *The Wizard of Oz* — Subject
  I. Hardest special effect: tornado — Main Topics
 II. Simple tricks
III. Simple tricks made difficult by unexpected problems

When you are satisfied with the organization of your main topics, study the information in your note cards again and add **subtopics** with capital letters under the Roman numerals. Then add **supporting points** with numbers under the subtopics and, if necessary to cover all the facts you gathered, add **supporting details** with lowercase letters under each point. Your outline should show how you intend to support your thesis and related claims.

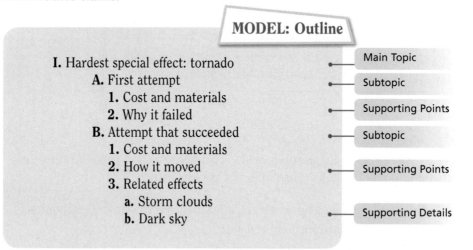

MODEL: Outline

I. Hardest special effect: tornado — Main Topic
  A. First attempt — Subtopic
    1. Cost and materials — Supporting Points
    2. Why it failed
  B. Attempt that succeeded — Subtopic
    1. Cost and materials
    2. How it moved — Supporting Points
    3. Related effects
      a. Storm clouds
      b. Dark sky — Supporting Details

Look over the expanded outline for a research report on the following page, and use it as a guide as you create your own outline.

MODEL: Expanded Outline for the Body of a Research Report

I. Hardest special effect: tornado   ← Main Topic
   A. First attempt   ← Subtopic
      1. Cost and materials   ← Supporting Points
      2. Why it failed
   B. Attempt that succeeded   ← Subtopic
      1. Cost and materials   ← Supporting Points
      2. How it moved
      3. Related effects
         a. Storm clouds   ← Supporting Details
         b. Dark sky

II. Simple tricks   ← Main Topic
   A. Lifting and dropping the house
   B. Crystal ball
   C. Glinda's glass bubble

III. Simple tricks made difficult by unexpected problems   ← Main Topic
   A. Flying monkeys
      1. Technique
      2. Problems
   B. Horse-of-a-different-color
      1. Technique
      2. Problems
         a. Objection of ASPCA
         b. Horses' licking off colored gelatin

PROJECT PREP *Prewriting* *Outline*

Review your categories and notes on your research topic and write an outline for the body of the report. Arrange your ideas in a logical order suited to your topic, audience, purpose, and context. Share your outline with your group for feedback.

The Power of Language ⚡

Adverbial Clauses: Tip the Scale

Since the elementary grades, you have been using adverbial clauses in your speech and writing. You create adverbial clauses by putting a subordinating word like *when, if, because, until, while, since,* or *although* in front of a sentence. (See pages 644–646.) Take, for example, this simple sentence:

The seeds had grown into stalks.

You can turn this sentence into a subordinate clause by adding the word *when*:

When the seeds had grown into stalks

But, of course, a subordinate clause is not a sentence, so the adverbial clause you've created cannot stand alone. An independent clause must be added to create a meaningful sentence, such as:

When the seeds had grown into stalks, we would pull them up.

You have now created a fully explanatory sentence with an adverbial clause at the beginning and an independent clause at the end. Writers often use adverbial clauses like these when they want to "tip the scale," subordinating one idea to another. Below are more examples from *When Heaven and Earth Changed Places* (pages 325–327).

After the hard crust had been turned and the clods broken up with mallets to the size of gravel, we had to wet it down with water conveyed from nearby ponds or rivers.

Although we grew many crops around Ky La, the most important by far was rice.

Because the rice was freshly cut, it had to dry in the sun for several days.

Punctuation Tip

When subordinate clauses **begin a sentence,** they should be **followed by a comma.** Usually a comma is not used if the subordinate clause comes at the end.

Try It Yourself

Write five sentences with adverbial clauses on the topic of your project. You may use the suggested subordinating words on this page, or you may draw from the list on page 645. If possible, use these sentences in your draft. Otherwise, during revision, see if there are places in your writing where subordinating one complete sentence to another in this way would have a strong effect.

As you draft, concentrate on getting your ideas down as clearly as you can without worrying about spelling or grammar. You will go back over your draft and polish your writing later, but for now, follow the steps below and start writing.

1 Refining Your Thesis Statement

Use your thesis statement, outline, and notes as you begin to structure your draft. In a research report, the introduction makes your thesis clear to readers. As you draft your introduction, refine your working thesis into a tight, appropriate statement of your main idea and/or the point you want to prove.

Guidelines for Refining a Thesis Statement

• Make the thesis statement specific enough so the main point of your research paper is clear to the readers.
• Make the thesis statement general enough to include all the main topics in your outline.

● Practice Your Skills

Refining Thesis Statements

Rewrite each thesis statement to include all the main topics in the outline.

1. Some lifesaving techniques are simple enough for anyone to learn.
    I. Heimlich maneuver
    II. Cardiopulmonary resuscitation (CPR)
    III. Techniques only doctors should use

2. The Constitution of the United States grew out of the Articles of Confederation.
    I. Summary of Articles of Confederation
    II. Changes from Articles to Constitution
    III. Constitution as model for other countries

PROJECT PREP *Drafting* **Refined Thesis Statement**

In your writing group, examine each author's thesis statement in light of the outline he or she has prepared for the research. Help each author refine the thesis statement so that it aligns with the research question and information gathered for the report.

2 Using Sources

As you consult your note cards for the details you will need to draft the body of your research paper, think of ways to work your source materials smoothly into your own writing. Remember that you need to cite your sources for all information you use in your report. The following tips may help you.

HERE'S HOW Tips for Using Sources

- Use a quotation to finish a sentence you have started.

- Quote a whole sentence. If you omit words from a quoted sentence, indicate the omission with an ellipsis (. . .).

- Quote only a few words as part of a sentence.

- Paraphrase information from a source. When you paraphrase, reword the text in your own words. When you summarize on note cards, you are often paraphrasing. Cite your source even if you are only paraphrasing.

EXAMPLE: Paraphrasing

Original Source "To match the appearance of the swirling pools of water in the real Yellowstone, Alex used evaporated milk and white poster paint, mixed with water and poured into the set's pools. The pressure of the steam caused just the proper amount of movement in the pale white whirlpools and eddies duplicated in this enormous outdoor set."

Paraphrase With condensed milk, paint, and steam, Alex made a model of a Yellowstone hot spring.

PROJECT PREP *Drafting* *Using Sources*

On your project topic, practice using sources as you draft by following these directions:

1. Write a sentence that ends with a quotation from one of your sources.

2. Write three sentences, making one of the sentences a direct quotation from the source.

3. Write a sentence that includes only a few words that are quoted from the source.

4. Write a sentence paraphrasing information from a source. If you can use these sentences in your draft, feel free to do so. If not, watch for opportunities to use quotations in all the ways described in the Tips above.

③ Studying a Model Draft of a Research Report

The following passage is the final draft of the research report on special effects in *The Wizard of Oz*. As you read it, notice how it follows both the **Structure of a Research Report** on page 363 and the outline on pages 368–369. You will also see how the writer added transitions—such as *although, instead, first,* and *meanwhile*—to connect the parts of the outline into coherent paragraphs.

Your report may be more complex or have a different purpose than this brief model. If you are trying to prove a certain thesis, identify the major issues and debates on the topic and present your ideas in a logical order. Present enough evidence to support the thesis and any related claims.

As you read, notice how the writer incorporated source material, with quotes and paraphrases worked into the sentences and paragraphs. You will see that sources are cited in parentheses in the body of the report. The writer chose this method of citing sources, called **parenthetical citation,** instead of using footnotes at the bottom of each page. A parenthetical citation briefly identifies the source and page number within each sentence in which the source of information must be credited. When you finish reading the model report, you will learn more about citing sources.

> **MODEL: Draft of a Research Report**
>
> ## The Wizardry of Oz   — Title
>
>   *The Wizard of Oz* was released in 1939 after two years in production at a cost of three million dollars. One reviewer remarked that "the wizards of Hollywood" had produced a "delightful piece of wonderworking" (Nugent). The "wonderworking" referred to the movie's special effects, such as the "realistically contrived cyclone" praised by *Newsweek* ("Fabulous Land of Oz" 23). Other reviewers raved about the Good Witch's arriving — Introduction in a golden bubble, the Wicked Witch's skywriting and her later melting away to nothing, the monkeys' flying, the trees' talking, and the horse's changing colors. The movie was nominated for an Oscar in 1939 for these creative effects by special effects director A. Arnold (Buddy) Gillespie (Dirks). Although these effects looked effortlessly magical, they were created without the computer animation familiar to viewers today (Berardinelli). Much real wizardry went into creating the special effects in *The Wizard of Oz*. — Thesis Statement

The most challenging effect was the twister. Gillespie knew he "couldn't go to Kansas and wait for a tornado to come down and pick up a house" (Harmetz 244). Instead he got an idea from watching cone-shaped wind socks used at airports to indicate wind direction. First he made a similar cone out of rubber at a cost of $8,000; but when the rubber did not twist properly, he had to start over. After several experiments he built a 35-foot miniature cyclone out of muslin. He attached it to a machine that moved along a track and blew a dusty substance through the model twister to create a dust cloud. The $12,000 machine moved and twisted the muslin cone in a convincing way. Meanwhile a worker perched above the machine made huge clouds of yellowish-black smoke from carbon and sulfur. In front of the cameras, glass panels covered with gray cotton gave the tornado scene a dark, menacing quality on film and at the same time hid all the machinery (Harmetz 244, 246–48).

First Body Paragraph (Roman numeral I in outline)

A much simpler effect was the illusion that the cyclone lifted Dorothy's house off the ground. Gillespie's crew filmed a three-foot-high model of the house falling onto a floor painted like the sky. Then the film was simply run in reverse (Harmetz 249). The crystal ball in the witch's castle was also a simple trick. It was a big glass bowl placed over a small screen. Film shot earlier was projected onto the screen, giving the illusion of real images appearing in the crystal ball. Another simple effect was the glass bubble that transports Glinda into Munchkinland. Gillespie's crew first filmed a silver ball, "just like a Christmas tree ornament, only bigger," by moving the camera closer and closer, making the ball seem to grow larger (Harmetz 254–55). Then, by layering the films, they added the scene of Munchkinland and Billie Burke, the actress playing Glinda.

Second Body Paragraph (Roman numeral II in outline)

Some effects that should have been simple became complicated because of unexpected problems. The flying monkeys, for example, were models suspended from a trolley, attached by 2,200 piano wires that moved them and their wings (McClelland 92). The wires kept breaking, however, which forced the crew to reshoot the scene repeatedly. Another problem was the horse-of-a-different-color, the creature that keeps changing hues. Six matching white horses were used for the trick photography—each

Third Body Paragraph (Roman numeral III in outline)

colored a different shade. When the crew proposed to paint the horses to achieve the desired effect, however, the American Society for the Prevention of Cruelty to Animals protested. As a creative solution, the horses were "painted" with colored gelatin, but the crew had to work fast because the horses kept licking it off (McClelland 92–93)!

While the cyclone was the most difficult effect, the melting disappearance of the Wicked Witch was the simplest of all. "As for how I melted," said Margaret Hamilton, the actress playing the witch, "I went down through the floor on an elevator . . . leaving some fizzling dry ice and my floor length costume" (McClelland 96–97). While the demise of the Wicked Witch was truly effortless, the other tricks and illusions in *The Wizard of Oz* required both effort and skill. One film critic describes the effects as "glorious in that old Hollywood way" (Ebert). Another concludes, "Because of the power of imagination, the film transcends the limitations of the techniques used" (Berardinelli). Most agree that it is the combination of the special effects and the universal appeal of the story that make *The Wizard of Oz* a truly magical film.

Conclusion

CHAPTER 11

Works Cited

Berardinelli, James. Rev. of *The Wizard of Oz,* dir. Victor Fleming. *Reelviews.net.* 1998. Web. 17 Mar. 2009.

Dirks, Tim. Rev. of *The Wizard of Oz,* dir. Victor Fleming. *Filmsite.org.* American Movie Classics, 2009. Web. 17 Mar. 2009.

Ebert, Roger. Rev. of *The Wizard of Oz,* dir. Victor Fleming. *RogerEbert.com.* Chicago Sun Times, 22 Dec. 1996. Web. 17 Mar. 2009.

"The Fabulous Land of Oz: Dream World via Cyclonic Ride Recreated in Technicolor." *Newsweek* 21 Aug. 1939: 23–24. Print.

Harmetz, Aljean. *The Making of* The Wizard of Oz. New York: Delta, 1989. Print.

McClelland, Doug. *Down the Yellow Brick Road: The Making of* The Wizard of Oz. New York: Bonanza, 1989. Print.

Nugent, Frank S. "The Screen in Review: 'The Wizard of Oz,' Produced by the Wizards of Hollywood, Works Its Magic on the Capitol's Screen." *New York Times* 18 Aug. 1939: 16. *ProQuest Historical Newspapers The New York Times (1851–2005)*. Web. 17 Mar. 2009.

● **Practice Your Skills**

Recognizing Transitions

Reread the research report draft. Answer the questions below.

1. What was the most challenging special effect in the film?
2. What transitional phrase is used to begin the second paragraph in the body?
3. Is "As a creative solution, the horses were 'painted' with colored gelatin," part of a transition sentence? Why or why not?
4. Think of another way to write the transition sentence used in the conclusion of this draft.

editing ☆

The following sentence has been paraphrased from the writer's note card and contains some solid information. However, it is needlessly wordy. Make the sentence more "fuel efficient."

> The wealth and richness of Latin American culture is the result of a great deal of bountiful influences, not the least of which can be seen as those coming from Pre-Columbian peoples.

PROJECT PREP *Drafting* *First Draft*

Following your outline, write a first draft of your report. Be sure your thesis statement achieves the goals outlined on pages 364 and 371. Add a parenthetical citation each time you include a quotation or an idea that is not your own. Simply identify the source and page number in parentheses, as in the model. As long as you know which source you mean, you can rewrite each citation in the proper form if necessary when you revise your draft. Share your work with your writing group and make notes on their feedback to use when you revise.

Citing Sources

Laws protect authors, illustrators, photographers, and publishers whose materials have been copyrighted. Using another person's words, pictures, or ideas without giving proper credit is called **plagiarism,** a serious offense. Whenever you use source materials, therefore, you must give credit to the authors—even if you only paraphrase. You have already taken steps to avoid plagiarism by taking notes in your own words and by recording the author, the page number, and the exact words of any quotation you plan to use. The chief methods of citing sources are parenthetical citations, as you have seen, and footnotes or endnotes.

PARENTHETICAL CITATIONS

The following guidelines and examples will help you use parenthetical citations correctly. Keep in mind that the citations in parentheses are intentionally brief. Their purpose is to provide the reader with only enough information to identify the source of the material you have borrowed. Readers then refer to the works-cited page at the end of your report for complete information about each source.

MODERN LANGUAGE ASSOCIATION (MLA) STYLE GUIDELINES	
Book by One Author	Give author's last name and a page reference: (Harmetz 244).
Book by Two or More Authors	Give both authors' names and a page reference: (Morella and Epstein 27).
Article; Author Named	Give author's last name and a page reference, unless the article is a single page: (Rhodes).
Article; Author Unnamed	Give shortened form of title of article (omit initial *A, An,* or *The*) and page reference: ("Fabulous Land of Oz" 24).
Article in a Reference Work; Author Unnamed	Give title (full or shortened) and page number, unless title is entered alphabetically in an encyclopedia: ("Special Effects").
Online Article; Author Named	Give author's last name; include a page or paragraph number only if the online source includes them; do not use page references from a print version of the article: (Nugent).
Online Article or Web Page; No Author Named	Give title of article or Web page, as used on the works-cited page: ("There's No Place Like Oz").

The *Chicago Manual of Style* uses a slightly different style of parenthetical citations. This style is recommended for research reports in the physical sciences and most social sciences. Parenthetical citations include the author's name, the date of publication, and a page reference. This style is similar to that in the *Publication Manual of the American Psychological Association*, which is now focused on professionals writing articles for publication.

A useful guide for these parenthetical citations is Kate Turabian, *A Manual for Writers of Research Papers, Theses, and Dissertations*, which is based on *The Chicago Manual of Style*.

TURABIAN *(Chicago Manual of Style)* GUIDELINES

Book or Article by One Author	Give author's last name and date of publication, then a page reference separated by a comma: (Harmetz 1989, 244).
Book or Article by Two Authors	Give both authors' names and date of publication, then a page reference: (Morella and Epstein 1969, 27).
Article; Author Unnamed	Use the name of the publication in place of the author, then give the date of publication and page reference: (*Newsweek* 1939, 24).

No matter which style you use, parenthetical citations should be placed as close as possible to the words or ideas being credited. To avoid interrupting the flow of the sentence, place them at the end of a phrase, a clause, or a sentence. If a parenthetical citation falls at the end of a sentence, place it before the period. If you are using quotation marks, the citation goes after the closing quotation mark but before the period.

FOOTNOTES AND ENDNOTES

If your teacher directs you to use footnotes or endnotes instead of parenthetical citations, you will use a different form. For either footnotes or endnotes, you put a small numeral halfway above the line immediately after the borrowed material. This numeral is called a **superscript.** It refers readers to a note at the bottom, or foot, of the page. As the examples show, the notes themselves are not introduced with a superscript number. Your teacher will tell you whether to number your notes consecutively throughout your report or to begin the first note on each page with the numeral *1*. Endnotes are the same as footnotes, except that they are listed at the end of the paper.

The Turabian *Manual* is also a useful guide for footnotes or endnotes. This *notes-bibliography* style of citations is used primarily in the humanities and some social sciences. See the following page for examples.

TURABIAN (Chicago Manual Of Style) GUIDELINES FOR FOOTNOTES AND ENDNOTES

General Reference Works	1. *World Book Encyclopedia*, 2009 ed., s.v. "Special Effects." [s.v. = "under the word"]
Books by One Author	2. Aljean Harmetz, *The Making of "The Wizard of Oz"* (New York: Delta, 1989), 244.
Books by Two or More Authors	3. Joe Morella and Edward Epstein, *Judy: The Films and Career of Judy Garland* (New York: Citadel Press, 1969), 34.
Articles in Magazines	4. Jesse Rhodes, "There's No Place Like Home," *Smithsonian*, January 2009, 25.
Articles in Newspapers	5. Neil Genzliger, "Dorothy and Her Friends, Bitten by the Jitterbug," *New York Times*, March 31, 2009.
Articles from Online Databases	6. Frank S. Nugent, "The Screen in Review: 'The Wizard of Oz,' Produced by the Wizards of Hollywood, Works Its Magic on the Capitol's Screen," *New York Times (1857-Current file)*, August 18, 1939, http://www.proquest.com/ (accessed March 17, 2009).
Articles from Web Sites	7. James Berardinelli, review of *The Wizard of Oz*, directed by Victor Fleming, Reelviews, 1998, http://www.reelviews.net/movies/w/wizard_oz.html (accessed March 17, 2009).

Whenever you cite a work that you previously cited in full, you can use a shortened form of footnote for all repeated references to that work.

First Reference   2. Aljean Harmetz, *The Making of "The Wizard of Oz"* (New York: Delta, 1989), 244.

Later Reference   8. Harmetz, 247.

WORKS-CITED PAGE

The sources you cited in your research paper should be listed on a works-cited page at the end of the report. In the research report on *The Wizard of Oz*, for example, the writer added a works-cited page to give a complete list of references for the parenthetical citations in the report (pages 375–376). A **works-cited page** is an alphabetical listing of sources cited in a research report.

On a works-cited page, sources are listed alphabetically by the author's last name or by the title if no author is given. Page numbers are given for articles but usually not for books. The following examples show the correct form for works-cited entries. In each example, note the order of information, the indentation, and the punctuation. When citing online sources, always give the date you accessed the site.

MLA GUIDE TO WORKS-CITED PAGE

General Reference Works	May, Jill P. "Baum, L. Frank." *World Book Encyclopedia.* 2009 ed. Print.
Books by One Author	Harmetz, Aljean. *The Making of* The Wizard of Oz. New York: Delta, 1989. Print.
Books by Two or More Authors	Morella, Joe, and Edward Epstein. *Judy: The Films and Career of Judy Garland.* New York: Citadel, 1969. Print.
Articles; Author Named	Rhodes, Jesse. "There's No Place Like Home." *Smithsonian* Jan. 2009: 25. Print.
Articles; Author Unnamed	"The Fabulous Land of Oz: Dream World via Cyclonic Ride Recreated in Technicolor." *Newsweek* 21 Aug. 1939: 23–24. Print.
Articles in Newspapers	Genzliger, Neil. "Dorothy and Her Friends, Bitten by the Jitterbug." *New York Times* 31 Mar. 2009: A3. Print.
Reviews	Rev. of *The Wizard of Oz*, dir. Victor Fleming. *Senior Scholastic* 18 Sept. 1939: 32–33. Print.
Articles from Online Databases	Nugent, Frank S. "The Screen in Review: 'The Wizard of Oz,' Produced by the Wizards of Hollywood, Works Its Magic on the Capitol's Screen." *New York Times* 18 Aug. 1939: 16. *ProQuest Historical Newspapers The New York Times (1851–2005).* Web. 17 Mar. 2009.
Articles from Web Sites	Berardinelli, James. Rev. of *The Wizard of Oz,* dir. Victor Fleming. *Reelviews.net.* 1998. Web. 17 Mar. 2009.

These entries follow the style recommended in the *MLA Handbook for Writers of Research Papers* (7th ed.). The MLA no longer recommends including URLs for most online sources because they change so frequently. If your teacher asks you to include a URL, enclose it in angle brackets, for example <http://www.reelviews.net/movies/w/wizard_oz.html>, as the last entry in the citation.

Turabian (*The Chicago Manual of Style*) recommends including URLs for most electronic sources. The next page gives examples for entries in a works-cited page using different citation styles.

PROJECT PREP   Drafting   Citations

Review what you have learned about citing sources. Reread your draft and write parenthetical citations in the proper form. Prepare a works-cited page for the end of your report. If you have a source that does not fit one of the categories described, refer to the *MLA Handbook for Writers of Research Papers* for information on how to cite the source.

TURABIAN *(Chicago Manual Of Style)*
BIBLIOGRAPHY STYLE FOR WORKS-CITED PAGE

Books by One Author	Harmetz, Aljean. *The Making of "The Wizard of Oz."* New York: Delta, 1989.
Books by Two or More Authors	Morella, Joe, and Edward Epstein. *Judy: The Films and Career of Judy Garland*. New York: Citadel Press, 1969.
Magazine Articles	Rhodes, Jesse. "There's No Place Like Home." *Smithsonian,* January 2009.
Articles from Online Databases	Nugent, Frank S. "The Screen in Review: 'The Wizard of Oz,' Produced by the Wizards of Hollywood, Works Its Magic on the Capitol's Screen." *New York Times (1857-Current file)*, August 18, 1939. http://www.proquest.com/ (accessed March 17, 2009).
Articles from Web Sites	Berardinelli, James. Review of *The Wizard of Oz*, directed by Victor Fleming. Reelviews, 1998. http://www.reelviews.net/movies/w/wizard_oz.html (accessed March 17, 2009).

TURABIAN *(Chicago Manual Of Style)*
REFERENCE-LIST STYLE FOR WORKS-CITED PAGE

Books by One Author	Harmetz, Aljean. 1989. *The making of "The Wizard of Oz."* New York: Delta.
Books by Two or More Authors	Morella, Joe, and Edward Epstein. 1969. *Judy: The films and career of Judy Garland*. New York: Citadel Press.
Magazine Articles	Rhodes, Jesse. 2009. There's no place like home. *Smithsonian,* January.
Articles from Online Databases	Nugent, Frank S. 1939. The screen in review: 'The Wizard of Oz,' produced by the wizards of Hollywood, works its magic on the Capitol's screen. *New York Times (1857-Current file)*, August 18. http://www.proquest.com/ (accessed March 17, 2009).
Articles from Web Sites	Berardinelli, James. 1998. Review of *The Wizard of Oz*, directed by Victor Fleming. Reelviews. http://www.reelviews.net/movies/w/wizard_oz.html (accessed March 17, 2009).

Use the Turabian bibliography style with footnotes or endnotes; use the reference-list style with parenthetical citations based on the Turabian style. Whatever style you use, use it consistently for all the citations in your paper.

Sometimes your teacher may ask you to include a works-consulted page—often called a **bibliography**—on which you include all the works you consulted but did not necessarily cite in your research report. A works-consulted page or bibliography uses the same form as the works-cited page.

When you finish your draft, do a taste test: Does the report need a little more of this flavor, a little different texture in places? Check first to see whether you have achieved the purpose of your research paper. Then ask yourself: Does the report inform or persuade the audience as fully and accurately as possible?

CHECKING FOR ACCURACY

Check for accuracy in your use of sources by examining all the quotes in your report. Have you accurately represented each source? Have you quoted any source out of context, thus distorting the author's real meaning? Have you used enough different sources so that you are not relying too heavily on one viewpoint? The more accurate and balanced your report is, the greater will be its power to inform or persuade.

CONFERENCING TO REVISE

A second opinion is valuable when you are preparing the final draft of your research report. If possible, ask a reader to review and critique your work. Specifically, ask your reviewer to summarize in his or her own words the main idea of your report and to point out any words, sentences, or paragraphs that seem unclear. Then, as you revise, take into account the reader's specific comments and suggestions. If your reviewer cannot summarize your main idea, you may need to make your focus or thesis clearer. The following checklist will help you in the revising stage.

 Evaluation Checklist for Revising

✓ Does your research report include an introduction with a thesis statement? (pages 363–364)
✓ Does the body adequately develop and support the thesis statement and related claims? (pages 363 and 365–366)
✓ Is your research paper accurate and balanced? (pages 377–382)
✓ Do the ideas in your research report follow a logical development? (pages 365–369 and 373)
✓ Does your research report reflect a clearly stated point of view? (page 364)
✓ Do your research paper and the paragraphs within it have unity, coherence, and clarity? (pages 82–83 and 134)
✓ Are your sentences concise and your words precise? (pages 46–54 and 63–66)
✓ Did you use and cite sources correctly? (pages 377–381)
✓ Does your report use graphics or illustrations if needed? (pages 478–480)
✓ Did you add a suitable conclusion? (page 363)
✓ Did you include a works-cited page? (pages 379–381)
✓ Did you add an appropriate title? (pages 231 and 363)
✓ Did you use a style manual to format written materials? (pages 30 and 377–379)

You can also use the rubric on the following page to help you make revisions.

Ideas	4 The text conveys a clear and original thesis statement with abundant supporting details and is well chosen for the purpose and audience.	3 The text conveys a thesis statement with ample details and suits the purpose and audience.	2 The text conveys a thesis statement with some supporting details and suits the purpose and audience.	1 The text does not convey a thesis statement and fails to suit the purpose and audience.
Organization	4 The organization is clear with abundant transitions.	3 A few ideas seem out of place or transitions are missing.	2 Many ideas seem out of place and transitions are missing.	1 The organization is unclear and hard to follow.
Voice	4 The voice sounds engaging and is appropriate for purpose and audience.	3 The voice sounds natural and is appropriate for purpose and audience.	2 The voice sounds mostly unnatural with some exceptions.	1 The voice sounds mostly unnatural.
Word Choice	4 Words are specific. All terms are explained or defined.	3 Words are specific and some terms are explained or defined.	2 Some words are overly general and some technical terms are not explained.	1 Most words are overly general.
Sentence Fluency	4 Varied sentences flow smoothly.	3 Most sentences are varied and flow smoothly.	2 Some sentences are varied but some are choppy.	1 Sentences are not varied and are choppy.
Conventions	4 Punctuation, usage, and spelling are correct. The Power Rules are all followed.	3 Punctuation, usage, and spelling are mainly correct and Power Rules are all followed.	2 Some punctuation, usage, and spelling are incorrect but all Power Rules are followed.	1 There are many errors and at least one failure to follow a Power Rule.

PROJECT PREP *Development, Accuracy, Style*

1. Evaluate your report using the checklist on page 382 and do more research if necessary to develop your ideas. Be sure you check the accuracy of any information you obtain, especially information from the Internet.

2. Then exchange papers with a partner and use the rubric above to assess the report before the final edit. When you have both finished your evulation, meet to discuss it. Make any further changes you feel are necessary after your conference.

As you edit your work, pay special attention, as always, to the Power Rules.

The Language of **Power**   *Sound-Alikes*

Power Rule: For sound-alikes and certain words that sound almost alike, choose the word with your intended meaning. (See pages 796–811.)

See It in Action In the first draft, the writer of *The Wizard of Oz* report wrote:

> The principle actor in the film, Judy Garland, who's voice is strongly associated with the song "Somewhere Over the Rainbow," had no idea initially weather she would get the role of Dorothy.

During editing, however, the writer recognized that several words that sound exactly like other words were used incorrectly. The main actor is the *principal* actor; *who's* is a contraction meaning *who is* while *whose* shows possession; and *weather* indicates atmospheric conditions while *whether* is a conjunction expressing doubt. None of these misuses would be discovered by a spell-check on a computer, so learn as many of these sound-alikes as you can.

Remember It Record this rule in the Power Rule section of your Personalized Editing Checklist.

Use It Read through your research report to make sure you have not used sound-alikes incorrectly. Be aware of such troublesome pairs as *piece/peace, course/coarse,* and *which/witch.*

PROJECT PREP **Editing** *Final Draft*

Check your work for grammar, usage, mechanics, and spelling and refer to your Personalized Editing Checklist. Review all the Power Rules and read your report one more time to catch any Power Rule errors you may have made. Also check for places where you can tighten and refine your writing by editing out needless words and substituting sharper, more precise words for vague and general words.

As you review your edited manuscript, consider where you might be able to use graphics and/or illustrations to explain concepts and ideas. Use a software tool to help you create graphics and illustrations and place them in your report. For example, stills or even video clips from *The Wizard of Oz* would clarify the effects, especially for people who may not remember the movie well or who may never have seen it.

CHAPTER 11

Publishing Options for Research Reports

- A magazine that publishes articles on the subject
- A Web site devoted to similar subjects
- A video using text from the report along with images illustrating the text
- An entry on a blog

PROJECT PREP **Publishing** *Peer Evaluation*

Produce a final draft of your research report using a style manual or the guidelines for correct manuscript form on page 32. Use graphics or illustrations to help explain concepts where appropriate. Exchange papers with a writing partner and read one another's reports carefully. Give any suggestions on how to improve the final version of the report for publishing. Use your writing partner's suggestions to prepare a final, publishable version of your research report. (See page 328).

 TIME OUT TO REFLECT

Think about the process you used in writing your research paper. What resources did you find useful? How will you go about finding new resources in the future? How have your research and writing skills improved?

In the Media

Documentaries

Video and film documentaries are images, interviews, and narration woven together to present a powerful research report. Their subjects may range from teeanagers who dream of being star basketball players to the unseen life of bugs. Some documentaries have helped bring about positive changes. A documentary highlighting the poor living conditions of migrant farm workers might spur change. Others may tell a moving true-life story.

Making a full-scale documentary is expensive and time-consuming. Yet anyone with a critical mind, an observant eye, a good team to work with, and access to video recording and editing tools can create a short documentary. The following activities will guide you. Work in groups of about six students each.

Begin by Viewing

As a first step, view as many documentaries as you can, either from the library or on television. As you watch, think about the following:

Who made the documentary and why?

What is the intended audience?

What messages or themes are stated directly and which are implied?

What might the effect be on its audience?

What effect did it have on you?

When group members have seen at least two documentaries, compare responses. Make a list of features common to the best. Write up this list and save it for later use.

Develop and Research the Concept

As a group, choose a concept for your documentary. Keep in mind that you will need to have access to places and people you want to capture on film. For example, does anyone you know work in a hospital emergency room? At your favorite restaurant? Who will be your intended audience and what distinctive point of view do you want to convey? Will your documentary be strictly informational, or will it be critical or praising? What theme do you want to express or imply? Summarize your concept in a paragraph. Then you can begin your research. Whom do you need to interview? Keep good notes as each team member gathers information. Assign each group member a job, such as writer, director, or editor. Draw upon each person's special skills in assigning roles.

Creating a Three-Minute Documentary

Use the section called *Electronic Publishing* (pages 473–487) as you follow the process sketched out below.

Prepare a **treatment** in which you organize your ideas and identify people to interview and live-action or background footage to shoot. Bear in mind that three minutes is a very short time.

Next, create a script that covers everything that is seen and heard in the film. For a documentary, the script contains all narration, dialogue, music, and sound effects, plus descriptions of the characters, any sets, props, or costumes, plus all camera shots and movements, special visual effects, and onscreen titles or graphic elements. Anything that is left out of the script will likely be overlooked and omitted from the final production. So write this document carefully.

Record your video footage, including live interviews, background, and live-action shots. Take more footage than you think you'll need. Remember, you can edit out all but the best. Keep "log sheets" to record everything you have shot. Also take any still photographs that may be needed and record any additional sounds.

View everything you have shot with a critical eye. Do you have what you need to flesh out your concept? If not, shoot what you need.

Using your treatment as a guide, do a **rough edit** of your footage. Once you see your shots in place, make sure they are ordered the way you want. Go back to your list of features that good documentaries share. Reshoot and re-edit as necessary.

Make a **final cut** that clarifies and enhances the message of your documentary.

Determine what else you may need to weave the shots together and make your points effectively. Music? Narration? Titles? Add these elements.

Showing Your Video

Share your documentary with your class and ask for feedback. Meet with your group after the showing and discuss those responses. Also discuss what you learned in the process and what you would do differently to improve your next documentary.

TIME OUT TO REFLECT

You are surrounded by electronic media—television, the Internet, radio—and receive hundreds of messages every day. Compare the impact of electronic media with that of the written word. What can electronic media do that print materials cannot do? What can the printed word do that eletronic media cannot? Record your thoughts in your Learning Log.

Writing Lab

Project Corner

Speak and Listen Discuss It

In groups of five, **plan and present a panel discussion** on the subject of cultural traditions. What purpose do they serve in the lives of the people who take part in them? What would be lost and what would be gained if the traditions were abandoned? In your discussion, be prepared to use specific details and examples so you can describe traditions effectively.

Collaborate and Create
Write a Summary

Work with two other students who wrote on the same topic as you did to **create a summary** of your projects. (See pages 337 and 397 for help with summarizing.) Figure out the process you will follow to complete the summary, and assign each group member a task. In the summary, use transitions to connect the various parts, and include direct quotes from each paper.

Experiment Try a Different Form

Review the suggested project forms on page 328. Think about how your project would be different if it were in one of those forms you didn't use or another that you can think of. Choose a part of your project and **recast it in that new form.** What changes would you need to make? Write a brief paragraph explaining those changes.

Get Visual Chart It

Create a chart that depicts the various traditions each class member wrote about in his or her research report. In doing so, decide what categories the topics should go in and how to represent them so that the chart clearly demonstrates some point with respect to the cultural traditions.

In the Workplace

Writing A Business Report

1. Your boss at the construction consulting company responds to the memo you wrote about his idea to build a highway through the Florida Everglades (see page 341). He wants more detail. *Write a brief report* based on the research and notes you prepared earlier. Your purpose is to persuade your boss to agree with your viewpoint. Begin with a thesis that states your position. Support your thesis with evidence from your research. Review the major issues and debates related to the topic. Conclude by restating your thesis in different words or by recommending a plan of action for the company.

In Oral Communication

Presenting A Research Report

2. Your clients at the athletic shoe and clothing company want to hear your recommendations about trends in athletic clothing (see page 341). *Give an oral report* to your classmates based on your earlier interviews. Summarize your research process and the information you learned. Conclude with some specific ideas about a new line of athletic clothing for the company. Consider using graphics or illustrations to help explain your ideas.

Timed Writing ⏱ Environmental Report

3. Return to the notes you took on a report about protecting the environment (see page 341). Complete the report by first developing a thesis. Identify the major issues and debates about the issue. Choose evidence that supports your thesis and use an outline or graphic organizer to order this information. You have 30 minutes to complete your work.

One way to begin a research report is to start with an introductory paragraph that gives background information and ends with your thesis. Develop your report by using facts and examples from your research. End with a strong conclusion so that the congresswoman you work for knows why the issue is important.

Before You Write Consider the following questions: What is the subject? What is the occasion? Who is the audience? What is the purpose?

After You Write Evaluate your work using the six-trait rubric on page 383.

Guide to 21st Century

School and Workplace Skills

The whole purpose of education is to turn mirrors into windows.
—Sydney J. Harris

Education begins with trying to understand yourself. You then apply what you learn to others—to those who are like you, and also to those whose cultures may be very different from yours. Transforming a mirror into a window will help give you the outlook and skills you need to succeed in the 21st century.

Critical Thinking and Problem Solving for Academic Success

Essential Skills

In Part I of this guide, you will learn how to apply your **critical thinking** and **problem-solving skills** in order to achieve academic success. These skills will also help you succeed in the workplace.

1 Critical Thinking

USING REASONING

Using sound reasoning is essential for every task you perform in school and in the workplace. You frequently use two basic types of reasoning: deductive and inductive. When you use the **deductive** method, you start with a general concept or theory and support it with or apply it to specifics. For instance, you use deductive reasoning when you defend your thesis on an essay test. When you use the **inductive** method, you start with specifics and build to a general point. You use inductive reasoning, for example, when you draw a conclusion based on close reading. Make sure the type of reasoning you use suits the task, and always check for flaws in your logic.

ANALYZING OUTCOMES

In your science class, you may be asked to examine how parts of an ecosystem work together. Your history class may examine the economic system, focusing on the factors that led to the global economic decline in 2009. Understanding relationships—among events, factors, or parts of a system—is essential for analyzing outcomes, both their causes and their significance. By analyzing interactions and cause-and-effect relationships, you will gain insight into how systems work.

Evaluating and Drawing Conclusions

To think critically, you must do much more than simply comprehend information. You need to analyze and evaluate evidence, claims, and different points of view. (See pages 228–229, 261–264, and 335–336.) You need to infer, interpret, make connections, and synthesize information. Then you must draw conclusions. (See page 103.) You should also reflect on your learning in order to evaluate your progress, skills, and methods. Learning how to evaluate information effectively and draw logical conclusions will help you make sound judgments and decisions in school and in the workplace.

The following activities will help you develop critical thinking skills.

Developing Vivid Comparisons, page 51	Evaluating Information for Relevance, page 219
Drawing Conclusions, page 103	Developing Counter-Arguments, page 264
Interpreting Experience, page 123	Making Inferences, page 302
Observing, page 155	Synthesizing, page 367
Imaging, page 180	

② Problem Solving

Your critical thinking skills—using sound reasoning, analyzing outcomes, evaluating and drawing conclusions—will help you solve problems effectively. Faced with a problem on a test, for example, look for connections between it and other problems you have solved in the past to see if the solution should follow certain conventions. Use reasoning and draw conclusions to determine the correct solution. To solve complex problems, ask questions. Then synthesize and evaluate information and different viewpoints to produce strong, creative solutions. Developing and applying your problem-solving skills in school will prepare you for resolving various types of problems in the workplace.

A. Learning Study Skills

Apply Critical Thinking Skills

Whether you are reading a chapter in your textbook, studying for a test, or participating in a class discussion, you should think critically. Thinking critically means thinking actively about what you read and hear. It involves asking questions, making connections, analyzing, interpreting, evaluating, and drawing conclusions. When you interpret a passage in a book or evaluate an author's argument, you are using your critical thinking skills.

Thinking critically also involves reflecting on your learning. Evaluating the methods you use to study and prepare for assignments and tests will help you identify your strengths. It will also help you determine how you can learn more effectively.

In this section, you will develop your study skills. Improving these skills will help you become a better critical thinker and help you succeed academically.

Developing Effective Study Skills

Adopting good study habits will help you complete your daily classroom assignments. Improve your study habits by using the following strategies.

Strategies for Effective Studying

- Choose an area that is well lighted and quiet.
- Equip your study area with everything you need for reading and writing. You can easily access a dictionary and thesaurus online, but you may want to have print versions of these resources on hand.
- Keep an assignment book for recording due dates.
- Allow plenty of time to complete your work. Begin your assignments early.
- Adjust your reading rate to suit your purpose.

❶ Adjusting Reading Rate to Purpose

Your reading rate is the speed at which you read. Depending on your purpose in reading, you may decide to read quickly or slowly. If your purpose is to get a general impression of the material, you may quickly read only parts of a page. If your purpose is to find the main point of a selection, you read more thoroughly. When you are reading to learn specific information, you slow your reading rate considerably to allow for close attention to facts and details.

SCANNING

Scanning is reading to get a general impression and to prepare for learning about a subject. Read the title, headings, subheadings, picture captions, words and phrases in boldface or italics, and any focus questions. You can quickly determine what the material is about and what questions to keep in mind.

SKIMMING

Skimming is reading quickly to identify the purpose, thesis, main ideas, and supporting details of a selection. After scanning a chapter, section, or article, you can skim the material. Quickly read the introduction, the topic sentence and summary sentence of each paragraph, and the conclusion. **Skimming** is useful for reading supplementary material and for reviewing material previously read.

CLOSE READING

Most of your assignments for school will require close reading, which is an essential step for critical thinking. You use **close reading** for locating specific information, following the logic of an argument, or comprehending the meaning or significance of information. After scanning a selection, read it more slowly, word for word, to understand the text's meaning fully. You can then apply your critical thinking skills to analyze and interpret information and ideas. Be sure to evaluate points and draw conclusions in order to make judgments and decisions. Pose questions based on your close reading to help you solve problems.

READING A TEXTBOOK

When you read a textbook, you should combine the techniques of scanning, skimming, and close reading by using the **SQ3R study strategy**. This method helps you understand and remember what you read. The *S* in SQ3R stands for *Survey*, the *Q* for *Question*, and the *3R* for *Read*, *Recite*, and *Review*.

THE SQ3R STUDY STRATEGY

Survey	First get a general idea of what the selection is about by scanning the title, headings, subheadings, and words that are set off in a different type or color. Also look at maps, tables, charts, and other illustrations. Then read the introduction and conclusion or summary.
Question	Decide what questions you should be able to answer after reading the selection. You can do this by turning the headings and subheadings into questions or by looking at any study questions in the book.
Read	Now read the selection. As you read, try to answer your questions. In addition, find the main idea in each section, and look for important information that is not included in your questions. After reading, review the important points in the selection and take notes. (See pages 397–399.)
Recite	Answer each question in your own words by reciting or writing the answers.
Review	Answer the questions again without looking at your notes or at the selection. Continue reviewing until you answer each question correctly.

● **Practice Your Skills**

Choosing a Reading Strategy

For each situation below, decide whether you would use scanning, skimming, close reading, or the SQ3R study strategy to complete the task. Explain your choice.

1. You want to review a chapter in your history textbook to prepare for a class discussion.

2. You are writing a research report about endangered species. You need to read a chapter in a reference book to gather information about rhinos.

3. You are about to start a new unit in your science class, and you have been assigned to read a chapter in your textbook.

4. You have been assigned to read a brief biographical essay about the poet Langston Hughes. Your purpose is to learn about his life and views on poetry.

5. You want to find out if a newsmagazine contains any articles related to the topic of your oral report on the Middle East.

❷ Taking Notes

Taking notes helps you to identify and remember the essential information in a textbook, reference book, or lecture. Note taking will prepare you to engage in critical thinking. Focusing on and recording key information will help you to make connections, evaluate points, and draw conclusions. Three methods for taking notes are the informal outline, the graphic organizer, and the summary.

In an **informal outline,** you use words and phrases to record main ideas and important details. This method is especially useful when you are studying for a multiple-choice test because it highlights the most important facts.

In a **graphic organizer,** words and phrases are arranged in a visual pattern to indicate the relationships between main ideas and supporting details. This is an excellent tool for studying information for an objective test, for preparing an open-ended assessment, or for writing an essay. The visual organizer allows you to see important information and its relationship to other ideas instantly.

In a **summary** you use sentences to express important ideas in your own words. A good summary should do more than restate the information. It should express relationships among the ideas and state conclusions. For this reason, summarizing is a good way to prepare for an essay test.

Whether you are using an informal outline or a summary to take notes, include only the main ideas and important details. In the following passage from a science textbook, the essential information is underlined.

MODEL: Essential Information

Characteristics of Fish

All fish have certain characteristics in common. For example, <u>all fish have backbones and are cold-blooded.</u> In addition, <u>most fish breathe through gills.</u> The gills, which are found on either side of a fish's head, take up oxygen that is dissolved in water. As a fish opens its mouth, water enters and passes over the gills, where oxygen molecules diffuse from the water into the fish's blood. At the same time, carbon dioxide passes out of its blood into the water.

<u>Other characteristics of most fish include scales,</u> which cover and protect their bodies, <u>and fins,</u> which aid fish in swimming. Certain fins act as steering guides, while others help a fish keep its balance in the water. Another aid in swimming that <u>most fish have is a streamlined body,</u> one in which the head and tail are smaller and more pointed than the middle part of the body. This streamlined shape helps fish swim by making it easier for them to push water aside as they propel themselves through the water.

Informal Outline

Characteristics of Fish

1. Have backbones and are cold-blooded (all)

2. Breathe through gills (most)

3. Have scales, fins, and streamlined bodies (most)

Graphic Organizer

Characteristics of Fish

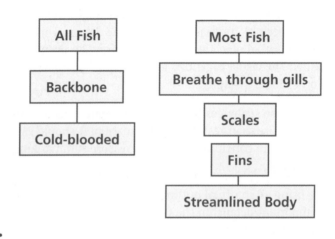

Summary

Characteristics of Fish

All fish share two common characteristics: backbones and cold-bloodedness. Most fish breathe through gills and have scales for protection. Most fish also have fins and streamlined bodies for efficient swimming.

No matter which note-taking method you use, the following strategies will help make your notes clear and useful.

Strategies for Taking Notes

- Label your notes with the title and page numbers of the chapter or the topic and date of the lecture.
- Record only the main ideas and important details, using key words and phrases.
- Use the title, headings, subheadings, and words in special type to help you select the most important information.
- Use your own words; do not copy word for word.
- Use as few words as possible.

● Practice Your Skills

Taking Notes

Choose a short portion of a reading assignment for one of your classes. Take notes on the reading in three ways. First make an informal outline. Next create a graphic organizer. Finally, write a summary. Then reflect on your note-taking process. Which method do you think was the most effective? Why?

③ Preparing Subject-Area Assignments

The strategies you have learned for reading textbooks and reference books and taking notes can be applied to assignments in any subject area.

Mathematics and science textbooks often list rules, formulas, equations, or models. In these subjects, you should focus on applying the rules or models to solve problems or to show the truth of scientific principles. Be sure to use sound mathematical and scientific reasoning.

History, government, and economics courses, on the other hand, emphasize reading and interpreting maps, charts, graphs, time lines, documents, and statistical data. In preparing for assignments or tests in these subjects, you should pay special attention to information provided in those formats. Remember to use your critical thinking skills to analyze outcomes and understand how systems work. Analyze and connect the information presented in different formats, and draw conclusions based on this information.

21ST CENTURY

Tips for Preparing Subject-Area Assignments

- Carefully read and follow directions.
- Adjust your reading rate to suit your purpose.
- In reading your textbook, use the SQ3R method. (See pages 395–396.)
- Take notes on your reading. Organize your notebook by keeping notes on the same topic together.
- For review, keep a separate list of vocabulary, key terms and concepts, or rules and equations.
- Keep a list of questions you think of as you read, listen, or review. Seek answers promptly.
- Participate in study groups, following the principles of cooperative learning.
- Leave ample time to study for tests. Anticipate and answer the questions you think will be asked.

B. Taking Standardized Tests

Applying Your Critical Thinking and Problem-Solving Skills

Applying your critical thinking skills is essential for success on standardized tests. Standardized test questions, such as analogies, require you to use reasoning to arrive at the correct answer. Other types, such as reading comprehension questions, ask you to analyze, infer, interpret, make connections, and draw conclusions. An essay test may ask you to evaluate ideas and give your opinion about a subject.

All types of test questions demand that you use your problem-solving skills. You must determine what a question is asking and how you should arrive at the correct answer. You should decide if a particular question is a familiar type and therefore if the answer should match certain conventions.

Learning to apply your critical thinking and problem-solving skills effectively will help you not only when taking tests but also when completing your daily classroom assignments. It will also prove essential in areas beyond the classroom—in all aspects of your daily life and career.

In this section, you will develop your skills in taking standardized tests. Improving these skills will help you do your best on classroom, school-wide, or statewide standardized tests.

Strategies for Taking Standardized Tests

Standardized tests measure your skills, progress, and achievement in such a way that the results can be compared with those of other students in the same grade. Standardized tests that measure your verbal or language skills are divided into two broad categories: analogy tests and tests of reading and writing ability.

Strategies for Taking Standardized Tests

- Read the test directions carefully. Answer sample questions to be sure you are following the instructions.
- Try to relax. You can expect to be a little nervous, but concentrate on doing your best.
- Skim the entire section to get an overview of the kinds of questions you will be asked.
- Plan your time carefully. Be aware of how much time you are allotted for each part of the test.
- Answer first the questions you find easiest. Skip questions you find too difficult, but come back to them later.
- Read all the choices before selecting the best answer. If you are not sure of an answer, eliminate choices that are obviously incorrect. Educated guessing often helps.
- If you have time, check your answers. Be sure you have correctly marked your answer sheet.

1 Analogies

Analogy questions test your skill at figuring out relationships between words. To complete an **analogy**, you need to use reasoning. The first step is to determine how the two words in the first pair are related (these words usually appear in capital letters). The second step is to decide which other pair has the same relationship as the words in the first pair.

In an analogy, the colon stands for *is to* and the pair of colons represent the word *as*.

> CLOCK : TIME :: thermometer : temperature

The example reads, "A *clock* is to *time* as a *thermometer* is to *temperature*." That is, a clock has the same relationship to time as a thermometer has to temperature. A clock measures time as a thermometer measures temperature.

In the following example, try to explain to yourself in one sentence the relationship between the two words in capital letters. You might say, "Handlebars are part of a bicycle." Then choose the correct answer.

> HANDLEBARS : BICYCLE ::
>
> (A) moose : antlers   (B) tire : fender
>
> (C) carpenter : hammer   (D) steering wheel : automobile
>
> (E) golf : sport
>
> (The answer is *(D) steering wheel : automobile* because the relationship between these two words is that of part to whole; a steering wheel is part of an automobile.)

Remember that the words in the answer must be in the same order as the words in the given pair. If the given pair of words in the analogy expresses a cause-to-effect relationship, the words in the correct answer should also be in order of cause to effect.

Rain is to *flood* as *virus* is to ▪ .

(A) computer   (B) drought

(C) illness   (D) energy

(E) nurse

(The first two italicized words are a cause and an effect: rain causes a flood. Therefore, the correct answer is *(C) illness*, an effect of a virus.)

Knowing some of the common types of analogies, like those in the following chart, will help you figure out word relationships. In the first step for completing an analogy, determining whether the relationship between the words is one of the familiar, conventional types will make it easier to select the correct answer.

COMMON TYPES OF ANALOGIES

Analogy	Example
word : synonym	plain : simple
part : whole	lens : camera
cause : effect	burn : pain
worker : tool	gardener : shovel
item : purpose	pencil : write

● **Practice Your Skills**

Recognizing Analogies

Write the letter of the word pair that has the same relationship as the word pair in capital letters.

1. DENTIST : DRILL ::

    (A) calendar : date   (B) sculptor : chisel

    (C) lumberjack : forest   (D) eyeglasses : sight

    (E) hammer : carpenter

2. HASTEN : HURRY ::

    (A) laugh : talk   (B) trust : doubt

    (C) stammer : whisper   (D) attempt : try

    (E) explain : understand

● **Practice Your Skills**

Completing Analogies

Complete the analogy by writing the letter of the word that best completes the sentence.

1. *Carelessness* is to *error* as *exploration* is to ▪ .

   (A) invention   (B) bravery

   (C) sailing   (D) artifacts

   (E) discovery

2. *Page* is to *book* as *card* is to ▪ .

   (A) king   (B) clubs

   (C) deck   (D) suit

   (E) joker

② Sentence-Completion Tests

Sentence-completion tests measure your ability to comprehend what you read and to use context correctly. Each item consists of a sentence with one or more words missing. First read the entire sentence. Then read the answer choices. Use logical reasoning to select the answer that completes the sentence in a way that makes sense.

The town of Odessa, Delaware, now has a population of only five hundred, but it was once a ▪ seaport.

(A) fascinating   (B) tiny

(C) Pacific   (D) bustling

(E) sleepy

(The answer is *(D) bustling*. The sentence contrasts the small size of the town today with its previous size.)

Some sentence-completion questions have two blanks in the same sentence, with each answer choice including two words.

Even today, the ▪ of the soldiers who bravely fought in World War II is remembered with ▪ .

(A) fear . . . scorn   (B) courage . . . horror

(C) honor . . . indifference   (D) story . . . anger

(E) heroism . . . pride

(The answer is *(E) heroism . . . pride*. None of the other choices fit the idea of remembering brave soldiers.)

Practice Your Skills

Completing Sentences

Write the letter of the word that best completes each of the following sentences.

1. Sharks do not have good eyesight, but their sense of smell is ▪.

(A) poor   (B) keen

(C) decisive   (D) huge

(E) inferior

2. After ten to fourteen days in its chrysalis, the monarch caterpillar ▪ as a beautiful monarch butterfly.

(A) transforms   (B) becomes

(C) emerges   (D) looms

(E) struggles

21ST CENTURY

Practice Your Skills

Completing Sentences with Two Blanks

Write the letter of the words that best complete each of the following sentences.

1. The ▪ empire fell shortly after a series of ▪ battles with an invading army.

(A) new . . . successful   (B) Roman . . . victorious

(C) mighty . . . easy   (D) crumbling . . . ruinous

(E) old . . . jubilant

2. The abandoned warehouse was an eyesore with its ▪ windows, ▪ paint, and sagging roof.

(A) gleaming . . . shining   (B) sparkling . . . fading

(C) open . . . bright   (D) cracked . . . peeling

(E) broken . . . vivid

③ Reading Comprehension Tests

Reading comprehension tests assess your ability to understand and analyze written passages. The information you need to answer the test questions may be either directly stated or implied in the passage. You must use your critical thinking skills to make inferences as you read, analyze and interpret the passage, and then draw conclusions in order to answer the questions. The following strategies will help you answer questions on reading comprehension tests.

HERE'S HOW

Strategies for Answering Reading Comprehension Questions

- Begin by skimming the questions that follow the passage so you know what to focus on as you read.
- Read the passage carefully and closely. Note the main ideas, organization, style, and key words.
- Study all possible answers. Avoid choosing one answer the moment you think it is a reasonable choice.
- Use only the information in the passage when you answer the questions. Do not rely on your own knowledge or ideas on this kind of test.

Most reading comprehension questions will focus on one or more of the following characteristics of a written passage.

- **Main Idea** At least one question will usually focus on the central idea of the passage. Remember that the main idea of a passage covers all sections of the passage—not just one section or paragraph.

- **Supporting Details** Questions about supporting details test your ability to identify the statements in the passage that back up the main idea.

- **Implied Meanings** In some passages not all information is directly stated. Some questions ask you to infer or interpret in order to answer questions about points that the author has merely implied.

- **Purpose and Tone** Questions on purpose and tone require that you interpret or analyze the author's attitude toward his or her subject and purpose for writing.

Reading for Comprehension

Read the following passage and write the letter of each correct answer.

Kidnapped by UFO Aliens

You have seen countless newspaper headlines or television stories like this. Although such tales are common today, hoaxes and rumors about space creatures go back many years. One famous example, the "*Sun* moon story," dates to 1835. In August of that year, the *New York Sun* announced that a distinguished British astronomer had made some wondrous discoveries while using a new telescope. The newspaper printed a series of articles describing the plants, animals, and winged men that lived on the moon. The stories helped make the *Sun* the best-selling daily newspaper in the world. Eventually reporter Richard Adams Locke admitted making up the articles. After the truth was discovered, Edgar Allan Poe abandoned a story he had begun about a man who flies to the moon in a balloon. He claimed to have been "outdone" by the newspaper's tales.

While readers of the *Sun* enjoyed the fantastic descriptions of life on the moon, listeners of another great hoax were terrified. Orson Welles's 1938 broadcast of "War of the Worlds" caused alarm all across the United States. In 1898, when the story was actually written, Mars was in close proximity to Earth. People could easily observe it and speculate about possible life on the planet. The writer, H. G. Wells, created a tale of Martian invaders with powerful new weapons resembling the nuclear, chemical, and biological weapons known to us today. When the story was broadcast over the radio in 1938, World War I was a recent event, and Hitler was menacing Europe. Most listeners were panic-stricken; few recognized the program as fiction. Today, we are less afraid of an alien invasion, but we are just as fascinated by the idea of meeting life from outer space.

1. The "*Sun* moon story" met with
   (A) contempt from the scientific community.
   (B) enthusiasm from readers worldwide.
   (C) skepticism from the public.
   (D) fear about an alien invasion.
   (E) jealousy from other American writers.

2. The passage indicates that space creature hoaxes

(A) are always believed.

(B) are usually treated as harmless practical jokes.

(C) often involve little green men.

(D) have existed for over 150 years.

(E) began in the 1930s.

3. This passage would most likely appear in

(A) a science fiction novel.

(B) a textbook on the solar system.

(C) a history of American newspapers.

(D) an article on the rise of NASA.

(E) a book on public fascination with life in outer space.

THE DOUBLE PASSAGE

You may also be asked to read a pair of passages and answer questions about each passage individually and about the way the two passages relate to each other. The two passages may present similar or opposing views or may complement each other in other ways. A brief introduction preceding the passages may help you anticipate the relationship between them. Questions about double passages require you to use your critical thinking skills in order to make connections and synthesize information.

● Practice Your Skills

Reading for Double-Passage Comprehension

These passages present two descriptions of tropical islands. The first passage is from an article called "An Aloha State of Mind" by William Ecenbarger. The second is from *In the South Seas* by Robert Louis Stevenson. Read each passage and answer the questions that follow.

Passage 1

Hot golden sunshine covers everything along Maui's southern coast, as though someone has spilled it. On the beaches, children, sugared in sand, whittle away at their parents' patience, while honeymooners stroll by, hand in hand, through the white lace left by the retreating surf. Coppery sunbathers stretch out like cookies on a baking sheet. . . .

Not far inland, Haleakala volcano begins its steep, 10,000-foot ascent, and about halfway up, there are thin layers of drifting clouds. It's twenty degrees cooler here, and the air is redolent with eucalyptus, woodsmoke, and the odors of earth and cattle. Looking down the slope you can see the beach five miles away. The sea appears as an immense blue fabric, rumpled and creased, and ends with the scrawling signature of the shore.

Passage 2

I have watched the morning break in many quarters of the world; it has been certainly one of the chief joys of my existence, and the dawn that I saw with the most emotion shone upon the Bay of Anaho. The mountains abruptly overhang the port with every variety of surface and of inclination, lawn, and cliff, and forest. Not one of these but wore its proper tint of saffron, of sulphur, of the clove, and of the rose. The lustre was like that of satin; on the lighter hues there seemed to float an efflorescence; a solemn bloom appeared on the more dark. The light itself was the ordinary light of morning, colourless and clean; and on this ground of jewels, pencilled out the least detail of drawing. Meanwhile, around the hamlet, under the palms, where the blue shadow lingered, the red coals of cocoa husk and the light trails of smoke betrayed the awakening business of the day. . . .

1. The tone of Passage 1 is
   (A) humorous
   (B) poetic
   (C) sarcastic
   (D) objective
   (E) ironic

2. The author of Passage 1 probably wrote the passage to
   (A) encourage people to visit Maui.
   (B) warn people about the dangers of sunbathing.
   (C) inform people about the volcanoes of Hawaii.
   (D) describe the tourists who visit the islands.
   (E) persuade people to write for travel magazines.

3. Which of the following best describes the author's purpose in Passage 2?
   (A) to argue for conservation of tropical islands
   (B) to persuade other travelers to visit the Bay of Anaho
   (C) to describe a beautiful morning scene
   (D) to show off his writing skills
   (E) to inform people what life is like for the people of the South Seas

4. Both authors would probably agree with which of the following statements?
   (A) The Bay of Anaho is a beautiful site.
   (B) Fewer people should visit Maui.
   (C) The richest colors on earth exist in the sunrise.
   (D) People in Hawaii do not appreciate where they live.
   (E) Tropical islands are wonderful to visit.

4 Tests of Standard Written English

Objective tests of Standard written English assess your knowledge of the language skills used for writing. They contain sentences with underlined words, phrases, and punctuation. The underlined parts will contain errors in grammar, usage, mechanics, vocabulary, and spelling. These tests ask you to use your problem-solving skills to find the error in each sentence or to identify the best way to revise a sentence or passage.

ERROR RECOGNITION

The most familiar way to test knowledge of grammar, usage, capitalization, punctuation, word choice, and spelling is through error-recognition questions. A typical test item of this kind is a sentence with five underlined choices. Four of the choices suggest possible errors. The fifth choice, *E*, states that there is no error.

Some scientists <u>believe</u> that the first <u>dog's</u> <u>were</u> tamed <u>over</u> 10,000 years
      A   B   C   D

ago. <u>No error</u>
        E

(The answer is *B*. The word *dogs* should not have an apostrophe because it is plural, not possessive.)

Some sentences have no errors. Before you choose *E (No error),* however, be sure that you have carefully studied every part of the sentence. The errors are often hard to notice.

Remember that the parts of a sentence not underlined are presumed to be correct. You can use clues in the correct parts of the sentence to help you search for errors in the underlined parts.

● Practice Your Skills

Recognizing Errors in Writing

Write the letter that is below the underlined word or punctuation mark that is incorrect. If the sentence contains no error, write *E*.

(1) Temperatures on summer nights <u>are</u> often <u>cooler</u> in the suburbs
                                         A   B

<u>then</u> <u>in</u> the city. **(2)** One reason for the difference <u>is</u> <u>that</u> suburbs have
  C   D   A   B

<u>less</u> buildings <u>than</u> the city has. **(3)** During the day city streets, sidewalks,
  C   D   A

and <u>buildings</u> <u>absorb</u> the <u>Summer</u> heat. **(4)** At night the suburbs <u>cool</u>
        B   C   D   A

down, but, the city <u>does</u> not. **(5)** Buildings and streets <u>release</u> the heat
   B   C   D   A
absorbed during the day, this heat <u>keeps</u> the city warmer throughout the
                       B   C
night. **(6)** The suburbs <u>have</u> more trees and grass that <u>hold</u> rainwater
    D   A   B   C   D
near the surface. **(7)** The water <u>evaporates</u> in the heat, and <u>cools</u> down
                          A   B   C
the temperature. **(8)** Furthermore, the trees, <u>like</u> a fan, <u>keeps</u> a breeze
             D   A B   C D
blowing. **(9)** Tall and unbending, the buildings in the city <u>retain</u> the warm
                      A   B
air <u>as</u> an oven <u>does</u>. **(10)** <u>Its</u> easy to understand why <u>people</u> often <u>try</u> to
   C   D   A   B   C
leave the city to visit the countryside on a hot <u>July</u> weekend.
                                           D

SENTENCE-CORRECTION QUESTIONS

Sentence-correction questions assess your ability to recognize appropriate phrasing. Instead of locating an error in a sentence, you must use your problem-solving skills to select the most appropriate way to write the sentence.

In this kind of question, a part of the sentence is underlined. The sentence is then followed by five different ways of writing the underlined part. The first way shown, (A), simply repeats the original underlined portion. The other four choices present alternative ways of writing the underlined part. The choices may differ in grammar, usage, capitalization, punctuation, or word choice. Consider all answer choices carefully. If there is an error in the original underlined portion, make sure the answer you choose solves the problem. Be sure that the answer you select does not introduce a new error and does not change the meaning of the original sentence.

Many colleges and universities in the United States, such as the College of William and Mary in <u>Virginia, is named after historical figures.</u>

    (A) Virginia, is named after historical figures.
    (B) Virginia. Is named after historical figures.
    (C) Virginia is named after historical figures.
    (D) Virginia, are named after historical figures.
    (E) Virginia are named after historical figures.

(The answer is *(D)*. The verb *is* must be changed to agree with the subject *colleges and universities*. Choices *(A)*, *(B)*, and *(C)* do not correct the subject-verb agreement problem. Choice *(E)* adds an error by removing the comma.)

Correcting Sentences

Write the letter of the most appropriate way of phrasing the underlined part of each sentence.

1. Is it true that Betsy Ross probably <u>didn't never sew the first American flag?</u>

(A) didn't never sew the first American flag?

(B) didn't ever sew the first american flag?

(C) didn't never sewed the first American flag?

(D) didn't sew the first American flag?

(E) did not never sew the first american flag?

2. <u>There is shiny white and gold fish</u> in the pool in my grandmother's garden.

(A) There is shiny white and gold fish

(B) There is shiny white, and gold fish

(C) There are shiny white and gold fish

(D) There are shiny white, and gold fish

(E) Here is shiny white and gold fish

REVISION-IN-CONTEXT

Another type of multiple-choice question that appears on some standardized tests is called revision-in-context. The questions following the reading ask you to choose the best revision of a sentence, a group of sentences, or the essay as a whole. To select the correct answer, use your critical thinking skills to evaluate the relative merits of each choice. You may also be asked to identify the writer's intention. To do so, you will need to analyze the text carefully to determine the writer's purpose.

Correcting Sentences

Carefully read the passage, which is the beginning of an essay about *The Jungle Book*. Answer the questions that follow.

> **(1)** Rudyard Kipling's collection of stories known as *The Jungle Book* features tales about animals and people living in India. **(2)** One story is about a mongoose named Rikki-Tikki-Tavi. **(3)** It is his job to protect his adopted family from two cobras. **(4)** The cobras are called Nag and Nagaina. **(5)** Threatening the other animals in the garden and the family in the house are the large and powerful cobras. **(6)** Despite the odds against him, the little mongoose must find a way to defeat the deadly cobras.

1. In relation to the rest of the passage, which of the following best describes the writer's intention in sentence 6?
   (A) to restate the opening sentence
   (B) to propose an analysis of the story
   (C) to explain a metaphor
   (D) to interest the reader in the outcome of the story
   (E) to summarize the paragraph

2. Which of the following best combines sentences 2, 3, and 4?
   (A) One story is about Rikki-Tikki-Tavi, a mongoose who must protect his adopted family from the cobras Nag and Nagaina.
   (B) One story is about Rikki-Tikki-Tavi, who must protect his adopted family from two cobras.
   (C) One story is about a mongoose who must protect his adopted family from Nag and Nagaina.
   (D) One story is about Rikki-Tikki-Tavi, who must protect his adopted family from Nag and Nagaina.
   (E) Protecting his adopted family from the cobras Nag and Nagaina is the mongoose Rikki-Tikki-Tavi.

C. Taking Essay Tests

Apply Critical Thinking Skills

Essay tests are designed to assess both your understanding of important ideas and your critical thinking skills. You will be expected to analyze, connect, and evaluate information and draw conclusions. You may be asked to examine cause-and-effect relationships and analyze outcomes. Some questions may address problems and solutions. Regardless of the type of question you are asked, your essay should show sound reasoning. You must be able to organize your thoughts quickly and express them logically and clearly.

In this section, you will develop your skills in taking essay tests. Your critical thinking skills are essential in performing well on these tests.

Doing Your Best on Essay Tests

1 Kinds of Essay Questions

Always begin an essay test by reading the instructions for all the questions. Then, as you reread the instructions for your first question, look for key words.

NARRATIVE, DESCRIPTIVE, AND PERSUASIVE PROMPTS

Following are some sample essay prompts and strategies for responding to them.

Narrative Writing Prompt

A friend loaned you a much-loved item. Although you promised nothing would happen to it, something did happen. Tell what happened and how you handled the problem with your friend.

Analyze the Question The key words in this question are "tell what happened." That is your cue that you will be relating a story.

Sketch Out the Key Parts You may want to make a chart like the following to be sure that you include all the necessary parts. Refer to the question for the headings in the chart.

STORY PLANNING SKETCH	
Item	
What happened to the item	
How you decided to handle it	
The outcome	

Use What You Know About Narrative Writing Think of other narratives you have written and remember their key features: an attention-getting beginning that introduces a conflict, a plot that unfolds chronologically and often includes dialogue, a resolution to the conflict. Draft accordingly.

Save Time to Revise and Edit Read over your essay and look for any spots where adding, deleting, rearranging, or substituting would improve your essay. Edit it for correct conventions. Pay special attention to punctuation with dialogue.

Descriptive Writing Prompt

Think of a place where you like to go when you want to take your mind off a problem. Write a well-organized detailed description of that place using words that appeal to the senses.

Analyze the Question The key words in this question are "detailed description." The directions to use "words that appeal to the senses" is another important item. It sets the stage for the expectation that you will include vivid sights, sounds, smells, tastes, and feelings.

Sketch Out the Key Parts You may want to make a chart like the following to be sure that you include all the necessary parts. Refer to the question for the headings in the chart.

DESCRIPTION PLANNING SKETCH	
Identification of place	
Vivid sights	
Vivid sounds	
Vivid smells, tastes, and feelings	

Use What You Know About Descriptive Writing Call to mind the key features of descriptive writing: a main idea that represents an overall attitude toward the subject; sensory details that support that overall feeling, often organized spatially; and a conclusion that reinforces the main impression of the place. Draft accordingly.

Save Time to Revise and Edit Read over your essay and look for any spots where adding, deleting, rearranging, or substituting would improve your essay. Edit it for correct conventions.

Persuasive Writing Prompt

Your class has received funding from the parents' organization to take a trip somewhere in your state. Write an essay expressing your opinion on which place would make the best destination.

Analyze the Question The key words in this question are "expressing your opinion." These words tell you that you will be writing a persuasive text to convince people that your opinion is worthwhile.

Sketch Out the Key Parts You may want to make a chart like the following to be sure that you include all the necessary parts. Refer to the question for the headings in the chart.

PERSUASIVE PLANNING SKETCH	
Your choice of place	
Reason #1	
Reason #2	
Reason #3	
Why other choices aren't as good	

Use What You Know About Persuasive Writing Call to mind the key features of persuasive writing: a main idea that expresses an opinion; facts, examples, reasons, and other supporting details arranged in logical order, often order of importance; a look at why other opinions are not as sound; and a conclusion that reinforces your opinion.

Save Time to Revise and Edit Read over your essay and look for any spots where adding, deleting, rearranging, or substituting would improve your essay. Edit it for correct conventions.

EXPOSITORY WRITING PROMPTS

Probably most of the essay tests you will take will ask you to address an expository writing prompt. Look for the key words in each of the following kinds of expository essay questions.

KINDS OF ESSAY QUESTIONS	
Analyze	Separate into parts and examine each part.
Compare	Point out similarities.
Contrast	Point out differences.
Define	Clarify meaning.
Discuss	Examine in detail.
Evaluate	Give your opinion.
Explain	Tell how, what, or why.
Illustrate	Give examples.
Summarize	Briefly review main points.
Trace	Show development or progress.

As you read the instructions, jot down what is required in your answer or circle key words and underline key phrases.

(Evaluate) the contributions of Louis Pasteur to the world of science in a short essay of three paragraphs. Use (specific examples.) Be sure to include his "germ theory of disease," which states that most infectious diseases are caused by germs.

The next lesson will take you through the process of answering this expository prompt.

Doing Your Best on Essay Tests **417**

② Writing an Effective Essay Answer

Writing an essay for a test is basically the same as writing any essay. Therefore, you should apply all you have learned about using the writing process to write an essay. The major difference is that you will have a very strict time limit.

PREWRITING

Because of the limited time in a test situation, you must carefully plan your essay. You should first brainstorm for ideas. Then decide what type of reasoning and organization would be most appropriate to use. For example, you may want to use deductive reasoning to build your argument. You may decide to use developmental order or chronological order to present your ideas. To help you organize your answer, write a simple informal outline or construct a graphic organizer. This plan will give structure to your essay and help you avoid omitting important points.

Outline **Louis Pasteur's Contributions to Science**

(thesis statement)
1. Contribution 1: "germ theory of disease"
2. Contribution 2: immunization
3. Contribution 3: pasteurization
(conclusion)

Your next step is to write a thesis statement. It is often possible to reword the test question into a thesis statement.

Essay Question Evaluate the contributions of Louis Pasteur to the world of science in a short essay of three paragraphs. Use specific examples. Be sure to include his "germ theory of disease," which states that most infectious diseases are caused by germs.

Thesis Statement Louis Pasteur was a great scientist whose contributions, including the "germ theory of disease," revolutionized the world of science.

DRAFTING

As you write your essay, keep the following strategies in mind.

Strategies for Writing an Essay Answer

- Write an introduction that includes the thesis statement.
- Follow the order of your outline, writing one paragraph for each main point.
- Provide adequate support for each main point—using specific facts, examples, and/or other supporting details.
- Use transitions to connect your ideas and/or examples.
- End with a strong concluding statement that summarizes the main idea of the essay.
- Write clearly and legibly.

MODEL: Essay Test Answer

Louis Pasteur was a great scientist whose contributions, including the "germ theory of disease," revolutionized the world of science. Before Pasteur proposed the "germ theory of disease," the causes of infectious diseases were unknown. After Pasteur discovered that tiny microbes passed from person to person, infecting each with disease, he argued for cleaner hospital practices. The germs of one patient were no longer passed to another through nonsterile instruments, dirty bed linens, and shared air.

Thesis Statement

Pasteur's research also led him to immunization. Although another scientist first created the vaccine for smallpox, Pasteur took the idea and applied it to other diseases, including rabies. He discovered that by using a weaker form of the virus that causes rabies, he could protect dogs from contracting the stronger form of the virus. Also, he was able to develop a cure for humans who had been bitten by rabid animals.

Pasteur's reputation as a great scientist led the Emperor Napoleon III to request his help with another problem. The French economy was suffering because French wine was diseased and unsellable. After some investigation, Pasteur discovered that the wine could be heated so that the germs were killed, but the wine remained unaffected. This process is now called pasteurization and is applied to many perishable foods, including beer and milk. Pasteur's research and discoveries have led to healthier lives all over the world.

Conclusion

REVISING

Always leave a few minutes to revise and edit your essay answer. As you revise, ask yourself the following questions.

Checklist for Revising an Essay Answer

✓ Did you follow the instructions completely?
✓ Did you interpret the question accurately?
✓ Did you begin with a thesis statement?
✓ Did you include facts, examples, or other supporting details?
✓ Did you organize your ideas and examples logically in paragraphs, according to your informal outline or graphic organizer?
✓ Did you use transitions to connect ideas and examples?
✓ Did you end with a strong concluding statement that summarizes your main ideas or brings your essay to a close?

EDITING

Once you have made revisions, quickly read your essay for mistakes in spelling, usage, or punctuation. Use proofreading symbols to make changes. As you edit, check for the following.

Check your work for:

✓ agreement between subjects and verbs (Chapter 22)
✓ forms of comparative and superlative adjectives and adverbs (Chapter 23)
✓ capitalization of proper nouns and proper adjectives (Chapter 24)
✓ use of commas (Chapter 25)
✓ use of apostrophes (Chapter 27)
✓ division of words at the end of a line (Chapter 27)

❸ Timed Writing

Throughout your school years, you will be tested on your ability to organize your thoughts quickly and to express them in a limited time. Time limits can vary from twenty to sixty to ninety minutes, depending upon the task. For a twenty-minute essay, you might consider organizing your time in the following way:

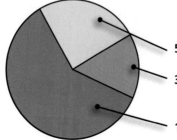

5 minutes: Brainstorm and organize ideas.

3 minutes: Revise your work and edit it for mistakes.

12 minutes: Write a draft.

Strategies for Timed Tests

- Listen carefully to instructions. Find out if you may write notes or an outline on your paper or in the examination book.
- Find out if you should erase mistakes or cross them out by neatly drawing a line through them.
- Plan your time, keeping in mind your time limit.

The more you practice writing under time constraints, the better prepared you will be for tests. You will find timed writing prompts on all of the following pages.

● **Practice Your Skills**

Completing a Timed Writing Assignment

You will have twenty minutes to write a complete essay on the following topic.

Discuss an important problem facing people of your age today. Explain why this problem is important and how you think it can best be solved.

Plan time for each stage of the writing process, set a timer, and write your response.

Communication and Collaboration

> **Part I** Critical Thinking and Problem Solving for Academic Success
>
> **Part II** Communication and Collaboration
>
> **Part III** Media and Technology

Essential Skills

In the 21st century, you live and work in a dynamic, global community. In Part II of this guide, you will learn effective communication and collaboration skills. These skills are essential for success, both in school and in the workplace.

 ## Communication

THE PURPOSE OF COMMUNICATION

In all areas of your life, you communicate for a variety of purposes—to inform, instruct, motivate, and persuade, for example. In school, you might motivate other students to reuse and recycle, or you might persuade them to elect you class president. At work, you might inform your boss about your research findings or instruct your colleagues on how to use new software. Having a clear purpose is essential for communicating your ideas successfully in both speech and writing.

EXPRESSING IDEAS EFFECTIVELY

Regardless of the form you are using to communicate (e-mail, a speech) or the context (a group discussion, a college interview), your goal is to express your thoughts and ideas as effectively as possible. Use words precisely and correctly, and articulate your ideas in a specific, concise manner. Suit your tone to your purpose and audience. Provide valid, relevant support for your ideas, and present information in a logical order. In a speech or presentation, use nonverbal communication skills to help convey your message.

USING MEDIA AND TECHNOLOGY EFFECTIVELY

Multiple forms of media and technology now exist to help you communicate. You can e-mail, text message, or Tweet a friend, and apply for a job online. To prepare a speech, you can look up technical terms in an online dictionary and research your subject on the Internet. You can use software to make a power presentation. To use media and technology effectively, make sure they suit the purpose and context of your communication. They should also help you make a positive impact on your audience by enhancing or facilitating your message.

LISTENING EFFECTIVELY

To listen effectively, you need to do much more than understand what words mean. Your goal is to gain knowledge and determine the speaker's purpose, values, and attitudes. Skillful listeners then evaluate and reflect on the speaker's message, views, and intentions. Listening effectively means listening actively—critically, reflectively, and appreciatively—and remembering what you have heard.

COMMUNICATING IN A DIVERSE WORLD

You probably attend school or work with people from diverse social and cultural backgrounds whose lifestyle, religion, and first language may be different from your own. To communicate effectively in these environments, listen actively in order to understand different traditions, values, and perspectives. Be sure to respect these differences when you express your thoughts and ideas.

② Collaboration

RESPECTING DIVERSITY

In school and in the workplace, you often collaborate with others on diverse teams. Open-mindedness is essential for being an effective team member. Make sure that all team members have an equal opportunity to be heard, and respect and value differences. By doing so, you will help create an environment in which ideas and opinions are freely shared. As a result, team members will benefit from each other's expertise, and you will produce sound, creative solutions.

ACHIEVING A COMMON GOAL

As a member of a team, you need to cooperate. Often, you may need to resolve conflicting opinions in order to achieve a common goal, whether it is completing a particular task or reaching a decision. Remember to maintain a positive attitude and put the group's needs before your own. Appreciate the merits of diverse viewpoints, and help the group work toward a compromise that all members can accept. Flexibility and openness are essential for successful collaboration.

SHARING RESPONSIBILITY

For true collaboration to take place, all team members must do their fair share. Complete your assigned tasks, come to meetings prepared, and remain actively engaged in the team's work. Respect the skills, expertise, and efforts of other team members, and provide constructive feedback as necessary. A sense of shared responsibility will lead to a successful collaborative process.

A. Vocabulary

Apply Communication Skills

Have you ever found yourself searching for just the right word to use in a speech or an e-mail? Have you ever been unsure of a writer's point because several key words were unfamiliar to you?

Successful communication depends on using language skillfully and understanding it thoroughly. As a writer and speaker, you want to choose words that best express your ideas and suit your purpose, audience, and the context. As a reader or listener, you must understand the precise meanings of words in order to comprehend an author's or a speaker's ideas and intentions.

In this chapter you will see how English developed into a language that is rich and varied. You will also learn strategies for expanding your storehouse of words. Developing your vocabulary will help you become a more effective communicator and a more skillful reader and listener in school and in the workplace.

Understanding the Development of the English Language

English is now the official language of several countries around the world, including Australia, the United States, Canada, and the Philippines. The heritage of the language explains how English became a rich, diverse language.

① English in the Past

OLD ENGLISH

Our language began to develop more than 1,500 years ago, in about A.D. 450. During this period England was part of the Roman Empire, and Latin was its written language. At that time three Germanic tribes—the Angles, the Saxons, and the Jutes—invaded England from the shores of the North Sea. After conquering the Celts who lived there, they stayed and settled on the land. These tribes discarded the older Celtic and Roman cultures. Soon their language became the language of the land.

The language those Germanic tribes spoke is now called **Old English,** although to English-speaking people today it would sound like a foreign language. Nevertheless, some Old English words are still part of the language. They include common nouns and verbs: *man, child, house, mother, horse, knee, eat, sing, ride, drink,* and *sell.* They also include most modern numbers such as *one, five,* and *nine;* pronouns such as *you, he, they,* and *who;* the articles *a, an,* and *the;* and prepositions such as *at, by, in, under, around,* and *out.*

MIDDLE ENGLISH

Old English began its change into **Middle English** when William the Conqueror invaded England from northwestern France in 1066 and made French the official language. Although the royal court and the upper classes spoke French, the common people continued to speak Old English. Nevertheless, English might eventually have faded out if the parliament had not started to use it in 1392. By 1450, Middle English, which included hundreds of French words, had evolved. At this time, Geoffrey Chaucer, a famous writer, wrote his works in Middle English.

> **MODEL: Middle English**
>
> ### The Knyghtes Tale
>
> Heere bygynneth the Knyghtes Tale
> Whilom, as olde stories tellen us,
> Ther was a duc that highte Theseus;
> Of Atthenes he was lord and governour,
> And in his tyme swich a conquerour,
> That gretter was ther noon under the sonne.
>
> —Geoffrey Chaucer, *The Canterbury Tales*

Here is the same passage, translated more than five hundred years later into modern language.

> **MODEL: Modern Translation**
>
> ## The Knight's Tale
>
> Here begins the Knight's Tale
> Once on a time, as old tales tell to us,
> There was a duke whose name was Theseus;
> Of Athens he was lord and governor,
> And in his time was such a conqueror,
> That greater was there not beneath the sun.
>
> —Geoffrey Chaucer, *The Canterbury Tales*

 Practice Your Skills

Analyzing Language

List ten similarities and differences you observe between the original Chaucer passage and the modern translation. Be specific, citing particular words and phrases. Next to each difference, write a statement, telling how the language has changed over time.

② English in the Present and Future

MODERN ENGLISH

Modern English started to evolve out of Middle English in the middle of the 1400s. During that time many writers and scholars borrowed words from Latin. In fact, it has been estimated that about half of the present words in modern English are from Latin. By the time Shakespeare was writing in the last half of the 1500s, English had become a versatile language that is understandable to modern speakers of English.

Read the following sonnet by William Shakespeare aloud. In comparison with Old or Middle English, notice how much closer this passage is to the English that you are used to speaking.

Shall I compare thee to a summer's day?
Thou art more lovely and more temperate;
Rough winds do shake the darling buds of May,
And summer's lease hath all too short a date:
Sometime too hot the eye of heaven shines,
And often is his gold complexion dimm'd;
And every fair from fair sometime declines,
By chance or nature's changing course untrimm'd;
But thy eternal summer shall not fade,
Nor lose possession of that fair thou owest;
Nor shall Death brag thou wander'st in his shade,
When in eternal lines to time thou grow'st;
      So long as men can breathe, or eyes can see,
      So long lives this, and this gives life to thee.

—William Shakespeare, "Sonnet XVIII"

● **Practice Your Skills**

Analyzing Language

With a partner, describe how Shakespeare's language is different from Old English and the English you speak today. Be specific, citing particular words and phrases as needed. Summarize what you discover, and report your findings to the class.

AMERICAN ENGLISH

The next phase in the history of the English language occurred when North America was settled. Separated from Europe, settlers began to develop a new kind of English, drawing on a variety of sources and influences. The language we, in America, know as English is truly a mosaic: it is a language that has been influenced by London merchants, Native American nations, enslaved Africans, Spanish and French colonists, and immigrants from many other nations. Many of the words we consider as "English" are, in fact, drawn from entirely different languages, and our language is all the richer because of it.

Cultural Origins

Words are often influenced by many different cultures. Next time you're eating some French fries, think of the origins of the word *potato*. When Columbus landed, he was met by the Taino tribe, who called this tuber *batata*. The Quechua people, another group indigenous to South America, called it *papa*. In Spanish, the word is *patata*. Next time you're at a cookout, consider the word *barbecue* (or the word's cousin, *bar-b-q*). The Taino people used a four-legged stand made from sticks to cook and roast meat. This stand was called a *barbacoa*.

Analyzing Language

The following English words were drawn from other languages: *cafeteria, chef, kayak, ketchup, pretzel*. Look up each word in a dictionary. Then create a chart or diagram to show the origins of the words.

ENGLISH IN THE NEW MILLENNIUM

English has become the dominant language in political diplomacy, science, technology, and trade. Every day new words are coined, and with every edition print dictionaries grow thicker and thicker and online dictionaries expand. Not only have different cultures influenced English, but computer technology has had a tremendous influence on the way we use English. No longer does *surf* apply only to the ocean; it now means "to skim television channels with the remote control," and it also means "to move quickly from one Web page to another on the Internet." No one can say with certainty exactly how English will change in the 21st century, but one thing is bound to be true: English will continue to evolve as cultures come into closer and closer contact and as technology continues to influence the way people around the world speak and think.

Computer Language

The technology revolution has had an enormous impact on the way we use language. Many computer terms are words that have taken on new meanings. The word *mouse*, for example, no longer means only "a small, furry mammal"; it also means "a handheld computer device." Here are other examples:

Word	Original Meaning	New Meaning
crash	collide	computer failure
hang	suspend	freeze up
enter	go in	add data to computer memory
twitter	make chirping sounds	real-time messaging service

The technology revolution has also generated a considerable number of new terms: *hyperlink, online, log on, Internet,* and *Web site*.

Using the Dictionary

A **dictionary** is your best resource for learning about all the words that make up the English language. You can access dictionaries, including specialized ones, more easily than ever before now that so many are available online. In this section you will review the wealth of information found in print and online dictionaries and learn how to use a dictionary for effective communication.

① Word Location

Understanding how a dictionary is organized will help you quickly find the information you need.

ALPHABETICAL ORDER

From beginning to end, the dictionary is a single, alphabetical list. Words beginning with the same letters are alphabetized by the next letter that is different, then the next, and so on. For example, *face* comes before *facet*. Compound words, abbreviations, prefixes, suffixes, and proper nouns also appear in alphabetical order. Note that compound words are alphabetized as if there were no space or hyphen between each word. Abbreviations are alphabetized letter by letter, not by the words they stand for. The following items are ordered as they would appear in a dictionary: *acrobatics, acute angle, AFL, –ally.*

GUIDE WORDS

If you look at the top of a dictionary page, you will see two words; these are called **guide words**. They show you, with just a glance, the first and last words defined on that page. For example, if the guide words are *ooze • or,* the word *operate* would be among the words that appear on the page. The word *orbit* would not be there.

② Information in an Entry

All the information provided for each word is called an **entry.** Each entry usually provides the spelling, pronunciation, parts of speech, definitions, and the origins of the word.

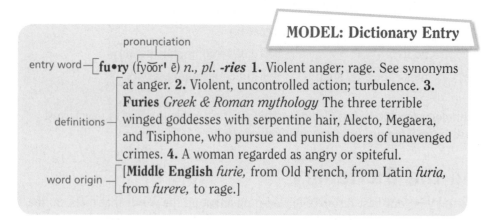

MODEL: Dictionary Entry

pronunciation

entry word — **fu•ry** (fyŏŏr′ ē) *n., pl.* **-ries** **1.** Violent anger; rage. See synonyms at anger. **2.** Violent, uncontrolled action; turbulence. **3.** **Furies** *Greek & Roman mythology* The three terrible winged goddesses with serpentine hair, Alecto, Megaera, and Tisiphone, who pursue and punish doers of unavenged crimes. **4.** A woman regarded as angry or spiteful.

definitions —

word origin — [**Middle English** *furie,* from Old French, from Latin *furia,* from *furere,* to rage.]

ENTRY WORD

The entry word in **bold** type tells you how to spell a word. In addition, an entry also shows any alternate spellings. The more common spelling, called the **preferred spelling**, is usually listed first. Plural nouns, comparatives and superlatives of adjectives, and principal parts of verbs are also given if these spellings are irregular. In the entry for *fury,* the plural form is provided.

The entry word is printed with a capital letter if it is capitalized. If it is capitalized only in certain uses, it will appear with a capital letter near the appropriate definition, as in the third definition in the entry for *fury.*

When writing, you sometimes need to divide a word at the end of a line. Because a word may be divided only between syllables, use a dictionary to check where each syllable ends. At the end of a line, you would divide *fury* after the *u.*

● **Practice Your Skills**

Using a Dictionary for Editing

Write the following paragraph, using a dictionary to help you correct the errors in spelling and capitalization. Underline each correction.

Starlit Skies

At night, thosands of stars appear accross the sky. Over the centurys, stargazers have observed that some stars form particular shapes. These star clusters are called constellations. Two of the most familar are ursa major, "great bear," and ursa minor, "little bear." Within these constellations are the big dipper, the little dipper, and the bright north star. Some constellations can be observed only durring certain seasons. Leo the Lion appears in Spring. During the winter, orion the Hunter is visable. At present, more than 80 constellations have been identifyed in the night sky.

PRONUNCIATION

The **phonetic spelling**, which directly follows the entry word, tells you how to pronounce the word. A pronunciation key at the front of the dictionary shows what sound each phonetic symbol stands for. Most dictionaries also place an abbreviated pronunciation key at the bottom of every other page.

To learn to pronounce a word, compare the phonetic spelling to the symbols in the key. Note that marks over vowels, called **diacritical marks**, indicate different vowel sounds. The key will tell you how to pronounce a vowel with a diacritical mark. For example, the phonetic spelling for *fury* tells you that the *y* should be pronounced like *e* in the word *be*.

In many words, one syllable receives more emphasis than the other syllables in the word. An accent mark indicates a syllable that should be stressed. In *fury,* the first syllable should be stressed.

In longer words, where two syllables should be stressed, the syllable receiving more stress is marked with a primary accent ('). The less emphasized syllable is marked with a secondary accent ('). In the example below, the third syllable receives the most stress in pronunciation.

en • er • get • ic (en' ər jĕt' ĭk) —— primary accent
—— secondary accent

Speaking Tip

With a partner, look up the pronunciations of the following words and practice pronouncing them until you feel comfortable with them: *abhor, exacerbate, hiatus, incorrigible, satiate, superfluous, reiteration, terrestrial.*

DEFINITIONS

A dictionary will list all the different meanings of a word. At the end of some entries, the dictionary will also list **synonyms**, or words that have similar definitions. This list can come in handy when you are writing or preparing a speech. Consult it to choose the most appropriate word to express your meaning and intention.

Consider the word *train.* It can be used as a noun ("I'll take the train") and as a verb ("I'm training for the race"). The dictionary entry for train shows these different uses with abbreviations, *n.* for *noun* and *v.* for *verb.* Dictionaries use the following abbreviations for the other parts of speech: *pron.* (pronoun), *adj.* (adjective), *adv.* (adverb), *prep.* (preposition), *conj.* (conjunction), *interj.* (interjection).

A dictionary also indicates the present usage of words by including such labels as *obsolete, informal, colloquial,* and *slang. Obsolete* means that a word is no longer used with this meaning. *Informal, colloquial* and *slang* indicate words that are used only in informal situations.

Choosing the Appropriate Definition

Look up the word *train* in a dictionary. Then write the definition from the dictionary entry that matches the use of *train* in each of the following sentences. After each definition, write the appropriate part of speech—noun or verb.

1. A train of horses led the parade.

2. I lost my train of thought during my speech.

3. Peter trained for two years to be an electrician.

4. Sara trained the horse's mane to curl.

5. The king tripped over the train of the queen's gown.

6. Julie trained her dog to jump two feet.

Expanding Your Vocabulary

When you hear or read words that are new to you, a dictionary is an invaluable tool for learning their definitions. However, there are several other ways that you can determine the meanings of new words and expand your vocabulary in the process.

① Context Clues

One of the best ways to learn the meaning of a word is through context clues. The **context** of a word is the sentence, the surrounding words, or the situation in which the word occurs. The following examples show the four most common kinds of context clues.

Definition or Restatement	During the storm, travelers took a detour because the isthmus, **a narrow strip of land connecting two larger landmasses,** was flooded. (The word *isthmus* is defined within the sentence.)
Example	You may find a fossil here, perhaps **like the one in our science lab that has an imprint of a leaf.** (The word *fossil* is followed by an example that is known to readers or listeners.)
Comparison	The mayor said that tax revenues, **like personal income,** should be spent wisely. (The word *like* compares *revenues* to its synonym *income*.)
Contrast	Contemporary students learn more about computers **than students did a few years ago.** (A contrast is drawn between today's students [*contemporary students*] and students of the past.)

Using Context Clues

Write the letter of the word or phrase that is closest in meaning to each underlined word. Then identify the type of context clue that helped you determine the meaning by writing *definition, restatement, example, comparison,* or *contrast.*

1. The team members gathered in a huddle but <u>dispersed</u> when the coach blew her whistle.

(A) cheered   (B) scattered   (C) exercised

(D) planned   (E) answered

2. The dogwood in our garden is a <u>perennial</u> source of delight, beautiful at every season of the year.

(A) perfect   (B) timid   (C) slippery

(D) victorious   (E) lasting

3. Like other protected land that cannot be turned into resorts and industrial plants, national parkland cannot be <u>exploited</u> for money-making projects.

(A) explored   (B) defended   (C) observed

(D) used   (E) donated

4. Have an expert <u>appraise</u>, or estimate the worth of, a major purchase before you buy it.

(A) record   (B) buy   (C) evaluate

(D) announce   (E) glorify

5. Winning the blue ribbon is her <u>incentive</u> to practice daily for the race.

(A) excuse   (B) reward   (C) payment

(D) idea   (E) motivation

Speaking Tip

Look up the pronunciations of all the underlined words in the exercise above. With a partner, practice pronouncing the words until you are comfortable with all the sounds within them.

● Connect to Writing: Paragraph

Use at least three of the five underlined words in the **Practice Your Skills** activity above in a brief paragraph.

Prefixes, Suffixes, and Roots

Words in English often have Latin or Greek roots, prefixes, and suffixes. These word parts offer clues to help you unlock the meanings of words. A **root** is the part of a word that carries the basic meaning. A **prefix** is one or more syllables placed in front of the root to modify the meaning of the root or to form a new word. A **suffix** is one or more syllables placed after the root to change its part of speech or meaning.

In the following examples, notice how the meaning of each word part is related to the meaning of the word as a whole.

USING WORD PARTS TO DETERMINE MEANINGS

Word	Prefix	Root	Suffix
dissimilarity (state of being unlike)	dis– (not)	–similar– (alike)	–ity (state of)
independence (state of not relying)	in– (not)	–depend– (to rely)	–ence (state of)
intergalactic (relating to area between galaxies)	inter– (between)	–galaxy– (star system)	–ic (relating to)
transporter (one who carries across)	trans– (across)	–port– (to carry)	–er (one who)
resourceful (able to use ways and means again)	re– (again)	–source– (ways and means)	–ful (full of)

Because word meanings in any language often change over years of use, you might not always find a perfect match between words and the meanings of their Latin and Greek word parts. Even so, knowing prefixes, roots, and suffixes can help you figure out the meanings of thousands of words. It will also help you remember these meanings and thus expand your vocabulary.

COMMON PREFIXES AND SUFFIXES

Prefix	Meaning	Example
com–, con–	with, together	con + join = conjoin = to join together
dis–	not, lack of	dis + harmony = a lack of agreement
extra–	outside, beyond	extra + curricular = outside the regular school courses
in–, il–, im–	in, into, not	im + migrate = to come into a country; il + legal = not lawful
inter–	between, among	inter + state = among or between states
post–	after	post + date = to give a later date
re–	again	re + occur = to happen again
sub–	under, below	sub + standard = below the standard
trans–	across	trans + Atlantic = across the Atlantic

Suffix	Meaning	Example
–ance, –ence	state of	import + ance = state of being important
–er	one who, that	foreign + er = one who is foreign
–ful	full of	hope + ful = full of hope
–ic	relating to	atom + ic = relating to atoms
–ite	resident of	Milford + ite = resident of Milford
–ity	state of	active + ity = state of being active
–less	without, lack of	pain + less = without pain

● **Practice Your Skills**

Understanding Prefixes and Suffixes

Write the prefix or the suffix that has the same meaning as the underlined word or words. Then write the complete word as it is defined after the equal sign.

Example   speech + <u>without</u> = without conversation

Answer   less - speechless

1. <u>together</u> + press = to squeeze together

2. patriot + <u>relating to</u> = relating to love of country

3. <u>across</u> + plant = to lift from one place and to reset in another

4. actual + <u>state of</u> = state of being real

5. <u>not</u> + frequent = not often

● Practice Your Skills

Using Prefixes

Write the letter of the phrase that is closest in meaning to each word in capital letters. Use the prefixes as clues to the word's meaning.

1. DISUNITY: (A) agreement with (B) agreement between (C) lack of agreement

2. SUBMERGE: (A) put underwater (B) place together (C) float across

3. EXTRAORDINARY: (A) after what is usual (B) beyond what is usual (C) among what is usual

4. REACTIVATE: (A) give energy again (B) be energetic with (C) take away energy

5. IMPARTIAL: (A) lacking parts (B) not favoring one side (C) after each part

● *Connect to Writing: Paragraph*

Write a paragraph using four of the five numbered words in the **Practice Your Skills** activity above.

③ Synonyms and Antonyms

A **synonym** is a word that has nearly the same meaning as another word. An **antonym,** on the other hand, is a word that means the opposite of another word. Slight differences exist among synonyms, as well as among antonyms. Expanding your vocabulary by learning synonyms and antonyms and understanding these differences can help you choose the most effective words when you write or speak.

Synonyms	affable : friendly	terminate : finish
Antonyms	affable : hostile	terminate : begin

Dictionaries contain information on synonyms and often explain the differences among them. A **thesaurus** is a kind of specialized dictionary for synonyms, available in print and online. A print thesaurus lists words and their synonyms alphabetically or provides an index of words for finding synonyms easily.

You can learn more about using a thesaurus and other specialized dictionaries on page 356.

● **Practice Your Skills**

Recognizing Synonyms

Write the letter of the word that is closest in meaning to the word in capital letters. Then check your answers in the dictionary.

1. DEBRIS: (A) ruins (B) corruption (C) debt (D) poverty (E) confidence

2. INTEGRITY: (A) honesty (B) cleverness (C) wealth (D) annoyance (E) fame

3. MUTUAL: (A) active (B) changed (C) deep (D) shared (E) solitary

4. NARRATE: (A) tell (B) judge (C) understand (D) separate (E) believe

5. OBSOLETE: (A) outdated (B) lost (C) hidden (D) wrecked (E) reversed

● **Practice Your Skills**

Recognizing Antonyms

Write the letter of the word that is most nearly opposite in meaning to the word in capital letters.

1. BREVITY: (A) briefness (B) wittiness (C) dullness (D) wordiness (E) slowness

2. CRUCIAL: (A) unimportant (B) required (C) stern (D) unbelievable (E) refined

3. ESSENTIAL: (A) unnecessary (B) secret (C) incorrect (D) tall (E) easy

4. IMPROVISE: (A) disprove (B) react (C) increase (D) plan (E) stop

5. OBSTRUCT: (A) refuse (B) assist (C) improve (D) suggest (E) obtain

Speaking Tip

Look up the words in items 1-5 in both **Practice Your Skills** activities above. With a partner, practice pronouncing the sounds in them, with special attention to long and short vowels, silent letters, and consonant clusters.

B. Letters, Applications, and Procedural Writing

Apply 21st Century Communication Skills

In the 21st century, people are communicating and sharing information much more than they have in the past. To communicate effectively, always have a clear purpose in mind and use technology wisely.

In this section, you will develop skills for making your communication with others suit your purpose, audience, and occasion.

Real-World Communication

1 Communicating for a Purpose

Communicating and sharing information in your personal life and in the business world can serve a variety of purposes: to inform, instruct, motivate, or persuade, for example. The purpose of a friendly letter might be to motivate your cousin to try out for the track team. When you complete a job application, your purpose is to inform the employer about your educational background, skills, and work experience. Always keep your purpose in mind. Your goal is to write in a clear, concise, focused manner because you want your readers to know exactly what you mean.

2 Using Technology to Communicate

In the 21st century, you can text or "tweet" a friend, e-mail a request, or post a complaint online. With all these options, electronic communication—particularly e-mail—has replaced letter writing to a great extent. However, writing a letter can be more effective or appropriate than sending an e-mail depending on your purpose, the context, and the impact you want to make. Use these guidelines to determine whether to send a letter or an e-mail.

Send a letter in the following circumstances:

- You want to express sincere, serious emotions, such as sympathy for a loss or thanks for a favor or a gift.
- You want to show that you have put thought and care into communicating.
- You want to introduce yourself formally or make an impact on your audience by using impressive stationery, for example.
- You are including private, confidential information. Keep in mind that e-mail is not a private form of communication, and you should never include confidential information in an e-mail. A recipient can forward an e-mail to others without your knowledge, and companies can read their employees' e-mails. Also, hackers can break into e-mail systems and steal information.
- You need to have formal documentation of your communication, or you are sending authentic documents.

Send an e-mail in the following circumstances:

- You want to communicate quickly with someone.
- You want to send a message, perhaps with accompanying documents, to several people at once.
- You have been instructed by a business or an organization to communicate via e-mail.

The Purpose and Format of Letters

Letters fall into two general categories: friendly letters and business letters. In both categories, letters can serve many different purposes. Regardless of your purpose, your goal when you write a letter is to make contact in a positive and clear way. Perhaps you want the recipient to write back, send you information, or interview you for a job.

For each category of letters, there is a correct format to use, which is demonstrated in this chapter. Using reader-friendly formatting techniques will help you to communicate clearly and create a positive impression.

① Friendly Letters

Some **friendly letters** are written to inform friends or relatives of news or to keep in touch. Others serve such special purposes as offering or responding to invitations, expressing congratulations or sorrow, or thanking. As a substitute for writing a friendly letter, texting is extremely useful if your message is brief and you want to communicate quickly. Sending an e-mail can be appropriate for quick, but more extended communication. However, if the occasion is formal or if you want to express your feelings or provide a personal touch, you should write a letter. Text a friend to say you will meet her at the movies in an hour. E-mail your cousin to tell him about your summer plans, but send a letter to thank your grandparents for the generous gift.

Each part of a friendly letter is explained in the chart below. An e-mail, like a letter, should contain a proper salutation and closing.

PARTS OF A FRIENDLY LETTER	
Heading	The heading includes your full address with the ZIP code. Use the two-letter abbreviation for your state. Always include the date after your address.
Salutation	The salutation is your friendly greeting and is followed by a comma. Capitalize the first word and any proper nouns.
Body	In the body of your friendly letter, include your conversational message. Indent the first line of each paragraph.
Closing	End your letter with a brief personal closing, followed by a comma. Capitalize the first word of the closing.
Signature	Your signature should be handwritten below the closing, even if the rest of the letter is typed.

The following model shows the correct form for a friendly letter.

The envelope for a friendly letter may be handwritten. It should contain the same information as that on the envelope of a business letter as shown on page 445. Be sure both addresses—yours and the recipient's—are clear and complete.

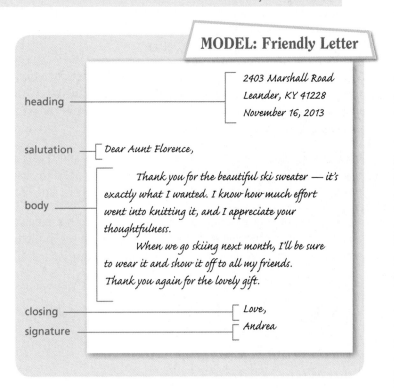

MODEL: Friendly Letter

heading
2403 Marshall Road
Leander, KY 41228
November 16, 2013

salutation
Dear Aunt Florence,

body
Thank you for the beautiful ski sweater — it's exactly what I wanted. I know how much effort went into knitting it, and I appreciate your thoughtfulness.
When we go skiing next month, I'll be sure to wear it and show it off to all my friends. Thank you again for the lovely gift.

closing
Love,

signature
Andrea

● **Practice Your Skills**

Achieving a Specific Purpose

Choose one of the following purposes for writing a friendly letter. Write the letter to a friend or relative. Make sure that your completed letter uses the correct format.

1. inviting someone to a surprise party

2. congratulating someone on earning an award

3. thanking a friend's parent after a weekend visit at their house

4. expressing sympathy for someone who broke a leg

5. declining an invitation to a Halloween party

2 Business Letters

Most of the **business letters** you will write call for some action on the part of the recipient. You may write to request information or to order merchandise. To make sure busy companies understand your point, keep your letter simple and direct.

You may wish to write a draft of your main message to make sure you have included all necessary information. Be sure the information is organized and accurately conveyed. Exclude any extraneous details. Check that your vocabulary, tone, and style are appropriate for business communication. Then prepare a neat final version that follows the correct format for a business letter.

Because a business letter is more formal than a friendly letter, it requires a more precise form. One of the most common forms is called **modified block form**. The heading, closing, and signature are positioned at the right, and the paragraphs are indented. The examples in this chapter follow this form.

Other techniques to make your letter professional and reader-friendly include using standard white paper, 8½-by-11 in size. Whenever possible, use a word-processing program to write your letters, leaving margins at least one inch wide.

Make a copy of your business letters in case you do not receive a reply in a reasonable amount of time and need to follow up by writing a second letter. If you are using a computer, be sure to save an electronic copy of your letters. If not, use a copying machine.

The parts of a business letter are explained in the chart below.

PARTS OF A BUSINESS LETTER	
Heading	The heading of a business letter is the same as the heading of a friendly letter. Include your full address, including two-letter state abbreviation and the full ZIP code, and, on the line below, the date.
Inside Address	A business letter includes a second address, called the inside address. Start the inside address two lines below the heading. Write the name of the person who will receive the letter if you know it. Use *Mr., Mrs., Ms.,* or *Dr.* If the person has a business title, such as Manager or Personnel Director, write it on the next line. Write the receiver's address, using the two-letter state abbreviation and the full ZIP code.
Salutation	Start the salutation, or greeting, two lines below the inside address. Use *Sir* or *Madam* if you do not know exactly who will read your letter. Otherwise, use the person's last name preceded by *Mr., Ms., Mrs., Dr.,* or other title. Use a colon after the salutation.
Body	Two lines below the salutation, begin the body or main message of your letter. Single-space each paragraph, and skip a line between paragraphs. If you enclose anything with your letter, such as a check, money order, or returned merchandise, mention this clearly and specifically.
Closing	In a business letter, use a formal closing such as *Sincerely, Sincerely yours, Very truly yours,* or *Yours truly.* Start the closing one line below the body. Line up the closing with the left-hand edge of the heading. Capitalize only the first letter and use a comma at the end of the closing.
Signature	In the signature of a business letter, your name appears twice. First type it—or print it if your letter is handwritten—four or five lines below the closing. Then sign your name in the space between the closing and your typed name. Use your full formal name but do not refer to yourself as *Mr.* or *Ms.*

When you are writing a business letter, always make sure it is clearly written, has a neat appearance, and follows the correct format, as in the sample that follows.

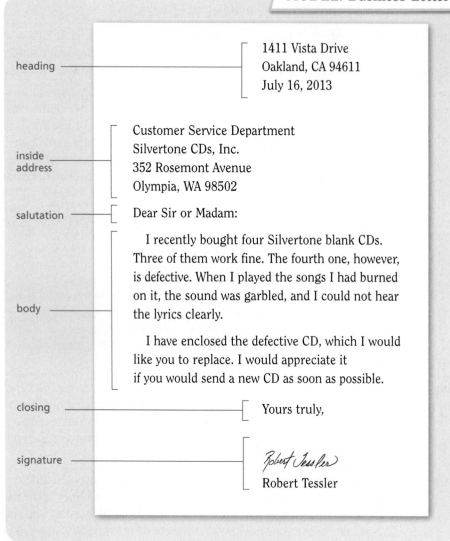

heading

1411 Vista Drive
Oakland, CA 94611
July 16, 2013

inside address

Customer Service Department
Silvertone CDs, Inc.
352 Rosemont Avenue
Olympia, WA 98502

salutation

Dear Sir or Madam:

body

I recently bought four Silvertone blank CDs. Three of them work fine. The fourth one, however, is defective. When I played the songs I had burned on it, the sound was garbled, and I could not hear the lyrics clearly.

I have enclosed the defective CD, which I would like you to replace. I would appreciate it if you would send a new CD as soon as possible.

closing

Yours truly,

signature

Robert Tessler
Robert Tessler

If you use a word-processing program to write your business letter, do the same for the envelope. Place your name and address in the upper left-hand corner. The recipient's address is centered on the envelope. Use the postal abbreviations for the state and include the ZIP code.

21ST CENTURY

Robert Tessler
1411 Vista Drive
Oakland, CA 94611

your name
and address

Customer Service Department
Silvertone CDs, Inc.
352 Rosemont Avenue
Olympia, WA 98502

recipient's
address

21ST CENTURY

BUSINESS E-MAILS

A business letter sent via e-mail should be just as formal as a letter sent by mail. Follow these guidelines when sending a business e-mail.

Guidelines for Writing a Business E-mail

- Include a formal salutation and closing. Format the body of the letter correctly.
- Use proper grammar and punctuation.
- Check your spelling. (Some e-mail programs have their own spell-check function. Use it!)
- Double-check the person's e-mail address to be sure you have typed it correctly.
- In the subject line of the e-mail, remember to specify the topic you are writing about.

LETTERS OF REQUEST

When writing a letter of request, be as accurate and specific as possible about the information you want to receive. To do so, include facts, details, and description. State your request politely; using *please* and *thank you* is essential. Notice how the format of a business letter is used to request information.

3412 Falcon Road
Mobile, AL 36619
May 29, 2014

Dr. Alan Morley
Membership Director
National Science Club
8880 Wilton Drive
Cooperstown, NY 13326

Dear Dr. Morley:

I learned about the National Science Club in a magazine, and I am eager to know more about it. Please send me information about activities the club sponsors, rules for membership, and annual dues. If a membership application is required, please send me the necessary form.

I would also be interested in learning whether there is a local chapter somewhere in the Mobile area. Thank you for your assistance.

Sincerely,

Carla Rodriguez

Carla Rodriguez

● Practice Your Skills

Requesting Information

Use the following information to write a letter of request. Be sure that you clearly state the information being requested and use a polite tone.

Heading:	364 Willow Street, Hainesburg, New Jersey 07832, January 10, 2014
Inside Address:	Ms. Sandra Hanson, Customer Service Representative, Quality Computer, Inc., 1167 Sequoia Boulevard, Belmont, California 94002
Request:	Arna Silverstein is shopping for a personal digital assistant (PDA). She has heard that the Vectronic7000 has all the features that she requires. She is writing to request a brochure and the current price of this computer.

21ST CENTURY

ORDER LETTERS

A business letter to order merchandise should give complete information—including the description, size, order number, price, and quantity of the items—in an organized manner. If you enclose payment for your order, the letter should state the amount enclosed.

MODEL: Order Letter

142 Harper Drive
Buffalo Gap, TX 79508
November 11, 2014

Capital Music Store
6554 Northwest Highway
Austin, TX 78756

Dear Sir or Madam:

Please send me the following items from your 2014 catalog:

1 Starlite music notebook, size 8½" by 11", Order #267-C	$ 3.95
1 music stand, Olympia model, order #383-F	$ 39.95
Shipping and handling	$ 8.50
TOTAL	$ 52.40

I have enclosed a money order for $52.40 to cover the cost of the merchandise, plus shipping and handling.

Sincerely yours,

Raymond Stevenson

Raymond Stevenson

● Practice Your Skills

Placing an Order

Use the following information to write an order letter. Be sure the information is organized and presented in a reader-friendly format, as in the model above.

Address: Order Department, The Cycle City, 4212 Emerson Street, Emporia, Kansas 66801

Merchandise: 2 rolls of Ace 1/2 inch handlebar tape, Item #33, $3.00 each; 4 Nite-Glow reflectors, Item #48, $5.95 each; $3.00 for shipping and handling

LETTERS OF COMPLAINT

If you have a complaint about a product, express yourself courteously in a letter to the company. Make sure your letter includes accurately conveyed information. The following letter provides specific facts and uses a polite but firm tone, which is appropriate for a letter of complaint.

MODEL: Letter of Complaint

313 Lavender Way
Millville, PA 17846
September 30, 2014

Subscription Department
Stars and Sky Magazine
36 Parkway Drive
Evanston, IL 60201

Dear Sir or Madam:

On August 4, I mailed an order form and a check for $19.95 to cover the cost of receiving your magazine for one year. Two weeks later I received a card indicating that my first issue would arrive by September 1. My check was cashed on August 21. So far I have not received a magazine.

Please look into this and let me know when I can expect my first magazine. Please resolve this issue as soon as possible. Thank you for your cooperation.

Very truly yours,

Michael Chin

Michael Chin

● Practice Your Skills

Making a Complaint

Rewrite the following body of an e-mail expressing a complaint. Revise the tone so that it is polite but firm. In rewriting, be sure to convey information accurately.

> I can't understand how anyone can be so careless! I ordered a kit for building a bird feeder (kit #BF-34) from your fall catalog, and you sent me a kit that doesn't include instructions. How do you expect a person to figure out how to put it together? I demand my money back or a set of instructions, immediately.

❸ Writing Procedures, Instructions, and Memos

Procedures and instructions are two other common forms of everyday writing. (You have already come across this kind of writing when you practiced writing how-to paragraphs, specifically when you were asked to describe a process or write a set of instructions on pages 240–243.) **Procedures** explain which steps and tasks are required to complete a job. **Instructions** tell you how to complete all the necessary steps.

A key difference between procedures and instructions is the scope of the task being described. Procedures can take place over a period of time and involve a number of people. Instructions are more focused. They involve smaller tasks that can be performed by one person.

WRITING PROCEDURES

The following model is taken from a booklet called "Student Discipline Rights and Procedures: A Guide for Advocates" published by the Education Law Center in New Jersey. Since the process is technical and must be followed precisely, the steps are each given a number for clarity. This reader-friendly formatting technique is often used in procedures and instructions, as are bullet points.

MODEL: Procedure

Procedural Requirements for Suspension of 10 Days or Less

A principal or his or her designee has the authority to impose a short-term suspension. The due process clause of the 14th Amendment to the U.S. Constitution has been interpreted to require the provision of the following procedural protections to a student facing short-term suspension:

1) Oral or written notice of what the student is accused of doing and the factual basis for the accusation.

2) An explanation of the evidence on which the charges are based, if the student denies the charges.

3) An informal hearing or meeting with the superintendent, principal, or other school administrator before the student is removed from school, during which time the student and his or her parent have the opportunity to explain the student's side of the story and request leniency in punishment. The hearing may immediately follow the notice.

WRITING INSTRUCTIONS

Written instructions are very direct. The following instructions from the San Antonio Public Library tell users how to renew books online.

How to Renew Checked Out Items Online

The due dates for checked out items can be extended in three different ways. In all cases the new due date will be three weeks from the date on which the item is renewed. Other restrictions may also apply.

- Click on the "My Account" button (above the red bar and on the left side) and enter your first or last name and your library card number. If you have problems logging into your account, please see "Logging into My Account" [link] for more information.

- In the "Summary" section of your patron account, click on "# items currently checked out."

- To renew **only** selected items, click in the checkbox next to each item you wish to renew and then click on the "Renew Selected" button at the top of the list.

- To renew **all** the items you have checked out, click on the "Renew All" button at the top of the list.

- If the renewal is successful, the due date section will show the new due date. If not, a brief message explaining why the item could not be renewed will be displayed. If you get a message that there is a "problem with your account," please call the library.

Well-written instructions and procedures share the following features.

Features of Good Procedures and Instructions

- They provide all the information necessary to complete a task or procedure.
- They anticipate the reader's questions, problems, and mistakes, and they address these issues.
- They explain unfamiliar terms or describe unfamiliar items.
- They present the steps in their sequential order.
- They use numbering systems, when appropriate, to separate the steps in the process. They may use other formatting structures, such as headings, to make the document user-friendly.
- They describe the task in accessible, concise language.

● Practice Your Skills

Writing Instructions

Think of a four- to five-step computer task that you know how to perform well. It might be hooking up a modem, logging on to the Internet, formatting a page, or manipulating graphics, for example. Write instructions for performing the task. Have a classmate evaluate the instructions by checking for the qualities listed in **Features of Good Procedures and Instructions**. If possible, ask your classmate to perform the task step-by-step to see if your instructions are easy to follow. Revise your instructions as necessary, based on your classmate's feedback.

WRITING MEMOS

A **memo** (short for memorandum) is a brief, somewhat informal communication. It is often used for communication among employees. It typically begins with the same four headings (shown in **boldface** type in the model below).

MODEL: Memo

Date: 6/14/13
To: All members of the secretarial staff
From: *Martin Burgess, Volunteer Coordinator, Tarryton Animal Shelter*
Subject: Training for new pet therapy

Please plan to attend a training workshop on our pet therapy program on Friday, 6/23, at 1:00 in the meeting room. The session will last until 3:00 and will include guidelines for handling the pets while at the retirement homes and for talking with the residents.

Memos are meant to be concise, usually running no longer than a single page, but they often contain complex information. The information should be well organized so that it is conveyed clearly to recipients who cannot spend much time reading the memo.

Guidelines for Writing Clear Memos

- Begin by writing a rough draft, an outline, notes, or a list of ideas.
- Refine these ideas to create a concise document with a clearly stated purpose. Make sure that all information is relevant.
- Use an organizational structure that is appropriate for your purpose and subject. Generally, put the most important information first. Divide complex information into small sections.
- Make the relationship among ideas explicit by using formatting structures such as headings, bullets, and numbers.
- Make sure the sentences in your final draft are short and focused. Phrasing in memos should be succinct and clear.
- Use accessible, direct language. Use jargon or technical terms specific to the subject when they suit your audience and the context.
- Maintain a polite, respectful, professional tone. This encourages others to adopt the same attitude when reading the memo.

Memos are used for all of the following purposes:

Common Purposes for Memos

1. To serve as notices or reminders of meetings. (See the model on page 451.)
2. To serve as transmittal sheets accompanying other materials. A transmittal memo should identify the materials being passed along (transmitted) and specify requests for action. For example:

    Attached is my report on how saxophone rental at Sharps and Flats compares in pricing and in other areas to rentals at other shops. Please let me know if there is any additional information that you would like to have.

3. To provide a written summary of a conversation in order to document specific agreements. For example:

    Thank you for working through the scheduling problem with me yesterday. We agreed that we will add a week to the schedule for the graphic arts department to complete its initial design, but we will shorten the turnaround time for page layout by one day per chapter. This change will keep our overall schedule on track.

4. To make a request. For example:

    I would like to take my vacation from July 15 to July 22. If these dates are acceptable, please add them to the vacation schedule and let me know so that I can move forward with my travel plans. Thank you.

5. To transfer information about a project, either to fellow workers within a company or to a client or employee working outside the company.

Although a memo can serve many purposes, there are times when a phone call or face-to-face conversation is preferable. Everything you put into writing can be read by anyone, whether or not the information is labeled "confidential". If you want to convey privileged information, either use the phone or meet with the person face-to-face. Also use the personal approach to resolve differences whenever possible. Human contact often promotes resolution.

E-MAIL VERSUS PAPER MEMOS

If you are sending a memo via e-mail, you should follow the same guidelines you would use for writing a paper memo. Express your ideas clearly, directly, and concisely and present well-organized information. Remember to use a formal, professional style when writing a business e-mail.

In memos sent via e-mail, "To", "From", and "Subject" are built into the e-mail format. You can send the same memo to many people, either by adding their e-mail addresses to the "To" entry field or by adding them to the "Cc" (carbon or courtesy copy) field.

● **Practice Your Skills**

Using an Appropriate E-mail Style

Rewrite the following e-mail message to make it suitable for a business communication.

> Hey Tina. What did you think of that presentation? Pretty awful, I'd say. :(
>
> I think we oughta tell the boss. "groan"

Completing a Job Application

When you apply for a job, you may be asked to fill out an application form. Some employers have you fill out a paper form; others require you to complete an application online. Application forms vary, but most of them ask for similar kinds of information. You may wish to prepare your information ahead of time so that you will be ready to complete the form when you apply for a job. Typically, you will be asked to supply the following information when completing a job application.

Information Often Requested on Job Applications

- the current date
- your complete name, address, and telephone number
- your date and place of birth
- your Social Security number
- names and addresses of schools you have attended and dates of attendance
- any special courses you have taken or advanced degrees you hold
- names and addresses of employers for whom you have worked and the dates you were employed
- any part-time, summer, and volunteer jobs you have held
- names and addresses of references (Obtain permission beforehand from each person you intend to list as a reference.)

When you fill out a job application, use the following guidelines.

Guidelines for Completing a Job Application

- Print or type all information neatly, accurately, and completely.
- Do not leave blanks. If a section does not apply to you, write or type N/A ("Not Applicable").
- List schools attended and work experience in order, giving the most recent first.
- If you mail the application form, include a brief cover letter, stating the job for which you are applying. The cover letter should follow the correct format for a business letter as shown on page 444.

● Practice Your Skills

Completing an Application

Think of a place where you would like to work in your community. Request an application, or download one from the company's or organization's Web site. Fill in the application. Then, with a partner, exchange completed applications. Check that your partner has filled in the application clearly and fully. Share your feedback with your partner.

APPLICATION FOR EMPLOYMENT

Barton's Department Store   *Please complete entire application to ensure processing.*

PERSONAL INFORMATION   (Please print)

Name	Last	First	Middle	Social Security/Social Insurance Number	Date (M/D/Y)
	Samuels	Paula	Jane	181-78-0945	11/15/15

Other names you are known by ___ N/A ___   Are you less than 18 years of age? Yes ✓ No ___ (Barton's is required to comply with federal, state, or provincial law.)

U.S. Applicant Only
Are you legally eligible for employment in the U.S.? Yes ✓ No ___
(proof of U.S. citizenship or immigration status will be required if hired for a position in the U.S.)

Have you been convicted of a felony in the last seven (7) years? Yes ___ No ✓
If Yes, list convictions that are a matter of public record (arrests are not convictions). A conviction will not necessarily disqualify you for employment.

Present Address	Street	City	State/Province		Zip Code/Postal Code
	414 Broad St.	Garfield	Pennsylvania		19015
Permanent Address	Street	City	State/Province		Zip Code/Postal Code
	same				

Phone Number   Daytime ___   Evening (555) 874-3198   Referred By ___

EMPLOYMENT DESIRED   (If you are applying for a retail hourly position, please keep in mind that the availability of hours may vary.)

Position *sales associate*   Location/Department *women's apparel*   Salary Desired *$7.50/hr*   Date You Can Start *immediately*

Specify hours available for each day of the week	Sunday	Monday	Tuesday	Wednesday	Thursday	Friday	Saturday
	Any	4p.m.–8p.m.	4p.m.–8p.m.	4p.m.–8p.m.	4p.m.–8p.m.	4p.m.–8p.m.	Any

Are you able to work overtime? *no*

Have you ever worked for Barton's Department Store? *no*   If yes, when? ___   Which store/department? *N/A*

EDUCATION

	Name and Address of School	Circle Last Years Completed	Did You Graduate?	Subjects Studied and Degrees Received
High School	Wilson High School	1 2 ③ 4	Y Ⓝ	in first year
College		1 2 3 4	Y N	N/A
Post College		1 2 3 4	Y N	N/A
Trade, Business, or Correspondence School		1 2 3 4	Y N	N/A

List skills relevant to the position applied for *can run a cash register; have computer experience*

SKILLS   *For Office/Administrative positions only*   Typing WPM: *45*   10-Key: ☐ Yes ☐ No

Computer Proficiency: ☐ Word for Windows   ☐ Excel   ☐ Others: ___

Have you ever visited a Barton's Department Store? Where? Describe your experience. *I went to the Barton's in Pittsburgh and was impressed by the selection of merchandise and the courtesy of the sales associates.*

What do you like about clothing? *I like to look nice and feel that I have a good fashion sense. I am good at helping people.*

Why would you like to work for Barton's Department Store? *It would be a convenient after-school location. I like working with people.*

Describe a specific situation where you have provided excellent customer service in your most recent position. Why was this effective? *When I worked at a bookstore I called around to all of our branches until I found a hard-to-find copy of a book a customer was looking for.*

FORMER EMPLOYERS List below current and last three employers, starting with most recent one first. Please include any non-paid/volunteer experience which is related to the job for which you are applying.

Date (M/D/Y) 11/15/15

	Current Employer (Name and Address of Employer – Type of Business)	Salary or Hourly	Position	Reason For Leaving
1. From 8/11/15 To 11/12/15	Della's Soup Kitchen 5 Gale Road, Garfield	Starting $5.75 Ending $6.50 If hourly, average # of hours per week 8 hrs.	Waitress	to gain more work experience

Duties Performed: serving soup; clearing; setting tables

Supervisor's Name	Phone Number	May We Contact?
Della Nathan	(555) 330-1234	yes

	Previous Employer (Name and Address of Employer – Type of Business)	Salary or Hourly	Position	Reason For Leaving
2. From 6/5/15 To 8/10/15	Reese's Candy Shop 55 Marsh Street, Garfield	Starting $5.75 Ending $5.75 If hourly, average # of hours per week 5 hrs.	Cashier	lack of hours

Duties Performed: working the register, opening the store

Supervisor's Name	Phone Number	May We Contact?
Dana Reese	(555) 774-2350	yes

	Previous Employer (Name and Address of Employer – Type of Business)	Salary or Hourly	Position	Reason For Leaving
3. From 12/7/14 To 5/1/15	Garfield Grocery 125 Main Street, Garfield	Starting $4.00 Ending $4.50 If hourly, average # of hours per week 10 hrs.	Cashier	insufficient wages

Duties Performed: working the register, straightening shelves, sweeping

Supervisor's Name	Phone Number	May We Contact?
Lovey Gaber	(555) 525-3725	yes

	Previous Employer (Name and Address of Employer – Type of Business)	Salary or Hourly	Position	Reason For Leaving
4. From To		Starting Ending If hourly, average # of hours per week		

Duties Performed:

Supervisor's Name	Phone Number	May We Contact?

REFERENCES Give below the names of three professional references, whom you have known at least one year.

	Name	Address & Phone Number	Business	Years Acquainted How Do You Know This Person?
1	Carl Smith	14 Main Street, Garfield (555) 705-2319	Principal	3, at school
2	Jane Bart	211 Main Street, Garfield (555) 858-2672	Manager	5, friend
3	Michael Reese	45 Dorand Road, Garfield (555) 646-2792	Accountant	7, friend's father

Date 11/15/15   Signature   Paula Samuels

WE ARE AN EQUAL OPPORTUNITY EMPLOYER COMMITTED TO HIRING A DIVERSE WORKFORCE.

Barton's Department Store

C. Speeches, Presentations, and Discussions

Apply 21st Century Communication and Collaboration Skills

True communication occurs when a speaker presents ideas in a clear, organized, and forceful way and the listeners are able to understand and respond to the speaker's message. Real collaboration takes place when people freely exchange ideas and share responsibility to achieve a common goal.

At the heart of good communication and collaboration lies respect. In the diverse world of the 21st century, you will learn and work with people from various social and cultural backgrounds who will have perspectives different from yours. Whether you are giving a speech, participating in a group discussion, or collaborating with a team to complete a task, respecting varied opinions and values will enrich your understanding and make you a more successful communicator and collaborator.

In this section, you will learn effective strategies for speaking, listening, and collaborating that will help you succeed in school and in the workplace.

Developing Your Public Speaking and Presentation Skills

In school and in the workplace, you may sometimes be asked to give a formal speech. As a student, you may make a speech to classmates, parents, or teachers. As a professional, you may make a formal presentation to a group of co-workers at a small meeting or a large convention. Learning to express your ideas well and use media and technology effectively will help you deliver a successful speech.

① Preparing Your Speech

A successful speech or presentation requires careful preparation. Putting thought, time, and effort into preparing your speech will pay off in the end.

CHOOSING A SUBJECT TO SUIT YOUR AUDIENCE AND PURPOSE

The purpose of a speech or presentation may be to inform, instruct, motivate, persuade, or entertain. Whether you are trying to inform experts in a field or entertain young children, you want to match your subject to your listeners and purpose in order to deliver a successful speech. The following strategies will help you choose a subject that suits your audience and purpose.

Strategies for Considering Audience and Purpose

- Determine your purpose. Is it to inform, instruct, motivate, persuade, or entertain?
- Find out the interests of your audience. Then choose a subject that matches your listeners' interests and your purpose. For example, if your purpose is to persuade a group of parents to vote for a particular candidate, then you might choose the candidate's views on education as your subject.
- You want your audience to have confidence in you, so choose a subject that you are very familiar with or can research thoroughly.

You can learn more about specific purposes for written and oral essays on pages 5–6, 15, and 124.

● Practice Your Skills

Identifying a Subject That Suits an Audience and Purpose

1. Write an example of a subject for a speech whose purpose is to inform. Your audience is a group of middle school students.
2. Write an example of a subject for a speech whose purpose is to persuade. Your audience is a group of officials in your community.
3. Write an example of a subject for a speech whose purpose is to entertain. Your audience is a group of parents.

LIMITING A SUBJECT

Once you choose your subject, you should limit and refine it. Limiting the subject enables you to present it fully to a given audience within a defined period of time. As a rule of thumb, it takes about as long to deliver a ten-minute speech as it does to read aloud slowly four pages of a typed, double-spaced, written composition. The strategies for limiting a subject for a speech are the same as the strategies you would use to limit a subject for an essay.

You can learn more about choosing and limiting a subject on pages 14–15 and 214–216.

Strategies for Limiting a Subject

- Limit your subject by choosing one aspect of it. For example, for a ten-minute speech about the planet Mars, you could limit the subject to the weather on Mars.
- Try to determine what your audience already knows about your subject, and consider what your audience may expect to hear. Then limit your subject to suit your listeners' expectations.
- Limit your subject to suit your purpose.

The following examples illustrate three ways to limit the subject of skiing according to the purpose of your speech.

LIMITING A SUBJECT

Purpose of Speech	Example
to inform	Explain the similarities and differences between downhill and cross-country skiing.
to persuade	Convince students to take up cross-country skiing.
to entertain	Tell about your experiences the first time you went downhill skiing.

● Practice Your Skills

Limiting a Subject

Choose a purpose and an audience, and then limit each subject to be suitable for a ten-minute speech.

1. pollution   **4.** explorers

2. parental problems   **5.** sports

3. the homeless   **6.** music trends

GATHERING AND ORGANIZING INFORMATION

After choosing and limiting your subject, you should begin to gather information. First, brainstorm with someone to list any information you already know about your subject. (See page 18). To learn more about your subject, research it in the library or media center or online. Think of knowledgeable people you might interview. Before the interview, prepare the questions you will ask.

Taking Notes Take notes on note cards throughout your research. Note cards are best for recording ideas because the information can be easily organized later as you prepare to make an outline of your speech. Use a separate card to summarize each important idea, and include facts and examples to support the idea. Record accurately any quotations you plan to use. If you conduct an interview, take notes or use an audio recorder and then transfer the information to note cards.

Collecting Audiovisual Aids Audiovisual aids, such as maps, pictures, power slides, CDs, and DVDs, can add to the impact of your speech. Choose aids that suit the purpose and context of your speech. Make sure the aids will help you communicate your message effectively and will not be distracting. Once you decide which of your main points to enhance with the use of audiovisual aids, gather or create these materials as you prepare your speech.

Strategies for Organizing a Speech

- Arrange your notes in the order in which you intend to present your information.
- Use the cards to make a detailed outline of your speech.
- Draft an introduction. To catch the interest of your audience, begin with an anecdote, an unusual fact, a question, or an interesting quotation. Be sure to include a thesis statement that makes clear the main point and the purpose of your speech.
- The body of your speech should include several ideas.
- Arrange the ideas in a logical order, and think of the transitions you will use.
- Support each idea or claim with facts, examples, and other types of valid evidence.
- Use appropriate and effective appeals to support points or claims.
- Write a conclusion for your speech that summarizes your important ideas. Try to leave your audience with a memorable sentence or phrase.

● Practice Your Skills

Gathering and Organizing Information for a Speech

Choose and limit a subject for a 10-minute speech in which the purpose is to inform. Write what you know about the subject on note cards. Next, find information for four more note cards by using Internet or library sources. Organize your cards, and write a detailed outline of your speech. Prepare any audiovisual aids you will use.

PRACTICING YOUR SPEECH

In most cases, you should not write out your speech in order to read it or memorize it. Instead, plan to use your outline to deliver your speech, or convert your outline and note cards into cue cards to use when making your presentation. Cue cards help you remember your main points, your key words and phrases, and any quotations you plan to include in your speech. Use the following strategies when practicing your speech.

Strategies for Practicing a Speech

- Practice in front of a long mirror so that you will be aware of your gestures, facial expressions, posture, and body language.
- Look around the room as if you were looking at your audience.
- As you practice, use your cue cards and any audiovisual aids that are part of your speech.
- If you intend to use a microphone, practice your technique.
- Time your speech. If necessary, add or cut information.
- Practice over a period of several days. Your confidence will grow each time you practice.

Revise your speech as you practice. You can do this by experimenting with your choice of words and your use of audiovisual aids. Add and delete information to make your main points clearer. Try practicing your speech with a friend. Listeners' comments may help you revise and improve your speech.

● Practice Your Skills

Practicing and Revising Your Informative Speech

Use your outline for your informative speech to make cue cards. Then, using the strategies above, practice your speech before a relative or classmate. Use your listener's comments to make improvements, and then practice your revised speech.

Developing Your Public Speaking and Presentation Skills   **461**

2 Delivering Your Speech

If you have followed the strategies for preparing your speech, you should feel confident when the time comes to stand up in front of your audience and deliver your speech. The following strategies will help you deliver an effective speech.

Strategies for Delivering a Speech

- Have ready all the materials you need, such as your outline or cue cards and audiovisual materials or equipment.
- Make sure that computer presentation equipment is assembled and running properly.
- Wait until your audience is quiet and settled.
- Relax and breathe deeply before you begin your introduction.
- Stand with your weight evenly divided between both feet. Avoid swaying back and forth.
- Look directly at the members of your audience, not over their heads. Try to make eye contact.
- Speak slowly, clearly, and loudly enough to be heard.
- Use good, clear diction.
- Use pitch and tone of voice to enhance the communication of your message.
- Be aware of using correct grammar and well-formed sentences.
- Use informal, technical, or standard language appropriate to the purpose, audience, occasion, and subject. Be sure to use respectful language when presenting opposing views.
- Use rhetorical strategies appropriate to the message, whether your purpose is to inform or to persuade.
- Use appropriate gestures and facial expressions to emphasize your main points.
- Make sure that everyone in your audience can see your audiovisual aids, such as charts and power slides.
- After finishing your speech, take your seat without making comments to people in the audience.

3 Evaluating an Oral Presentation

The ability to evaluate an oral presentation will help you and your classmates improve your future speeches. The following Oral Presentation Evaluation Form may be useful. When evaluating a classmate's speech and completing the form, be honest but remember to make your comments positive, respectful, and helpful. Your comments should be specific in order to help the speaker understand your suggestions. Use listener feedback to evaluate the effectiveness of your speech and to help you set goals for future speeches.

ORAL PRESENTATION EVALUATION FORM

Subject: _____

Speaker: _____ Date: _____

Content

Were the subject and purpose appropriate for the audience?

What was the speaker's point of view?

Was the main point clear?

Were there enough details and examples?

Did all the ideas clearly relate to the subject?

Were the speaker's reasoning and use of evidence sound?

If not, where was the fallacious reasoning and/or distorted or exaggerated evidence?

Was the speaker's rhetoric appropriate and effective?

Was the length appropriate (not too long or too short)?

Organization

Did the speech begin with an interesting introduction?

Did the ideas in the body follow a logical order?

Were transitions used between ideas?

Did the conclusion summarize the main points?

Presentation

Did the speaker use a good choice of words?

Was the speech sufficiently loud and clear?

Was the rate appropriate (not too fast or too slow)?

Did the speaker make eye contact with the audience?

Did the speaker make effective use of pitch and tone of voice?

Did the speaker use gestures and pauses effectively?

Were cue cards or an outline used effectively?

Were audiovisual aids used effectively?

Comments

● Practice Your Skills

Delivering and Evaluating an Informative Speech

Deliver your informative speech to your classmates. They should evaluate your presentation by using the Oral Presentation Evaluation Form. In addition, complete a form for the speeches presented by your classmates. Use your listeners' feedback to improve your future speeches.

Delivering and Evaluating an Entertaining Speech

Next week you will be a contestant on the game show *Crack That Grin.* Contestants compete to tell stories that will make the stone-faced panelists laugh. Prepare an entertaining speech that will make the panelists "crack grins." Be sure to include vivid and humorous details in a logical and clear order. Practice your speech before a friend or family member, and then present it to your classmates. Did you use effective strategies to make your speech entertaining? Have your classmates evaluate your performance.

Delivering and Evaluating a Persuasive Speech

Your school is constructing a new gymnasium. The plan is to demolish the old gym. Prepare a speech to persuade the faculty that the old gym should be converted into a student activities center instead. Support your argument by discussing useful, informative, and enjoyable activities that could be held in the student center. Draw on personal experiences or the experiences of others. Be sure to use a tone and style that suits your audience. Consider using audiovisual aids to enhance your message. Present your speech to your classmates. Then write a brief assessment of your performance. Describe your strengths and the areas that need improvement.

Developing Your Critical Listening Skills

Skillful listening requires that you pay close attention to what you hear. You must comprehend, evaluate, and remember the information. Good listeners engage in critical, reflective, and appreciative listening. They also engage in **empathic listening,** or listening with feeling. Skills that you have practiced while learning how to prepare and present a speech will be invaluable to you as you work to develop and sharpen your critical listening skills.

1 Listening Appreciatively to Presentations and Performances

You may have occasion to attend a public reading or an oral interpretation of a written work, such as an essay, a poem, a play, a chapter of a novel, or an excerpt from a memoir. **Oral interpretation** is the performance or expressive reading of a literary work. As a listener, you must judge how successfully the performer has expressed the intentions, style, and meaning of the work through the use of verbal and nonverbal techniques. The following guidelines will help you listen appreciatively to oral presentations and performances.

Strategies for Listening Appreciatively

- Be alert to the expressive power of the dramatic pause.
- Observe the use of gestures, voices, and facial expressions to enhance the message.
- Listen for changes in volume, intonation, and pitch used to emphasize important ideas.
- Listen for rhymes, repeated words, and other sound devices.
- Listen for rhetorical strategies and other skillful uses of language.
- Take time to reflect upon the message, and try to experience, with empathy, the thoughts and feelings being expressed.

● Practice Your Skills

Listening to Presentations and Performances

Perhaps your local bookstore hosts readings of prose and poetry by well-known authors. A nearby theater group might be performing a dramatic work that you have read for school. You may also have occasion to attend original artistic performances by your peers. You will get the most out of the experience by preparing a listening strategy suited to the speaker's subject and purpose.

Prepare your own strategies for listening to and evaluating the following oral presentations. Identify what you would listen for in each case.

1. an actor reading a dramatic monologue from a play

2. a poet reading a collection of new poetry

3. a writer reading a selection from a novel

4. a classmate reading John F. Kennedy's inauguration speech

● Practice Your Skills

Presenting an Oral Interpretation

Perform a reading of a scene for your class. Form a small group, and choose a scene from a play, such as *The Price,* that you have read for school. Then follow these steps to prepare and present your oral interpretation.

1. Sit in a circle and read through the scene. Discuss the most important ideas in the scene. Using the *5 W*s and *H,* analyze the scene for an understanding of character, purpose, and situation.

2. Prepare a script of the scene. Highlight the lines that you are going to perform. Mark key words that you want to emphasize through gestures, tone, or facial expressions.

3. Rehearse the scene. Try out different readings of your lines until you arrive at the best interpretation. Listen carefully to the other characters as they speak, and respond to them as though you were holding a real conversation. Use the techniques that you have learned to assess your performance and those of your peers.

4. Perform the reading for your classmates. Instruct them to take notes and analyze whether you successfully conveyed the meaning of the scene.

② Listening to Directions

When you are assigned a task, listen carefully to the instructions. Do not assume you know what to do or what the speaker will say. Then follow the strategies below for understanding directions.

Strategies for Listening to Directions

• Write down the directions as soon as the speaker gives them. You may not remember them as well as you think.

• Ask specific questions to clarify the directions.

• When you finish an assignment, review the directions to make sure you have followed them correctly.

● Practice Your Skills

Following and Evaluating Directions

To practice giving and following directions, think of a simple task that can be completed in the classroom, such as making a book cover out of a paper bag or putting new laces in a pair of sneakers. Write step-by-step directions for completing the task. Read your directions to a partner, and have your partner follow them using the Strategies for Listening to Directions. Repeat the process, but this time follow your partner's directions. You and your partner should then evaluate the effectiveness of each process. Were the directions clear and complete? Did you listen effectively?

❸ Listening for Information

When you listen to a speech or a lecture, pay close attention so that you can understand and evaluate what you hear. Listening for the purpose of learning requires extra concentration. You may find the following strategies helpful.

Strategies for Listening for Information

- Sit comfortably but stay alert. Try to focus on what the speaker is saying, without being distracted by people and noises.
- Determine the speaker's purpose, whether it is to inform, instruct, motivate, or persuade.
- Listen for verbal clues to identify the speaker's main ideas. Often, for example, a speaker emphasizes important points by using such phrases as *first, later, also consider, most importantly, remember that,* or *in conclusion.*
- Watch for nonverbal clues such as gestures, pauses, or changes in the speaking pace. Such clues often signal important points.
- Determine the speaker's values and point of view about the subject. For example, is the speaker expressing positive or negative attitudes or arguing for or against an issue?
- Use your knowledge of vocabulary to interpret accurately the speaker's message.
- As you listen, note anything that seems confusing or unclear.
- Ask relevant questions to monitor and clarify your understanding of ideas.
- Take notes to organize your thoughts and to help you remember details. Your notes provide a basis for further discussion. You may also want to use your notes to outline the speech or write a summary of it. If the speech is a course lecture, notes will help you study for a test on the subject.

● Practice Your Skills

Listening and Taking Notes

Organize a classroom experiment. The following test will show how well you communicate, how well your audience listens, and the extent to which note taking helps. Prepare a short speech for the purpose of informing. Write a few key questions that you think your listeners should be able to answer after listening to your talk. Deliver the speech while one half of the class listens without taking notes and the other half of the class takes notes while listening. Instruct all the students to write answers to your questions. Then have the class evaluate whether note taking helped students answer the questions correctly.

LISTENING CRITICALLY

Critical listeners carefully evaluate the information in a speech. They judge whether the information and ideas are valid. Be on the lookout for the following propaganda techniques, which a speaker may use to mislead or manipulate you.

TECHNIQUE	DEFINITION	FURTHER INFORMATION
Confusing Fact and Opinion	an opinion presented as a fact	To learn more, see page 274.
Bandwagon Appeal	an invitation to do or think the same thing as everyone else	To learn more, see page 274.
Testimonial	a statement, usually given by a famous person, that supports a product, candidate, or policy	To learn more, see page 274.
Unproved Generalization	a generalization based on only one or two facts or examples	To learn more, see page 274.
Glittering Generality	a word or phrase usually associated with virtue and goodness	To learn more, see page 275.

Developing Your Group Discussion Skills

Group discussion is a way for you to share your ideas and learn from others. In both formal and informal group discussions, you communicate ideas, exchange opinions, solve problems, and reach decisions. Learning group discussion skills will help you to state your own ideas effectively and to listen carefully to others' ideas.

1 Participating in Group Discussions

Discussing ideas with your classmates plays an important role in the learning process. In the writing process, group brainstorming can help you in the prewriting stage—particularly in generating ideas for subjects. Peer conferencing can help you in the revising stage, when you are looking for ways to improve an essay. In addition, you may use discussion skills when you practice a speech or prepare for a test with others. Use the following strategies to help you participate effectively in group discussions.

Strategies for Participating in Group Discussions

- Listen carefully and respond respectfully to others' views.
- Keep an open mind and appreciate diverse perspectives.
- Ask questions and clarify, verify, or challenge the ideas of others.
- Propel conversations by relating the discussion to broader themes.
- Express your ideas clearly. Present examples or evidence to support your ideas.
- Make sure your contributions to the discussion are constructive and relevant to the subject.
- Actively incorporate others into the discussion.
- Formulate and provide effective verbal and nonverbal feedback.
- Be flexible and try to help your group draw a conclusion or reach a consensus.

2 Leading Group Discussions

Sometimes the teacher will lead the discussion to make sure that it does not stray from the agenda. Other times a group appoints its own leader to focus the discussion and keep it on track. Such discussions are called **directed discussions**. If you are chosen to be the leader, or moderator, of a directed discussion group, use the following strategies to help you conduct the discussion effectively.

Strategies for Discussion Leaders

- Introduce the topic, question, or problem. With the group's help, state the purpose or goal of the discussion.
- Keep the discussion on track to help the group reach agreement and accomplish its goals.
- Encourage everyone to participate, and establish a tone of respect. Make sure that everyone has an equal opportunity and equal time to speak.
- Keep a record of the group's main points and decisions, or assign this task to a group member.
- At the end of the discussion, summarize the main points, and restate any conclusions or decisions the group reached.

● **Practice Your Skills**

Conducting a Directed Discussion

Form small groups for a directed discussion. Choose a subject related to school, and establish a goal. Take turns serving as discussion leader.

③ Cooperative Learning

A special kind of discussion group is the **cooperative learning** group, sometimes called a **task group.** In a cooperative learning group, you work with others to achieve a particular goal. Each member of the group is assigned a task to help meet the goal. For example, members of a cooperative learning group in a social studies class may work together to prepare an oral presentation on Saudi Arabia. One member of the group may research the geography and economy of Saudi Arabia, another member may concentrate on the history and government of that country, and a third member may explore its religion and art.

Each member may also have a particular role to play in the group, such as **group leader**. The leader not only leads discussions but also coordinates the group members' efforts. The success of the project depends on the effective collaboration of group members. Work with your peers to set rules, goals, deadlines, and roles for the discussion.

Strategies for Cooperative Learning

- Follow the **Strategies for Participating in Group Discussions** (page 469).
- Participate in planning the project and assigning tasks.
- When you have been assigned a task, do not let your group down by coming to a meeting unprepared.
- Value the contributions of other team members.
- Cooperate with others in the group to resolve conflicts, solve problems, reach conclusions, or make decisions.
- Help your group achieve its goals by taking your fair share of responsibility for the group's success.

● **Practice Your Skills**

Organizing a Cooperative Learning Group

Form groups of three to five, and plan a presentation on deserts. Choose a leader. Follow the **Strategies for Cooperative Learning** above. Prepare an oral presentation, and deliver it to the class. Remember to follow the steps for preparing and delivering an oral presentation.

Media and Technology

Part I	Critical Thinking and Problem Solving for Academic Success
Part II	Communication and Collaboration
Part III	Media and Technology

Essential Skills

You already understand the importance of literacy, or the ability to read and write. In the 21st century, literacy—meaning "knowledge of a particular subject or field"—in the areas of information, media, and technology is also essential. Part III of this guide will help you develop literacy in these three areas. This knowledge will help you succeed in school and in your future jobs.

① Information Literacy

Today, a tremendous amount of information is available at your fingertips. To acquire information literacy, you must know how to access, manage, evaluate, and use this wealth of information. Learning advanced search strategies will help you locate information efficiently and effectively from a range of relevant print and electronic sources. Evaluating the reliability and validity of sources will help you assess their usefulness. Then you can synthesize information in order to draw conclusions or to solve a problem creatively. Understanding the difference between paraphrasing and plagiarism and knowing how to record bibliographic information will ensure that you use information in an ethical, legal manner. Part III of this guide will help you build your information literacy skills by showing you how to use the Internet to access information.

You can learn more about information literacy on pages 324–389.

② Media Literacy

Media messages serve a variety of purposes. They can have a powerful influence on your opinions, values, beliefs, and actions. Part III of this guide will help you develop your media literacy skills by showing you how to use both print and nonprint media to communicate your message. You will learn how to use these media to create effective messages that suit your audience and purpose. You will also learn about the types of tools available for creating media products.

You can learn more about media literacy on pages 54, 68, 98, 132, 153, 200, 227, 267, 276, 342–361, and 386.

③ Technology Literacy

In the 21st century, knowing how to use technology to research, evaluate, and communicate information is essential. You must also know how to use different forms of technology, such as computers and audio and video recorders, to integrate information and create products. Part III of this guide will show you how to use technology effectively to access information and to publish and present your ideas in different media.

You can learn more about technology literacy on pages 386–387.

A. Electronic Publishing

Apply Media and Technology Literacy

Everything you may ever have to say or write requires some medium through which you express it and share it with others. The ability to use available media and technology to their fullest potential will enable you to communicate your ideas effectively and to a widespread audience. For now, most academic and workplace communication still depends on print technology. By using that to its full capability, you will prepare yourself for the inevitable improvements and upgrades that will be a feature of communication in the future.

In this section, you will develop your skills in using available technology in your communication.

Digital Publishing

The computer is a powerful tool that gives you the ability to create everything from newsletters to multimedia reports. Many software programs deliver word-processing and graphic arts capabilities that once belonged only to professional printers and designers. Armed with the knowledge of how to operate your software, you simply need to add some sound research and a healthy helping of creativity to create an exciting paper.

WORD PROCESSING

Using a standard word-processing program, such as Microsoft Word™, makes all aspects of the writing process easier. Use a word-processing program to

- create an outline
- save multiple versions of your work
- revise your manuscript
- proof your spelling, grammar, and punctuation
- produce a polished final draft document

USING A SPELL CHECKER

You can use your computer to help you catch spelling errors. One way is to set your Preferences for a wavy red line to appear under words that are misspelled as you type. You can also set your Preferences to correct spelling errors automatically.

A second way to check your spelling is to choose Spelling and Grammar from the Tools menu. Select the text you want to check and let the spell checker run through it looking for errors. While a spell checker can find many errors, it cannot tell you if a correctly spelled word is used correctly. For example, you might have written *The books were over their.* The spell checker will not identify an error here, even though the correct word is *there*, not *their*.

FASCINATING FONTS

Once your written material is revised and proofed, you can experiment with type as a way to enhance the content of your written message and present it in a reader-friendly format. Different styles of type are called **fonts** or **typefaces**. Most word-processing programs feature more than 30 different choices. You'll find them listed in the Format menu under Font.

Or they may be located on the toolbar at the top left of your screen.

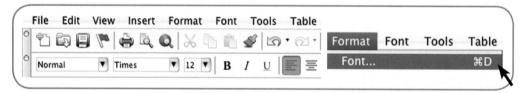

Most fonts fall into one of two categories: **serif** typefaces or **sans serif** typefaces. A serif is a small curve or line added to the end of some of the letter strokes. A typeface that includes these small added curves is called a serif typeface. A font without them is referred to as sans serif, or in other words, without serifs.

Times New Roman is a serif typeface.

Arial is a sans serif typeface.

In general, sans serif fonts have a sharp look and are better for shorter pieces of writing, such as headings and titles. Serif typefaces work well for body copy.

Each typeface, whether serif or sans serif, has a personality of its own and makes a different impression on the reader. Specialized fonts, like the examples in the second paragraph on the next page, are great for unique projects (posters, invitations, and personal correspondence) but less appropriate for writing assignments for school or business.

Since most school writing is considered formal, good font choices include Times New Roman, Arial, Helvetica, or Bookman Antiqua. These type styles are fairly plain. They allow the reader to focus on the meaning of your words instead of being distracted by the way they appear on the page.

With so many fonts to choose from, you may be tempted to include a dozen or so in your document. Be careful! Text pɾiNtᵉd *in* multiple fonts *caɴ* **ᵇᵉ EXTREMELY** *confusing* **to** *read*. Remember that the whole idea of using different typefaces is to enhance and clarify your message, not muddle it!

A SIZABLE CHOICE

Another way to add emphasis to your writing and make it reader-friendly is to adjust the size of the type. Type size is measured in points. One inch is equal to 72 points. Therefore, 72-point type would have letters that measure one inch high. To change the point size of your type, open the Format menu and click Font.

Or use the small number box on the toolbar at the top left side of your screen.

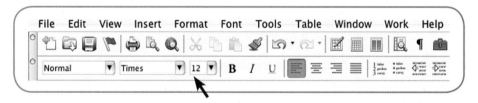

For most school and business writing projects, 10 or 12 points is the best size of type for the main body copy of your text. However, it's very effective to increase the type size for titles, headings, and subheadings to highlight how your information is organized. Another way to add emphasis is to apply a style to the type, such as **bold,** *italics,* or underline. Styles are also found in the Format menu under Font.

Or look for them—abbreviated as **B** for bold, *I* for italics, and U for underline—in the top center section of the toolbar on your screen.

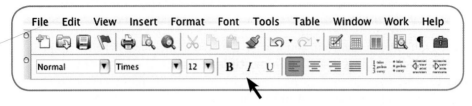

If you have access to a color printer, you may want to consider using colored type to set your heading apart from the rest of the body copy. Red, blue, or other dark colors work best. Avoid yellow or other light shades that might fade out and be difficult to read.

Use different type sizes, styles, and colors sparingly and consistently throughout your work. In other words, all the body copy should be in one style of type. All the headings should be in another, and so on. Doing so will give your work a unified, polished appearance.

TEXT FEATURES

Text features such as **bulleted lists** and **numbered lists** are useful ways to organize information and give it a reader-friendly format. If you create pages of text in which information isn't broken up in any way, your readers may lose focus or have trouble identifying your main points. Instead, use bulleted or numbered lists to highlight important information and present it clearly and simply. To create these lists, open the Format menu and click on Bullets and Numbering. You can also click on the numbered or bulleted list on the toolbar at the top right of your screen.

A sidebar is another useful text feature for presenting information. A **sidebar** is a section of text that is placed alongside the main copy. Often the text in a sidebar appears in a box. Use sidebars to present additional, interesting information that relates to your main topic but doesn't belong in the body of your report or paper.

LAYOUT HELP FROM YOUR COMPUTER

One way to organize the information in your document is to use one of the preset page layouts provided by your word-processing program. All you have to do is write your document using capital letters for main headings and uppercase and lowercase letters for subheadings. Set the headings apart from the body copy by hitting the "return" key. Then open the Format menu and click the Autoformat heading. Your copy will probably look like the illustration on the next page.

You can probably use this automatic, preset format for most of the writing you do in school. You'll also find other options available in the File menu under Page Setup.

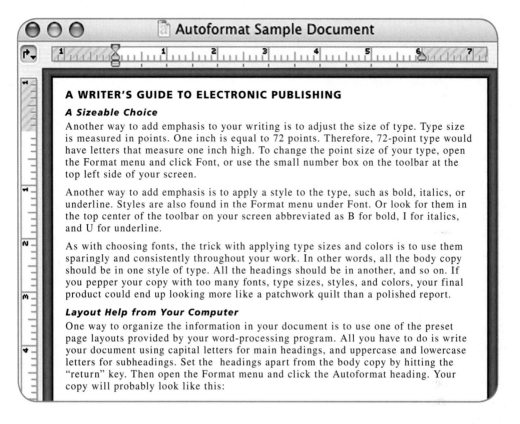

A WRITER'S GUIDE TO ELECTRONIC PUBLISHING

A Sizeable Choice

Another way to add emphasis to your writing is to adjust the size of type. Type size is measured in points. One inch is equal to 72 points. Therefore, 72-point type would have letters that measure one inch high. To change the point size of your type, open the Format menu and click Font, or use the small number box on the toolbar at the top left side of your screen.

Another way to add emphasis is to apply a style to the type, such as bold, italics, or underline. Styles are also found in the Format menu under Font. Or look for them in the top center of the toolbar on your screen abbreviated as B for bold, I for italics, and U for underline.

As with choosing fonts, the trick with applying type sizes and colors is to use them sparingly and consistently throughout your work. In other words, all the body copy should be in one style of type. All the headings should be in another, and so on. If you pepper your copy with too many fonts, type sizes, styles, and colors, your final product could end up looking more like a patchwork quilt than a polished report.

Layout Help from Your Computer

One way to organize the information in your document is to use one of the preset page layouts provided by your word-processing program. All you have to do is write your document using capital letters for main headings, and uppercase and lowercase letters for subheadings. Set the headings apart from the body copy by hitting the "return" key. Then open the Format menu and click the Autoformat heading. Your copy will probably look like this:

21ST CENTURY

Here you can change the margins and add headers, footers, and page numbers. Headers and footers are descriptive titles that automatically appear at the top or bottom of each page without your having to retype them each time. For example, you may wish to add the title of your project and the date as a header or footer to each page.

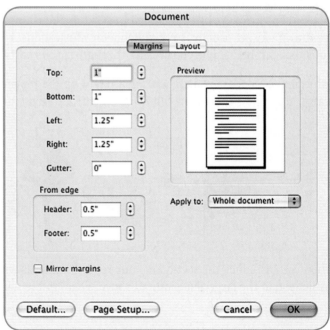

To insert a header or a footer, go to View and click on Header and Footer. Note that page numbers may also be inserted by way of the Insert option on your menu bar.

```
Header
Project Title Here ¶
Date Here ¶
```

LET'S GET GRAPHIC

The old saying "A picture is worth a thousand words" is particularly true when it comes to spicing up papers and reports. Publishing and presentation software programs give you the ability to include photographs, illustrations, and charts in your work that can express your ideas more clearly and succinctly than words alone.

The key to using graphics effectively is to make sure each one conveys a message of importance. Don't use them just for decoration. Be sure they add something meaningful, or you'll actually detract from your written message.

Drawings Many paint and draw programs allow you to create an illustration or **import** (bring in from another program) one into your document. Drawings can help illustrate concepts that are difficult to describe, such as mechanical parts or procedures. Cartoons can also add a nice touch. If you use them sparingly, they can lighten up an otherwise dry, technical report.

Clip Art Another kind of drawing is called clip art. These simple, black-and-white or color line pictures are often included in desktop publishing or word-processing programs. Pre-drawn clip art usually is not suitable for illustrations, but it does work well as graphic icons that can help guide your reader through various parts of a long report.

For example, suppose you are writing a report on the top arts programs in the United States. You might choose the following clip art for each of the sections:

When you introduce the section of your report that deals with music, you might use the music icon at the large size pictured above. Then, in the headings of all the following sections that deal with music, you might use a smaller version of the icon that looks like this:

Music Trends

Using clip art as icons in this manner lets your readers know at a glance which part of the report they are reading.

Charts and Graphs One of the best ways to communicate information about numbers and statistics is by using charts and graphs. Programs such as Microsoft PowerPoint™ allow you to create bar graphs, pie charts, and line graphs that can communicate fractions, figures, and comparative measurements much more powerfully than written descriptions.

Photographs With the widespread availability of digital cameras and scanners, adding photos to your project is an easy and effective way to enhance your content. Using a digital camera or a scanner, you can load photos directly into your computer. Another option is to shoot photographs with a regular camera, but when you have them developed, specify that they be returned to you as "pictures on disc," which you can open on your computer screen.

Photographic images are stored as bits of data in an electronic file. Once you have the photos in your computer, you can use a graphics program to manipulate the images in a variety of ways and create amazing visual effects. You can crop elements out of the photo, add special filters and colors, combine elements of two different pictures into one—the possibilities are endless.

After you have inserted the edited photo into your document, be careful when you print out your final draft. Standard printers often don't reproduce photographs well. You may want to take your document on disc to a professional printing company and have it printed out on a high-resolution printer to make sure you get the best quality.

Captions and Titles While it's true that a single photo can say a great deal, some pictures still need a little explanation in order to have the strongest impact on your reader. Whenever you include an illustration or photograph in a document, also include a simple caption or title for each image.

Add captions in a slightly smaller type size than the body copy and preferably in a sans serif typeface. Use the caption to add information that isn't immediately apparent in the photo. If there are people in the picture, tell readers who they are. If the photo features an odd-looking structure, explain what it is. Be smart with your captions. Don't tell readers the obvious. Give them a reason to read your caption.

Stand-Alone Graphics Occasionally you may include well-known graphics or logos in a report. These graphics convey powerful messages on their own and don't require captions. Examples of these logos or symbols include:

Nonprint Media—Audio and Video

The world we live in is becoming increasingly more multimedia-savvy. Many businesses rely extensively on multimedia presentations to market their products or convey messages to consumers and employees. Exciting opportunities exist for people who can produce clear, concise messages in audio and visual formats.

PRE-PRODUCTION—PUT IT ON PAPER FIRST

Although the final presentation of your subject material may be an audio recording or a video, your project needs to begin on paper first. When you write down your ideas, you do four things:

- Organize your thoughts.
- Narrow your focus.
- Isolate the main messages.
- Identify possible production problems.

Resist the urge to grab an audio recorder or camcorder and run off to record your project. That's a sure-fire way to create an unorganized mess. Take the time to plan your production.

Concept Outline The first task in the writing process is a short, one-page document that describes the basic idea of the project. Ideally this should be three paragraphs—one paragraph each describing the beginning, the middle, and the end. Do not go forward until you have clearly identified these three important parts of your project.

Brief Next write one to two pages that describe in detail the point of your project: how it will be used, who the intended audience is, what the purpose is, and what you hope to achieve with the presentation. Do you want your audience to be informed about something? Motivated to do something? Emotionally moved in some way?

Treatment The next phase of the writing process fleshes out the ideas you expressed in your outline and brief. The treatment is several pages long. It contains descriptions of the characters, dialogue, and settings and describes the presentation scene by scene. Include in your treatment descriptions of the mood and the tone of your piece. If your project is a video, set the stage by describing the overall look and feel of the production.

Script Once you've completed the first three steps, you are ready to go to script. Everything that is mentioned in the script will wind up in the audio recording or on the screen. Conversely, anything that is left out of the script will likely be overlooked and omitted from the final production. So write this document carefully.

For an audio recording, the script contains all narration, dialogue, music, and sound effects. For a video, it contains all of these elements plus descriptions of the characters, any sets, props, or costumes, plus all camera shots and movements, special visual effects, and onscreen titles or graphic elements. In short the audio script encompasses everything that is heard, and the video script covers everything that is seen and heard.

Storyboard Last, for video productions, it's also helpful to create storyboards—simple frame-by-frame sketches with explanatory notes jotted underneath—that paint a visual picture of what the video will look like from start to finish.

Pre-production Tasks The final stages of pre-production include assembling all the elements you will need before you begin producing your audio recording or video. Here's a general checklist.

 Pre-Production Checklist

Audio Tasks

✓ Arrange for audio recording equipment

✓ Cast narrator/actors

✓ Find music (secure permission)

✓ Arrange for sound effects

✓ Set up recording schedule

✓ Coordinate all cast and crew

✓ Arrange for transportation if needed

✓ Rehearse all voice talent

Video Tasks

✓ Arrange for video equipment (including lighting and sound recording equipment)

✓ Cast narrator/host/actors

✓ Find music (secure permission)

✓ Arrange for sound/visual effects

✓ Set up shooting schedule

✓ Coordinate all cast and crew

✓ Arrange for transportation if needed

✓ Set up shooting locations (secure permission)

✓ Arrange for costumes, props, sets

✓ Arrange for make-up if needed

✓ Rehearse all on-camera talent

Video Production Schedule Tucked into the list of pre-production tasks is "Set up recording/shooting schedule." For a video, this means much more than just deciding what day and time you will begin shooting.

During the video production phase of your project, the idea is to shoot everything that your script calls for in the final production. Often the most efficient way to do this is what is called "out-of-sequence" filming. This means that, rather than shooting scenes sequentially (that is, in the order that they appear in the script), you shoot them in the order that is most convenient. Later you will edit them together in the correct order in post-production.

For example, your video might begin and end in the main character's office. Rather than shoot the first office scene, then move the cast and crew to the next location, then later at the end of the day return to the office, it might be easier to shoot both office scenes back-to-back. This will save a great deal of time and effort involved in moving people, lights, and props back and forth.

Lighting may be a factor in the order in which you shoot your scenes. For example, scenes 3, 4, and 7 may take place in the daytime, and scenes 1, 2, 5, and 6 may take place at night.

To accommodate all of these factors, you will need to plan your shooting schedule carefully. The difference between a smooth shoot day and chaos is a well thought-out shooting schedule.

Last, for video or audio recording, it's also a good idea to assemble your team for a pre-production meeting before you begin. This is your chance to read through the script together, go over time schedules, review responsibilities of each person involved, and answer any questions or discuss potential problems before you begin the production process.

PRODUCTION

At last, it's production time! There are a number of different formats you can use for audio and video recording. Talk to the AV expert in your school or check with the media center for help in selecting the best format to use. Get tips, as well, for how to use the audio or video equipment to achieve the best results and produce a polished, professional project.

Next, if you are producing a video, think carefully about how you will shoot it. Consider the kinds of camera shots, camera moves, and special effects you will use.

Camera Shots To hold the interest of your audience, use a variety of camera shots and angles. Check your local library or media center for good books on camera techniques that describe when and how to use various shots—from long shots to close-ups, from low angles to overhead shots. As a rule, every time you change camera shots, change your angle slightly as well. This way, when the shots are edited together, you can avoid accidentally putting two nearly identical shots side-by-side, which creates an unnerving jarring motion called a "jump cut."

Do some research on framing techniques as well to make sure you frame your subjects properly and avoid cutting people's heads off on the screen.

Camera Moves Learn about ways to move the camera in order to keep your audience interested. Three common, but effective camera moves are panning, tracking, and zooming. **Panning** means moving the camera smoothly from one side of the scene to another. Panning works well in an establishing shot to help orient your audience to the setting where the action takes place.

Tracking means moving the camera from one place to another in a smooth action as well, but in tracking, the camera parallels the action, such as moving alongside a character as he or she walks down the street. It's called tracking because in professional filmmaking, the camera and the operator are rolled forward or backward on a small set of train tracks alongside the actor or actress.

Zooming means moving the camera forward or back, but zooming actually involves moving the lens, rather than the camera. By touching the zoom button, you can focus in on a small detail that you would like to emphasize, or you can pull back to reveal something in the background.

The important factor in any kind of camera move is to keep the action fluid and, in most cases, slow and steady. Also, use camera movement sparingly. You want to keep your audience eager and interested, not dizzy and sick!

Cuts Another good way to keep your presentation moving is to use frequent cuts. While the actual cuts will be done during post-production, you need to plan for them in production. Professional filmmakers use the word *coverage* for making sure they have ample choices for shots. You can create coverage for your production by planning shots such as those on the following pages.

Here are three kinds of video shots:

establishing shot   This shot sets up where the action of the story will take place. For example, if your story takes place inside an operating room, you might begin with an establishing shot of the outside of the hospital.

reaction shot   It's a good idea to get shots of all on-camera talent even if one person does not have any dialogue but is listening to, or reacting to, another character. This gives you the chance to break away from the character who is speaking to show how his or her words are affecting other people in the scene.

cutaway shot   The cutaway shot is a shot of something that is not included in the original scene, but is somehow related to it. Cutaways are used to connect two subjects. For example, the first shot may be of a person falling off a boat. The second shot could be a cutaway of a shark swimming deep below the water.

Special Effects If you are adventurous, you may want to try some simple special effects. For instance, dry ice can create smoke effects. You can also have your actors freeze; then stop the camera, remove an object from the set, and restart the camera. This technique will make objects seem to disappear as if by magic. Other effects can be achieved by using false backdrops, colored lights, and filters.

Technology Tip

You may already have video editing tools on your computer or your school's computer. Many computers come equipped with free video editing software. These programs are simple to use and can produce very effective videos or slide shows that are coordinated with music and narration and that feature interesting transitional elements like fades and dissolves. (See next page.) These programs also allow you to edit your video in a way that makes for easy uploading to video file-sharing sites. There are also free video editing tools online. Check out the computer you use most often to see what video tools it may have on it, and follow a tutorial to learn how to use the tool.

POST-PRODUCTION—THE MAGIC OF EDITING

Once all of your video recording is complete, it's time to create the final cut—that is, your choice of the shots you wish to keep and the shots you wish to discard. Be choosy and select the footage with only the best composition, lighting, focus, and performances to tell your story.

There are three basic editing techniques:

in-camera editing	In this process you edit as you shoot. In other words, you need to shoot all your scenes in the correct sequence and in the proper length that you want them to appear. This is the most difficult editing process because it leaves no margin for error.
insert editing	In insert editing you transfer all your footage to a new video. Then you record over any scenes that you don't want with scenes that you do want in the final version.
assemble editing	This process involves electronically copying your shots from the original source in your camera onto a new blank source, called the edited master, in the order that you want the shots to appear. This method provides the most creative control.

Consider including effects such as a dissolve from one shot to another instead of an abrupt cut. A *dissolve* is the soft fading of one shot into another. Dissolves are useful when you wish to give the impression that time has passed between two scenes. A long, slow dissolve that comes up from black into a shot, or from a shot down to black, is called a *fade* and is used to open or close a show.

In addition to assembling the program, post-production is the time to add titles to the opening of your program and credits to the end of the show. Computer programs, such as Adobe Premiere™, can help you do this. Some cameras are also equipped to generate titles. If you don't have any electronic means to produce titles, you can always mount your camera on a high tripod and focus it downward on well-lit pages of text and graphics placed on the floor. Then edit the text frames into the program.

Post-production is also the time to add voiceover narration and music. Voiceovers and background music should be recorded separately and then edited into the program on a separate sound track once the entire show is edited together. Video editing programs for your computer, such as Adobe Premiere™, allow you to mix music and voices with your edited video.

After post-production editing, your video production is ready to present to your audience or upload to a video file-sharing site.

Publishing on the Web

You can become a part of the Web community by building and publishing a Web site of your own. In fact, you may already have a Web presence with your account on a social network such as Facebook, which provides a medium for publishing your thoughts and linking to the sites of those you have designated as your "friends." Maybe you have even created your own social network through Ning or communicated with other members of your school on Twitter. Many businesses now have a presence in one or more social networks, appreciating the opportunity to interact with customers and collaborators.

Traditional Web sites, however, are still the main medium through which most organizations or businesses communicate. Web sites have universal access; the ability to use photos, illustrations, audio, and video; unlimited branching capabilities; and the ability to link with related content.

If you are going to create a Web site, take advantage of all of these features. Your goal should be to make your site interesting enough that visitors will want to stay, explore, and come back to your site again—and that takes thought and planning.

PLANNING YOUR SITE

First you need to capture your thoughts and ideas on paper before you publish anything. Start with a one-page summary that states the purpose of your Web site and the audience you hope to attract. Describe in a paragraph the look and feel you think your site will need in order to accomplish this purpose and hold your audience's attention.

Make a list of the content you plan to include in your Web site. Don't forget to consider any graphics, animation, video, or sound you may want to include.

Next go on a Web field trip. Ask your friends and teachers for the URLs of their favorite Web sites. (URL stands for Universal Resource Locator.) Visit these sites, and ask yourself, "Do I like this site? Why or why not?" Determine which sites are visually appealing to you and why. Which sites are easy to navigate and why? Chances are the sites you like best will have clean, easy-to-read layouts, be well written, contain visually stimulating graphic elements, and have intuitive **interfaces** that make it simple to find your way around.

One sure drawback in any Web site is long, uninterrupted blocks of text. Decide how to break up long passages of information into manageable sections. Will there be separate sections for editorial content? News? Humor? Feedback? Which sections will be updated periodically and how often?

Make a few rough sketches for your site. How do you envision the home page of your site? What will the icons and buttons look like? Then give careful thought to how the pages will connect to each other, starting with the home page. Your plan for connecting the pages is called a **site map**.

Because the Web is an interactive medium, navigation is critical. Decide how users will get from one page to another. Will you put in a navigation bar across the top of the page or down the side? Will there be a top or home page at the beginning of each section?

Once you have planned the content, organized your material into sections, and designed your navigation system, you are ready to begin creating Web pages.

PUTTING IT ALL TOGETHER

Writing for the Web is different from writing for print. The Web is a fast medium. Keep your messages succinct and to the point. Use short, punchy sentences. Break up your copy with clever subheads. Try not to exceed 500 to 600 words in any single article on any one page.

In order to turn text into Web pages, you need to translate the text into a special language that Web browsers can read. This language code is called HTML—HyperText Markup Language. There are three methods available:

- You can use the Save As Web Page feature in the File menu of most word-processing programs.
- You can import your text into a Web-building software program and add the code yourself if you know how.
- You can easily find free software programs online that will do the work for you. Web-building software programs are referred to as WYSIWYG (pronounced "Wiz-E-Wig"), which stands for "What You See Is What You Get."

Web-building software also allows you to create links to other Web pages using a simple process called **drag and drop**. Be sure to read the directions that come with your software package for complete instructions.

BLOGS

Blogs (short for weblogs) are a type of Web page. In many ways, they are like online diaries or journals, where "bloggers" post the latest events of their lives and their thoughts and feelings on a wide range of subjects. Some blogs have other purposes, such as to promote community among speakers of certain languages or to influence politics. Among the most popular blogs are those devoted to celebrity news and to animal photos with funny captions. The most popular blog software is free and easy enough to use so that anyone with Web space can build one.

B. Using the Internet

Apply Information and Technology Literacy

The "age of information" dawned in the last half of the 20th century. Success in the 21st century requires the ability to access, evaluate, and wisely use the abundance of information made available by advances in technology. Developing an understanding of the changing technologies and skill in putting them to work for your purposes are key competencies for the rest of your schooling and for your adult life ahead.

In this section, you will develop your skills for understanding and making the most of what the Internet has to offer.

How Does the Internet Work?

The Internet is made up of thousands of networks all linked together around the globe. Each network consists of a group of computers that are connected to one another to exchange information. If one of these computers or networks fails, the information simply bypasses the disabled system and takes another route through a different network. This rerouting is why the Internet is so valuable to agencies such as the U.S. Department of Defense.

No one "owns" the Internet, nor is it managed in a central place. No agency regulates or censors the information on the Internet. Anyone can publish information on the Internet as he or she wishes.

In fact, the Internet offers such a vast wealth of information and experiences that sometimes it is described as the Information Superhighway. So how do you "get on" this highway? It's easy. Once you have a computer, a modem, and a telephone or cable line, all you need is a connection to the Internet.

THE CYBERSPACE CONNECTION

A company called an Internet Service Provider (ISP) connects your computer to the Internet. Examples of ISPs that provide direct access are Microsoft

Network, Earthlink, Comcast, and AT&T. You can also get on the Internet indirectly through companies such as America Online (AOL).

ISPs charge a flat monthly fee for their service. Unlike the telephone company, once you pay the monthly ISP fee, there are no long-distance charges for sending or receiving information on the Internet—no matter where your information is coming from, or going to, around the world.

ALPHABET SOUP—MAKING SENSE OF ALL THOSE LETTERS

Like physical highways, the Information Superhighway has road signs that help you find your way around. Each specific group of information on the World Wide Web is called a **Web site** and has its own unique address. Think of it as a separate street address of a house in your neighborhood. This address is called the URL, which stands for Uniform Resource Locator. It's a kind of shorthand for where the information is located on the Web.

Here's a typical URL: **http://www.perfectionlearning.com.**

All addresses, or URLs, for the World Wide Web begin with **http://.** This stands for HyperText Transfer Protocol and is a programming description of how the information is exchanged.

The next three letters—**www**—let you know you are on the World Wide Web. The next part of the URL—**perfectionlearning**—is the name of the site you want to visit. The last three letters, in this case **com**, indicate that this Web site is sponsored by a **com**mercial company. Here are other common endings of URLs you will find:

- "org" is short for **org**anization, as in http://www.ipl.org, which is the URL of the Web site for the Internet Public Library, ipl2: Information You Can Trust.

- "edu" stands for **edu**cation, as in the Web address for the Virtual Reference Desk, http://thorplus.lib.purdue.edu/reference/index.html, featuring online telephone books, dictionaries, and other reference guides.

- "gov" represents **gov**ernment-sponsored Web sites, such as http://www.whitehouse.gov, the Web site for the White House in Washington, D.C.

To get to a Web site, you use an interface called a **browser**. Two popular browsers are Microsoft Internet Explorer and Mozilla Firefox. A browser is like a blank form where you fill in the information you are looking for. If you know the URL of the Web site you want to explore, all you have to do is type it in the field marked Location, click Enter on your keyboard, and wait for the information to be delivered to your computer screen.

BASIC INTERNET TERMINOLOGY

Here are some of the most frequently used words you will hear associated with the Internet.

address
The unique code given to information on the Internet. This may also refer to an e-mail address.

bookmark
A tool that lets you store your favorite URL addresses, allowing you one-click access to your favorite Web pages without retyping the URL each time.

browser
Application software that supplies a graphical interactive interface for searching, finding, viewing, and managing information on the Internet.

chat
Real-time conferencing over the Internet.

cookies
A general mechanism that some Web sites use both to store and to retrieve information on the visitor's hard drive. Users have the option to refuse or accept cookies.

cyberspace
The collective realm of computer-aided communication.

download
The transfer of programs or data stored on a remote computer, usually from a server, to a storage device on your personal computer.

e-mail
Electronic mail that can be sent all over the world from one computer to another.

FAQs
The abbreviation for Frequently Asked Questions. This is usually a great resource to get information when visiting a new Web site.

flaming
Using mean or abusive language in cyberspace. Flaming is considered to be in extremely poor taste and may be reported to your ISP.

FTP
The abbreviation for File Transfer Protocol. A method of transferring files to and from a computer connected to the Internet.

home page
The start-up page of a Web site.

HTML	The abbreviation for HyperText Markup Language—a "tag" language used to create most Web pages, which your browser interprets to display those pages. Often the last set of letters found at the end of a Web address.
http	The abbreviation for HyperText Transfer Protocol. This is how documents are transferred from the Web site or server to the browsers of individual personal computers.
ISP	The abbreviation for Internet Service Provider—a company that, for a fee, connects a user's computer to the Internet.
keyword	A simplified term that serves as subject reference when doing a search.
link	Short for hyperlink. A link is a connection between one piece of information and another.
network	A system of interconnected computers.
online	To "be online" means to be connected to the Internet via a live modem connection.
plug-in	Free application that can be downloaded off the Internet to enhance your browser's capabilities.
podcast	An audio or video file on the Internet that is available for downloading to a personal media device.
real time	Information received and processed (or displayed) as it happens.
RSS	A format for distributing content to people or Web sites. It stands for "Really Simple Syndication." With an RSS "feed," users can get updates from sites of interest without having to go to the sites for the information.
search engine	A computer program that locates documents based on keywords that the user enters.
server	A provider of resources, such as a file server.
site	A specific place on the Internet, usually a set of pages on the World Wide Web.
social network	An online community of people who share interests and activities, usually based on the Web.

spam	Electronic junk mail.
surf	A casual reference to browsing on the Internet. To "surf the Web" means to spend time discovering and exploring new Web sites.
upload	The transfer of programs or data from a storage device on your personal computer to another remote computer.
URL	The abbreviation for Uniform Resource Locator. This is the address for an Internet resource, such as a World Wide Web page. Each Web page has its own unique URL.
Web 2.0	The so-called second generation of the World Wide Web, which promotes programming that encourages interaction and collaboration.
Web site	A page of information or a collection of pages that is being electronically published from one of the computers in the World Wide Web.
Wiki	Technology that holds together a number of user-generated web pages focused on a theme, project, or collaboration. Wikipedia is the most famous example. The word *wiki* means "quick" in Hawaiian.
WWW	The abbreviation for the World Wide Web. A network of computers within the Internet capable of delivering multimedia content (images, audio, video, and animation) as well as text over communication lines into personal computers all over the globe.

Communicating on the Internet

E-mail, mailing lists, and newsgroups are all great ways of exchanging information with other people on the Internet. Here's how to use these useful forms of communication, step-by-step.

21ST CENTURY

1 Using E-mail

Any writer who has ever used e-mail in his or her work will agree that sending and receiving electronic messages is one of the most useful ways of gathering information and contacts for writing projects.

Once you open your e-mail program, click on the command that says Compose Mail or New Message. This will open a new blank e-mail similar to the one pictured below. Next, fill in the blanks.

Type the person's e-mail address here. There is no central listing of e-mail addresses. If you don't have the person's address, the easiest way to get it is to call and ask the person for it. You can address an e-mail to one or several people, depending on the number of addresses you type in this space.

Cc stands for courtesy copy. If you type additional e-mail addresses in this area, you can send a copy of the message to other people.

Bcc stands for blind courtesy copy. By typing one or more e-mail addresses here, you can send a copy of the message to others without the original recipient knowing that other people have received the same message. Not all e-mail programs have this feature.

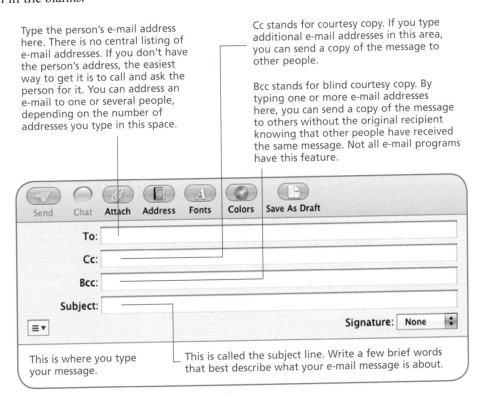

This is where you type your message.

This is called the subject line. Write a few brief words that best describe what your e-mail message is about.

SAY IT WITH STYLE

Like regular letters, e-mail can assume different tones and styles, depending on to whom you are writing. Usually informal e-mails and instant messages (IMs) to close friends are light, brief, and to the point. In the case of more formal e-mails, such as a request for information from an expert or a museum, keep the following guidelines in mind.

Guidelines for Writing E-mails

- Make sure your message is clear and concise.
- Use proper grammar and punctuation.
- Check your spelling. (Some e-mail programs have their own spell-check function—use it!)
- Double-check the person's e-mail address to be sure you've typed it correctly.

ATTACH A LITTLE SOMETHING EXTRA

When you send e-mail, you can also send other information along with your message. These are called **attachments**. Depending on your e-mail program's capabilities, you can attach documents, photos, illustrations—even sound and video files. Click Attach, and then find and double-click on the document or file on your computer that you wish to send.

After you have composed your message and added any attachments you want to include, click the Send button. Your message arrives in the other person's mailbox seconds later, regardless of whether that person lives right next door or on the other side of the world.

FOLLOW UP

Just because you have sent a message, you shouldn't automatically assume that the other person has received it. Internet Service Providers (ISPs) keep all messages that are sent until the recipient requests them. The person you sent your e-mail to might be away from his or her computer or may not check messages regularly.

Also, the Internet is still an imperfect science. From time to time, servers go down or other "hiccups" in electronic transmissions can occur, leaving your message stranded somewhere in cyberspace. If you don't get a reply in a reasonable amount of time, either resend your original e-mail message or call the person and let him or her know that your message is waiting.

YOU'VE GOT MAIL

When someone sends you an e-mail message, you have several options:

Reply Click Reply, and you can automatically send back a new message without having to retype the person's e-mail address. (Be sure you keep a copy of the sender's e-mail address in your Address Book for future use.)

Forward Suppose you receive a message that you would like to share with someone else. Click Forward, and you can send a copy of the message, plus include a few of your own comments, to another person.

Print In some instances, you may need to have a paper copy of the e-mail message. For example, if someone e-mails you directions to a party, click Print to take a hard copy of the instructions with you.

Store Do you want to keep a message to refer to later? Some e-mail programs allow you to create folders to organize stored messages.

Delete You can discard a message you no longer need just by clicking Delete. It's a good idea to throw messages away regularly to keep them from accumulating in your mailbox.

② Other Online Communication

Another way to communicate online is Internet Relay Chat (IRC), or "chat rooms" for short. Chat rooms focus on a large variety of topics, so it's possible you'll be able to find a chat room where people are discussing the subject you are writing about.

"Chat" is similar to talking on the telephone except, instead of speaking, the people in the chat room type their responses back and forth to each other. As soon as you type your comment, it immediately appears on the computer screen of every person involved in the "conversation." There are also more advanced forms of chat available on the Net, such as video chat and voice chat.

One-to-one chatting, or instant messaging, is probably something you do frequently. With instant messaging, you need to "accept" as a buddy or contact each person you will communicate with.

In contrast, anyone in a chat room can talk to you, and the anonymous nature of a chat room can make people less inhibited than they might otherwise be in person. If you sense that one of the participants in your chat room is responding inappropriately, ask your parents or teacher to step in, or simply sign off.

JOIN THE GROUP

Mailing lists and newsgroups are larger discussion forums that can help you get even more information about a specific subject.

Mailing Lists To find a directory of available mailing lists, enter "mailing list directory" in a search engine. If you find a mailing list that interests you and wish to subscribe to it, just send a message to the administrative address. You will start to receive messages from the mailing list within a few days.

Remember, mailing lists use e-mail to communicate, so be sure to check your e-mail often because once you subscribe to a list, it's possible to receive dozens of messages in a matter of days.

Another good idea is to read the messages in your new mailing list for a week or so before submitting a message of your own. This will give you a good idea of what has already been discussed so you can be considerate about resubmitting old information.

You can reply to a message any time you wish. However, it doesn't do anyone any good to respond by saying "Yes, I agree." Get in the habit of replying to messages only when you have something important to add. Also, be sure to repeat the original question in your reply so that people understand which message you are responding to.

Be sure that you really want to belong to a mailing list before you subscribe. Unwanted e-mail can be a nuisance. Fortunately, if you change your mind, you can always unsubscribe to mailing lists at any time.

Newsgroups To join a newsgroup, check with your ISP. Service providers frequently list available topics under the heading "Newsgroups." Newsgroups are named with two or more words separated by a period. For example, there is a newsgroup named rec.sport.baseball. college. The first three letters—"rec"—defines the main subject, in this case recreation. Each word that follows—sport, baseball, and college—narrows the scope of the subject to an increasingly more specific area of interest.

As with mailing lists, you can always unsubscribe to newsgroups at any time.

As in any social setting, there are a few guidelines to follow when you are talking to people online—via e-mail, in a chat room, or in a newsgroup. This conduct is called **netiquette**. Netiquette requires that you refrain from harsh or insulting language and from writing in all uppercase letters, which can feel like shouting. It requires you to respect other people's privacy, ideas, and work. Don't forward a message or attach documents written by someone else without first asking the author's permission. Don't send spam, unwanted messages for the purpose of selling something.

Online Collaboration and Web 2.0

The Web is always changing. One big change from its earliest days is the ease with which people can collaborate online. For example, your writing group could use Google Docs (http://docs.google.com) to work together on writing projects: to share drafts, to edit your peers' work, and to set schedules and guidelines. Through Google Docs, everyone who is invited to do so can have access to documents and edit them online.

Another useful tool for collaboration is the **wiki**, a platform for creating linked pages on a common theme or for a common project. Wikipedia is the best known example. You can start your own free wiki at wiki.com and explore how you can use it in your learning.

Cyberbullying

More than half of teenagers recently surveyed reported that they have been the victim of online bullying, also called cyberbullying, or know someone who has been. **Cyberbullying** is the use of such technology as the Internet and cell phones to deliberately hurt or embarrass someone. Cyberbullies often assume fake identities to trick people. They also knowingly spread lies and often post pictures of someone without his or her permission. Cyberbullies can trick their victims into revealing personal information which is then abused.

Victims react in different ways. Some take such reasonable measures as blocking an offending user or refusing to read comments that might be hurtful and deleting them as soon as they arrive. Some seek help from adults, who sometimes help the victim report the problem to the appropriate authorities. Other teens have a more negative and painful reaction. They might withdraw from their usual pastimes and suffer from problems with self-esteem. Or they might get caught up in the negative swirl and try to bully back.

The National Crime Prevention Council (NCPC) makes these suggestions to teens to stop cyberbullying.

- Refuse to pass along cyberbullying messages.
- Tell friends to stop cyberbullying.
- Block communication with cyberbullies.
- Report cyberbullying to a trusted adult.

The NCPC developed a slogan to summarize what to do: "Delete cyberbullying. Don't write it. Don't forward it."

Unit 4

Grammar

You can admire anything, such as a tree, from afar. You can observe its general shape, color, and size. But as John Dryden suggests, to know a thing "distinctly," you must climb into it and examine its unique structure. To climb the "grammar tree" of the English language is to learn its parts—the nouns, the verbs, the participles. From your position among its branches, you will begin to see how the parts work together. When you climb down, your new knowledge will help you use your language with skill, clarity, and power.

Who climbs the grammar-tree, distinctly knows where noun, and verb, and participle grows. — John Dryden

Nouns and Pronouns

Susan B. Anthony in 1900

How can you use nouns and pronouns to create lively and precise prose?

Nouns and Pronouns: Pretest 1

Read the following draft paragraph about Susan B. Anthony and her work for women's suffrage. The paragraph is hard to read because it contains noun and pronoun errors. Revise the paragraph so that it reads more smoothly. Several of the errors have been corrected as examples.

In the <u>united</u> <u>states</u>, Susan b. Anthony devoted their life to Women's Suffrage. At the time when Anthony began her work, they had few legal rights. When African American Men were given the right to vote in 1869, anthony began a movement to secure the same rights for women. In 1869, the territory of wyoming was the first area in the United States to allow their Female Citizens to vote. Anthony was President of the American Woman Suffrage association until her was eighty. Anthony voted in the election of 1872, but Anthony was fined $100 for breaking the Law. Susan B. Anthony refused to pay the fine. Few people were as devoted to the cause as her. American Women did not gain her right to vote until 1920.

Nouns and Pronouns: Pretest 2

Directions

Write the letter of the term that correctly identifies the underlined word in each sentence. The paragraph is about the Culinary Institute of America (CIA).

(1) At the CIA, <u>chefs</u> teach the classes. (2) Each <u>class</u> learns a different kind of cooking. (3) The <u>classrooms</u> are equipped with stoves and refrigerators. (4) The students are responsible for cleaning <u>their</u> workstations. (5) <u>Each</u> must pass an intensive cooking examination to graduate. (6) The students get great <u>satisfaction</u> from learning cooking skills. (7) <u>Those</u> are the skills they will use all their lives. (8) <u>Who</u> will go on to cook professionally? (9) They <u>themselves</u> do not know the answer until after graduation. (10) They must prepare <u>themselves</u> for a difficult job search.

1. A common noun
  B collective noun
  C abstract noun
  D proper noun

2. A proper noun
  B abstract noun
  C compound noun
  D collective noun

3. A abstract noun
  B collective noun
  C compound noun
  D proper noun

4. A personal pronoun
  B reflexive pronoun
  C intensive pronoun
  D indefinite pronoun

5. A intensive pronoun
  B indefinite pronoun
  C personal pronoun
  D reflexive pronoun

6. A compound noun
  B proper noun
  C abstract noun
  D collective noun

7. A interrogative pronoun
  B indefinite pronoun
  C reflexive pronoun
  D demonstrative pronoun

8. A demonstrative pronoun
  B intensive pronoun
  C interrogative pronoun
  D personal pronoun

9. A intensive pronoun
  B interrogative pronoun
  C indefinite pronoun
  D reflexive pronoun

10. A indefinite pronoun
  B reflexive pronoun
  C demonstrative pronoun
  D intensive pronoun

Nouns Lesson 1

Every word can be categorized into one of the eight parts of speech listed below. A word's part of speech is determined by the job it does in a sentence.

THE EIGHT PARTS OF SPEECH	
noun (names)	**adverb** (describes, limits)
pronoun (replaces a noun)	**preposition** (relates)
verb (states action or being)	**conjunction** (connects)
adjective (describes, limits)	**interjection** (expresses strong feeling)

In English, there are more nouns than any other part of speech.

12 A A **noun** is a word that names a person, place, thing, or idea.

Concrete and Abstract Nouns

Nouns can be divided into **concrete nouns** and **abstract nouns**.

12 A.1 A **concrete noun** names people, places, and things you can usually see or touch. An **abstract noun** names ideas and qualities.

CONCRETE NOUNS	
People	sailor, brother, Mrs. Wong, singers, Heather
Places	forest, mountain, amusement park, Texas, Empire State Building
Things	rug, flower, explosion, flu, chipmunk, color, guitar, slogan, list
ABSTRACT NOUNS	
Ideas and Qualities	freedom, fun, love, inflation, bravery, anger, honesty, sickness, faith

Nouns can also be divided into **general** and **specific nouns**.

GENERAL NOUN	SPECIFIC NOUN
fruit	apple, pear, orange, apricot, mango
insect	grasshopper, mosquito, beetle, moth, mayfly

Finding Nouns

Write the nouns in each sentence.

(1) During springtime, flowers bloom. **(2)** The fragrance of the buds fills the air. **(3)** Bees are attracted to the perfume of flowers. **(4)** These insects see color, pattern, and movement. **(5)** Bees taste blooms with their front legs and antennae. **(6)** These creatures have short bodies covered with hair. **(7)** Pollen clings to the hair on the body of the insect. **(8)** Bees make honey from the nectar of flowers. **(9)** Humans have harvested honey for many centuries. **(10)** Our appreciation of this golden liquid continues today.

● *Connect to Writing:* **Revising**

Using Specific Nouns

Rewrite the following sentences, changing the underlined general noun to a specific noun that creates a clearer picture.

1. The <u>tree</u> was covered with <u>insects</u>.
2. <u>Fruit</u> hung from its branches.
3. A <u>bird</u> circled above the <u>building</u>.
4. A cool <u>wind</u> blew across the <u>land</u>.

➤ Common and Proper Nouns

12 A.2   A **common noun** names any person, place, or thing. A **proper noun** names a particular person, place, or thing.

All nouns are either common nouns or proper nouns. Every proper noun begins with a capital letter.

COMMON NOUN	PROPER NOUN
woman	Maria Chavez
city	Paris
building	Taj Mahal
team	Houston Astros

A proper noun sometimes includes more than one word. For example, even though *Taj Mahal* is two words, it is considered one noun. It is the name of one place.

You can learn more about the capitalization of proper nouns on pages 819–827.

Finding Common and Proper Nouns

Make two columns on your paper. Label the first column **Common Nouns** and the second column **Proper Nouns.** Then, in the appropriate column, write the nouns from the following sentences.

(1) In Colombia, ants are sold as snacks by vendors on the street. (2) Fried worms are eaten in Mexico. (3) People in Uganda crush flies and shape them into pancakes. (4) In other parts of Africa, termites are munched like pretzels. (5) Certain spiders are roasted in New Guinea. (6) Some insects taste like nuts. (7) Restaurants in New York City serve ants dipped in chocolate. (8) In recent years, North American Bait Farms, Inc. has held a cooking contest using worms. (9) In some cookbooks, you can find a recipe for peppers stuffed with earthworms. (10) Actually, insects give people necessary protein and vitamins.

Compound and Collective Nouns

12 A.3 A noun that includes more than one word is called a **compound noun.**

Some nouns include more than one word. *Post* is one noun, *office* is one noun, but *post office* is also one noun. *Post office* is an example of a compound noun. It is not always easy to know how to write a particular compound noun. The best way to find out is to check in a dictionary. Compound nouns can take one of three forms: separate words, hyphenated, and combined.

COMPOUND NOUNS	
Separate Words	living room, home run, peanut butter, ice cream
Hyphenated	break-in, attorney-at-law, bird's-eye, great-grandmother
Combined	birdhouse, headband, flashlight, crosswalk, brainpower

You can learn more about punctuation of compound nouns on pages 910–911.

12 A.4 A **collective noun** names a group of people or things.

COMMON COLLECTIVE NOUNS			
band	crew	flock	nation
committee	crowd	herd	orchestra
colony	family	league	swarm

● Practice Your Skills

Finding Compound and Collective Nouns

Make two columns on your paper. Label the first column **Compound Nouns** and the second column **Collective Nouns.** Then, in the appropriate column, write each noun.

(1) My classmates and I listened to presentations by members of an environmental group. **(2)** One speaker discussed water pollution and how it affects a species of wild ducks. **(3)** Another pair of presenters warned of the decline in the population of the grasshopper. **(4)** According to the organization, a number of animals have recently been declared endangered. **(5)** Because the group was so interesting, the entire faculty of the high school came to hear them.

● *Connect to Writing:* Editing

Writing Nouns Correctly

Edit the following advertisement copy to eliminate errors in capitalization of proper nouns and misspellings of compound nouns. Write the corrected paragraph.

(1) Let ollie's outdoor expeditions take you to visit mothernature for the day! **(2)** Join our group as we travel to the st. francis river, where we will spend the day discussing the flora and fauna, as well as the wild-life of the area. **(3)** Birdwatchers will enjoy viewing the flock of geese that live in the area, while animallovers will appreciate the herd of deer that often come to drink at the river. **(4)** Children will enjoy building bird houses while their parents become fossilhunters for the day. **(5)** Stop by ollie's outdoor expeditions at 211 sunnyvale street for more details.

Power Your Writing: Who or What?

You can strengthen your writing by adding details that elaborate on the nouns you use. As you draft or edit, add descriptive information about a person, place, or thing by using an **appositive phrase**—a group of words that adds information about another word in the sentence (see pages 617–618). Notice how Charles G. Finney uses an appositive phrase to add an interesting detail about the rattlesnake he describes in "The Life and Death of a Western Gladiator" (pages 71–74).

On the other hand, he had a pit, **a deep pock mark between eye and nostril.** Unique, this organ was sensitive to animal heat.

Revise a composition you completed recently by adding at least two appositive phrases.

● *Connect to Writing:* **Personal Message**

Using Proper Nouns

You have invited a friend to come for dinner. Compose an e-mail to her. Include the day, time, details about the meal, and directions to your home. Take special care to capitalize the proper nouns in the message.

12 B A **pronoun** is a word that takes the place of one or more nouns.

Speaking and writing would be very repetitious if there were no words to take the place of nouns. Pronouns do this job. The second example below reads more smoothly and is easier to understand because pronouns have been used in the place of two of the nouns.

Holly took Holly's sweater with Holly on the class trip.

Holly took **her** sweater with **her** on the class trip.

➤ Pronoun Antecedents

12 B.1 The noun a pronoun refers to or replaces is called its **antecedent.**

In the following examples, an arrow has been drawn from the pronoun to its antecedent or antecedents. Notice that the antecedent usually comes before the pronoun.

Dion said that **he** couldn't go to the zoo.

Lynn asked **Sandy,** "Did **we** miss the dolphin show?"

You can learn more about pronouns and antecedents on pages 736–742.

● Practice Your Skills

Finding Antecedents

Write the antecedent for each underlined pronoun.

1. Juanita brought <u>her</u> camera on the trip to the zoo.
2. Steve asked Juanita to take a picture of <u>him</u>.
3. Linda said, "<u>I</u> enjoy the reptiles."
4. Gretchen and Margo said <u>they</u> were looking for the penguins.
5. Ms. Jackson told Henry that <u>she</u> liked to watch the monkeys.
6. The monkey cage had a tire swing in <u>it</u>.
7. Jeff asked Ms. Jackson, "Did <u>you</u> bring the monkeys a banana?"
8. Chris and Jesse asked the teacher, "Are <u>we</u> leaving now?"
9. Juanita said that <u>she</u> wanted one more picture of the peacocks.
10. Ms. Jackson's students enjoyed <u>their</u> trip to the zoo.

Replacing Nouns with Pronouns

Rewrite the paragraph, replacing nouns with pronouns where they are needed.

(1) Investigations into the intelligence of gorillas show that gorillas are much smarter than people once thought gorillas were. **(2)** Gorillas will stack boxes to help gorillas reach bananas that are too high to pick. **(3)** Gorillas will use sticks as tools to pull food into gorillas' cages. **(4)** One scientist, Dr. James White, trained a female gorilla named Congo to perform various actions. **(5)** When the scientist returned some years later, Congo remembered the scientist. **(6)** Congo also repeated some of the actions the scientist had taught Congo. **(7)** Congo's behavior in these instances helped convince scientists of gorillas' intelligence.

 Personal Pronouns

Personal pronouns can be divided into the following three groups.

PERSONAL PRONOUNS	
First Person	(the person speaking)
Singular	I, me, my, mine
Plural	we, us, our, ours
Second Person	(the person spoken to)
Singular	you, your, yours
Plural	you, your, yours
Third Person	(the person or thing spoken about)
Singular	he, him, his, she, her, hers, it, its
Plural	they, them, their, theirs

The following sentences use personal pronouns.

First-Person	**I** want to take **my** notebook with **me** to the convention.
	We think **our** plan of political action is best for **us.**
Second-Person	Did **you** bring **your** list of questions for the candidate?
Third-Person	The reporter took **his** camera and film with **him.**
	They enjoyed **their** new leader's speech to the delegates.

Reflexive and Intensive Pronouns

12 B.2   **Reflexive pronouns** and **intensive pronouns** refer to or emphasize another noun or pronoun.

These pronouns are formed by adding –*self* or –*selves* to certain personal pronouns.

REFLEXIVE AND INTENSIVE PRONOUNS	
Singular	myself, yourself, himself, herself, itself
Plural	ourselves, yourselves, themselves

A **reflexive pronoun** reflects back to a noun or a pronoun mentioned earlier in the sentence. An **intensive pronoun** is used directly after its antecedent to intensify, or emphasize, a statement. A reflexive pronoun is necessary to the meaning of the sentence; an intensive pronoun is not. Never use reflexive or intensive pronouns by themselves. They must be used with antecedents.

Reflexive	Pioneers organized **themselves** into wagon trains before their long westward journey.
Incorrect	**Myself** could not have survived the hardships of such a trek.
Intensive	I **myself** could not have survived the hardships of such a trek.

● Practice Your Skills

Finding Pronouns

Write the personal, reflexive, and intensive pronouns in these sentences and label them *P* for personal, *R* for reflexive, and *I* for intensive.

(1) In the early 1840s, adventurous settlers readied themselves for the overland trip to the West. **(2)** Life in the Oregon country held new promise for them. **(3)** The settlers themselves could never have anticipated all the hardships they encountered on the two-thousand-mile Oregon Trail. **(4)** When it was loaded, a covered wagon often weighed thousands of pounds. **(5)** It was pulled across various types of terrain by teams of horses, mules, or oxen. **(6)** The wagons were uncomfortable for the passengers themselves. **(7)** On many occasions, settlers might walk beside them rather than ride. **(8)** The journey was hard for the travelers, but many nights they sang by their campfires. **(9)** The route was mapped in 1804 by Lewis and Clark themselves. **(10)** Today, we can drive our cars along modern roads beside the historic trail.

Add intensive pronouns to the following sentences to make the statements stronger.

> **(1)** On many days, a woman rode alone in the covered wagon. **(2)** She often drove the long miles and cared for her children at the same time. **(3)** Sometimes on the trail, disputes arose among the settlers. **(4)** The wagon master often served as the mediator of these disputes. **(5)** He knew how dangerous fights among the settlers could be.

Other Kinds of Pronouns

There are five other kinds of pronouns: indefinite pronouns, demonstrative pronouns, interrogative pronouns, reciprocal pronouns, and relative pronouns.

Indefinite Pronouns

12 B.3   **Indefinite pronouns** refer to unnamed people, places, things, or ideas.

Indefinite pronouns often do not have definite antecedents as personal pronouns do.

Several have qualified for the contest.

Many collected the newspapers.

I've gathered **everything** now.

COMMON INDEFINITE PRONOUNS	
Singular	another, anybody, anyone, anything, each, either, everybody, everyone, everything, much, neither, nobody, no one, nothing, one, somebody, someone, something
Plural	both, few, many, others, several
Singular/Plural	all, any, more, most, none, some

CHAPTER 12

A pronoun must agree with its antecedent. When singular indefinite pronouns serve as antecedents to other pronouns, all the pronouns must be singular. When plural indefinite pronouns serve as antecedents to other pronouns, all the pronouns must be plural.

Everything was in **its** place. (singular)

Everyone at the gym has **his** or **her** own locker. (singular)

Each of the girls ate **her** lunch. (singular)

Several brought **their** lunches. (plural)

Look at a recent composition, and check to be sure you have used indefinite pronouns correctly.

You can learn more about indefinite pronouns as antecedents on pages 738–740.

Practice Your Skills

Finding Indefinite Pronouns

Write the indefinite pronouns in these sentences.

1. Many feel they cannot help the environment.
2. Some say the problem is too large.
3. However, anyone can recycle.
4. Almost everything has more than one use.
5. Everybody can conserve natural resources.
6. A small action is better than none.
7. We should encourage others in this pursuit.
8. Nothing is wrong with thanking citizens who recycle their trash.
9. Anyone can join the effort.
10. No one should forget to recycle.
11. Each can make a difference.
12. Everyone can learn how to recycle.
13. We should do anything to reduce waste.
14. All have a right to a cleaner environment.
15. Most have access to recycling bins these days.

Demonstrative Pronouns

12 B.4 **Demonstrative pronouns** point out a specific person, place, thing, or idea.

DEMONSTRATIVE PRONOUNS			
this	that	these	those

This is Mary's coat on the hanger.

Are **these** John's glasses?

Interrogative Pronouns

12 B.5 **Interrogative pronouns** are used to ask questions.

INTERROGATIVE PRONOUNS				
what	which	who	whom	whose

What is known about the case?

Who is coming to the party?

Reciprocal Pronouns

12 B.6 The **reciprocal pronouns** *each other* and *one another* show that the action is two-way.

You can use the reciprocal pronoun *each other* to simplify sentences or combine short, repetitive sentences when referring to two people.

> Veronica e-mailed Larry last night. Larry e-mailed Veronica last night.
>
> Veronica and Larry e-mailed **each other** last night.

You can use the reciprocal pronoun *one another* to refer to two or more people.

> The players congratulated **one another** after the big win.
>
> The writers and editors cooperated with **one another** to meet the deadline.

You can learn about another type of pronoun, the relative pronoun, on pages 647–650.

● Practice Your Skills

Finding Demonstrative, Interrogative, and Reciprocal Pronouns

Write the demonstrative pronouns, the interrogative pronouns, or the reciprocal pronouns. Use the label *D* for demonstrative, *I* for interrogative, and *R* for reciprocal.

1. Who is going to the dance on Saturday?

2. That is the most important question on our minds.

3. This is my outfit for the dance.

4. Of all my shoes, these will match my dress best.

5. The girls took pictures of one another before the dance.

6. What is the first song going to be?

7. Those are great tunes for dancing.

8. Which is your favorite?

9. That is a good example of rap.

10. Robert and Linda danced with each other.

● *Connect to Writing:* **Drafting**

Using Pronouns

Add pronouns to complete the following sentences. Choose personal, reflexive, indefinite, demonstrative, or interrogative pronouns.

(1) The little girl found __ all alone in the department store. **(2)** __ began to cry. **(3)** __ in the store turned to look at __. **(4)** Suddenly, __ felt a hand on __ small shoulder. **(5)** __ had found her? **(6)** __ mother smiled down at her. **(7)** "__ was a scary feeling," she told her mother. **(8)** __ is why little girls should not wander from __ mothers. **(9)** "Well, __ are safe now," said the mother. **(10)** "May __ get two ice cream cones for __?" asked the little girl. **(11)** "Should __ eat lunch first?" asked her mother. **(12)** "__ should we eat for lunch?" she also asked the girl. **(13)** "__ good," the girl decided.

✔ *Check Point:* **Mixed Practice**

Write the pronouns in the following sentences. Label each *P* for personal, *Ind* for indefinite, *D* for demonstrative, *Int* for interrogative, or *R* for reciprocal.

1. That was the year when we built the tree house in our backyard.

2. Whose was it?

3. Ryan and Marcus actually helped each other build it for their younger brothers and sisters.

4. This was the block where we used to live when all of us were in grade school.

5. These are the streets where we played ball with one another.

6. Which is the school where you and the rest of your family went?

7. What were the subjects you studied with my older brother?

8. Whom among all of your mathematics teachers did you like the best?

9. Those were the days when no one realized how our lives would change.

10. We spent summer evenings playing ball—that used to be great fun.

● *Connect to Speaking and Writing:* **Peer Interaction**

Reviewing Content

With a partner, review the vocabulary you have learned in this chapter. (Hint: New terms are printed in purple.) Quiz each other until you understand the definitions of all the new words and concepts.

Assess Your Learning

■ Identifying Nouns and Pronouns

Write each noun and pronoun in the following sentences. Then label each one **N** for noun or **P** for pronoun. Note: A date, such as 1533, is a noun.

1. Born in 1533, Elizabeth I was one of the most famous rulers of England.

2. Her court was well known for its artists and playwrights.

3. When she was a young girl, Elizabeth was locked up in the Tower of London by her half-sister Mary.

4. When Mary died, Elizabeth came to the throne of England and ruled for forty-five years.

5. Born in 1769, Napoleon was a famous ruler of France.

6. He conquered large parts of Europe and made himself emperor over them.

7. He was born on the island of Corsica.

8. Eventually he became the most powerful man in the French army and won many victories throughout Europe.

9. He reorganized France and improved the law, banks, trade, and education.

10. When his enemies in Europe invaded France, Napoleon was exiled to an island off the coast of Italy.

11. He eventually returned to France with his soldiers, but he was finally defeated at the Battle of Waterloo.

12. Whom do you remember from centuries ago?

13. Only a few stand out in our history books for their bravery, great deeds, or incredible lives.

14. In the modern world, however, people instantly become famous because of television, movies, and newspapers.

15. Of course, few of these instant celebrities will be remembered next month.

Recognizing Pronouns and Their Antecedents

Write each personal pronoun and its antecedent in the following sentences.

1. Because Jamie was absent, he missed the field trip.

2. When the twins dress alike, they look identical.

3. An anteater can extend its tongue about two feet.

4. Lisa told Tim, "If you bring your racket, we can play a game."

5. Ken took his raincoat with him to the baseball game.

6. Mr. Ash told Nancy, "You should give your report now."

7. Bill and Ron rode their bicycles to school today.

8. "I didn't see you at the mall," Pam told Terry.

9. Linda said she is making her own dinner tonight.

10. "My friends asked me to visit them," Daniel told his dad.

Using Nouns and Pronouns

Write ten sentences that follow the directions below. (The sentences may include other nouns and pronouns besides those listed, and they may come in any order.) Write about one of the following topics or a topic of your own choice: a famous leader, sports figure, or musician. Write *N* above each noun and *P* above each pronoun.

Write a sentence that . . .

1. includes nouns that name a person, a place, and a thing.

2. includes a noun that names an idea.

3. includes a common noun and a proper noun.

4. includes a collective noun.

5. includes a compound noun.

6. includes several personal pronouns.

7. includes a reflexive pronoun.

8. includes one or two indefinite pronouns.

9. includes a demonstrative pronoun.

10. includes an interrogative pronoun.

Using Reciprocal Pronouns

Write a sentence that simplifies or combines each sentence or set of sentences using reciprocal pronouns.

1. Snoopy chases Frisky up the tree. Frisky chased Snoopy back down the tree.

2. Despite a minor tussle now and then, Frisky gets along with Snoopy and Snoopy gets along with Frisky.

3. Snoopy likes to curl up with Frisky. Frisky likes to clean Snoopy's fur.

4. My neighbor likes to tell me stories about her cat Sam. I like to tell her about Snoopy and Frisky.

Nouns and Pronouns: Posttest

Directions

Write the letter of the term that correctly identifies the underlined word or words in each sentence. The paragraph is about fires in Indonesia.

(1) <u>Indonesia</u> had been in the grip of a long drought throughout the year. (2) The <u>rain forests</u> were drier than we remembered them ever being before. (3) <u>They</u> burned with a hot intensity day and night for months. (4) <u>This</u> produced a severe smog over much of the country and surrounding areas. (5) <u>What</u> were the results of this disaster? (6) <u>Everything</u> in the country came to a halt. (7) Farm <u>families</u> were left without livelihoods. (8) <u>Sickness</u> and hunger were rampant. (9) If they stayed outdoors, people found <u>themselves</u> wheezing and fainting. (10) Indonesia <u>itself</u> lost over a billion dollars in farm and other products.

1. A abstract noun
   B proper noun
   C common noun
   D collective noun

2. A compound noun
   B proper noun
   C collective noun
   D abstract noun

3. A reflexive pronoun
   B intensive pronoun
   C personal pronoun
   D demonstrative pronoun

4. A personal pronoun
   B demonstrative pronoun
   C intensive pronoun
   D indefinite pronoun

5. A intensive pronoun
   B indefinite pronoun
   C interrogative pronoun
   D demonstrative pronoun

6. A reflexive pronoun
   B demonstrative pronoun
   C intensive pronoun
   D indefinite pronoun

7. A compound noun
   B collective noun
   C abstract noun
   D proper noun

8. A abstract noun
   B compound noun
   C proper noun
   D collective noun

9. A intensive pronoun
   B indefinite pronoun
   C reflexive pronoun
   D interrogative pronoun

10. A indefinite pronoun
    B reflexive pronoun
    C intensive pronoun
    D demonstrative pronoun

Writer's Corner

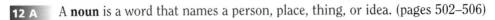

Snapshot

12 A A **noun** is a word that names a person, place, thing, or idea. (pages 502–506)

12 B A **pronoun** is a word that takes the place of one or more nouns. The noun that a pronoun refers to or replaces is called its **antecedent.** (pages 507–514)

Power Rules

 Use standard ways to make nouns possessive. When you use a **noun to show ownership,** add an *'s* to singular nouns and to plural nouns that don't end in an *s.* Add only an apostrophe to plural nouns ending in an *s.* (pages 895–897)

Before Editing

I wore my *boyfriends* jersey to the football game.

The *players's* uniforms were covered in mud after the game.

After Editing

I wore my *boyfriend's* jersey to the football game.

The *players'* uniforms were covered in mud after the game.

 Use **subject forms of pronouns** in subject position. Use the **object form** when the pronoun is a direct object, indirect object, or object of a preposition. (pages 716–725)

Before Editing

Rebecca and *him* went to the snack bar.

Them wanted some nachos.

Rebecca also bought popcorn for *we* to share.

After Editing

Rebecca and *he* went to the snack bar.

They wanted some nachos.

Rebecca also bought popcorn for *us* to share.

Editing Checklist

Use this checklist when editing your writing.

✓ Did I use specific nouns to make my writing more lively? (See page 502.)
✓ Did I capitalize proper nouns? (See pages 819–827.)
✓ Did I write compound nouns correctly? (See pages 504–505.)
✓ Did I use pronouns to avoid repetition? (See pages 507–514.)
✓ Did I replace nouns with the correct pronouns? (See pages 507–514.)

Use the Power

Use specific nouns to create vivid pictures in your writing. Use this graphic to help you turn general nouns into specific nouns.

Notice how the second sentence below becomes more vivid when general nouns are replaced with specific nouns.

The **boy** raced to **work** in his **car.**

Harold raced to the **courthouse** in his **Ferrari.**

Look at a recent composition, and check to be sure you have used specific nouns rather than general nouns.

Verbs

How can you make your writing sing by adding just the right verbs?

Verbs: Pretest 1

Read the following draft paragraph about birds. The paragraph is dull because it contains several ineffective action verbs. One of the verbs has been replaced as an example. Revise the rest of the paragraph so that it is more interesting to read.

      Scientists watch *study* birds to learn about their behavior. Falcons fly down on their prey at speeds of more than 200 miles per hour. Eagles have the same nests throughout their lives. Robins move in the winter. Ibises often take materials for their nests from other birds. Snow buntings lose their brown feathers in the winter. Penguins move their wings like flippers in the water. A bobwhite eats up to 15,000 seeds a day.

Verbs: Pretest 2

Directions

Write the letter of the term that correctly identifies the underlined word or words in each sentence.

(1) The class <u>has selected</u> a play. (2) The students <u>chose</u> William Shakespeare's *Julius Caesar* for their class play. (3) Carlos very much <u>wanted</u> the part of Caesar in the school production. (4) He <u>would have been</u> a great Caesar. (5) Instead, the rest of the class <u>chose</u> Nick for the part of the famous Roman leader. (6) Nick <u>was</u> good in rehearsals. (7) No one <u>could have worked</u> harder. (8) Julia <u>designed</u> the sets for the play. (9) She <u>painted</u> after school every day. (10) Raul and Ashley <u>were</u> the costume designers as well as the make-up artists.

1. **A** transitive verb
   B helping verb
   C intransitive verb
   D linking verb

2. **A** transitive verb
   B intransitive verb
   C linking verb
   D helping verb

3. **A** linking verb
   B transitive verb
   C helping verb
   D intransitive verb

4. **A** helping verb
   B linking verb
   C transitive verb
   D action verb

5. **A** linking verb
   B intransitive verb
   C helping verb
   D transitive verb

6. **A** action verb
   B helping verb
   C linking verb
   D transitive verb

7. **A** helping verb
   B linking verb
   C transitive verb
   D intransitive verb

8. **A** intransitive verb
   B helping verb
   C linking verb
   D transitive verb

9. **A** helping verb
   B intransitive verb
   C transitive verb
   D linking verb

10. **A** action verb
    B transitive verb
    C linking verb
    D helping verb

Action Verbs **Lesson 1**

Verbs are essential to every sentence. They breathe life into your writing.

13 A   A **verb** is a word that expresses action or a state of being.

One kind of verb, an **action verb,** gives a subject action and movement.

13 A.1   An **action verb** tells what action a subject is performing.

Most action verbs show physical action.

> Marine biologists **observe** the creatures of the sea.
>
> Many fish **swim** in the world's oceans.

Some action verbs show mental action; others show ownership or possession.

> Our class **studied** water mammals.
>
> The teacher **has** a photograph of a killer whale.

13 A.2   A **verb phrase** includes a main verb plus any helping, or auxiliary, verbs.

A verb phrase may contain more than one helping verb. It may also be interrupted by other words.

> The whales **will have migrated** by October.
>
> The students **could** certainly **learn** more about the sea.
>
> I **have** never **seen** a killer whale.

Below is a list of the most common helping verbs.

COMMON HELPING VERBS	
be	am, is, are, was, were, be, being, been
have	has, have, had
do	do, does, did
Others	may, might, must, can, could, shall, should, will, would

You can learn about regular and irregular verbs on pages 684–690.

When You Speak and Write

When you speak or write, the verbs you use can appeal to all five senses. Use verbs to make your audience see, feel, hear, taste, and smell what is happening.

Weak Sensory Appeal	The windsurfers **moved** through the water.
Strong Sensory Appeal	The windsurfers **sliced** through the water.

Look at a recent composition, and check to be sure you have used verbs that appeal to the senses.

● **Practice Your Skills**

Finding Action Verbs

Write the verb or verb phrase in the following sentences. Remember, words that interrupt a verb phrase are not part of the verb.

1. Dr. John C. Lilly, a scientist from California, studied dolphins for many years.
2. He had made some of the following claims about them.
3. Dolphins can mimic human speech patterns.
4. Their language contains at least fifty thousand words.
5. Their brains can handle four different conversations at one time.
6. They can also judge between right and wrong.
7. Dolphins can remember sounds and series of sounds.
8. They can even communicate among themselves.
9. They use a series of clicks, buzzes, and whistles.
10. Dolphins have discharged some of these sounds at the rate of seven hundred times a second.

Finding Verb Phrases

Write the verb or verb phrase in the following sentences.

1. Humans have been fascinated by the whale for centuries.

2. Whales can be divided into two basic types.

3. They are classified by scientists as either baleen or toothed whales.

4. Some small whales must surface for air several times each hour.

5. The larger creatures can remain underwater for an hour or more.

6. One species of baleen whale, the blue whale, can weigh up to fifteen hundred tons.

7. This species of whale was almost hunted to extinction in the early 1900s.

8. Didn't early whale hunters see their beauty and grace?

9. Some of them may not have realized the consequences of their actions.

10. Today, many wildlife organizations protect whales from hunters.

● *Connect to Writing:* **Revising**

Replacing Verbs

Change the underlined verbs in the following sentences to help the reader "hear" rather than "see" the action.

1. The waterfall <u>ran</u> over the rocks.

2. Children <u>have been playing</u> in the water throughout the morning.

3. The tugboat <u>moved</u> through the water.

4. The waves <u>hit</u> against the rocks.

5. The whale <u>blew</u> water from its spout.

● *Connect to Writing:* **Postcard**

Using Action Verbs

You are vacationing at the seashore. Your younger brother has never been to the beach. Write a postcard to him describing your first day on the beach. Remember to include vivid action verbs to make your writing interesting.

Transitive and Intransitive Verbs

13 B   All action verbs fall within two general classes: **transitive** or **intransitive**.

13 B.1   A **transitive verb** is an action verb that passes the action from a doer to a receiver. An **intransitive verb** expresses action or states something about the subject but does not pass the action from a doer to a receiver.

You can determine whether a verb is transitive or intransitive by identifying the subject and the verb. Then ask, *What?* or *Whom?* A word that answers either question is called an object. An action verb that has an object is transitive. An action verb that does not have an object is intransitive.

Transitive	Many birds **eat** insects.
	(Birds eat what? *Insects* is the object. *Eat* is a transitive verb.)
Intransitive	Most geese **travel** in flocks.
	(Geese travel what? Since there is no object, *travel* is an intransitive verb.)

The same verb may be transitive in one sentence and intransitive in another.

Transitive	We **hung** birdhouses in the trees.
	(We hung what? *Birdhouses* is the object.)
Intransitive	The birdhouse **hung** from a rope in the oak tree.
	(Birdhouse hung what? There is no object.)

You can learn about objects that follow transitive verbs on pages 592–595.

● Practice Your Skills

Finding Transitive and Intransitive Verbs

Write the action verb in each sentence. Then label each one *T* for transitive or *I* for intransitive.

1. Birds live in trees, on the ground, and in the sides of cliffs.

2. Many different birds nest near the seashore.

3. Some owls build their nests in burrows.

4. Hummingbirds sometimes fly backward.

5. Lice live on some birds and mammals.

6. Humans pose the greatest danger to the bird population.

● *Connect to Writing:* **Editing**

Using Action Verbs

Supply an action verb for each of the following sentences. Label each one *T* for transitive or *I* for intransitive.

1. During autumn many birds ▨ from the north to the south.

2. Most adult birds ▨ their young from dangers.

3. In forests you ▨ birds' songs all around you.

4. Two cardinals ▨ across the wooded path.

5. Most birds ▨ the nest when they are a few months old.

6. Many people around the world ▨ birds as pets.

● *Connect to Speaking and Writing:* **Vocabulary Review**

Using the Vocabulary of Grammar

With a partner, talk about the difference between transitive and intransitive verbs. Then write a short definition of the grammar terms *transitive verb* and *intransitive verb*.

Power Your Writing: Getting into the Action

You are not limited to verbs when adding action to your writing. You can also use participles. A **participle** is a word formed from a verb. It "gets into the action" by modifying a noun, just as an adjective does.

A participle can be turned into a **participial phrase** by joining it with other words. Present participial phrases, or "–*ing* modifiers," describe a person, thing, or action. (See pages 621–622.) Read how Maya Angelou uses –*ing* phrases at the beginning of a sentence in *I Know Why the Caged Bird Sings* (pages 37–40).

Participial Phrase at Beginning of Sentence	**Remembering my manners**, I took nice little lady-like bites off the edges.

You can also add an –*ing* modifier to the end of a sentence as Angelou does in this example.

Participial Phrase at End of Sentence	She had the grace of control to appear warm in the coldest weather, and on the Arkansas summer days it seemed she had a private breeze which swirled around, **cooling her.**

Look at a recent composition, and check to see if you can use participial phrases to add a sense of action to your descriptions.

526 Verbs

Lesson 3

13 C   A **linking verb** links the subject with another word in the sentence. The other word either renames or describes the subject.

The farm **is** my home.

(*Is* links *home* with *farm*. *Home* renames the subject.)

Have you **been** sad lately?

(Turn a question into a statement: *You have been sad lately*. Then you can easily see that *have been* links *sad* and the subject *you*. *Sad* describes the subject.)

Here is a list of common linking verbs. They are all forms of the verb *be*. Any verb phrase ending in *be* or *been* is a form of *be* and can be used as a linking verb.

COMMON FORMS OF *BE*		
be	shall be	have been
is	will be	has been
am	can be	had been
are	could be	will have been
was	should be	should have been
were	would be	may have been
	may be	might have been
	might be	must have been

The forms of *be* are not always linking verbs. To be a linking verb, a verb must link the subject with another word that renames or describes it. The word that renames or describes the subject is known as the **subject complement.**

In the examples below, the verbs simply make statements and are not linking verbs.

Our farm **is** over that hill.

The cows **will be** in the barn.

You can learn more about subject complements on pages 595–598.

Finding Linking Verbs

Write the linking verb in each sentence. Then write the words that the verb links.

1. My childhood on the farm was great.

2. Childhood memories should be happy for everyone.

3. My mother had been a city girl.

4. My father could have been a doctor.

5. Instead, he was a farmer.

➤ Additional Linking Verbs

A few other verbs besides *be* can be linking verbs.

ADDITIONAL LINKING VERBS			
appear	grow	seem	stay
become	look	smell	taste
feel	remain	sound	turn

These verbs also link the subject with a word that describes or renames it.

The air **feels** humid today.

(*Humid* describes the *air*.)

The tornado **remains** a destructive force of nature.

(*Force* renames *tornado*.)

● **Practice Your Skills**

Finding Linking Verbs

Write the linking verb in each sentence. Then write the two words that the verb links.

1. The weather suddenly turned colder.

2. The sky looks dark today.

3. The clouds have grown thicker.

4. The gentle breeze became a strong wind.

5. The raindrops felt cold against my skin.

● *Connect to Writing:* **Revising**

Changing Questions into Statements

Change the following questions into statements. Underline the linking verb in each of your sentences.

1. Does the rain seem heavier?

2. Are you afraid of storms?

3. Are the windows in your bedroom very large?

4. Do I look pale?

5. Was that the worst storm ever in your town?

➤ Linking Verb or Action Verb?

Most linking verbs can also be action verbs.

Linking Verb   The darkness **felt** oppressive to us.
                     (*Oppressive* describes the subject.)

Action Verb   In the darkness my little sister **felt** for my hand.
                     (*Felt* shows action. It tells what *sister* did.)

You can decide whether a verb is a linking verb or an action verb by asking two questions: *Does the verb link the subject with a word that renames or describes the subject? Does the verb show action?*

Linking Verb   My little sister **looked** afraid.

Action Verb   My mother **looked** for the candles.

● *Connect to Writing and Speaking:* **Descriptive Paragraph**

Using Linking Verbs

Your town has just experienced a devastating tornado. You are standing in a neighborhood looking at the damage. A radio reporter walks up to you and asks you to describe how the neighborhood looked before the storm. Write a paragraph describing the neighborhood. Underline the linking verbs you use in your description.

CHAPTER 13

Distinguishing Between Linking Verbs and Action Verbs

Write the verb in each sentence. Then label each one *A* for action or
L for linking.

1. Suddenly the room grew dark.
2. Did you turn off the light?
3. I looked for the light switch.
4. The night turned darker.
5. The phone rang suddenly.
6. My sister grew afraid in the dark.
7. Tall vines grew outside the window.
8. In the moonlight, the vines appear human.
9. The clock sounded loud in the darkness.
10. We felt better with the lights on.

● *Connect to Writing:* **Drafting**

Writing Sentences

Write a sentence using each verb as a linking verb. Then use the verb as an
action verb. Label each one *A* for action or *L* for linking.

1. taste   2. grow   3. appear   4. turn   5. smell

✓ *Check Point:* **Mixed Practice**

Write the verb or verb phrase in each sentence. Then label the verb *A* for action
verb or *L* for linking verb. If the verb is an action verb, label it *T* for transitive or
I for intransitive.

1. Cryogenics is the study of cold.
2. At very cold temperatures, your breath will turn into a liquid.
3. At colder temperatures, it actually freezes into a solid.
4. Cold steel becomes very soft.
5. A frozen banana can serve as a hammer.
6. Shivers can raise a person's body temperature seven degrees.
7. People with a low body temperature feel lazy.
8. One should wear layers of clothing for protection from cold.
9. Chipmunks have found a good solution to the cold.
10. They hibernate all winter long!

Chapter Review

Assess Your Learning

■ Identifying Verbs and Verb Phrases

Write each verb or verb phrase in the following sentences. Then label each one *action verb* or *linking verb.*

1. The world is filled with incredible creatures.
2. Facts about these creatures will be equally incredible.
3. A dragonfly is extremely small.
4. Dragonflies, however, have been clocked at fifty miles per hour.
5. The largest animal in the world actually swims in the ocean.
6. The blue whale can weigh more than thirty elephants.
7. Your pet goldfish might live as long as thirty or forty years!
8. Does a goldfish ever look old?
9. The fastest land animal probably would be given a ticket on a highway.
10. The cheetah can actually run faster than sixty miles per hour.
11. Cockroaches are the oldest species on earth.
12. They looked similar more than 320 million years ago.
13. Do baby cockroaches appear beautiful to their mothers?
14. A skunk can hit something twelve feet away with its smell.
15. Have you ever smelled a skunk's scent?
16. The spray of a skunk smells absolutely horrible!
17. The ostrich egg is by far the biggest egg.
18. Some have actually weighed almost four pounds.
19. An ostrich egg must cook for at least two hours.
20. Have you read about any other incredible creatures?

■ Understanding Transitive and Intransitive Verbs

Write the verb or verb phrase in each sentence. Then label each verb or verb phrase *T* for transitive or *I* for intransitive.

1. Most of the apples fell from the tree during the storm.
2. Spiders have transparent blood.
3. Dad is reading on the porch.
4. Most American car horns beep in the key of F.
5. I usually answer the phone on the second ring.

6. Did you read this book for your book report?

7. Cut the grass tomorrow.

8. The robot will always answer politely.

9. Thomas Jefferson invented the calendar clock.

10. The fire engine rushed through the red light.

Using Verbs

Write sentences that follow the directions below. (The sentences may come in any order.) Write about one of the following topics or a topic of your own choice: a pet you have had, a pet you would like to have, a wild animal, or an endangered animal. You also could write about what animal you would like to be and why.

Write a sentence that . . .

1. includes an action verb.

2. includes a linking verb.

3. includes a verb phrase.

4. includes an interrupted verb phrase.

5. includes *taste* as an action verb.

6. includes *taste* as a linking verb.

7. includes *look* as an action verb.

8. includes *look* as a linking verb.

9. includes *appear* as an action verb.

10. includes *appear* as a linking verb.

11. includes *smell* as an action verb.

12. includes *smell* as a linking verb.

Underline each verb or verb phrase.

Verbs: Posttest

Directions

Write the letter of the term that correctly identifies the underlined word or words in each sentence.

(1) Jesse's family <u>has</u> visited the same cabin in Maine every summer for eight years. (2) Jesse and his father <u>fish</u> for their dinner each day. (3) They <u>have caught</u> some enormous bass and pickerel that Jesse's father cooks on the grill. (4) Ducks and loons <u>swim</u> on the lake in the pleasant summer evenings. (5) The loon's call <u>sounds</u> eerie. (6) Sometimes the family <u>will hear</u> the loon calls for hours into the night. (7) The water <u>is</u> great for swimming, boating, and skipping stones, too. (8) Jesse's mother <u>can</u> swim for miles. (9) The whole family <u>canoes</u> around the lake in a sturdy craft built by Jesse's grandfather. (10) Sometimes they <u>will paddle</u> the canoe to the small island in the center.

1. **A** transitive verb
   B intransitive verb
   C helping verb
   D linking verb

2. **A** transitive verb
   B intransitive verb
   C helping verb
   D linking verb

3. **A** helping verb
   B intransitive verb
   C transitive verb
   D linking verb

4. **A** linking verb
   B helping verb
   C transitive verb
   D intransitive verb

5. **A** transitive verb
   B helping verb
   C linking verb
   D action verb

6. **A** intransitive verb
   B linking verb
   C transitive verb
   D helping verb

7. **A** linking verb
   B transitive verb
   C action verb
   D helping verb

8. **A** transitive verb
   B helping verb
   C linking verb
   D intransitive verb

9. **A** intransitive verb
   B linking verb
   C transitive verb
   D helping verb

10. **A** linking verb
    B transitive verb
    C helping verb
    D intransitive verb

Writer's Corner

Snapshot

13 A   A **verb** is a word that expresses action or a state of being. An **action verb** tells what action a subject is performing. (pages 522–524)

13 B   **Transitive verbs** are action verbs that express action toward a person or a thing. **Intransitive verbs** do not direct action at a person or a thing. (pages 525–526)

13 C   A **linking verb** links the subject with another word in the sentence. The other word either renames or describes the subject. (pages 527–530)

Power Rules

 Use the helping verb *have* or the contraction *'ve* with *could, might,* or *should* **instead of the word** *of.* (pages 160 and 801)

Before Editing	**After Editing**
I *should of* studied for the test.	I *should have* studied for the test.
I *could of* gotten a better grade.	I *could've* gotten a better grade. (*could have*)

Be sure that the **subject and verb always agree.** (pages 750–767)

Before Editing

The *dog run* in the park.

The *boy* and *girl throws* balls to the dog.

After Editing

The *dog runs* in the park.

The *boy* and *girl throw* balls to the dog.

Editing Checklist

Use this checklist when editing your writing.

✓ Did I use action verbs effectively? (See pages 522–524.)
✓ Did I use the correct helping verbs in verb phrases? (See pages 522–524.)
✓ Did I use the correct form of the verb *to be?* (See page 527.)
✓ Did I use linking verbs effectively? (See pages 527–530.)

Use the Power

Use the illustration below to help remember how action verbs can appeal to your readers' five senses. Choosing the right verb will make your writing interesting, lively, and exact.

	buzz, roar, crack, shout, cry, whir, sing, bellow, crash, drum, stomp, whisper, stutter, smash, smear, babble, croak, flap, flutter
	loom, tower, shrink, crawl, creep, race, speed, limp, gallop, bolt, halt, cringe, peer, scamper, scatter, sweep
	grasp, shiver, catch, caress, stroke, brush, huddle, scratch, sting, smooth, rumple, crinkle, crumble
	chomp, gobble, crunch, gulp, nibble, pepper, quench, savor, sip, swig, spice
	breathe, emit, exhale, perfume, reek, sniff, stink

Look at a recent composition, and check to be sure you have used verbs that appeal to the senses.

Adjectives and Adverbs

How can you add interest and detail to your writing with adjectives and adverbs?

Adjectives and Adverbs: Pretest 1

The following draft paragraph about a trip to Yellowstone National Park lacks interesting adverbs and adjectives. Revise the paragraph so that it expresses more excitement. One adjective has been replaced as an example.

My trip to Yellowstone this past summer was ~~nice~~ *extraordinary*. I met many friendly, interesting people. I slept in a tent with other campers and enjoyed being surrounded by the sights and sounds of the natural world. The park is full of sites. I liked the geysers. Some of us went fishing for trout and salmon. The water in the stream was cold. Later we climbed a rock face. It was a hard climb to the top. I also saw the Morning Glory Pool, which was very clear. The time flew by that week. Although I enjoyed my trip, I was glad to return home. I missed my friends, and it felt good to sleep in my own bed.

Adjectives and Adverbs: Pretest 2

Directions

Write the letter of the term that correctly identifies the underlined word in each sentence.

The County Fair

(1) At the county fair, there are <u>wild</u> rides near the carnival section. **(2)** Sometimes young children become <u>nervous</u> or frightened. **(3)** The food section <u>always</u> features exotic treats from around the world. **(4)** The <u>deep-dish</u> pizza is a real favorite among the carnivalgoers. **(5)** Many people enjoy the <u>Greek</u> salads topped with feta cheese. **(6)** In long barns the <u>farm</u> animals are judged on appearance and merit. **(7)** The cows and horses behave <u>well</u>. **(8)** Last year <u>several</u> of the sheep got loose from their pens. **(9)** The sheep led their owners on a <u>merry</u> chase around the fair. **(10)** Needless to say, <u>those</u> sheep did not win prizes.

1. A adjective
   B adverb
   C pronoun
   D compound adjective

2. A adjective
   B adverb
   C pronoun
   D article

3. A adjective
   B pronoun
   C adverb
   D article

4. A article
   B proper adjective
   C adverb
   D compound adjective

5. A adverb
   B compound adjective
   C proper adjective
   D article

6. A article
   B adjective
   C adverb
   D noun

7. A adverb
   B adjective
   C article
   D pronoun

8. A adverb
   B pronoun
   C proper adjective
   D article

9. A article
   B compound adjective
   C adjective
   D pronoun

10. A pronoun
   B adverb
   C article
   D adjective

Your sentences would be very short and dull with only nouns and pronouns.

> The girls watched movies.

You can use adjectives and adverbs to give color and sharper meaning to sentences and paragraphs.

> The **teenage** girls **avidly** watched the **classic** movies **yesterday.**

Adjectives modify, or make more precise, the meanings of nouns and pronouns. For example, what is your favorite movie like? Is it *long, short, happy, interesting*, or *scary?* All these possible answers are adjectives. They make the meaning of the word *movie* more precise.

14 A   An **adjective** is a word that modifies a noun or a pronoun.

To find an adjective, first find each noun and pronoun in a sentence. Then ask yourself, *What kind? Which one(s)? How many?* or *How much?* about each one. The answers will be adjectives.

What Kind?	The **silent** crowd watched the film.
	Do you like **scary** movies?
Which One(s)?	**That** role was written for the actress.
	I like the **funny** parts.
How Many?	**Thirty** people stood in line to buy a ticket.
	I have seen the movie **many** times.
How Much?	He deserves **much** praise for his performance.
	Few seats in the theater were empty.

Practice Your Skills

Finding Adjectives

Write the adjectives from the following sentences. Do not include *the* or *a*.

(1) For more than 100 years, people have been entertained in dark theaters. (2) Movies have a rich and interesting history. (3) Thomas Edison and a helpful assistant were among the first people to use transparent film to create images. (4) Early movies amazed most audiences. (5) Because of a sunny climate, California became the home of modern movies. (6) After many years, the first permanent studio was built in Los Angeles in 1911. (7) Because early films did not have sound, a pianist would play musical pieces to accompany the action of the silent film. (8) One of the first filmmakers to shoot different angles with a camera was D. W. Griffith. (9) The lavish costumes and elaborate settings of early films cost a lot of money. (10) Even so, most people went to early movies not to see beautiful costumes but to see popular stars of the era.

Connect to Writing: Drafting

Supplying Adjectives

Write an adjective to complete each sentence.

1. The ▨ movie will be opening soon.
2. Do you want a ▨ seat or one at the back of the room?
3. It was hard to find my friend in the ▨ theater.
4. If we are late, there will be ▨ seats available.
5. I love to eat the ▨ popcorn from the concession stand.

Different Positions of Adjectives

Adjectives can modify different nouns or pronouns, or they can modify the same noun or pronoun.

> **Different Nouns**   Mandy wore a **red** vest with a **white** shirt.
>
> **The Same Noun**   The vest had **big blue** buttons.

PUNCTUATION WITH TWO ADJECTIVES

Sometimes you will write two adjectives before the noun they describe. If the adjectives are not connected by a conjunction—such as *and* or *or*—you might need to put a comma between them.

To decide whether a comma belongs, read the adjectives and add the word *and* between them.

- If the adjectives make sense, put a comma in to replace the *and*.
- If the adjectives do not make sense with the word *and* between them, do not add a comma.

> **Comma Needed**   The **soft, furry** vest is on the hanger.
>
> **No Comma Needed**   The **red corduroy** vest is in the drawer.

You can learn more about placing commas between multiple adjectives that come before nouns on pages 850–851.

Usually an adjective comes before the noun or pronoun it modifies. An adjective can also follow a noun or pronoun, or it can follow a linking verb.

> **Before a Noun**   She wore the **latest** fashion.
>
> **After a Noun**   His shirt, **big** and **baggy,** hung down to his knees.
>
> **After a Linking Verb**   Ron looks quite **handsome** today.

You can learn more about adjectives that follow linking verbs on pages 597–598.

Professional writers use a variety of positions for adjectives, placing some of them before the nouns they modify and others after the nouns they modify. This is one of the ways that writers add variety to their descriptions and make their writing more interesting. Notice the position of the underlined adjectives in Ray Bradbury's description of Martian spaceships.

In the <u>blowing</u> moonlight, like <u>metal</u> petals of some <u>ancient</u> flower, like <u>blue</u> plumes, like <u>cobalt</u> butterflies <u>immense</u> and <u>quiet</u>, the <u>old</u> ships turned and moved over the <u>shifting</u> sands, the masks <u>beaming</u> and <u>glittering</u>, until the <u>last</u> shine, the <u>last</u> <u>blue</u> color, was lost among the hills.

—*Ray Bradbury,* The Martian Chronicles

Revise a recent descriptive passage you have written by moving some adjectives after the nouns they modify.

CHAPTER 14

● Practice Your Skills

Finding Adjectives

Write the adjectives in each sentence. Then beside each adjective, write the word it modifies. Do not include *the* or *a*.

(1) For several centuries, men dressed with more color and greater style than women. **(2)** During the 1600s, men wore lacy collars and fancy jackets with shiny buttons. **(3)** Curly long hair reached their shoulders. **(4)** Men even carried small purses on huge belts. **(5)** After all, there were no pockets in the warm, colorful tights they wore. **(6)** By 1850, men's clothing had become drab and conservative. **(7)** Gone were the elegant white silk shirts, purple vests, lacy cuffs, and stylish black boots. **(8)** Men's clothing stayed colorless and dreary until the Beatles came along in the 1960s. **(9)** Clothes of the 1960s, bright and informal, created a new style for men. **(10)** Today, people don't follow one style; everyone dresses to suit personal taste. **(11)** Still, we are all influenced by current trends. **(12)** Who can guess the strange and wonderful clothes we will be wearing in 2050?

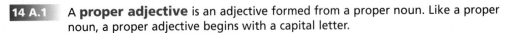

Proper Adjectives

14 A.1   A **proper adjective** is an adjective formed from a proper noun. Like a proper noun, a proper adjective begins with a capital letter.

Some proper adjectives keep the same form as the proper noun; others change form.

Proper Noun	Proper Adjective Keeps Same Form
New York	**New York** restaurant
Monday	**Monday** dinner
Thanksgiving	**Thanksgiving** holiday

Proper Noun	Proper Adjective Changes Form
Greece	**Greek** salad
France	**French** bread
Mexico	**Mexican** fiesta

You can learn more about capitalizing proper adjectives on page 828.

Compound Adjectives

You have learned that compound nouns are nouns made up of two or more words.

14 A.2   **Compound adjectives** are made up of two or more words.

COMPOUND ADJECTIVES	
rooftop café	**household** word
faraway lands	**record-breaking** sprint

Articles

14 A.3   *A, an,* and *the* form a special group of adjectives called **articles.**

A comes before words that begin with consonant sounds and *an* before words that begin with vowel sounds.

A new theater showed **an** old movie.

You will not be asked to list the articles in the exercises in this book.

● **Practice Your Skills**

Finding Proper and Compound Adjectives

Write the proper adjectives and the compound adjectives in each sentence below. Then beside each adjective, write the word it modifies.

(1) That popular restaurant offered a variety of dishes from faraway lands. **(2)** The straightforward waitress described the European delicacies in simple language. **(3)** While Caribbean music played, diners enjoyed Russian caviar served with Italian bread. **(4)** One couple ate a Caesar salad with Greek olives. **(5)** Some Japanese tourists ate Indian food and drank Turkish coffee. **(6)** The restaurant recently received a five-star rating in an American travel magazine. **(7)** Our after-dinner treat was some Hawaiian pineapple. **(8)** The tuxedo-clad waiter brought a Chinese fortune cookie with our check. **(9)** When they visit, our Canadian friends and I will probably dine at the award-winning restaurant. **(10)** Of course, I usually prefer a hamburger with Swiss cheese from a fast-food restaurant.

● *Connect to Writing:* **Editing**

Capitalizing Proper Adjectives

Find the proper adjective in each sentence and rewrite it with a capital letter.

1. Our european vacation took us to some historic places.
2. The london subway system was quite a marvel.
3. Our english hotel was once a famous poet's home.
4. My favorite activity was visiting ancient roman ruins.
5. We even had the opportunity to ski in the swiss Alps.

Adjective or Noun?

The same word can be an adjective in one sentence and a noun in another sentence.

Adjective	I hope to finish my **school** assignment before dinner.
	(*School* tells what kind of assignment.)
Noun	I left my English book at **school.**
	(*School* is the name of a place.)
Adjective	While setting the table, I broke a **dinner** plate.
Noun	My father often cooks **dinner.**

Distinguishing Between Adjectives and Nouns

Write the underlined word in each sentence. Then label each word **A** for adjective or **N** for noun.

1. Dad put our dinner in the <u>oven</u>.

2. We sat down to watch a <u>television</u> show.

3. We watched our favorite <u>news</u> program.

4. The reception on our set was bad, so the <u>picture</u> was fuzzy.

5. I put on <u>oven</u> mitts to take the casserole out of the oven.

6. As I brought out the casserole, I dropped the <u>glass</u> dish.

7. My brother and I cleaned up the <u>glass</u>.

8. My mom turned off the <u>television</u>.

9. The <u>news</u> was over.

10. Instead of casserole, we ate sandwiches as we looked out the <u>picture</u> window.

Adjective or Pronoun?

The following words can be used as adjectives or pronouns.

WORDS USED AS ADJECTIVES OR PRONOUNS				
Demonstrative	**Interrogative**		**Indefinite**	
this	what	all	either	neither
these	which	another	few	other
that	whose	any	many	several
those		both	more	some
		each	most	

These words are adjectives when they modify a noun; they are pronouns when they stand alone.

Adjective   I have been to **this** camp before.

Pronoun   Do you like **this?**

Adjective   **What** time is it?

Pronoun   **What** is planned for today?

Adjective   I called you **several** times before we left.

Pronoun   **Several** of the campers got poison ivy.

Sometimes the possessive pronouns *my, your, his, her, its, our,* and *their* are called adjectives because they answer the question *Which one?* Throughout this book, however, these words will be considered pronouns.

● **Practice Your Skills**

Distinguishing Between Adjectives and Pronouns

Write the underlined word in each sentence. Then label each word **A** for adjective or **P** for pronoun.

(1) <u>Both</u> of my brothers came to camp with me last summer. **(2)** <u>Some</u> friends came along as well. **(3)** I prefer <u>this</u> camp to the one I attended two years ago. **(4)** <u>These</u> mosquitoes will not stop biting me! **(5)** <u>Which</u> of the canoes do you want? **(6)** I dropped <u>both</u> paddles into the water. **(7)** <u>These</u> are designed to float. **(8)** After <u>this</u>, let's go horseback riding. **(9)** <u>Which</u> horse is the most gentle? **(10)** <u>Some</u> of them are very well trained.

✔ *Check Point:* **Mixed Practice**

Write each adjective and the word it modifies. Do not include *the, a,* or *an.*

Nikolai, a Russian athlete, helped the American team win the Olympic ice hockey championship in 1960. The Americans had beaten the Canadian team and the Russian team. Now all they had to do was defeat the Czechs in the final game. After two periods, the Americans were losing. The thin air in the California mountains was slowing them down. Between the second period and the third period, Nikolai visited the weary Americans. Unfortunately, he didn't speak any English. Through many gestures, however, he told them to inhale some oxygen. The team immediately felt lively and energetic. For the first time, an American team won the title.

● *Connect to Writing:* **Advertisement**

Using Adjectives

You have been hired by an advertising agency to write an ad for a summer camp for teenagers. Decide first what kind of camp you will advertise. Is it a camp in the country, a sports camp, a space camp, or another type of camp? Remember to make the camp appealing to someone like you, but also try to describe a summer experience for which parents would gladly pay. Describe activities, meals, and other aspects of the camp that are enticing. Underline all the adjectives you use in your description.

Adverbs Lesson 2

14 B   An **adverb** is a word that modifies a verb, an adjective, or another adverb.

Just as adjectives add more information about nouns and pronouns, **adverbs** make verbs, adjectives, and other adverbs more precise. You probably know that many adverbs end in -*ly*.

Recently my family voted **unanimously** for a vacation in the national forest.

We strolled **casually** through the woods.

Following is a list of common adverbs that do not end in -*ly*.

CHAPTER 14

COMMON ADVERBS			
afterward	far	not (n't)	soon
again	fast	now	still
almost	hard	nowhere	straight
alone	here	often	then
already	just	outside	there
also	late	perhaps	today
always	long	quite	tomorrow
away	low	rather	too
before	more	seldom	very
down	near	so	well
even	never	sometimes	yesterday
ever	next	somewhat	yet

You probably use many contractions in casual conversation. *Not* and its contraction *n't* are always adverbs.

We could **not** find our binoculars.

Do**n't** disturb the other campers.

Adverbs That Modify Verbs

Most adverbs modify verbs. To find these adverbs, first find the verb. Then ask yourself *Where? When? How?* or *To what extent?* about the verb. The answers to these questions will be adverbs. The adverbs in the following examples are in bold type. An arrow points to the verb each adverb modifies.

Where?	Look **everywhere** for wildlife.
	Wild animals are **there.**
When?	We **frequently** camp in the forest.
	I **sometimes** sleep in a tent.
How?	I **carefully** approached the deer.
	The animal **swiftly** and **surely** jumped over the boulder.
To What Extent?	My sister **completely** enjoys the experience.
	We have **almost** arrived at the waterfall.

An adverb can come before or after the verb or in the middle of a verb phrase.

● Practice Your Skills

Finding Adverbs That Modify Verbs

Write the adverbs in each sentence. Then beside each adverb, write the verb it modifies.

1. Porcupines never shoot their quills.

2. Usually the quills catch on something.

3. Then they fall out.

4. Porcupines always use their quills for protection.

5. Occasionally another animal will greatly disturb a porcupine.

6. The porcupine's quills will immediately stand upright.

7. Often the porcupine will bump the other animal.

8. The quills do not miss.

9. They stick swiftly and securely in the animal's skin.

10. An animal rarely bothers a porcupine twice.

Adverbs That Modify Adjectives and Other Adverbs

A few adverbs modify adjectives and other adverbs.

> **Modifying an Adjective** Visiting national parks is **always** fun.

> **Modifying an Adverb** You should approach wild animals **very** cautiously.

To find adverbs that modify adjectives or other adverbs, first find the adjectives and the adverbs in a sentence. Then ask yourself *To what extent?* about each one. Notice in the preceding examples that the adverbs that modify adjectives or other adverbs usually come before the word they modify.

● **Practice Your Skills**

Finding Adverbs that Modify Adjectives and Other Adverbs

Write each adverb that modifies an adjective or another adverb. Then beside each adverb, write the word it modifies.

(1) Yellowstone National Park is an exceptionally beautiful place. **(2)** The drive through the park can be rather long. **(3)** As they drive, tourists go very slowly as they attempt to see wildlife. **(4)** Bison and moose are quite abundant in the park. **(5)** Bears are almost never seen from the roadways. **(6)** Geysers are surprisingly common attractions in the park. **(7)** Old Faithful, a large geyser, is the most famous one in the park. **(8)** The benches around Old Faithful are extremely full of tourists. **(9)** Due to minerals in the water, a sulfur smell is very strong throughout the park. **(10)** If you decide to go, plan your vacation very early in the summer. **(11)** The park is unusually busy in July. **(12)** May is most assuredly the best month to visit the park.

When You Read and Write

Writers often use the placement of adverbs to create an effect on their audiences. In this passage from *The Great Gatsby*, F. Scott Fitzgerald used adverb placement to heighten the tension between two of the main characters.

> The telephone rang <u>inside</u>, <u>startlingly</u>, and as Daisy shook her head <u>decisively</u> at Tom the subject of the stables, in fact all subjects, vanished into thin air. Among the broken fragments of the last five minutes at the table I remember the candles being lit <u>again</u>, <u>pointlessly</u>.

Look at a recent composition. Are there ways you can change the position of adverbs to create an effect?

Adverb or Adjective?

As you have seen in the previous section, many adverbs end in *-ly*. You should be aware, however, that some adjectives end in *-ly* as well. In addition, many words can be used as either adverbs or adjectives. Always check to see how a word is used in a sentence before you decide what part of speech it is.

Adverb	We visit my Aunt Sylvia **yearly.**
Adjective	Our **yearly** visits to Aunt Sylvia are filled with fun.
Adverb	My cousin hit the baseball quite **hard.**
Adjective	The **hard** ball broke Aunt Sylvia's window.

You can learn about the comparison of adverbs and adjectives on pages 776–782.

● **Practice Your Skills**

Distinguishing Between Adjectives and Adverbs

Write the underlined word in each sentence. Then label each one as *adverb* or *adjective*.

1. My <u>early</u> memories are filled with visits to Aunt Sylvia's house in the country.

2. She had a <u>warm</u> smile and lively eyes.

3. I <u>especially</u> loved her delicious apple pies.

4. Her house was high on a hill overlooking an <u>open</u> field of wildflowers.

5. My cousins and I <u>joyfully</u> roamed the countryside near her home.

6. <u>Sometimes</u> we swam in the lake.

7. We knew the area <u>very</u> well.

8. We would run <u>loudly</u> through Aunt Sylvia's house.

9. After a big supper on the porch, we would go to bed <u>early</u>.

10. It was <u>easy</u> for us to fall asleep.

● *Connect to Writing:* **Description**

Using Adverbs

Recall a memorable holiday gathering. Write a description of the scene as if you were talking to a friend. Remember to include details such as the reason for the gathering, the time of year, the activities, and the interactions between the people. Use adverbs in your description to make your description come alive. Underline each adverb.

✔ *Check Point:* **Mixed Practice**

Write the adverbs in the following paragraphs. Then beside each adverb, write the word or words it modifies.

(1) The first pair of roller skates appeared in 1760 and were unsuccessfully worn by Joseph Merlin. **(2)** Merlin had unexpectedly received an invitation to **(3)** a very large party. **(4)** Quite excitedly, he planned a grand entrance. **(5)** The night finally arrived. **(6)** Merlin rolled unsteadily into the ballroom on skates as he played a violin. **(7)** Unfortunately, he couldn't stop. **(8)** Merlin crashed into an extremely large mirror, which broke into a million pieces. **(9)** Merlin also smashed his violin and hurt himself severely.

(10) Roller skates were never used again until 1823. **(11)** Robert Tyers eventually made another attempt. **(12)** His skates had a single row of five very small wheels. **(13)** In 1863, James Plimpton finally patented the first pair of four-wheel skates. **(14)** With these skates, people could keep their balance easily. **(15)** They could even make sharp turns. **(16)** In-line skates would not be reinvented for many years.

● *Connect to Speaking and Writing:* **Peer Interaction**

Reviewing Content

With a partner, review the vocabulary you have learned in this chapter. (Hint: New terms are printed in purple.) Quiz each other until you understand the definitions of all the new words and concepts.

Diagraming Adjectives and Adverbs

Adjectives and adverbs are diagramed on slanted lines below the words they modify.

My small brother swam.

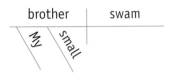

He swam skillfully.

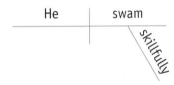

My small but strong brother swam fast and skillfully.

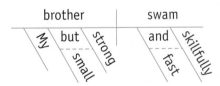

An adverb that modifies an adjective or another adverb is written on a line parallel to the word it modifies.

The extremely smart child won.

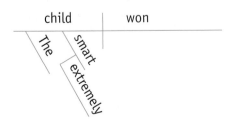

CHAPTER 14

She ate too quickly.

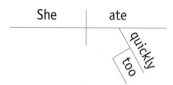

A rather large cat purred very softly.

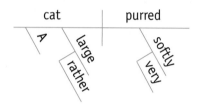

● **Practice Your Skills**

Diagraming Adjectives and Adverbs

Diagram the following sentences or copy them. If you copy them, draw one line under each subject and two lines under each verb. Then label each modifier *adj.* for adjective or *adv.* for adverb.

1. A large octopus appeared.

2. It paused briefly.

3. Octopuses can move very quickly.

4. They also swim forward and backward.

5. The extremely large arms stretched forward.

6. Suddenly an inky fluid squirted out.

7. Some small fish were blinded.

8. Others were even poisoned.

9. Then this large but flexible creature turned.

10. Suddenly it swam away forever.

Assess Your Learning

■ Identifying Adjectives and Adverbs

For each sentence below, draw a line under each modifier and label each one *adj.* for adjective or *adv.* for adverb. Do not include articles (*a, an,* and *the*).

1. Recently thirty students and several teachers took a bus trip from South Carolina to Everglades National Park in the southern part of Florida.
2. This national park uniquely combines prairies, swamps, saltwater marshes, and freshwater lakes.
3. The Everglades is actually a river, a very unusual river.
4. It flows from Lake Okeechobee southward to the Gulf of Mexico.
5. Everyone carefully got into canoes for a tour of the Everglades.
6. Initially the landscape seemed somewhat monotonous to these first-time visitors.
7. Then they looked closely and saw hundreds of unusual things.
8. The park is the home to a large variety of animals.
9. Alligators are the most famous occupants of the park.
10. The ranger pointed to the tall, dense grasses.
11. Students immediately and excitedly saw two huge alligators in the grass.
12. Suddenly everyone looked up into the cloudless blue sky.
13. A roseate spoonbill, large and graceful, landed nearby on a park pond.
    (*Roseate spoonbill* is the whole name of the bird.)
14. The pink color of the bird comes from the many shrimp it eats.
15. Every South Carolina student also saw many different birds, fish, turtles, and snakes.

■ Distinguishing Among Different Parts of Speech

Write the underlined words in each sentence. Then label each one *N* for noun, *P* for pronoun, *adj.* for adjective, or *adv.* for adverb.

1. Your apple pie tastes much better than this.
2. Both of my brothers went to the play rehearsal.
3. Most drivers couldn't see the street sign.
4. Some of the fawns stood close to their mothers.

5. I have waited a long time to see <u>this</u> <u>play</u>.

6. The <u>car</u> roared down the <u>street</u>.

7. The <u>kindly</u> gentleman offered <u>some</u> good advice.

8. <u>Most</u> of the <u>car</u> dealers are holding sales.

9. <u>Apples</u> were given to <u>both</u> children.

10. She spoke <u>kindly</u> of her <u>close</u> friend.

■ Using Adjectives and Adverbs

Write ten sentences that follow the directions below. (The sentences may come in any order.) Write about one of the following topics or a topic of your own choice: a place you have visited or a place you would like to visit.

Write a sentence that. . .

    1. includes two adjectives before a noun.

    2. includes an adjective after a linking verb.

    3. includes two adjectives after a noun.

    4. includes a proper adjective.

    5. includes a compound adjective.

    6. includes *that* as an adjective.

    7. includes an adverb at the beginning of a sentence.

    8. includes the adverb *very*.

    9. includes *daily* as an adjective.

    10. includes *daily* as an adverb.

Adjectives and Adverbs: Posttest

Directions

Read the passage. Write the letter of the answer that each underlined adjective or adverb modifies.

Flying Squirrels

(1) The wooly flying squirrel is very <u>rare</u>. (2) It is found only in <u>the</u> Himalayan Mountains of northern Pakistan. (3) It is <u>much</u> larger than other flying squirrels and may be the largest squirrel in the world. (4) It sails <u>gracefully</u> off cliff ledges and (5) glides to the stand of trees <u>below</u>. (6) Skin membranes between its wrists and hind legs allow it to glide <u>long</u> distances. (7) It uses its <u>flat</u> tail to guide its flight. (8) For <u>many</u> years, scientists thought the wooly flying squirrel was extinct. (9) Scientists <u>recently</u> rediscovered it, (10) and its <u>high-altitude</u> habitat is now being preserved.

1. A the
  B flying squirrel
  C is
  D very

2. A Himalayan Mountains
  B it
  C Pakistan
  D only

3. A it
  B other
  C larger
  D squirrels

4. A cliff
  B sails
  C it
  D glides

5. A glides
  B stand
  C trees
  D to

6. A allow
  B it
  C distances
  D glide

7. A uses
  B tail
  C guide
  D flight

8. A scientists
  B years
  C squirrel
  D extinct

9. A rediscovered
  B scientists
  C it
  D habitat

10. A its
  B scientists
  C preserved
  D habitat

Writer's Corner

Snapshot

14 A An **adjective** is a word that modifies a noun or a pronoun. An adjective answers the question *What kind? Which one(s)? How many?* or *How much?* about the word it modifies. (pages 538–545)

14 B An **adverb** is a word that modifies a verb, an adjective, or another adverb. Adverbs make the words they modify more precise. (pages 546–550)

Power Rules

Avoid double negatives—using negative words with adverbs that have negative meanings. (pages 789–790)

Before Editing	After Editing
Jane *doesn't hardly* care where they sit as long as she gets to see the concert.	Jane *doesn't* care where they sit as long as she gets to see the concert.
They *couldn't scarcely* see the stage because their seats were so far away.	They *could scarcely* see the stage because their seats were so far away.
She was so excited after the show that she *wasn't barely* able to sleep.	She was so excited after the show that she *was barely* able to sleep.

Editing Checklist

Use this checklist when editing your writing.

✓ Did I use adjectives that appeal to the senses? (See pages 146–148 and 557.)
✓ Did I capitalize proper adjectives? (See page 828.)
✓ Did I use commas to separate adjectives when necessary? (See pages 540–541 and 850–851.)
✓ Did I use adverbs to make verbs, adjectives, and other adverbs more precise? (See pages 546–550.)
✓ Did I vary my sentence structure by beginning some sentences with adverbs? (See page 546.)

Use the Power

Use adjectives and adverbs to make your sentences appeal to the five senses. Look at the images. Which burger and sentence is more appealing?

Shelley made a burger and ate it for dinner.

Shelley carefully made a burger with melted American cheese, garden-fresh lettuce, juicy tomatoes, crispy onions, and tangy mustard and eagerly ate it for dinner.

Revise a composition you have worked on recently by adding details through the use of well-placed adjectives and adverbs.

Other Parts of Speech

How can prepositions, conjunctions, and interjections help you add detail, fluency, and variety to your writing?

Other Parts of Speech: Pretest 1

The draft paragraph about the effect of music on plants contains several errors in the use of interjections, conjunctions, and prepositions. Two such errors have been corrected. Revise the draft to be sure all parts of speech are used correctly.

Caution
~~Great!~~ Music may wilt your leaves. In 1969, Dorothy Retallack ran some experiments with plants to̸ and music. Her experiments proved that music affects the growth of plants. On one test loud rock music stunted the growth of corn, squash, or several flowers. Under another test several of the plants grew tall, so their leaves were small. Also, they needed water, and their roots grew very short. Within several weeks, the marigolds on one experiment died! Identically healthy flowers, though, bloomed nearby. These flowers had been listening about classical music!

Other Parts of Speech: Pretest 2

Directions
Write the letter of the term that correctly identifies the underlined word in each sentence.

Danielle Throws a Dinner Party

(1) Danielle had never cooked a whole dinner before, <u>but</u> she was eager to try. **(2)** Danielle began <u>at</u> noon. **(3)** <u>First</u> she baked an apple pie. **(4)** <u>Not only</u> did she put too much flour in the crust, <u>but</u> she <u>also</u> forgot the sugar. **(5)** She then placed a large rump roast on a tray <u>in</u> the oven. **(6)** First she forgot to turn on the oven, <u>and</u> then she turned it on too high. **(7)** <u>Oh, no!</u> The smoke alarm went off! **(8)** At the same time, two pots on the stove boiled <u>over</u>. **(9)** <u>In spite of</u> these disasters, Danielle remained cool and collected. **(10)** Before the guests could figure out what had happened, Danielle whisked them off <u>to</u> a pizza parlor.

1. **A** coordinating conjunction
   B preposition
   C correlative conjunction
   D adverb

2. **A** coordinating conjunction
   B correlative conjunction
   C interjection
   D preposition

3. **A** preposition
   B interjection
   C adverb
   D adjective

4. **A** coordinating conjunctions
   B correlative conjunctions
   C prepositions
   D adverbs

5. **A** interjection
   B coordinating conjunction
   C preposition
   D adverb

6. **A** adverb
   B coordinating conjunction
   C correlative conjunction
   D preposition

7. **A** interjection
   B preposition
   C adverb
   D adjective

8. **A** interjection
   B adjective
   C adverb
   D preposition

9. **A** coordinating conjunction
   B preposition
   C correlative conjunction
   D interjection

10. **A** adjective
    B correlative conjunction
    C coordinating conjunction
    D preposition

If you were discussing a letter you had just received, prepositions would help you discuss the letter, telling who it was *from,* who it was *to,* and what it was *about.*

15 A **A preposition** is a word that shows the relationship between a noun or a pronoun and another word in the sentence.

The three words in **bold** print in the following sentences are prepositions. Each of these prepositions shows a different relationship between Lori and the letter. As a result, changing only the preposition will alter the meaning of the whole sentence.

> The letter **to** Lori was lost.
>
> The letter **from** Lori was lost.
>
> The letter **about** Lori was lost.

Following is a list of common prepositions.

COMMON PREPOSITIONS				
aboard	before	down	off	till
about	behind	during	on	to
above	below	except	onto	toward
across	beneath	for	opposite	under
after	beside	from	out	underneath
against	besides	in	outside	until
along	between	inside	over	up
among	beyond	into	past	upon
around	but (except)	like	since	with
as	by	near	through	within
at	despite	of	throughout	without

15 A.1 A preposition that is made up of two or more words is called a **compound preposition.**

COMMON COMPOUND PREPOSITIONS

according to	by means of	instead of
ahead of	in addition to	in view of
apart from	in back of	next to
as of	in front of	on account of
aside from	in place of	out of
because of	in spite of	prior to

● **Practice Your Skills**

Finding Prepositions

Write the prepositions from the following sentences.

1. The legendary Pony Express rode its way into American history.

2. The riders' trail began at St. Joseph, Missouri.

3. A weary rider would often reach California in ten days.

4. Wild Bill Cody was one of the riders for this early mail system.

5. In spite of its popularity, the Pony Express lasted only eighteen months.

6. Because of its expense, the Pony Express cost its owners $200,000.

7. Later, dromedary camels were imported from the Middle East.

8. However, the camels were not used for regular mail service.

9. These dromedaries delivered salt between several western towns.

10. Today, the United States mail is transported by airplanes and trucks.

● *Connect to Writing:* **Drafting**

Supplying Prepositions

Write each sentence twice, using a different preposition to fill each blank.

1. The mail plane flew ___ the storm clouds.

2. The package ___ the chair is mine.

3. Caleb should go ___ the post office.

4. A letter came ___ Christopher.

5. ___ that package you will find the tape dispenser.

Prepositional Phrases

A preposition is always part of a group of words called a **prepositional phrase.**
The noun or pronoun that ends the prepositional phrase is called the **object of the preposition.** Any number of modifiers can come between a preposition and its object.

15 A.2 A **prepositional phrase** begins with a preposition and ends with a noun or a pronoun.

> **Prepositional Phrases**
>
> England is the setting **of** this suspenseful *mystery.*
> (*Mystery* is the object of the preposition *of.*)
>
> The detective chases the criminal **through** London's *streets.*
> (*Streets* is the object of the preposition *through.*)

A sentence can have several prepositional phrases, and the phrases can come anywhere in the sentence.

> ***Without*** *a moment's hesitation,* the detective leaped ***into*** *the criminal's path.*
> ***Before*** *the end* ***of*** *books* ***by*** *Agatha Christie,* I usually can identify the criminal.

When You Write

You can create sentence variety by starting some sentences with prepositional phrases.

> The true villain is always discovered **by** *the book's end.*
> **By** *the book's end,* the true villain is always discovered.
> I like mysteries **because of** *the suspense.*
> **Because of** *the suspense,* I like mysteries.

Revise a recent composition by moving some of the prepositional phrases to the beginning of the sentence.

Practice Your Skills

Finding Prepositional Phrases

Write the prepositional phrases in the following sentences.

1. A nurse at a London hospital had a young girl in her ward.

2. None of the doctors could find a cure for her.

3. Before work the nurse read a chapter in a mystery by Agatha Christie.

4. After several pages she put the book into her bag and hurried to the hospital.

5. According to the book, someone had taken a rare poison called thallium.

6. The description of the victim's symptoms matched the symptoms of the young girl.

7. The nurse placed the book in front of the doctors.

8. She told them about her suspicions.

9. Within minutes the doctors prescribed a new series of treatments for the girl.

10. Because of a mystery by Agatha Christie, a young girl's life was saved.

● *Connect to Writing:* **Drafting**

Creating Sentence Variety

Use each preposition below in a sentence. Then rewrite each sentence, changing the position of the prepositional phrase to create a variation on the original sentence.

1. next to   **2.** through   **3.** because of   **4.** beyond   **5.** in back of

Preposition or Adverb?

The same word can be used as a preposition in one sentence and an adverb in another. A word's usage in a sentence determines its part of speech. A word such as *up* is a preposition only if it is part of a prepositional phrase. It is an adverb if it stands alone and answers the question *Where?*

Preposition	***Below*** *the stairs* is the storage area for our new sleds.
	(*Below the stairs* is a prepositional phrase.)
Adverb	The snow fell from the roof to the ground **below.**
	Below is an adverb that tells where the snow fell.
Preposition	We raced ***up*** *the hill.*
Adverb	Pull your sled **up** onto the porch.

You can learn more about prepositional phrases on pages 610–616.

● Practice Your Skills

Distinguishing Between Prepositions and Adverbs

Write the underlined word in each sentence. Then label it *P* for preposition or *A* for adverb.

1. Last week, a blizzard raged <u>outside</u> our warm house.
2. Snow accumulated <u>around</u> the town.
3. The flakes drifted <u>off</u> our roof.
4. Today the weather <u>outside</u> is perfect for sledding.
5. My friends and I looked <u>around</u> for our sleds.
6. I went <u>before</u> Jaime.
7. <u>Down</u> the hill I raced on my sled.
8. I fell <u>off</u> near the bottom of the hill.
9. Jaime had never been sledding <u>before</u>.
10. He squealed as his sled raced <u>down</u>.

● *Connect to Writing:* **Drafting**

Writing Sentences

Write two sentences using each of the words below. In the first sentence, use the word as a preposition. In the second sentence, use it as an adverb.

| **1.** near | **2.** across | **3.** out | **4.** aboard | **5.** within |

✔ *Check Point:* **Mixed Practice**

Write the prepositional phrases from the following paragraph.

(1) In the Beartooth Mountains of Montana, there is a most unusual glacier. (2) Within the ice of the glacier are frozen millions of grasshoppers. (3) According to scientists, an immense swarm of grasshoppers made a forced landing on the glacier two centuries ago! (4) They were then quickly frozen by a snowstorm. (5) Today the grasshoppers are still well preserved. (6) During the warm weather, birds and animals throughout the region flock to the glacier for an addition to their normal sources of food. (7) When the ice melts, the grasshoppers provide them with a most unusual meal.

Conjunctions · Lesson 2

Conjunctions help pull words together. There are three kinds of conjunctions: coordinating, correlative, and subordinating.

15 B A **conjunction** connects words or groups of words.

 ## Coordinating Conjunctions

A **coordinating conjunction** is a single connecting word. The conjunctions in the following list are used to connect single words or groups of words.

COORDINATING CONJUNCTIONS						
and	but	for	nor	or	so	yet

Connects Single Words

An astronomer observes **stars *and* planets.**
(connects nouns)

He *or* she watches the night sky.
(connects pronouns)

They **watch** asteroids ***and* chart** their courses.
(connects verbs)

The astronomer's job is **difficult *but* interesting.**
(connects adjectives)

Now *and* then, they discover a new comet.
(connects adverbs)

Connects Groups of Words

He looked **through the telescope *and* into space.**
(connects prepositional phrases)

Earth has one moon, *but* Neptune has eight satellites.
(connects sentences)

Correlative Conjunctions

Correlative conjunctions are pairs of conjunctions. Like coordinating conjunctions, these conjunctions connect words and groups of words.

15 B.1   **Correlative conjunctions** are pairs of connecting words.

CORRELATIVE CONJUNCTIONS		
both/and	either/or	neither/nor
not only/but also	whether/or	

Connecting Words

Both Gretta *and* Emmaline own telescopes. (connects nouns)

Those asteroids are *neither* close *nor* familiar.
(connects adjectives)

Connecting Groups of Words

Either I will attend a university in the United States, *or* I will study physics abroad. (connects sentences)

You can learn about the third type of conjunction, a subordinating conjunction, on pages 59 and 645–646.

When You Write

When you revise your writing, you can often use conjunctions to make your writing more interesting. You can combine sentences or elements of sentences to make your writing less repetitive.

The moon is bright tonight. We can see only a few stars.

The moon is bright tonight, **so** we can see only a few stars.

Our group can study the moon. We can study the planets.

Our group can study **either** the moon **or** the planets.

Revise a recent composition by combining related short sentences by using conjunctions.

● Practice Your Skills

Finding Conjunctions

Write the coordinating or correlative conjunctions in each sentence.

1. Neither Mercury nor Venus has its own natural satellite.
2. After Mars and before Jupiter, there lies an asteroid belt.
3. Earth rotates on its axis and revolves around the sun.
4. Neptune is an ocean blue color, so it was named for the god of the sea.
5. Each planet is classified as either an inner or an outer planet.
6. Ceres is a large asteroid, but most asteroids are relatively small.
7. Both beautiful and mysterious, Saturn's rings can be observed from Earth through binoculars.
8. Slowly but surely, the planets make their way around the sun.
9. A meteor is a rock or a metal fragment that enters Earth's atmosphere.
10. Humans have studied the heavens for centuries, yet many mysteries remain.

● *Connect to Writing:* Revising

Using Conjunctions to Combine Sentences

Combine each pair of sentences into one sentence using coordinating or correlative conjunctions.

1. Carmen wrote a report about black holes. Maria wrote a report about black holes.
2. You can read a book about quasars. You can see a video about quasars.
3. My dad knows nothing about space. My mom took astronomy in college.
4. Tell Jesse about meteors. Tell Jesse about comets.
5. Mercury is my favorite planet. I wrote a play about Mercury.

● *Connect to Writing:* Directions

Using Conjunctions

You are writing directions to your house for a new friend. Write directions that begin at your school and explain the best way to reach your home. Remember to be specific and make the directions easy to follow. Use at least two coordinating conjunctions and one correlative conjunction. After completing your directions, underline the conjunctions you used in your writing. Then write a brief definition of the grammar term *conjunction*.

Interjections Lesson 3

Surprise, disbelief, joy, disappointment—these and other emotions or feelings are often expressed by interjections. An interjection at the beginning of a sentence is immediately followed by an exclamation point or a comma.

15 C An **interjection** is a word that expresses strong feeling or emotion.

COMMON INTERJECTIONS			
aha	oh	ugh	yes
goodness	oops	well	yikes
no	ouch	wow	yippee

Good writers use interjections sparingly for greater impact.

Hurrah! Our team won.

Gosh, they pulled off an amazing win!

Yes, now they compete for the championship!

Wow! I can't believe it.

● Practice Your Skills

Finding Interjections

Write the interjections from the following sentences.

1. Oh, did you see that pass?
2. Whew! I can't believe Jim caught it.
3. Hurrah, he's running down the field!
4. Great, he made a touchdown!
5. Gee, what a great play that was!
6. Hey, wait for me!
7. Goodness, what a heavy suitcase this is.
8. No! What more can go wrong?
9. Ugh! This is awful.
10. Yeah, I'm on my way.

Parts of Speech Review

This section reviews the eight parts of speech. How a word is used in a sentence determines its part of speech. The word *near* can be used as four different parts of speech.

Verb	The plant will **near** its full growth soon.
Adjective	I will plant my flower garden in the **near** future.
Adverb	The best planting time is drawing **near.**
Preposition	Plant the flowers **near** the house.

The following series of questions will help you determine a word's part of speech.

Noun Is the word naming a person, place, thing, or idea?

Nathaniel bought **plants** at the **nursery.**

Pronoun Is the word taking the place of a noun?

This is **my** favorite flower.

Verb Is the word showing action?

Kiki **planted** the rose bush.

Does the word link a noun, pronoun, or adjective to the subject?

The daisy **is** a simple flower.

Adjective Is the word modifying a noun or a pronoun? Does it answer the question *What kind? How many? How much?* or *Which one?*

Three yellow tulips bloomed today.

Adverb Is the word modifying a verb, an adjective, or another adverb? Does it answer the question *How? When? Where?* or *To what extent?*

The seedling grew **very quickly** in the **extremely** rich soil.

Preposition Is the word showing a relationship between a noun or pronoun and another word in the sentence?

Because of the sunlight, the plant grew well **on** the windowsill.

Conjunction Is the word connecting words or groups of words?

Kiki **and** I grow **neither** fruits **nor** vegetables.

I planted marigolds, **but** they didn't grow.

Interjection Is the word expressing strong feelings?

Wow! The petunias in the window box are blooming.

● *Connect to Writing:* **Drafting**

Writing Sentences

Write two sentences using the word as directed.

1. Use *light* as a verb and a noun.

2. Use *that* as a pronoun and an adjective.

3. Use *below* as a preposition and an adverb.

4. Use *these* as a pronoun and an adjective.

5. Use *secret* as an adjective and a noun.

● *Connect to Writing:*

Correctly Using the Parts of Speech

Look at the sentences you wrote based on the exercise above. Write a cohesive paragraph based on these sentences, fixing any parts of speech that you may have used incorrectly.

● *Connect to Speaking and Writing:* **Peer Interaction**

Reviewing Content

With a partner, review the vocabulary you have learned in this chapter. (Hint: New terms are printed in purple.) Quiz each other until you understand the definitions of all the new words and concepts.

Assess Your Learning

▨ Identifying Prepositions, Conjunctions, Interjections, and Prepositional Phrases

Write each sentence. Then label each of the following parts of speech: *preposition, conjunction,* and *interjection.* Finally, underline each prepositional phrase.

1. Wow! You have a really big test ahead of you on Friday.
2. Never wait until the last minute.
3. Start two nights before any test.
4. Review both your material and your notes from class.
5. Yes! Study with a friend or classmate.
6. Not only review old tests throughout your notebook, but also look for certain kinds of familiar questions.
7. During the night before the test, review the most important points and the main topics.
8. Neither study late nor stay up late.
9. According to many studies, your brain will need proper food and rest for the best results.
10. Avoid sweets like doughnuts around the time of the test.

▨ Determining Parts of Speech

Write the underlined words. Then beside each word, write its part of speech using the following abbreviations.

noun = *n.*	pronoun = *pron.*	preposition = *prep.*
adjective = *adj.*	adverb = *adv.*	interjection = *interj.*
conjunction = *conj.*	verb = *v.*	

In 1928, a farmer was planting horseradishes in a field in West Virginia. He noticed a greasy, shiny stone. He picked it up and took it home. Ten years later he made a startling discovery. The stone was a thirty-two-carat diamond. Wow!
Diamonds, however, are not necessarily rare in the United States. The Eagle diamond was found in Wisconsin. Other large stones have also been discovered in Ohio, Illinois, and Indiana.

◼ Determining Parts of Speech

Write the underlined words. Then beside each word, write its part of speech using the following abbreviations.

noun = *n.*   pronoun = *pron.*   preposition = *prep.*
adjective = *adj.*   adverb = *adv.*   interjection = *interj.*
conjunction = *conj.*   verb = *v.*

1. <u>Steel</u> workers were laid off because demand for <u>steel</u> dropped.

2. Did <u>those</u> horses really eat <u>those</u>?

3. Turn <u>left</u> because a <u>left</u> turn will take you to the park.

4. Will you <u>water</u> the plants with the <u>water</u> in this can?

5. Everyone drew <u>near</u> and sat <u>near</u> the fire.

◼ Completing Sentence Skeletons

Make up five sentences matching the parts of speech indicated below. You can use an article *(a, an,* or *the)* for an adjective. The following abbreviations are used: noun *(n.)*, pronoun *(pron.)*, verb *(v.)*, adjective *(adj.)*, adverb *(adv.)*, preposition *(prep.)*, conjunction *(conj.)*, and interjection *(interj.)*. Use the example below to help guide you.

Example   *adj. n. prep. adj. n. v. adj.*

Possible Answer   **The winner of the contest was happy.**

1. n. v. adj. adj. n.

2. pron. v. adv.

3. adj. adj. n. prep. adj. n. v. adj.

4. n. conj. n. v. adv.

5. n. v. adj. prep. adj. n.

Other Parts of Speech: Posttest

Directions

Read the passage. Write the letter of the term that correctly identifies the underlined word or words after each number.

For hundreds of years, historians have wondered what happened to the two sons **(1)** of the **(2)** English king, Edward IV. When Edward IV died, his eldest son **(3)** should have become king. However, Edward's brother Richard took the throne **(4)** and put his nephews in the Tower of London. **(5)** After July of 1483, no one ever saw the boys again. **(6)** Either they were killed on Richard's orders, or they were sent away in exile. Richard III's supporters **(7)** claimed that someone else killed the princes. **(8)** Well, that may be true, **(9)** but there is no way to prove it. No one but Richard himself will **(10)** ever know the truth.

1. **A** adverb
   B preposition
   C verb
   D interjection

2. **A** proper adjective
   B compound adjective
   C preposition
   D adverb

3. **A** action verb
   B adverb
   C linking verb
   D adjective

4. **A** interjection
   B correlative conjunction
   C preposition
   D coordinating conjunction

5. **A** verb
   B adverb
   C preposition
   D adjective

6. **A** prepositions
   B adverbs
   C correlative conjunctions
   D interjections

7. **A** verb
   B preposition
   C adjective
   D correlative conjunction

8. **A** adverb
   B article
   C interjection
   D preposition

9. **A** correlative conjunction
   B coordinating conjunction
   C article
   D interjection

10. **A** adjective
    B preposition
    C coordinating conjunction
    D adverb

Writer's Corner

Snapshot

15 A A **preposition** is a word that shows the relationship between a noun or a pronoun and another word in the sentence. (pages 560–564)

15 B A **conjunction** connects words or groups of words. The most common **coordinating conjunctions,** or single connecting words, are *and, but, for, nor, or, so,* and *yet.* (pages 565–567)

15 C An **interjection** is a word that expresses strong feeling or emotion. (page 568)

Power Rules

 Revise run-on sentences. Use the best conjunction and/or punctuation for the meaning when connecting two sentences. (pages 672–674)

Before Editing	**After Editing**
Carmen had trouble with her science project, her mother helped her.	Carmen had trouble with her science project, *so* her mother helped her.
Jackson thought he'd win first place, he came in second.	Jackson thought he'd win first place, *but* he came in second.
After the fair, we can have pizza for dinner we can have hamburgers.	After the fair, we can have pizza for dinner, *or* we can have hamburgers.

 When using pronouns with conjunctions, use subject forms of pronouns in subject position. Use object forms of pronouns in object position. (pages 717–725)

Before Editing	**After Editing**
Robin sent a text to Juan and *they*.	Robin sent a text to Juan and *them*.
According to the text, Kara and *him* won the election.	According to the text, Kara and *he* won the election.
Ask Juan and *she* the reason for the victory.	Ask Juan and *her* the reason for the victory.

Editing Checklist

Use this checklist when editing your writing.

✓ Did I use precise prepositions to show relationships? (See pages 560–561.)
✓ Did I write sentences using prepositions and adverbs? (See pages 563–564.)
✓ Did I use coordinating and correlative conjunctions to combine sentences and make my writing less repetitive? (See pages 565–567.)
✓ Did I use interjections when necessary to show strong emotions or feelings? (See page 568.)
✓ Did I use all the the parts of speech correctly? (See pages 569–570.)

Use the Power

Prepositions are words that show relationships between a noun or pronoun and another word in a sentence. To choose the most effective preposition when you write, picture the relationship between the words in your mind and what you want the reader to "see."

Conjunctions can help you combine sentences or elements of sentences to make your writing more fluid and interesting. Use the acronym FANBOYS to remember the coordinating conjunctions.

F	A	N	B	O	Y	S
for	and	nor	but	or	yet	so

Interjections carry a lot of punch, so use them ONLY when you want your sentence to convey a "WOW" factor.

Look at a recent composition, and check to be sure you have used prepositions, conjunctions, and interjections correctly.

CHAPTER 16

The Sentence Base

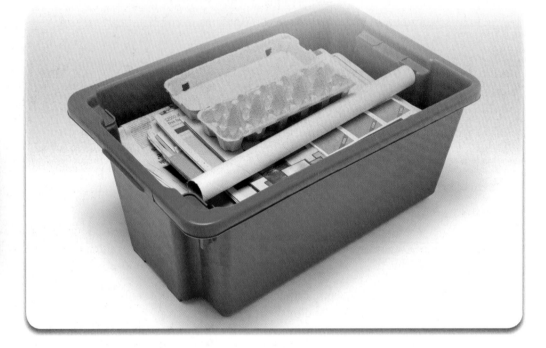

How can you use a variety of sentences to increase fluency in your writing?

The Sentence Base: Pretest 1

The following draft paragraph about recycling is hard to read because it contains several sentence errors and unnecessary repetition. Revise the paragraph so that it reads more smoothly. Two corrections have been made as an example.

Our county has a mandatory recycling program. ~~Our county~~ *and* provides each household. ✕With special bins. You can put cans in the green bin. You can put bottles in the green bin. You can save your newspapers. In the orange bin. The county collects plastic drink containers. Refuses all other plastic containers. Yard waste is also picked up. Tree limbs are also picked up. Must be in special bags. Bundled together with rope. Batteries are considered hazardous materials. Should not be put with regular trash. You should not throw away computers. You should not throw away cell phones. Batteries should be taken to special collection centers. Computers and cell phones should be taken to special collection centers.

The Sentence Base: Pretest 2

Directions

Write the letter of the term that correctly identifies the underlined word or words in each sentence.

(1) Last summer my aunt <u>invited</u> me to her farm in New Mexico. (2) One morning I <u>cooked</u> some toast and <u>made</u> some orange juice. (3) I <u>shoved a rack with sliced bread into the oven and burned my finger.</u> (4) <u>Aunt May</u> broke off a piece of a spiny plant on her windowsill. (5) She <u>squeezed</u> a gooey substance from the plant and <u>rubbed</u> it on my burn. (6) In no time my <u>finger</u> felt as good as new. (7) <u>Learned the name of this miraculous plant—aloe.</u> (8) Aloe <u>looks somewhat like a cactus but belongs to the lily family.</u> (9) <u>Many gardeners in the southern and southwestern parts of the United States.</u> (10) <u>Have you ever seen the leaves of an aloe plant?</u>

1. **A** simple subject
   B complete subject
   C simple predicate
   D complete predicate

2. **A** complete subject
   B complete predicate
   C compound subject
   D compound verb

3. **A** simple subject
   B complete subject
   C complete predicate
   D simple predicate

4. **A** complete predicate
   B complete subject
   C compound subject
   D compound verb

5. **A** complete subject
   B complete predicate
   C compound subject
   D compound verb

6. **A** simple subject
   B complete subject
   C simple predicate
   D complete predicate

7. **A** sentence fragment
   B inverted order
   C simple predicate
   D compound subject

8. **A** complete subject
   B complete predicate
   C compound subject
   D simple predicate

9. **A** sentence fragment
   B inverted order
   C simple predicate
   D compound subject

10. **A** sentence fragment
    B inverted order
    C simple predicate
    D compound subject

16 A   A **sentence** is a group of words that expresses a complete thought.

In conversation, people sometimes express their ideas incompletely.

> **Kim:** Do you want to play a game of football?
>
> **Allen:** In this weather? No way!

Kim easily understood Allen's reply, even though he used only parts of a sentence to answer her. Indeed, Allen would have sounded unnatural if he had used complete sentences. In standard written English, however, you need to use complete sentences to be sure your message is clear and your reader understands it accurately.

The following groups of words are incomplete thoughts:

> The player in the torn jersey.
>
> Made a touchdown.
>
> Blocking the defense.
>
> When the game ended.

16 A.1   A group of words that expresses an incomplete thought is a **sentence fragment.**

To change fragments into sentences, you need to add the missing information.

> The player in the torn jersey **is the team's best player.**
>
> **The running back** made a touchdown.
>
> Blocking the defense **allowed the running back to score.**
>
> When the game ended, **the team celebrated.**

You can learn more about fragments on pages 666–671.

Recognizing Sentences and Fragments

Label each group of words *S* if it is a sentence or *F* if it is a fragment.

1. The fans at the football game cheered wildly.

2. Because the weather turned cold.

3. Brought a blanket to the game.

4. The quarterback for the winning team.

5. My family watched the game from the fifty-yard line.

6. Buying hot chocolate from the concession stand.

7. Since we know the coach of the team.

8. Practices for four hours each day.

● *Connect to Writing:* **Revising**

Writing Complete Sentences from Fragments

Add information to expand each fragment in the Practice Your Skills above into a sentence. When you write your sentences, remember to begin each sentence with a capital letter and end it with a punctuation mark.

Power Your Writing: Let It Flow

To make your paragraphs flow invitingly, vary the length and structure of your sentences. Notice how the length of the sentences varies in the example below from "Say It with Flowers" by Toshio Mori (pages 285–291).

> We watched Teruo talking to the young lady. The boss shook his head. Then it came. Teruo came back to the rear and picked out a dozen of the very fresh white roses and took them out to the lady.

The shortest sentence (highlighted in yellow) prepares readers for what is about to happen and provides a sharp contrast to the sentence that follows it.

Notice how the concluding paragraph of the story combines sentences of different lengths with sentences of different structures.

> On the way out, Teruo remembered our presence. He looked back. "Good-bye, Good luck," he said cheerfully to Tommy and me. He walked out of the shop with his shoulders straight, head high, and whistling. He did not come back to see us again.

A sentence has two main parts: a subject and a predicate.

16 B The **subject** names the person, place, thing, or idea that the sentence is about. The **predicate** tells something about the subject.

	Subject	Predicate
Person	Albert Einstein	was a very famous scientist.
Place	The United States	became his home.
Thing	Many inventions	came from his ideas.
Idea	His intelligence	made him a celebrity.

➤ Complete and Simple Subjects

16 B.1 A **complete subject** includes all the words used to identify the person, place, thing, or idea that the sentence is about.

To find a complete subject, ask yourself *Whom?* or *What?* the sentence is about.

> **The tour guide at the science museum** told us about atoms. (Who told us about atoms? *The tour guide at the science museum* is the complete subject.)
>
> **Microscopes with powerful lenses** magnify the atoms. (What magnifies the atoms? *Microscopes with powerful lenses* is the complete subject.)

● **Practice Your Skills**

Finding Complete Subjects

Write the complete subject in each sentence.

(1) Young Albert Einstein showed an interest in math and science. **(2)** His grades in other subjects were poor. **(3)** The future scientist finished high school and technical college in Switzerland. **(4)** The Swiss patent office hired Einstein in 1902. **(5)** Scholarly journals gave Einstein a forum for his ideas. **(6)** A German physics journal published some of his articles. **(7)** These articles discussed radical theories about the nature of matter. **(8)** Publication of these articles changed scientists' view of the universe. **(9)** The theory of relativity was Einstein's most important contribution. **(10)** The Nobel Prize in physics was awarded to Einstein in 1921.

 # Simple Subjects

16 B.2   A **simple subject** is the main word in the complete subject.

The simple subject is the one word that directly answers the question *Who?* or *What?*

> **Many <u>immigrants</u>** arrived at Ellis Island in the early part of the 20th century.
>
> **<u>Officials</u> at the station** processed more than twelve million immigrants.

Sometimes a complete subject and a simple subject are the same.

> **<u>Albert Einstein</u>** came to the United States in 1933.
>
> **<u>He</u>** became a United States citizen seven years later.

Throughout the rest of this book, the word subject refers to the simple subject.

● **Practice Your Skills**

Finding Complete and Simple Subjects

Write the complete subject in each sentence. Then underline each simple subject.

1. New York Harbor is home to the Statue of Liberty.

2. This figure of a woman with a torch stands at the entrance to the harbor.

3. She holds a tablet in her left hand.

4. Seven rays surround her head.

5. Broken chains lie at her feet.

6. The statue weighs 225 tons.

7. The people of France gave the statue to the United States.

8. A formal presentation occurred in 1886.

9. Major repairs were made to the statue in the 1980s.

10. Tourists from around the world visit this famous lady.

● *Connect to Writing:* **Drafting**

Writing Complete Subjects

Add a complete subject to each of the following sentences.

1. ___ work very hard at their jobs.

2. ___ could be considered dangerous.

3. ___ may mean hours of extra work.

4. ___ makes the effort worthwhile.

5. ___ is not finished.

6. ___ will be admired by many people.

Complete and Simple Predicates

16 B.3 A **complete predicate** includes all the words that tell what the subject is doing or that tell something about the subject.

To find a complete predicate, first find the subject. Then ask, *What is the subject doing?* or *What is being said about the subject?*

Wild horses roamed across the prairie.

(The subject is *horses*. What did the horses do? *Roamed across the prairie* is the complete predicate.)

Simple Predicates

16 B.4 A **simple predicate,** or **verb,** is the main word or phrase in the complete predicate.

In the following examples, the simple predicate, or verb, is underlined:

Everyone in the park **enjoyed** the fireworks.

The Roman candle **burned** beautifully in the night sky.

Sometimes verbs are hard to find because they do not show action; instead, they tell something about a subject. Such verbs are called linking verbs.

COMMON LINKING VERBS	
Be **Verbs**	is, am, are, was, were, be, being, been, shall be, will be, can be, should be, would be, may be, might be, has been, have been, had been
Others	appear, become, feel, grow, look, remain, seem, sound, stay, taste, turn

You can learn more about linking verbs on pages 527–530.

Finding Complete and Simple Predicates

Write the complete predicate in each sentence. Then underline the verb.

1. Millions of Americans watch displays of fireworks on the Fourth of July.
2. Pyrotechnics is another name for fireworks.
3. Fireworks are not a recent invention.
4. The Chinese invented fireworks centuries ago.
5. They used them for celebrations.
6. Fireworks existed before the invention of guns and gunpowder.
7. The Italians manufactured fireworks during the 1500s.
8. Gases propel the fireworks into the air.
9. The fireworks explode in an array of colors.
10. The bright colors of fireworks come from different metallic salts.

● *Connect to Writing:* **Revising**

Using Vivid Verbs

Write each sentence, replacing each verb with a more vivid verb.

1. The fireworks went into the night sky.
2. The colors of the rockets showed against the dark sky.
3. My sister ran to the edge of the water.
4. The colors appeared on the surface of the lake.
5. The firecrackers popped loudly.

● *Check Point:* **Mixed Practice**

Write the subject and verb in each sentence.

(1) In 1848, a settler discovered gold in northern California's mountains. (2) That discovery transformed San Francisco from a frontier town into a busy city. (3) People on the East Coast heard of the discovery of gold. (4) Thousands of gold prospectors invaded the city on their way to the mountains. (5) Two steamship companies brought an endless stream of people to San Francisco. (6) Other people arrived by stagecoach. (7) The Pony Express brought mail to the population. (8) Soon, telegraph lines provided additional communication to the city. (9) Few prospectors found gold in San Francisco. (10) However, many of them settled there.

 **Verb Phrases**

16 B.5   A **verb phrase** includes the main verb plus any helping, or auxiliary, verbs.

The helping verb or verbs are underlined in the following examples.

> Kerry **is choosing** plants for the garden.
>
> Those seeds **can be planted** next month.
>
> The tulip bulbs **should have been planted** in the fall.

As you can see from the examples above, a verb phrase may include as many as three helping verbs. The following verbs are often used as helping verbs.

COMMON HELPING VERBS	
be	am, is, are, was, were, be, being, been
have	has, have, had
do	do, does, did
Others	may, might, must, can, could, shall, should, will, would

● **Practice Your Skills**

  Finding Verb Phrases

  Write the verb phrase in each sentence.

  1. Trees are known as the largest of all plants.

  2. They have been identified as the oldest living things.

  3. Some giant sequoia trees have lived for thousands of years.

  4. The fruit of the coconut palm can be eaten.

  5. You might bake a tasty pie from the fruit of apple trees.

  6. Pine trees will remain green all year long.

  7. Evergreen trees do not lose their leaves in winter.

  8. Trees can prevent the loss of topsoil.

  9. For a very long time, people have used trees for wood.

  10. Malaria is treated with quinine from the bark of the cinchona tree.

Sometimes a verb phrase is interrupted by other words.

> A bloodhound **can** easily **follow** a day-old scent.
>
> Most household pets **have** never **hunted** for food.

In a question the subject may come in the middle of a verb phrase.

> **Is** Toto **scratching** at the door?

When You Write

The word *not* and its contraction, *n't*, often interrupt verb phrases. Neither is part of the verb.

> Health laws **do** not **allow** dogs in grocery stores.
>
> The pet store in the mall **isn't selling** fish.

In formal and academic writing, you should spell out the word *not*. You should use the contraction *n't* only in speaking and in informal writing.

Throughout the rest of this book, the word verb *also refers to the verb phrase.*

● **Practice Your Skills**

Finding Verbs

Write the verb in each sentence. Remember that words that interrupt a verb phrase are not part of the verb.

(1) German shepherds are often trained as guide dogs. **(2)** Guide dogs are always allowed in public places with their owners. **(3)** The guide dog must quickly adjust to the leather harness and stiff handle. **(4)** The dog doesn't obey all commands from its owner. **(5)** A command could sometimes place an owner in a dangerous situation. **(6)** A dog will not lead its owner into the middle of a busy street. **(7)** Labrador retrievers and golden retrievers are also used as guide dogs. **(8)** Golden retrievers have often been recommended as the best dog for a family. **(9)** Dogs do not usually live longer than twelve to fifteen years. **(10)** Have you ever had a dog for a pet?

Using Verb Interrupters

Verb interrupters change the meaning of sentences. Add verb interrupters to the following sentence and write five new sentences, each with a different meaning.

Cats have threatened dogs.

Compound Subjects

16 B.6   A **compound subject** is two or more subjects in one sentence that have the same verb and are joined by a conjunction.

The conjunctions that usually join compound subjects are *and, or,* or *nor.* Pairs of conjunctions, such as *either/or, neither/nor, not only/but also,* and *both/and* may also be used. In the following examples, each subject is underlined once, and the verb is underlined twice. Notice that the conjunction is not part of a compound subject.

Janice spent the hot day at the beach.

Janice and Kate spent the hot day at the beach.

Janice, Kate, and Sue spent the hot day at the beach.

Either Kate or Sue had brought the food.

Neither Janice nor Kate ate much dessert.

Not only Kate but also Janice went swimming.

When You Speak and Write

To make your writing smoother and less repetitious, you can combine two or more sentences that have the same verb but different subjects.

Jon has a surfboard. **Rick** has a surfboard. **Tammy** has a surfboard.

Jon, Rick, and **Tammy** have surfboards.

To add emphasis to a speech, you might want to keep the repetition. For example, if you are trying to persuade your parents to let you have a surfboard, you might want to repeat the verb phrase.

Jon **has a surfboard.** Rick **has a surfboard.** Tammy **has a surfboard.**

● Practice Your Skills

Finding Compound Subjects

Write the subject in each sentence.

1. Rick and Tammy brought their surfboards to the beach.
2. Both the wind and the waves were impressive.
3. Jamie and Rob rented jet skis.
4. Their beach towels and sandals were almost swallowed up by the tide.
5. Two baby crabs and a starfish washed up on shore.
6. The sandwiches and fruit in the lunches were a target for the seagulls.
7. Neither Tammy nor Rick stayed up on a surfboard for very long.
8. Thunder and lightning signaled a storm in the distance.
9. The beach patrol and the lifeguards ordered everyone out of the water.
10. Jamie, Rob, Tammy, and Rick quickly gathered up their belongings and headed for the car.

● *Connect to Writing:* Revising

Combining Sentences

Combine each pair of sentences into one sentence with a compound subject. Use *and* or *or* to connect your sentences.

1. Cod feed along the ocean bottom. Flounder feed along the ocean bottom.
2. Clams live on the sea floor. Lobsters live there, too.
3. Manatees stay in the ocean for their entire lives. Whales also stay in the ocean for their entire lives.
4. Sea lions spend time on land. Walruses spend time on land.
5. Winds cause ocean waves. Earthquakes cause ocean waves.

Compound Verbs

16 B.7   A **compound verb** is formed when two or more verbs in one sentence have the same subject and are joined by a conjunction.

Conjunctions such as *and, or, nor,* and *but* are used to connect the verbs. In the following examples, each subject is underlined once, and each verb is underlined twice.

> Jeff pours the juice into his glass.
>
> Jeff pours the juice into his glass and rinses the bottle.
>
> Jeff pours the juice into his glass, rinses the bottle, and places it in the recycling bin.

Some sentences have both a compound subject and a compound verb.

> Nancy and Pete save their newspapers and bring them to the collection center.

● **Practice Your Skills**

Finding Compound Verbs

Write the verbs in the following sentences.

(1) Many people drink the last sip of soda and throw the can away. (2) You should save your cans and deliver them to a recycling center. (3) An employee will take the cans and give you some money. (4) Trucks collect the old cans and unload them at a recycling plant. (5) Machines at the plant flatten the cans and dump them onto conveyor belts. (6) The cans are then shredded and cleaned. (7) Next, workers load the pieces into a hot furnace and soften them. (8) The soft metal is made into long sheets and cooled. (9) Beverage companies buy the sheets and make new cans out of them. (10) With these new cans, the beverage companies have prevented extra waste and thereby have saved everyone money.

 # Natural and Inverted Order

16 B.8   When the subject in a sentence comes before the verb, the sentence is in **natural order.** When the verb or part of a verb phrase comes before the subject, the sentence is in **inverted order.**

To find the subject and verb in a sentence that is in inverted order, put the sentence in its natural order. To do this, first find the verb. Then ask who or what is doing the action. In the following examples, each subject is underlined once, and each verb is underlined twice.

Into the dungeon marched the prisoners.

The prisoners marched into the dungeon.

Questions are often in inverted order. To find the subject in a question, turn the question around so that it makes a statement.

Do you like mystery stories?

You do like mystery stories.

Sentences that begin with *here* or *there* are often in inverted order. To find the subject of this kind of sentence, drop the word *here* or *there*. Then put the rest of the words in their natural order. Remember that *here* or *there* can never be the subject.

Here comes the librarian with my favorite book.

The librarian comes with my favorite book.

There are several mysteries in the book.

Several mysteries are in the book.

● **Practice Your Skills**

   Finding Subjects in Sentences in Inverted Order

   Write the subject and verb in each sentence.

   1. Do you enjoy Edgar Allan Poe's short stories?

   2. From "The Cask of Amontillado" comes a scary scene.

   3. There is no happy ending for Fortunato.

   4. Behind a wall of Montresor's house lie Fortunato's bones.

   5. How did the bones get behind the wall?

   6. From the brain of a madman came the plot.

   7. There were many wrongs done to Montresor.

   8. Had Montresor really been the victim of slights by Fortunato?

   9. Did Fortunato deserve his fate?

   10. There exists scant evidence against Fortunato.

   11. Have you ever read "The Pit and the Pendulum"?

   12. In that story are some very macabre events.

   13. There is a pendulum with a sharp scythe.

   14. For the squeamish reader, there are even some rats.

Varying Sentence Beginnings

Add interest to this paragraph by varying five sentence beginnings.

(1) The band marched onto the football field. **(2)** Two helicopters flew directly overhead. **(3)** The helicopters hovered over the crowd. **(4)** The noise from the helicopters was loud. **(5)** The band could not be heard. **(6)** The helicopters finally rose higher into the sky. **(7)** They flew away. **(8)** The crowd cheered in grateful response.

➤ Understood Subjects

16 B.9   When the subject of a sentence is not stated, the subject is an **understood *you*.**

The subject of a command or a request is an understood *you*.

(You) Meet me in the cafeteria at lunchtime.

(You) Please wait for me.

In the following example, *you* is still the understood subject.

Danielle, (you) please be there also.

● **Practice Your Skills**

Finding Subjects

Write the subject and verb in each sentence. If the subject is an understood *you*, write (you).

1. The lunch line is always long.
2. Hand me a tray, please.
3. Save a place for me at your table.
4. May I have a slice of pizza?
5. Ken, have your money ready.
6. Please pass me some milk.
7. Do the potatoes need some salt?
8. Pile the empty trays by the kitchen window.
9. Take this ticket for your lunch.
10. Maria, try some of this strawberry applesauce.

● *Connect to Writing:* **Revising**

Using Understood You

Instructions are usually easier to follow when an understood *you* is the subject. Revise these instructions for washing a car, using the understood *you.*

1. First, you should have a bucket with soap and hot water.

2. Then, you wet the car with a hose.

3. You put the sponge in the bucket and soap it well.

4. Next, you wash the car with the sponge.

5. The hose is used to rinse away the soap.

6. Last, you dry the car with a soft cloth.

✅ *Check Point:* **Mixed Practice**

Write the subject and verb in each sentence. If the subject is an understood *you,* write (you).

1. Have you ever been to an automobile museum?

2. Visit one soon.

3. There are cars from every era on display.

4. Do not sit in any of the cars, though.

5. By each car is usually found an information card.

6. Read the card for interesting facts.

7. There was an old Rolls-Royce in the center of the floor.

8. To the right of it was a Model T Ford.

9. Does the crank on that car turn?

10. Please crank it for me.

● *Connect to Writing:* **Directions**

Using the Understood You

Do you know how to change a flat tire? Do you know how to make a tasty pizza? Perhaps you know how to make a great-looking holiday decoration. Share what you know with your classmates by writing directions for what you can do well. Use sentences with an understood *you* so that your directions are easy to follow.

Sometimes a complete thought can be expressed with just a subject and a verb. At other times a subject and a verb need another word to complete the meaning of the sentence.

> Greg likes.   Ruth seems.

16 C A **complement** is a word or group of words that completes the meaning of subjects or verbs.

> Greg likes **snakes.**   Ruth seems **wary.**

There are four common kinds of complements: direct objects, indirect objects, predicate nominatives, and predicate adjectives. Together, a subject, a verb, and a complement are called the **sentence base.**

 Direct Objects

16 C.1 A **direct object** is a noun or pronoun that receives the action of the verb.

Direct objects complete the meaning of action verbs. To find a direct object, first find the subject and the action verb in a sentence. Then ask yourself, *What?* or *Whom?* after the verb. The answer to either question will be a direct object. In the following sentences, subjects are underlined once, and verbs are underlined twice.

> d.o.
> Dylan saw a **snake** in the river.
> (Dylan saw what? He saw a snake. *Snake* is the direct object.)
> d.o.
> He called **Nicole** over to the water.
> (He called whom? *Nicole* is the direct object.)

Verbs that show ownership are action verbs and take direct objects.

> d.o.
> Anna owns a **python.**

Sometimes two or more direct objects, called a **compound direct object,** will follow a single verb. On the other hand, each part of a compound verb may have its own direct object. The verbs are underlined in the examples on the next page.

Did you <u>see</u> a **cobra** or a **viper** at the zoo? *(d.o. on cobra, viper)*

I <u>took</u> **pictures** at the zoo and <u>developed</u> the **film** later.

A direct object can never be part of a prepositional phrase.

At the petting zoo, Caroline touched **one** of the snakes.

(*One* is the direct object. *Snakes* is part of the prepositional phrase *of the snakes.*)

Our class walked around the zoo.

(*Zoo* is part of the prepositional phrase *around the zoo.* Even though this sentence has an action verb, it has no direct object.)

You can learn more about transitive verbs, or verbs that take direct objects, on pages 525–526.

● **Practice Your Skills**

Finding Direct Objects

Write each direct object. If a sentence does not have a direct object, write *none.*

1. Many people fear snakes because of their slimy appearance and slithery movements.
2. Thousands of people die from venomous snakebites each year.
3. Humans kill many of them each year.
4. However, some snakes serve a useful purpose.
5. Snakes eat rats and other small mammals.
6. Some people buy nonvenomous reptiles and keep them as pets.
7. Snakes are found throughout the world.
8. Boa constrictors suffocate their prey.
9. Rattlesnakes periodically shed their fangs.
10. The rattlesnake gets its name from the noisemaking rattles on its tail.

➤ Indirect Objects

16 C.2 An **indirect object** answers the questions *To* or *For whom?* or *To* or *For what?* after an action verb.

If a sentence has a direct object, it also can have another complement, called an indirect object. To find indirect objects, first find the direct object. Then ask yourself, *To whom? For whom? To what?* or *For what?* about each direct object. The answers to these questions will be an indirect object. An indirect object always comes before a direct object in a sentence.

>   i.o.   d.o.
> Daniel sent his **friends** invitations to his birthday party.
> (*Invitations* is the direct object. Daniel sent invitations to whom? *Friends* is the indirect object.)
>   i.o.   d.o.
> Daniel gave his **pets** a bath before the party.
> (*Bath* is the direct object. Daniel gave a bath to what? *Pets* is the indirect object.)

A verb in a sentence can have two or more indirect objects called a **compound indirect object.**

>   i.o.   i.o.   d.o.
> Daniel's aunt read **Daniel** and his **friends** a poem about birthdays.
>   i.o.   i.o. d.o.
> Daniel should not have given his **dog** and **cat** cake.

Keep in mind that an indirect object is never part of a prepositional phrase.

>   i.o.   d.o.
> Daniel's dad showed **us** a baby picture of Daniel.
> (*Us* is the indirect object. It comes between the verb and the direct object, and it is not a part of a prepositional phrase.)
>   d.o.
> Daniel's dad showed a baby picture of Daniel to us.
> (*Us* is not an indirect object. It does not come between the verb and the direct object. It follows the direct object and is part of the prepositional phrase *to us*.)

You cannot have an indirect object without a direct object in a sentence.

Finding Indirect Objects

Write the indirect objects from the sentences below. If a sentence does not have an indirect object, write **none.**

1. The whole class came to the party.

2. Daniel gave all his friends party favors.

3. Show his mother those beautiful pictures of our recent class trip.

4. I already gave the pictures to his sister.

5. Daniel's mom showed us some home movies.

6. We told his aunt and uncle a story about Daniel and his dog.

7. I handed him my present first.

8. I gave Daniel a collar for his dog.

9. My sister sent him a card.

10. We will visit his family again.

● *Connect to Writing:* **Revising**

Adding Indirect Objects to Sentences

Add indirect objects to the following sentences by changing each underlined prepositional phrase into an indirect object.

1. Daniel also sent an invitation <u>to our homeroom teacher</u>.

2. Mrs. Jenkins brought some delicious lemon cookies <u>for Daniel</u>.

3. Cindi and Josh taught some great new tricks <u>to Daniel's dog</u>.

4. Will you show the presents <u>to me</u>?

5. We will send a note of thanks <u>to his parents</u>.

6. Have you made a present <u>for Aunt Liz</u> yet?

7. I will mail the present <u>to her</u>.

➤ Predicate Nominatives

16 C.3   A **predicate nominative** is a noun or a pronoun that follows a linking verb and identifies, renames, or explains the subject.

Direct objects and indirect objects follow action verbs. Two other kinds of complements follow linking verbs. They are called **subject complements** because they either rename or describe the subject. One subject complement is a predicate nominative.

To find a predicate nominative, first find the subject and the verb. Check to see if the verb is a linking verb. Then find the noun or the pronoun that identifies, renames, or explains the subject. This word will be a predicate nominative. Notice in the second example that a predicate nominative can be a compound.

> p.n.
> The cat has become America's favorite **pet.** (pet = cat)
>
> p.n.   p.n.
> Two common house cats are the **Manx** and the **Burmese.**
>
> (Manx = cats, Burmese = cats)

Like a direct object and an indirect object, a predicate nominative cannot be part of a prepositional phrase.

> p.n.
> The Siamese is **one** of the most exotic breeds.
>
> (*One* is the predicate nominative. *Breeds* is part of the prepositional phrase *of the most exotic breeds.*

You can learn more about linking verbs on pages 527–530 and 582.

● **Practice Your Skills**

Finding Predicate Nominatives

Write the predicate nominatives from the sentences below.

1. The cat can be an excellent companion.
2. The two classifications of cats are the long-haired Persian cat and the short-haired domestic feline.
3. Cats were sacred creatures to the ancient Egyptians.
4. Until recently, the most popular pet in America was the dog.
5. Some house cats can be rather large animals.
6. The cat's most effective weapon might be its claws.
7. Its claws are excellent tools for defense.
8. Its whiskers can be sense organs of touch.
9. The Siberian tiger is the largest member of the cat family.
10. Is the cheetah the fastest land animal?

CHAPTER 16

Predicate Adjectives

16 C.4   A **predicate adjective** is an adjective that follows a linking verb and modifies the subject.

The second kind of subject complement is a predicate adjective. Notice the difference between a predicate nominative and a predicate adjective in the following examples.

> p.n.
> The test was a long **one.**
>
> (A predicate nominative renames the subject.)
>
> p.a.
> The test was **long.**
>
> (A predicate adjective modifies or describes the subject.)

To find a predicate adjective, first find the subject and the verb. Check to see if the verb is a linking verb. Then find an adjective that follows the verb and describes the subject. This word will be a predicate adjective. Notice in the second example that there is a compound predicate adjective.

> p.a.
> Does our assignment for history seem **easy** to you?
>
> (*Easy* describes the assignment.)
>
> p.a.   p.a.
> The project for science was **fun** and **interesting.**
>
> (*Fun* and *interesting* describe the project.)

Do not confuse a regular adjective with a predicate adjective. Remember that a predicate adjective must follow a linking verb and describe the subject of a sentence.

> **Regular Adjective**   Some dinosaurs were **great** hunters.
>
> **Predicate Adjective**   The dinosaurs were **great** as hunters.

You can learn more about adjectives on pages 776–790.

● *Connect to Speaking and Writing:* **Peer Interaction**

Reviewing Content

With a partner, review the vocabulary you have learned in this chapter. (Hint: new terms are printed in purple.) Quiz each other until you understand the definitions of all the new words and concepts.

● Practice Your Skills

Finding Predicate Adjectives

Write each predicate adjective. If the sentence does not have a predicate adjective, write *none.*

1. Today was the first day of school.

2. This year most of my classes will be difficult.

3. I was very nervous.

4. The hallways at my new high school are long and narrow.

5. Most classrooms appeared large.

6. In my science class, the lab tables are high off the floor.

7. For some reason the seniors in the auditorium seemed very tall.

8. The locker room in the gym smelled bad.

9. The cafeteria food tastes delicious.

10. After the first day, I felt better.

✔ *Check Point:* Mixed Practice

Write each complement. Then label each one *direct object, indirect object, predicate nominative,* or *predicate adjective.* If there is no complement, write *none.*

(1) The 1960s were an interesting decade. (2) In 1960, Chubby Checker started a new dance craze. (3) Dancers loved the twist. (4) The Beach Boys were also popular. (5) Their songs filled the heads of young people with dreams of California sun and surf. (6) The most popular rock group was The Beatles. (7) At that time The Beatles' hair was fairly short. (8) By the end of the decade, this band was legendary. (9) Americans watched more and more television. (10) *American Bandstand* was popular with the teenagers of the day. (11) *Sesame Street* taught young children letters and numbers. (12) Other popular television programs were *Captain Video* and *Captain Midnight.* (13) Elephant jokes were the rage in the early 1960s. (14) For example, why do elephants wear green sneakers? (15) Their blue ones are dirty. (16) The miniskirt became the fashion rage. (17) Christiaan Barnard transplanted a human heart. (18) Olympic officials gave Peggy Fleming a gold medal for figure skating. (19) President Kennedy had wanted an astronaut on the moon by the end of the decade. (20) In 1969, humans landed on the moon.

Diagraming Subjects and Verbs

A **sentence diagram** is a picture made up of lines and words. It can help you clearly see the different parts of a sentence. These parts make up the structure of your sentences. By varying your sentence structure, you can make your writing more interesting.

Subjects and Verbs All sentence diagrams begin with a baseline. A straight, vertical line then separates the subject (or subjects) on the left from the verb (or verbs) on the right. Notice in the following diagram that the capital letter in the sentence is included, but not the punctuation. Also notice that the whole verb phrase is included on the baseline.

She has remembered.

She	has remembered

Inverted Order A sentence in inverted order, such as a question, is diagramed like a sentence in natural order.

Were you talking?

you	Were talking

Understood Subjects When the subject of a sentence is an understood *you*, put parentheses around it in the subject position. When a name is included with the understood subject, place it on a horizontal line above the understood subject.

Ted, listen.

Ted

(you)	listen

Compound Subjects and Verbs Place compound subjects and verbs on parallel lines. Put the conjunction connecting them on a broken line between them. Notice in the following example that two conjunctions are placed on either side of the broken line.

Both cameras and computers were displayed.

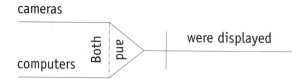

Jan has gone but will return.

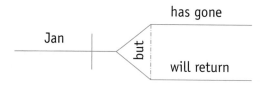

Balloons, hats, and horns were bought but have been lost.

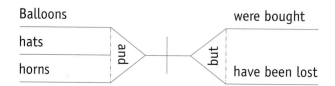

Diagraming Complements

Together, a subject, a verb, and a complement are called the sentence base. Since complements are part of the **sentence base,** they are diagramed on or below the baseline.

Direct Objects A direct object is placed on the baseline after the verb. It is separated from the verb by a vertical line that stops at the baseline.

Some sharks have no natural enemies.

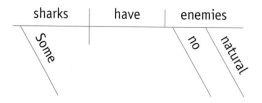

Indirect Objects An indirect object is diagramed on a horizontal line that is connected to the verb.

Phil prepared his friends a big dinner.

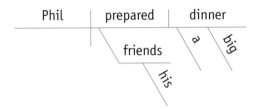

Subject Complements Both subject complements are diagramed in the same way. They are placed on the baseline after the verb. They are separated from the verb by a slanted line that points back toward the subject.

This tree is an oak.   The painting is very old.

The winners are two freshmen and one senior.

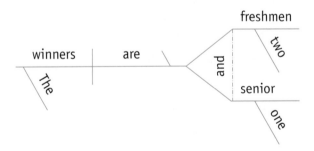

● **Practice Your Skills**

Diagraming Subjects and Verbs

Diagram the following sentences or copy them. If you copy them, draw one line under each subject and two lines under each verb. If the subject is an understood *you,* write *you* in parentheses.

1. Pigeons are landing.

2. Look!

3. Both males and females are eating.

4. Are you looking?

5. Birds leave but return.

6. Ben and Zach have come and are watching.

7. Zach, listen.

8. Birds are cooing.

9. Do pigeons migrate?

10. They might stay or leave.

● **Practice Your Skills**

Diagraming Complements

Diagram the following sentences or copy them. If you copy them, draw one line under each subject and two lines under each verb. Then label each complement *d.o.* for direct object, *i.o.* for indirect object, *p.n.* for predicate nominative, or *p.a.* for predicate adjective.

1. My soft sculpture won first prize.

2. Don gave me a new notebook.

3. The director is a wonderful man.

4. I have visited pretty gardens and parks.

5. That flower looks very delicate.

6. Will you show Jan and me your coin collection?

7. Haven't you given him your answer yet?

8. The books were very old and dusty.

9. Sing us another song. (You)

10. My favorite sports are basketball and baseball.

Assess Your Learning

▪ Finding Subjects and Verbs

Write the subjects and verbs in the following sentences. If the subject is an understood *you,* write the word *you* in parentheses.

1. Do you know anything about elephants?

2. Look at this book about elephants.

3. Here are many very interesting facts.

4. Elephants, for example, are the largest land animals in the world.

5. An elephant can run at a rate of twenty-four miles per hour!

6. The trunk of an elephant is longer than the nose of any other animal.

7. There are forty thousand muscles and tendons in the elephant's trunk.

8. With its trunk, an elephant can pick a single flower or carry a huge log.

9. For centuries the elephant has been a good friend to people throughout the world.

10. Read more about elephants on your own.

▪ Identifying Complements

Write each complement. Then label each one, using the following abbreviations.

direct object = *d.o.*   predicate nominative = *p.n.*
indirect object = *i.o.*   predicate adjective = *p.a.*

  (1) I will tell you an unusual story. **(2)** During World War I, a Canadian pilot was flying a small military plane over Germany. **(3)** Of course, in those days, military planes were open. **(4)** Captain J. H. Hedley was the other person in the plane. **(5)** Suddenly an enemy plane attacked their plane. **(6)** The pilot took the plane into a nearly vertical dive, and Hedley shot out of his seat and into the air. **(7)** Several hundred feet lower the plane was finally level again. **(8)** Then, incredibly, Hedley grabbed the tail of the plane. **(9)** Apparently the extremely powerful suction of the steep dive had pulled Hedley back to the plane. **(10)** With tremendous relief, he eventually reached his seat on the plane.

Writing Sentences

Write five sentences that follow the directions below. (The sentences may come in any order.) Write about one of the following topics or a topic of your choice: an animal in the natural world or an event in nature.

1. Write a sentence with a compound subject.

2. Write a sentence with a compound verb.

3. Write a sentence that starts with the word *there*.

4. Write a question.

5. Write a sentence with an understood *you* as the subject.

Underline each subject once and each verb twice. Remember to add capital letters and end punctuation.

Using Complements

Write five sentences that follow the directions below. (The sentences may come in any order.) Write about one of the following topics or a topic of your choice: the funniest present you ever gave or the funniest present you ever received.

Write a sentence that . . .

1. includes a direct object.

2. includes an indirect object and a direct object.

3. includes a predicate nominative.

4. includes a predicate adjective.

5. includes a compound predicate adjective.

Underline and label each complement.

The Sentence Base: Posttest

Directions

Write the letter of the term that correctly identifies the underlined word or words in each sentence.

   (1) <u>Fruits</u> and <u>vegetables</u> can spoil if they become too ripe. **(2)** Many <u>foods</u> need to be refrigerated so they will be safe for eating. **(3)** <u>A candy maker in France</u> developed the method of canning in the 1790s. **(4)** <u>Made it possible for fruits and vegetables to be stored for a long time.</u> **(5)** He <u>cooked</u> the foods and <u>poured</u> them into clean glass bottles. **(6)** <u>He</u> sealed and sterilized the bottles by heating them in boiling water. **(7)** <u>High temperatures</u> will destroy organisms in food. **(8)** <u>Charles Birdseye</u>, a scientist, developed a way to keep foods fresh. **(9)** <u>Did he freeze the foods?</u> **(10)** <u>Today routinely freeze the foods.</u>

1. **A** complete subject
   B complete predicate
   C compound subject
   D compound verb

2. **A** simple subject
   B complete subject
   C simple predicate
   D complete predicate

3. **A** simple subject
   B complete subject
   C simple predicate
   D complete predicate

4. **A** sentence fragment
   B inverted order
   C simple predicate
   D compound subject

5. **A** complete subject
   B complete predicate
   C compound subject
   D compound verb

6. **A** simple subject
   B compound subject
   C simple predicate
   D complete predicate

7. **A** sentence fragment
   B inverted order
   C simple predicate
   D complete subject

8. **A** simple subject
   B complete predicate
   C compound subject
   D compound verb

9. **A** sentence fragment
   B inverted order
   C simple predicate
   D compound subject

10. **A** sentence fragment
    B inverted order
    C simple predicate
    D compound subject

Writer's Corner

Snapshot

16 A A **sentence** is a group of words that expresses a complete thought. (pages 578–579)

16 B A **subject** names the person, place, thing, or idea that the sentence is about. The **predicate** tells something about the subject. (pages 580–591)

16 C A **complement** is a word or group of words that completes the meaning of subjects and verbs. There are four kinds of complements: **direct objects, indirect objects, predicate nominatives,** and **predicate adjectives.** (pages 592–598)

Power Rules

 Be sure that the **subject and verb of a sentence agree.** (pages 750–767)

Before Editing	**After Editing**
He *don't* know.	He *doesn't* know.
Mai or the twins *was* working on that.	Mai or the twins *were* working on that.

 Revise a **run-on sentence** by adding a conjunction, by adding the proper punctuation, by subordinating a clause, or by writing it as two sentences. (pages 672–674)

Before Editing	**After Editing**
I liked the movie, I don't think, however, it will win any awards.	I liked the movie, but I don't think it will win any awards.
	While I liked the movie, I don't think it will win any awards.
	I liked the movie. I don't think, however, it will win any awards.

Editing Checklist

Use this checklist when editing your writing.

✓ Did I write sentences that express complete thoughts? (See pages 578–579.)
✓ Did I correct any sentence fragments? (See pages 666–671.)
✓ Did I use verb phrases correctly? (See pages 584–586.)
✓ Did I use compound subjects and/or compound predicates to combine simple sentences? (See pages 586–588.)
✓ Did I make my writing interesting by varying the beginnings of sentences and using different sentence patterns? (See pages 579 and 588–589.)
✓ Did I use direct objects and indirect objects to complete the meaning of action verbs? (See pages 592–595.)
✓ Did I use predicate adjectives and predicate nominatives to complete the meaning of linking verbs? (See pages 595–598.)

Use the Power

Study the diagram below. It shows the correct way to diagram this sentence:

Snoopy gave Bear a swat on the nose.

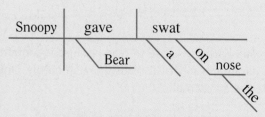

Now diagram this nonsense sentence.

Rufus zvamled Reester u plee un za uncus.

Create two nonsense or imaginative sentences for your partner to diagram. Go over each other's diagrams and share them with your teacher and classmates.

CHAPTER **17**

Phrases

How can you add precision and variety to your writing with phrases?

Phrases: Pretest 1

The following draft paragraph about Amelia Earhart is hard to read because it contains several misplaced modifiers. Revise the paragraph so that it reads more smoothly. One of the misplaced phrases has been corrected as an example.

gaining fame in 1928,

    Amelia Earhart was the first woman to fly across the Atlantic Ocean gaining fame in 1928. Of that plane she was not the pilot. She was riding as a passenger. Earhart first soared across the Atlantic Ocean in 1932 flying solo. Earhart who was greatly interested in commercial aviation worked for an early airline service. Earhart left Miami, Florida, in June of 1937, flying with navigator Fred Noonan. Earhart flew a twin-engine plane attempting an around-the-world flight. Surrounding her disappearance, people still debate the mystery. The plane was never found vanishing near Howland Island. Some historians suspecting foul play believe that Earhart and Noonan were forced down and killed by the Japanese. Others believing a different story claim that she and Noonan crashed on a Pacific island.

Phrases: Pretest 2

Directions

Write the letter of the term that correctly identifies the underlined phrase in each sentence.

(1) <u>In the West</u> coyotes have been considered pests for decades. (2) These animals, <u>the subject of many Native American legends</u>, have spread eastward. (3) There were no coyotes in the East <u>until the twentieth century</u>. (4) Coyotes have managed <u>to spread quickly</u>. (5) Hunters <u>with permits</u> kill hundreds each year. (6) Coyotes have been known <u>to eat cats and small dogs</u>. (7) <u>Yipping loudly</u> is the way the coyote announces its presence. (8) <u>Adapting easily to harsh conditions</u>, the coyote is a survivor. (9) Coyotes could not flourish when there were wolves <u>to compete with them</u>. (10) The wolf, <u>a relative of the coyote</u>, is a better predator.

1. **A** participial
   B infinitive
   C appositive
   D prepositional

2. **A** gerund
   B appositive
   C participial
   D prepositional

3. **A** gerund
   B participial
   C appositive
   D prepositional

4. **A** participial
   B gerund
   C infinitive
   D prepositional

5. **A** participial
   B appositive
   C adjectival
   D infinitive

6. **A** infinitive
   B prepositional
   C adverbial
   D participial

7. **A** gerund
   B infinitive
   C participial
   D prepositional

8. **A** infinitive
   B prepositional
   C participial
   D gerund

9. **A** prepositional
   B gerund
   C participial
   D infinitive

10. **A** appositive
    B gerund
    C prepositional
    D participial

Prepositional Phrases

17 A   **A phrase** is a group of related words that function as a single part of speech. A phrase does not have a subject and a verb.

You know that a prepositional phrase begins with a preposition and ends with a noun or pronoun called the object of the preposition.

Why don't you go **with Jennifer?**

The man **beneath the tightrope** was a famous person **in New York.**

On Monday we will ride **around the stadium** when we get **out of school.**

Following is a list of common prepositions.

COMMON PREPOSITIONS			
about	beneath	inside	over
above	beside	instead of	past
across	between	into	since
after	beyond	near	through
against	by	next to	throughout
ahead of	down	of	to
along	during	off	toward
among	except	on	under
around	for	on account of	until
at	from	onto	up
before	in	out	with
behind	in addition to	out of	within
below	in back of	outside	without

You can learn more about prepositions and prepositional phrases on pages 560–564.

Finding Prepositional Phrases

Write the prepositional phrases in this paragraph.

(1) In 1859, Charles Blondin walked across Niagara Falls on a tightrope. **(2)** He was high above the water. **(3)** Later, he crossed with a blindfold over his eyes. **(4)** Then he crossed on stilts. **(5)** Finally, he really amazed everyone. **(6)** Halfway across the falls, he stopped for breakfast. **(7)** He cooked some eggs, ate them, and continued to the other side!

➤ Adjectival Phrases

17 A.1 An **adjectival phrase** is a prepositional phrase that is used to modify a noun or a pronoun.

Like a single adjective, an adjectival phrase answers the question *Which one(s)?* or *What kind?* about a noun or pronoun.

Which One(s)	The dog **with the short legs** is a dachshund.
What Kind?	Please give me that bag **of dog food.**

An adjectival phrase usually modifies the noun or the pronoun directly in front of it. Occasionally, an adjectival phrase will modify a noun or a pronoun in another phrase.

The story ***about*** the dog ***with*** a broken leg was sad.

Two adjectival phrases can also modify the same noun or pronoun.

That spaniel ***with*** the red collar ***on*** the porch is mine.

When You Write

You can combine sentences by using adjectival phrases.

Have you seen that movie? It's about two dogs and a cat.
Have you seen that movie **about two dogs and a cat?**

As you compose, look for ways to combine short sentences with adjectival phrases.

Recognizing Adjectival Phrases as Modifiers

Write each adjectival phrase. Then beside each phrase, write the word it modifies. Some sentences have more than one adjectival phrase.

(1) Dogs can be great friends to humans. **(2)** There are many breeds of dogs. **(3)** The smallest type of canine is the Chihuahua. **(4)** One of the largest breeds in the American Kennel Club is the Irish wolfhound. **(5)** Some of these dogs are taller than their owners!

● *Connect to Writing:* Revising

Using Adjectival Phrases to Combine Sentences

Combine each pair of sentences, putting some information into an adjectival phrase.

1. Have you read this book? It is about dog training.

2. That dog protects their home. He has a scary bark.

3. A beautiful dog is the collie. The collie has long fur.

4. My cousin lives on a farm. He has many dogs.

5. I took a picture. The photo showed dogs at the shelter.

➤ Adverbial Phrases

17 A.2 An **adverbial phrase** is a prepositional phrase that is used to modify a verb, an adjective, or an adverb.

The following examples show how adverbial phrases may be used to modify verbs.

Single Adverb	A mosquito buzzed **by.**
Adverbial Phrase	A mosquito buzzed **by my ear.**
Single Adverb	Everyone came **here.**
Adverbial Phrase	Everyone came **to the picnic.**

Like a single adverb, an adverbial phrase answers the question *Where? When? How? To what extent?* or *To what degree?* Most adverbial phrases modify the verb. Notice that an adverbial phrase modifies the whole verb phrase, just as a single adverb does.

Where?	We should meet **at the park.**
When?	We will meet **by noon.**
How?	We planned the picnic **with excitement.**

Adverbial phrases also modify adjectives and adverbs.

Modifying an Adjective	Liz was happy **with her new kite.**
	The picnic blanket was soft **against my skin.**
Modifying an Adverb	The picnic continued late **into the evening.**
	Liz's kite soared high **into the sky.**

An adverbial phrase does not necessarily come next to the word it modifies. Also, several adverbial phrases can modify the same word.

On Saturday meet us *by* noon *at* the park entrance.

During our vacation we will go **to the zoo on Monday afternoon.**

PUNCTUATION WITH ADVERBIAL PHRASES

If a short adverbial phrase comes at the beginning of a sentence, no comma is needed. You should place a comma after an introductory phrase of four or more words or after several introductory phrases.

No Comma	At noon we met at the park.
Comma	**Because of the heavy traffic,** Dee was late.
	In the shade under the tree, we ate our picnic lunch.

Recognizing Adverbial Phrases as Modifiers

Write each adverbial phrase. Then beside each phrase, write the word it modifies. Some sentences have more than one adverbial phrase.

(1) Since Monday we have been planning a picnic. (2) On Saturday I awakened with happy anticipation. (3) My brother drove me across town to the park. (4) I brought sandwiches and cold drinks in a large blue ice chest. (5) Before noon my friends had arrived at the park. (6) We put a blanket on the ground over the rocks. (7) Near our picnic blanket, Amanda tossed a baseball to her little brother. (8) For a while, we watched the many joggers. (9) After that, Luke and Brittany flew their kites into the wind. (10) After a long day, we put our trash into the garbage cans and left the park.

Power Your Writing: Scene Setters

Examine the following sentences. Consider the placement of the highlighted phrases.

> We're portrayed too many times as hostile and criminal, as some kind of blood-thirsty savages.

> We're proud to acknowledge and foster the legacy of Sockalexis today, 79 years later.

Now consider what Kimble and DiBiasio actually wrote in "Are Native American Team Nicknames Offensive?" (pages 255–258)

> Too many times, we're portrayed as hostile and criminal, as some kind of blood-thirsty savages.

> Today, 79 years later, we're proud to acknowledge and foster the legacy of Sockalexis.

The authors put the highlighted phrases at the beginning of their sentences, where they act like "scene setters" for the main part of the sentence. More than one such phrase can occur together as in the two prepositional phrases below.

> On Monday afternoon, in the very heart of Times Square, he let out a blood-curdling yell.

Misplaced Modifiers

Because a prepositional phrase is used as a modifier, it should be placed as close as possible to the word it describes.

17 A.3 When a phrase is too far away from the word it modifies, the result may be a **misplaced modifier.**

Misplaced modifiers create confusion and misunderstanding for readers.

Misplaced	On the stage the audience applauded for the performers.
Correct	The audience applauded for the performers **on the stage.**
Misplaced	The actor told us about his career in his dressing room.
Correct	**In his dressing room,** the actor told us about his career.

Practice Your Skills

Identifying Misplaced Modifiers

Write **MM** for misplaced modifier if the underlined prepositional phrase is too far away from the word it modifies. Write **C** for correct if the underlined prepositional phrase is correctly placed.

1. From the script the actor practiced his lines.
2. Tonight the audience will see the actor's first performance in the play.
3. The cast waited for the start of the play behind the curtain.
4. The character actor heard a strange noise from the back row.
5. The actors bowed to the appreciative audience in their costumes.
6. We looked in the program for the names of the talented cast.
7. From a blue glass, the villain took a long drink.

Connect to Writing: Revising

Correcting Misplaced Modifiers

Rewrite the sentences in the preceding exercise that have misplaced modifiers.

✓ *Check Point:* Mixed Practice

Write each prepositional phrase. Then label each one *adjective* or *adverb.*

1. The Braille family lived in a village near Paris, France.

2. As a boy, Louis Braille played in his father's shop.

3. On one fateful afternoon, young Louis was playing with an awl.

4. Without any warning, the awl accidentally went into Louis's left eye.

5. After several days an infection in this injured eye spread to his good eye.

6. Because of the accident, Louis became totally blind.

7. At the age of ten, he entered a school for the blind in Paris.

● *Connect to Writing:* Persuasive Letter

Using Adjectival and Adverbial Phrases

You wish to adopt a puppy from the local shelter. Make a list of some possible objections a parent might have to having a puppy. Then, try to answer your parent's concerns by making a list of the positive changes a dog will bring to your life. After that, write a letter to your parent in which you attempt to persuade him or her to let you adopt a dog. Use at least two adjectival phrases and two adverbial phrases in your letter and underline them.

17 B An **appositive** is a noun or a pronoun that identifies or explains another noun or pronoun in the sentence.

Sometimes a noun or a pronoun is followed immediately by another noun or pronoun that identifies or explains it. This identifying noun or pronoun is called an appositive.

My brother **Pat** returned from his trip.

On vacation he visited his favorite city, **Washington, D.C.**

17 B.1 An appositive with modifiers is called an **appositive phrase.**

The president, **the nation's leader,** lives in the White House.

The nation's capital is named for George Washington, **the first president.**

Notice that a prepositional phrase can be part of an appositive phrase.

Washington's nickname, **the Father of Our Country,** is familiar to all Americans.

PUNCTUATION WITH APPOSITIVES AND APPOSITIVE PHRASES

If the information in an appositive is essential to the meaning of the sentences, no commas are needed. The information is usually essential if it names a specific person, place, or thing.

A comma is needed before and after an appositive or an appositive phrase if the information is not essential to the meaning of the sentence.

| **Essential (Restrictive)** | Last year in American history, we read Abraham Lincoln's speech "The Gettysburg Address." |
| **Nonessential (Nonrestrictive)** | "The Gettysburg Address," a speech by Abraham Lincoln, is read by many students of history. |

Essential elements are sometimes called *restrictive;* nonessential elements are sometimes called *nonrestrictive.*

CHAPTER 17

● Practice Your Skills

Finding Appositives and Appositive Phrases

Write the appositive or appositive phrase in each sentence. Then, beside each one, write the word or words it identifies or explains.

1. We know many interesting details about the men of America's highest office, the presidency.
2. One president, Grover Cleveland, entered the White House as a bachelor.
3. While in office, he married Frances Folsom, a beautiful young woman.
4. Thomas Jefferson, the author of the Declaration of Independence, was an architect, a writer, and a politician.
5. William Henry Harrison, our ninth president, died after only one month in office.
6. His vice president, John Tyler, succeeded him as president.
7. Woodrow Wilson, a great intellectual, led America through World War I.
8. Bill Clinton played the saxophone, a woodwind instrument.
9. Ronald Reagan, a former actor, was elected president in 1980.
10. Theodore Roosevelt, a sickly child, grew up to become a war hero.

Theodore Roosevelt

● *Connect to Writing:* **Editorial**

Using Appositives

You are a newspaper reporter who has been asked to write an opinion piece about leadership. Consider the qualities that are important in a leader. What does one need to be effective in that role? Describe three characteristics of a good leader. In your editorial, use specific examples of effective leaders—either people from history or people you have known. Use at least three appositives or appositive phrases in your editorial and underline them. Then write a brief definition of the grammar term *appositive phrase*.

You are already familiar with some of the information you will cover in this section. For example, you already know that the words *exhausted* and *cheering* in the following sentence are used as adjectives.

> The **exhausted** singers bowed before the **cheering** fans.

What you may not know is that they belong to a special group of words called **verbals.** In the example above, for instance, *exhausted* and *cheering* look like verbs, but they are actually used as adjectives.

17 C   A **verbal** is a verb form that is used as some other part of speech. There are three kinds of verbals: **participles, gerunds,** and **infinitives.**

All of these verbals are important writing tools. They add variety when placed at the beginning of a sentence, and they add conciseness when they are used to combine two simple sentences.

Participles

17 C.1   A **participle** is a verb form that is used as an adjective.

The words *exhausted* and *cheering* in the example above are participles. To find a participle, ask the adjective questions *Which one?* or *What kind?* about each noun or pronoun. If a verb form answers one of these questions, it is a participle. The participles in the following examples are in **bold** type. An arrow points to the noun or pronoun each participle modifies.

> The **screaming** fans surrounded the **delighted** musicians.
>
> Their manager, **surprised** and **frightened,** pulled them
> away from the **adoring** crowd.

There are two kinds of participles. **Present participles** end in *-ing.*
Past participles usually end in *-ed,* but some have irregular endings
such as *-n, -t,* or *-en.*

PARTICIPLES	
Present Participle	adoring, screaming, cheering
Past Participle	surprised, frightened, torn, bent, fallen

Everyone enjoyed the sound of the **singing** group.

Their voices filled the **hushed** stadium.

● **Practice Your Skills**

Recognizing Participles as Modifiers

Write each participle that is used as an adjective. Then, beside each one, write the
word it modifies.

(1) The rock band stepped into the blinding spotlights. **(2)** Their fans,
applauding wildly, welcomed their entrance. **(3)** One musician struck a loud,
ringing chord on his guitar. **(4)** The drummer and the bass player joined the
screaming melody. **(5)** After the first song, the dancing crowd yelled for more.
(6) The obliging band played another great song. **(7)** The pleased crowd sang
along with the band. **(8)** After the concert, many fans stayed to meet the
exhausted band. **(9)** These loyal fans held up crumpled pieces of paper to the
performers. **(10)** The band members signed the papers and handed them back
to the thrilled fans.

Participle or Verb?

Because a participle is a verb form, you must be careful not to confuse it with the verb
in a verb phrase. When a participle is used in a verb phrase, it is part of the verb, not
an adjective.

Participle	The **burning** forest poses a threat to nearby homes.
Verb	The fire is **burning** out of control.
Participle	Many **injured** animals escaped the blaze.
Verb	No campers were **injured** by the fire.

Also be careful not to confuse a participle with the main verb. Sometimes the participle form is the same as the past tense verb form.

Participle   The **charred** trees were black against the blue sky.

Verb   The fire **charred** many acres of forest.

● Practice Your Skills

Distinguishing Between Participles and Verbs

Write the underlined word in each sentence. Then label it **P** for participle or **V** for verb.

1. The firefighter is <u>caring</u> for an injured deer.

2. <u>Caring</u> campers thoroughly douse their campfires.

3. The <u>questioning</u> reporter inquired about the cause of the fire.

4. The police officer was <u>questioning</u> several nearby residents.

5. The paramedic <u>discarded</u> her dirty gloves.

6. A <u>discarded</u> cigarette started the blaze.

7. The man's <u>camping</u> gear was destroyed in the fire.

8. That couple had been <u>camping</u> near the man.

9. A man was <u>talking</u> to the couple in a quiet voice.

10. The <u>talking</u> man was a park ranger.

➤ Participial Phrases

17 C.3   A **participial phrase** is a participle with its modifiers and complements—all working together as an adjective.

Because a participle is a verb form, it can have modifiers or a complement. A participle plus any modifiers or complements form a **participial phrase.** The following examples show three variations of a participial phrase. Notice that a participial phrase can come at the beginning, the middle, or the end of a sentence.

Participle with an Adverb   **Flying low,** the plane circled the airport.

Participle with a Prepositional Phrase   The crowd **standing on the ground** watched the airplane.

Participle with a Complement   A cheer went up for the woman **piloting the small craft.**

PUNCTUATION WITH PARTICIPIAL PHRASES

A participial phrase that comes at the beginning of a sentence is always followed by a comma.

> **Slowly turning the plane,** Amelia Earhart flew away.

Participial phrases that come in the middle or at the end of a sentence may or may not need commas. If the information in the phrase is **essential,** no commas are needed. Information is essential if it identifies a person, place, or thing in the sentence.

If the information is **nonessential,** commas are needed to separate it from the rest of the sentence. A participial phrase is nonessential if it can be removed without changing the meaning of the sentence.

> **Essential (Restrictive)**   The photograph **hanging on the wall** is of Amelia Earhart.
>
> **Nonessential (Nonrestrictive)**   The picture, **given to me as a gift,** was taken in 1937.

Essential phrases are often called *restrictive;* nonessential phrases are often called *nonrestrictive.*

● Practice Your Skills

Recognizing Participial Phrases as Modifiers

Write the participial phrase in each sentence. Then beside each one, write the word it modifies.

(1) Charles Lindbergh, born in 1902, was raised in Minnesota. **(2)** Known by the nickname "Lucky Lindy," Lindbergh was a pioneer of aviation. **(3)** In 1927, he flew solo across the Atlantic in a plane called *Spirit of St. Louis.* **(4)** Departing from Long Island, the plane flew into a stormy sky. **(5)** Awaiting Lindbergh in Paris, the crowd grew extremely anxious. **(6)** Two Frenchmen, attempting the same feat, had recently lost their lives. **(7)** The enthusiastic crowd cheered the plane landing on the strip. **(8)** Emerging a hero, Lindbergh waved to the crowd. **(9)** Marrying Anne Morrow in 1929, Charles Lindbergh gained more than a wife. **(10)** Flying with Lindbergh, Anne Morrow Lindbergh served as his copilot and navigator on later flights.

Gerunds

17 C.4   A **gerund** is a verb form that is used as a noun.

Both the gerund and the present participle end in *-ing*. A gerund, however, is used as a noun, not as an adjective. A gerund is used in all the ways in which a noun is used.

Subject	**Swimming** is my favorite activity.
Direct Object	Do you enjoy **skiing?**
Indirect Object	I gave **diving** my full attention.
Object of the Preposition	The lifeguard saved her from **drowning.**
Predicate Nominative	My sister's favorite pastime is **boating.**
Appositive	I have a new hobby, **sailing.**

● **Practice Your Skills**

Finding Gerunds

Write the gerund in each sentence. Then label it *subject, direct object, indirect object, object of the preposition, predicate nominative,* or *appositive.*

1. In the summer swimming is a great way to stay cool.

2. I just finished a book about sailing.

3. Another enjoyable activity at the lake is water skiing.

4. The hardest part of skiing is balance.

5. Kim has always enjoyed boating.

6. My new exercise, rowing, keeps me fit.

7. The little child gave swimming a try.

8. At first, the sound of laughing came from the water's edge.

9. Suddenly I heard yelling from that direction.

10. By running, the lifeguard was able to reach the child first.

Gerund or Participle?

It is easy to confuse a gerund and a present participle because they both end in -*ing*. Just remember that a gerund is used as a noun. A participle is used as an adjective.

Gerund	My best friend earns extra money by **sewing.** (*Sewing* is the object of the preposition.)
Participle	I might take a **sewing** class. (*Sewing* modifies *class*.)

● **Practice Your Skills**

Distinguishing Between Gerunds and Participles

Write the underlined word in each sentence. Then label it **G** for gerund or **P** for *participle.*

(1) Many teenagers start <u>working</u> to make extra money. **(2)** Others become <u>working</u> people to help out their families.
(3) <u>Cooking</u> is one way to earn money. **(4)** Meg took a <u>cooking</u> class to improve her skills. **(5)** Jason's <u>singing</u> helps bring in some cash. **(6)** People pay him to hear his beautiful <u>singing</u> voice. **(7)** Can you get paid for <u>reading</u>? **(8)** There are some <u>reading</u> services for the visually impaired. **(9)** If you're good at <u>swimming</u>, you could be a lifeguard. **(10)** My cousin teaches <u>swimming</u> classes.

Gerund Phrases

17 C.5   A **gerund phrase** is a gerund with its modifiers and complements—all working together as a noun.

Like a participle, a gerund can be combined with modifiers or a complement to form a gerund phrase. There are four variations of a gerund phrase.

Gerund with an Adjective	**His heavy breathing** was due to an intense workout.
Gerund with an Adverb	**Exercising daily** is important for everyone.
Gerund with a Prepositional Phrase	**Jogging in the park** is a pleasant form of exercise.
Gerund with a Complement	**Walking a mile** every day will help keep you healthy.

Be sure to use the possessive form of a noun or pronoun before a gerund. A possessive form before a gerund is considered part of the gerund phrase.

> We were not surprised by **Keisha's** winning the marathon.
>
> The family has always encouraged **her** running.

● **Practice Your Skills**

Finding Gerund Phrases

Write the gerund phrase in each sentence. Then underline the gerund.

(1) At the mall many people choose riding the escalator. **(2)** You can stay fit by walking up the stairs. **(3)** Exercising regularly is not just good for your body. **(4)** Doing a little workout each day helps fight depression. **(5)** Most athletes do not go for a day without working their bodies. **(6)** Lifting weights is a good way to build muscles. **(7)** Another way is rowing a boat. **(8)** Many people work out by aerobic dancing. **(9)** Playing basketball daily helps many people stay fit. **(10)** Making a daily workout goal will focus your mind on fitness.

● **Practice Your Skills**

Understanding the Uses of Gerund Phrases

Write the gerund phrase in each sentence. Then label the use of each one, using the following abbreviations. Not every label will be used.

subject = *subj.*   direct object = *d.o.*
indirect object = *i.o.*   object of the preposition = *o.p.*
predicate nominative = *p.n.*   appositive = *appos.*

1. Every four years the world enjoys watching the Summer Olympics.
2. Breaking records is the goal of many Olympic athletes.
3. One event, long-distance running, captures a great deal of attention.
4. Another exciting event is the jumping of the hurdles.
5. Successful hurdlers win by barely skimming the barrier.
6. Running fast between hurdles also helps a competitor win the race.
7. Throwing the discus takes a very strong arm.
8. An especially difficult event is competing in the two-day decathlon.
9. Data tables are used in this event for comparing the athletes' performances.
10. Competing in the Olympics is the dream of many athletes.

➤ Infinitives

17 C.6 An **infinitive** is a verb form that usually begins with *to*. It is used as a noun, an adjective, or an adverb.

An infinitive looks different from a participle or a gerund because it usually begins with the word *to*. An infinitive is used in almost all the ways in which a noun is used. It can also be used as an adjective or an adverb.

Noun	**To succeed** was his only goal in life.
	(subject)
	He wanted **to win** more than anything else.
	(direct object)
Adjective	That is a difficult goal **to accomplish.**
	(*To accomplish* modifies the noun *goal*.)
	His desire **to win** was very strong.
	(*To win* modifies the noun *desire*.)
Adverb	He was eager **to triumph.**
	(*To triumph* modifies the adjective *eager*.)
	He worked hard **to succeed.**
	(*To succeed* modifies the verb *worked*.)

● **Practice Your Skills**

Finding Infinitives

Write the infinitive in each sentence.
Then label it *noun, adjective,* or *adverb.*

(1) In the 1960s and 1970s, Muhammad Ali was the boxer to see. (2) His life is interesting to research. (3) He had one goal, to win. (4) As a young child, he learned to box. (5) For his opponents, his punches were too fast to avoid. (6) For several years, he was not allowed to compete. (7) When he was drafted by the army, he refused to go. (8) He refused on religious grounds to fight. (9) In 1979, Muhammad Ali decided to retire. (10) Later, he came out of retirement to fight again.

Infinitive or Prepositional Phrase?

Because an infinitive usually begins with the word *to,* it is sometimes confused with a prepositional phrase. Just remember that an infinitive is *to* plus a verb form. A prepositional phrase is *to* plus a noun or a pronoun.

Infinitive	I am learning **to drive.**
	(ends with the verb form *drive*)
Prepositional Phrase	My mom drove me **to school.**
	(ends with the noun *school*)

● Practice Your Skills

Distinguishing Between Infinitives and Prepositional Phrases

Write the underlined words in each sentence. Then label them *I* for infinitive or *PP* for prepositional phrase.

1. We need some time <u>to rest</u>.
2. What do you want <u>to do</u>?
3. Now I would like <u>to go</u>.
4. Should I take my bag with me <u>to gym</u>?
5. That bag is too heavy <u>to carry</u>.
6. Give your bag <u>to Dylan</u>.
7. Take my bag <u>to class</u> with you.
8. Let's go <u>to band</u>.
9. I think the drums are the most fun <u>to play</u>.
10. Let's walk <u>to lunch</u> together.

● *Connect to Writing:* **Drafting**

Using Infinitives in Sentences

Use the following infinitives in complete sentences. Use at least one as a noun, one as an adjective, and one as an adverb.

1. to glow
2. to spin
3. to shriek
4. to see
5. to ride

→ Infinitive Phrases

17 C.7   An **infinitive phrase** is an infinitive with its modifiers and complements—all working together as a noun, an adjective, or an adverb.

The following examples show three variations of an infinitive phrase.

Infinitive with an Adverb	My friends have learned **to read quickly.**
Infinitive with a Prepositional Phrase	Alexandra and I plan **to go to the library.**
Infinitive with a Complement	Haley went to the library **to get a book.**

Sometimes *to* is omitted when an infinitive follows such verbs as *dare, feel, hear, help, let, need, see,* and *watch.*

Will you and Jesse help me **find** the library's reference section? (*to find*)

No one dared **talk** in the quiet reading room. (*to talk*)

Molly helped her little sister **read** an illustrated children's book. (*to read*)

Will the librarian let you **check out** five books? (*to check out*)

● Practice Your Skills

Recognizing Infinitive Phrases as Modifiers

Write the infinitive phrase in each sentence. Then label it *noun, adjective,* or *adverb.*

(1) In English classes, many students are asked to read the novels of John Steinbeck. (2) After high school Steinbeck left Salinas to attend Stanford University. (3) He did not stay to earn his degree. (4) To support himself, Steinbeck worked as a laborer. (5) He began to publish novels in 1929. (6) In 1935 with *Tortilla Flat,* he managed to gain critical acclaim. (7) Critics consider his greatest work to be *The Grapes of Wrath.* (8) Steinbeck traveled to North Africa to serve as a war correspondent. (9) Throughout his life, he continued to write novels and short stories. (10) In 1962, Steinbeck was honored to win the Nobel Prize for Literature.

Misplaced and Dangling Modifiers

Participial phrases and infinitive phrases can be used as modifiers. Therefore, they should be placed as close as possible to the word they modify.

17 C.8 When participial and infinitive phrases are placed too far from the word they modify, they become **misplaced modifiers.**

Misplaced	We saw an elk **hiking along with our cameras.**
Correct	**Hiking along with our cameras,** we saw an elk.
	(The participial phrase modifies *we.*)

Notice that to correct a misplaced modifier, you simply move the verbal phrase closer to the word it modifies.

17 C.9 A verbal phrase that has nothing to describe is called a **dangling modifier.**

Dangling	**To go on the camping trip,** a permission slip must be signed.
Correct	**To go on the camping trip,** you must bring a signed permission slip. (The infinitive phrase modifies *you.*)

Notice that to correct a dangling modifier, you must add words or change the sentence so that the verbal phrase has a noun or pronoun to modify.

● **Practice Your Skills**

Recognizing Misplaced and Dangling Modifiers

Label the underlined verbal phrases in the following sentences *MM* for misplaced modifier or *DM* for dangling modifier. If there is no mistake in the placement of the verbal, write *C* for correct.

1. To avoid last-minute problems, our teacher made plans for the field trip well in advance.

2. We saw a deer riding along on the bus.

3. Studying the plants and wildlife around us, we collected data for a report.

4. We admired the autumn leaves gliding along in our canoe.

5. Weighed down by our packs, the trail seemed endless.

6. Jack noticed two woodpeckers hiking through the woods.

7. Lost on the trail, my compass was a big help.

8. We ate our lunches sitting on the ground.

● *Connect to Writing:* **Revising**

Correcting Misplaced and Dangling Participles

Rewrite the incorrect sentences in the previous activity so that the modifiers are used correctly.

☑ *Check Point:* **Mixed Practice**

Write each verbal or verbal phrase from the following sentences. Then label it **P** for participle, **G** for gerund, or **I** for infinitive.

(1) Weighing over 300 pounds, Louis Cyr may have been the strongest man in history. **(2)** Lifting a full barrel of cement with one arm was an easy task for him. **(3)** One story, known to everyone in Quebec, tells about his pushing a freight car up an incline. **(4)** To entertain townspeople, Cyr also would lift 588 pounds off the floor by using only one finger! **(5)** Pitting himself against four horses in 1891 was, however, his greatest feat. **(6)** Standing before a huge crowd, Cyr was fitted with a special harness. **(7)** The horses, lined up two on each side, were attached to the harness. **(8)** Planting his feet wide apart, Cyr stood with his arms on his chest. **(9)** The signal was given and the horses began to pull. **(10)** Moving either arm from his chest would disqualify him. **(11)** After minutes of tugging, the winner was announced. **(12)** Louis Cyr bowed before the cheering crowd.

● *Connect to Speaking and Writing:* **Peer Interaction**

Reviewing Content

With a partner, review the vocabulary you have learned in this chapter. (Hint: new terms are printed in purple.) Quiz each other until you understand the definitions of all the new words and concepts.

Diagraming Phrases

In a diagram a prepositional phrase is connected to the word it modifies. The preposition is placed on a connecting slanted line. The object of a preposition is placed on a horizontal line that is attached to the slanted line.

Adjectival Phrase An adjectival phrase is connected to the noun or pronoun it modifies. Notice that sometimes a phrase modifies the object of a preposition of another phrase.

The squirrel with the fluffy tail gathered acorns from the ground under the oak tree.

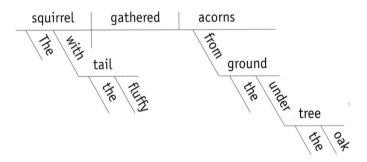

Adverbial Phrase An adverbial phrase is connected to the verb, adjective, or adverb it modifies.

We drove to the park on Saturday.

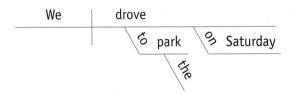

Notice in the next example that an adverbial phrase that modifies an adjective or an adverb needs an additional line.

CHAPTER 17

The score was tied early in the inning.

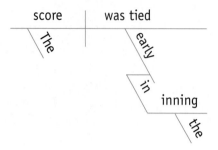

Appositive and Appositive Phrase An appositive is diagramed in parentheses next to the word it identifies or explains.

I bought a new calendar, one with pictures of horses.

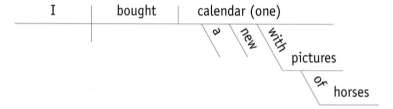

● **Practice Your Skills**

Diagraming Phrases

Diagram the following sentences or copy them. If you copy them, draw one line under each subject and two lines under each verb. Then put parentheses around each phrase and label each one *adj.* for adjective, *adv.* for adverb, or *appos.* for appositive.

1. Many children can swim at an early age.

2. I just bought a new radio, a small portable one.

3. The posters for the dance are beautiful.

4. I went to Mexico with my sisters.

5. My friend Bert collects stamps from foreign countries.

6. The tips of the daffodils showed through the snow.

7. Meg left the store with the groceries.

8. Wendy, my best friend, went to the horse show.

9. At the signal every swimmer dived into the water.

10. The summit of Mount McKinley is always covered with snow.

Diagraming Verbal Phrases

How a verbal phrase is used in a sentence will determine how it is diagramed.

Participial Phrases Because a participial phrase is always used as an adjective, it is diagramed under the word it modifies. The participle, however, is written in a curve.

Hiking through the mountains, we used the trails marked by the rangers.

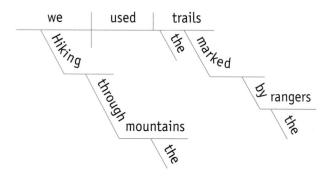

Gerund Phrases Because a gerund phrase is used as a noun, it can be diagramed in any noun position. In the following example, a gerund phrase is used as a direct object. Notice that the complement *plants* and a prepositional phrase are part of the gerund phrase.

José enjoys growing plants in his room.

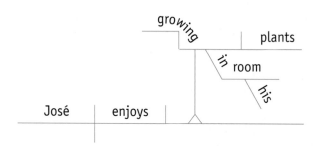

Infinitive Phrases Because an infinitive phrase may be used as an adjective, an adverb, or a noun, it is diagramed in several ways. The following example shows how an infinitive phrase used as an adjective is diagramed.

This is the best place to stop for lunch.

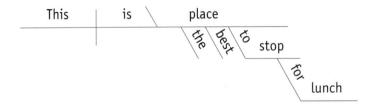

An infinitive phrase used as a noun can be diagramed in any noun position. In the following example, an infinitive phrase is used as the subject of the sentence.

To arrive on time is important.

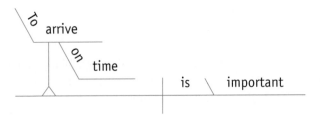

● **Practice Your Skills**

Diagraming Verbal Phrases

Diagram the following sentences or copy them. If you copy them, draw one line under each subject and two lines under each verb. Then put parentheses around each verbal phrase and label each one *part.* for participial, *ger.* for gerund, or *inf.* for infinitive.

1. Sitting on the doorstep, the dog waited for its owner.

2. Spilled by accident, the milk dripped from the counter.

3. No one noticed Sally tiptoeing down the stairs.

4. I enjoy speaking before an audience.

5. The team practiced kicking the football between the goalposts.

6. Eating food in the halls is not permitted.

7. This is the best shovel to use for that job.

8. To rush into a decision is a mistake.

9. The uniform to wear to the banquet is the blue one.

10. We want to watch this movie.

Assess Your Learning

▪ Identifying Prepositional and Appositive Phrases

Write each prepositional phrase and each appositive phrase. Then label each one *adj.* for adjectival, *adv.* for adverbial, or *appos.* for appositive.

1. The *ZIP* in *ZIP code* stands for "zone improvement plan."
2. The Abyssinian, a beautiful short-haired feline, developed entirely from the African wildcat.
3. The largest of the python family of snakes grows to a length of 25 feet.
4. The center of the earth, a ball of solid iron and nickel, has a temperature of 9,000°F.
5. Lungfish of Africa sleep out of water for an entire summer.
6. A famous art museum in New York City has a collection of 200,000 baseball cards.
7. A completely blind chameleon will still change to the color of its environment.
8. A year is 88 days on Mercury, the planet closest to the sun.
9. A grasshopper's sense of hearing is centered in its front knees.
10. James Naismith, the inventor of basketball, was a YMCA instructor in Massachusetts.

▪ Identifying Verbal Phrases

Write each verbal phrase. Then label each one *participial, gerund,* or *infinitive.*

1. Steam is water expanded 1,600 times.
2. The first apples to reach America arrived from England in 1629.
3. A house cat can be expected to live from eight to twenty years.
4. Ancient Egyptian boats were constructed by binding together bundles of papyrus stems.
5. One out of every four human beings living in the world today is Chinese.

CHAPTER 17

6. Pumping blood steadily through our bodies, our hearts never take a rest.

7. Eating honey from a beehive has provided nourishment for lost hikers.

8. It takes approximately ten seconds to slice six cucumbers in a food processor.

9. Long ago doctors used leeches for sucking blood from patients.

10. Polo is the oldest game played with a stick and ball.

◼ Using Phrases

Write five sentences that follow the directions below. (The sentences may come in any order.) Write about one of the following topics or a topic of your own choice: a singer at a concert, a score at a hockey game, or the final lap of a car race.

Write a sentence that . . .

    1. includes at least two prepositional phrases.

    2. includes an appositive phrase.

    3. includes an introductory participial phrase.

    4. includes a gerund phrase.

    5. includes an infinitive phrase.

Underline and label each phrase. Then check for correct punctuation in each sentence.

Phrases: Posttest

Directions

Write the letter of the term that correctly identifies the underlined phrase in each sentence.

Service Dogs

(1) Service dogs are trained <u>to aid people with problems of mobility, strength, or coordination</u>. **(2)** They help people in many ways <u>in their homes</u>. **(3)** Dogs help people <u>to get to the bathroom</u>. **(4)** <u>Using a dog for support</u>, a disabled person can keep his or her balance. **(5)** Dogs help deaf people <u>recognize important sounds</u>. **(6)** They alert their owners to <u>the ringing of a phone</u>. **(7)** <u>Noticing a dog with a person in a wheelchair</u>, people are more likely to be friendly. **(8)** A well-trained assistant, <u>a service dog</u>, can allow a disabled person to interact with others more fully. **(9)** Service dogs usually work <u>for eight years</u> before they are replaced. **(10)** <u>Overlapping with a new dog</u>, the old service dog can help the young one.

1. A prepositional
   B gerund
   C appositive
   D infinitive

2. A infinitive
   B prepositional
   C participial
   D gerund

3. A participial
   B infinitive
   C gerund
   D prepositional

4. A gerund
   B participial
   C prepositional
   D infinitive

5. A prepositional
   B participial
   C infinitive
   D gerund

6. A adjectival
   B adverbial
   C participial
   D gerund

7. A prepositional
   B participial
   C appositive
   D gerund

8. A adjectival
   B adverbial
   C appositive
   D prepositional

9. A gerund
   B infinitive
   C prepositional
   D participial

10. A participial
   B prepositional
   C appositive
   D gerund

Writer's Corner

Snapshot

17 A A **phrase** is a group of related words that function as a single part of speech. **Adjectival** and **adverbial phrases** are prepositional phrases that modify another part of speech. (pages 611–614)

17 B An **appositive phrase** is made up of a noun or pronoun and its modifiers. An appositive phrase identifies or explains another noun or pronoun in the sentence. (pages 617–618)

17 C A **verbal** is a verb form that is used as a noun, an adjective, or an adverb. There are three kinds of verbals: **participles, gerunds,** and **infinitives.** (pages 619–630)

Power Rules

 Fix phrase fragments by adding words to turn the phrase into a sentence or by attaching the phrase to an existing sentence. (pages 668–670)

Before Editing	**After Editing**
Clara got the best grade on the test. *The smartest girl in class*.	Clara, the smartest girl in class, got the best grade on the test.
Because he didn't study. Johan got a *C* on the test.	*Because he didn't study,* Johan got a *C* on the test.
Clara was always willing. *To help other students.*	Clara was always willing *to help other students.*

Use the **objective case** when the pronoun is an object of a prepositional phrase. (pages 716–717 and 722–725)

Before Editing	**After Editing**
Between you and I, Cassady is the best singer in school.	*Between you and me,* Cassady is the best singer in school.
She sang *for Hank and I* the other day.	She sang *for Hank and me* the other day.

Editing Checklist

Use this checklist when editing your writing.

✓ Did I use phrases to combine sentences? (See pages 611–612.)
✓ Did I use correct punctuation with phrases? (See pages 613, 617, and 622.)
✓ Did I use commas to set off nonrestrictive phrases? (See pages 617 and 622.)
✓ Did I avoid dangling and misplaced modifiers? (See pages 615–616 and 629–630.)
✓ Did I use a variety of verbal phrases to create interesting sentences?
   (See pages 619–630.)

Use the Power

Think of phrases as colors. Adding phrases to sentences makes your writing more vivid just as adding colors to a room makes it come alive.

appositive phrase	**infinitive phrase**
participial phrase	**adverbial phrase**
gerund phrase	**adjectival phrase**

On Friday, Caige and Ryan went to Alpine Stadium to see the Cubs, their favorite team. Standing on their seats, Caige and Ryan were able to watch the pitchers in the bullpen. During the game, they joined the crowd by chanting and clapping.

Clauses

How can you connect related ideas with clauses?

Clauses: Pretest 1

The following draft paragraph about the *Titanic* is hard to read because it contains several misplaced clauses. Revise the paragraph so that it reads more smoothly. One of the misplaced clauses has been corrected as an example.

> In 1912, where icebergs were a constant threat, the *Titanic* was crossing the North Atlantic. The passengers, because they felt secure on this great ship, were enjoying themselves. What they didn't know was that their lives were in danger. The crew ignored several iceberg warnings that should have been heeded. An iceberg suddenly appeared in front of the ship whose size was tremendous. A slight impact had actually struck the ship a fatal blow, which scarcely disturbed the passengers. Who were unaware of their danger, the passengers chatted casually about the accident. The lifeboats could carry only a fraction of the passengers that were on board. Some of the lifeboats that were launched were not filled completely. The panic overcame the passengers at the end. The disaster will never be forgotten, which resulted in a loss of 1,513 lives.

Clauses: Pretest 2

Directions

Write the letter of the term that correctly identifies each sentence or underlined part of a sentence.

(1) Because I have neat handwriting, Maisie asked me to design a farewell card. **(2)** I used my calligraphy pen and blue ink. **(3)** Before I made a final version, I practiced on a separate sheet of paper. **(4)** The card was for a teacher who was leaving in June. **(5)** She had been there twenty years, and everyone would miss her. **(6)** Because she was so well-liked, we expected a big turnout, and we were not disappointed. **(7)** Mrs. Strout was the person <u>who taught me calligraphy</u>. **(8)** <u>When I first met her</u>, I was just starting middle school. **(9)** Her art class was harder <u>than I had expected</u>. **(10)** <u>That I'd had art in the past</u> did not prepare me for Mrs. Strout's class.

1. A simple sentence
   B compound sentence
   C complex sentence
   D compound-complex sentence

2. A simple sentence
   B compound sentence
   C complex sentence
   D compound-complex sentence

3. A simple sentence
   B compound sentence
   C complex sentence
   D compound-complex sentence

4. A simple sentence
   B compound sentence
   C complex sentence
   D compound-complex sentence

5. A simple sentence
   B compound sentence
   C complex sentence
   D compound-complex sentence

6. A simple sentence
   B compound sentence
   C complex sentence
   D compound-complex sentence

7. A independent clause
   B adverbial clause
   C adjectival clause
   D noun clause

8. A independent clause
   B adverbial clause
   C adjectival clause
   D noun clause

9. A independent clause
   B adverbial clause
   C adjectival clause
   D noun clause

10. A independent clause
   B adverbial clause
   C adjectival clause
   D noun clause

Independent and Subordinate Clauses

In the preceding chapter, you learned about a group of words called a phrase that can be used as a noun, an adjective, or an adverb. In this chapter you will learn about another group of words called a **clause,** which can also be used as a noun, an adjective, or an adverb.

> **18 A**   A **clause** is a group of words that is part of a sentence and that has a subject and a verb.

Notice that in the examples below, the clause has a subject and a verb.

Phrase	I wrote a letter **after dinner.**
	(*After dinner* is a prepositional phrase that modifies the verb *wrote.*)
Clause	I wrote a letter **after dinner was finished.**
	(*Dinner* is the subject of the clause; *was finished* is the verb.)

There are two kinds of clauses: **independent clauses** and **subordinate,** or **dependent, clauses.**

➤ Independent Clauses

> **18 A.1**   An **independent (main) clause** can stand alone as a sentence because it expresses a complete thought.

An independent clause is called a sentence when it stands by itself. It is called a clause when it appears in a sentence with another clause.

The first example below is a sentence with two independent clauses. In the second example, the clauses are shown as two sentences.

Independent Clauses	I will write a few sentences, and you can analyze my handwriting.
Two Sentences	I will write a few sentences. You can analyze my handwriting.

Subordinate Clauses

18 A.2 A **subordinate (dependent) clause** cannot stand alone as a sentence because it does not express a complete thought.

The subordinate clause in each of the following examples does not express a complete thought—even though it has a subject and a verb.

```
 ┌─subordinate clause─┐ ┌──────── independent clause ────────┐
 If you are interested, you can read about handwriting analysis.

 ┌─independent clause──┐ ┌────subordinate clause────┐
 My friends read a book that was about graphology.
```

When You Write

When writers want to persuade an audience to adopt a particular viewpoint, they often acknowledge the opposing point of view by presenting it in a subordinate clause.

Although some argue that art and music classes take valuable time and budget resources away from basic academic subjects, new findings indicate that art and music instruction adds to a student's overall intelligence.

By placing the opponent's point of view in a subordinate clause, the writer both acknowledges it and subordinates it under her own point of view.

● Practice Your Skills

Differentiating Between Kinds of Clauses

Write each underlined clause. Then label each one *I* for independent or *S* for subordinate.

(1) Graphology, which is the study of handwriting, has existed for many years. **(2)** Many people think that handwriting can reveal personality traits. **(3)** Because some businesses accept this theory, they analyze job applicants' handwriting. **(4)** When you apply for a job, watch your handwriting. **(5)** You can always go back to your old ways after you have been hired. **(6)** If your writing slants to the right, you are probably friendly and open. **(7)** If your writing slants to the left, you might very well be a nonconformist. **(8)** Writing uphill indicates an optimist, and writing downhill suggests a reliable person. **(9)** Capital letters that are inserted in the middle of a word reveal a creative person. **(10)** An i dotted with a circle shows an artistic nature, and a correctly dotted *i* indicates a careful person.

18 B A **subordinate clause** can function as an adverb, an adjective, or a noun.

Adverbial Clauses

18 B.1 An **adverbial clause** is a subordinate clause that is used like an adverb to modify a verb, an adjective, or an adverb.

A subordinate clause can be used like a single adverb or like an adverbial phrase. When it functions in one of those ways it is called an adverbial clause.

Single Adverb	Our plane left **early.**
Adverbial Phrase	Our plane left **at dawn.**
Adverbial Clause	Our plane left **as the sun came up over the horizon.**

An adverbial clause answers the adverb questions *How? When? Where? How much?* or *To what extent?* as well as the questions *Under what condition?* or *Why?*

When?	We will travel **until we have seen all of England.**
Under What Condition?	**If our flight is late,** the tour guide will wait for us.
Why?	We took an early flight **because it was less expensive.**

The adverbial clauses in the preceding examples all modify verbs. Notice that they modify the whole verb phrase. Adverbial clauses can also modify adjectives and adverbs.

Modifying an Adjective	I am happy **whenever I am traveling.**
Modifying an Adverb	The flight lasted longer **than I had expected.**

CHAPTER 18

Subordinating Conjunctions

18 B.2   All adverbial clauses begin with a **subordinating conjunction.**

Keep in mind that *after, as, before, since,* and *until* can also be prepositions.

COMMON SUBORDINATING CONJUNCTIONS

after	as soon as	in order that	until
although	as though	since	when
as	because	so that	whenever
as far as	before	than	where
as if	even though	though	wherever
as long as	if	unless	while

Unless you hear from me, I will return at six o'clock.

The flight has not changed **as far as** I know.

PUNCTUATION WITH ADVERBIAL CLAUSES

Always place a comma after an adverbial clause that comes at the beginning of a sentence.

Before we visited Ireland, we saw the sights of London.

Sometimes an adverbial clause will interrupt an independent clause. If it does, place a comma before and after the adverbial clause.

Our schedule**, as far as I can tell,** seems reasonable.

When an adverbial clause follows an independent clause, no comma is needed.

We will drive **so that we can see the countryside.**

CHAPTER 18

● **Practice Your Skills**

Recognizing Adverbial Clauses as Modifiers

Write the adverbial clause in each sentence. Then beside it, write the verb, adjective, or adverb that it modifies.

(1) After Ferdinand V. Hayden surveyed Yellowstone, Congress established the country's first national park. **(2)** So that the country would have public lands, the government has created more national parks. **(3)** These lands are protected so that all Americans can see the beauty of nature. **(4)** Campers are happy when they sleep under the stars of California's Yosemite National Park. **(5)** The drive through Glacier National Park takes longer than most tourists realize. **(6)** The Grand Canyon in Arizona stretches farther than the eye can see. **(7)** Because it is unusually beautiful, many tourists visit Arches National Park in Utah. **(8)** When people visit Big Bend National Park in Texas, they are surprised by the mountains. **(9)** If you like mountains, you will love Rocky Mountain National Park in Estes Park, Colorado. **(10)** Because they belong to all of us, Americans should visit these magnificent places.

● *Connect to Writing:* **Drafting**

Writing Sentences Using Adverbial Clauses

Write sentences about taking a trip that follow the directions below. Then underline each adverbial clause. Include commas where needed in your sentences.

1. Include an adverbial clause that begins with *than*.
2. Include an adverbial clause that begins with *even though*.
3. Start a sentence with an adverbial clause that begins with *because*.
4. Use an adverbial clause that begins with *unless* that interrupts an independent clause.
5. Start a sentence with an adverbial clause that begins with *whenever*.

Power Your Writing: Tip the Scales

Writers often use adverbial clauses to "tip the scales," subordinating one idea or position to another. In this example from *When Heaven and Earth Changed Places* (pages 325–327), the importance of the rice crop is emphasized over the other crops.

> Although we grew many crops around Ky La, the most important by far was rice.

Look at a recent persuasive essay, and check to be sure you have used subordinate clauses to tip the scales toward your position.

 **Adjectival Clauses**

18 B.3 An **adjectival clause** is a subordinate clause that is used like an adjective to modify a noun or a pronoun.

A subordinate clause used like a single adjective or an adjectival phrase is called an **adjectival clause.**

Single Adjective	My great-uncle witnessed a **famous** disaster.
Adjectival Phrase	My great-uncle witnessed a disaster **of air travel.**
Adjectival Clause	My great-uncle witnessed a disaster **that is still remembered today.**

An adjectival clause answers the adjective question *Which one?* or *What kind?*

Which One?	He saw one man **who jumped to the ground.**
What Kind?	The airship, **which was a zeppelin,** came down in flames.

Relative Pronouns

Most adjectival clauses begin with a relative pronoun and are often called relative clauses.

18 B.4 A **relative pronoun** relates an adjectival clause to its antecedent—the noun or pronoun it modifies.

RELATIVE PRONOUNS				
who	whom	whose	which	that

The crash, **which occurred in 1937,** destroyed the *Hindenburg*.

The zeppelin carried a fuel **that was highly flammable.**

CHAPTER 18

Sometimes a word such as *where* or *when* can also introduce an adjectival clause.

Frankfurt, Germany, is the place **where the *Hindenburg's* flight originated.**

This was an era **when commercial air travel was just beginning.**

● **Practice Your Skills**

Finding Relative Pronouns

Write the adjectival clause in each sentence. Then underline the relative pronoun.

(1) The *Hindenburg,* which was a magnificent zeppelin, left Frankfurt, Germany, for a two-day flight to the United States. **(2)** The passengers who made the journey enjoyed great comfort on the airship. **(3)** The world was interested in the flight of the *Hindenburg,* which was the largest human-made object ever to fly. **(4)** The passengers had a glorious view from the windows that lined the zeppelin. **(5)** In the United States, the people who gathered at the naval air station awaited the *Hindenburg's* arrival. **(6)** The *Hindenburg* was over Lakehurst, New Jersey, which was its destination, when a spark ignited the airship. **(7)** Some spectators who had family members on board began to scream in horror. **(8)** The zeppelin was filled with hydrogen, which is a very combustible gas. **(9)** Another cause for the blaze may have been the flammable material that covered the outside of the airship. **(10)** About one third of the people who were on board the *Hindenburg* died in the disastrous accident.

● *Connect to Writing:* **News Article**

Using Adjectival Clauses

Using the information in the activity above, write a brief news account of the *Hindenburg* accident. Use at least four adjectival clauses in your account and underline them. Then write a brief definition of the grammar term *adjectival clause.*

Functions of a Relative Pronoun

In addition to introducing an adjectival clause, a **relative pronoun** has another function. It can serve as a subject, a direct object, or an object of a preposition within the adjectival clause. It can also show possession.

Subject	The Great Depression, **which began in 1929,** was a bleak time in American history.
	(*Which* is the subject of *began.*)
Direct Object	The economic confidence **that most Americans enjoyed** was shattered.
	(*That* is the direct object of *enjoyed.*)
Object of a Preposition	The time period **about which I am writing** lasted for eleven years.
	(*Which* is the object of the preposition *about.*)
Possession	Few were the Americans **whose lives were unaffected.**
	(*Whose* shows possession of *lives.*)

Sometimes the relative pronoun *that* is omitted from an adjectival clause. Nevertheless, it still has its function within the clause.

The Grapes of Wrath is a novel **John Steinbeck wrote about the Depression.**

(*That John Steinbeck wrote about the Depression* is the adjectival clause. *That* [understood] is the direct object within the adjectival clause.)

Restrictive and Nonrestrictive Clauses

Not all relative clauses are essential to the meaning of a sentence.

18 B.5   A **restrictive (essential) clause** contains information that is essential to identifying a person, place, or thing in a sentence.

A restrictive clause answers the question *Which one?* Do not use commas to set off an essential clause.

Dorothea Lange's photograph **that shows a tired-looking mother with her children** is on display at the museum.

(No commas are used because the clause is essential to identify which photograph is on display.)

A **nonrestrictive (nonessential) clause** adds additional information and can be removed without changing the main information of a sentence.

A nonrestrictive clause answers the question *What kind?* Use a comma or commas to set off a nonrestrictive clause.

> The photograph**, which was taken in 1936,** is striking.
> (Commas are needed because the clause could be removed from the sentence without changing its meaning.)

To determine if you should use commas to set off a clause, read the sentence without the clause. If the sentence is meaningful without the clause, set the clause off with commas. It is customary to use the relative pronoun *that* in a restrictive clause and *which* in a nonrestrictive clause.

> The photograph, **which** was taken in 1936, shows an image **that** is striking.

● **Practice Your Skills**

Determining the Function of a Relative Pronoun

Write each adjectival clause and underline the relative pronoun. Label its use in the adjectival clause as **subject, direct object, object of the preposition,** or **possessive.** Write an **R** next to restrictive clauses and an **NR** next to nonrestrictive clauses.

(**1**) The stock market crash that occurred on Tuesday, October 24, 1929, was the beginning of the Great Depression. (**2**) The Great Depression devastated America's farmers, who were contending with a terrible drought. (**3**) The drought was in the Great Plains region, which became known as the "Dust Bowl." (**4**) Farmers headed west to California, which offered many job opportunities. (**5**) In large cities, soup kitchens that fed hungry people had long lines at every meal. (**6**) Woody Guthrie was an American folksinger who sang about the Depression. (**7**) One song that he wrote is still familiar to almost every American. (**8**) "This Land Is Your Land" is a song whose words still resonate with Americans. (**9**) Herbert Hoover, on whom the blame for the economic disaster was placed, was not reelected in 1932. (**10**) Franklin Roosevelt, whose 1932 election brought him to the presidency, enacted programs to put Americans back to work.

Misplaced Modifiers

An adjectival clause should be placed as near as possible to the word it modifies.

18 B.7 A clause that is too far away from the word it modifies is called a **misplaced modifier.**

Misplaced	Mark plays the guitar **who lives down the street.**
Correct	Mark, **who lives down the street,** plays the guitar.

● Practice Your Skills

Identifying Misplaced Modifiers

Each sentence below contains an adjectival clause. If the clause is correctly placed, write **C** for correct. If the clause is too far away from the noun or pronoun it modifies, write **MM** for misplaced modifier.

1. Some kids started a rock band who live in my neighborhood.

2. Heather's garage is very small where they practice each evening.

3. I can hear them from my house, which is way down the street.

4. Shelby plays the bass guitar who is my age.

5. Heather's father works at a factory that makes amplifiers.

6. The neighbors call Heather's unconcerned parents who hate the noise.

7. The songs were written by Mark that their rock band plays.

8. Mark's guitar screams across the neighborhood which is electric.

9. We will have a big party on my sixteenth birthday, which is in June.

10. The band will play at my party, which will really be fun.

Noun Clauses

18 B.8 A **noun clause** is a subordinate clause that is used like a noun.

A noun clause can be used like a single noun.

Single Noun	I just learned an interesting **fact.**
Noun Clause	I just learned **that Russia was once ruled by tsars.**

A noun clause can be used in all the ways in which a single noun can be used.

Subject	**Whatever you read** is fine with our English teacher.
Direct Object	Does anybody know **when Leo Tolstoy was born?**
Indirect Object	Give **whoever comes to class** a copy of the reading list.
Object of a Preposition	I was intrigued by **what our teacher said.**
Predicate Nominative	The literature of Russia is **what interests me most.**

The chart below shows words that are commonly used to introduce noun clauses.

COMMON INTRODUCTORY WORDS FOR NOUN CLAUSES			
how	whatever	which	whomever
if	when	who	whose
that	where	whoever	why
what	whether	whom	

Keep in mind that the words *who, whom, whose, which,* and *that* may also begin an adjectival clause. Therefore, do not rely on the introductory words themselves to identify a clause. Instead, decide how a clause is used in a sentence.

Noun Clause	**That Leo Tolstoy is a great Russian writer** is common knowledge. (used as a subject)
Adjectival Clause	The short story **that I like best** is "The Death of Ivan Ilych." (used to modify *story*)

● **Practice Your Skills**

Finding Noun Clauses

Write the noun clause from each sentence.

1. That Leo Tolstoy is revered today is a testament to his genius.
2. Many critics believe that *War and Peace* is Tolstoy's greatest novel.
3. The contention of others is that *Anna Karenina* is his greatest work.
4. His works bring great pleasure to whoever reads them.

5. That Tolstoy was a member of the Russian upper class is obvious in his novels.

6. He did, however, write about what the peasants' lives were like.

7. His novels and short stories give whoever reads them a taste of Russian life.

8. Why *Anna Karenina* is known as a psychological novel is easy to explain.

9. The reason for this label is that Tolstoy reveals the thoughts of all the characters in the book.

10. What makes Tolstoy's novels so realistic is their mixture of tragedy and happiness.

● **Practice Your Skills**

Determining the Uses of Noun Clauses

Label each noun clause in the preceding sentences as *subject, direct object, indirect object, object of a preposition,* or *predicate nominative.*

✔ *Check Point:* **Mixed Practice**

Write each subordinate clause in the following paragraphs and label each one *adverbial, adjectival,* or *noun.* (There are 14 subordinate clauses.)

(1) The Panama Canal, which connects two oceans, is the greatest constructed waterway in the world. (2) Because it was completed around 100 years ago, few people can remember the tragic problems that occurred during its construction. (3) In 1881, a French firm that was headed by Ferdinand de Lesseps began to dig the canal. (4) Although the work was hard, it was possible. (5) What wasn't possible was finding a way to overcome the mosquitoes that infested the whole area. (6) Within eight years, nearly 20,000 men had died of malaria as they worked on the canal. (7) The French company that had first built the Suez Canal finally went bankrupt after it had lost $325 million.

(8) After 18 years some Americans tried their luck. (9) They first found a plan that wiped out the mosquitoes. (10) Their work then proceeded without the hazard that had doomed the French. (11) The construction, which began at both ends, moved inland through the dense jungle. (12) Finally, after ten billion tons of earth had been removed, the canal was opened in 1914.

18 C   There are four kinds of sentences: **simple, compound, complex,** and **compound-complex.** The kind of sentence depends on the type and number of clauses in it.

18 C.1   A **simple sentence** consists of one independent clause.

The subject and the verb in a simple sentence can be compound. In the following examples, each subject is underlined once and each verb is underlined twice.

> The blueberry <u>pie</u> <u>cooled</u> on the windowsill.
>
> <u>Tyrone</u> and <u>Lili</u> <u>prepared</u> and <u>baked</u> the blueberry pie.

18 C.2   A **compound sentence** consists of two or more independent clauses.

> ┌————independent clause————┐   ┌—independent clause—┐
> <u>Dad</u> just <u>baked</u> an angel food cake, and <u>I</u> <u>can't wait</u> to taste it.
>
> ┌————independent clause————┐ ┌————— independent clause —————┐
> <u>Mom</u> and <u>Tyrone</u> <u>set</u> the table; <u>Lili</u> <u>poured</u> the milk and <u>served</u> the food.

PUNCTUATION WITH COMPOUND SENTENCES

You can join independent clauses in a compound sentence with a comma and a conjunction.

> The pie had baked for a while, **but** it still was not done.

You can also join independent clauses with a semicolon and no conjunction.

> A hot cake is impossible to ice; you must wait for it to cool.

---

18 C.3   A **complex sentence** consists of one independent clause and one or more subordinate clauses.

┌──subordinate clause──┐ ┌────independent clause────┐
Since I learned to cook, I have made dinner each Friday.

┌──subordinate clause──┐ ┌──independent clause──┐ ┌──subordinate clause──┐
After the game is over, we can go to my house, where we can eat dinner.

18 C.4   A **compound-complex sentence** consists of two or more independent clauses and one or more subordinate clauses.

┌────independent clause────┐ ┌────independent clause────┐ ┌────subordinate clause────┐
Baking a cake is easy for me, so I baked three of them so that we could sell them

┌────subordinate clause────┐
when we had our bake sale.

To punctuate compound-complex sentences, follow the rules for both compound and complex sentences.

● *Connect to Writing:* **Commercial**

Using Different Types of Sentences

Write a commercial about your favorite food. Begin by writing four sentences about this food that explain why it is better than any other food. Use variety in your sentence structure. Write one simple, one compound, one complex, and one compound-complex sentence. Then use the four sentences in your commercial. Be prepared to point out the four sentence types.

Kinds of Sentence Structure • Lesson 3   **655**

Classifying Sentences

Label each sentence *simple, compound, complex,* or *compound-complex.*

1. Hamburger meat may have originated in Hamburg, Germany, and hot dogs supposedly originated in Frankfurt.

2. The idea of placing meat on a bun, however, came from the United States.

3. When hamburger meat first arrived in the United States, it was eaten raw.

4. The French still prefer their meat rare, but the Germans eat raw hamburger meat.

5. Hamburger was popular among German immigrants who lived in Cincinnati.

6. Hamburger meat wasn't placed on a bun until the twentieth century.

7. According to many, the first hamburger sandwich appeared in 1904 in St. Louis, Missouri, which is also the birthplace of the ice-cream cone.

8. Today the hamburger remains popular, and the hot dog is right there with it.

9. Chopped meat now accounts for about thirty percent of all meat sales.

10. Because people have become more health conscious, they are eating less meat, so many stores now sell hamburger patties made from soybeans.

● *Connect to Writing and Speaking:* **Peer Interaction**

Reviewing Content

With a partner, review the vocabulary you have learned in this chapter. (Hint: New terms are printed in purple.) Quiz each other until you understand the definitions of all the new words and concepts.

➤ Diagraming Clauses

The simple sentences that you diagramed earlier in this book had only one baseline. In the diagrams for compound, complex, and compound-complex sentences, each clause has its own baseline.

Compound Sentences These sentences are diagramed like two simple sentences, except that they are joined by a broken line on which the conjunction is placed. The broken line connects the verbs.

Mysteries are interesting, but I prefer biographies.

Mysteries | are \ interesting

but

I | prefer | biographies

Complex Sentences In a complex sentence, an adverbial clause is diagramed beneath the independent clause. The subordinating conjunction goes on a broken line that connects the verb in the adverbial clause to the word the clause modifies.

I read my report after I typed it.

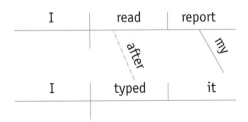

An adjectival clause is also diagramed beneath the independent clause. The relative pronoun is connected by a broken line to the noun or pronoun the clause modifies.

This song is one that I will never forget.

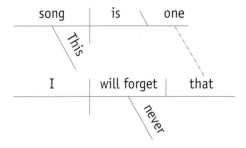

A noun clause is diagramed on a pedestal in the same place a single noun with the same function would be placed. The noun clause in the following diagram is used as the subject.

What the teacher said pleased Jane.

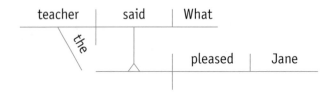

Compound-Complex Sentences To diagram this kind of sentence, apply what you just learned about diagraming compound and complex sentences.

● **Practice Your Skills**

Diagraming Clauses

Diagram the following sentences or copy them. If you copy them, draw one line under each subject and two lines under each verb. Put parentheses around each subordinate clause. Label each clause *adverbial, adjectival,* or *noun.*

1. *Skylab* orbited Earth in the 1970s, and from *Skylab* astronauts studied the sun.

2. A million planets that are the size of Earth could be squashed inside the sun.

3. If the sun were dark for a few days, most life-forms on Earth would die.

4. Some scientists believe that the sun will grow hotter.

5. Never look at the sun because the light could blind you.

Assess Your Learning

■ Identifying Subordinate Clauses

Write the subordinate clause in each sentence. Then label each one *adverbial, adjectival,* or *noun.*

1. Do you know what metal is used to make most cans?

2. If you can crush a can, it probably was made from aluminum.

3. Aluminum, which makes up nearly eight percent of Earth's crust, is the most common metal in the world.

4. Although aluminum is so abundant, it has been used for only about 100 years.

5. The problem is that aluminum is found only in combination with other substances in the rocks.

6. In 1886, it was Charles Hall who finally separated the aluminum from these other substances.

7. What he accomplished changed the canning industry forever.

8. Today you see aluminum products wherever you look.

9. Aluminum is useful because it is strong and lightweight.

10. Some aluminum products that you have heard of are pots and pans and parts for airplane and automobile engines.

11. Aluminum is also useful in wiring because it is a good conductor of heat and electricity.

12. Pure aluminum is soft and lacks strength although its alloys have many useful properties.

13. Another good thing about aluminum is that you can recycle it.

14. You should save empty soda cans until you can take them to a recycling center.

15. Did you know that you can earn money by recycling aluminum cans?

Classifying Sentences

Label each sentence *simple, compound, complex,* or *compound-complex.*

1. Does color affect you in any way?

2. Color experts say that different colors make a big difference in people's lives.

3. For example, people won't buy ice cream in a red carton because they associate red with meat.

4. Pink calms people, and yellow makes them nervous.

5. As a result, you should never paint your bedroom yellow.

6. People will eat less from blue plates, but they will eat more from red plates.

7. People who like candy prefer it in pink boxes.

8. Younger children go mainly for colors that are bright, but as teenagers they prefer softer colors.

9. Do you know what is the most popular color?

10. Most Americans pick blue as their favorite color, and red comes next.

Using Sentence Structure

Write five sentences that follow the directions below. (Clauses may come in any order.) Write about one of the following topics or a topic of your choice: your favorite color, your favorite game, or your favorite food.

1. Write a simple sentence.

2. Write a complex sentence with an introductory adverbial clause.

3. Write a complex sentence with an adjectival clause.

4. Write a compound sentence.

5. Write a complex sentence with a noun clause.

Label each sentence and check its punctuation.

Clauses: Posttest

Directions

Write the letter of the term that correctly identifies each sentence or underlined part of a sentence.

Dinner Cruise

(1) The evening dinner cruise was considerably more fun than I had expected. **(2)** We traveled up the west shore of Seneca Lake. **(3)** After we had been aboard for half an hour, dinner finally was served. **(4)** The food was unexciting, but the exotic atmosphere was truly delightful. **(5)** When dinner was over, we all went downstairs, and a band serenaded us. **(6)** The man <u>who led the band</u> was really a showman. **(7)** <u>How he danced around</u> made everyone laugh. **(8)** <u>As the band took a break</u>, I watched a nearby sailboat. **(9)** I asked the two women next to me <u>whether they enjoyed sailing</u>. **(10)** As it turned out, <u>one of them was a sailing instructor</u>.

1. **A** simple sentence
   B compound sentence
   C complex sentence
   D compound-complex sentence

2. **A** simple sentence
   B compound sentence
   C complex sentence
   D compound-complex sentence

3. **A** simple sentence
   B compound sentence
   C complex sentence
   D compound-complex sentence

4. **A** simple sentence
   B compound sentence
   C complex sentence
   D compound-complex sentence

5. **A** simple sentence
   B compound sentence
   C complex sentence
   D compound-complex sentence

6. **A** independent clause
   B adverbial clause
   C adjectival clause
   D noun clause

7. **A** independent clause
   B adverbial clause
   C adjectival clause
   D noun clause

8. **A** independent clause
   B adverbial clause
   C adjectival clause
   D noun clause

9. **A** independent clause
   B adverbial clause
   C adjectival clause
   D noun clause

10. **A** independent clause
    B adverbial clause
    C adjectival clause
    D noun clause

Writer's Corner

Snapshot

18 A   A **clause** is a group of words that has a subject and verb. An **independent clause** expresses a complete thought. A **subordinate clause** does not express a complete thought and cannot stand alone as a sentence. (pages 642–643)

18 B   A **subordinate clause** can function as an adverb, an adjective, or a noun. (pages 644–653)

18 C   There are four types of sentence structures: **simple, compound, complex,** or **compound-complex.** The sentence structure depends on the number and the kind of clauses in it. (pages 654–656)

Power Rules

Fix a clause fragment by joining it with an independent clause or by adding words to make it a complete sentence. (pages 670–671)

Before Editing	After Editing
Although Kendall left a few minutes late. She arrived right on time.	*Although Kendall left a few minutes late,* she arrived right on time.
Kendall takes the subway to work. *Because she works downtown.*	Kendall takes the subway to work *because she works downtown.*
Why she doesn't live downtown. Is easy to explain.	*Why she doesn't live downtown* is easy to explain.

Editing Checklist

Use this checklist when editing your writing.

✓ Did I use subordinating conjunctions to show relationships between ideas? (See pages 645–646.)

✓ Did I use noun clauses to add detail to my sentences? (See pages 651–653.)

✓ Did I use adverbial and adjectival clauses to add variety and detail to my sentences? (See pages 644–650.)

✓ Did I avoid misplaced modifiers? (See page 651.)

✓ Did I use commas correctly with adjectival and adverbial clauses? (See pages 644–650.)

✓ Did I use a combination of simple, compound, complex, and compound-complex sentences to add variety and interest to my writing? (See pages 654–656.)

Use the Power

A subordinate clause isn't a complete thought; it doesn't make sense on its own. You need to combine a subordinate clause with an independent clause to get an entire story. Study the photos below to see how joining clauses completes a story.

While the girls waved good-bye to their parents

While the girls waved good-bye to their parents, both their mom and dad were already concentrating on the trip.

As you compose, make sure your subordinate clauses are joined with independent clauses.

Sentence Fragments and Run-ons

How can you clarify your meaning by fixing unintended sentence fragments and run-ons?

Sentence Fragments and Run-ons: Pretest 1

The following draft paragraphs about comic books are hard to read because they contain several sentence fragments and run-on sentences. Revise the paragraphs so that they read more smoothly. The first error has been corrected as an example.

If you owned Marvel Comics #1. You could be a rich person. In 1939, it cost a dime today it is worth $15,000. No one knows. Exactly which comic books to save. There are, however, a few things. To look for when you're buying them. Buy the first issue. Of any comic book and hold onto it. Origin issues are also available, they are the issues in which a character is born or comes into being.

Do you have any old comic books? Lying around the house? You can find out how much they are worth by looking in a book it's called *The Comic Book Price Guide* by Robert Overstreet. It can be found. In most public libraries.

Directions

Read the passage. Write the letter of the best way to write each underlined section. If the underlined section contains no error, write D.

(1) Pythagoras was a Greek <u>philosopher. Lived</u> in the sixth century B.C. The Pythagoreans, his followers, were skilled mathematicians. (2) They were the first to <u>teach. That</u> Earth rotates daily on its axis. (3) Pythagoras is famous for a <u>theorem. We</u> studied this year. (4) It involves <u>triangles geometry</u> depends on it. (5) According to the <u>theorem, the</u> square of the length of the hypotenuse of a right triangle equals the sum of the squares of the lengths of the other two sides.

CHAPTER 19

1. A philosopher. Who lived
　 B philosopher he lived
　 C philosopher who lived
　 D No error

2. A teach that
　 B teach that. Earth
　 C teach, and Earth
　 D No error

3. A theorem. Which we
　 B theorem we
　 C theorem, we
　 D theorem; we

4. A triangles and geometry
　 B triangles, and geometry
　 C triangles, geometry
　 D No error

5. A theorem. The
　 B theorem; the
　 C theorem the
　 D No error

Sentence Fragments Lesson 1

19 A **A sentence fragment** is a group of words that does not express a complete thought.

Some sentence fragments are missing either a subject or a verb. These are fragments due to incomplete thoughts.

> **No Subject** Was running and catching snowflakes on her tongue.
>
> Skate at the ice rink.
>
> **No Verb** Gretchen and her two little sisters.
>
> The snow shovel next to the snowblower in the garage.

Some sentence fragments result from incorrect punctuation.

> **Part of a Compound Verb** Will you wait for us? **Or come back to get us?**
>
> We rushed to the ice. **And started to skate.**
>
> **Items in a Series** We will have to take warm clothes with us. **Coats, wool scarves, and gloves.**
>
> Rachel brought snacks for us. **Pretzels, chips, and hot chocolate.**

 ## Ways to Correct Sentence Fragments

When you edit your writing, always check specifically for missing subjects or missing verbs. You can fix such fragments by adding a subject or verb.

> **Fragment** Was running and catching snowflakes on her tongue.
>
> **Sentence** **My little sister** was running and catching snowflakes on her tongue.
>
> (A complete subject, *My little sister,* was added.)
>
> **Fragment** The snow shovel next to the snowblower in the garage.
>
> **Sentence** The snow shovel **is** next to the snowblower in the garage.
>
> (The verb *is* was added.)

Another way to correct a sentence fragment is to attach it to a related group of words near it. Sometimes you can simply include the information from the fragment in another sentence. At other times you can write two separate sentences.

Sentence and Fragment	Will you wait for the two of us? **Or come back to get us?**
Attached	Will you wait for the two of us **or come back to get us?**
Separate Sentences	Will you wait for the two of us? Will you come back to get us?
Sentence and Fragment	Rachel brought snacks for us. **Pretzels, chips, and hot chocolate.**
Attached	Rachel brought **pretzels, chips, and hot chocolate** for us.
Separate Sentences	Rachel brought snacks for us. She brought pretzels, chips, and hot chocolate.

You can learn more about complete sentences on pages 578–598.

● Practice Your Skills

Recognizing Fragments

Label each group of words *sentence* or *fragment.*

1. Each winter, I go ice-skating with friends from my neighborhood.
2. We hurry to the ice.
3. And skate as fast as possible.
4. Try to catch each other.
5. Sometimes I fall down.
6. And go sliding across the ice.
7. Usually bring our own skates.
8. Yesterday, however, Katie had to rent skates.
9. Her feet had grown since last winter.
10. Her old skates too small.

● *Connect to Writing:* Revising

Correcting Sentence Fragments

Rewrite each fragment from the previous exercise as a complete sentence. You may add words or attach the fragment to another sentence.

19 B   Phrases and clauses punctuated as sentences are also fragments.

Phrase Fragments

A phrase does not have a subject and a verb; therefore, it can never stand alone as a sentence.

19 B.1   When phrases are written alone, they are called **phrase fragments.**

Following are examples of different phrase fragments (in **bold** type). Notice that they are capitalized and punctuated as if they were sentences.

Prepositional Phrases	Mandy and Grant Saunders vacationed in Africa. **During the winter just after Christmas.**
	Before their trip to Zimbabwe and South Africa. Grant read about the continent.
Appositive Phrases	Mandy was fascinated by the African elephant. **The largest land mammal.**
	Have you seen Grant's books? **The ones about Africa.**
Participial Phrases	**Traveling by canoe on a wild river.** They saw a crocodile.
	Their canoe glided through a river. **Teeming with dangerous animals.**
Infinitive Phrases	Grant and Mandy bought a new camera. **To bring along on the trip.**
	They went to their doctor for vaccinations. **To prevent illness.**

When You Write

In fiction and drama and in informal writing, authors sometimes use sentence fragments in dialogue and for emphasis. Fragments should not be used, however, in most formal and academic writing.

CHAPTER 19

Ways to Correct Phrase Fragments

When you find phrase fragments, correct them in one of two ways: (1) add words to turn the phrase into a sentence; or (2) attach the phrase to a related group of words that has a subject and a verb.

Sentence and Phrase Fragment	Mandy was fascinated by the African elephant. **The largest land mammal.**
Separate Sentences	Mandy was fascinated by the African elephant. **Elephants are the largest land mammals.**
Attached	Mandy was fascinated by the African elephant, **the largest land mammal.**
Sentence and Phrase Fragment	Their canoe glided through a river. **Teeming with dangerous animals.**
Separate Sentences	Their canoe glided through a river. **The water was teeming with dangerous animals.**
Attached	Their canoe glided through a river **teeming with dangerous animals.**
Sentence and Phrase Fragment	They went to their doctor for vaccinations. **To prevent illness.**
Separate Sentences	They went to their doctor for vaccinations. **These shots help prevent illness.**
Attached	They went to their doctor for vaccinations **to prevent illness.**

● **Practice Your Skills**

Recognizing Phrase Fragments

Label each group of words **S** for sentence or **PF** for phrase fragment.

1. To learn more about wild animals.

2. Living in bushes and forest areas.

3. Gorillas are herbivores.

4. Scavengers like jackals and hyenas.

5. Lionesses raise their cubs together.

6. Found in Africa on game reserves.

7. One interesting animal in Africa is the zebra.

8. The lemur is found only in Madagascar.

9. On a photographic safari with an African guide.

10. Seeing animals in their natural habitats.

Correcting Phrase Fragments

Rewrite each phrase fragment from the previous exercise as a complete sentence. You may add words or attach the fragment to another sentence.

➤ **Clause Fragments**

All clauses have a subject and a verb, but only an independent clause can stand alone as a sentence. As you know, a subordinate clause does not express a complete thought.

19 B.2   When a subordinate clause stands alone, it is known as a **clause fragment.**

Following are examples of clause fragments (in **bold** type). Notice that they are punctuated and capitalized as if they were complete sentences.

Adverbial Clause Fragment	You will miss the exhibit. **If you don't purchase advance tickets.**
Adjectival Clause Fragment	This is a masterpiece. **That Pablo Picasso painted.**

Ways to Correct Clause Fragments

Looking for fragments should always be a part of your editing process. If you find a clause fragment, you can correct it in one of two ways: (1) add words to make it into a separate sentence; or (2) attach it to the sentence next to it.

Sentence and Clause Fragment	You will miss the exhibit. **If you don't purchase advance tickets.**
Separate Sentences	You will miss the exhibit. **You should purchase advance tickets.**
Attached	You will miss the exhibit **if you don't purchase advance tickets.**
Sentence and Clause Fragment	This is a masterpiece. **That Pablo Picasso painted.**
Separate Sentences	This is a masterpiece. **Pablo Picasso painted it.**
Attached	This is a masterpiece **that Pablo Picasso painted.**

Practice Your Skills

Recognizing Clause Fragments

Label each group of words **S** for sentence or **CF** for clause fragment.

1. Pablo Picasso who was born in 1881.

2. He led the artistic movement against naturalism.

3. Which is realism in art.

4. His father was an art teacher.

5. Who realized very early his son's great talent.

6. Picasso's painting evolved throughout his life.

7. When he was a young man.

8. He painted more realistic works.

9. As he matured, he experimented with line, form, and color.

10. Which allowed him to create amazing pieces of art.

Connect to Writing: Revising

Correcting Clause Fragments

Rewrite each clause fragment from the previous exercise as a complete sentence. You may add words or attach the fragment to another sentence.

Check Point: Mixed Practice

Rewrite the following paragraphs, correcting all sentence fragments. Add capital letters and punctuation marks as needed.

When Jesse Owens graduated from East Technical High School in Cleveland, Ohio. He had established three national high school records in track. At Ohio State University, Jesse broke a few more world records. Then in the 1936 Olympic Games at Berlin. He acquired world fame by winning four gold medals.

Owens's performance on May 25, 1935, at the Big Ten Conference championships, however, will always be remembered. Getting up from a sickbed. He ran the 100-yard dash in 9.4 seconds. To tie the world record. Ten minutes later in the broad jump. He leaped 26 feet 8.25 inches on his first try. To beat a world record. When the 220-yard dash was over. Owens had smashed another world record. He then negotiated the hurdles in 22.6 seconds. And shattered another record. Within three quarters of an hour. Jesse Owens had established himself as one of the greatest track athletes of all time.

Run-on Sentences

A common writing mistake is combining several thoughts into one sentence. This sometimes results in a run-on sentence.

19 C   **A run-on sentence** is two or more sentences that are written together and are separated by a comma or no mark of punctuation at all.

Generally, run-on sentences are written in either of two ways: separated by a comma **(comma splice),** or separated by no punctuation.

Comma Splice	The class trip was in April, **we went to Washington, D.C.**
With No Punctuation	On the trip we visited four museums **the Smithsonian was the best.**

⯈ Ways to Correct Run-on Sentences

To correct a run-on sentence, you can turn it into (1) separate sentences; (2) a compound sentence; or (3) a complex sentence.

Run-on Sentence	I walked all over the city my feet were very tired at the end of the day.
Separate Sentences	I walked all over the city. My feet were very tired at the end of the day.
	(separated with a period and a capital letter)
Compound Sentences	I walked all over the city, so my feet were very tired at the end of the day.
	(clauses combined with a comma and a conjunction)
	I walked all over the city; my feet were very tired at the end of the day.
	(clauses combined with a semicolon)
Complex Sentence	Because I walked all over the city, my feet were very tired at the end of the day.
	(clauses combined by changing one of them into a subordinate clause)

A good way to edit for sentence errors is to use two highlighting markers. Highlight your first sentence in one color; highlight your second sentence in another color. Continue alternating. You can then easily see the length of each sentence. If a group of words looks short, read it carefully to be sure it is a complete sentence. If a sentence looks long, read closely to be sure it is not a run-on.

Power Your Writing: The Power of 3s

When editing run-on sentences, be careful not to create monotony by composing sentences of the same length and kind. Your writing does not have to plod along, one sentence after another. It can be enlivened with a variety of grammatical options. Consider the power of three, or **parallelism.** In this device, the writer uses the same kind of word or group of words, grammatically speaking, in a series of three or more.

Charles Finney amply demonstrates parallelism in his descriptive piece about the rattlesnake (pages 71–74). Notice the impact of the series of verbs.

> This cuckoo, or road runner as it is called, found the baby [rattlesnake] amid some rocks, uttered a cry of delight, scissored it by the neck, shook it until it was almost lifeless, banged and pounded it upon a rock until life had indeed left it, and then gulped it down.

Review a recent composition, and look for places you might use the power of three to your advantage.

● Practice Your Skills

Recognizing Run-on Sentences

Label each group of words *S* for sentence or *RO* for run-on.

1. George Washington was the first president he was not the first to live in the White House.
2. The second president, John Adams, was the first head of state to live in the White House.
3. In 1800, John and Abigail Adams moved in the builders had completed only six rooms.
4. Still, Abigail Adams was impressed by the place she was glad to live in such a beautiful mansion.
5. The White House wasn't always white, it started out gray.
6. During the War of 1812, British troops invaded Washington they burned the structure on August 24, 1814.
7. Only a shell was left standing.
8. Under the direction of the original architect, the building was restored.
9. The work was completed in 1817.
10. "The White House" did not become its official name until 1902, Theodore Roosevelt adopted it.

● *Connect to Writing Process:* Revising

Correcting Run-on Sentences

Correct each run-on sentence from the previous exercise. Add capital letters and punctuation marks where needed.

Assess Your Learning

Correcting Sentence Fragments and Run-on Sentences

Write the following sentences, correcting each sentence fragment or run-on sentence. Use capital letters and punctuation marks as needed.

1. A large tree had fallen. At the end of the road leading to the lake.
2. We have three kinds of trees growing in our yard. Oak, maple, and spruce.
3. Smith is a very common name. Appearing in more than 40 languages.
4. In 1946, there were 10,000 television sets in the United States, there were twelve million five years later.
5. Of all the ore dug in a diamond mine. Only one carat in every three tons proves to be a diamond.
6. Yesterday I mowed the lawn. And trimmed the bushes and hedges.
7. If the moon were placed on the surface of the United States. It would extend from California to Ohio.
8. The hardiest of all the world's insects is the mosquito, it can be found in all parts of the world.
9. South American Indians introduced tapioca to the world it comes from the root of a poisonous plant.
10. We must have loaned the snowblower to Uncle Pete I can't find it.

Correcting Sentence Fragments and Run-on Sentences

Rewrite the following paragraph, correcting all sentence fragments and run-on sentences. Be sure to correct the errors in a variety of ways. Add capital letters and punctuation as needed.

According to a common superstition. The groundhog is supposed to come out of its underground home on February 2. National Groundhog Day. If the animal sees its shadow. It hurries back to its snug bed. For another six weeks. This means that there will be six more weeks of winter, people should not put their winter coats away. Of course, if the little critter stays out of its burrow, spring will soon begin. Should you believe this superstition? The National Geographic Service says that the groundhog. Has been right only 28 percent of the time that's not a very good record. Still, next February 2, hundreds of reporters will be waiting. To see if the groundhog will see its shadow.

CHAPTER 19

◼ Writing Sentences

Write five sentences that follow the directions below. Beware of sentence fragments and run-ons. Write about your favorite holiday or about a topic of your choice.

1. Write a sentence that contains only a subject and a verb.

2. Write a sentence that consists of a simple sentence with an attached phrase.

3. Write a sentence that consists of a simple sentence with an attached dependent clause.

4. Write a compound sentence containing the word *and*.

5. Write a compound sentence with a semicolon.

Sentence Fragments and Run-ons: Posttest

Directions

Read the passage. Write the letter of the best way to write each underlined section. If the underlined section contains no error, write **D**.

(1) At its peak the Incan empire controlled the entire Andean mountain region. Despite the rough terrain, the Incas were able to grow crops. They did this by terracing the (2) ground. and they irrigated. The Incas (3) raised llamas and alpacas. (4) With their heavy coats. These unusual animals are well suited to the mountain climate. The Incan civilization was quite advanced. They built extraordinary structures. (5) Artwork still admired today.

1. A At, its peak the
   B At its peak. The
   C At its peak of the
   D No error

2. A ground and they irrigated
   B ground and irrigating
   C ground and, they irrigated
   D No error

3. A raised llamas, and alpacas.
   B raised, llamas and alpacas,
   C raised: llamas and alpacas.
   D No error

4. A With their heavy coats, these unusual
   B With their heavy coats these, unusual
   C With their heavy, coats these unusual
   D No error

5. A Artwork is still
   B Their artwork is still
   C artwork still
   D No error

Writer's Corner

Snapshot

19 A A **sentence fragment** is a group of words that is punctuated like a sentence but does not express a complete thought. (pages 666–667)

19 B A **phrase fragment** is a phrase that is punctuated like a sentence. A **clause fragment** is a subordinate clause that is punctuated like a sentence. (pages 668–671)

19 C A **run-on sentence** is two or more sentences that are written together and are separated by a comma or by no punctuation mark. (pages 672–674)

Power Rules

 Fix phrase and clause fragments by using punctuation and conjunctions to join them to independent clauses or by adding words to make them complete sentences. (pages 669–671)

Before Editing	After Editing
Marcus and Dustin went to Cancun, Mexico. *For spring break.*	Marcus and Dustin went to Cancun, Mexico, *for spring break.*
Because they're not old enough to travel alone. They went with Marcus's parents.	*Because they're not old enough to travel alone,* they went with Marcus's parents.
Marcus's father. *Who is a teacher.* Was on spring break, too.	Marcus's father, *who is a teacher,* was on spring break, too.

 Edit **run-on sentences** by separating the sentences or by joining them with a conjunction and/or punctuation to form complex or compound sentences. (pages 672–674)

Before Editing	After Editing
Marcus and Dustin spent the day snorkeling and swimming, they were too tired to go out that night.	*Because Marcus and Dustin spent the day snorkeling and swimming,* they were too tired to go out that night.
They spent a few days sightseeing, they enjoyed the Mayan ruins the best.	They spent a few days sightseeing. *They enjoyed the Mayan ruins the best.*

Editing Checklist

Use this checklist when editing your writing.

✓ Did I check my work for sentence fragments? (See pages 666–671.)

✓ Did I fix phrase fragments by adding words to turn them into sentences or by correctly attaching them to independent clauses? (See pages 669–670.)

✓ Did I fix any clause fragments by joining them to sentences or by adding words to make them separate sentences? (See pages 670–671.)

✓ Did I fix run-on sentences by separating the sentences or by adding a conjunction and/or punctuation to form complex or compound sentences? (See pages 672–674.)

Use the Power

Study the chart below for ways to fix sentence fragments and run-ons.

What's the Problem?	Fix It Up
Phrase Fragment During the storm.	**Add a subject and verb.** A tree fell during the storm.
Clause Fragment Because the tree was blocking the road.	**Join it to an independent clause.** No one could get to work or school because the tree was blocking the road.
Run-on with Missing Punctuation A crew came out to remove the tree it took them the entire day.	**Separate the sentences.** A crew came out to remove the tree. It took them the entire day.
Comma Splice I was thrilled to have the day off, my mother was upset because she missed an important meeting.	**Add a conjunction.** I was thrilled to have the day off, but my mother was upset because she missed an important meeting.
	Change one clause to a subordinate clause. Although I was thrilled to have the day off, my mother was upset because she missed an important meeting.

Write a paragraph about an event that took place in your neighborhood recently.

Unit 5

Usage

Every language is as alive as the humans who speak and write it. English is no exception. Each community of English speakers changes and shapes the language to fit its needs. Each pattern of usage is as powerful as any other. Conventional usage, however—the pattern of English presented in this unit— is useful to learn because it can help you communicate effectively in schools and workplaces. It can help you communicate with the many people all over the world who have learned this form of English in addition to their own language. Opening yourself to mastering this usage, and any other, will help you learn, work, and speak in the world community.

The English language is nobody's special property. It is the property of the imagination: it is the property of the language itself.
— *Derek Walcott*

Using Verbs

How can you use verbs to improve your writing?

Using Verbs: Pretest 1

The first draft below contains several errors in the use of verbs. The first error is corrected for you. How would you revise the draft so that all verbs are used correctly?

> The ghostly remains of once-glorious sailing vessels now litters the sea floor. These sunken ships often contain treasures that has been preserved in the salty water. The water is an excellent protector of glass objects, but glass often shrink and become brittle when it is brang to land. A way has been discovered by scientists to preserve these artifacts. The objects are submerged in silicone polymers, which invades the pores of the glass. Then a thin layer of polymers are applied to further strengthened the glass and kept it from breaking. These techniques has saved many glass artifacts, including jars from a sixteenth-century sunken pirate ship discovered in Jamaica.

Using Verbs: Pretest

Directions

Read the passage and choose the word or group of words that belongs in each underlined space. Write the letter of the correct answer.

Moving day __(1)__ at last! Yesterday I __(2)__ all my belongings into boxes. Later, when my friend Jason arrives, I __(3)__ them into the back of a rental truck. He __(4)__ his help. I __(5)__ him at the door now. Jason __(6)__ used to moving because he moves to a new apartment every other year. He __(7)__ some old blankets for us to use today. Before Jason arrived, I __(8)__ to protect my furniture with towels. He __(9)__ some blankets over the piano, and we are ready to go. I feel a little sad to leave because I __(10)__ in this apartment a long time.

1. **A** will have been coming
   B had been coming
   C has been coming
   D has come

2. **A** packed
   B pack
   C will pack
   D am packing

3. **A** had loaded
   B loaded
   C will load
   D have loaded

4. **A** will have offered
   B has offered
   C will have been offering
   D offers

5. **A** will hear
   B hear
   C had heard
   D will have heard

6. **A** will be
   B will have been
   C is being
   D is

7. **A** has been bringing
   B has brought
   C will have brought
   D had been bringing

8. **A** will try
   B try
   C had been trying
   D will have tried

9. **A** lays
   B will lay
   C had laid
   D will have laid

10. **A** live
    B will live
    C have lived
    D will have lived

The Principal Parts of a Verb

Even though verbs can be the most informative—and most powerful—words in the English language, they can also be difficult to master.

20 A The **principal parts of a verb** are the **present**, the **present participle**, the **past**, and the **past participle**.

The principal parts of the verb *jog* are used in the following examples. Notice that the present participle and the past participle must have a helping verb when they are used as verbs.

Present	I **jog** two miles every day.
Present Participle	I *am* **jogging** to the lake and back.
Past	Today I **jogged** with Ashley.
Past Participle	I *have* **jogged** every day for a year.

Regular Verbs

20 A.1 A **regular verb** forms its past and past participle by adding *-ed* or *-d* to the present.

Most verbs form their past and past participle just like the verb *jog*—by adding *-ed* or *-d* to the present. These verbs are called *regular verbs*.

The following chart shows the principal parts of the regular verbs *paint, share, stop,* and *trim*. Notice that the present participle is formed by adding *-ing* to the present form and the past participle is formed by adding *-ed* or *-d* to the present form.

REGULAR VERBS			
Present	**Present Participle**	**Past**	**Past Participle**
paint	(is) painting	painted	(have) painted
share	(is) sharing	shared	(have) shared
stop	(is) stopping	stopped	(have) stopped
trim	(is) trimming	trimmed	(have) trimmed

When endings such as *-ing* and *-ed* are added to some verbs, such as *share, stop,* and *trim*, the spelling changes. If you are unsure of the spelling of a verb form, look it up.

Determining the Principal Parts of a Verb

Make four columns on your paper. Label them *Present, Present Participle, Past,* and *Past Participle.* Then, using all four columns, write the four principal parts of each of the following regular verbs.

1. ask	**6.** climb	**11.** shout	**16.** gaze
2. use	**7.** wrap	**12.** stare	**17.** call
3. hop	**8.** jump	**13.** check	**18.** talk
4. row	**9.** taste	**14.** drop	**19.** shop
5. share	**10.** weigh	**15.** cook	**20.** look

Irregular Verbs

20 A.2   An **irregular verb** does not form its past and past participle by adding *-ed* or *-d* to the present form.

The irregular verbs have been divided into six groups, according to the way they form their past and past participle. Remember, though, that the word *is* is not part of the present participle and the word *have* is not part of the past participle. They have been added to the lists of irregular verbs to remind you that all the present and past participles must have a form of one of these helping verbs when they are used as a verb in a sentence.

Group 1   These irregular verbs have the same form for the present, the past, and the past participle.

GROUP 1			
Present	**Present Participle**	**Past**	**Past Participle**
burst	(is) bursting	burst	(have) burst
cost	(is) costing	cost	(have) cost
hit	(is) hitting	hit	(have) hit
hurt	(is) hurting	hurt	(have) hurt
let	(is) letting	let	(have) let
put	(is) putting	put	(have) put
set	(is) setting	set	(have) set

Group 2 These irregular verbs have the same form for the past and past participle.

GROUP 2			
Present	**Present Participle**	**Past**	**Past Participle**
bring	(is) bringing	brought	(have) brought
buy	(is) buying	bought	(have) bought
catch	(is) catching	caught	(have) caught
feel	(is) feeling	felt	(have) felt
find	(is) finding	found	(have) found
get	(is) getting	got	(have) got or gotten
hold	(is) holding	held	(have) held
keep	(is) keeping	kept	(have) kept
lead	(is) leading	led	(have) led
leave	(is) leaving	left	(have) left
lose	(is) losing	lost	(have) lost
make	(is) making	made	(have) made
say	(is) saying	said	(have) said
sell	(is) selling	sold	(have) sold
send	(is) sending	sent	(have) sent
teach	(is) teaching	taught	(have) taught
tell	(is) telling	told	(have) told

● **Practice Your Skills**

Using the Correct Verb Form

Write the past or past participle of each verb in parentheses.

1. The left fielder has (hit) his second long, high fly ball.

2. Dee (win) the prize for most valuable player.

3. She (put) the trophy on her bookshelf at home.

4. Our coach (tell) us about good sportsmanship.

5. I (find) my lucky bat in the coach's bag.

6. Amanda has (leave) our baseball team.

7. The batter blew a bubble that (burst) all over his face.

8. The concession stand has always (sell) the players bubble gum for half price.

9. Our coach (lead) us to five straight victories.

10. Vince (keep) striking out player after player.

Group 3 These irregular verbs form their past participle by adding -*n* to the past form.

GROUP 3			
Present	**Present Participle**	**Past**	**Past Participle**
break	(is) breaking	broke	(have) broken
choose	(is) choosing	chose	(have) chosen
freeze	(is) freezing	froze	(have) frozen
speak	(is) speaking	spoke	(have) spoken
steal	(is) stealing	stole	(have) stolen

Group 4 These irregular verbs form their past participle by adding -*n* to the present.

GROUP 4			
Present	**Present Participle**	**Past**	**Past Participle**
blow	(is) blowing	blew	(have) blown
draw	(is) drawing	drew	(have) drawn
drive	(is) driving	drove	(have) driven
give	(is) giving	gave	(have) given
grow	(is) growing	grew	(have) grown
know	(is) knowing	knew	(have) known
see	(is) seeing	saw	(have) seen
take	(is) taking	took	(have) taken
throw	(is) throwing	threw	(have) thrown

Determining the Correct Verb Form

Write the correct verb form for each sentence.

1. I have just (chose, chosen) the seeds for our garden.

2. Last year I planted too early, so the seedlings (froze, frozen).

3. Tomatoes have always (grew, grown) well in this soil.

4. By the end of last season, I had (gave, given) many vegetables to our neighbors.

5. The wind (blew, blown) very hard last night!

6. It (broke, broken) some of my small tomato plants.

7. Last summer rabbits (stole, stolen) carrots from my garden.

8. They (took, taken) the carrots before they were mature.

9. I have never (saw, seen) them in the act.

10. I (knew, known) that rabbits were the culprits because of their tracks.

● **Practice Your Skills**

Using the Correct Verb Form

Write the past or past participle of each verb in parentheses.

1. Mr. Foster has (grow) vegetables for more than 15 years.

2. He (speak) to me about my rabbit problem.

3. He (drive) rabbits away from his garden by playing a portable radio in the garden at night.

4. Then he (draw) them away from his yard by putting vegetable scraps on the other side of his fence.

5. He said that many farmers have (throw) a party after ridding themselves of rabbits.

● *Connect to Writing:* **Making a Radio Announcement**

Correcting Improperly Used Verbs

Read the following radio announcement aloud to a classmate or your teacher. Correct any verb errors you find. The sentence numbers are for reference only.

(1) Have you ever drove your car on an icy driveway? **(2)** Have you ever threw salt on your sidewalk to make ice melt? **(3)** Well, those days are over. **(4)** We are introducing new Bye-Ice. **(5)** Bye-Ice will broke up ice like nothing you've ever saw! **(6)** Just sprinkle some on icy sidewalks or driveways. **(7)** It clears any cement or asphalt that has froze over. **(8)** Buy Bye-Ice today!

Group 5 These irregular verbs form their past and past participles by changing a vowel.

GROUP 5			
Present	**Present Participle**	**Past**	**Past Participle**
begin	(is) beginning	began	(have) begun
drink	(is) drinking	drank	(have) drunk
fling	(is) flinging	flung	(have) flung
ring	(is) ringing	rang	(have) rung
shrink	(is) shrinking	shrank	(have) shrunk
sing	(is) singing	sang	(have) sung
sink	(is) sinking	sank	(have) sunk
sting	(is) stinging	stung	(have) stung
swim	(is) swimming	swam	(have) swum

Group 6 These irregular verbs form the past and the past participle in other ways.

GROUP 6			
Present	**Present Participle**	**Past**	**Past Participle**
come	(is) coming	came	(have) come
do	(is) doing	did	(have) done
eat	(is) eating	ate	(have) eaten
fall	(is) falling	fell	(have) fallen
fly	(is) flying	flew	(have) flown
go	(is) going	went	(have) gone
ride	(is) riding	rode	(have) ridden
run	(is) running	ran	(have) run
tear	(is) tearing	tore	(have) torn
wear	(is) wearing	wore	(have) worn
write	(is) writing	wrote	(have) written

● **Practice Your Skills**

Determining the Correct Verb Form

Write the correct verb form for each sentence.

1. My friends and I have (went, gone) to the lake every weekend this year.

2. Juan (swam, swum) from the boat to the pier.

3. Mindy has (wrote, written) for a sample of that new sunscreen lotion.

4. I always (wear, worn) a hat to shade my eyes from the sun.

5. My hat has (fell, fallen) in the lake before.

6. Leslie has (sank, sunk) her brother's boat!

7. Cali (rode, ridden) on the inner tube behind the ski boat.

8. Our water polo match has not (began, begun) yet.

9. On the dock my cell phone (rang, rung) so loudly that everyone stared at me.

10. I dropped my phone, and it (sank, sunk) to the bottom of the lake.

● *Connect to Writing:* **Editing**

Correcting Improperly Used Verbs

Edit the following passage to correct verb errors.

(1) Each spring in Austin, Texas, the Mexican free-tail bats have came to the Congress Avenue Bridge to make their homes underneath. (2) The Austin bats are welcomed by this city, where they have eat large numbers of pesky mosquitoes. (3) Tourists have began to come to see the bats, which constitute the largest urban bat colony in the United States. (4) Many joggers have ran under the bridge to see the bats. (5) Local musicians have sang songs about the flying mammals. (6) For years the bats have teared across the darkening sky at sunset. (7) Throughout the summers, Austinites have came down to watch the spectacle. (8) In the fall, disappointed tourists find that the bat population has shrank due to the bats' migration to Mexico.

20 B The verbs *lie* and *lay, rise* and *raise,* and *sit* and *set* are often confused.

Lie and *Lay*

20 B.1 *Lie* means "to rest or recline." *Lie* is never followed by a direct object. *Lay* means "to put or set (something) down." *Lay* is usually followed by a direct object.

You can learn about direct objects on pages 592–593 and 722–723.

Present	Present Participle	Past	Past Participle
lie	(is) lying	lay	(have) lain
lay	(is) laying	laid	(have) laid

Lie	Our puppies always **lie** near the fireplace in the living room.
Lay	**Lay** the puppies' mats on the floor.

Rise and *Raise*

20 B.2 *Rise* means "to move upward" or "to get up." *Rise* is never followed by a direct object. *Raise* means "to lift (something) up," "to increase," or "to grow something." *Raise* is usually followed by a direct object.

Present	Present Participle	Past	Past Participle
rise	(is) rising	rose	(have) risen
raise	(is) raising	raised	(have) raised

Rise	**Rise** out of that bed!
Raise	**Raise** the litter of puppies carefully.

Sit and *Set*

20 B.3 *Sit* means "to rest in an upright position." *Sit* is never followed by a direct object. *Set* usually means "to put or place (something)." *Set* is usually followed by a direct object.

Present	Present Participle	Past	Past Participle
sit	(is) sitting	sat	(have) sat
set	(is) setting	set	(have) set

Sit	**Sit** down by the fire and get warm.
Set	**Set** the dogs' dishes on the kennel floor.
	(You set what? *Dishes* is the direct object.)

You can learn more about other problem verbs on pages 796–809.

Connect to Writing: Editing

Correcting Verb Usage

Write each sentence, correcting the underlined verb. If the verb in the sentence is correct, write *C*.

1. Most hens <u>lay</u> at least one egg each day.
2. They <u>set</u> on the eggs in order to keep them warm enough to hatch.
3. They <u>raise</u> from their nests to eat, but return to the eggs as soon as possible.
4. The eggs <u>lay</u> in the nest, waiting for the hen's speedy return.
5. If the eggs have been fertilized, the hen will soon be <u>rising</u> baby chicks.
6. Chicks usually are <u>risen</u> on farms.
7. Some farmers also <u>rise</u> cows.
8. Baby calves do not <u>lie</u> in a nest as baby chicks do.
9. Some ranchers will <u>sit</u> hay in a field for their cows to eat.
10. On hot days cows will <u>set</u> in the shade.

Connect to Writing: Drafting

Determining the Correct Verb Form

Write the correct form of each verb in parentheses.

(1) The magician (raised, rose) from a deep bow to the audience. (2) He (sat, set) a tall top hat on the table at the front of the stage. (3) His lovely assistant (lay, laid) a feather inside the hat on the table. (4) Then she (set, sat) a blue, silk handkerchief over the hat. (5) The magician (rose, raised) his wand over the hat three times. (6) The hat that was (lying, laying) on the table began to shake violently. (7) The top hat tumbled from the table on which it had (set, sat). (8) As the hat fell, a beautiful dove (rose, raised) from inside it. (9) The audience could not (set, sit) still at the sight of the graceful dove. (10) They (rose, raised) from their seats, applauding the magnificent magician.

Verb Tense Lesson 3

20 C The time expressed by a verb is called the **tense** of a verb.

20 C.1 The six tenses of a verb are the **present, past, future, present perfect, past perfect,** and **future perfect.**

In the following examples, the six tenses of *run* are used to express action at different times.

Present	I **run** a mile every day.
Past	I **ran** a mile yesterday.
Future	I **will run** a mile tomorrow.
Present Perfect	I **have run** a mile every day since June.
Past Perfect	I **had** not **run** that much before.
Future Perfect	I **will have run** almost 200 miles before the end of the year.

 ## Uses of Tenses

Verbs in the English language have six basic tenses: three simple tenses and three perfect tenses. All these tenses can be formed from the four principal parts of a verb and the helping verbs *have, has, had, will,* and *shall.*

Present tense is the first of the three simple tenses. It is used to express an action that is going on now. To form the present tense, use the present form (the first principal part of the verb) or add *-s* or *-es* to the present form.

Present Tense	I **watch** music videos.
	Megan **sings** along with the videos.
	Even her parents **enjoy** some of the videos.

Past tense expresses an action that has already taken place or was completed in the past. To form the past tense of a verb, add *-ed* or *-d* to the present form. To form the past of an irregular verb, check a dictionary for the past form or look for it on pages 685–689.

Past Tense	I **watched** the music awards program on television.
	Megan **sang** beautifully at the concert last night.
	Her parents **enjoyed** the concert.

Future tense is used to express an action that will take place in the future. To form the future tense, use the helping verb *shall* or *will* with the present form.

> **Future Tense**
> I **shall watch** the awards program again this year.
>
> Megan **will sing** at the concert tomorrow night.
>
> Her parents probably **will enjoy** the concert.

In formal English, *shall* is used with *I* and *we,* and *will* is used with *you, he, she, it,* or *they*. In informal speech, however, *shall* and *will* are used interchangeably with *I* and *we,* except for questions, which still use *shall*.

You can learn more about shall *and* will *on page 805.*

Present perfect tense is the first of the three perfect tenses. The present perfect tense expresses an action that was completed at some indefinite time in the past. It also expresses an action that started in the past and is still going on. To form the present perfect tense, add *has* or *have* to the past participle.

> **Present Perfect Tense**
> I **have watched** the awards program for several years now.
>
> Megan **has sung** here before now.
>
> Her parents **have enjoyed** watching her perform.

Past perfect tense expresses an action that took place before some other action in the past. To form the past perfect tense, add *had* to the past participle.

> **Past Perfect Tense**
> I **had watched** my video before I watched yours.
>
> Megan **had sung** the national anthem before the concert.
>
> Her parents **had enjoyed** listening to her rehearse.

Future perfect tense expresses an action that will take place before another future action or time. To form the future perfect tense, add *shall have* or *will have* to the past participle.

> **Future Perfect Tense**
> I **shall have watched** more than ten videos by Friday.
>
> By Saturday Megan **will have sung** at the concert.
>
> By Saturday Megan's parents **will have enjoyed** listening to all the music.

 **Verb Conjugation**

One way to see or study all the tenses of a particular verb is to look at a conjugation of that verb.

20 C.2   A **conjugation** is a list of all the singular and plural forms of a verb in its various tenses.

Irregular verbs are conjugated like regular verbs. The only variations result from the differences in the principal parts of the verbs themselves. Following is a conjugation of the irregular verb *ride,* whose four principal parts are *ride, riding, rode,* and *ridden.*

SIMPLE TENSES OF THE VERB *RIDE*	
Present	
Singular	**Plural**
I ride	we ride
you ride	you ride
he, she, it rides	they ride
Past	
Singular	**Plural**
I rode	we rode
you rode	you rode
he, she, it rode	they rode
Future	
Singular	**Plural**
I shall/will ride	we shall/will ride
you will ride	you will ride
he, she, it will ride	they will ride

PERFECT TENSES OF THE VERB *RIDE*

Present Perfect Tense

Singular	Plural
I have ridden	we have ridden
you have ridden	you have ridden
he, she, it has ridden	they have ridden

Past Perfect Tense

Singular	Plural
I had ridden	we had ridden
you had ridden	you had ridden
he, she, it had ridden	they had ridden

Future Perfect Tense

Singular	Plural
I shall/will have ridden	we shall/will have ridden
you will have ridden	you will have ridden
he, she, it will have ridden	they will have ridden

The present participle is used to conjugate only the progressive forms of a verb. You can learn more about those verbs on pages 699–701.

Since the principal parts of the verb *be* are highly irregular, the conjugation of that verb is different from other irregular verbs. Following is the conjugation of the verb *be,* whose four principal parts are *am, being, was,* and *been.*

SIMPLE TENSES OF THE VERB *BE*

Present

Singular	Plural
I am	we are
you are	you are
he, she, it is	they are

Past

Singular	Plural
I was	we were
you were	you were
he, she, it was	they were

Future

Singular	Plural
I shall/will be	we shall/will be
you will be	you will be
he, she, it will be	they will be

PERFECT TENSES OF THE VERB *BE*

Present Perfect Tense

Singular

I have been
you have been
he, she, it has been

Plural

we have been
you have been
they have been

Past Perfect Tense

Singular

I had been
you had been
he, she, it had been

Plural

we had been
you had been
they had been

Future Perfect Tense

Singular

I shall/will have been
you will have been
he, she, it will have been

Plural

we shall/will have been
you will have been
they will have been

When You Write

You have probably noticed that most folk literature is written in the past tense, as is this excerpt from "Hansel and Gretel."

> Hard by a great forest dwelt a poor wood-cutter with his wife and his two children. The boy was called Hansel and the girl Gretel. He had little to bite and to break, and once when great dearth fell on the land, he could no longer procure even daily bread.
>
> —Grimm Brothers, "Hansel and Gretel"

When you write about the literature you read, however, it is proper to write about it in the present tense. For example, if you were to write about the passage above, you might say:

> The story of "Hansel and Gretel" opens with a description of the sad state of the children's family. Hansel and Gretel live in the forest with their father and his wife. The woodcutter is no longer able to feed his family.

Choose a fairy tale that you enjoy. Write a short paragraph about the story using the present tense.

● Practice Your Skills

Identifying Verb Tense

Write the tense of each underlined verb.

1. Today popular bands <u>make</u> videos for each of their hit songs.
2. Prior to 1980, filming music videos <u>was</u> rare.
3. Before that year musicians <u>had recorded</u> only audio albums.
4. Even today, many bands <u>have</u> never <u>produced</u> any professional recordings of their music.
5. Recording an album in a music studio <u>costs</u> a great deal of money.
6. Writers <u>have composed</u> many songs for other musicians to play.
7. Most people <u>will</u> probably never <u>hear</u> these songs on the radio.
8. Famous singers and bands <u>earn</u> a considerable amount of money.
9. By age eighteen, you <u>will have seen</u> many music videos on television.
10. You <u>will</u> likely <u>watch</u> even more after that.

● Practice Your Skills

Using Tenses of the Verb Be

For each blank, write the tense of the verb *be* that is indicated in parentheses.

1. The history of the monarchy in England ▨ (present) truly interesting.
2. Many scholars ▨ (present) experts in this area of British history.
3. Many men and women ▨ (past perfect) rulers of England.
4. King John always ▨ (future) famous as the signer of the Magna Carta.
5. Lady Jane Grey ▨ (past) queen of England for only nine days.
6. Henry VIII's son Edward ▨ (past perfect) ruler before her.
7. Mary ▨ (past) queen of England before her half-sister Elizabeth I.
8. King James I ▨ (present) famous for the English version of the Bible, begun during his reign.
9. In the year 2010, Elizabeth I ▨ (future perfect) dead for over four hundred years.
10. Who ▨ (future) the next monarch of Britain?

Using Verb Tenses

Imagine that you are an Egyptian king or queen. Write a letter to your friend, who will be coming to visit you soon. Describe for her what a typical day is like at your palace. What do you do to occupy your time? What will you and your friend do when you are together? Use your imagination to make the letter seem realistic. After you have written your letter, underline seven verbs you have used. Above each verb, label its tense.

Progressive Verb Forms

20 C.3   Each of the six verb tenses has a **progressive form**. The progressive form is used to express continuing or ongoing action.

To form the progressive, add a form of the *be* verb to the present participle. Notice in the following examples that all the progressive forms end in *-ing*.

Present Progressive	I am riding.
Past Progressive	I was riding.
Future Progressive	I will (shall) be riding.
Present Perfect Progressive	I have been riding.
Past Perfect Progressive	I had been riding.
Future Perfect Progressive	I will (shall) have been riding.

The **present progressive form** shows an ongoing action that is taking place now.

I am eating very hot soup.

CHAPTER 20

Occasionally the present progressive can be used to show action in the future when the sentence contains an adverb or a phrase that indicates the future—such as *tomorrow* or *next month*.

> I **am eating** at a restaurant tomorrow night.

The **past progressive form** shows an ongoing action that took place in the past.

> I **was eating** hot French onion soup when I burned my tongue.

The **future progressive form** shows an ongoing action that will take place in the future.

> By six o'clock tonight, I **will be eating** Grandma's delicious soup.

The **present perfect progressive form** shows an ongoing action that is continuing in the present.

> I **have been eating** Grandma's soup my whole life.

The **past perfect progressive form** shows an ongoing action in the past that was interrupted by another past action.

> I **had been eating** Grandma's soup when the doorbell rang.

The **future perfect progressive form** shows a future ongoing action that will have taken place by a stated future time.

> I **will have been eating** Grandma's soup for at least 21 years by the time I graduate from college.

Identifying Progressive Verb Forms

Write the verbs in the following sentences. Then write which progressive form of the verb is used.

1. Grandma has been cooking famous dishes for more than 40 years.
2. She was serving a variety of great soups and stews before my mother's birth.
3. Until recently, her neighbors had been begging her for the recipes.
4. Now I am helping Grandma with her latest project.
5. We have been writing down all her recipes.
6. Next year a local company will be publishing her recipes in a cookbook.
7. By then Grandma will have been serving her soups for a half century.
8. We are hoping the cookbook will sell well.
9. Grandma has been dreaming of a trip to Paris.
10. My entire family will be joining her on the trip.

Connect to Writing: Studying Writer's Craft

Analyzing the Use of the Past Progressive Form

In the paragraph below from *The Liar's Club,* Mary Karr describes an incident at the beach when her sister Lecia was stung by a jellyfish. Read the paragraph and then identify the progressive verbs. Be careful not to confuse gerunds (verb forms used as nouns) with progressive verbs.

(1) The guy in the camouflage pants had dragged Lecia out of the water while I was fetching my parents. (2) He was kneeling beside her with his pink grandma gloves on when we came up. (3) Lecia sat on the sand with her legs straight out in front of her like some drugstore doll. (4) She had stopped squealing. (5) In fact, she had a glassy look, as if the leg with the man-of-war fastened to it belonged to some other girl. (6) She wasn't even crying, though every now and then she sucked in air through her teeth like she hurt. (7) The camouflaged guy with the pink gloves was trying to peel the tentacles off her, but it was clumsy work. (8) Mother was looking at Daddy and saying what should they do. (9) She said this over and over, and Daddy didn't appear to be listening.

—Mary Karr, *The Liar's Club*

→ Shifts in Tense

When you write, it is important to keep your tenses consistent. For example, if you are telling a story that took place in the past, use the past tense of verbs. If you suddenly shift to the present, you will confuse your readers.

20 C.4   Avoid unnecessary shifts in tense within a sentence or with related sentences.

Incorrect	I **opened** the front door, and something **flies** past me.
	past ··· present
Correct	I **opened** the front door, and something **flew** past me.
	past ··· past
Correct	I **open** the front door, and something **flies** past me.
	present ··· present
Incorrect	When the excitement **had passed**, I **looked** around in the hallway. I **find** a baseball on the floor.
	past perfect ··· past ··· present
Correct	When the excitement **had passed**, I **looked** around in the hallway. I **found** a baseball on the floor.
	past perfect ··· past ··· past

● Practice Your Skills

Identifying Shifts in Tense

If the sentence contains a shift in tense, change the second verb to the correct tense. If a sentence is correct, write **C**.

1. Babe Ruth was born in 1895, and his birth name is George Herman Ruth.

2. Ruth learned to play baseball in school, and a priest helps him get his first job with the Baltimore Orioles.

3. When Ruth started his professional career, he earned 600 dollars for his first season.

4. Babe Ruth began his career as a pitcher, but he is later shifted to the outfield.

5. Because he was such an amazing hitter, the manager wants him to play every game.

6. The Orioles sold him to the Boston Red Sox, who later sell him to the New York Yankees.

7. He had his best year in 1927, when he hits a season record of 60 home runs.

8. Even though he was famous and popular on the field, Babe Ruth has problems off the field.

9. He got in trouble, and in 1925 he is suspended for his behavior off the field.

10. In 1935, he joined the Boston Braves, but before the end of that season, he has quit playing the game.

11. Today baseball is still the popular sport it has been in the past.

12. Each year thousands of fans have flocked to stadiums across the country.

13. Fans always eagerly await the playoffs because the games were so intense.

14. Do you hope the team you watched last year also will have won this year?

15. Whichever team wins the World Series will have had an excellent year.

Connect to Writing: Revising

Correcting Shifts in Tense

Rewrite the following paragraph, correcting shifts in tense.

(1) Modern baseball was once named "town ball." It first become popular in the United States in the 1830s. (2) Wooden stakes are the bases, and the playing field is square. (3) A pitcher is called a feeder, and a batter was called a striker. (4) After a batter hits the ball, he ran clockwise. (5) After a fielder catches the ball, he gets a runner out by hitting him with the ball. (6) In the early days of baseball, balls are soft and are made by winding yarn around a piece of rubber.

Check Point: Mixed Practice

Rewrite the paragraph below, correcting any incorrect verb forms or shifts in tense.

(1) Mozart's father play in a string quartet. (2) One day the quartet had planned to practice at his home. (3) When the second violinist did not appear, Mozart takes his place. (4) Even though he had never saw the music before, Mozart plays it perfectly. (5) Mozart was only five years old at the time! (6) Three years later Mozart written his first complete symphony. (7) No one has ever doubted that Mozart is the greatest musical genius of his time.

In addition to tense, a verb is in either the active voice or the passive voice. Writers can use either the active voice or the passive voice to tell about an action.

20 D The **active voice** indicates that the subject is performing the action. The **passive voice** indicates that the action of the verb is being performed upon the subject.

In the following examples, the same verb is used in the active voice in one sentence and the passive voice in the other. The verb in the active voice has a direct object. The verb in the passive voice does not have a direct object.

Active Voice   Our world history class **studied** the history of Chile.
                     (*History* is the direct object.)

Passive Voice   The history of Chile **was studied** by our world
                     history class. (There is no direct object.)

You can learn more about direct objects on pages 592–593 and 722–723.

Use of the Active and Passive Voice

Only transitive verbs—verbs that take direct objects—can be used in the passive voice. When an active verb is changed to passive, the direct object of the active verb becomes the subject of the passive verb. The subject of the active verb can be used in a prepositional phrase.

                                    ┌─direct object─┐
Active Voice   Pedro de Valdivia founded **Santiago, Chile,** in 1541.
                     ┌──────subject──────┐
Passive Voice   **Santiago, Chile,** was founded by Pedro de Valdivia in 1541.

A verb in the passive voice consists of a form of the verb *be* plus a past participle.

Early explorers **were startled** by Chile's unfamiliar animals.
Llamas **are** still **used** as beasts of burden in South America.

Use the active voice as much as possible. It adds greater directness and forcefulness to your writing. However, you should use the passive voice when the doer of the action is unknown or unimportant. Also use it when you want to emphasize the receiver of the action.

CHAPTER 20

Notebooks of the early Spanish explorers **will be displayed** at our local museum. (The doer is unknown.)

Grand descriptions of llamas and other animals **were recorded** by early explorers. (Emphasis is on the receiver, *descriptions*.)

Practice Your Skills

Recognizing Active and Passive Voice

Write the verb in each sentence and label it *A* for active or *P* for passive.

1. Literature is respected by Chileans.

2. Many poems were written by Chile's most famous poet, Pablo Neruda.

3. He continued his education in Santiago.

4. His life was devoted to writing poetry.

5. Neruda also served the government of Chile as a diplomat.

6. Neruda is remembered for such poems as "General Song."

7. Many critics consider that poem to be his greatest work.

8. Pablo Neruda was awarded the prestigious Nobel Prize in 1971.

Connect to Writing: Revising

Changing Verbs to Active Voice

Rewrite the following paragraph, changing passive-voice verbs to active voice, if appropriate.

In 1814, the small South American country of Chile had been ruled by Spain for centuries. At that time, the country's freedom was being fought for by a small band of Chilean patriots. Independence was gained in 1818. Chile has been ruled by dictators at different times throughout its history. In 1989, the constitution was reformed and civil liberties were restored. In 2006, Michelle Bachelet was elected the first female president of Chile. Today, Chile is being led by a democratically elected president. By 2018, Chile will have been freed from Spanish rule for 200 years.

20 E The **mood** of a verb is the feature that shows the speaker's attitude toward the subject. Verbs have three moods: indicative, imperative, and subjunctive.

The Indicative Mood

The indicative mood is the one you will probably use most often. When you want to present facts, state opinions, or ask questions, the indicative is the mood to use.

20 E.1 The **indicative mood** is used to is make a statement of fact or to ask a question.

I **am** 5´4″ tall.

How tall **are** you?

The Imperative Mood

The imperative gives advice or orders, often with the subject *you* not stated, but understood.

20 E.2 The **imperative mood** is used to give a command or make a request. In imperative statements, the subject *you* is understood though not stated.

Wear your hat when you are outside in winter.

Please **shovel** the sidewalk before you go to school.

CHAPTER 20

Much, if not most, of your writing will use the indicative mood. Here are some examples of how it might be used in different kinds of writing.

Personal Narrative	We could not have moved to a neighborhood less like the barrio. — Ernesto Galarza, *Barrio Boy* (page 118)
Expository Writing	What makes 12-24 year olds happy?—"The Future of Happiness" (page 211)
Short Story	He came into the room to shut the windows while we were still in bed and I saw he looked ill. — Ernest Hemingway, "A Day's Wait" (page 167)

In some kinds of writing, you might be more likely to use imperative mood.

How-To Text	To conduct a successful interview with an expert, follow these steps. (pages 240–241)
Persuasive Writing	Stand up for what you believe in and vote "Yes" on the recycling initiative.

➤ The Subjunctive Mood

The present subjunctive uses the base form of the verb for all persons and numbers, including the third-person singular, but indicative verbs use the *-s* form.

20 E.3 The **subjunctive mood** is used to express ideas contrary to fact, such as a wish, doubt, or possibility; or to express a proposal, demand, or request after the word *that*.

Indicative	Tanya is the captain of the cheerleading squad.
Subjunctive	Mrs. Stein proposed that Tanya **be** the captain of the cheerleading squad.

In the present subjunctive, the verb *to be* is always *be,* as in the sentence above. The **past subjunctive** form of the verb *to be* is *were* for all persons and numbers.

Past Subjunctive	If Alex **were** smart, he'd take Lindsay's advice.

Using the Subjunctive Mood

Write the correct form of the verb in parentheses.

1. If I (was, were) you, I would try out for quarterback.
2. I wish I (was, were) qualified for the position.
3. I suggest that he (is, be) nominated for treasurer.
4. If she (was, were) older, she could get a driver's permit.
5. I wish I (was, were) old enough to drive.

● Practice Your Skills

Using the Subjunctive Mood

Write the correct form of the verb in parentheses.

1. Chico brags as if he (was, were) king of the world!
2. If Angelo (was, were) here, he'd set him straight.
3. Tell the commander he (be, is) the one I want.
4. After hiking, my knee felt as if it (was, were) twisted.
5. The leaves covering the pond (be, are) like a carpet.
6. Coach Hill asked that the team (are, be) packed to board the train.
7. If Ansel requested that he (be, is) the captain, we'll agree to that.
8. I wish I (was, were) taller than my younger sister.
9. A deep pond (be, is) a good fishing hole.
10. If wishes (was, were) snowflakes, the blizzard would never end.

● *Connect to Writing:* Revising

Using Subjunctive and Indicative Mood in Sentences

Write each sentence using either the subjunctive or the indicative mood of the verb form. Then write *S* for *subjunctive* or *I* for *indicative*.

1. Yellowstone National Park (be) a sacred place to certain tribes.
2. The young brave wished he (be) old enough to join the men.
3. If I (be) older, I could ride my pony there.
4. Little Flower demanded that she (be) allowed to chant with the boys.
5. She (be) sure that no snakes are on the trail.

CHAPTER 20

Assess Your Learning

Using the Correct Verb Form

Write the past or past participle form of each verb in parentheses.

1. Ten minutes after the downpour, the sun (come) out.

2. How long have you (know) about the party?

3. The sun (rise) at 5:36 yesterday.

4. Lake Erie has never (freeze) over completely.

5. My sister has (sing) twice on television.

6. Have you (write) your history report yet?

7. Who (write) the screenplay for that movie?

8. The telephone hasn't (ring) all day.

9. You should have (go) to the dance last night.

10. Dana has already (take) those books back to the library.

11. Before World War II, the United States had (give) the Philippines a guarantee of independence.

12. I should have (do) my homework earlier.

13. Until 1875, no one had ever successfully (swim) the English Channel.

14. My wallet hadn't been (steal) after all.

15. Who (choose) brown as the color for this room?

16. Tom (fall) off his skateboard yesterday, but fortunately he was wearing a helmet.

17. Have you ever (wear) those hiking boots on a hike of more than two miles?

18. Who (draw) that picture of Mr. Turner's barn?

19. Lately I have (grow) more confident using the laptop computer.

20. Waiting on the windy corner, we nearly (freeze).

Understanding Tenses

Write the tense of each underlined verb.

1. I <u>am going</u> to the library.
2. Lenny <u>has seen</u> Sarah somewhere before.
3. On Monday Mrs. Saunders <u>will announce</u> the names of the new class officers.
4. Tim <u>was</u> enthusiastic about the project.
5. I <u>have been practicing</u> for my recital every night for a month.
6. Next year will be the third year he <u>will have played</u> for the soccer team.
7. Laura <u>discovered</u> that she <u>had left</u> the tickets at home.
8. Pilar <u>knows</u> that we <u>will be working</u> together on the dance committee.
9. Marie <u>has been</u> happy ever since she <u>won</u> the CD player.
10. Susan and Greg <u>were riding</u> the bus when they first <u>met</u>.

Writing Sentences

Write ten sentences that follow the directions below. Write about a pet or a topic of your choice.

Write a sentence that . . .

1. includes the past tense of *choose*.
2. includes the past perfect tense of *become*.
3. includes the future tense of *take*.
4. includes the present perfect tense of *lie*.
5. includes the past tense of *lay*.
6. includes the present progressive tense of *rise*.
7. includes the future progressive tense of *set*.
8. includes the present tense of *be*.
9. includes any verb in the passive voice.
10. includes any verb in the subjunctive mood.

Using Verbs: Posttest

Directions

Read the passage and choose the word or group of words that belongs in each underlined space. Write the letter of the correct answer.

Yesterday my sister and I __(1)__ the movie *A Wild Ride*. The story __(2)__ on an actual event. Joe, the main character, __(3)__ money from his boss for years until he was caught. My sister __(4)__ the movie three times already. She probably __(5)__ to the same movie again! She __(6)__ to one movie a week since last June. My favorite scene __(7)__ at the end of the movie. Three police officers __(8)__ Joe in a dense forest after he had made his break from prison. He __(9)__ to escape through a secret tunnel before they made their move. Since yesterday I __(10)__ to tell everyone I know how the movie ends.

1. A see
   B saw
   C will see
   D will be seeing

2. A is basing
   B was basing
   C will be based
   D is based

3. A steals
   B is stealing
   C had been stealing
   D will steal

4. A sees
   B will see
   C has been seeing
   D has seen

5. A goes
   B will go
   C will have been going
   D went

6. A is going
   B has gone
   C will go
   D will be going

7. A has happened
   B will have happened
   C happened
   D is happening

8. A will surround
   B will have surrounded
   C surrounded
   D will be surrounding

9. A was hoping
   B hopes
   C will hope
   D is hoping

10. A will want
   B have been wanting
   C am wanting
   D will have been wanting

Writer's Corner

Snapshot

20 A   The **principal parts of a verb** are the present, the present participle, the past, and the past participle. (pages 684–690)

20 B   *Lie* and *lay*, *rise* and *raise*, **and** *sit* and *set* **are especially tricky** because their principle parts are often confused. (pages 691–692)

20 C   The time expressed by a verb is called the **tense** of a verb. (pages 693–703)

20 D   The **active voice** indicates that the subject is performing the action. (pages 704–705) The **passive voice** indicates that the action of the verb is being performed upon the subject. (pages 704–705)

20 E   The **mood** of a verb—indicative, imperative, or subjunctive—shows the manner of the action. (pages 706–708)

Power Rules

Use mainstream **past tense verb forms**. (pages 684–703)

Before Editing	**After Editing**
A recent study *show* that video games had a positive effect.	A recent study *showed* that video games had a positive effect.
The debate could have *went* on longer.	The debate could have *gone* on longer.

Use **verbs that agree with the subject**. (pages 750–767)

Before Editing	**After Editing**
A newborn baby *don't* even know how to smile.	A newborn baby *doesn't* even know how to smile.
One of the monkeys *were* always up to something.	One of the monkeys *was* always up to something.

Editing Checklist

Use this checklist when editing your writing.

✓ Did I use the correct verb forms of both regular and irregular verbs?
(See pages 684–690.)
✓ Did I avoid shifts in tense? (See pages 702–703.)
✓ Did I use the progressive verb forms correctly? (See pages 699–701.)
✓ Did I use the active voice to add power? (See pages 704–705.)
✓ Did I use the subjunctive mood instead of the indicative or imperative when
appropriate? (See pages 706–708.)

Use the Power

Communicate precisely the time of an action and whether it is completed or ongoing by using the appropriate principle part of a verb.

Communicate certainty or doubt by using the appropriate mood of a verb.

Communicate action with the appropriate voice of a verb. Strengthen your writing by using the **active voice** whenever possible. The active voice shows the subject engaged in action and breathes life into a text. Avoid the passive voice, which robs the subject of its power to act and instead shows the subject being acted upon. Look back at a recent composition, and be sure you have used verbs that communicate just what you want them to.

Using Pronouns

Why is it important to avoid unclear, missing, or confusing pronoun references?

Using Pronouns: Pretest 1

The following cover letter is a draft intended for a prospective employer. The draft contains several pronoun errors. The first error is corrected. How would you revise the letter so that all pronouns are used correctly?

To who it may concern:

My friend and me read your classified advertisement in Sunday's newspaper. It says that your looking for two high school girls to work at you day-care center. Clara and me have always wanted to work with children. She has two brothers. As for myself, I have ten cousins.

Please read the attached resumés and call her or I if you think the qualifications needed can be found in she and I. Although we have never worked in a preschool, her and me would be really good at that. We have references. Them numbers are on the resumé of myself. We would like to one day find us working in your day-care center.

Sincerely,

Tiffany Washington and Clara Jones

Using Pronouns: Pretest 2

Directions

Read the passage and choose the pronoun that belongs in each underlined space. Write the letter of the correct answer.

The students in Ms. Key's class knew that __(1)__ would have to study hard for the test. Jan and Marisa asked Jeff, __(2)__ they always called for help, to study with __(3)__. __(4)__ all agreed to meet at Jan's house that afternoon. Both Marisa and Jeff brought __(5)__ review notes. Marisa gave __(6)__ to Jan to look over. Jan, __(7)__ notes were messy, was relieved that her friend took better notes. Jan was also glad to study with Jeff, __(8)__ knew more about solving equations than __(9)__. However, neither Jeff nor Marisa could match __(10)__ skill at graphing.

CHAPTER 21

1. A they
   B it
   C them
   D he

2. A he
   B whose
   C whom
   D who

3. A they
   B them
   C she
   D her

4. A He
   B She
   C They
   D Them

5. A them
   B their
   C her
   D our

6. A her
   B his
   C them
   D hers

7. A whose
   B who
   C whom
   D whomever

8. A him
   B he
   C who
   D she

9. A her
   B hers
   C she
   D him

10. A they
   B their
   C her
   D hers

21 A   **Case is the form of a noun or a pronoun that indicates its use in a sentence.**

You avoid using the same nouns over and over again by using pronouns instead of nouns. *She* and *her* are personal pronouns. In the first example below, these pronouns take the place of *Tracy*. In the second example, *his* and *him* are personal pronouns that take the place of *Durrell*.

> Tracy said **she** was going to teach **her** little sister how to ride a bicycle.
>
> Durrell brought **his** cello with **him** to the party.

All nouns and pronouns have a case. There are three cases: the **nominative case,** the **objective case,** and the **possessive case.** Unlike nouns, personal pronouns usually change form for each of the three cases.

NOMINATIVE CASE	
(Used for subjects and predicate nominatives)	
Singular	I, you, he, she, it
Plural	we, you, they
OBJECTIVE CASE	
(Used for direct objects, indirect objects, and the objects of a preposition)	
Singular	me, you, him, her, it
Plural	us, you, them
POSSESSIVE CASE	
(Used to show ownership or possession)	
Singular	my, mine, your, yours, his, her, hers, its
Plural	our, ours, your, yours, their, theirs

● **Practice Your Skills**

Determining Case

Write the pronouns in each sentence. Then identify the case of each pronoun, using *N* for nominative, *O* for objective, and *P* for possessive.

1. Why wasn't he invited to Anila's party?

2. I hope Anila left me directions to her house.

3. My sister will pick us up after Anila's party.

4. Did my brother go with them to the party?

5. Our friends like to go to your parties rather than ours.

6. You should speak to them about the awful music they play.

7. She knew that the best present was mine.

8. Are the decorations yours or theirs?

9. That party was more successful than our other parties have been.

10. When the party ended, we thanked them for coming.

Nominative Case

The personal pronouns in the nominative, or **subjective,** case are *I, you, he, she, it, we,* and *they.*

21 A.1 The **nominative case** is used for subjects and predicate nominatives.

Pronouns Used as Subjects

Pronoun subjects are always in the nominative case.

Subjects   If **they** are late, **we** will keep the food warm for at least an hour.

She and **I** are chopping the vegetables.

Choosing the right case for a single subject does not usually present any problem. Errors occur more often, however, when the subject is compound. There is a test that will help you check your choice.

Eric and (she, her) are cooking dinner tonight for 27 guests.

To find the correct answer, say each choice separately as if it were a single subject.

> **She** is cooking dinner tonight for 27 guests.
>
> **Her** is cooking dinner tonight for 27 guests.

Separating the choices makes it easier to see and hear which pronoun is correct. The nominative case *she* is the correct form to use.

> Eric and **she** are cooking dinner tonight for 27 guests.

You can learn more about compound subjects on pages 758–760.

You can also use this test when both parts of a compound subject are pronouns.

> (He, Him) and (she, her) planned the menu.
>
> (She, Her) and (I, me) enjoyed the food.

Try each choice alone as the subject of the sentence.

> **He** planned the menu.
>
> **Him** planned the menu.
>
> **She** planned the menu.
>
> **Her** planned the menu.
>
> **She** enjoyed the food.
>
> **Her** enjoyed the food.
>
> **I** enjoyed the food.
>
> **Me** enjoyed the food.

You can see that the correct choices are *he* and *she* in the first sentence, and *she* and *I* in the second.

> **He** and **she** planned the menu.
>
> **She** and **I** enjoyed the food.

A pronoun that is used as a subject can also have a noun appositive. An **appositive** is a word that comes right after the pronoun and identifies or renames it. The appositive in each of the following sentences is underlined.

We <u>siblings</u> worked together to cook dinner.

I, <u>the assistant chef,</u> worked hard.

An appositive, however, will never affect the case of a pronoun. In fact, you can check whether you have used the correct pronoun by dropping the appositive.

We worked together to cook dinner.

I worked hard.

You can learn more about appositives on pages 617–618.

Practice Your Skills

Using Nominative Pronouns as Subjects

Write the correct form of the pronoun in parentheses.

1. My brother Chris and (I, me) love to cook together.

2. (Him, He) can cook great Italian specialties.

3. (They, Them) are his most delicious dishes.

4. When our mom works late, (us, we) prepare the meals.

5. When (he, him) cooks, our neighbor always calls.

6. (Her, She) can smell Chris's lasagna baking.

7. (We, Us) all learned how to cook from our mom.

8. (She, Her) felt that both boys and girls should have this skill.

9. When (we, us) were tall enough to reach the counter, (her, she) put us to work in the kitchen.

10. Before my little brother could walk, (he, him) was tossing salads.

11. Before my dad met my mom, (him, he) had never touched a stove.

12. When Mom married Dad, (her, she) taught him to cook better too.

13. (She, Her) and (he, him) like to cook spicy dishes.

14. (Us, We) sisters are all good cooks.

Connect to Speaking and Listening: Language Acquisition

Using and Identifying Case

To demonstrate your understanding of the English terms *nominative case, objective case,* and *possessive case,* define each of them with a partner. Then take turns creating sentences such as "You and I have something in common" or "His mother and my mother are friends with them." After you say a sentence, your partner must identify all pronouns, stating whether they are nominative, objective, or possessive.

Pronouns Used as Predicate Nominatives

21 A.2 A **predicate nominative** is a noun or a pronoun that follows a linking verb and identifies or renames the subject. Pronouns used as predicate nominatives are always in the nominative case.

Predicate Nominative	The best speller on the team was **he.**
	(speller = he)
	The finalists were **she** and Greg.
	(finalists = she and Greg)

Sometimes using a pronoun as a predicate nominative sounds awkward even though the pronoun is correct. When you write, you can avoid awkwardness if you reword a sentence, making the predicate nominative the subject.

Awkward	The team captain last year was **she.**
	The last person to join the team was **he.**
Natural	**She** was the team captain last year.
	He was the last person to join the team.

When You Speak and Write

In everyday conversation, people do not always use the nominative case for predicate nominatives. It is common to hear someone say, "It's *me*" instead of "It is *I*," or "That's *him*" instead of "That is *he*." While this usage is common in conversation, you should avoid it when you write.

You can find a list of linking verbs on pages 527–528 and 582. You can find out more about predicate nominatives on pages 595–596.

● Practice Your Skills

Pronouns as Predicate Nominatives

Write the correct form of the pronoun in parentheses.

1. Action movies are great. My favorite genre are (they, them).

2. My favorite actor in these movies is (he, him).

3. By far the most exciting films are (they, them).

4. When a new action movie is showing, the first people in line are (us, we).

5. Two other big fans of these movies are Kassidy and (he, him).

6. The best actress to watch is (her, she).

7. The finest director of action movies is (he, him).

8. The most realistic movies of the genre are (they, them).

Practice Your Skills

Supplying Pronouns in the Nominative Case

Complete each sentence by writing an appropriate pronoun in the nominative case.

1. We won't know who our class officers are until ___ have voted.

2. The only people voting will be ___ students in the ninth grade.

3. The person who ran for class president was ___.

4. ___ had to wait in line to vote.

5. The two most popular candidates for vice president were Fallon and ___.

6. Neither Antoine nor ___ ran for an office.

7. No one can predict whether ___ will be elected.

8. If ___ are patient, we will know the answer soon.

9. The votes have been counted, and the new class president is ___.

10. ___ students are all glad that we voted.

Connect to Writing: Editing

Using Nominative Case Pronouns

Rewrite the sentences, correcting any errors in pronoun usage. If the sentence is correct, write **C**.

1. Us girls decided to start a neighborhood swim team.

2. Our weakest swimmer is either Sammi or she.

3. We will practice hard before the first meet.

4. The best teams in the league are that group of boys and them.

5. The other teams and us will work hard to win the tournament.

Connect to Writing: Supportive Letter

Using Nominative Case Pronouns

Your friend has just suffered a great disappointment. Perhaps he or she just lost an election or an important game. Write a letter to your friend, giving him or her support by sharing a similar experience that you have had or read about. Include at least four nominative pronouns in the letter. Use two of these pronouns as predicate nominatives. After you write, underline all of the nominative pronouns you have used.

Objective Case

The **objective case** is used for direct objects, indirect objects, and objects of a preposition. The table below shows the personal pronouns that are object pronouns.

OBJECT PRONOUNS		
	Singular	Plural
First Person	me	us
Second Person	you	you
Third Person	him, her, it	them

21 A.3 **Object pronouns** are used as direct objects, indirect objects, and objects of prepositions.

Pronouns Used as Direct and Indirect Objects

A direct object answers the question *What?* or *Whom?* after an action verb. If a sentence has a direct object, it also can have an indirect object. An indirect object answers the questions *To* or *For whom?* or *To* or *For what?*

> **Direct Object**   Carlos will join **us** when he returns.
> (Carlos will join whom? *Us* is the direct object.)
> Mom took **him** to the dentist.
>
> **Indirect Object**   Dr. Garcia showed **him** X-rays of his teeth.
> (*X-rays* is the direct object. Dr. Garcia showed the X-rays to whom? *Him* is the indirect object.)

Use the same test you used for compound subjects to find the correct pronoun in a compound direct or indirect object.

> Please take Carlos and (he, him) with you.
> Please take **he** with you.
> Please take **him** with you.

Once more, it is easy to both see and hear that the objective case pronoun *him* is correct.

Pronouns in the objective case can also have appositives.

> Dr. Garcia's explanations really helped **us** patients.

● **Practice Your Skills**

Using Pronouns as Direct and Indirect Objects

Write the correct form of the pronoun in parentheses.

1. Mom told (us, we) that it was time for our dental appointments.
2. Dr. Garcia, our dentist, always tells (I, me) jokes.
3. It helps (me, I) to relax.
4. He gives (we, us) new toothbrushes and dental floss.
5. Dr. Garcia also offers my brother and (I, me) advice about cavity prevention.
6. My dad knew (him, he) in college.
7. My mother met (they, them) both when she visited their college campus.
8. Mom and Dad always tell (us, we) stories about Dr. Garcia in college.
9. My brother Carlos, who wants to be a dentist, especially admires (he, him).
10. Dr. Garcia lets Carlos watch (him, he) as he works.

Pronouns Used as Objects of Prepositions

21 A.4 An **object of a preposition** is always a part of a prepositional phrase. A pronoun used as the object of a preposition is in the objective case.

> **Objects of Prepositions**
>
> That song was written for Pat and **me.**
> (*For Pat and me* is a prepositional phrase. *Pat* and *me* are the objects of the preposition *for.*)
> Singers like **her** are very rare.

If an object of a preposition is compound, use the same test by saying each pronoun separately. The correct form to use in the sentence below is *me.*

> Isn't Marta going with Jeff and (I, me) to the concert?
> Isn't Marta going with **I** to the concert?
> Isn't Marta going with **me** to the concert?

You can find a list of commonly used prepositions on pages 560–561.

A common mistake occurs with the preposition *between*. In trying to sound formal or correct, people will often use nominative-case pronouns after *between*. However, all pronouns used as objects of a preposition should be in the objective case. In this case, the more common-sounding expression is correct.

Incorrect	The agreement is between **he** and **I**.
Correct	The agreement is between **him** and **me**.

Look over a recent composition to be sure you have used all pronouns correctly, particularly any object of a preposition.

● **Practice Your Skills**

Using Pronouns as Objects of Prepositions

Write the correct form of the pronoun in parentheses.

1. For help, there is no one like Madison or (he, him).

2. They have been very helpful to my friends and (I, me).

3. Madison and Will are leaders in our class and role models for (we, us).

4. Our class sponsors divide many of the class's duties between (they, them).

5. People like (she, her) are fun to have around.

6. Madison comes to every game and gives her support to Will and (I, me).

7. The rest of the team also looks to (she, her) for support.

8. No other freshman can come close to (she, her) in school spirit.

9. Let's do something to recognize the efforts of (he, him) and (she, her).

10. When we are seniors, I hope that scholarships will be presented to (they, them).

● **Practice Your Skills**

Supplying Pronouns in the Objective Case

Complete each sentence by writing an appropriate pronoun in the objective case. (Do not use *you* or *it*.) Then indicate how each pronoun is used by writing *D* for direct object, *I* for indirect object, or *O* for object of the preposition.

1. Aunt Laura gave ____ good advice.

2. Her point of view always comes as a big surprise to ____.

3. Uncle Fred usually agrees with ____.

4. After our visit he drove ____ back home.

5. He took ____ with us.

6. Did we send ____ a thank-you note for their hospitality?

7. Aunt Laura always gives ____ lots of attention.

8. Our family respects ____ immensely.

9. We wanted to do something special for ____.

10. He and I are throwing ____ a big birthday party next month.

● *Connect to Writing:* **Drafting**

Writing Sentences

Write ten sentences that use the expressions correctly.

1. Corey and I

2. us students

3. him and me

4. she and Jan

5. Don and he

6. you and me

7. we players

8. Mom, Dad, and I

9. she and I

10. Alex and her

☑ *Check Point:* **Mixed Practice**

Write each pronoun that is in the wrong case. Then write each pronoun correctly. If a sentence is correct, write **C**.

1. Without you and I, the trip would have been boring.

2. We told Aaron and she funny stories as we drove.

3. During that trip, we friends visited the city's boardwalk.

4. You and me rode the big, wooden roller coaster.

5. We bought saltwater taffy and had some shipped to our cousins and they.

6. Aaron invited we three for a picnic on the beach.

7. Our group ate a picnic lunch packed by Julie and he.

8. We shared a bag of chips among Aaron, you, and me.

Possessive Case

The **possessive case** is used to show ownership or possession.

The personal pronouns in the possessive case are *my, mine, your, yours, his, her, hers, its, our, ours, their,* and *theirs.* Some possessive pronouns can be used to show possession before a noun or a gerund. Others can be used by themselves.

Before a Noun	Kylie shared **her** latest set of poems with Alyssa.
Before a Gerund	Ryan takes **his** writing seriously.
By Themselves	This pencil could be **mine.**

Personal possessive pronouns are not written with an apostrophe. Sometimes an apostrophe is incorrectly included because possessive nouns are written with an apostrophe.

Possessive Noun	**Alyssa's** journal is on the table.
Possessive Pronoun	The notebook is **hers.** (not her's)

Do not confuse a contraction with a possessive pronoun. *Its, your, their,* and *theirs* are possessive pronouns. *It's, you're, they're,* and *there's* are contractions.

Possessive Pronoun	I like the story because of **its** characters.
Contraction	**It's** (It is) time to share our ideas.

● *Connect to Writing:* **Basic Vocabulary**

Using the Possessive Case

It is important that you understand the possessive case and how to use it when you are writing in English. Look over the examples above carefully. Then, write six sentences, each of which contains one of the following:

• a personal pronoun before a noun

• a personal pronoun before a gerund

• a possessive noun

• a possessive pronoun

Read your sentences to a partner, but leave out the pronoun or the noun, and ask your partner to supply the missing word, for example: "If the book belongs to Peter, then it is —— book."

When you use an apostrophe with a pronoun, check whether you have written a contraction or a possessive pronoun. You can do this by removing the apostrophe and adding the letter that it replaced back into the word. Then read the sentence to see if the contraction was used properly or if you really needed to use a possessive pronoun.

Correct	You're such a good writer. (You are such a good writer.)
Incorrect	I am you're writing partner.
	("I am you are writing partner" does not make sense.)
Correct	It's his turn to walk the dogs. (It is his turn to walk the dogs.)
Incorrect	We cannot find it's leash.
	("We cannot find it is leash" does not make sense.)

Reread a recent essay and apply the suggestion above to be sure you have used the possessive pronouns you intended to use and not contractions.

● **Practice Your Skills**

Possessive Pronoun or Contraction?

Read the following sentences aloud. Then write the correct word in parentheses.

1. (Its, It's) a beautiful poem.

2. Are all of (your, you're) poems like this one?

3. (Your, You're) going to keep writing.

4. Is (your, you're) story finished?

5. When did you send (your, you're) manuscript to them?

6. Are (their, they're) poems well written?

7. (Your, You're) article is due tomorrow.

8. That box of old writings is (hers, her's).

9. Joining the writers' group has improved (me, my) writing.

10. The poem that Ryan wrote doesn't fit (its, it's) title.

● **Practice Your Skills**

Supplying Pronouns in All Cases

Complete the sentences by writing appropriate pronouns. (Do not use *you* or *it*.)

1. Read ___ and ___ your poem.

2. ___ listened to ___ and Melissa read.

3. ___ helped ___ with new ideas for a story.

4. ___ thanked Ryan and ___.

5. Latice showed ___ and ___ the new literary magazine.

6. ___ was writing with Moira and ___.

7. ___ went to the library with ___ for books about poets and playwrights.

● *Connect to Writing:* Drafting

Using Possessive Pronouns and Contractions

Write sentences using the following words correctly.

1. your

2. they're

3. its

4. ours

5. their

6. it's

7. hers

8. we're

✓ *Check Point:* Mixed Practice

Write the correct word in parentheses.

1. Both wild and domesticated animals are very protective of (their, they're) young.

2. You should cautiously approach (your, you're) pet if (she, her) is a new parent.

3. (She, Her) is likely to act differently toward you and (your, you're) family.

4. You should give (she, her) a comfortable, secluded place to care for (her, hers) newborns.

5. A wild animal is even more likely to attack humans who come near (its, it's) young.

6. Each spring hikers are mauled by female bears protecting (their, they're) cubs.

7. The bear is just following (she, her) natural instincts.

8. The one to blame for such attacks is not (she, her).

9. (We, Us) hikers endanger ourselves when (we, us) come between a cub and (its, it's) mother.

10. Careful hikers make lots of noise to warn bears of (their, they're) presence when (they, them) walk through the wilderness.

Pronoun Problems Lesson 2

Pronoun choice can be a problem. Should you say, "Who is calling?" or "Whom is calling?" Should you say, "Is Jim taller than I?" or "Is Jim taller than me?"

21 B Common pronoun problems include the misuse of *who* and *whom* and incomplete comparisons.

Who or *Whom*?

21 B.1 The correct case of *who* is determined by how the pronoun is used in a question or a clause.

Who is a pronoun that changes its form depending on how it is used in a sentence.

WHO OR WHOM?	
Nominative Case	who, whoever
Objective Case	whom, whomever
Possessive Case	whose

Who and its related pronouns are used in questions and in subordinate clauses.

In Questions

21 B.2 Forms of *who* are often used in questions. Use *who* when the pronoun is used as a subject. Use *whom* when the pronoun is used as a direct object or an object of the preposition.

Nominative Case   **Who** planned the school dance? (subject)

Objective Case   **Whom** did you call for that information?
(direct object)

To whom is the invitation addressed?
(object of the preposition *to*)

When deciding which form to use, turn a question around to its natural order.

Question   **Whom** did you ask?

Natural Order   You did ask **whom.**

When You Speak and Write

While *whom* is not used as much today in everyday speaking and writing, it is important to know its proper use. When you write formal papers and letters or prepare speeches and debates, be sure to use *whom* instead of *who* whenever appropriate.

● **Practice Your Skills**

Using Forms of **Who** in Questions

Write the correct form of the pronoun in parentheses. Then indicate how each pronoun is used by writing **S** for subject, **D** for direct object, and **O** for object of the preposition.

1. (Who, Whom) is on the telephone?

2. (Who, Whom) told you that Ashley was going with me to the dance?

3. With (who, whom) did Paige say she was going?

4. (Who, Whom) will play the music at the dance?

5. From (who, whom) did you get an invitation to the dance?

6. (Who, Whom) sent you that note about the dance?

7. (Who, Whom) will you take to the dance?

8. (Who, Whom) is the best dancer in the ninth grade?

9. (Who, Whom) is designing the decorations?

10. With (who, whom) did you go to the dance last year?

In Clauses

Forms of *who* can be used in both adjectival clauses and noun clauses.

21 B.3   The form of *who* you use depends on how the pronoun is used within the clause. Use *who* when the pronoun is used as the subject of the clause. Use *whom* when the pronoun is used as a direct object or an object of the preposition in the clause.

The following examples show how *who* and *whom* are used in adjectival clauses.

Nominative Case   Dr. Rush is the woman **who will serve as marshal of the parade.**
(*Who* is the subject of *will serve.*)

Objective Case   She is the woman **whom you met yesterday.**
(You met whom yesterday? *Whom* is the direct object of *met.*)

Have you met Mr. Keats, **from whom we got our idea for the freshman float?**
(We got our idea from whom? *Whom* is the object of the preposition *from.*)

The following examples show how forms of *who* are used in noun clauses.

Nominative Case   The prize winners will be **whoever builds the best float.**
(The entire noun clause is the predicate nominative of the sentence. *Whoever* is the subject of the noun clause.)

Do you know **who organizes the homecoming parade?**
(The entire noun clause is the direct object of the sentence. *Who* is the subject of the noun clause).

Objective Case   I don't know **from whom she got the idea.**
(The entire noun clause is the direct object. *Whom* is the object of the preposition in the noun clause.)

Invite **whomever you want to the homecoming game.**
(The entire noun clause is the direct object of the sentence. *Whomever* is the direct object of *want.*)

Using Forms of Who in Clauses

Write the correct form of the pronoun in parentheses. Then, using the following abbreviations, write how each pronoun is used in the clause.

subject = **subj.**   object of the preposition = **o.p.**

direct object = **d.o.**

1. Bailey doesn't know (who, whom) will lead the parade.
2. The organizers of the parade accept (whoever, whomever) they wish.
3. They couldn't tell to (who, whom) the entry form belonged.
4. (Whoever, Whomever) is named homecoming queen rides on the float.
5. The person (who, whom) the most students vote for will win the title.
6. Does Shelly know (who, whom) will judge the competition for best float?
7. I spoke with the committee (who, whom) organized the parade.
8. They want all (who, whom) are participating to line up by three o'clock.
9. The people to (who, whom) I spoke said that the parade route changed.
10. The parade will be led by two drum majors (who, whom) will be dressed in gold and white.

Connect to Writing: Drafting

Writing Sentences Using Forms of Who

Write a sentence using the correct form of *who* or *whom* in the indicated construction.

1. as the object of a preposition
2. as the subject of a sentence
3. as the predicate nominative in a sentence
4. as the direct object of the verb in a noun clause
5. as the subject in an adjectival clause

Connect to Writing: Essay

Writing Sentences Using Forms of Who

Your history teacher has asked you to write a 150-word essay titled "The Greatest Person Who Ever Lived." Choose a person—living or dead, famous or obscure—who you feel deserves this designation. Write a short essay for your teacher, explaining why you feel that this person is important. As you write, use the following forms of *who* correctly at least once: *who, whom, whoever, whomever.*

✔ Check Point: Mixed Practice

Write the correct form of the pronoun in parentheses.

1. (Who, Whom) was the first president of the United States?
2. There are few Americans (who, whom) could not answer that question.
3. George Washington, (who, whom) is known as "the father of his country," was the first president.
4. He is a person about (who, whom) much history has been written.
5. Even in his own day, Washington did not fail to impress (whoever, whomever) he met.
6. Legend tells us it was George Washington (who, whom) could not lie to his father about chopping down a cherry tree.
7. History tells us that Washington led the Continental Army, against (who, whom) the British and their loyalists fought.
8. (Who, Whom) was the first vice president of the United States?
9. Few Americans know to (who, whom) this distinction belongs.
10. John Adams, (who, whom) was America's second president, was the nation's first vice president.

Pronouns in Comparisons

Over the years, writers have introduced shortcuts into the language. One such shortcut is an elliptical clause. An **elliptical clause** is a subordinate clause in which words are omitted but are understood to be there. Elliptical clauses begin with *than* or *as.*

Delisa takes more classes **than I.**

Noah takes as many classes **as she.**

21 B.4   In an **elliptical clause,** use the form of the pronoun you would use if the clause were completed.

In the following examples, both expressions in bold type are elliptical clauses. Both are also correct because they have two different meanings.

Delisa studies with us more **than he.**

Delisa studies with us more **than him.**

He is correct in the first example because it is used as the subject of the elliptical clause.

> Delisa studies with us more **than he (does).**

Him is correct in the second example because it is used as an object of a preposition.

> Delisa studies with us more **than she studies with him.**

Because the meaning of a sentence with an elliptical clause sometimes depends upon the case of a pronoun, be careful to choose the correct case. One way to do this is to complete the elliptical clause mentally before you say it or write it. Then choose the form of the pronoun that expresses the meaning you want.

> Noah helps her as much as (I, me).
>
> Noah helps her as much **as *I* (do).**
>
> Noah helps her as much **as he helps *me*.**

In the previous example, decide which meaning you want. Then choose either *I* or *me*.

● Practice Your Skills

Completing Elliptical Clauses

Read the sentence aloud, completing the elliptical clause.

1. Olivia is a better student than he ___.
2. She spends more time on her homework than I ___.
3. Jesse knows her better than we ___.
4. They study together more than we ___.
5. Emma and Jake make better grades than we ___.
6. We work just as hard as they ___.
7. Jadyn likes math better than you ___.
8. Clare and Leonardo have won just as many awards as I ___.

● Practice Your Skills

Using Pronouns in Elliptical Clauses

Write each sentence, completing the elliptical clause. Then write the correct form of the pronoun in parentheses.

1. Ben spends more time at the library and in the computer lab than (I, me).
2. Our teacher didn't review the test with us as much as (they, them).
3. I studied longer and harder than (they, them).

4. The topic we covered sounds more exciting to them than (we, us).

5. Did you answer as many questions on the math test as (they, them)?

6. No one was more prepared than (I, me) for the last history quiz.

7. The professor from the university talked to us longer than (them, they).

8. That grade means more to Noah than (she, her).

9. Everyone should be as studious as (he, him).

10. I think Jesse is a better test taker than (I, me).

● *Connect to Writing:* Drafting

Writing Sentences with Elliptical Clauses

Write sentences that follow the instructions. Each sentence should contain an elliptical clause.

1. Compare a history class with a math class.

2. Compare two basketball players.

3. Compare two sports.

4. Compare two foods.

5. Compare two television shows.

6. Compare two Hollywood superstars.

7. Compare a summer vacation you had with an ideal winter vacation.

8. Compare your two favorite bands.

9. Compare two kinds of animals as pets.

10. Compare board games with video games.

● *Connect to Writing:* Paragraph of Comparison

Using Elliptical Clauses

Your parents cannot understand why you like the music you do. They constantly ask you to turn down the volume on your stereo. Write a paragraph for your parents in which you compare and contrast your music to the music of their generation. Be sure to use elliptical clauses that begin with *than* or *as* to explain the differences and similarities between your music and that of your parents.

In Lesson 1 you learned that a pronoun takes the place of a noun. That noun is called the pronoun's **antecedent.**

21 C   A pronoun must agree in **number** and **gender** with its antecedent.

In the first example below, *Duke Ellington* is the antecedent of *his*. In the second example, *orchestra* is the antecedent of *its*.

Duke Ellington left **his** mark on American music.

Ellington's **orchestra** had **its** own sound.

21 C.1   **Number** is the term used to indicate whether a noun or pronoun is singular or plural. Singular indicates one, and plural indicates more than one. **Gender** is the term used to indicate whether a noun or a pronoun is masculine, feminine, or neuter.

Remember that the forms of *I, you,* and *they* do not show gender because they can be either masculine or feminine.

GENDER			
Masculine	he	him	his
Feminine	she	her	hers
Neuter	it	its	

If the antecedent of a pronoun is one word, there usually is no problem with agreement.

The **man** playing the trumpet lowered **his** horn.

The **listeners** showed **their** appreciation of the music.

If the antecedent of a pronoun is more than one word, there are two rules you should remember.

21 C.2   If two or more singular antecedents are joined by *or, nor, either/or,* or *neither/nor,* use a singular pronoun to refer to them.

These conjunctions indicate a choice. In the following example, Maria will play her long clarinet solo *or* Lacey will play hers.

> Either **Maria** or **Lacey** will play **her** long clarinet solo next.

21 C.3   If two or more singular antecedents are joined by *and* or *both/and,* use a plural pronoun to refer to them.

These conjunctions always indicate more than one. In the following example, Maria and Lacey—together—volunteered their help with the musical project.

> Both **Maria** and **Lacey** volunteered **their** help with the musical project.

Sometimes you will not know whether an antecedent is masculine or feminine. Standard written English solves this problem by using *his or her* to refer to such vague antecedents.

> Each orchestra **member** will donate two hours of **his or her** time to help with the project.
>
> Each **violinist** must practice **his or her** solo many times before the opening performance.

You can avoid this problem completely if you rewrite such sentences, using plural forms.

> All orchestra **members** will donate two hours of **their** time to help with the project.
>
> The **violinists** must practice **their** solos many times before the opening performance.

WORD ALERT

The words *gender* and *sex* both indicate the state of being male or female. However, they are typically used in slightly different ways. *Sex* is used to refer to biological differences, while *gender* tends to refer to cultural or social differences.

Making Pronouns and Antecedents Agree

Write the pronoun that correctly completes each sentence. Make sure that the pronoun agrees in both number and gender with its antecedent.

1. Either Felix or Jason left ___ trombone on the stage after practice.
2. All the orchestra members should wear ___ best outfits to the show.
3. Tricia and Max will sing ___ songs while the orchestra accompanies them.
4. Neither Aura nor Tricia remembered to take ___ music stand.
5. Felix took three music stands with ___ on our orchestra's tour.
6. Each player is responsible for ___ own instrument.
7. After the orchestra members left the stage, ___ went to the bus.
8. Jason carried his trombone and put ___ on the bus for the trip home.
9. Either Jane or Tricia will play ___ own song tomorrow night.
10. The trumpet was placed carefully in ___ case after the performance.

Indefinite Pronouns as Antecedents

Sometimes an indefinite pronoun is the antecedent of a personal pronoun. Making the personal pronoun and the indefinite pronoun agree can be confusing because some singular indefinite pronouns suggest a plural meaning. Other indefinite pronouns can be either singular or plural. The table below lists singular indefinite pronouns.

SINGULAR INDEFINITE PRONOUNS			
anybody	either	neither	one
anyone	everybody	nobody	somebody
each	everyone	no one	someone

21 C.4   Use a singular pronoun if the antecedent is a singular indefinite pronoun.

One of the girls left **her** bike unlocked.

Sometimes the gender of a singular indefinite pronoun is not indicated. You can solve this problem by using *his or her*.

Everyone must keep **his or her** bike locked up.

The use of *he or she, his or her,* or *him or her* can make your writing awkward. You can often eliminate this problem by rewriting the sentences in the plural form.

All students must keep **their** bikes locked up.

PLURAL INDEFINITE PRONOUNS			
both	few	many	several

21 C.5 Use a plural pronoun if the antecedent is a plural indefinite pronoun.

Many of the younger children have **their** own bikes.

SINGULAR OR PLURAL INDEFINITE PRONOUNS				
all	any	most	none	some

21 C.6 Agreement with an indefinite pronoun that can be either singular or plural depends upon the number and gender of the object of the preposition that follows it.

Some of the **chrome** on Stevie's bike has lost **its** shine.

Most of his **friends** keep **their** bikes out of the sun.

● **Practice Your Skills**

Making Personal Pronouns Agree with Indefinite Pronouns

Write the pronoun that correctly completes each sentence.

1. All of the boys in my apartment complex received bicycles for ___ birthdays.

2. Each of them had ___ bike painted a different color.

3. Not one of the boys in the apartment complex painted ___ bike red.

4. Many of the neighbors near our complex let the boys ride in ___ driveways.

5. One of our local organizations put up fliers about ___ bicycle races.

6. All of the boys decided ___ would enter.

7. Some of us in the complex gave them ___ encouragement to enter the race.

8. Someone in the boys' group had ___ bike stolen.

9. The winner of the race bought that boy a new bike with ___ prize money.

10. All of the younger boys were glad ___ friend had a bike again.

● *Connect to Writing:* Revising

Correcting Pronoun Agreement Errors

Rewrite the following sentences, correcting any problems with pronoun agreement. If a sentence is correct, write **C.**

1. Each of the girls won their softball letter.

2. No one on the girls' team liked her uniform.

3. Neither of the boys received their trophy for baseball.

4. Both of the Randall sisters practice batting in their backyard.

5. One of the girls lost their baseball glove.

✓ *Check Point:* Mixed Practice

Write the pronoun in the parentheses that correctly completes each sentence.

1. The high school band prepared for (their, its) first performance.

2. (All, Each) of the band members were a little nervous, but they were ready.

3. Alicia was the only one (who, whom) did not seem prepared.

4. Consuela helped (her, his) friend get ready.

5. Ali was more prepared than (I, me).

6. Our director, Mrs. Chandler, gave us (their, our) usual pre-game instructions.

7. After Mrs. Chandler's speech, (each, all) in the band gave a cheer as the crowd joined in.

8. Because we had practiced so hard, (we, us) in the band thought we would do our best.

9. As we walked onto the field, the crowd cheered the players and (us, them).

10. That night the band played (its, their) best.

● *Connect to Writing:* Personal Description

Using Pronouns

If you were to write a description of yourself doing something that best represents you, what written images would you include? How would you tie those images together? Write a one-page description that uses these images and any others that you feel get to the heart of you. Use as many pronouns as you can, and write your description in the first person, using the pronoun *I.* Include insights into your personality and your unique way of seeing things.

Unclear, Missing, or Confusing Antecedents

21 D   **Every personal pronoun should clearly refer to a specific antecedent.**

Missing antecedents and unclear references can be confusing.

Unclear	We tried to call the employment agency, but **it** was busy. (The antecedent of *it* is not clear, but the context of the sentence suggests that the pronoun *it* refers to the telephone line.)
Clear	We tried to call the employment agency, but **its telephone** was busy.
Unclear	I checked the Internet for job listings because **you** can always get good information there. (*You* is incorrect. It is unclear whether *you* is the speaker or the person being spoken to. Pronouns must agree with their antecedents in person—first, second, or third.)
Clear	I checked the Internet for job listings because **I** can always get good information there.
Missing	In the newspaper **it** lists the requirements for every job. (What does *it* refer to in this sentence? The antecedent in this sentence is missing.)
Clear	The **newspaper** lists the requirements for every job.
Missing	**It** had many job listings for entry-level computer positions. (*It* is unclear. The antecedent is missing.)
Clear	The **employment section of the newspaper** had many job listings for entry-level computer positions.
Confusing	My mother drove Liza to the interview, but **she** didn't go into the office. (Who didn't go into the office, the mother or Liza?)
Clear	My mother drove Liza to the interview, but **Mom** didn't go into the office.
Confusing	Liza put the business card into her purse, but now she can't find **it.** (Does *it* refer to the business card or the purse?)
Clear	Liza put the business card into her purse, but now she can't find **the card.**

Identifying Antecedent Problems

Label the antecedent problems in the sentences below as *unclear, missing,* or *confusing,* and rewrite the sentences correctly. If the sentence is written correctly, write **C**.

1. Almost all teenagers can find a job if you try hard enough.

2. My dad helped Elizabeth get a job, but she didn't like it very much.

3. Almost everyone I know likes to work if it is interesting.

4. I like dog walking because you get lots of outdoor exercise.

5. The employment agent stared at the boy, but he said nothing.

6. To earn extra money, Michael took the rugs off the floor and cleaned them.

7. Sarah wants to work at a veterinarian's office because you can learn a lot about animals.

8. My sister told Jenni about the job, and then she applied for it.

✔ *Check Point:* Mixed Practice

Each sentence below contains an error in pronoun usage. Rewrite the sentence, correcting the error.

1. During the national election, many of the citizens cast his or her votes early.

2. According to the polls, they said the incumbent president will win.

3. Several of the candidates gave his or her speeches.

4. I read the newspaper articles about the candidates, because you can learn a lot.

5. Neither of my parents has cast their vote yet.

6. My parents went to vote, and it was crowded.

7. During the town meeting, our neighbors asked the candidates their questions.

8. My mom took Granny to the debate, but she didn't listen to the candidates.

9. The candidates were responsible for raising his or her campaign money.

10. Depending upon who wins the mayoral election, Ms. Sands or Mr. Stone will try their hand at running our city.

● *Connect to Writing:* Response Letter

Using Pronoun References

You have found a job listing that interests you. Write a response letter to the contact person. Remember to mention the position you are applying for, the reason it interests you, and your qualifications. Be sure to use correct pronoun references.

Assess Your Learning

◼ Using Pronouns Correctly

Write the correct form of the pronoun in parentheses.

1. Neither Sue nor Rebecca has had (her, their) turn at bat.
2. One of the girls left (her, their) tennis shoes in the gym.
3. Please explain to (we, us) students how to get a pass.
4. To (who, whom) should I send the invitation?
5. Do other students study as hard as (we, us)?
6. (They, Them) made a delicious dinner for us.
7. Sandra went to the movies with David and (I, me).
8. Both Raul and Ted forgot (his, their) skates.
9. Our debaters will be Jorge and (he, him).
10. It was (she, her) who won the local marathon.
11. Jessica and (he, him) went to the game with us.
12. (Whoever, Whomever) draws the best picture will win a prize.
13. That was quick thinking for an inexperienced quarterback like (he, him).
14. No one types as fast as (she, her) on a word processor.
15. Between you and (I, me), we're never going to get there on time.
16. She is the only person (who, whom) arrived early.
17. (We, Us) joggers need to pay special attention to the traffic lights.
18. I think that's (she, her) in the blue coat.
19. Yes, I think she dives as well as (I, me).
20. Mr. Pentose is someone (who, whom) we met in Florida last year.

◼ Making Personal Pronouns Agree with Their Antecedents

Write the personal pronoun that correctly completes each sentence.

1. Either Mary or Suzanne will bring ▨ guitar.
2. One of my brothers just received ▨ diploma.
3. Both Heidi and John turned in ▨ reports early.
4. The tire has lost most of ▨ air.

5. All of the students will be assigned to  homerooms.

6. Several of my friends want to add biology to ▢ schedules.

7. Both of the girls think that ▢ will compete in the race.

8. Either Sam or Ernesto should drive ▢ car to the game.

9. After we painted the posters, we hung ▢ in the halls.

10. None of the silver pieces had lost ▢ shine.

11. Either of the boys will share ▢ lunch.

12. Several of the tourists lost ▢ way.

13. That tree is beginning to lose ▢ leaves.

14. Neither Mindy nor Sue can finish ▢ picture.

15. Either Claire or Erica will have ▢ camera at the game.

▇ Writing Sentences

Rewrite these sentences so there is a clear antecedent for each pronoun.

1. Rita tried to call her friend, but she did not feel like talking.

2. Rita drove to Lisa's house and listened to her new CD.

3. Then Rita drove her sister to the library, but she forgot her library card.

4. Rita put her book in a bag, but she left it on the counter at the library.

5. Rita's book fell on the floor, and it was damaged.

Using Pronouns: Posttest

Directions

Read the passage and choose the pronoun that belongs in each underlined space. Write the letter of the correct answer.

It was the big night of the talent show. Everybody in school watched as Jerome approached the microphone. __(1)__ singing partner Juan, __(2)__ was already on the stage, handed __(3)__ the guitar. Jerome immediately felt calmer. He began to strum the guitar strings, and __(4)__ began to sing. "__(5)__ have chosen a ballad for __(6)__ first selection," Juan said, as Jerome continued to play the guitar. When they finished the song, all of the students clapped and cheered loudly. Mr. Watkins, the principal, went to the microphone. "__(7)__ knew that __(8)__ had such talent right here under __(9)__ noses?" __(10)__ asked.

1. A His
   B Our
   C Him
   D Their

2. A whoever
   B whom
   C who
   D whomever

3. A him
   B he
   C who
   D whom

4. A they
   B its
   C his
   D their

5. A Us
   B We
   C Our
   D Ours

6. A my
   B we
   C us
   D our

7. A Whom
   B Whose
   C Who
   D Whomever

8. A we
   B us
   C our
   D ours

9. A us
   B our
   C ours
   D we

10. A his
    B him
    C he
    D them

Writer's Corner

Snapshot

21 A **Case** is the form of a noun or a pronoun that indicates its use in a sentence. (pages 716–719)

21 B **Common pronoun problems** include the misuse of *who* and *whom* and incomplete comparisons. (pages 729–735)

21 C A pronoun must agree in **number** and **gender** with its **antecedent.** (pages 736–740)

21 D Every personal pronoun should clearly refer to a specific **antecedent.** (pages 741–742)

Power Rules

 Use **subject forms of pronouns** in subject position. Use **object forms of pronouns** in object position. (See pages 716–725.)

Before Editing

Billy went with *he* and *I.*

Them and *us* want you to go with *she.*

After Editing

Billy went with *him* and *me.*

They and *we* want you to go with *her.*

For **homophones** and certain words that sound almost alike, choose the word with your intended meaning. (See pages 796–811.)

Before Editing

Where is *you're* cookbook? (*You're* is a contraction of *you are.*)

Their helping Alyssa make dinner. (*Their* is the possessive form of *they.*)

Please put the salad over *their.* (*Their* is the possessive form of *they.*)

Its time for dinner. (*Its* is the possessive form of *it.*)

After Editing

Where is *your* cookbook? (*Your* is the possessive form of *you.*)

They're helping Alyssa make dinner. (*They're* is the contraction of *they are.*)

Please put the salad over *there.* (*There* means "in that place.")

It's time for dinner. (*It's* is a contraction of *it is.*)

Editing Checklist

Use this checklist when editing your writing.

✓ Did I use nominative pronouns as subjects? (See pages 716–721.)

✓ Did I use objective pronouns as objects of prepositions, direct objects, and indirect objects? (See pages 722–725.)

✓ Did I use possessive pronouns to show ownership? (See pages 726–728.)

✓ Did I use *who* and *whom* correctly in questions? (See pages 729–730.)

✓ Did I use pronouns correctly when making comparisons? (See pages 733–735.)

✓ Does each pronoun agree with its antecedent in number and gender? (See pages 736–740.)

✓ Did I make sure all pronouns have clear antecedents? (See pages 741–742.)

Use the Power

The **nominative case** is used for subject and predicate nominatives. The **objective case** is used for direct objects, indirect objects, and objects of prepositions. Use the diagram below to understand the case and gender of pronouns. Read the dialogue at the right below (loosely based on Abbott and Costello's "Who's on First?") for a humorous look at pronouns.

THE PLAYERS

Pitcher = HE

Batter = YOU

First Base = HIM

Second Base = SHE

Third Base = HER

Catcher = WHO

Outfielders = ANYONE, SOMEONE, NO ONE

CATCHER: **WHO** is the catcher?

PITCHER TO BATTER: **HE** pitches to **YOU.**

OUTFIELD: **SOMEONE** drops the ball.

OUTFIELD TO THIRD BASE: **ANYONE** picks it up and throws it to HER.

SECOND BASE TO FIRST BASE: **SHE** throws it to **HIM.**

UMPIRE TO BATTER AT FIRST BASE: **YOU** are out!

Subject and Verb Agreement

How can you make your subjects and verbs work together so that your ideas are clear?

Subject and Verb Agreement: Pretest 1

The first draft of the essay below contains several errors in subject and verb agreement. The first error has been corrected. Revise the paragraph to correct the remaining errors in subject and verb agreement.

Everyone from Houston to Hong Kong ~~have~~ *has* read folktales about cunning wolves. Movies and television depicts wolves endlessly attacking innocent victims. Do you think any of these stories about wolves is true? Science writer Boyce Rensberger say that a wolf don't like to fight. In fact, wolves often goes out of their way to avoid harming humans. Rensberger also says that each wolf pack are a tightly-knit families. Both mother and father wolf raises the young. When both of the parents goes out to hunt, another wolf will baby-sit the pups. We all can learn something from the lives of wolves.

Subject and Verb Agreement: Pretest 2

Directions
Read the passage. Write the letter of the correct answer.

    All geologists <u>categorizes</u> rocks according to origin. Sometimes magma <u>move</u> up
               (1)   **(2)**
through cracks in the earth's crust and <u>cools</u>. This action creates igneous rocks.
                                        (3)
Sedimentary rocks <u>is made</u> from pieces of rocks, sand, and other material. These
                    (4)
sediments <u>is washed</u> into oceans, and they <u>settle</u> to the bottom. Then the layers of
             (5)   **(6)**
sediment <u>is pressed</u> together to create rocks. The third group <u>are</u> metamorphic rocks.
           (7)   **(8)**
Heat and pressure <u>creates</u> these rocks from igneous and sedimentary rocks. Both of
                    (9)
these sometimes <u>becomes</u> metamorphic rocks.
              (10)

1. **A** is categorizing
   B categorize
   C has categorized
   D No error

2. **A** moves
   B are moving
   C have moved
   D No error

3. **A** cool
   B are cooling
   C have cooled
   D No error

4. **A** is being made
   B was made
   C are made
   D No error

5. **A** is washing
   B are washed
   C washes
   D No error

6. **A** settles
   B are settles
   C is settled
   D No error

7. **A** are pressed
   B is pressing
   C has been pressed
   D No error

8. **A** is
   B is being
   C are being
   D No error

9. **A** has created
   B create
   C is creating
   D No error

10. **A** become
   B has become
   C is becoming
   D No error

Language is like a jigsaw puzzle. You must put all the elements together to create a complete picture. In the English language, when a subject and a verb fit together, they are said to be *in agreement*.

This chapter will show you how to make subjects and verbs agree so that you can communicate complete, clear pictures. One basic rule applies to this entire chapter.

22 A   A **verb** must agree with its subject in **number**.

➤ Number

You know that **number** refers to whether a noun or a pronoun is singular or plural. Verbs also have number. The number of a verb must agree with the number of its subject. A singular subject takes a singular verb. A plural subject takes a plural verb.

The Number of Nouns and Pronouns

In English the plural of most nouns is formed by adding *-s* or *-es* to the singular form. However, some nouns form their plurals in other ways. You should always check a dictionary to see whether a noun has an irregular plural.

NUMBER			
Singular	floor	tax	child
Plural	floors	taxes	children

Pronouns have singular and plural forms. For example, *I, he, she,* and *it* are singular, and *we* and *they* are plural.

You can find lists of pronoun forms on pages 722, 726, and 729.

● **Practice Your Skills**

Determining the Number of Nouns and Pronouns

Write each word and label it *S* for singular or *P* for plural.

1. Jessica   **6.** hats   **11.** they

2. everyone   **7.** mice   **12.** both

3. children   **8.** trucks   **13.** women

4. several   **9.** anyone   **14.** cap

5. schools   **10.** lights   **15.** we

The Number of Verbs

The singular and plural forms of nouns and pronouns are fairly easy to recognize. You can easily see, for example, that *eagle* and *it* refer to only one, while *eagles* and *they* refer to more than one.

The number of verbs, however, is not so easy to recognize. Only the form of the verb indicates its number. Most verbs form their singulars and plurals in exactly the opposite way that nouns form their singulars and plurals.

22 A.1   Most verbs in the present tense add *-s* or *-es* to form the singular. Plural forms of verbs in the present tense drop the *-s* or *-es*.

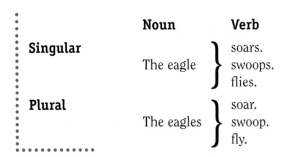

	Noun	**Verb**
Singular	The eagle	soars. / swoops. / flies.
Plural	The eagles	soar. / swoop. / fly.

Most verbs have the same form for both singular and plural when the verbs are used in the past tense.

Singular   The eagle **soared.**

Plural   The eagles **soared.**

22 A.2   The irregular verb *be* indicates number differently from other verbs. The singular is not formed by adding *-s* or *-es*.

FORMS OF *BE*			
Singular Forms	am/is	was	has been
Plural Forms	are	were	have been

Singular   The eagle **is** a majestic bird.

Plural   Eagles **are** majestic birds.

Determining a Verb's Number

Write each verb and label it *S* for singular or *P* for plural.

1. breaks	**6.** works	**11.** is
2. freezes	**7.** was	**12.** tear
3. are	**8.** reads	**13.** look
4. have been	**9.** am	**14.** sings
5. keep	**10.** has	**15.** walk

➤ Singular and Plural Subjects

Because a verb must agree in number with its subject, you need to remember two rules.

22 A.3   A singular subject takes a singular verb, and a plural subject takes a plural verb.

To make a verb agree with its subject, ask yourself two questions: *What is the subject?* and *Is the subject singular or plural?* Then choose the correct verb form.

In the following examples, each subject is underlined once and each verb is underlined twice. Notice the difference in the spelling of the verb in its singular and plural form.

Singular	A geologist studies rocks and minerals.
Plural	Geologists study rocks and minerals.
Singular	She examines layers of the earth.
Plural	They examine layers of the earth.
Singular	The emerald is a beautiful gemstone.
Plural	Emeralds are beautiful gemstones.

The pronouns *you* and *I* are the only exceptions to these agreement rules.

22 A.4   The pronoun *you*, whether singular or plural, always takes a plural verb.

Singular	You use a shovel.	You are a geologist.
Plural	You two use shovels.	You are scientists.

22 A.5 The pronoun *I* also takes a plural verb—except when it is used with a form of *be*.

Singular Verb	I am a researcher.	I was her assistant.
Plural Verb	I like minerals and gems.	I have some rock samples.

When You Write

Many errors in subject and verb agreement occur when writers do not edit their work. Never turn in a first draft without reading through your work and correcting errors. Reading a piece aloud to yourself or to a friend can help you find errors more easily than reading your work silently.

● **Practice Your Skills**

Making Subjects and Verbs Agree

Write the subject in each sentence. Next to each, write the form of the verb in parentheses that agrees with the subject.

1. Jewelers (place, places) a high value on emeralds of good quality.
2. Emeralds (is, are) a rarer find than diamonds.
3. An emerald (is, are) a special type of the mineral beryl.
4. Geologists (know, knows) the minerals that make up all precious stones.
5. Geology also (involve, involves) the study of Earth's landforms and surface features.
6. You (see, sees) these features wherever you look in nature.
7. A volcano (interest, interests) some specialized scientists called volcanologists.
8. Magma (is, are) molten rock contained within the earth.
9. When it comes to the surface, magma (become, becomes) lava.
10. I (study, studies) stones and minerals more than land features.

● *Connect to Writing:* **Editing**

Correcting Errors in Subject and Verb Agreement

Write the verbs that do not agree with their subjects. Then write the verbs correctly. If a sentence is correct, write **C**.

1. Diamonds is the world's favorite gem.
2. You finds them in most countries of the world.

3. South Africa exports the most diamonds.

4. A diamond's brilliance determine its value.

5. Most diamonds have color.

6. Blue and pink stones is the most valuable.

7. When found, these precious stones resembles glass.

8. It take a diamond to cut a diamond and other hard surfaces.

Agreement with Verb Phrases

If a sentence contains a verb phrase, make the first helping verb agree with the subject.

22 A.6   The first helping verb must agree in number with the subject.

In the following sentences, each subject is underlined once and each verb is underlined twice.

Kristy was writing a poem.
(*Kristy* is singular, and *was* is singular.)
They have been writing all afternoon.
(*They* is plural, and *have* is plural.)

The following chart shows the singular and plural forms of common helping verbs.

COMMON HELPING VERBS	
Singular	am, is, was, has, does
Plural	are, were, have, do

In the following sentences, each subject is underlined once and each verb is underlined twice. The helping verb agrees with the subject.

Singular	Kristy **is** writing a sonnet.
	The teacher **does** not have a dictionary of rhymes.
Plural	The poetry books **are** located in this section of the library.
	Our poems **have** been published in the local newspaper.

Making Subjects and Verb Phrases Agree

Write the subject in each sentence. Next to each, write the form of the verb in parentheses that agrees with the subject.

1. Sonnets (has, have) been written for centuries according to certain rules.

2. A new poet (is, are) often intimidated by the sonnet's rigid structure.

3. This particular poetic form (was, were) made popular by Petrarch in the 1300s.

4. His mystery woman Laura (has, have) become immortal through Petrarch's sonnets.

5. Sonnets (was, were) also written by William Shakespeare.

6. Other poets (do, does) often attempt this type of verse.

7. They (has, have) tried to write sonnets of Shakespeare's quality.

8. However, Shakespeare's sonnets (is, are) considered to be the finest collection by a single person.

9. I (was, were) awed when I read Shakespeare's sonnets.

10. When you read them aloud, you (do, does) hear the beauty in his words.

● *Connect to Writing:* **Revising**

Correcting Errors in Agreement

Rewrite correctly the sentences in which the verb phrases do not agree with their subjects. If a sentence is correct, write **C**.

1. You was really missed at the poetry reading.

2. They has finished sharing their poems.

3. The poem do sound familiar to me.

4. She have read it to us before.

5. Kevin have submitted three sonnets for publication.

6. His poems is often chosen as our group's best.

7. I were just reading one of his poems.

8. The college coffeehouse does have poetry readings.

➡ Agreement and Interrupting Words

Subjects and verbs are often interrupted by phrases or clauses. A common mistake is making the verb agree with the object of a preposition or the word closest to the verb, instead of the subject. However, interrupting phrases and clauses should not affect the subject and verb agreement.

22 A.7   The agreement of a verb with its subject is not changed by any interrupting words.

In the following examples, notice that the subjects and verbs agree in number—despite the words that come between them. Each subject is underlined once, and each verb is underlined twice.

> A bouquet of roses **was** given to the skater.
> (*Was* agrees with the singular subject *bouquet*. The verb does not agree with *roses*, the object of the prepositional phrase, even though *roses* is closer to the verb.)
> The skaters who won medals at the competition **were** invited to the White House.
> (*Were* agrees with the subject *skaters*—not with *competition*, the object of the prepositional phrase.)

Compound prepositions, such as *in addition to, as well as,* and *along with,* often begin interrupting phrases.

> The gold medal winner, along with her teammates, **was** called back to the ice.
> (*Was* agrees with the subject *winner*—not with *teammates*, the object of the compound preposition *along with*.)

You can avoid mistakes in agreement by reading the sentence without the interrupting phrase or clause. Then it's easy to see which word is the subject and to choose the verb form that agrees with it.

> A bouquet of roses **was** given to the skater.
> A bouquet **was** given to the skater.

● Practice Your Skills

Making Interrupted Subjects and Verbs Agree

Write the subject in each sentence. Next to each, write the form of the verb in parentheses that agrees with the subject. (If you're having trouble, try reading the sentence without the interrupting words.)

1. The blades on a pair of ice skates (is, are) called runners.

2. The runners on the earliest ice skates (was, were) probably made of bone.

3. The original purpose of ice skates (was, were) for travel.

4. Competition lovers in Scotland (is, are) credited with turning ice skating into a sport.

5. The invention of roller skates (was, were) probably the work of ice skaters.

6. Today, skaters from around the globe (compete, competes) for the fans.

7. Figure skating at the modern Olympics (is, are) one popular event.

8. In 2006, Sasha Cohen, together with her teammates, (was, were) a delight to Olympic audiences.

9. Ice dancing in pairs (has, have) been an Olympic sport since 1976.

10. Speed skating by men and women also (draw, draws) a large Olympic audience.

Connect to Writing: Editing

Correcting Errors in Subject and Verb Agreement

Write the verbs that do not agree with their subjects. Then write the verbs correctly. If a sentence is correct, write **C.**

1. The best athletes in the world competes at the Olympic Games.

2. A team is sent to compete by almost every country.

3. The modern spectacle of competing athletes were named for contests held in ancient Greece.

4. The original Olympic Games in Greece was banned in 394 A.D.

5. The modern international competition of athletes was revived in 1896.

✔ Check Point: Mixed Practice

Write the verbs that do not agree with their subjects. Then write the verbs correctly. If a sentence is correct, write **C.**

(1) My dog Muscles chases squirrels in our backyard. **(2)** Right now, a squirrel on the back steps are chattering at Muscles. **(3)** The squirrel really seem to love to tease him. **(4)** Muscles, like most dogs, hate to be teased. **(5)** Muscles starts moving toward the squirrel. **(6)** The squirrel, aware of the danger, jump quickly to a nearby tree. **(7)** Muscles, standing at the bottom of the tree, bark angrily at the intruder. **(8)** The squirrel, now safe in the branches, resume his chattering.

Connect to Writing: Persuasive Letter

Making Subjects and Verbs Agree

Imagine that the Olympic committee has decided to remove basketball from the list of Olympic sports. Write a letter to the committee either supporting or challenging its decision. Include at least three strong reasons why basketball should or should not remain an Olympic sport. After completing your letter, read it again to be sure all subjects and verbs agree.

When you edit your written work, look for agreement problems. They are often the result of quickly written first drafts. Some common problems are explained in the following section.

22 B   **Compound subjects, indefinite pronouns as subjects, and subjects in inverted order can present agreement problems.**

Compound Subjects

Agreement between a verb and a compound subject can sometimes be confusing. The following rules will help you avoid errors of agreement.

22 B.1   When subjects are joined by *or, nor, either/or,* or *neither/nor,* the verb agrees with the subject that is closer to it.

This rule applies even when one subject is singular and the other subject is plural. In the following examples, notice that the subjects closest to the verbs agree in number. Each subject is underlined once, and each verb is underlined twice.

> Either rain <u>showers</u> or <u>sleet</u> **is** <u>expected</u> tomorrow.
>
> (*Is,* the helping verb, is singular because *sleet,* the subject closer to it, is singular.)
>
> <u>Wind</u> or rising <u>temperatures</u> <u>dispel</u> fog.
>
> (The verb is plural because the subject closer to it is plural.)
>
> Neither my <u>brother</u> nor my <u>parents</u> <u>like</u> to drive in wet weather.
>
> (The verb is plural because the subject closer to it is plural—even though the other subject *brother* is singular.)

22 B.2   When subjects are joined by *and* or *both/and,* the verb is plural—whether the subjects are singular, plural, or a combination of singular and plural.

> Both <u>hail</u> and high <u>wind</u> <u>accompany</u> many storms.
>
> (Two things—*hail* and *wind*—accompany storms. The verb must be plural to agree.)
>
> My <u>brother</u> and his <u>roommates</u> <u>were</u> not <u>injured</u> in the storm.
>
> (Even though one subject is singular, the verb is still plural because *brother* and *roommates*—together—are more than one.)

There are two exceptions to the second rule. Sometimes two subjects that are joined by *and* refer to only one person or thing. Then a singular verb must be used.

My family's weather expert and storm lover **is** my sister.

(The *weather expert* and *storm lover* is the same person.)

Thunder and lightning **does** not frighten her.

(*Thunder* and *lightning* is considered one thing.)

The other exception occurs when the word *every* or *each* comes before a compound subject whose parts are joined by *and*. Since each subject is being considered separately in these sentences, a singular verb is called for.

Every thunderclap and lightning bolt **delights** my sister exceedingly.

(*Thunderclap* and *lightning bolt* are considered separately. The verb must be singular to agree.)

Each fall and spring **brings** the increased possibility of severe weather.

(*Fall* and *spring* are considered separately. The verb must be singular to agree.)

● **Practice Your Skills**

Making Verbs Agree with Compound Subjects

Write the correct form of the verb in parentheses.

1. Climate conditions and soil types (combine, combines) to affect vegetation.
2. Every animal and plant (react, reacts) to the surrounding environment.
3. For instance, moisture and warm air (is, are) needed to make orchids grow.
4. A tropical plant or flower (do, does) not grow in the desert.
5. Due to their white pelts, polar bears and arctic hares (thrive, thrives) in snowy climates.
6. Today, great ice caps and glaciers (cover, covers) one tenth of the earth's surface.
7. Dark clouds and high winds (alert, alerts) people to changing weather.
8. The air currents and weather patterns (change, changes) constantly.
9. Neither a lightning strike nor a tornado (is, are) easy to predict.
10. Snow or showers (is, are) easier to forecast.

● *Connect to Writing:* **Editing**

Correcting Errors in Agreement

Write the verbs that do not agree with their subjects. Then write the verbs correctly. If a sentence is correct, write **C**.

1. Earthquakes and volcanoes has caused cities to sink beneath the sea.

2. Broken dams or volcanic activity sometimes follows earthquakes.

3. Often fires or floods is caused by earthquakes.

4. Each collapsed building or damaged home presents a danger after a quake.

5. Tsunamis in coastal areas and landslides in mountainous regions is also associated with earthquakes.

6. Both Japan and Indonesia has been the site of disastrous tsunamis.

7. In Alaska in 1958, ice and rock was broken off a glacier by the jolt of an earthquake.

8. The force and fury of the resulting splash were responsible for a tsunami.

➡ Indefinite Pronouns as Subjects

In the last chapter, you learned that not all indefinite pronouns have the same number.

COMMON INDEFINITE PRONOUNS	
Singular	anybody, anyone, each, either, everybody, everyone, neither, nobody, no one, one, somebody, someone
Plural	both, few, many, several
Singular/Plural	all, any, most, none, some

22 B.3   A verb must agree in number with an indefinite pronoun used as a subject.

Singular   Everyone in the room owns a dog.

Plural   Many of the dogs are poodles.

The number of an indefinite pronoun in the last group in the box is determined by the object of the prepositional phrase that follows the pronoun.

Singular or Plural	Most of the training **has** been effective.
	(Since *training,* the object of the prepositional phrase, is singular, the verb is also singular.)
	Most of the dogs **have** learned a lot in obedience school.
	(Since *dogs,* the object of the prepositional phrase, is plural, the verb is also plural.)
	None of the dog owners **were unhappy** with the program.
	(Since *owners,* the object of the prepositional phrase, is plural, the verb is also plural.)

● Practice Your Skills

Making Verbs Agree with Indefinite Pronouns

Write the subject in each sentence. Next to each, write the correct form of the verb in parentheses that agrees with the subject.

1. Several of her dogs (is, are) collies.
2. Each of you (is, are) needed to train the dogs.
3. Some of the new leashes (is, are) in the closet.
4. One of the dogs in the class (was, were) a beagle.
5. Many of the dogs (has, have) been adopted at the shelter.
6. None of the owners (was, were) disappointed in the class.
7. Nobody (want, wants) a badly behaved dog.
8. Both of her puppies (walk, walks) on a leash together.
9. Most of the dogs (was, were) fast learners.
10. Either of these classes (is, are) a good one to take next.

● *Connect to Writing:* **Drafting**

Writing Sentences

Write ten sentences, each using one of the phrases below as a beginning.

1. Both of the dogs
2. Anybody at the shelter
3. Few of the older dogs
4. All of the kittens
5. None of the volunteers
6. Each of the cages
7. No one at the desk
8. Several of the stores
9. Some of the pets
10. Neither of the cats

➤ Subjects in Inverted Order

In an inverted sentence, the verb comes before the subject. This structure does not affect subject and verb agreement.

22 B.4   The subject and the verb of an inverted sentence must agree in number.

There are several types of inverted sentences. To find the subject in an inverted sentence, turn the sentence around to its natural order, placing the subject first.

Inverted Order	At the bottom of the trunk <u>were</u> my great uncle's <u>medals</u>.
	(My great uncle's <u>medals</u> <u>were</u> at the bottom of the trunk.)
Questions	<u>Are</u> the <u>medals</u> from World War II?
	(The <u>medals</u> <u>are</u> from World War II.)
Sentences Beginning with *Here* or *There*	There <u>were</u> many <u>letters</u> in the trunk.
	(Many <u>letters</u> <u>were</u> in the trunk. The word *there* is dropped from the sentence.)

You can learn more about inverted sentences on pages 588–589.

● Practice Your Skills

Making Subjects and Verbs in Inverted Order Agree

Write the subject in each sentence. Next to each, write the form of the verb in parentheses that agrees with the subject. (If you're having trouble, rewrite the sentence in natural order.)

1. There (was, were) many countries involved in World War II.

2. In Europe (was, were) the locations of many of the battles.

3. (Do, Does) any war have only one cause?

4. At the core of the fighting (was, were) many factors.

5. There (was, were) much tension remaining in Europe after World War I.

6. In the numerous battles of the war (was, were) men from all countries.

7. (Was, Were) anyone able to predict that Hitler would gain such power?

8. (Have, Has) the world learned anything from these world wars?

9. At the end of the war, there (was, were) a struggle for political power in Europe.

10. (Is, Are) there any good results that come from such wars?

Writing Sentences

Write five sentences, each using one of the phrases below as a beginning. Be sure that the subject you choose agrees with the verb.

1. There are

2. In the newspaper was

3. At the top of the page were

4. There is

5. On the front page are

Power Your Writing: Who or What?

An **appositive phrase** is a group of words with no subject or verb that adds information about another word in the sentence. You use an appositive phrase to give your reader insight into who someone is or what something is like. In the following sentence from Ernesto Galarza's *Barrio Boy* (pages 117–120), for example, readers would not know who the Harrisons are without the appositive phrase, which comes between the subject (the proper noun *Harrisons*) and the verb phrase *(were cordial)*. Notice that the appositive phrase is set off by commas.

Appositive Phrase	The Harrisons, **the people across the street,** were cordial to us.

In a similar way, Galarza uses an appositive to elaborate on the school he attended by using descriptive details. This time the appositive phrase comes after the verb *(transferred)* and the object of the preposition *(Bret Harte School)*. A single comma is needed to separate the appositive phrase from the rest of the sentence.

Appositive Phrase	I transferred to Bret Harte School, **a gingerbread two-story building.**

Provide more detail to a composition you have completed recently by adding at least two appositive phrases.

Other Agreement Problems Lesson 3

Certain other subjects and verbs require special attention as well.

| 22 C | Some contractions, collective nouns, and other issues can present agreement problems. |

➤ *Doesn't or Don't?*

Doesn't, don't, and other contractions often present agreement problems. When you write a contraction, always say the two words that make up the contraction. Then check for agreement with the subject.

| 22 C.1 | The verb part of a contraction must agree in number with the subject. |

Doesn't, isn't, wasn't, and *hasn't* are singular and agree with singular subjects. *Don't, aren't, weren't,* and *haven't* are plural and agree with plural subjects.

> He **does**n't know any musicians.
> (He *does* not know.)
>
> **Do**n't they know anyone?
> (They *do* not know.)

➤ Collective Nouns

A collective noun names a group of people or things.

COMMON COLLECTIVE NOUNS			
band	congregation	flock	orchestra
class	crew	gang	swarm
colony	crowd	herd	team
committee	family	league	tribe

Most of the time, a collective noun is singular, but the way in which the noun is used will determine its agreement with the verb.

| 22 C.2 | Use a singular verb with a collective noun subject that is thought of as a unit. Use a plural verb with a collective noun subject that is thought of as individuals. |

The <u>committee</u> **is** <u>planning</u> to hire a band for the big event.

(The committee is working as a single unit. Therefore, the verb is singular.)

The <u>committee</u> **are** <u>unable</u> to agree on the band for the big event.

(The individuals on the committee are acting separately. Therefore, the verb is plural.)

➤ Words Expressing Amounts

Words that express amounts of time or money or that express measurements or weights are usually considered singular.

22 C.3   A subject that expresses an amount, a measurement, a weight, or a time is usually considered singular and takes a singular verb.

Subjects expressing amounts can be confusing because they are sometimes plural in form.

Amounts	Five <u>dollars</u> <u>is</u> the price of admission to the dance.
	(one sum of money)
Time	Nine <u>tenths</u> of Adriana's spare time **has** been spent planning the dance.
	(one segment of time)

Once in a while, an amount is thought of as individual parts. When this happens, a plural verb must be used.

Three <u>quarters</u> **were** left in the cash box.

● Practice Your Skills

Making Subjects and Verbs Agree

Write the subject in each sentence. Next to each, write the form of the verb in parentheses that agrees with the subject.

1. (Aren't, Isn't) you going to the dance?

2. A group (has, have) been chosen to perform.

3. Those singers (is, are) a big hit now.

4. The swim team (has, have) a meet on the same night as the dance.

5. Invitations to join the dance committee (was, were) extended to them.

6. Three fourths of the refreshment table (was, were) covered with plates of cookies.

7. Thirty dollars (was, were) donated to our class to purchase decorations.

8. Three days (was, were) spent looking for a purple banner for the wall.

9. They (wasn't, weren't) interested in hiring Daria's band for the dance.

10. One result of their choice of bands (is, are) that her feelings were hurt.

● *Connect to Writing:* **Drafting**

Writing Sentences

Write a sentence using each phrase. Be sure that your subjects and verbs agree.

1. The pack of wolves

2. Seventy-five percent of the forest

3. Three fifty-dollar bills

4. The Sierra Club

5. Three tablespoons of sugar

Singular Nouns That Have Plural Forms

Although words like *measles, mathematics, economics,* and *news* each end in *-s,* they name single things, such as one disease or one area of knowledge.

22 C.4   Use a singular verb with certain subjects that are plural in form but singular in meaning.

In middle school, mathematics was Arnetta's best subject.

The news is that she now likes English better.

Subjects with Linking Verbs

Sometimes a sentence will have a subject and a predicate nominative that do not agree in number.

22 C.5   A verb agrees with the subject of a sentence, not with the predicate nominative.

In the following examples, the number of the predicate nominative does not affect the number of the verb.

Felicia's topic of discussion was the novels of Jane Austen.

The novels of the Victorian period are Juan's passion.

 **Titles**

Titles may have many words, and some of those words may be plural. Nevertheless, a title is the name of only one book or work of art.

22 C.6 A title takes a singular verb.

Wuthering Heights by Emily Brontë <u>is</u> my favorite Victorian novel.

A print of Van Gogh's *Irises* <u>hangs</u> next to the bookshelf in our living room.

● **Practice Your Skills**

Making Subjects and Verbs Agree

Write the subject in each sentence. Next to each, write the form of the verb in parentheses that agrees with the subject.

1. *Sense and Sensibility* (was, were) much easier to read than I had expected it to be.
2. One challenge in reading the book (is, are) that many words are unfamiliar to us.
3. The news that we would read the book (was, were) not welcomed by the class.
4. Manners in Jane Austen's time (is, are) a fascinating topic.
5. The main focus of our discussion (was, were) the characters in the novel.
6. One result of our discussions (was, were) our reading more of Austen's novels.
7. Pablo Picasso's *Three Musicians* (is, are) our next discussion topic.
8. *The Martian Chronicles* by Ray Bradbury (follow, follows) a study of Picasso's art.

● *Connect to Writing:* **Editing**

Correcting Errors in Agreement

Write the verbs that do not agree with their subjects. Then write the verbs correctly. If a sentence is correct, write **C**.

1. Economics are my hardest class this semester.
2. One problem in the class are lots of homework.
3. The news of a stock market crash were exciting to discuss.
4. Problems in the stock market is a common phenomenon.
5. *Investing Dollars with Sense* are the title of our economics textbook.
6. There is many trading simulation games on the Internet.
7. Blue-chip stocks usually has the highest money value.
8. Prices usually rise in a bull market.

✅ *Check Point:* Mixed Practice

Write the verbs that do not agree with their subjects. Then write the verbs correctly. If a sentence is correct, write **C.**

1. The groundhog for years have been used to predict the arrival of spring.

2. The fuzz on woolly bear caterpillars are used to determine how hard a winter will be.

3. Neither a groundhog nor caterpillars is really dependable for forecasting, though.

4. Many of the predictions are wrong.

5. There are reports that some kinds of animals can sense earthquakes.

6. Ten catfish in a research laboratory was observed for two years.

7. During that time, 20 earthquakes was experienced in the area.

8. Most of the earthquakes was inaccurately forecast by humans.

● *Connect to Writing:* Vocabulary Application

Writing About Yourself

You have learned a number of new vocabulary terms used to describe how subjects and verbs work together. Go over that vocabulary once again. Then apply what you have learned as you write a short essay about yourself. Begin with a physical description, including your height, hair and eye color, and other distinguishing features. Then move on to the most important part— who you are inside. What do you love? What do you dislike? What makes you angry? What makes you joyful? As you write, try to include at least one of each of the following:

• the word *doesn't* used with a noun

• the word *don't* used with a pronoun

• a collective noun and an appropriate verb

• a title and an accompanying verb

• a subject and a linking verb

Assess Your Learning

Making Subjects and Verbs Agree

For each sentence write the subject and the verb that agrees with it.

1. (Isn't, Aren't) these four loaves of bread enough?
2. There (is, are) still horse ranches within the city limits of San Diego.
3. Neither of the loudspeakers (was, were) working by the end of the concert.
4. Two members of the golf team (was, were) able to finish the course at five under par.
5. Off the coast of Maine (is, are) many rocky islands.
6. Ten dollars (was, were) a fair price for the used tennis racket.
7. My height and weight (is, are) average for my age.
8. (Doesn't, Don't) you think we can win?
9. The team (was, were) fighting among themselves over the choice of a new captain.
10. *Incredible Athletic Feats* (is, are) an interesting book by Jim Benagh.
11. Every student and teacher (was, were) at the dedication ceremony.
12. Ellen's sister, along with my cousin, (is, are) at the University of Wisconsin.
13. One fourth of the world's population (lives, live) on less than two thousand dollars a year.
14. (Wasn't, Weren't) you able to solve the math problem?
15. One of our best pitchers (was, were) unable to play in the county championships.

Subject and Verb Agreement

Find the verbs that do not agree with their subjects and write them correctly. If a sentence is correct, write **C**.

1. Was you with Ben in the crowd after the game?
2. In the picnic basket were sandwiches for everyone.
3. Fifty dollars were contributed by my family.
4. Crackers and cheese are my favorite snack.

5. Either red or green looks good on you.

6. Every actor and dancer were dressed in a colorful costume.

7. Don't that dripping faucet bother you?

8. There are few poisonous snakes in northern regions.

9. Each of the members are assigned to a committee.

10. Is your father and mother at home this evening?

■ Writing Sentences

Write ten sentences that follow the directions below. The verb in each sentence should be in the present tense.

Write a sentence that...

1. includes *dogs in the park* as the subject.

2. includes *a game of dominoes* as the subject.

3. includes *Mom and Dad* as the subject.

4. includes *neither bats nor balls* as the subject.

5. includes *don't* at the beginning of a sentence.

6. includes *here* at the beginning of a sentence.

7. includes *many* as the subject.

8. includes *team* as the subject.

9. includes *three fourths* as the subject.

10. includes *Romeo and Juliet,* the title of the play, as the subject.

Subject and Verb Agreement: Posttest

Directions

Read the passage. Write the letter of the correct answer.

According to a United States survey, there really <u>is</u> no surefire ways to predict
(1)

an earthquake. Seismologists, nevertheless, <u>is continuing</u> to work on this problem.
(2)

For example, some people <u>have observed</u> unusual animal behavior before a quake: a
(3)

pet sometimes <u>become</u> agitated; a swarm of bees <u>have been seen</u> evacuating its hive
(4)   (5)

in a panic; catfish in a lake <u>has leaped</u> onto dry land. Many earthquake researchers
(6)

throughout the world <u>is seeking</u> a scientific explanation for these events. Fluctuations
(7)

in the earth's magnetic field, for example, <u>occurs</u> at the epicenter of an earthquake, and
(8)

certain animals <u>is</u> sensitive to electromagnetic changes. Some seismologists studying the
(9)

problem <u>hopes</u> to develop instruments for detecting earthquakes.
(10)

1. A has been
   B are
   C be
   D No error

2. A are continuing
   B continues
   C has continued
   D No error

3. A observes
   B is observing
   C has observed
   D No error

4. A is becoming
   B are becoming
   C becomes
   D No error

5. A has been seen
   B are seen
   C are being seen
   D No error

6. A have leaped
   B is leaping
   C leaps
   D No error

7. A are seeking
   B has been seeking
   C seeks
   D No error

8. A occur
   B is occurring
   C has occurred
   D No error

9. A has been
   B are
   C is being
   D No error

10. A hope
   B is hoping
   C has hoped
   D No error

Writer's Corner

Snapshot

22 A A **verb** must agree with its **subject** in number. A singular subject takes a singular verb. A plural subject takes a plural verb. (pages 750–757)

22 B Compound subjects, indefinite pronouns as subjects, and subjects in inverted order can present agreement problems. (pages 758–763)

22 C Some contractions, collective nouns, and other issues can present agreement problems. (pages 764–768)

Power Rules

 Use **verbs that agree with the subject.** (pages 750–768)

Before Editing	After Editing
Each of the players *are* responsible for equipment.	Each of the players *is* responsible for equipment.
The team *are* excited about tomorrow's game.	The team *is* excited about tomorrow's game.
Either Lola or Suzie *are* going to play center.	Either Lola or Suzie *is* going to play center.
Jeni and Stephanie *is* the team captains.	Jeni and Stephanie *are* the team captains.

 Use **mainstream past tense forms** of regular and irregular verbs. (pages 684–703)

Before Editing	After Editing
The whole class *vote* after school.	The whole class *voted* after school.
She *brung* her little dog along,	She *brought* her little dog along.
They *come* to see me yesterday.	They *came* to see me yesterday.

Editing Checklist

Use this checklist when editing your writing.

- ✓ Did I make singular subjects take singular verbs and plural subjects take plural verbs? (See pages 750–754.)
- ✓ Did I make verbs agree with compound subjects? (See pages 758–760.)
- ✓ Did I use singular verbs with singular indefinite pronouns and plural verbs with plural indefinite pronouns? (See pages 760–761.)
- ✓ Did I make subjects and verbs in inverted order agree? (See pages 762–763.)
- ✓ Did I use verbs that agree with collective nouns? (See pages 764–765.)
- ✓ Did I make verbs agree with singular nouns that have plural forms? (See page 766.)

Use the Power

Some subjects and verbs fit together, and others do not. Use these diagrams to help you understand rules for subject and verb agreement.

Rule: Singular subjects take singular verbs.	
The girl watch the dolphins swim.	[not]
The girl watches the dolphins swim.	[match]

Rule: Plural subjects takes plural verbs.	
Dolphins is very intelligent animals.	[not]
Dolphins are very intelligent animals.	[match]

Rule: When subjects are joined by *or, nor, either/ or,* or *neither/nor,* the verb agrees with the closer subject.	
Neither Jo nor her sisters has seen a dolphin.	[not]
Neither Jo nor her sisters have seen a dolphin.	[match]

Rule: The verb part of a contraction must agree in number with the subject.	
We doesn't understand how they train dolphins.	[not]
We don't understand how they train dolphins.	[match]

Rule: A verb must agree in number with an indefinite pronoun used as a subject.	
All of them is excited to see it.	[not]
All of them are excited to see it.	[match]

Rule: The subject and verb of an inverted sentence must agree in number.	
Were the show exciting?	[not]
Was the show exciting?	[match]

Using Adjectives and Adverbs

How can you create colorful prose with adjectives and adverbs?

Using Adjective and Adverbs: Pretest 1

The first draft below contains errors in the use of adjectives and adverbs. The first error is corrected. How would you revise the draft to correct other errors in using adjectives and adverbs?

. As my uncle and I explored Fairview, we decided that using a map made finding locations

easier.

~~more easy~~ I think Fairview has the most interestingest history of any other city in the state. The city is most picturesque than most other cities its size and age. My favoritest building is the bank. It is the more striking building in the city. Everywhere the sidewalks are constructed of the beautifulest cobblestones. After lunch, I took Uncle Al to hear the mayor speak. To get to the lecture on time, my uncle and I had to walk more faster than we'd been walking. I didn't want to miss a word of the lecture because the mayor knows the city's history good. The talk was really fascinating, but it lasted longer than we'd expected.

Using Adjectives and Adverbs: Pretest

Directions

Read the passage and choose the word or group of words that belongs in each underlined space. Write the letter of the correct answer.

The __(1)__ audience in the history of the performance hall filled the auditorium. Robyn and Alison's seats were __(2)__ than seats they had the year before. However, the man in front of Alison was __(3)__ than she. Luckily, the girls found empty seats that were __(4)__ to the front.

The six musicians wore hats with the __(5)__ colors Robyn had ever seen. The __(6)__ guitarist was the one with a purple and pink top hat. The __(7)__ hat, with sequined antlers, belonged to the drummer.

Robyn said, "I've never been __(8)__ than I am right now!" She pointed out that the drummer seemed __(9)__ than the lead guitarist. The girls decided that, as the leader of the band, the guitarist had to be __(10)__.

CHAPTER 23

1. **A** largest
   B larger
   C most large
   D large

2. **A** good
   B more good
   C better
   D gooder

3. **A** tall
   B taller
   C more tall
   D most tall

4. **A** more close
   B close
   C closest
   D closer

5. **A** brightest
   B most bright
   C more bright
   D bright

6. **A** more interesting
   B interestingest
   C most interesting
   D interesting

7. **A** most funny
   B funniest
   C funnier
   D more funny

8. **A** most excited
   B excited
   C more excited
   D exciteder

9. **A** most animated
   B more animated
   C animateder
   D animated

10. **A** more serious
    B seriouser
    C most serious
    D seriousest

Before you buy a bicycle, you probably do some comparison shopping. You might find out, for example, that one make of bicycle is a *good* buy. A second make, however, is a *better* buy, and a third make is the *best* buy of all. *Good, better,* and *best* are the different forms of a modifier that show comparisons.

Most adjectives and adverbs have three forms: the positive, the comparative, and the superlative. These forms are used to show differences in degree or extent.

23 A   **Adjectives** and **adverbs** are modifiers. Most modifiers show degrees of comparison by changing form.

23 A.1   The **positive degree** is the basic form of an adjective or an adverb. It is used when no comparison is being made.

This is a **hot** summer.

Carla is **mature.**

Eric is a **tall** basketball player.

23 A.2   The **comparative degree** is used when two people, things, or actions are being compared.

This summer is **hotter** than last summer.

Carla is **more mature** than her sister.

Eric is **taller** than Josh.

23 A.3   The **superlative degree** is used when more than two people, things, or actions are being compared.

This is the **hottest** summer of the past three years.

Carla is the **most mature** of all her sisters.

Eric is the **tallest** player on the team.

Following are additional examples of the three degrees of comparison.

Positive   Today's game is a **big** one.

                      Josh practices **often.**

Comparative   Today's game is **bigger** than last week's game.

                      Josh practices **more often** than Eric.

Superlative   Tomorrow's game will be the **biggest** game of the year.

                      Josh practices the **most often** of all the team members.

Some adverbs, such as *too, somewhere, very*, and *never*, cannot be compared.

If you want to review how adjectives and adverbs are used in a sentence, go to pages 538–550.

● **Practice Your Skills**

Determining Degrees of Comparison

Write the underlined modifier in each sentence. Then label its degree of comparison **P** for positive, **C** for comparative, or **S** for superlative.

1. Mario ran <u>hurriedly</u> to the locker room with his uniform in hand.

2. The team was dressing for the <u>most important</u> game of the season.

3. This week's game will be <u>more difficult</u> than last week's game.

4. The coach sent in his <u>fastest</u> runners, and Mario led them out.

5. A player on the other team sauntered <u>lazily</u> down the field.

6. Mario, who was <u>quicker</u> than that player, took the ball from him.

7. Eric worked <u>harder</u> than Josh to defend Mario as he ran down the field.

8. Josh, however, was the <u>most helpful</u> member of the team.

9. He played a <u>wonderful</u> game.

10. He had <u>fewer</u> chances to score than Mario, but he played great defense.

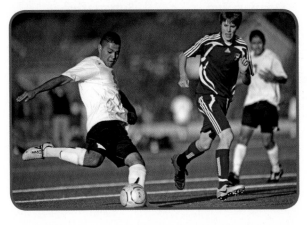

Regular Comparisons

The number of syllables in a modifier determines how you form its comparative and superlative degrees.

One-Syllable Modifiers

23 A.4   Add –*er* to form the comparative degree and –*est* to form the superlative degree of one-syllable modifiers.

ONE-SYLLABLE MODIFIERS		
Positive	**Comparative**	**Superlative**
brave	braver	bravest
kind	kinder	kindest
soon	sooner	soonest
old	older	oldest

Two-Syllable Modifiers

The comparative and superlative degrees of many two-syllable modifiers are formed the same way. However, some two-syllable modifiers sound awkward when –*er* or –*est* is added. For these modifiers, *more* or *most* should be used to form the comparative and superlative degrees. (*More* and *most* are always used with adverbs that end in –*ly*.)

23 A.5   Use –*er* or *more* to form the comparative degree and –*est* or *most* to form the superlative degree of many two-syllable modifiers.

TWO-SYLLABLE MODIFIERS		
Positive	**Comparative**	**Superlative**
happy	happier	happiest
helpful	more helpful	most helpful
quickly	more quickly	most quickly
easy	easier	easiest

Let your ear be your guide when deciding between *–er/–est* and *more/most* with two-syllable modifiers. If adding *–er* or *–est* makes a word difficult to pronounce, use *more* or *most* instead. It is obvious, for example, that you would never say "helpfulest."

Look back at a recent composition to see that you have used two-syllable modifiers correctly.

Modifiers with Three or More Syllables

23 A.6   Use *more* to form the comparative degree and *most* to form the superlative degree of modifiers with three or more syllables.

MODIFIERS WITH THREE OR MORE SYLLABLES

Positive	Comparative	Superlative
trivial	more trivial	most trivial
serious	more serious	most serious
vigorously	more vigorously	most vigorously
sympathetic	more sympathetic	most sympathetic

23 A.7   Because *less* and *least* mean the opposite of *more* and *most,* use these words to form negative comparisons.

NEGATIVE COMPARISONS

trivial	less trivial	least trivial
serious	less serious	least serious
vigorously	less vigorously	least vigorously
sympathetic	less sympathetic	least sympathetic

● **Practice Your Skills**

Forming the Comparison of Modifiers

Write each modifier. Then write its comparative and superlative forms. Do not write the negative comparisons.

1. quick

2. sure

3. muddy

4. hastily

5. heavy

6. safe

7. high	**12.** exuberant
8. loudly	**13.** fast
9. secure	**14.** slow
10. lofty	**15.** seasick
11. lively	**16.** dark

● **Practice Your Skills**

Forming the Negative Comparison of Modifiers

1.–5. Write the first five modifiers in the previous exercise. Then write the negative comparative and superlative forms, using *less* and *least*.

● *Connect to Writing:* **Drafting**

Writing Sentences with Comparisons

Write sentences using the indicated form of the words below.

1. positive form of *high*
2. comparative form of *low*
3. superlative form of *eagerly*
4. positive form of *definite*
5. comparative form of *hasty*
6. superlative form of *close*
7. positive form of *serious*
8. comparative form of *sunny*
9. superlative form of *swiftly*

When You Write

Use a dictionary if you are unsure of the comparative or superlative form of an adjective or adverb. The dictionary will list the various forms and show *–er* or *–est* changes to base word spelling. A good collegiate dictionary can be a writer's best friend.

Go back over a recent composition to be sure you have used comparative and superlative forms correctly in your writing.

● *Connect to Writing:* **Tall Tale**

Using Comparison with Adjectives and Adverbs

Pecos Bill is a hero of American tall tales. Write a tall tale that has a hero like him. Remember that tall-tale characters often use their extraordinary powers to perform great feats, such as creating the Grand Canyon. Use adjectives and adverbs in the positive form, the comparative form, and the superlative form. Underline and label each.

Irregular Comparison

The comparative and superlative degrees of a few modifiers are formed irregularly. You might want to memorize these forms.

IRREGULAR MODIFIERS		
Positive	**Comparative**	**Superlative**
bad/badly/ill	worse	worst
good/well	better	best
little	less	least
many/much	more	most

23 A.8 The endings *–er* and *–est* should never be added to the comparative and superlative forms of irregular modifiers.

The word *worse* is the comparative form of *bad*. Never use *worser*. *Least* is the superlative form of *little*. Never use *most little*.

● **Practice Your Skills**

Forming the Comparison of Irregular Modifiers

Write the comparative and superlative forms of the underlined modifier to complete the sentences.

1. That movie was really <u>bad</u>.

It was _____ than the movie we saw last week.

In fact, it was the _____ movie I have seen in my entire life.

2. Felipe showed <u>much</u> concern about the poor quality of the movie.

Belinda showed even _____ concern than Felipe.

Amazingly, Juana showed the _____ concern of all.

3. <u>Many</u> movies are filmed in Texas.

_____ movies are filmed in New York.

The _____ movies are filmed in California.

4. The movie we rented this morning was <u>good</u>.

The movie we rented yesterday was _____.

The movie we rented last month was the _____ I had ever seen.

5. I have <u>little</u> interest in watching another movie this week.

I have _____ interest in watching television.

I have the _____ interest in listening to music.

Practice Your Skills

Writing Forms of Comparison

Write each modifier below. Then write its comparative and superlative forms. (If you are unsure of the form or its spelling, look up the word in a dictionary.)

1. mad

2. lovely

3. timely

4. far

5. hot

6. fun

7. easy

8. homey

9. lonely

10. malevolent

Connect to Writing: Editing

Using Forms of Comparison

Write each incorrect modifier and then write it correctly. If a sentence is correct, write **C**.

1. I have the baddest cold I have ever had.

2. One morning I felt a little run down, but by the afternoon I was iller.

3. I wanted to get better in the littlest amount of time possible.

4. My sister called the doctor, who gave me many instructions.

5. In fact, it was the manyest instructions I had ever received from a doctor.

✔ Check Point: Mixed Practice

Write each incorrect modifier and then write it correctly. If the modifier in a sentence is correct, write **C**.

1. Spending the day at an amusement park is the more enjoyable thing to do.

2. Amusement parks are one of the better places on Earth!

3. The more exciting ride of all is the roller coaster.

4. When the car drops down from the tallest hill on the ride, you almost fly.

5. Roller coasters seem quickest than sports cars.

6. A most crowded place than the roller coaster is the midway.

7. Kids love to try to win the bigger stuffed animals at the ring-toss booth.

23 B When you compare people or things, avoid **double comparisons, illogical comparisons,** and **comparing a thing with itself.**

➤ Double Comparisons

Use only one method of forming the comparative and superlative degree of a modifier.

23 B.1 Do not use both *–er* and *more* to form the comparative degree, or both *–est* and *most* to form the superlative degree.

Double Comparison	Our city is **more larger** than most.
Correct	Our city is **larger** than most.
Double Comparison	I have the **most usefulest** map of the city.
Correct	I have the **most useful** map of the city.

➤ Illogical Comparisons

Only similar things should be compared. If you compare different things, you end up with an illogical comparison—a comparison that does not make sense.

23 B.2 Compare only items of a similar kind.

Illogical Comparison	This building's roof is steeper than the bank. (A roof is being compared to a bank.)
Logical Comparison	This building's roof is steeper than the bank's. (A roof is being compared with another roof.)
Illogical Comparison	The tour guide's description of the building's history was better than the girls. (The description is being compared to girls.)
Logical Comparison	The tour guide's description of the building's history was better than the girls' description. (The description is being compared to a description.)

You can learn about the use of an apostrophe with possessive nouns on pages 895–897.

CHAPTER 23

Other and *Else* in Comparisons

Do not make the mistake of comparing one thing with itself when it is part of a group. You can avoid this mistake by adding *other* or *else* to your comparison.

23 B.3 Add *other* and *else* when comparing a member of a group with the rest of the group.

Incorrect	The bank building is taller than any structure in the city. (Since the bank building is a structure, it is being incorrectly compared with itself.)
Correct	The bank building is taller than any **other** structure in the city. (When the word *other* is added, the building is being compared only with other structures.)
Incorrect	The bank president delivers more speeches than anyone in the company. (Since the bank president works in the company, he or she is being compared with himself or herself.)
Correct	The bank president delivers more speeches than anyone **else** in the company. (With the addition of the word *else,* the bank president no longer is being compared to himself or herself.)

● Practice Your Skills

Making Comparisons

Write *I* if the comparison in the sentence is incorrect. Write *C* if it is correct. Rewrite any sentences that are incorrect.

1. Our map of the downtown area made locations more clearer for my visiting uncle.

2. Our city has a more interesting history than any city in the state.

3. Our city is more picturesque than most other cities its size and age.

4. The architecture of the bank is more interesting than that of the library or city hall.

5. The sidewalks were constructed of the most beautiful cobblestones.

6. The town hall is more farther south than any building except the old courthouse at the end of Alexandria Street.

Write each incorrect modifier and then write it correctly. If a sentence is correct, write **C.**

1. Norman Rockwell was one of America's best known illustrators.

2. Of these two pictures, I enjoyed this one the most.

3. The painting with the boy and the Santa Claus suit is the most cutest picture I have ever seen.

4. The most versatile artist in our class is Roberta.

5. In our class, the person with the less interest in art is Anthony.

6. His painting is messier than any painting in the class.

7. This museum's exhibit is better than any exhibit in town.

8. These paintings are more abstracter than other paintings.

9. We enjoyed this exhibit the most of all that we have seen.

10. Eli thinks that painting with oils is hardest than painting with watercolors.

● *Connect to Writing:* **Comparing and Contrasting**

Using Adjectives and Adverbs

Look at the image next to this paragraph. Think about the people, situation, and attitudes revealed in the photograph. Next, choose another image in this book, and take a good look at it. Compare and contrast the two images. Describe what you finding pleasing about each, and why. Then, point by point, write a paragraph in which you compare and contrast the two images.

Most words that end in *–ly* are adverbs. However, some adjectives such as *friendly* and *lovely* also have this ending.

23 C   **It is important to know whether a word is an adjective or an adverb in order to form the comparisons correctly.**

Adjective or Adverb?

Adjectives and adverbs are both modifiers because they describe other words. Remember that an adjective describes a noun or pronoun. It usually comes before the noun or pronoun it describes, or it follows a linking verb. Adjectives are easy to recognize because they answer the following questions:

Which One?	The **yellow** taxi is pulling away.
What Kind?	My bicycle is a **new** model.
How Many?	**Two** cherries sat atop my sundae.
How Much?	The trip sounds **expensive**.

Remember that some verbs—such as *look, feel,* and *sound*—can be either linking verbs or action verbs. When these verbs are used as linking verbs, they are often followed by an adjective.

Linking Verb	The roses in his garden **look** beautiful.
	(*Look* links *beautiful* and *roses*—beautiful roses.)
Action Verb	We **looked** at the beautiful roses in his garden.
	(The subject is *We*. What did we do? *Looked* is the action verb.)

You can find lists of linking verbs on pages 527–528 and 582.

Adverbs describe verbs, adjectives, and other adverbs. Adverbs can be placed almost anywhere in a sentence. You can find them by asking the questions below.

Where?	We looked **everywhere** for her missing shoe.
When?	Debbie **sometimes** whistles when she is nervous.
How?	Please speak **slowly.**
To What Extent?	My vacation was **very** enjoyable.
	He writes me e-mails **quite** often.

Because so many adverbs end in *–ly,* they are usually easy to recognize. Remember, however, that a few adjectives also end in *–ly.*

Adverb	On the weekends I get up very **early.**
	(*Early* tells when I get up.)
Adjective	On Saturday, I had an **early** dentist appointment.
	(*Early* tells what kind of appointment.)

A few words—such as *first, hard, high, late,* and *long*—are the same whether they are used as adjectives or adverbs.

Adverb	She worked **late** to finish her homework.
	(*Late* tells when she worked.)
Adjective	We met at two for a **late** lunch.
	(*Late* tells what kind of lunch it was.)

● *Connect to Writing:* **Content-Based Vocabulary**

Using Adjectives and Adverbs in Comparisons

Write an explanatory paragraph describing what you have learned about the the problems involved in using adjectives and adverbs in comparisons. Give a short definition of the problem in your own words. Then give examples of how these problems might occur. Write two original sentences using an adjective as a modifier and two original sentences using an adverb as a modifier. Finally, write a sentence using *high* as an adjective and *hard* as an adverb.

⟱ Special Problems

Some adjectives and adverbs present special problems.

Good or Well?

23 C.1   *Good* is always used as an adjective. *Well* is usually used as an adverb. However, when *well* means "in good health" or "attractive," it is an adjective.

Adjective	That baking bread smells **good.**
Adverb	The bread machine ran **well.**
Adjective	I like **good,** homemade bread!
Adjective	This recipe was a **good** test of bread-making skills.
Adverb	I think we all baked very **well.**
Adjective	You feel **well** when you eat healthy foods, (in good health)

Bad or Badly?

23 C.2   *Bad* is an adjective and often follows a linking verb. *Badly* is used as an adverb.

Adjective	This bland white bread tastes **bad.**
Adverb	I'm afraid I prepared the meal **badly.**

When You Speak and Write

In casual conversation it is acceptable to use *bad* or *badly* after the verb *feel.* In writing, however, use *bad* as an adjective and *badly* as an adverb.

In Conversation	I feel **bad** about what I said to him. or I feel **badly** about what I said to him.
In Writing	I feel **bad** about what I said to him.

Double Negatives

Words such as *hardly, never, nobody,* and *nothing* are **negative words.** Never use two negative words to express one negative idea. The chart below shows common negatives.

COMMON NEGATIVES	
but (meaning "only")	none
hardly	not (and its contraction *n't*)
never	nothing
no	only
nobody	scarcely

23 C.3   Avoid using a **double negative.**

A double negative often cancels itself out, leaving a positive statement. For example, if you say, "There isn't no more time," you are really saying, "There is more time."

Double Negative	Do**n't never** cook while Mom is gone.
Correct	Do**n't ever** cook while Mom is gone.
Correct	**Never** cook while Mom is gone.
Double Negative	There is**n't hardly** any milk left.
Correct	There is **hardly** any milk left.
Double Negative	I did**n't** drink **nothing** all morning.
Correct	I did**n't** drink **anything** all morning.
Correct	I drank **nothing** all morning.

● *Connect to Writing:* **Persuasive Speech**

Using Modifiers

Your school board has proposed ending physical education at your school. You plan to give a five-minute talk to the board explaining your opinion of this proposal. List specific reasons and examples that support your position. Then arrange your notes in logical order and write a speech. Edit your work, paying attention to comparative and superlative forms of modifiers. Write a final draft, and practice reading your speech aloud.

Writers may use double negatives to make dialogue seem real and natural. The rock group Pink Floyd used the speech of school children in writing the following sarcastic double negative for the song "Another Brick in the Wall."

We don't need no education.

We don't need no thought control.
    —Pink FLoyd, from the album *The Wall*

Practice Your Skills

Comparing with Problem Modifiers

Write *I* if the comparison in the sentence is incorrect. Write **C** if it is correct.

1. I didn't go nowhere near the stove today.
2. I haven't done nothing about preparing our dinner.
3. I would have cooked, but I wasn't feeling good.
4. Mom's business trip went good, but she will be glad to be home.
5. I'm a good cook, and I don't mind cooking.
6. When I'm well, there is not nothing I'd rather do than cook.

Connect to Writing: Revising

Using Modifiers Correctly

Rewrite correctly the preceding sentences that contain errors in comparison.

Check Point: Mixed Practice

Rewrite the following paragraph, correcting each mistake in the use of comparisons.

(1) The Olympic decathlon is held in greater esteem than any event in sports. **(2)** The champion of this event is generally considered the most greatest athlete in the world. **(3)** The performances in the decathlon are watched more than those in any Olympic event. **(4)** The athletes competing in this event must be well at several different activities. **(5)** They can't hardly go even one day without practicing their sport. **(6)** A decathlon performer must be able to jump the highest, run the fastest, and throw the javelin the most farthest. **(7)** The winner must be the bestest at everything.

Assess Your Learning

Using Modifiers Correctly

Write the following sentences, correcting each error. If a sentence is correct, write **C**.

1. For its size the honeybee is much more stronger than a person.

2. Paul hasn't done nothing yet about the garden.

3. Rainbow Bridge in Utah is larger than any other natural arch.

4. Woodworking is the bestest class I have this year.

5. Sean hasn't never seen *Star Wars*.

6. English contains more words than any language.

7. There isn't no more hamburger for the picnic.

8. The Great Dane is among the most largest of all dogs.

9. I think Molly is smarter than anyone in her class.

10. The copies seem brightest than the originals.

11. Which is hardest, ice-skating or roller-skating?

12. Do people in the United States have a higher standard of living than anyone in the world?

13. Nobody knew nothing about the defective fuse.

14. The flood last week was the worst yet.

15. That was the less expensive gift I could find.

16. Even an expert could hardly tell the difference between the real and the counterfeit bill.

17. Lee plays the drums better than anyone in his band.

18. Of Sarah's parents, her dad is most easygoing.

19. Tulips haven't never done well on that side of the house.

20. Of the two finalists, Carl has the best chance of winning.

Writing with Modifiers

Write the correct form of each modifier below.

1. the comparative of *quickly*

2. the comparative of *wide*

3. the superlative of *good*

4. the superlative of *generous*

5. the comparative of *little*

6. the superlative of *bright*

7. the comparative of *carefully*

8. the superlative of *bad*

9. the comparative of *brave*

10. the comparative of *many*

11. the superlative of *angry*

12. the superlative of *evenly*

13. the comparative of *zany*

14. the negative superlative of *courageous*

15. the comparative of *nervous*

16. the comparative of *easily*

17. the comparative of *swiftly*

18. the superlative of *heavy*

19. the negative comparative of *abrupt*

20. the superlative of *surely*

21. the superlative of *thin*

22. the negative comparative of *seasick*

23. the comparative of *ill*

24. the superlative of *much*

25. the comparative of *fast*

Writing Sentences

Write a paragraph that compares three pets or three desserts. Use modifiers in the positive, comparative, and superlative degrees.

Using Adjectives and Adverbs: Posttest

Directions

Read the passage and choose the word or group of words that belongs in each underlined space. Write the letter of the correct answer.

The new car was __(1)__ than Jim's old car. With four-wheel drive, it also had __(2)__ brakes for his trips to the mountains. However, it was __(3)__ than what Jim could afford.

Later Jim went to the mall. He saw two jackets. One was __(4)__ than the other. The __(5)__ jacket had __(6)__ buttons. Although they were both blue, the more formal one was a __(7)__ shade. The more formal jacket also had the __(8)__ sleeves. Jim decided to buy the __(9)__ jacket. "Buying a jacket is certainly __(10)__ than buying a car," he thought.

1. **A** powerful
   B more powerful
   C most powerful
   D powerfulest

2. **A** better
   B more better
   C more good
   D best

3. **A** expensive
   B more expensive
   C most expensive
   D more expensiver

4. **A** formaler
   B most formal
   C more formal
   D formal

5. **A** least formal
   B less formal
   C unformal
   D formal

6. **A** more fewer
   B fewest
   C fewer
   D most fewer

7. **A** more deeper
   B most deep
   C deepest
   D deeper

8. **A** most wide
   B more wide
   C widest
   D wider

9. **A** lightest
   B lighter
   C more lighter
   D most lightest

10. **A** affordable
    B affordabler
    C most affordable
    D more affordable

Writer's Corner

Snapshot

23 A Adjectives and adverbs are **modifiers.** Most modifiers show the degree of comparison by changing form. (pages 776–782)

23 B When you compare people or things, avoid **double comparisons, illogical comparisons,** and comparing a thing with itself. (pages 783–785)

23 C It is important to know whether a word is an adjective or an adverb in order to form comparisons correctly. (pages 786–788)

Power Rules

Avoid using double negatives. Use only one negative form for a single negative idea. (pages 789–790)

Before Editing	**After Editing**
Sally *won't* finish *nothing*.	Sally *won't* finish *anything*.
We *couldn't* think of *nothing* to say to the new neighbors.	We *couldn't* think of *anything* to say to the new neighbors.
There *isn't hardly* any milk left.	There *is hardly* any milk left.
We *couldn't scarcely* see the road because it was so foggy.	We *could scarcely* see the road because it was so foggy.
She *didn't never* ask my opinion.	She *didn't ever* ask my opinion.

Editing Checklist

Use this checklist when editing your writing.

✓ Did I use the correct forms of adjectives and adverbs to show degrees of comparison? (See pages 776–782.)

✓ Did I avoid double comparisons and illogical comparisons? (See page 783.)

✓ Did I use *other* or *else* when comparing a member of a group with the rest of the group? (See pages 784–785.)

✓ Did I use adverbs and adjectives correctly in comparisons? (See pages 786–788.)

✓ Did I generally use *good* as an adjective that follows a linking verb and *well* as an adverb that follows an action verb? (See page 788.)

✓ Did I avoid using double negatives? (See pages 789–790.)

Use the Power

Use these graphics to help you understand the regular and irregular comparative and superlative forms.

Regular Comparative: The Singapore Flyer is shorter than the Great Dubai Wheel.

Regular Superlative: When completed, the Beijing Great Wheel will be the tallest wheel in the world.

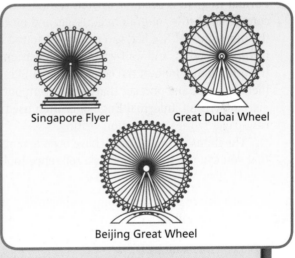

Singapore Flyer   Great Dubai Wheel

Beijing Great Wheel

Irregular Comparative: The Singapore Flyer can carry many people, but the Beijing Great Wheel will carry even more people.

Irregular Superlative: Singapore sounds like a good city, but Beijing sounds like the best of all cities.

A Writer's Glossary of Usage

In the last four chapters, you covered the fundamental elements of usage. A Writer's Glossary of Usage presents some specific areas that might give you difficulty. Before you use the glossary, though, there are some terms that you should know.

You will notice references in the glossary to various levels of language. Two of these levels of language are Standard English and nonstandard English. **Standard English** refers to the rules and the conventions of usage that are accepted and used most widely by English-speaking people throughout the world. **Nonstandard English** has many variations because it is influenced by regional differences and dialects, as well as by current slang. Remember that *nonstandard* does not mean that the language is wrong, but that the language may be inappropriate in certain situations. Because nonstandard English lacks uniformity, you should use Standard English when you write.

You will also notice references to formal and informal English. **Formal English** is used for written work because it follows the conventional rules of grammar, usage, and mechanics. Examples of the use of formal English can usually be found in business letters, technical reports, and well-written compositions. **Informal English,** on the other hand, follows the conventions of Standard English but might include words and phrases that would seem out of place in a formal piece of writing. Informal English is often used in magazine articles, newspaper stories, and fiction writing.

The items in this glossary have been arranged alphabetically so that you can use this section as a reference tool.

a, an Use *a* before words beginning with consonant sounds and *an* before words beginning with vowel sounds.

> Did you buy **a** new CD?
>
> No, it was given to me as **an** early birthday gift.

accept, except *Accept* is a verb that means "to receive with consent." *Except* is usually a preposition that means "but" or "other than."

> Everyone **except** Bernie **accepted** the news calmly.

advice, advise *Advice* is a noun that means "a recommendation." *Advise* is a verb that means "to recommend."

> I usually follow my doctor's **advice.**
>
> He **advised** me to exercise more often.

affect, effect *Affect* is a verb that means "to influence" or "to act upon." *Effect* is usually a noun that means "a result" or "an influence." As a verb, *effect* means "to accomplish" or "to produce."

> Does the weather **affect** your mood?
>
> No, it has no **effect** on me.
>
> The medicine **effected** a change in my disposition.

● *Connect to Speaking and Writing*

> Professional writers sometimes use *ain't* to enhance a dialect and create a humorous effect. Notice the effectiveness of this device in Mark Twain's writing.
>
> Tom's most well now, and got his bullet around his neck on a watch-guard for a watch, and is always seeing what time it is, and so there **ain't** nothing more to write about, and I am rotten glad of it, because if I'd 'a' knowed what a trouble it was to make a book I wouldn't 'a' tackled it, and **ain't** a-going to no more.
> —Mark Twain, *The Adventures of Huckleberry Finn*

ain't This contraction is nonstandard English. Avoid it in your formal writing.

> **Nonstandard**   Ken **ain't** here yet.
>
> **Standard**   Ken **isn't** here yet.

all ready, already *All ready* means "completely ready." *Already* means "previously."

> We were **all ready** to go by seven o'clock.
>
> I had **already** told my parents that we were going to the movies.

all together, altogether *All together* means "in a group." *Altogether* means "wholly" or "thoroughly."

> Let's try to sing **all together** for a change.
>
> The traditional song will sound **altogether** different if we do.

a lot People very often write these two words incorrectly as one. There is no such word as "alot." *A lot,* however, even when it is written as two words, should be avoided in formal writing.

> **Informal**   Famous movie stars usually receive **a lot** of fan mail.
>
> **Formal**   Famous movie stars usually receive **a large quantity** of fan mail.

among, between These words are both prepositions. *Among* is used when referring to three or more people or things. *Between* is used when referring to two people or things.

> Put your present **among** the others.
>
> Then come and sit **between** Judith and me.

amount, number *Amount* refers to a singular word. *Number* refers to a plural word.

> Although there were a **number** of rainy days this month, the total **amount** of rain was less than usual.

● *Connect to Speaking and Writing*

To avoid confusion in usage between *amount* and *number* when speaking and writing, remember that *amount* refers to things in bulk or mass that cannot be counted, whereas *number* refers to things that can be counted.

I was surprised at the **amount** of coffee he drank. (Coffee cannot be counted.)

He put a large **number** of coffee beans into the machine. (Coffee beans can be counted.)

anywhere, everywhere, nowhere, somewhere Do not add –*s* to any of these words.

> I looked **everywhere** but could not find my keys.

at Do not use *at* after *where*.

> **Nonstandard**   Do you know **where** we're **at?**
>
> **Standard**   Do you know **where** we are?

a while, awhile *A while* is made up of an article and a noun; together, they are mainly used after a preposition. *Awhile* is an adverb that stands alone and means "for a short period of time."

> We can stay on the job for **a while.**
>
> After we work **awhile,** we can take a break.

● Practice Your Skills

Finding the Correct Word

Write the word in parentheses that correctly completes each sentence.

1. The junior varsity team has (all ready, already) started football practice.
2. (Accept, Except) for a few players, the team is in excellent condition.
3. This year's team has (a, an) difficult schedule.
4. Their coaches offer the players useful (advice, advise) (everywhere, everywheres) the team plays.
5. In addition, they teach the eager squad a large (amount, number) of plays.
6. Loyalty (among, between) the members of the football team is encouraged.
7. (A lot, A large amount) of time is spent in daily practice.
8. Players arriving late (affect, effect) the practice schedule.
9. The players meet (all together, altogether) before practice (a while, awhile) for a pep talk.
10. It (ain't, isn't) long before the first game will be played.

Recognizing Correct Usage

Add interest to this paragraph by replacing the term *a lot* with a more precise word or phrase. As you rewrite the paragraph, use a different word or phrase each time.

A lot of students waited eagerly for the first football game. When the day arrived, a lot of the ninth grade class met for a pep rally. The teachers advised the students not to wander around a lot. After cheering and applauding a lot, they returned to class, a lot satisfied with their class spirit.

bad, badly *Bad* is an adjective and often follows a linking verb. *Badly* is used as an adverb. In the first two examples, *felt* is a linking verb.

Nonstandard	Luke felt **badly** all day.
Standard	Luke felt **bad** all day.
Standard	Luke **badly** needs a haircut.

bring, take *Bring* indicates motion toward the speaker. *Take* indicates motion away from the speaker.

Bring me the stamps.

Now, please **take** this letter to the post office.

can, may *Can* expresses ability. *May* expresses possibility or permission.

I **can** baby-sit for you tonight.

May I watch TV after Kenny is asleep?

doesn't, don't *Doesn't* is singular and must agree with a singular subject. *Don't* is plural and must agree with a plural subject, except when used with the singular pronouns *I* and *you*.

This article **doesn't** make sense to me.
(singular subject)

These articles **don't** make sense to me.
(plural subject)

double negative Words such as *barely, but* (when it means "only"), *hardly, never, no, none, no one, nobody, not* (and its contraction *n't*), *nothing, nowhere, only,* and *scarcely* are all negatives. Do not use two negatives to express one negative meaning.

Nonstandard	I **hardly never** see you anymore.
Standard	I **hardly ever** see you anymore.
Standard	I **never** see you anymore.

etc. *Etc.* is an abbreviation for the Latin phrase *et cetera,* which means "and other things." Never use the word *and* with *etc.* If you do, what you are really saying is "and and other things." You should not use this abbreviation at all in formal writing.

Informal	Before moving, we had to pack our clothes, books, records, **etc.**
Formal	Before moving, we had to pack our clothes, books, records, **and other belongings.**

fewer, less *Fewer* is plural and refers to things that can be counted. *Less* is singular and refers to quantities and qualities that cannot be counted.

There seem to be **fewer** hours in the day.

I seem to have **less** time to get my homework done.

good, well *Good* is an adjective and often follows a linking verb. *Well* is an adverb and often follows an action verb. However, when *well* means "in good health" or "satisfactory," it is used as an adjective.

The biscuits smell **good.** (adjective)

Janice cooks **well.** (adverb)

I feel quite **well** after eating the chicken soup. (adjective meaning "in good health")

have, of Never substitute *of* for the verb *have.* When speaking, many people make a contraction of *have.* For example, they might say, "We should've gone." Because *'ve* may sound like *of, of* is often mistakenly substituted for *have* in writing.

Nonstandard	We should **of** started earlier.
Standard	We should **have** started earlier.

hear, here *Hear* is a verb that means "to perceive by listening." *Here* is an adverb that means "in this place."

> I can't **hear** the music from **here.**

hole, whole A *hole* is an opening. *Whole* means "complete" or "entire."

> Have you noticed the **hole** in your coat?
>
> Did you leave your coat on for the **whole** movie?

in, into Use *in* when you are referring to a stationary place. Use *into* when you want to express motion from one place to another.

> Is the money **in** your coat pocket?
>
> Why don't you transfer it **into** your wallet?

its, it's *Its* is a possessive pronoun and means "belonging to it." *It's* is a contraction for *it is.*

> The dog returned home to **its** owner.
>
> **It's** fun to watch **its** happy expression.

● **Practice Your Skills**

Finding the Correct Word

Write the word in parentheses that correctly completes each sentence.

1. Who (doesn't, don't) enjoy an interesting detective story?

2. It (can, may) also be referred to as a mystery story or whodunit.

3. Some writers use (fewer, less) clues than others, but all detective stories contain clues designed to solve a crime.

4. The detective story made (its, it's) first appearance in Edgar Allan Poe's writings.

5. Poe also wrote essays, poems, short stories, (etc., and other works).

6. His fictional detective, C. Auguste Dupin, (may have, may of) been based on a real-life detective.

7. Poe wrote a (hole, whole) group of stories that featured Detective Dupin.

8. Detective Dupin first appeared (in, into) Poe's "The Murders in the Rue Morgue."

● *Connect to Writing:* **Revising**

Recognizing Correct Usage

Rewrite the following paragraph, changing the words that are used incorrectly.

In fiction an author don't often leave readers in suspense. Usually the hole case is carefully tied together into a neat package. Hardly ever is a crime left unsolved in a fictional detective story. In real life, however, its often not what we hear about. On television, for example, news programs sometimes bring us to the scene of a unsolved mystery and try to recreate it. Some shows present the facts good while others present them bad. Regardless of the way the program is presented, the crime don't have a final resolution as fictional detective stories do.

● **Practice Your Skills**

Explanatory Writing: Adjectives and Adverbs

You have been asked to tutor a student who is experiencing difficulty with the following terms: *bad/badly* and *good/well*. In your own words, write an explanation to offer the student for the choice(s) underlined in each of the following sentences.

1. Interest in a detective story often depends on whether the plot is <u>bad</u> or <u>good.</u>

2. Clues that are presented <u>well</u> prevent the reader from solving the crime too quickly.

3. If the description of a possible suspect is presented <u>badly</u>, it detracts from the story.

4. A writer might present a suspect as being in <u>bad</u> health to gain sympathy from the reader for that particular character.

5. Most people feel <u>good</u> at the end of a detective story because justice has been served.

knew, new *Knew,* the past tense of the verb *know,* means "was acquainted with." *New* is an adjective that means "recently made" or "just found."

Michael's sneakers looked so clean and white that I **knew** they were **new.**

learn, teach *Learn* means "to gain knowledge." *Teach* means "to instruct" or "to show how."

I just **learned** how to use that computer program that Mom bought for us.

Now I can **teach** you how to use it.

leave, let *Leave* means "to depart." *Let* means "to allow" or "to permit."

> **Nonstandard**   **Leave** me help you carry those packages into the house.
>
> **Standard**   **Let** me help you carry those packages into the house.
>
> **Standard**   Don't **leave** before you help me carry in my packages.

lie, lay *Lie* means "to rest or recline." *Lie* is never followed by a direct object. Its principal parts are *lie, lying, lay,* and *lain. Lay* means "to put or set (something) down." *Lay* is usually followed by a direct object. Its principal parts are *lay, laying, laid,* and *laid.*

> **Lie**   Our kittens always **lie** on the sofa.
>
> They are **lying** there now.
>
> They **lay** there all morning.
>
> They have **lain** there for a long time.
>
> **Lay**   **Lay** their food dish on the floor. (*Dish* is the direct object.)
>
> Jill is **laying** the dish on the floor.
>
> Molly **laid** the dish on the floor yesterday.
>
> Until recently Gary always has **laid** the dish on the floor.

You can learn more about using the verbs lie *and* lay *on page 691.*

like, as *Like* is a preposition that introduces a prepositional phrase. *As* is usually a subordinating conjunction that introduces an adverb clause.

> **Standard**   Betty should read stories **like** these.
> (prepositional phrase)
>
> **Nonstandard**   Betty usually does **like** she is told.
> (clause)
>
> **Standard**   Betty usually does **as** she is told.

passed, past *Passed* is the past tense of the verb *pass.* As a noun *past* means "a time gone by." As an adjective *past* means "just gone" or "elapsed." As a preposition *past* means "beyond."

> In the **past** I have **passed** all math tests. (*past* as a noun and *passed* as a verb)
>
> I have walked **past** my math class for the **past** few days, hoping to see my final grade posted. (*past* as a preposition and then as an adjective)

rise, raise *Rise* means "to move upward" or "to get up." *Rise* is never followed by a direct object. *Raise* means "to lift (something) up," "to increase," or "to grow something." *Raise* is usually followed by a direct object.

> Dad will **rise** at 7:00 A.M.
>
> At that time, he will **raise** the shades. (*Shades* is the direct object.)

You can learn more about using the verbs rise *and* raise *on page 691.*

shall, will Formal English used to use *shall* with first-person pronouns and *will* with second- and third-person pronouns. Today, *shall* and *will* are used interchangeably with *I* and *we,* except that *shall* should be used with *I* and *we* for questions.

> **Shall** I invite her to join the club?
>
> I **will** ask her tonight.

sit, set *Sit* means "to rest in an upright position." *Sit* is not followed by a direct object. *Set* means "to put or place (something)." *Set* is usually followed by a direct object.

> After Mom has **set** the timer, we will **sit** and wait thirty minutes for dinner.
> (*Timer* is the direct object of *set.*)

You can learn more about using the verbs sit *and* set *on pages 691–692.*

suppose to, supposed to Be sure to add the *d* to *suppose* when it is followed by *to.*

> **Nonstandard**   We are **suppose to** arrive one hour early to practice.
>
> **Standard**   We are **supposed to** arrive one hour early to practice.

than, then *Than* is a subordinating conjunction and is used for comparisons. *Then* is an adverb and means "at that time" or "next."

> **Nonstandard**   Jupiter is much larger **then** Saturn.
>
> **Standard**   After learning that Jupiter is much larger **than** Saturn, we **then** learned more interesting facts about our solar system.

that, which, who All three words are relative pronouns. *That* refers to people, animals, or things; *which* refers to animals or things; and *who* refers to people.

> The airline tickets **that** I bought for the trip were expensive.
>
> The flight attendant **who** was on my plane pointed out the cows, **which** looked like little dots.

A Writer's Glossary of Usage   **805**

● Practice Your Skills

Finding the Correct Word

Write the word in parentheses that correctly completes each sentence.

1. The family (shall, will) go on their annual family picnic tomorrow.

2. Leslie and David (knew, new) they could each invite one friend.

3. They invited the twins (which, who) live in the house down the road.

4. The family members will (raise, rise) early and pack the car.

5. Leslie (lain, laid) out the tablecloth and the paper plates the night before the picnic.

6. Their parents always (leave, let) them help prepare food for the picnic basket and decide on the sporting equipment to use at the picnic.

7. David first wanted Dad to (learn, teach) him to make deviled eggs.

8. His cooking (passed, past) inspection after the family sampled the eggs.

9. Leslie declared that they tasted exactly (like, as) the ones from the deli.

10. (Than, Then) she began baking brownies.

11. Later they took out the sporting equipment, (which, who) was in the garage.

12. Leslie and David (sit, set) a variety of sporting equipment next to the car.

13. David remembered to include his (new, knew) baseball and glove.

14. Leslie and David decided to (teach, learn) the twins how to play volleyball.

15. The whole family agreed they would have a better time (than, then) last year.

● *Connect to Writing:* Drafting

Writing Correct Forms of Verbs

Rewrite the following paragraph, changing the words that are used incorrectly.

On the day of the picnic, Leslie had sat her alarm for 7:00 A.M. After the alarm rang, she set up on the side of the bed. Next, she slowly raised the blinds to see if the sun had raised. Deciding to rest another few minutes, she reset the alarm and lied down on the bed again, carefully laying her head on the pillow. When the alarm sounded, she went downstairs to help sit the picnic items inside the basket. Before sitting down to eat, she called David. David came to the table and set down. He saw Leslie rise the blinds so that they could watch the sunrise while they ate. After breakfast, David lay an old blanket on the floor and quickly folded it before the dog could lay down on it.

Practice Your Skills

Description: Verbs

Pretend you have arrived at the beach or park for a family picnic. Write a well-developed paragraph in which you describe the day's events. In your description, include at least four of the phrases listed below, making sure you use the correct principal parts of the verbs in parentheses.

- on the blanket *(lie, lay)*
- the golden sun *(sit, set)*
- food to the picnic area *(bring, take)*
- the volleyball net *(sit, set)*
- the picnic basket to the car *(bring, take)*
- on the picnic bench *(sit, set)*

their, there, they're *Their* is a possessive pronoun. *There* is usually an adverb, but sometimes it begins an inverted sentence. *They're* is a contraction for *they are*.

Tell them to take **their** time.

There will be many reporters gathered in the hall.

They're meeting at seven o'clock for the press conference.

theirs, there's *Theirs* is a possessive pronoun. *There's* is a contraction for *there is*.

These messages are ours; those messages are **theirs.**

There's a message for you in the office.

them, those Never use *them* as a subject or as an adjective.

Nonstandard	**Them** are freshly picked tomatoes. (subject)
Standard	**Those** are freshly picked tomatoes.
Nonstandard	Did you like **them** tomatoes? (adjective)
Standard	Did you like **those** tomatoes?

this here, that there Avoid using *here* or *there* in addition to *this* or *that*.

Nonstandard	**That there** chair is very comfortable.
Standard	**That** chair is very comfortable.
Nonstandard	**This here** sofa matches your chair.
Standard	**This sofa** matches your chair.

threw, through *Threw* is the past tense of the verb *throw*. *Through* is a preposition that means "in one side and out the other."

Denny **threw** the ball over the fence.

He's lucky that it didn't go **through** the window of the house.

to, too, two *To* is a preposition. *To* also begins an infinitive. *Too* is an adverb that modifies a verb, an adjective, or another adverb. *Two* is a number.

Keith went **to** the gym **to** practice.

Two members of the team arrived **too** late.

Only one was asked **to** play in the game, but the other played **too**.

use to, used to Be sure to add the *d* to *use* when it is followed by *to*.

Nonstandard	I **use to** have three cats, but now I have one.
Standard	I **used to** have three cats, but now I have one.

When You Use Technology

The spell check feature on your word processing or e-mail software can be very helpful. It can help you check your spelling as you compose or edit your writing. Be careful, however, because a spelling check will not edit your work. For example, spell check will not flag your writing when you incorrectly use *affect* when *effect* is the right choice. You can usually find the spelling feature in the Edit or the Tools menu of your software. You can also set most current programs to mark misspelled words as you type. Look in the Preferences menu to activate this feature.

way, ways Do not substitute *ways* for *way* when referring to a distance.

> **Nonstandard**   We have gone a long **ways** since noon.
>
> **Standard**   We have gone a long **way** since noon.

when, where Do not use *when* or *where* directly after a linking verb in a definition.

> **Nonstandard**   A *presbyope* is **when** a person is farsighted.
>
> **Standard**   A *presbyope* is a farsighted person.
>
> **Nonstandard**   A *domicile* is **where** people live.
>
> **Standard**   A *domicile* is a place **where** people live.

where Do not substitute *where* for *that*.

> **Nonstandard**   I heard **where** crime rates are going down.
>
> **Standard**   I heard **that** crime rates are going down.

who, whom *Who*, a pronoun in the nominative case, is used as either a subject or a predicate nominative. *Whom*, a pronoun in the objective case, is used as a direct object, an indirect object, or an object of a preposition.

> **Who** is coming to your party? (subject)
>
> **Whom** did you choose? (direct object)

You can learn more about using who *and* whom *on pages 729–733.*

whose, who's *Whose* is a possessive pronoun. *Who's* is a contraction for *who is*.

> **Whose** bicycle did you borrow?
>
> **Who's** going to ride with you?

your, you're *Your* is a possessive pronoun. *You're* is a contraction for *you are*.

> Are these **your** campaign posters?
>
> **You're** the one we want for president of the class.

Finding the Correct Word

Write the word in parentheses that correctly completes each sentence.

1. Edward J. Smith, (who, whom) was called the "Millionaire's Captain" by some, commanded the *Titanic* on its fateful journey.
2. Captain Smith, (whose, who's) reputation for experience and safety were excellent, planned to retire after this voyage.
3. (Their, There) have been many accounts written about the sinking of the *Titanic*.
4. Most people believed the ship (to, too) be unsinkable.
5. Regulations never (use to, used to) require lifeboat space for every person.
6. The *Titanic* had traveled a long (way, ways) from Southampton, England, when it struck an iceberg.
7. Some hours later, passengers were instructed to put on (their, there) life jackets.
8. There were 16 wooden lifeboats; at first, only women and children were allowed on (them, those) lifeboats.
9. Hundreds of passengers (threw, through) themselves into the freezing water.
10. Today the ship's (too, two) main sections lie on the ocean floor.

Connect to Writing: Revising

Recognizing Correct Usage

Rewrite the following paragraph, changing the words that are used incorrectly.

Imagine the excitement on that day in 1912 when the *Titanic* left port. On shore their would have been many who bid they're farewells by waving, while others through flowers and kisses too their loved ones. Many passengers were used to traveling on large ships. Few, however, could imagine those lavish staterooms that awaited them when they walked threw the corridors. One such passenger, who's name was well known, was John Jacob Astor, a fur trader and American millionaire. The happy excitement tragically ended on the night of the sinking of the *Titanic*. Astor was among the approximately 1,500 passengers to who death came that fateful night.

✔ *Check Point:* Mixed Practice

Write the word in parentheses that best completes each sentence.

1. The *Titanic* tragedy was difficult to (accept, except) because of the ship's "unsinkable" reputation.
2. Everyone (who, whom) had helped design and build the *Titanic* believed it to be unsinkable.
3. In spite of the (advice, advise) of the original designer, only sixteen wooden lifeboats were on board.
4. The (amount, number) of luxury features onboard impressed even those in first class.
5. (There, Their, They're) was even a kennel for the dogs of first-class passengers.
6. First-class passengers could walk (in, into) a gymnasium for a workout or exercise on the tennis court.
7. The ship featured a swimming pool (that, who) was filled with seawater.
8. (A lot of, A great many) features on the *Titanic* were inspired by the French.
9. (Among, Between) the ship's many remarkable features was its spectacular Grand Staircase.
10. Even second-class and third-class accommodations were better (than, then) those on other ships.
11. None of the passengers (knew, new) that iceberg alerts had been received on several occasions during the voyage.
12. Even after the *Titanic* had hit an iceberg, passengers throughout the (hole, whole) ship believed themselves to be safe.
13. Many of the passengers boarded the lifeboats (like, as) they were told, but others refused to leave their families.
14. As the water was (raising, rising), the band courageously continued to play.
15. (Fewer, Less) than fifteen people were saved from the freezing water.

● *Connect to Writing:* Writing a Narrative

Using Glossary Words

Read over this writer's glossary (pages 796–809), paying particular attention to items that give you trouble in your writing. Then write a short account of a place you would like to visit in the future. Describe what you know about the place, and explain why you would like to go there. Try to use as many of the words you find troublesome as you can. Read your narrative to a friend.

Unit 6

Mechanics

Your readers are like drivers on a journey through your thoughts and ideas. Punctuation and the other mechanics of language are like the traffic signals that guide them safely to their destination. A comma, for instance, can warn readers to pause or slow down as other ideas and information merge into the sentence. A semicolon signals the end of a complete thought, yet also directs readers to keep "rolling" toward the next, closely related thought. Only the period demands a full stop. It asks readers to take a moment to consider the meaning of the recently completed thought. Help your readers navigate through your thoughts with clear and precise mechanics.

A period is a stop sign. A semicolon is a rolling stop sign;
a comma is merely an amber light.

— *Andrew Offutt*

Capital Letters

How can you use capital letters to clarify your meaning when you write?

Capital Letters: Pretest 1

The following description contains several errors in capitalization. The first error is corrected by capitalizing the *e* in *Europe*. How would you revise the paragraph so that all words that should be capitalized are and so that three words that shouldn't be aren't?

My sister Juanita went to europe recently. she brought back more stories and souvenirs than i've ever seen. while visiting madrid, she went to view the art at the prado museum. She also saw an actual spanish Flamenco dance. then she traveled to great britain for a walking tour of the Countryside. after buying my Mother some beautiful gifts, she flew to france and toured notre dame in paris. juanita also visited a world war II memorial. next, She skied in the swiss alps. jaunita has promised to take Me on her next trip across the atlantic. in the meantime, I am going to read books by French authors, such as *The Little Prince*. i'm also going to search the internet for travel articles in publications such as *the New York Times*.

Capital Letters: Pretest 2

Directions

For each sentence, choose the word or words that should be capitalized. Write the letter of your answer. If the sentence contains no error, write *D*.

(1) Last year I took a class called poetry I. (2) It was taught by a real poet, winifred smith. (3) She is the author of *down time*. (4) Though she is american, she spoke with a foreign accent. (5) I think she grew up in france. (6) Now she teaches during the year at hampshire college. (7) She read us poems from different eras; I especially liked the ones from the renaissance. (8) I love hearing ms. smith read her poems with her french accent. (9) My favorite poem begins, "did i miss something?/my back was turned for just a moment...." (10) My friend anita and i wrote a lot of poetry for the class.

1. **A** Class, Poetry
   B Class
   C Poetry
   D No error

2. **A** Poet, Winifred Smith
   B Poet, Smith
   C Winifred Smith
   D No error

3. **A** Author
   B *Down Time*
   C Author, *Down Time*
   D No error

4. **A** American, Foreign
   B Foreign
   C American
   D No error

5. **A** France
   B She
   C Up
   D No error

6. **A** Hampshire
   B College
   C Hampshire College
   D No error

7. **A** Renaissance
   B Eras, Renaissance
   C Eras
   D No error

8. **A** Ms. Smith
   B French
   C Ms. Smith, French
   D No error

9. **A** Did
   B Did, I, My
   C I
   D No error

10. **A** Anita
    B Poetry
    C Anita, I
    D No error

You know that a capital letter signals the beginning of a new idea, but there are additional ways that capitals are used. This chapter will cover them all.

24 A   Capitalize first words and the pronoun *I*.

➤ First Words and the Pronoun *I*

Sentences and Poetry

24 A.1   Capitalize the first word of a sentence and of a line of poetry.

Sentences	**A** lone rose stood in the vase.
	Crystal vases are beautiful.
	Roses have a special fragrance.
Lines of Poetry	**S**he went as quiet as the dew
	From a familiar flower.
	Not like the dew did she return
	At the accustomed hour!

—Emily Dickinson

When you are quoting lines of poetry, copy them exactly as the poet has written them, including any nonstandard capitalization or punctuation. Some poets intentionally break conventional rules of grammar and the poetic form.

You can learn about capitalizing quotations on pages 878–879.

Parts of Letters

24 A.2   Capitalize the first word in the greeting of a letter and the first word in the closing of a letter.

SALUTATIONS AND CLOSINGS		
Salutations	**T**o whom it may concern:	**D**ear Ashley,
	Dear Sir or Madam:	**D**ear boys and girls,
Closings	**Y**ours truly,	**T**hank you,
	With love,	**S**incerely,

Outlines

24 A.3   Capitalize the first word of each item in an outline and the letters that begin major subsections of the outline.

Wildflowers

I. Stonecrop family
  A. Pigmyweed
  B. Stonecrop
    1. Rose-flowered sedum
    2. Yellow stonecrop
  C. Echeveria
    1. Savior flower
    2. Bluff weed
II. Saxifrage family
  A. Saxifrage
    1. Mountain lettuce
    2. Tufted saxifrage
  B. Sullivantia
  C. Boykinia
III. Fireweed family
  A. Purple-leaved willowherb
  B. Pink fireweed
  C. Orange paintbrush

The Pronoun *I*

24 A.4   Capitalize the pronoun *I*, both alone and in contractions.

I hope I've picked enough greenery for the flower arrangement.

I know I'll enjoy seeing those flowers bloom when spring arrives.

Last spring I planted daisies, but this year I'm going to plant bluebonnets.

I'd like to grow roses, but they require a great deal of care.

Using Capital Letters

Rewrite the following items, correcting the errors in capitalization.

1. shall i compare thee to a summer's day?

thou art more lovely and more temperate…

—William Shakespeare, *sonnet XVIII*

2. i went to the play, and i really enjoyed it.

3. Types of Poems

    I. rhyming

        A. Limerick

        B. Sonnet

           1. petrarchan

           2. shakespearean

        c. Ballad

Connect to Writing: Editing

Correcting Errors in Capitalization

Rewrite the following letter, correcting the errors in capitalization.

Dear Mrs. Wallace,

  i enjoyed your recent Lecture on the sonnets of Shakespeare. i would like to find one of his sonnets, but i'm not sure what number it is. the first two lines are as follows:

When in disgrace with fortune and men's eyes,

i all alone beweep my outcast state. . .

  would you please let me know which of Shakespeare's sonnets this is? you may write me back at the address i've enclosed.

thank You,

Mikayla Simpson

Connect to Speaking and Writing: Peer Consultation

Using Correct Capitalization

Discuss with a partner the elements of an outline. Together, write a short outline of the plot of a favorite movie. Find a third person to whom you can read your outline. Tell the person that whenever a word in your outline should be capitalized, he or she should say "Cap!" Discuss how many capitalized words the person recognized.

Proper Nouns Lesson 2

24 B **Capitalize proper nouns and their abbreviations.**

24 B.1 Names of persons and animals should be capitalized. Also capitalize initials that stand for people's names.

NAMES OF PERSONS AND ANIMALS

Persons	Eli, Tiffany Jones, Susan **B.** Anthony, Ming Li, **T. H.** Murphy Jr.
Animals	Spot, Muffin, Rover, Scout, Buttercup

24 B.2 Geographical names, which include particular places and bodies of water and their abbreviations, initials, and acronyms, are capitalized.

GEOGRAPHICAL NAMES

Streets, Highways	Maple Avenue (**Ave.**), the Pennsylvania Turnpike (**Tpk.**), Route (**Rt.**) 30, Forty-second Street (**St.**) (The second part of a hyphenated numbered street is not capitalized.)
Towns, Cities	San Francisco, Dallas, Minneapolis, Cheyenne, Phoenix, Atlanta
Counties, Parishes, etc.	Dade County, Iberia Parish, Orange County, Township 531, Hidalgo County
States	Texas (**TX**), Maine (**ME**), Wyoming (**WY**), New Mexico (**NM**) (In a phrase such as "the state of Ohio," *state* is not capitalized.)
Countries	Canada, the United States (**US**), France
Sections of a Country	the Midwest, New England, the Sunbelt, the East, the Southwest (Compass directions are not capitalized: *Go east on Lee St.*)
Continents	Africa, South America, Antarctica, Asia
World Regions	Northern Hemisphere, South Pole, Scandinavia, the Middle East
Islands	the Hawaiian Islands, Long Island, the Galapagos Islands
Mountains	the Himalayas, the Rocky Mountains, Mount Everest, the Andes
Parks	Serengeti National Park, Grand Canyon National Park, Yellowstone
Bodies of Water	the Nile River, the Indian Ocean, the Black Sea, the Great Lakes, Victoria Falls

Words like *street, lake, ocean,* and *mountain* are capitalized only when they are part of a proper noun.

Which is the smallest **l**ake of the **G**reat **L**akes?

Mount **M**c**K**inley is the tallest **m**ountain in North America.

● **Practice Your Skills**

Capitalizing Geographical Names

Write the term that is correctly capitalized in each of the following pairs.

1. New delhi, india
New Delhi, India

2. Thirty-third Street
Thirty-Third Street

3. Great smokey mountains
Great Smokey Mountains

4. lake Michigan
Lake Michigan

5. Ft. Lauderdale
Ft. lauderdale

6. the South
the south

7. Central Park
Central park

8. north on Route 20
North on Route 20

9. the Indian Ocean
the indian ocean

10. Catalina island
Catalina Island

● *Connect to Writing:* **Directions**

Using Capitalization

You have invited a new friend to your home. Since she has never been to your house before, you must give her directions. Beginning at your school, write the directions to your house. Remember to be very specific so that your friend does not get lost. Include the names of streets and landmarks. After you have written your directions, check to make sure that you have used capital letters correctly.

Practice Your Skills

Using Capital Letters

Rewrite each sentence, correcting errors in capitalization.

1. here are some facts about the western hemisphere.

2. did you know that quito is the capital of ecuador?

3. lake titicaca in south america is the highest large lake above sea level.

4. on one of his voyages for spain, christopher columbus discovered the virgin islands.

5. brazil, the largest country in south america, is also the most populous country in latin america.

6. la salle, an early explorer, discovered the mouth of the mississippi river.

7. in order to fly to antarctica, a plane usually leaves from chile.

8. charles darwin studied bird species after visiting the galapagos islands.

Connect to Writing: Editing

Correcting Errors in Capitalization

Rewrite the following paragraph, correcting the errors in capitalization.

(1) high in the lofty, snow-covered andes mountains, the amazon river begins. **(2)** it runs eastward across the continent of south america, flowing through the jungles of brazil. **(3)** finally it empties into the atlantic ocean. **(4)** the mighty amazon river has more water flowing through it than the mississippi river, the nile river, and the yangtze river—all put together! **(5)** the reason for this amazing fact is that the drainage basin of this giant river lies in one of the rainiest regions of the world.

---

24 B.3 Capitalize historically important nouns, which include the names of historical events, periods, and documents and their associated initials and acronyms.

HISTORIC NAMES	
Events	World War II (**WWII**), the Battle of Bull Run
Periods	the Renaissance, the Middle Ages, the Shang Dynasty, the Industrial Revolution
Documents	the Magna Carta, the Declaration of Independence, the Treaty of Versailles

Prepositions that are part of a proper noun are not usually capitalized.

24 B.4 Names of groups, such as organizations, businesses, institutions, government bodies, teams, and political parties, should be capitalized.

NAMES OF GROUPS	
Organizations	the American Red Cross, the United Nations **(UN)**, the Girl Scouts of America **(GSA)**
Businesses	the Dahl Motor Company (Co.), the Leed Corporation (Corp.), Lexington Lumber
Institutions	the University of Chicago (U of C), Emerson High School, Memorial Hospital (Words such as *high school* and *hospital* are not capitalized unless they are a part of a proper noun: *The nearest hospital is Mercy General Hospital.*)
Government Bodies/Agencies	Congress, the State Department, the Bureau of Land Management
Teams	the Boston Red Sox, the Los Angeles Lakers, the Lake Brandon High School Patriots
Political Parties	the Republican Party, the Labor Party, a Republican, a Democrat

24 B.5 Specific time periods and events, including the days of the week, the months of the year, civil and religious holidays, and special events, should be capitalized.

TIME PERIODS AND EVENTS	
Days, Months	Tuesday (Tues.), Friday (Fri.), February (Feb.), October (Oct.)
Holidays	Valentine's Day, Kwanzaa, the Fourth of July, Veteran's Day
Special Events	the Rose Bowl Parade, the Boston Marathon, the Junior Prom
Time Abbreviations	400 B.C. or 400 B.C.E., A.D. 1185, 7:15 AM or 7:15 a.m., 9:45 PM or 9:45 p.m.

However, do not capitalize a season of the year unless it is part of a proper noun.

I like **w**inter best.

Did you go to the **W**inter **F**air?

Capitalizing Proper Nouns

Write the term that is correctly capitalized in each of the following pairs.

1. Thanksgiving day
Thanksgiving Day

2. summer
Summer

3. december
December

4. the Stone Age
the stone age

5. the united way
the United Way

6. Acme brick company
Acme Brick Company

7. the Monroe doctrine
the Monroe Doctrine

8. the Defense Department
the defense department

9. the library of Congress
the Library of Congress

10. the Statue of Liberty
the statue of liberty

● Practice Your Skills

Using Capital Letters

Identify each word that should begin with a capital letter and then rewrite the words correctly.

1. The declaration of independence is an important document in the history of the united states.

2. The treaty of paris ended the american revolution.

3. The signing of a treaty, such as the treaty of neuilly, is an important event.

4. In the winter of 1918, woodrow wilson announced his fourteen points as the basis for the peace settlement of world war I.

5. Wilson was warmly received in paris, where he traveled to sign the treaty of versailles after world war I.

6. Wilson helped establish the league of nations, the precursor of the modern united nations.

7. The republican party controlled congress, and wilson's political enemies refused to allow the united states to enter the league of nations.

● *Connect to Writing:* Editing

Correcting Errors in Capitalization

Rewrite the following paragraphs, correcting the errors in capitalization.

(1) winning the greatest battle in baseball, the world series, is the goal of every professional baseball player. (2) the first game of the modern world series was played in 1903. (3) in that series the boston pilgrims, who would later become known as the red sox, defeated the pittsburgh pirates.

(4) the first player to be named Most Valuable Player was johnny podres of the brooklyn dodgers in 1955. (5) that was the first world championship for the dodgers, who defeated their rivals from across the city, the new york yankees. (6) just two years later, the dodgers would disappoint their brooklyn fans by moving the team out of new york to los angeles, california.

24 B.6   Names of nationalities, races, and languages should be capitalized.

NATIONALITIES, RACES, AND LANGUAGES

Nationalities	an American, a German, Canadians
Races and Ethnic Groups	Caucasian, Asian, Hispanic
Languages	Spanish, English, Mandarin, Russian
Computer Languages	Java, Cobol, C++, Visual Basic

24 B.7   Religions, religious holidays, and religious references, such as the names referring to the Deity, the Bible, and divisions of the Bible, should be capitalized. Also, capitalize pronouns that refer to the Deity.

RELIGIOUS NAMES

Religions	Christianity, Buddhism, Judaism, Islam
Religious Holidays	Hanukkah, Christmas, Ramadan, Epiphany, Purim, Passover, Easter
Religious References	God, the Lord, God and His children, the Bible, Exodus, the Scriptures, the Koran, Allah, Buddha , the Torah

Notice that the word *god* is not capitalized when it refers to gods in polytheistic religions.

> Neptune, who was also called Poseidon, was the god of the sea.

24 B.8   Names of stars, planets, and constellations are capitalized.

ASTRONOMICAL NAMES	
Stars	the Dog Star, Canopus, the North Star
Planets	Mars, Saturn, Venus, Neptune, Jupiter
Constellations	the Big Dipper, Orion's Belt, the Milky Way

The words *sun* and *moon* are not capitalized. *Earth* is not capitalized if it is preceded by the word *the*.

24 B.9   Other proper nouns—such as the names of aircraft, awards, brand names, and buildings—should also begin with capital letters.

OTHER PROPER NOUNS	
Aircraft, Spacecraft	the *Concorde, Titan II, Apollo 13*
Awards	the Nobel Prize, the Heisman Trophy
Brand Names	New Foam soap, Silkie shampoo, Crunchies cat food
Technological Terms	Internet, Web, World Wide Web, Web site, Web page
Bridges and Buildings	the Golden Gate Bridge, the Empire State Building, the Eiffel Tower
Memorials, Museums, Monuments	the Lincoln Memorial, the Holocaust Museum, the Statue of Liberty
Ships, Trains, Planes	the *Mayflower, the Wabash Cannonball, the Spirit of St. Louis*
Names of Courses	English I, History IA, Art II, Latin III (Names of general subjects, such as math, social studies, and history are not capitalized.)

Do not capitalize the name of an unnumbered course, such as *history, math,* or *biology,* unless it is the name of a language.

Last year I studied **h**istory, **a**rt, and **J**apanese.

When You Write

When you are unsure whether to capitalize a word, use a reference source. A good dictionary will include most proper nouns. Many dictionaries contain specific sections with geographical and biographical information where you can find the correct spelling and capitalization of the names of famous people and places. An encyclopedia will also give you such information. A good writer always has up-to-date, reliable reference sources available.

Find a composition you have previously written or one currently in progress. Highlight all the proper nouns and check their capitalization. Refer to a dictionary or other sources to check any items about which you are unsure.

● **Practice Your Skills**

Using Capital Letters

Identify each word that should begin with a capital letter and then rewrite the words correctly.

1. The middle ages was a historical period in western europe that lasted from about A.d. 500 to A.d. 1400.

2. During the middle ages, common people worked only 260 days per year.

3. They did not work on religious holidays, such as easter and christmas.

4. On december 6, people would celebrate st. nicholas's day, a children's holiday.

5. On most days between 9 a.m. and noon, people living in a castle would eat dinner, a very large meal.

● *Connect to Writing:* **Editing**

Correcting Errors in Capitalization

Rewrite the following paragraph, correcting the errors in capitalization.

(1) every few years a city in a major country like canada, japan, france, or the united states hosts a world's fair. **(2)** the united states has hosted fairs in major cities like new york, chicago, and st. louis. **(3)** one of the earliest fairs, however, was held in london, england, in 1851. **(4)** that was during the early reign of queen victoria. **(5)** joseph paxton, an english architect, designed the exhibition hall in london's hyde park that the queen called "extraordinary." **(6)** he created the largest glass building ever made. **(7)** it contained 3,300 columns to support its three stories. **(8)** after the exhibition it was taken down and moved to a different part of london. **(9)** there it became known as the crystal palace. **(10)** unfortunately, it was destroyed by a fire in 1936.

✔ *Check Point:* **Mixed Practice**

In each of the following trivia questions, find the words that should be capitalized and write the words correctly. Then see if you can answer the questions!

1. was william sherman a general in the civil war or the american revolution?

2. was andrew wyeth a painter or a united states senator?

3. was george c. scott a composer or the winner of an oscar?

4. did captain james kirk or captain bligh command the starship enterprise?

5. who paid for the statue of liberty in new york by giving donations: the french or the americans?

6. did thomas edison or george eastman invent the first camera?

7. did tara lipinski win a gold medal for ice skating or for gymnastics?

8. in 1848, was gold found in california or in colorado?

● *Connect to Writing:* **Formal Letter of Inquiry**

Using Capital Letters

You are writing a report on a European country, focusing on the art and architecture of one of its major cities. You must write about how the city's history, culture, politics, and social structure influenced its art and architecture. Do a bit of research, and then write a letter or an e-mail to a history or art museum in the country requesting information. After you have finished writing, check that you have capitalized all the proper nouns correctly.

Proper Adjectives  Lesson 3

Proper adjectives are formed from proper nouns. Like proper nouns, proper adjectives begin with capital letters.

24 C   **Capitalize most proper adjectives.**

Proper Nouns	Proper Adjectives
France	French doors
Rome	Roman numerals
Alaska	Alaskan cruise
Boston	Boston baked beans

Some adjectives that originated from proper nouns are so common that they are no longer capitalized.

> Be careful not to drop the china plate.

● **Practice Your Skills**

Capitalizing Proper Adjectives

Write the following items, adding capital letters where needed.

1. a chinese restaurant

2. a british naval officer

3. a former french colony

4. an ancient egyptian tomb

5. irish stew

6. new england weather

7. a german clock

8. a turkish towel

9. maine lobster

10. a swedish ship

Capital letters indicate the importance of titles of people, written works, and other works of art.

24 D   **Capitalize certain titles.**

Titles Used with Names of Persons

24 D.1   Capitalize a title showing office, rank, or profession when it comes directly before a person's name.

Before a Name	Have you met **D**r. Anna Richman?
After a Name	Jennifer Kemp is also a **d**octor.
Before a Name	Dr. Richman voted for **G**overnor Harper.
After a Name	Did you think Jennifer Kemp would be elected **g**overnor?

Titles Used Alone

24 D.2   Capitalize a title that is used alone when the title is being substituted for a person's name in direct address.

Used as a Name	Please, **G**overnor, may I speak with you?
	I didn't see the sign, **O**fficer.

Titles of high government officials, such as the *President, Vice President, Chief Justice,* and *Queen of England,* are almost always capitalized when they stand alone.

I have come to see the **Q**ueen of England.

The **P**resident visited Governor Harper.

President and vice president are capitalized when they stand alone only if they refer to the current president or vice president.

CHAPTER 24

Titles Showing Family Relationships

24 D.3   Capitalize a title showing a family relationship when it comes directly before a person's name. When the title is used as a name, or when the title is substituted for a person's name in direct address, it is also capitalized.

Before a Name	I am going to see **A**unt Lori.
Used as a Name	I told **M**om that I would vacuum my room tomorrow.
Substituted for a Person's Name in Direct Address	May I borrow the car for just a few hours, **D**ad?
	Will you come, **G**randpa, to my game on Saturday?

Do not capitalize titles showing family relationships when they are preceded by possessive nouns or pronouns—unless the titles are considered part of someone's name.

Have you met Kristen's **a**unt?

Have you met Kristen's **A**unt Diane?

● **Practice Your Skills**

Capitalizing the Titles of Persons

Write the term that is correctly capitalized In each of the following pairs.

1. our family doctor
   our family Doctor

2. Senator Barrientos
   senator Barrientos

3. aunt Ruthie
   Aunt Ruthie

4. a Governor
   a governor

5. Granny Taylor
   granny Taylor

6. my uncle
   my Uncle

7. a state senator
   a state Senator

8. a president of Egypt
   a President of Egypt

9. Mayor Wilson
   mayor Wilson

10. president Nixon
   President Nixon

Correcting Errors in Capitalization

Rewrite the following letter, correcting the errors in capitalization.

> dear grandma hazel,
>
>   i hope you are doing well. i heard from aunt linda that you had been ill. did you go to the doctor? i enjoyed meeting dr. williams when i visited you last summer. i'm sure she would take good care of you if you would make an appointment.
>
>   well, i'd better close this letter. i promised mom and uncle denny that i would take out the trash before the president's state of the union address on television tonight.
>
> love always,
samantha

➤ Titles of Written Works and Other Works of Art

24 D.4 Capitalize the first word, the last word, and all important words in the titles of books, newspapers, periodicals, stories, poems, movies, plays, musical compositions, and other works of art.

However, do not capitalize a preposition, a conjunction, or an article (*a, an,* and *the*) unless it is the first word of a title.

Books and Chapter Titles	I finished reading a chapter called "**T**he **M**an on the **T**or" in the book *The Hound of the Baskervilles*.
Short Stories	I enjoyed Truman Capote's story "**C**hildren on **T**heir **B**irthdays."
Poems	My favorite poems are "**F**rom **B**lossoms" and "**T**he **W**eight of **S**weetness" by Li-Young Lee.
Newspapers and Newspaper Articles	I read an article called "**L**ocal **W**riter **H**as **N**ovel **P**ublished" in today's issue of the *Chicago Tribune*. (Generally, do not capitalize *the* as the first word of a newspaper or magazine title. *The New York Times* is an exception.)
Magazines and Magazine Articles	I read "**I**nterview with the **N**ew **T**alent" about that author in *People* magazine last week.
Television Series	Two popular British television comedy series were *Keeping Up Appearances* and *As Time Goes By*.

You can learn more about the punctuation of titles on pages 873–876.

Capitalizing Titles of Written Works and Other Works of Art

Write the title that is correctly capitalized in each of the following pairs.

1. the sculpture *The thinker*
the sculpture *The Thinker*

2. the poem "The Raven"
the poem "the Raven"

3. the song "This land is your land"
the song "This Land Is Your Land"

4. the magazine *seventeen*
the magazine *Seventeen*

5. the painting *American Gothic*
the painting *american gothic*

6. the film *The return of the Jedi*
the film *The Return of the Jedi*

7. the book *The Great Gatsby*
the book *The great gatsby*

8. the newspaper the *Dallas Morning News*
the newspaper the *Dallas morning news*

9. the song "Singin' in the Rain"
the song "Singin' in the rain"

10. the book *The Count of Monte Cristo*
the book *The count of monte Cristo*

● *Connect to Writing:* **Compile a list**

Using Capital Letters

You are going to be stationed on a desolate island in the Pacific for several months. You will be allowed to take along videos, books, CDs, and magazines to entertain yourself. Using what you have read about how to capitalize titles, list ten of these items that you would take along on your island adventure.

CHAPTER 24

Correcting Errors in Capitalization

Rewrite the following paragraph, correcting the errors in capitalization.

(1) the 1950s was an interesting time in the history of entertainment. (2) In the music world, rock 'n' roll was born. (3) elvis presley recorded hit songs like "hound dog" and "that's all right." (4) he also made a historic appearance on *the ed sullivan show.* (5) other popular television shows at that time included the comedy *i love lucy* and *the twilight zone.* (6) suspense was popular in the movies and TV shows of alfred hitchcock. (7) two of Hitchcock's most famous movies of the 1950s were *strangers on a train* and *rear window.* (8) in the literary world, a new generation of writers was heralded by jack kerouac and allen ginsberg. (9) kerouac's *on the road* tells stories of crossing and recrossing the highways of the united states, far outside the mainstream 1950s culture.

✔ *Check Point:* **Mixed Practice**

In each of the following trivia questions, find the words that should be capitalized and write the words correctly. Then see if you can answer the questions!

1. which god in greek mythology held the world on his shoulders: apollo or atlas?

2. which fictional reporter worked at the *daily planet* in the city of metropolis: clark kent or bruce wayne?

3. is the name of the football team in dallas, texas, the cowboys or the broncos?

4. does the initial in president john f. kennedy's name stand for *fitzgerald* or *franklin*?

5. which television series has run longer: meet the press or days of our lives?

6. did ernest hemingway or stephen crane write *the red badge of courage*?

7. in the united states, which holiday is celebrated on the first monday in september: labor day or memorial day?

8. which separates scandinavia from the rest of europe: the baltic sea or the mediterranean sea?

● *Connect to Writing:* Composing an Advertisement

Using Correct Capitalization

You are the owner of the first intergalactic travel agency to take people on tours of the planets and outer space. Write an advertisement for an upcoming tour. Inform prospective clients of the travel accommodations, such as the comfort and safety of your spacecraft and its name, the sites they will see, the cost of space travel, the activities they might enjoy, and departure days and times. In your advertisement, be sure to give your company a name. After you have finished writing your ad, check to make sure that you have used proper capitalization.

Chapter Review

Assess Your Learning

▰ Using Capital Letters Correctly

Correctly write each word that should begin with a capital letter.

1. let's turn back the clock to the year 1900 and look at the united states at the turn of that century.

2. the population had reached nearly 76 million, and the center of the population was near columbus, indiana.

3. the united states had about ten miles of concrete pavement and fewer than 8,000 automobiles.

4. the first well-organized automobile race was held at springfield, long island, on april 15.

5. in the presidential election, president william mckinley was re-elected for a second term.

6. r. a. fessenden, an american scientist, became the first person to transmit human speech through radio waves.

7. the united states and england inaugurated a tennis competition for the davis cup.

8. casey jones, the famous engineer in song and legend, died on april 30 at the throttle of his locomotive, the *cannonball,* trying to save his passengers' lives.

9. the wright brothers, wilbur and orville, built their first full-scale glider and flew it at kitty hawk, nc.

10. among rising young novelists of the day were such writers as zane grey, edgar rice burroughs, and theodore dreiser.

11. irving bacheller wrote the novel *eben holden,* a best-seller.

12. ray c. ewry won eight olympic gold medals in the 1900, 1904, and 1908 games.

13. a notable painter of the time was albert pinkham ryder, whose famous painting, *toilers of the sea,* is a ghostly sea scene.

14. famous archeologist arthur evans discovered artifacts from the minoan culture in his excavations in crete.

15. the largest railroad was the new york central.

Editing for the Correct Use of Capital Letters

Write each sentence using capital letters correctly.

1. the world's largest church is st. peter's in rome.

2. the *voyager* missions studied jupiter and saturn.

3. required courses for juniors are english, math II, biology, and american history.

4. in his novel *the grapes of wrath,* john steinbeck tells about the problems of the poor in oklahoma.

5. the houston oaks hotel is in the southwest.

6. did michigan ever beat nebraska in the cotton bowl?

7. yes, senator parks will speak at logan high school.

8. the west indies form an island arc in the atlantic ocean.

9. the irish potato originated in south america.

10. the snake river flows from wyoming to washington.

Writing Sentences

At the library, find a fact that pertains to each of the following topics. Each fact should include a proper noun, a proper adjective, or a title.

1. geography

2. political parties

3. the presidency

4. astronomy

5. art

6. literature

7. holidays

8. history

9. space exploration

10. languages

Capital Letters: Posttest

Directions

For each sentence, choose the word or words that should be capitalized. Write the letter of your answer. If the sentence contains no error, write **D.**

(1) My friend speaks flemish most of the time at her home near the city of bruges. **(2)** She also knows the english language well enough to write great letters. **(3)** Her name is helen. **(4)** She told me that belgium became a country only in modern times. **(5)** Long ago during the renaissance, the part of the country where she lives was known as flanders. **(6)** Some great painters such as hans memling lived there. **(7)** I've seen one of his paintings, *adoration of the magi,* which now hangs in a museum within a hospital in bruges. **(8)** almost every month i get a letter from helen. **(9)** She begins them all, "dear American friend." **(10)** I write back to her, "Dear belgian friend."

1. A Flemish, Bruges
   B Home
   C Flemish, Home
   D No error

2. A English
   B Language
   C English Language
   D No error

3. A Name
   B Helen
   C Name, Helen
   D No error

4. A Modern Times
   B Belgium, Modern
   C Belgium
   D No error

5. A Renaissance
   B Renaissance, Flanders
   C Flanders
   D No error

6. A Memling
   B Hans Memling
   C Hans
   D No error

7. A *Adoration*
   B *Adoration, Of, Magi*
   C *Adoration, Magi,* Bruges
   D No error

8. A Almost, I
   B Helen
   C Almost, I, Helen
   D No error

9. A Dear
   B Dear, Friend
   C Friend
   D No error

10. A Belgian, Friend
   B Belgian
   C Friend
   D No error

Writer's Corner

Snapshot

24 A Capitalize first words and the pronoun *I*. (pages 816–818)

24 B Capitalize proper nouns and their abbreviations. (pages 819–827)

24 C Capitalize most proper adjectives. (page 828)

24 D Capitalize certain titles. (pages 829–834)

Power Rules

 Every statement that begins with a capital letter should be a **complete sentence,** not a sentence fragment. (pages 666–671)

Before Editing	After Editing
After I finish school. I work at the hardware store.	*After I finish school,* I work at the hardware store.
Although I've been saving money for a year. I still don't have enough for a new bike.	*Although I've been saving money for a year,* I still don't have enough for a new bike.
I love my friend's new bike. *Which he bought on sale.*	I love my friend's new bike, *which he bought on sale.*

 Check for **run-on sentences** and separate them by capitalizing the first word of the second sentence or adding a conjunction and/or punctuation. (pages 672–674)

Before Editing	After Editing
The trip will take two hours, we have to travel 120 miles.	The trip will take two hours. We have to travel 120 miles.
Wanda's car is new it is not very reliable.	Wanda's car is new, *but* it is not very reliable.
Still, we are leaving on Sunday, we are returning on Friday.	Still, we are leaving on Sunday, *and* we are returning on Friday.

Editing Checklist

Use this checklist when editing your writing.

✓ Did I capitalize the first word in each sentence? (See page 816.)
✓ Did I capitalize the pronoun *I*? (See pages 817–818.)
✓ Did I capitalize proper nouns and their abbreviations? (See pages 819–827.)
✓ Did I capitalize proper adjectives? (See page 828.)
✓ Did I capitalize the titles of persons, written works, and works of art? (See pages 829–834.)
✓ Did I edit my work for mistakes in capitalization? (See pages 816–834.)

Use the Power

Capitalization draws attention to certain words and the beginnings of sentences. Use the graphics and rules below to help you understand how to use correct capitalization in your writing.

RULE	EXAMPLE
Capitalize the **first word** in every sentence.	One of my favorite activities is hiking.
Always capitalize the pronoun *I*.	I try to organize hiking trips as often as I can.
Capitalize **proper nouns**.	Some of the best hiking is in the Rocky Mountain National Park.
Capitalize **proper adjectives**.	The Colorado mountain air is fresh and invigorating.
Capitalize most **titles**.	Maybe I'll write a book about hiking and call it *Hardy Hiking with Greg*.

Write a paragraph about your favorite activity. Be sure to capitalize proper nouns and adjectives, titles, the pronoun *I*, and the first word in every sentence.

CHAPTER 25

End Marks and Commas

How can you create meaning through the careful use of end marks and commas?

End Marks and Commas: Pretest 1

The first draft below contains errors in the use of end marks and commas. The first error is corrected. How would you revise the draft so that all end marks and commas are used correctly?

Because of its proximity to the San Andreas Fault, San Francisco experiences frequent earthquakes! Although not all are violent, several have devastated the city which is a beautiful place to live! Yes the 1906 quake was especially destructive. In that earthquake a total of 450 or more people perished. That's such a tragedy? Throughout the city for three long days fires ravaged homes and buildings. People lost all their furniture clothing and family treasures. Coming together to help one another the citizens rebuilt their devastated city. From the rubble and ashes of the earthquake and fires rose a city determined to host the Panama-Pacific International Exhibition in 1915. In October of 1989 60,000 excited loyal baseball fans were shaken in Candlestick Park when the city's next severe earthquake occurred during the World Series? The highest number of deaths 42 occurred in Oakland on that day due to the collapse of a portion of the Nimitz Freeway.

End Marks and Commas: Pretest 2

Directions

Write the letter of the term that correctly identifies each type of sentence.

(1) The winds started rising during the night. (2) How frightening they were! (3) The police and other emergency workers patrolled the streets and made loudspeaker announcements. (4) "Evacuate the island!" (5) Would we suffer a direct hit? (6) Our home would be completely submerged! (7) By midday most people had packed up and left the island. (8) We were packed and ready to go, but my sister couldn't find her cat. (9) Where was he hiding? (10) My father ordered her to get into the car.

1. **A** declarative
   B imperative
   C interrogative
   D exclamatory

2. **A** declarative
   B imperative
   C interrogative
   D exclamatory

3. **A** declarative
   B imperative
   C interrogative
   D exclamatory

4. **A** declarative
   B imperative
   C interrogative
   D exclamatory

5. **A** declarative
   B imperative
   C interrogative
   D exclamatory

6. **A** declarative
   B imperative
   C interrogative
   D exclamatory

7. **A** declarative
   B imperative
   C interrogative
   D exclamatory

8. **A** declarative
   B imperative
   C interrogative
   D exclamatory

9. **A** declarative
   B imperative
   C interrogative
   D exclamatory

10. **A** declarative
    B imperative
    C interrogative
    D exclamatory

Imagine New York City without any traffic lights or stop signs. There would be utter confusion. The result of writing sentences without end marks or commas would be very much the same.

A sentence may have one of four different purposes or functions. The purpose of a sentence determines the punctuation mark that goes at the end.

25 A A sentence may be **declarative, imperative, interrogative, or exclamatory.**

One purpose of a sentence is to make a statement or to express an opinion.

25 A.1 A **declarative sentence** makes a statement or expresses an opinion and ends with a period.

The following examples are declarative sentences. Notice that the second sentence makes a statement, even though it contains an indirect question.

> My brothers were going to the tennis courts.
> I asked them what time they were leaving home.
> (A direct question would be *What time are they leaving home?*)

A second purpose of a sentence is to give directions, make requests, or give commands. The subject of these kinds of sentences is usually an understood *you.*

25 A.2 An **imperative sentence** gives a direction, makes a request, or gives a command. It ends with either a period or an exclamation point.

Although all of the following examples are imperative, two are followed by a period, and one is followed by an exclamation point.

> Turn left when you see the tennis courts.
> Please take me with you.
> Call the police!
> (This command would be stated with great excitement or emphasis.)

A third purpose of a sentence is to ask a question.

25 A.3   An **interrogative sentence** asks a question and ends with a question mark.

The following examples are interrogative sentences. Notice that the second example is phrased as a statement but is intended as a question.

> Where is my tennis racket**?**
> You have played tennis eight times this weekend**?**

Some questions are not expressed completely; nevertheless, they are followed by a question mark.

> You have decided not to play tennis. Why**?**

A fourth purpose of a sentence is to express a feeling—such as excitement, joy, anger, fear, or surprise.

25 A.4   An **exclamatory sentence** expresses strong feeling or emotion and ends with an exclamation point.

The following examples are exclamatory sentences. Notice they express strong feeling.

> What a fantastic tennis match**!**
> I feel fabulous**!**

Use exclamatory sentences sparingly when you write. They lose their impact when they are used too often. Remember that an exclamation point also follows an interjection.

> Wow**!** That was my best match ever.

You can learn more about interjections on page 568.

● *Connect to Reading, Speaking, and Listening:* **Vocabulary**

Using Inflection to Understand Sentences

You use the inflection of your voice to make meaning clear when speaking. In writing, you use end marks. Play this game: Read a few statements from a written text without inflection, such as "This is a new opportunity" or "Indeed." Have a partner say each as a simple statement, a question, and an exclamation. You must suggest the mark that would be used at the end of each sentence.

● Practice Your Skills

Classifying Sentences

Label each sentence *declarative, imperative, interrogative,* or *exclamatory* according to the meaning of the sentence.

1. I love tennis!

2. Please bring me my racket.

3. Are you ready to play?

4. I began playing tennis when I was eight years old.

5. Stand behind the baseline to serve.

6. What a powerful forehand!

7. Drive the ball across the net.

8. Would you like to play again?

● *Connect to Writing:* Editing

Correcting End Punctuation

Write the correct end punctuation for each sentence. Then label each sentence *declarative, imperative, interrogative,* or *exclamatory.*

1. Have you heard of the "Battle of the Sexes"

2. Bobby Riggs challenged Billie Jean King to a winner-take-all match in 1973

3. America watched the amazing tennis match with great excitement

4. Riggs had declared that there was no way a woman could beat a man

5. Wow King showed him in no uncertain terms how wrong he was

6. King defeated Riggs in each set to handily win the match

7. Look at any magazine of the time

8. You will see how this tennis match captured America's attention

9. Can you imagine how this victory affected the future of women's tennis

10. Find out more about this event by looking at newspapers from that time

● *Connect to Writing:* Instructions

Creating Sentence Variety

Your coach has asked you to explain the rules of your favorite sport to someone who has never played the game before. Write a paragraph in which you explain the basics that every beginner should know. Try to give detailed directions while also conveying how much fun the sport is. Use at least one of each type of sentence—declarative, interrogative, exclamatory, and imperative.

Other Uses of Periods

25 A.5 A period may be used in places other than at the ends of sentences.

Periods in Abbreviations

Abbreviations are as old as the written word. They came about in order to make words shorter and easier to write. Most abbreviations should not be used in formal writing.

ABBREVIATIONS					
Titles with Names	Mr. Mrs.	Ms. Dr.	Rev. Gen.	Sgt. Lt.	Jr. Sr.
Initials for Names	R. L. Rosen, Sarah E. Campbell, J. J. Jackson, K. Petra Beck				
Times with Numbers	AM or a.m. (*ante meridiem*—before noon) PM or p.m. (*post meridiem*—after noon) B.C. (before Christ) or B.C.E. (before the common era) A.D. (*anno Domini*—in the year of the Lord)				
Addresses	Ave.	St.	Blvd.	Rt.	Dept.
Organizations and Companies	Co.	Inc.	Corp.	Assn.	

Many organizations and companies use abbreviations without periods to indicate their names. A few other common abbreviations also do not include periods.

> FAA = Federal Aviation Administration
>
> UN = United Nations
>
> CIA = Central Intelligence Agency
>
> IQ = intelligence quotient
>
> km = kilometer

If an abbreviation is the last word of a statement, only one period is used. Use two marks when a sentence ends with an abbreviation and a question or exclamation.

> I would like to introduce you to Ronald Franklin, Jr.
>
> Should I meet you at 10:00 p.m.?

Today almost everyone uses the U.S. Postal Service's two-letter state abbreviations. These abbreviations do not include periods. A list of these abbreviations can be found in the front of most telephone books. The following are a few examples.

AK = Alaska	MD = Maryland	NY = New York
AL = Alabama	ME = Maine	OH = Ohio
CT = Connecticut	MI = Michigan	TX = Texas
HI = Hawaii	NV = Nevada	UT = Utah

Periods in Outlines

Use a period after each number or letter that shows a division in an outline.

I. Guitars
    A. Electric
        1. Hollow body
        2. Solid body
    B. Acoustic
II. Drums
    A. Hand
    B. Zylo

● **Practice Your Skills**

Using End Marks

Write the abbreviations that stand for the following items. Be sure to end them with a period whenever appropriate. If you are not sure of the abbreviation, use a dictionary.

1. dozen

2. major

3. ounce

4. latitude

5. mountain

6. Fahrenheit

7. Rhode Island

8. television

9. association

10. incorporated

11. before Christ

12. Bachelor of Arts

13. miles per hour

14. post meridiem

Rewrite the following sentences, adding end punctuation and periods to abbreviations if needed. Then label each sentence *declarative, imperative, interrogative,* or *exclamatory.*

1. Have you called Dr Wilson

2. Dr Barry Wilson, Jr has been our family physician for years

3. Please get the phone book

4. Call him right this minute

5. Mrs Smith, the school nurse, thinks that my right arm is broken

6. Ouch, it hurts

7. I fell off the auditorium stage during Mr Miller's drama class

8. When did it happen

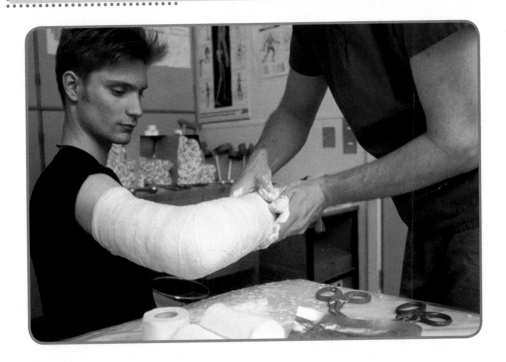

● *Connect to Writing:* **Outline**

Using Periods

Write an outline of what you ate yesterday. Use a separate Roman numeral for each meal and snack. Be sure to list all the food you had at each meal. As you make your outline, be sure that you place periods appropriately throughout.

Commas That Separate   Lesson 2

25 B **Commas** are used to prevent confusion and to keep items from running into one another.

The following are specific rules for commas that are used to separate items.

➤ Items in a Series

Three or more similar items—words, phrases, or clauses—that are placed together form a series.

25 B.1 Use commas to separate items in a **series**.

Words	**Blackberries, raspberries,** and **strawberries** are all members of the rose family. (nouns)
	We **picked, washed,** and **ate** as many fresh berries as we could. (verbs)
	At the end of the day, we were **tired, dirty,** and **full.** (adjectives)
Phrases	The buckets for the berries could be **in the garage, in the pantry,** or **on the porch.**
	Are they going **to the picnic, to the park,** or **to the campground?**
Clauses	We know **where the berries are, if they are ripe,** and **when they should be picked.**
	She told us **where to go, how to get there,** and **what to wear.**

When a conjunction connects the last two items in a series, some writers omit the last comma. Although this is acceptable, it can be confusing. Therefore, it is better to get into the habit of including the comma before the conjunction.

Confusing	We bake cakes, pies and cobblers.
Clear	We bake cakes, pies, and cobblers.

When conjunctions connect all items in a series, no commas are needed.

> We ate **and** rested **and** ate some more.

Some pairs of words, such as *bacon and eggs,* are thought of as a single item. If one of these pairs of words appears in a series, consider it one item.

> For dinner you can have a burger and fries, fish and chips, or pork and sauerkraut.

● **Practice Your Skills**

Commas in a Series

Rewrite each sentence, adding commas where needed. If the sentence is correct, write **C.**

1. Combine flour shortening pecans and cold water to make a tasty pie crust.
2. Preheat the oven oil the pan and prepare the crust.
3. Shall we bake raisin and nut or apple and cinnamon or butter and oatmeal muffins?
4. Whipped cream ice cream and cheddar cheese make excellent toppings for apple pie.
5. Please mix the batter pour it into a pan, and place it in the oven.
6. Use soap and hot water and a fresh towel to clean your hands before cooking.
7. I enjoy a glass of milk or a small dessert or a piece of fruit after lunch.
8. The best cakes are made with fresh butter milk and eggs.

● *Connect to Writing:* **Drafting**

Writing Sentences

Finish each sentence with a series of three or more appropriate items. Add commas where needed.

1. When I make a hamburger, I like to add ___.
2. This year in school I am studying ___.
3. When we have a holiday dinner, my favorite foods are ___.
4. I ___ to stay in shape.
5. Before leaving for school each morning, I usually like to ___.
6. Three places in the United States I would like to visit are ___.
7. ___ are the friends whom I trust the most to help me in difficult situations.

Adjectives Before a Noun

If a conjunction is missing between two adjectives that come before a noun, a comma is sometimes used to take its place.

> The rabbits disappeared into the tall, thick grass of the Nebraska plain.
>
> That is the oldest, most beautiful tree in the redwood forest.
>
> Several delicate, fragrant flowers blossomed from the desert cactus.

25 B.2   A comma is sometimes needed to separate two adjectives that precede a noun and are not joined by a conjunction.

A useful test can help you decide whether a comma is needed between two adjectives. If the sentence reads sensibly with the word *and* between the adjectives, a comma is needed.

> **Comma Needed**   Mississippi is a damp, lush place.
> (*A damp and lush place* reads well.)
>
> **Comma Not Needed**   Today was a damp spring day.
> (*A damp and spring day* does not read well.)

Usually no comma is needed after a number or after an adjective that refers to size, shape, or age. For example, no commas are needed in the following expressions.

ADJECTIVE EXPRESSIONS	
six oak trees	his old brown guitar
a large green meadow	the ancient oral saga
one hundred beautiful butterflies	two leafy willow trees

● **Practice Your Skills**

Using Commas with Adjectives

Rewrite each sentence, adding commas where needed. If the sentence is correct, write **C.**

1. America is a land of diverse colorful regions.

2. Prickly cactus produces beautiful delicate flowers in the harsh deserts of Arizona.

3. Some parts of California are famous for sturdy redwood trees.

4. The golden wheat fields of Kansas are a glorious sight to behold.

5. The city of Chicago offers many great vistas of Lake Michigan.

6. The lovely quaint villages of New England attract many tourists.

7. Florida has large sandy beaches along both the Atlantic Ocean and the Gulf of Mexico.

8. Central Texas contains dark rich farmland and a good supply of water.

Compound Sentences

A comma is usually used to separate the independent clauses in a compound sentence.

25 B.3   Use a comma to separate the independent clauses of a compound sentence if the clauses are joined by a conjunction.

A coordinating conjunction most often combines the independent clauses in a compound sentence.

COORDINATING CONJUNCTIONS						
and	but	for	nor	or	so	yet

Notice in the following examples that the comma comes before the conjunction.

I play the flute, and my sister plays the guitar.

Pick up my guitar, or it might get left behind.

A comma is not needed in a very short compound sentence.

Lisa played and I sang.

Do not confuse a compound sentence with a sentence that has a compound verb. No comma comes between parts of a compound verb unless there are three or more verbs.

Compound Sentence	We waited for twenty minutes, but Lisa never appeared on stage.
Compound Verb	We waited for twenty minutes and then left.

A compound sentence can also be joined by a semicolon. You can learn more about compound sentences on pages 654–656.

● **Practice Your Skills**

Using Commas with Compound Sentences

Read the paragraph below. Write **C** if a sentence is punctuated correctly. Write **I** if it is punctuated incorrectly.

(1) Musicologists study the history of music and analyze its meaning to society. **(2)** The history of rap music is interesting and so many musicologists are beginning to examine it. **(3)** In 1979, Sugar Hill Gang recorded "Rappers' Delight" and this song changed the music world. **(4)** The song "Rappers' Delight" was a breakthrough and its lyrics provided the term hip hop. **(5)** Hip hop is related to rap music but they are different in some ways. **(6)** Rap is the spoken words of the song and hip hop refers to the background music. **(7)** Rappers speak the words of their songs rapidly and accent some phrases more than others. **(8)** In 1982, the first rap song with a political message was recorded and this song gave a social conscience to rap. **(9)** Sampling pieces of other songs began in 1986 and opened rap music to many lawsuits. **(10)** In 1986, rap videos began to appear on TV and attracted a new audience.

 # Introductory Structures

Some words, phrases, and clauses at the beginning of a sentence need to be separated from the rest of the sentence by a comma.

25 B.4 Use a comma after certain **introductory structures**.

The following are examples of introductory words that should be followed by a comma.

Words	**No,** I have not heard about the earthquake.
	Yes, it was a bad one.
	(Other words include *now, oh, well,* and *why*—except when they are part of the sentence. *Why didn't you tell me?*)
Prepositional Phrase	**After the earthquake in San Francisco,** neighbors joined together to help one another.
	In just a few seconds, people's lives changed dramatically.
	(A comma comes after two or more prepositional phrases or a single phrase of four or more words.)
Participial Phrase	**Feeling the ground begin to rumble,** residents ran nervously from their homes and offices into the street.
Adverbial Clause	**As one man exited his home,** the roof caved in.

Notice that the punctuation of shorter phrases varies. Also, never place a comma after a phrase or phrases followed by a verb.

Others	**In Room 37,** 19 students were injured.
	(A comma is usually used after an introductory phrase that ends in a number.)
	In the road, blocks of wood were a hazard.
	(The comma prevents confusion.)
	On the floor of a destroyed home lay a child's teddy bear.
	(The phrases are followed by the verb.)

● *Connect to Writing:* **Drafting**

Writing Sentences

Write a sentence using each of the following introductory words or phrases. Add commas where needed.

1. After the long thunderstorm

2. As the sky began to clear

3. Well

4. Hearing the raindrops on our roof

5. In Room 206

6. When the sounds stopped

7. Because the lights went out

8. Hiding under her desk

9. In the heat of the day

10. When we went outside

➤ Commonly Used Commas

When you tie your shoelaces, you do not have to think about how to do it as you did when you were little. You do it automatically. There are some comma rules you have been using for so many years that they probably have also become automatic. The following is a brief review of those rules for using commas.

Commas with Dates and Addresses

For clarity, commas are used to separate the various elements in a date or an address from one another.

25 B.5   Use commas to separate the elements in dates and addresses.

Notice in the following examples that a comma is also used to separate a date or an address from the rest of the sentence.

Date   On Tuesday, February 2, 1941, my grandmother was born.

Address   Her parents lived at 29 Bank Street, Long Beach, California, at the time.

A comma is not used to separate the state and the ZIP code.

Send your request for information to Genealogy Research, 500 West 52nd Street, New York, NY 10019.

Commas in Letters

25 B.6   Use a comma after the salutation of a friendly letter and after the closing of all letters.

SALUTATIONS AND CLOSINGS		
Salutations Dear Uncle Joe,	Dear Emily,	Dearest Grandma,
Closings Love,	Yours truly,	Sincerely,
Thank you,	Regards,	Best wishes,

When You Write

Using too many commas can be as confusing as not using enough commas. Use commas only where a rule indicates they are needed and only where they make the meaning of your writing clearer. If you cannot find a rule that says you need a comma, try reading the sentence aloud with a comma and without a comma. If the pause seems natural or if the sentence is confusing without it, keep the comma. You can also follow this saying: "When in doubt, leave it out."

Practice Your Skills

Using Commas

Write *a* or *b* to indicate which phrase in each pair shows the correct use of commas.

1. a. Dear Felipe,

   b. Dear Felipe

2. a. Wednesday, June 2, 1999

   b. Wednesday June 2, 1999

3. a. With love,

   b. With love

4. a. Dr. Tonya Jackson 21 Jewel Road Park City Idaho 92714

   b. Dr. Tonya Jackson, 21 Jewel Road, Park City, Idaho 92714

5. a. Thank you

   b. Thank you,

6. a. Dear Darla,

   b. Dear, Darla

7. a. December 7, 1941

   b. December 7 1941

8. a. El Paso, Texas

   b. El Paso Texas,

Connect to Writing: Revising

Correcting Comma Errors

Rewrite the following letter, adding commas where needed.

May 2 2006

Dear Grandma

    I am trying to get some information for a family-tree project that I have to do for social studies. I know that your father was born on March 26 1919. His place of birth was his aunt's home on 26 Lasso Lane Bozeman Montana. What can you tell me about your father's parents?

    Please send a response to me at my school address, which is Lake Travis High School 3322 Ranch Road Austin, Texas 78734.

                       Love

                       Elias

Read the paragraphs below. Write each word that should be followed by a comma.

(1) Pinnipeds are fin-footed mammals with limbs that are used as paddles or flippers. **(2)** The three main kinds of pinnipeds are the walrus the sea lion and the seal. **(3)** All pinnipeds are meat eaters and they all live in the water. **(4)** Most pinnipeds live in the cold waters of the Arctic and they have become well adapted to this kind of existence. **(5)** Their tapered streamlined bodies make them excellent swimmers. **(6)** Their thick layer of blubber gives them added buoyancy and helps keep them warm.

(7) Searching for food pinnipeds can dive two or three hundred feet below the water's surface. **(8)** When they are underwater their nostrils close. **(9)** Most pinnipeds have sharp backward-pointing teeth. **(10)** This feature makes it possible for a pinniped to seize prey and direct it down its throat. **(11)** Because pinnipeds are sociable animals they live together in large herds.

(12) The walrus is one type of pinniped. **(13)** Some scientists classify the walrus as a type of large seal. **(14)** Having tusks to defend itself the walrus can protect itself from the threat of the much larger polar bear. **(15)** When walruses climb onto ice they can also use their tusks as hooks.

(16) The sea lion lives in the northern Pacific Ocean and parts of the Southern Hemisphere. **(17)** Using all four flippers sea lions can walk on land. **(18)** Their thick blubbery layers keep them warm.

● *Connect to Writing:* **Informative Note**

Using Commas

You are applying for a job as a counselor in a summer camp. Your prospective employer, Ms. Smythe, has asked that you send her a note that contains all the following information:

- your full name
- your date of birth
- your current address
- your previous work experience
- the date on which you can begin work

Because Ms. Smythe is a prospective employer, you want to make a good impression. Use complete sentences and check your work for the proper use of commas.

Some expressions interrupt the flow of a sentence. These expressions generally add important information, but are not necessary to understanding the main idea of the sentence.

25 C **Commas are used to enclose words that interrupt the main idea of a sentence.**

If an interrupting expression comes in the middle of a sentence, a comma is placed before and after the expression to set it off. If an interrupting expression comes at the beginning or the end of a sentence, only one comma is used to separate it from the rest of the sentence.

Commas in Middle	The movie**,** to tell the truth**,** was boring.
Comma at Beginning	**To tell the truth,** the movie was boring.
Comma at End	The movie was boring**,** to tell the truth.

 ## Direct Address

Names, titles, or words that are used to address someone are set off by commas. These expressions are called nouns of direct address.

25 C.1 Use commas to enclose **nouns of direct address.**

Shelli, what is your opinion?

Your explanation**,** **Marc,** was excellent.

Did you like the movie**,** **Maria?**

When You Read and Write

Writers often use commas when writing dialogue to indicate pauses in their characters' words. What do the pauses in the following dialogue tell you about what is happening?

"What in the world happened here?" our father asked in disbelief.
"Well, uh, we were just, uh, playing."

Using Commas with Direct Address

Read the sentences below. Write **C** if the sentence is punctuated correctly. Write **I** if it is punctuated incorrectly.

1. As our drama teacher, Mrs. Washburn, will you explain that movie to us?

2. Certainly Shelli but the explanation is lengthy.

3. We thought the movie was boring Mrs. Washburn.

4. The plot was complicated, class.

5. Marc, would you like to explain it to the class?

6. The plot, Mrs. Washburn was actually one big story with two smaller subplots.

7. Yes, Marc, that is very true.

8. Mrs. Washburn why did the director make the movie so hard to understand?

➤ Parenthetical Expressions

A **parenthetical expression** provides additional or related ideas. It is related only loosely to the rest of the sentence. The parenthetical expression could be removed without changing the meaning of the sentence.

25 C.2   Use commas to enclose, or set off, **parenthetical expressions.**

COMMON PARENTHETICAL EXPRESSIONS		
after all	for instance	of course
at any rate	generally speaking	on the contrary
by the way	I believe	on the other hand
consequently	I guess (hope, expect)	moreover
however	in fact	nevertheless
for example	in my opinion	to tell the truth

By the way, did you bring your binoculars?

The indigo bunting, **in my opinion,** is a beautiful bird.

We can watch the birds a little longer, **I guess.**

Nicole, **on the other hand,** has to leave.

We, **however,** just arrived.

Other expressions, as well, can be used as parenthetical expressions.

The roseate spoonbill, **although it looks like a flamingo,** is a different bird.

According to my book, puffins are not found in Florida.

Birds, **it is known,** communicate with one another.

25 C.3   **Contrasting expressions,** which usually begin with the word *not,* are also considered parenthetical expressions and should be set off by commas.

The mockingbird, **not the cardinal,** is the state bird of Texas.

The seagull is found inland, **not just by the ocean.**

My sister, **not I,** is the family bird expert.

● **Practice Your Skills**

Using Commas with Parenthetical Expressions

Rewrite each sentence, adding commas where needed. If the sentence is correct, write **C.**

1. Generally speaking birds are animals that have wings and fly.

2. Not all birds however fit this description.

3. In fact, many birds are unable to fly but have wings.

4. Consequently, birds are classified as animals with both wings and feathers.

5. Nevertheless birds are among nature's most interesting creatures.

6. Burrowing owls for example are ingenious birds.

● *Connect to Writing:* **Drafting**

Using Parenthetical Expressions

Write a paragraph about a favorite bird or other animal. Use a variety of parenthetical expressions, including contrasting expressions, in your paragraph. Be sure to use commas correctly.

Appositives

An **appositive** with its modifiers identifies or explains a noun or a pronoun in the sentence. Notice in the example that an appositive is enclosed in commas.

> The Greenville firehouse, **a town landmark,** has finally been restored.

25 C.4 Use commas to enclose most **appositives** and their modifiers.

Notice in the following examples that an appositive can come in the middle of a sentence or at the end of a sentence. If an appositive comes in the middle of a sentence, two commas are needed to enclose it.

> Greenville, **an old Western town,** is an interesting place to visit.
>
> Hannah bought me a beautiful gift, **some Greenville turquoise.**

Titles and degrees that follow a person's name are a type of appositive and should also be set off by commas. Contemporary usage does not treat *Jr.* as an appositive. Use , *Jr.,* in cases where the person named has traditionally used it, however.

> Rose Watts, **Ph.D.,** is a well-known expert on the history of Greenville.
>
> Harry Jackson, **Jr.,** was the first sheriff in Greenville.
>
> Mr. Smith, **CEO,** joined the Greenville Historical Society in 1999.

Commas are not used if an appositive identifies a person or thing by telling which one or ones when there is more than one possibility. Usually these appositives are names and have no modifiers.

> My friend **Greta** will travel to Greenville with us.
>
> The book *Western History* devotes two pages to a description of the town.
>
> We **students** studied the Old West last year.

You can learn more about appositives on pages 617–618.

Using Commas with Appositives

Rewrite each sentence, adding commas where needed. If the sentence is correct, write **C.**

1. Manifest Destiny the belief that it was America's mission to expand westward inspired many explorers in the 1800s.

2. The explorers Lewis and Clark set out to cross the unmapped continent in 1804.

3. The third president Thomas Jefferson had purchased a large portion of that land from France.

4. Jefferson secured $2,500 a grant from the Congress to support the Lewis and Clark expedition.

5. The Native American guide Sacajawea helped the party cross the unfamiliar terrain.

6. Lewis and Clark also hired Sacajawea's husband, Toussaint Charbonneau to guide them.

7. Sacagawea, a Shoshone, was fluent in many native languages.

✔ Check Point: Mixed Practice

Rewrite the paragraph below, adding commas where needed.

(1) A man who lived in California constructed a musical robot. **(2)** The amazing thing about this achievement however is that the man made it in 1940! **(3)** The robot by the way looked like a woman. **(4)** Sitting on a couch the robot would play the zither. **(5)** The zither a musical instrument has 30 to 40 strings.

(6) Anyone who was within a twelve-foot radius could ask it to play any of about 3,000 tunes. **(7)** A person's voice not a switch touched off its controls. **(8)** The machinery inside it included 1,187 wheels and 370 electromagnets. **(9)** No one has discovered in spite of extensive research whatever happened to Isis the world's first robot musician.

Nonrestrictive and Restrictive Elements

Sometimes a particular phrase or a clause is not essential to the meaning of a sentence. These phrases and clauses are called **nonrestrictive**.

25 C.5   Use commas to set off **nonrestrictive** participial phrases and clauses.

A participial phrase or a clause is nonrestrictive if it provides extra information that is not essential to the meaning of the sentence.

> **Nonrestrictive**   Dallas, **lying in the eastern part of Texas,** receives quite a bit of rain. (participial phrase)
>
> **Nonrestrictive**   Carol, **wearing a raincoat but no hat,** likes the rain. (participial phrase)
>
> **Nonrestrictive**   Three inches is the annual rainfall in Yuma, Arizona, **which is in the southwestern part of the state.** (relative clause)

If the nonrestrictive phrase and clause in the preceding examples were dropped, the main idea of the sentences would not be changed in any way.

> Dallas receives quite a bit of rain.
>
> Carol likes the rain.
>
> Three inches is the annual rainfall in Yuma, Arizona.

A **restrictive** phrase or clause usually identifies a person or thing and answers the question *Which one?* when there might be confusion otherwise.

25 C.6   If a participial phrase or a clause is **restrictive**—essential to the meaning of a sentence—no commas are used.

Clauses that begin with *that* are usually restrictive; clauses that begin with *which* are often nonrestrictive.

> **Restrictive**   We enjoyed the program **presented by the meteorologists.** (participial phrase)
>
> **Restrictive**   The speaker **who closed the program** is my father. (relative clause)
>
> **Restrictive**   His prediction **that the summer would be very dry** proved accurate. (relative clause)

CHAPTER 25

If the restrictive phrases and clauses in the preceding examples were dropped, necessary information would be missing. The main idea of the sentence would be incomplete.

We enjoyed the program. (*Which* program?)

The speaker is my father. (*Which* speaker?)

His prediction proved accurate. (*Which* prediction?)

Nonrestrictive and restrictive elements are sometimes called nonessential and essential elements.

● **Practice Your Skills**

Using Commas with Nonrestrictive Phrases and Clauses

Rewrite each sentence, adding commas where needed. If the sentence is correct, write **C**.

1. Lightning that strikes in dry forests can cause forest fires.

2. Often thunderstorms produce lightning that ignites dry areas.

3. Lightning which occurs all over the world is an amazing phenomenon.

4. Thunder which can be quite loud follows a lightning flash.

5. Lightning which is caused by streams of electricity can also strike humans.

6. A bolt of lightning striking a person usually causes very serious injury or death.

7. The phenomenon of lightning bolts traveling between two clouds is quite common.

8. Animals alarmed by the loud noises usually find cover during thunderstorms.

9. Lightning rods placed on the roof protect buildings from lightning damage.

10. Thunder occurring after a lightning flash is not dangerous in itself.

Rewrite the paragraphs below, adding commas where needed.

(1) The bald eagle of course is not bald. **(2)** It was named at a time when bald meant "white." **(3)** Because it has white feathers on its head the adult eagle has its present name. **(4)** In contrast to its white head and tail the bald eagle's body and wings are brown. **(5)** Its eyes beak and feet are yellow. **(6)** An eagle can be over three feet long and its wingspan may be over seven feet. **(7)** Its toes end in talons which are strong claws.

(8) An eagle is a hunter. **(9)** It feeds mainly on dead or dying fish but sometimes will eat small animals. **(10)** It swoops down picks up its prey in its talons and flies off. **(11)** An eagle that weighs eight to twelve pounds is able to carry an animal weighing as much as seventeen pounds!

(12) Even though the bald eagle is the national emblem it had become an endangered species by the 1960s. **(13)** After years of federal action and nationwide attention this magnificent bird was declared out of danger in 1999.

Assess Your Learning

▰ Understanding Kinds of Sentences and End Marks

Write each sentence and its appropriate end mark. Then label each one **D** for declarative, **IM** for imperative, **IN** for interrogative, or **E** for exclamatory.

1. Listen to these interesting facts about your body

2. No one else in the whole world has the same fingerprints or voiceprint as you do

3. If it takes 14 muscles to smile, how many muscles does it take to frown

4. The answer is 20, which means that it's easier to smile than to frown

5. Wait until you hear this next fact

6. Particles in a sneeze can travel at speeds of over 100 miles per hour

7. Did you ever cry when you cut an onion

8. A cut onion releases a gas that irritates your eyes

9. Then your tears automatically come to your eyes to wash away the gas—like windshield wipers

10. There are 206 bones in the human body

11. Do you know the name of the longest bone

12. The longest is the femur, or the thigh bone

13. Take care of your bones by drinking plenty of milk

14. What have we learned from these facts

15. Without a doubt, the workings of the human body are extraordinarily amazing

Using Commas Correctly

Write each sentence, adding a comma or commas where needed. If a sentence needs no commas, write **C**.

1. Pablo is your birthday on Tuesday March 6?

2. Gazelles and prairie dogs seldom drink water.

3. The Marianas Trench in the Pacific the lowest point on Earth is 36,198 feet below sea level.

4. Jennifer is only one day older than her cousin.

5. An old farmhouse owned by Ito stands near a meadow.

6. On Monday my brother will enter the Army at Fort Dix New Jersey.

7. Before locking up the custodian turned off the lights.

8. In Switzerland official notices are printed in French German Italian and Romansch.

9. Generally speaking a worker bee may live for six months but a queen bee may live for six years.

10. No Leslie doesn't live in Louisville Kentucky anymore.

Writing Sentences

Write ten sentences that follow the directions below.

Write a sentence that...

1. includes a series of nouns.

2. includes two adjectives before a noun.

3. has two independent clauses joined by a coordinating conjunction.

4. includes an introductory participial phrase.

5. includes an introductory adverbial clause.

6. includes a direct address.

7. includes a parenthetical expression.

8. includes an appositive.

9. includes a nonrestrictive adjectival clause.

10. includes a street number and name, city, and state.

End Marks and Commas: Posttest

Directions

Write the letter of the mark of punctuation that correctly completes each sentence. If the sentence contains no error, write **D.**

(1) The Alistairs have ten children, whose ages range from fifteen years to six months. (2) How do they manage a shopping trip (3) They load the kids into two vans and they drive to a large shopping mall. (4) Then the fun begins (5) Each older wiser kid takes charge of a younger one. (6) The Alistairs go to clothing stores shoe stores, and stationery stores. (7) Don't lose anyone (8) By the end of the day everyone is exhausted and ready to go home. (9) They meet in a pizza restaurant inside the mall. (10) With a little bit of luck all of the children and their parents will have accomplished their shopping on time.

1. A period
   B comma
   C question mark
   D No error

2. A period
   B comma
   C question mark
   D No error

3. A period
   B comma
   C exclamation point
   D No error

4. A exclamation point
   B comma
   C question mark
   D No error

5. A period
   B comma
   C question mark
   D No error

6. A period
   B comma
   C question mark
   D No error

7. A exclamation point
   B comma
   C question mark
   D No error

8. A period
   B comma
   C question mark
   D No error

9. A period
   B comma
   C question mark
   D No error

10. A period
   B comma
   C question mark
   D No error

Writer's Corner

Snapshot

25 A   A sentence may be **declarative, imperative, interrogative,** or **exclamatory.** (pages 842–844)

25 B   **Commas** are used to prevent confusion and to keep items from running into one another. (pages 848–856)

25 C   **Commas** enclose words that interrupt the main idea of a sentence. (pages 857–864)

Power Rules

 Be sure that every statement in your writing is a **complete sentence, not a fragment.** Each sentence should begin with a capital letter and end with the correct punctuation mark. You can fix a fragment by adding a conjunction and/or a comma to join it to an independent clause. (pages 666–671)

Before Editing	**After Editing**
If I go to the game. I'll pick you up.	*If I go to the game,* I'll pick you up.
My cousin. *A soccer fanatic.* Will probably want to come along too.	My cousin, *a soccer fanatic,* will probably want to come along too.
I will try to get to this game. *Because it will determine the final play-off.*	I will try to get to this game *because it will determine the final play-off.*

Check for **run-on sentences** and fix them by adding a conjunction and/or a comma or by separating the sentences into two complete sentences with the proper end marks. (pages 672–674)

Before Editing	**After Editing**
Sara decided to go to the picnic, her sister went to the movies.	Sara decided to go to the picnic, *and* her sister went to the movies.
They met in the late afternoon, they were going to look for a birthday gift for their cousin.	They met in the late afternoon. *They were going to look for a birthday gift for their cousin.*
They found a gift, they had an early dinner.	*After* they found a gift, they had an early dinner.

Editing Checklist

Use this checklist when editing your writing.

✓ Did I use a period to end sentences that make a statement or express an opinion? (See page 842.)

✓ Did I use a period or exclamation point to end a sentence that gives a direction or a command or makes a request? (See page 842.)

✓ Did I use a question mark to end a sentence that asks a question? (See page 843.)

✓ Did I use an exclamation point to end a sentence that expresses strong feelings? (See page 843.)

✓ Did I correctly use commas to separate items in a series? (See pages 848–849.)

✓ Did I use commas between two adjectives when they were needed to make my writing clear? (See pages 850–851.)

✓ Did I use commas to set off expressions that interrupt the flow of the sentence? (See pages 857–864.)

✓ Did I use commas correctly to set off nonrestrictive phrases and clauses? (See pages 862–864.)

Use the Power

When you know the purpose of your sentence, you know which end punctuation to use. Use the sentences and the image at the right to help you remember how different end marks can sometimes completely change the meaning or clarity of a sentence.

| **Imperative** | Add green food coloring to the milk. |
| **Interrogative** | Add green food coloring to the milk? |

Italics and Quotation Marks

How can you create voice in your writing with italics and quotation marks?

Italics and Quotation Marks: Pretest 1

The following first draft contains several errors in the use of italics and quotation marks. The first error has been corrected. How would you revise the draft to correct other errors?

"We're leaving bright and early. Are you all packed?" asked Dad.
Almost called Jerry
Be sure to bring *The Hiker's Survival Guide* and the map said Dad.
Will do.
Did you grab some CDs to listen to on the ride up? asked Dad. I've got "Come Another Day" and "Ten to One."
Cool. I love the first track. I think it's called *"What's Next?"* Jerry said.
"Do we need anything else"? asked Dad. If not, let's get this show on the road.

Italics and Quotation Marks: Pretest 2

Directions

Read the passage and write the letter of the answer that correctly punctuates each underlined part. If the underlined part contains no error, write **D**.

(1) "Are you taking advanced English, Jay" Ellie asked?

(2) "No," Jay replied, "math is what interests me."

(3) Ellie said, "I hope we do some of Emily Dickinson's poems, such as 'I Am Nobody.'"

(4) "We have to write five papers"! Anthony exclaimed.

Ellie couldn't believe her ears. Did she just hear him say, **(5)** "We have to write five papers"?

1. **A** "Are you taking advanced English, Jay"? Ellie asked.
   B "Are you taking advanced English, Jay?" Ellie asked.
   C "Are you taking advanced English, Jay Ellie asked"?
   D No error

2. **A** "No." Jay replied, "Math is what interests me."
   B "No." Jay replied. "Math is what interests me."
   C "No," Jay replied. "Math is what interests me."
   D No error

3. **A** Ellie said, "I hope we do some of Emily Dickinson's poems, such as 'I Am Nobody."
   B Ellie said, "I hope we do some of Emily Dickinson's poems, such as I Am Nobody.
   C Ellie said, "I hope we do some of Emily Dickinson's poems, such as 'I Am Nobody.'
   D No error

4. **A** "We have to write five papers" Anthony exclaimed!
   B "We have to write five papers." Anthony exclaimed.
   C "We have to write five papers!" Anthony exclaimed.
   D No error

5. **A** 'We have to write five papers'?
   B 'We have to write five papers?'
   C "We have to write five papers?"
   D No error

Italics (Underlining)  Lesson 1

26 A   **Italics** are printed letters that slant to the right. Italics are used for titles of long works, foreign words, and words or numbers used as words. When you are writing by hand, underline words that should be in italics.

> **Italics**   My mom read *Charlie and the Chocolate Factory* to my little sister.
>
> **Underlining**   My mom read <u>Charlie and the Chocolate Factory</u> to my little sister.

➤ Letters, Numbers, and Words

Certain letters, numbers, and words should be italicized (underlined).

26 A.1   Italicize (underline) letters, numbers, and words when they are used to represent themselves. Also italicize (underline) foreign words that are not generally used in the English language.

When you use the computer, you should italicize; when you write, you should underline. Do not do both. If the number or letter is plural, do not italicize (underline) the *s*.

> **Letters**   My little sister has trouble writing *5*s and *B*s.
>
> or
>
> My little sister has trouble writing <u>5</u>s and <u>B</u>s.
>
> **Words, Phrases**   She cannot pronounce the word *teeth*.
>
> or
>
> She cannot pronounce the word <u>teeth</u>.
>
> **Foreign Words**   We call our German grandmother *Oma*.
>
> or
>
> We call our German grandmother <u>Oma</u>.

There may be times when you want to emphasize a word for a specific reason. You can do so by italicizing or underlining the word. Example: She insists that she heard *two* explosions.

 # Titles

26 A.2 Italicize (underline) the titles of long written or musical works that are published as a single unit. Also italicize (underline) the titles of periodicals, movies, radio and television series, paintings and sculptures, and the names of vehicles. All words in the title should be italicized.

	TITLES	
Books	*Jane Eyre*	White Fang
Newspapers	*Chicago Tribune*	Sacramento Bee
Periodicals	*Seventeen*	the Reader's Digest
	(In general, do not italicize or underline *the*, which often appears before newspaper or periodical titles.)	
Plays, Movies	*Romeo and Juliet*	The Wizard of Oz
Book-Length Poems	*Evangeline*	Odyssey
Radio and Television Series	*The Shadow*	Law and Order
Long Musical Works	*Faust*	La Traviata
Works of Art	*Mona Lisa*	Venus de Milo
Ships, Planes, Other Craft	*Titanic*	Spirit of St. Louis
	Voyager 2	Discovery

You can learn about capitalization of titles on pages 829–832.

● **Practice Your Skills**

Using Italics (Underlining)

Write *a* or *b* to indicate which item in each pair shows the correct use of italics.

1. a. the novel *The Mill* on the *Floss*
   b. the novel *The Mill on the Floss*

2. a. the opera The Barber of Seville
   b. the opera *The Barber of Seville*

3. a. the magazine *Boy's Life*
   b. *the magazine Boy's Life*

4. a. the newspaper the *Los Angeles Times*
   b. the newspaper *the Los Angeles Times*

Italics (Underlining) • Lesson 1   **873**

5. **a.** the painting The *Last Supper*

   b. the painting *The Last Supper*

6. **a.** the musical *The Phantom of the Opera*

   b. the musical *The Phantom* of the *Opera*

7. **a.** the film *Citizen Kane*

   b. *the film Citizen Kane*

8. **a.** *Shakespeare's play Twelfth Night*

   b. Shakespeare's play *Twelfth Night*

9. **a.** the television show *The X-Files*

   b. the television show The *X-Files*

10. **a.** the aircraft carrier USS *Enterprise*

   b. the *aircraft carrier* USS *Enterprise*

● *Connect to Writing:* Editing

Using Underlining

Rewrite the following sentences, underlining the words that should be italicized.

1. I love adventure books like 20,000 Leagues Under the Sea by Jules Verne.

2. I can imagine myself on a submarine like the Nautilus.

3. This book was written before transportation innovations like the Concorde.

4. In The Wonderful Wizard of Oz, published in 1900, tornadoes, horses, and hot-air balloons are all used for transportation.

5. In 1912, the allegedly unsinkable ship Titanic sank after striking an iceberg.

6. The word titanic actually means "colossal."

7. It is derived from the Greek word titanikos, which relates to the mythological Titans.

8. Other famous vehicles that suffered a tragic end include the zeppelin Hindenburg and the ocean liner Lusitania.

9. The history of steamships, such as the Queen Mary, is rich.

10. Magazines like Aviation History and Collectible Automobile regularly feature stories about the history of transportation.

● *Connect to Writing and Speaking:* Peer Consultation

Using Italics

Write a paragraph about the television programs and films you most enjoy. Then consult with a partner about your preferences. Together, write a new paragraph that combines examples that you both admire. Be sure you use italics correctly.

26 B **Quotation marks** always come in pairs. They are placed at the beginning and at the end of certain titles and uninterrupted quotations.

Quotation Marks with Titles

You have learned that titles of long works are italicized (underlined). Most long works are made up of smaller parts. For example, books are composed of chapters, and magazines contain articles. The titles of these smaller parts should be enclosed in quotation marks.

26 B.1 Use quotation marks to enclose the titles of chapters, articles, stories, one-act plays, short poems, and songs. The entire title should be in quotation marks.

Chapters	Read **"**I Am Born,**"** the first chapter in my favorite book, *David Copperfield.*
Articles	Have you seen the article **"**Charles Dickens's England**"** in *Newsweek?*
Stories	I read **"**Everyday Use**"** by Alice Walker yesterday.
One-Act Plays	Sherry is going to be in the school's performance of **"**Drama Club.**"**
Short Poems	My favorite poem in the book *Famous Twentieth Century Poetry* is **"**Sea Lullaby.**"**
Songs	My mother told us that they used to sing a song called **"**Puff, the Magic Dragon.**"**

You will learn more about other punctuation, such as commas and periods, with quotation marks later in this chapter.

● **Practice Your Skills**

Punctuating Titles

Write *a* or *b* to indicate which title in each pair is correctly punctuated.

1. a. the short story *The Lottery*
   b. the short story "The Lottery"
2. a. the poem *The Elegance of Memory*
   b. the poem "The Elegance of Memory"

CHAPTER 26

3. a. the song "Somewhere Over the Rainbow"

   b. the song "Somewhere Over" the "Rainbow"

4. a. the short story "The Washwoman"

   b. the short story The "Washwoman"

5. a. the chapter title The "Romantic" Poets

   b. the chapter title "The Romantic Poets"

6. a. the song *Twinkle, Twinkle Little Star*

   b. the song "Twinkle, Twinkle Little Star"

7. a. the poem "The Road Not Taken"

   b. the poem The "Road Not Taken"

8. a. the short story "The Rocking-Horse Winner"

   b. the short story *The Rocking-Horse Winner*

9. a. the chapter title *The Art of Georgia O'Keefe*

   b. the chapter title "The Art of Georgia O'Keefe"

10. a. the song "Frozen"

   b. the song *Frozen*

✔ *Check Point:* **Mixed Practice**

Write each sentence, adding quotation marks or underlining where needed.

1. The Roots of Old Verse is the lead article in the Atlantic Literary Journal.

2. The familiar lullaby Rock-a-Bye Baby dates from the Elizabethan period.

3. Ring Around the Roses is an old rhyme from the Middle Ages.

4. No, I read Mending Wall in the book Selected Poems of Robert Frost.

5. I read an article about him called Frost's New England in Newsweek.

6. Do you know the song I Can't Choose by John Knight?

7. It is based on The Road Not Taken, which was also written by Frost.

● *Connect to Writing:* **Persuasive Letter**

Using Quotation Marks with Titles

Your choral director has asked for song suggestions for an upcoming performance. Write a letter suggesting two songs for the performance. They can be popular songs or songs from opera or musicals. Give convincing reasons why the chorus should sing these two songs. When you have finished your letter, check that you have punctuated the song titles correctly.

Quotation Marks with Direct Quotations

The most important thing to remember when writing direct quotations is that quotation marks enclose only the *exact words* of a speaker. In other words, quotation marks are used only with a **direct quotation.**

26 B.2   Use quotation marks to enclose a person's exact words.

> **"**I just finished my homework,**"** Zoe said.
>
> Will said, **"**I'll be glad to check it for you.**"**

Sometimes, when you write, you may paraphrase what someone has said—without using his or her exact words. When you paraphrase, you are indirectly quoting a person. Do not use quotation marks with **indirect quotations.**

> Zoe said that she had just finished her homework.
> (The word *that* signals the indirect quotation.)
> Will said he would check it for her.
> (The word *that* is understood.)

A one-sentence direct quotation can be written in several ways. It can be placed before or after a speaker tag, such as *she said* or *Mr. Billings asked.* In both cases quotation marks enclose the person's exact words—from beginning to end.

> **"**Yesterday I left my homework in my locker,**"** Zoe added.
>
> Zoe added, **"**Yesterday I left my homework in my locker.**"**

For variety or emphasis, a quotation can also be interrupted by a speaker tag. When this interruption occurs, you need two pairs of quotation marks because quotation marks enclose only a person's exact words, not the speaker tag.

> **"**Yesterday,**"** Zoe added, **"**I left my homework in my locker.**"**

To quote more than one sentence, put quotation marks at the beginning and at the end of the entire quotation. Do not put quotation marks around each sentence within a quotation—unless a speaker tag interrupts.

Zoe added, "Yesterday I left my homework in my locker. Mrs. Cash was very nice about it. She wrote a hall pass so that I could retrieve it."

"Yesterday I left my homework in my locker," Zoe said. "Luckily, Mrs. Cash wrote a hall pass so I could retrieve it."

Notice in the examples that the comma or period that follows the quotation is placed *inside* the closing quotation marks. Of course, if the sentence ends with the speaker tag, then the period follows the speaker tag.

"I got my homework and returned to class," said Zoe.

● **Practice Your Skills**

Using Quotation Marks with Direct Quotations

Write *I* If a sentence is punctuated incorrectly. Write **C** if a sentence is punctuated correctly.

1. Joey told Mrs. Cash that the dog ate his homework.

2. That's the oldest excuse there is, said Mrs. Cash.

3. Mrs. Cash asked us to get out our math books.

4. "I wonder what our topic is today," said Zoe.

5. "Today, Mrs. Cash said, we'll be discussing real-life math."

6. She said that "we were going to discuss how to count a customer's change back to him or her."

7. Our teacher continued, We will also talk about how to determine sales tax.

8. "Mrs. Cash, Will said, most cash registers indicate the correct change."

Capital Letters with Direct Quotations

26 B.3   Begin each sentence of a direct quotation with a capital letter.

"Usually, bees swarm in the spring," my teacher said.

My teacher said, "Usually, bees swarm in the spring."

If a single-sentence quotation is interrupted by a speaker tag, use only one capital letter—at the beginning of the sentence.

"Usually," my teacher said, "bees swarm in the spring."

Using Capital Letters with Direct Quotations

Read the sentences below. Write *I* if the sentence is capitalized incorrectly. Write **C** if the sentence is capitalized correctly.

1. "When honey bees swarm," said Mr. Johnson, "They are usually engorged with honey."
2. Maya asked, "Will they sting people then?"
3. "Yes, they might," replied the teacher, "But they are less likely to sting than at other times."
4. "Bees are not native to America," Mr. Johnson said.
5. Greg said, "in a magazine, I read an article that said they were brought here from Europe."

Commas with Direct Quotations

When you are reading quoted material aloud, your voice naturally pauses between the speaker tag and the direct quotation. In written material these pauses are indicated by commas.

| 26 B.4 | Use a comma to separate a direct quotation from a speaker tag. Place the comma inside the closing quotation marks. |

"The ice cream isn't frozen yet," Jordan cautioned.

Jordan cautioned, "The ice cream isn't frozen yet."

"The ice cream," Jordan cautioned, "isn't frozen yet."

In the second and third examples above, note that the comma before the opening quotation marks is placed after the speaker tag, outside the opening quotation marks.

● Practice Your Skills

Using Commas with Direct Quotations

If the use of commas in the sentence is incorrect, write *I.* If the use of commas is correct, write **C.**

1. "I love making homemade ice cream", said Jordan.
2. Lori admitted, "I've never done that before."
3. "It's not hard," said Jordan "as long as you have an ice-cream maker."
4. "My grandfather has one of the old ones," said Lori, "with a crank."
5. "Ours is electric", said Jordan "but either one will do."

CHAPTER 26

End Marks with Direct Quotations

End marks come at the end of a quoted sentence, just as they do in a sentence that is not a quotation. Commas and periods always come within quotation marks.

26 B.5   Place a period inside the closing quotation marks when the end of the quotation comes at the end of the sentence.

> Carlos said, "This afternoon we'll hike in the Grand Canyon."
>
> "This afternoon," Carlos said, "we'll hike in the Grand Canyon."

If a quotation comes at the beginning of a sentence, the period follows the speaker tag.

> "This afternoon we'll hike in the Grand Canyon," Carlos said.

A period comes at the end of each sentence in a quotation of two or more sentences.

> "This afternoon we'll hike in the Grand Canyon," Carlos said. "Tomorrow we'll visit an archaeological dig. The next day we'll go home."

Follow these two rules when dealing with quotations, questions, and exclamations.

26 B.6   Place a question mark or an exclamation point inside the closing quotation marks when the question or exclamation is part of the quotation.

> Madison asked, "Is the canyon close or will we drive there?"
>
> "Is the canyon close," Madison asked, "or will we drive there?"
>
> "Is the canyon close or will we drive there?" Madison asked.
>
> Dani screamed, "Watch out for that snake!"
>
> "Watch out for that snake!" Dani screamed.

26 B.7   When a question mark or exclamation mark is part of the whole sentence, it is placed *outside* the closing quotation marks.

> Did I hear the guide say, "That snake is not harmful"?
>
> (The whole sentence—not the quotation—is the question.)
>
> It was the happiest moment of my life when Carlos said, "It's time for a break"!
>
> (The whole sentence is exclamatory, not the quotation.)

Connect to Writing: Editorial

Using Quotations

What is love? Why do people fall in love? Nikki Giovanni once said, "We love because it's the only true adventure." Collect two quotations about love from two people you know. Then using the quotation above and the two you collect, write an editorial about the meaning of love. After you write your article, read it to correct any errors. Don't forget to punctuate the quotations properly. Around the time of Valentine's Day, send your article to your local paper for inclusion in the special holiday section.

Practice Your Skills

Using End Marks with Direct Quotations

Write **I** if the end mark in the sentence is incorrect. Write **C** if the sentence is correct.

1. "Hiking the Grand Canyon can be fun," said Carlos. "However, you have to be careful."
2. "Going down is much easier than coming up," exclaimed Madison!
3. Carlos said, "It's also hotter down by the river than at the rim".
4. "Bring plenty of water," warned the guide. "It's also important to wear proper shoes."
5. Did you hear that ranger say, "Some trails are closed?"

Check Point: Mixed Practice

Write each sentence, adding capital letters, quotation marks, and other punctuation marks where needed.

1. a cat has absolute honesty Ernest Hemingway noted
2. someone once said it's nice for children to have pets—until the pets start having children
3. if things went by merit Mark Twain announced you would stay out and your dog would go in
4. Samuel Butler said the hen is an egg's way of producing another egg
5. all animals are equal wrote George Orwell but some are more equal than others
6. what modest claim do kittens make David Irvine asked they claim the ownership of humans

Other Uses of Quotation Marks

Once you know how to punctuate a direct quotation correctly, you will be able to apply what you know to the following situations.

Dialogue

In writing, dialogue is treated in a special way so that a reader always knows who is speaking, even if there are no speaker tags such as "he said" or "she asked."

26 B.8 When writing dialogue, begin a new paragraph each time the speaker changes.

In the following excerpt from *Oliver Twist* by Charles Dickens, a new paragraph begins each time the housekeeper or Oliver speaks. They are discussing a painting of a beautiful woman that has been taken from the wall.

> "Ah!" said the housekeeper, watching the direction of Oliver's eyes. "It is gone, you see."
>
> "I see it is, ma'am," replied Oliver. "Why have they taken it away?"
>
> "It has been taken down, child, because Mr. Brownlow said, that as it seemed to worry you, perhaps it might prevent your getting well, you know," rejoined the old lady.
>
> "Oh, no, indeed. It didn't worry me, ma'am," said Oliver. "I liked to see it. I quite loved it."

When You Write

When you write dialogue or direct quotations, it is important not to repeat the word *said* too often in the speaker tags. Try to convey to your reader the tone or mood of the speaker or character by using vivid speaker tags. You can do this by using a different word for *said* or by adding an adverb showing how the words are spoken.

> "You're finally here," **laughed** Jennifer.
>
> "You're finally here," **whined** Jennifer.
>
> "You're finally here," **snapped** Jennifer **impatiently.**

Notice how changing the speaker tags changes the meaning of the quotation and helps readers understand the speaker's or character's emotions.

Long Passages

When you write a report and want to support a point, you may want to quote more than one paragraph from a book. If this is the case, you use quotation marks in a slightly different manner.

26 B.9   When quoting a passage of more than one paragraph, place quotation marks at the beginning of each paragraph—but at the end of only the last paragraph.

Closing quotation marks are omitted at the end of each paragraph, except the last one, to indicate to a reader that the quotation is continuing.

> **"**Charles Dickens wrote some of the most popular books of the nineteenth century. He was one artist who enjoyed as much fame during his lifetime as after his death.
> (no closing quotation marks)
>
> **"**The characters created by Dickens still resonate with modern readers of all ages. From the rags-to-riches-to-rags Pip of *Great Expectations* to the tragic Sydney Carton of *A Tale of Two Cities,* Dickens wrote remarkable accounts of the human condition.
> (no closing quotation marks)
>
> **"**Known after his first novel *The Pickwick Papers* as a writer of humor, Dickens turned to the darker side of orphanages and the Victorian workhouse in *Oliver Twist,* his second book. Through Oliver's eyes, readers experience the ugliness of poverty and the cruelty of adults to children.**"**
> (closing quotation marks)

Another way to quote a long passage is to set it off from the rest of the text by indenting both left and right margins. When you use this method of quoting a long passage—called the **block quote**—no quotation marks are needed.

> As Donna Russell notes in her article "The Overtaxed Brain," people, particularly young people, can become overtaxed:
>> I really do believe that most people want to do the right thing. From earliest childhood, we do our best to please others and to fit in. The problem arises when we don't fully understand the right thing to do. Our wiring becomes overtaxed, and we get a bit frazzled. How can we do right when we are so confused?

Quotations Within Quotations

A quotation within a quotation follows all the rules covered previously in this chapter. However, to avoid confusion, use single quotation marks to make a distinction between the two quotations.

> **26 B.10** To distinguish a quotation within a quotation, use single quotation marks to enclose the inside quotation.

> "Is the song 'Food, Glorious Food' from the musical *Oliver!* by Lionel Bart?" Li asked.
>
> Mr. Sanders said, "The most famous of Oliver Twist's lines in Dickens's book and Bart's musical is 'Please, Sir, I want some more.'"

Notice in the second example that the closing single quotation mark and the closing double quotation marks come together.

Quote Marks to Show Irony or Sarcasm

Have you ever seen a speaker make a hand gesture to mimic the use of quotation marks? These finger quotes often indicate the person is using a term sarcastically or in an unusual way. In writing, you can use quotation marks in the same way.

> **26 B.11** Quotation marks can be used to alert readers to sarcasm or irony or to signal an unusual use of a term.

> Bob's a real "expert" when it comes to cooking. He can boil water and make toast.
>
> I saw the "chef" in action yesterday. He made me macaroni and cheese from a box.

Quotation marks can also be used to indicate jargon or slang. Be careful not to overuse quote marks to show irony or sarcasm. The usage can become tiresome if overdone.

When You Write

Most professional writers express sarcasm or irony through the structure of their sentences and the context of their words. Sometimes they use scare quotes, quotation marks around a word that indicate some special status. These quotation marks are often used to express humor, doubt, sarcasm, irony, or jargon. Compare these two sentences:

Quote Marks: Suddenly the room was filled with extremely loud pulsating "music."

Sentence structure: Suddenly the room was filled with extremely loud pulsating music apparently created by musicians beating their amplifiers to death with rocks. —Dave Barry

Write two sentences: One that expresses sarcasm by using scare quotes and one that uses only words to express a sarcastic idea.

● **Practice Your Skills**

Using Quotation Marks Correctly

Write *I* if the quotation marks in a sentence are used incorrectly. Write **C** if the quotation marks in a sentence are used correctly.

1. Mr. Sanders explained, "Charles Dickens's works have now become a part of our everyday language."
2. He continued, "Few educated people do not recognize these opening lines from *A Tale of Two Cities*. It was the best of times; it was the worst of times."
3. "Mr. Sanders," Li interrupted, "who is your favorite character from *Great Expectations?*"
4. "That's hard to say," answered Mr. Sanders, "but I do love the blacksmith Joe."
5. Cindi said, "I love it when Sydney Carton says, It is a far, far better thing I do than I have ever done."
6. "Yes, that's the beginning of the last sentence in *A Tale of Two Cities*," said Mr. Sanders.
7. "Why does Mr. Grimwig keep saying I'll eat my head in *Oliver Twist?*" asked Cindi.

● *Connect to Writing:* Drafting

Using Scare Quotes

Write three sentences using quotation marks to indicate irony, sarcasm, or jargon.

● *Connect to Writing:* Editing

Using Quotation Marks to Show Sarcasm

Edit the following descriptive paragraph about a student's summer vacation. Put quotation marks around words or phases used ironically or with sarcasm and remove quotation marks that have been used incorrectly.

> This summer my mother decided we would go on what she called a minivacation. Mini is right, particularly when it came to "fun." We drove about "twenty" miles and checked into a hotel in the "neighboring city." Our beach was the hotel swimming pool and our arcade was the game console in our room, which my brothers "hogged" the whole time. The only "benefit" of this vacation: I completed my summer reading "assignment" two months early.

● *Connect to Writing:* Scene

Using Quotations Marks to Show Sarcasm

Imagine a character who pretends to be something he or she isn't. For example, Bob in the two examples on page 884 might think he is a chef, but he certainly isn't one. Create a short scene in which your character reveals his or her "knowledge" or "skill." Be sure to use quotation marks to show sarcasm where appropriate.

Assess Your Learning

▪ Punctuating Quotations

Write each sentence, adding capital letters, quotation marks, and other punctuation marks where needed.

1. Abigail Adams once wrote to her husband we have many high sounding words, and too few actions that correspond to them

2. trees are swayed by winds, but men are swayed by words wrote the author Joan Aiken

3. she went on to say words are like spices too many is worse than too few

4. in the book Little Women, the character Jo said I like good strong words that mean something

5. look was Pa's favorite word it meant admire, wonder, goggle at the beauty and excitement all around us said Lucy in the book The Ballad of Lucy Whipple

6. Scrooge said bah! humbug! in Charles Dickens's A Christmas Carol

7. words can destroy said Jeane Kirkpatrick what we call each other ultimately becomes what we think of each other, and it matters

8. the ballpoint pen said Noah in the book The View from Saturday has been the biggest single factor in the decline of Western Civilization it makes the written word cheap, fast, and totally without character

9. the famous artist Georgia O'Keeffe once said I found I could say with color and shapes what I couldn't say in any other way

10. polite words open iron gates says a Serbo-Croatian proverb

■ Punctuating Quotations Correctly

Write each sentence, adding underlining, capital letters, quotation marks, and other punctuation marks where needed.

1. where asked Ina did you find those incredible, fluorescent earrings?

2. A hairstylist's sign on Bradbury St. read we curl up and dye for you.

3. I just read Oliver Twist, Jan said it was better than any movie version I have ever seen.

4. News Ben Bradlee once said is the first rough draft of history.

5. Have you ever read the Christian Science Monitor Dan asked.

6. Cathleen asked is the ocean rough today

7. Ken declared I'm going to be the new class president

8. Please don't break us apart the sign over the bananas read

9. Arlene remarked we grew up together

10. That was an incredible pass exclaimed Dave

11. Work is the best escape from boredom Eleanor Dean once said

12. Who said little things affect little minds

13. Defeat is not the worst of failures said G. E. Woodberry not to have tried is the true failure

14. We saw a production of the Shakespearean play As You Like It at the Lyric State Theatre Cheryl announced

15. Life shrinks or expands in proportion to one's courage Anaïs Nin commented

■ Writing Sentences

Follow the directions below.

1. Write a dialogue between you and a fictional person: a superhero, a character in a book, a cartoon character, or someone created in your imagination. Punctuate the dialogue correctly.

2. After an introductory paragraph, quote a long passage.

Italics and Quotation Marks: Posttest

Directions

Read the passage and write the letter of the answer that correctly punctuates each underlined part. If the underlined part contains no error, mark D.

The show got a favorable review in our **(1)** newspaper, the Enquirer. In the first show, Kayla's only line was, **(2)** "Coming, Mother"!

Kayla was also interviewed in our newspaper. **(3)** "How," the reporter asked, "did you get this part"?

Kayla answered, **(4)** "In my tryout, I read from the poem The Lake Isle of Innisfree. The director told me that his favorite poet is Yeats!"

"Really, it was just luck, then," the reporter said.

"Oh, no," Kayla protested, **(5)** "he really liked my work."

1. **A** newspaper, the "Enquirer"
   B newspaper, the *Enquirer*
   C newspaper, the *"Enquirer"*
   D No error

2. **A** "Coming, Mother!"
   B *"Coming, Mother"!*
   C *"Coming, Mother"*
   D No error

3. **A** "How," the reporter asked, "did you get this part?"
   B "How?" the reporter asked, "did you get this part?"
   C "How," the reporter asked? "did you get this part?"
   D No error

4. **A** "In my tryout, I read from the poem "The Lake Isle of Innisfree."
   B "In my tryout, I read from the poem *The Lake Isle of Innisfree.*
   C "In my tryout, I read from the poem 'The Lake Isle of Innisfree.'
   D No error

5. **A** "He really liked my work."
   B he really liked my work."
   C He really liked my work."
   D No error

Writer's Corner

Snapshot

26 A **Italics** are printed letters that slant to the right. Italics are used for titles of long works, foreign words, and words or numbers used as words. When you are writing by hand, underline whatever should be italicized. (pages 872–874)

26 B **Quotation marks** come in pairs. They are placed at the beginning and at the end of the titles of certain works and uninterrupted quotations. Quotation marks are also used to indicate dialogue. (pages 875–886)

Power Rules

 When you write dialogue, you can use sentence fragments to imitate the way people actually speak. In **all other types of writing, check for sentence fragments.** Fix a fragment by adding words to make it a complete sentence or by adding a conjunction and/or punctuation to join it to an independent clause. (pages 666–670)

Before Editing	**After Editing**
Uncle Leo. *Who lives in California.* Is visiting us for a month.	Uncle Leo, *who lives in California,* is visiting us for a month.
I'll finish my homework. *After we have dinner.*	I'll finish my homework *after we have dinner.*

 In speech, people sometimes use double negatives to stress a point. In formal writing, however, you should avoid double negatives. Instead, **use italics or underlining** to add emphasis. (page 872)

Before Editing	**After Editing**
The writer does *not* do *nothing* to prove his point.	The writer does *nothing* to prove his point.
The editor of this magazine does *not* care for *nobody* else's opinion.	The editor of this magazine cares for *nobody* else's opinion.

Editing Checklist

Use this checklist when editing your writing.

✓ Did I italicize or underline the titles of long works, like books, newspapers, magazines, and movies? (See pages 873–874.)

✓ Did I use quotation marks to enclose the titles of shorter works, like poems and songs? (See pages 875–876.)

✓ Did I use quotation marks to enclose a person's exact words? (See page 877.)

✓ Did I punctuate quotations and dialogue correctly? (See pages 877–886.)

✓ Did I use a comma to separate a quotation from a speaker tag? (See page 879.)

✓ Did I begin each sentence of a direct quotation with a capital letter? (See pages 878–879.)

✓ Did I use single quotation marks to enclose an inside quotation to distinguish a quotation within a quotation? (See page 884.)

CHAPTER 26

Use the Power

Read the dialogue below to help you learn how to use italics and quotation marks. Notice how sentence fragments are used to imitate the way people talk.

Where are you going? Didn't Mom say, and I quote, "No leaving the house"?

She said I could run to the mall to get that new CD *Anything in Between*.

Oh, yeah. That song "Come On, Come On" is awesome!

Totally. *Spin* magazine gave it five stars.

Hey, while you're out, will you get me a copy of *Newsweek*? I need it for class.

Me too. I have to read the article "Teens and Politics."

Other Punctuation

How can you use apostrophes, semicolons, colons, hyphens, and other punctuation to communicate precisely and enhance your writing style?

Other Punctuation: Pretest 1

The first draft below contains punctuation errors. The first error, in which an apostrophe was missing from a possessive noun, is corrected. Revise the remaining errors.

I love spending summers at my Aunt Betty's farm. Every morning we have a huge breakfast bacon, eggs, hash browns, and fresh-squeezed orange juice. Aunt Betty who grew up on a ranch loves to have lots of animal's around. She has three horses Im allowed to ride them whenever I want. She taught me how to: tie a lasso; mend a saddle; and brush a horse so she expects me to help out when I visit. Its hard work: nevertheless, I enjoy doing it. I could spend all day brushing the horses manes. My sister in law shes allergic to horses takes care of the hogs. Aunt Betty says pigs are smarter than dogs so they're easier to train. Shes trained one pig named Milo to fetch a ball.

Other Punctuation: Pretest 2

Directions

Write the letter of the answer that correctly punctuates the underlined part in each sentence. If the underlined part contains no error, write **D.**

(1) This summer was the <u>camps first year</u>. (2) The counselors were all <u>nervous many of us</u> had never worked with kids before. (3) Our day began at <u>9:30 am</u> (4) The <u>kids at least most of them</u> were eager to play. (5) In my group one girl was incredibly <u>self assured</u>. (6) She organized groups for <u>games helped me</u> hand out lunches, snacks, and drinks; and soothed nervous kids. (7) She was the <u>camp directors niece</u>, so I shouldn't have been surprised at her maturity. (8) <u>I couldnt have</u> done my job without Anna's help. (9) I like to think that it was <u>Annas and my work</u> that made the third-grade group do so well. (10) The <u>Matthews family</u> were new to the area and had seven children in the camp.

1. A camp's first year
   B camps' first year
   C camp's first-year
   D No error

2. A nervous; many of us
   B nervous: many of us
   C nervous (many of us)
   D No error

3. A 9:30 (AM).
   B 93:0 A.M.
   C 9:30 a.m.
   D No error

4. A kids—at least most of them—
   B kids—at least most of them
   C kids: at least most of them
   D No error

5. A self; assured
   B self-assured
   C selfassured
   D No error

6. A games; helped me
   B games: helped me
   C games—helped me
   D No error

7. A camp directors—niece
   B camp directors-niece
   C camp director's niece
   D No error

8. A I couldn't have
   B I could'nt have
   C I couldnt' have
   D No error

9. A Annas, and my work
   B Annas' and my work
   C Anna's and my work
   D No error

10. A Matthews family,
   B Matthew's family
   C Matthews' family
   D No error

The most costly punctuation error of all time occurred in 1962. A hyphen was omitted from a set of directions sent to the rocket powering the *Venus* space probe. As a result of the omission, the rocket self-destructed. Most errors that are made in punctuation do not have such disastrous results. Nevertheless, correct punctuation is necessary for clear communication—right here on Earth.

Omitting a tiny apostrophe can make a big difference in a sentence. In fact, including apostrophes in certain words is as important as spelling those words correctly. Without an apostrophe, the first sentence in the following examples does not make sense. With an apostrophe the meaning of the sentence instantly becomes clear.

> Well go with you to the game tonight.
>
> We'll go with you to the game tonight.

27 A **An apostrophe (') is used with nouns and some pronouns to show ownership or relationship, to represent missing letters in contractions, and with certain plurals and some dates.**

Apostrophes to Show Possession

One of the most common uses of an apostrophe is to show that someone or something owns something else.

> Lani's softball = the softball of Lani
>
> a woman's house = the house of a woman
>
> the Spensers' garage = the garage of the Spensers
>
> the Jones's new dog = the new dog belonging to the Jones

As you can see from the examples above, some nouns have a special form to show possession. An apostrophe or an apostrophe and an *s* are added to the noun.

Possessive Forms of Singular Nouns

To form the possessive of a noun, first decide whether the noun is singular or plural.

27 A.1   Add **'s** to form the possessive of a singular noun.

There is no need to add or omit a letter. Just write the word and put 's at the end.

> baby + **'s** = baby**'s**   Give me the baby**'s** blanket.
>
> Joey + **'s** = Joey**'s**   That is Joey**'s** little sister.

The 's is added to the last word of compound words and the names of most businesses and organizations.

> The passerby**'s** gaze fell on the cute child.
>
> The baby broke the jack-in-the box**'s** spring.
>
> The YMCA**'s** advertisements appeal to young families.

When You Write

Publishers vary as to whether to add an *-s* to a personal name ending in *s* to show possession. In such cases, be sure that you use the form that is expected and that you are consistent in its use.

Often Used   The **Prentiss's** house is on the corner.

Also Used   The **Prentiss'** house is on the corner.

● Practice Your Skills

Forming Possessive Singular Nouns

Write the possessive form of each noun.

1. apple	**5.** cat	**9.** sailor
2. Pep Club	**6.** mother-in-law	**10.** Bess
3. starfish	**7.** brother	
4. Georgia	**8.** Mike	

Possessive Forms of Plural Nouns

There are two rules to follow to form the possessive of plural nouns.

27 A.2   Add only an apostrophe to form the possessive of a plural noun that ends in *s*.

27 A.3   Add *'s* to form the possessive of a plural noun that does not end in *s*.

Deciding which rule to follow is simple if you take two steps. First, write the plural of the noun. Second, look at the ending of the word. If the word ends in *s*, add only an apostrophe. If it does not end in *s,* add an apostrophe and an *s*.

POSSESSIVE FORMS OF PLURAL NOUNS			
Plural	**Ending**	**Add**	**Possessive**
babies	s	'	= babies'
foxes	s	'	= foxes'
mice	no *s*	's	= mice's
children	no *s*	's	= children's
sheep	no *s*	's	= sheep's

● **Practice Your Skills**

Forming Possessive Plural Nouns

Write the plural form of each noun. Then write the plural possessive form.

1. friend   **6.** wolf   **11.** waltz

2. box   **7.** tomato   **12.** store

3. house   **8.** city   **13.** cloud

4. deer   **9.** book   **14.** woman

5. boy   **10.** goose   **15.** Ryan

Forming Possessive Nouns

Write the possessive form, singular or plural, of each underlined word.

1. We went to the hospital to see my <u>sister-in-law</u> new baby.

2. My <u>brother</u> first child is a girl.

3. My <u>parents</u> excitement was obvious as they gazed at their first grandchild.

4. The <u>hospital</u> policy allowed the newborn to sleep in her <u>mother</u> room.

5. The <u>infant</u> cries were certainly loud for such a small baby.

6. I helped my sister-in-law write comments in the baby <u>book</u> pages.

7. Several <u>nurses</u> comments were complimentary.

8. My new <u>niece</u> name is Sabrina.

Possessive Forms of Pronouns

Unlike nouns, personal pronouns do not use an apostrophe to show possession. Here is a list of the possessive forms of the personal pronouns: *my, mine, your, yours, his, her, hers, its, our, ours, their,* and *theirs.*

27 A.4   Do not add an apostrophe to form the possessive of a personal pronoun.

> The camera is **hers.**
>
> The dog wagged **its** tail for the photographer.

Indefinite pronouns, however, form the possessive the same way singular nouns do—by adding *'s.*

27 A.5   Add *'s* to form the possessive of an indefinite pronoun.

> This seems to be everyone**'s** favorite photo.
>
> Someone**'s** film cartridge was left under the seat.

You can find a list of common indefinite pronouns on page 760.

Using the Possessive of Pronouns

Write the correct form of the pronoun in parentheses.

1. Are these photographs (yours, your's)?

2. (Anyone's, Anyones') photos may be entered in the contest.

3. The album is beautiful with (its, it's) photos of the Rocky Mountains.

4. They looked at my portfolio, but Heather hasn't submitted (hers, her's) yet.

5. (No one's, No ones') photographs were chosen for the prize.

6. I hope (everybody's, everybodys') photos are published.

7. Those cameras are (ours, our's).

8. Has (everyones, everyone's) film been developed?

9. It was (nobody's, nobodys') fault that the film was ruined.

10. The best photographs are (their's, theirs).

Apostrophes to Show Joint and Separate Ownership

Sometimes it is necessary to show that something belongs to more than one person.

27 A.6 To show joint ownership, make only the last word possessive in form.

These are Nan and Faron**'s** compact discs.
(The compact discs belong to both Nan and Faron.)

The only exception to this rule occurs when one word showing joint ownership is a possessive pronoun. In such cases the noun must also show possession.

This is Hannah**'s** and **my** stereo.

Separate ownership is shown in a different way from joint ownership.

27 A.7 To show separate ownership, make each word possessive in form.

These are Nan**'s** and Faron**'s** compact discs.
(Each girl has her own compact discs.)

Apostrophes with Nouns Expressing Time or Amount

When you use a noun that expresses time or amount as an adjective, write it in the possessive form.

27 A.8   Use an apostrophe with the possessive form of a noun that expresses time or amount.

> That compact disc player cost Nan two week**s'** salary.
>
> Nan really got her money**'s** worth.

Other words that express time include such words as *minute, hour, day, month,* and *year.* Other words that express amount include such words as *dollar, quarter, dime, nickel,* and *penny.*

● Practice Your Skills

Using Apostrophes Correctly

Add an apostrophe and *s,* if needed, to each underlined word to make it possessive. If the word is correct as is, write **C**.

1. The <u>woman</u> and man's voices on that compact disc sound great together.
2. The woman on the recording was <u>Nan</u> and my music teacher.
3. I picked up two more compact discs for <u>Jason</u> and Dad's birthdays.
4. <u>Dawn</u> and Tiffany's song was recorded by a professional group.
5. My family spent a <u>week</u> vacation watching them record in the studio.
6. The band we watched earns a <u>month</u> rent in one night at a concert.
7. The crew brought in the <u>guitarist</u> and the drummer's instruments.
8. <u>Nan</u> and my excitement was very high!

● *Connect to Writing:* **Dialogue**

Possessive Nouns and Pronouns

Imagine that you are playing a board game with some friends or with your family. Write a brief dialogue between the players. In your dialogue use (and underline) at least three possessive nouns and three possessive pronouns.

● *Connect to Writing:* Editing

Using Possessive Forms Correctly

Write the possessive forms that are used incorrectly in the following sentences. Then write the correct possessive forms. If a sentence does not contain any errors in the use of possessives, write **C**.

1. My moms brother Ryan has a ranch that is a days drive from Rock Springs.

2. On almost all ranches, there are many workers.

3. During our visit, my brothers and I stayed in the workers bunkhouse.

4. Everyone's is coming to my uncles' ranch for a big dance tonight.

5. Dad's and Mom's suggestions for party decorations were accepted.

6. Have you seen Uncle Ryan's new hat?

7. My efforts at learning to square dance were finally rewarded.

8. Her's were not.

✔ *Check Point:* **Mixed Practice**

Write the following paragraph, correcting any errors in the use of possessives.

One of the most popular childrens books of all times is L. Frank Baum *The Wonderful Wizard of Oz*, published in 1900. While many people have read the book, most are more familiar with Metro-Goldwyn Mayer 1939 movie version, *The Wizard of Oz*.

Both the book and the movie feature Dorothy Gayle and friends of her—the Scarecrow, the Tin Woodsman, and the Cowardly Lion. Everybody favorite little dog Toto is also in both versions. The makers of the movie were true to Baum book in many other ways.

One major change in the movie version is the color of Dorothy shoes. In the movie they are ruby red. In the book they are silver. Technicolor was new to Hollywoods studios in 1939. While silver didn't show up well on the big screen, red looked dazzling. The filmmakers decision changed forever how many people would remember Baum work.

● *Connect to Writing:* Friendly Letter

Using Apostrophes

A young child you know is having difficulty learning to write his or her letters and numbers. Write a short letter to this child encouraging him or her to keep trying. Share your experiences learning to write. As you compose your letter, use at least two examples of apostrophes showing possession and one example of an apostrophe that expresses time or amount. Be sure to punctuate them properly.

Other Uses of Apostrophes

Apostrophes have other uses besides showing the possessive of nouns and some pronouns.

Apostrophes with Contractions

A **contraction** is a shortcut. It usually combines two words into one. An apostrophe is added to take the place of one or more missing letters.

27 A.9 Use an apostrophe in a contraction to show where one or more letters have been omitted.

These examples show how some contractions are formed.

CONTRACTIONS	
do not = don't	there is = there's
we are = we're	who is = who's
of the clock = o'clock	let us = let's

In most contractions, no letters are added or changed around. There is one common exception: *will + not = won't.*

Do not confuse the contractions *it's, you're, they're, there's,* and *who's* with the possessive pronouns *its, your, their, theirs,* and *whose.*

● **Practice Your Skills**

Using Apostrophes with Contractions

Write the contraction for each pair of words.

1. are not	**6.** is not	**11.** that is
2. will not	**7.** let us	**12.** I would
3. did not	**8.** I have	**13.** they had
4. you are	**9.** we have	**14.** there is
5. do not	**10.** we will	**15.** I am

Distinguishing Between Contractions and Possessive Pronouns

Write the correct word in parentheses to complete each sentence.

1. If (were, we're) going to breakfast, we should go now.

2. Please tell the server how you would like (your, you're) eggs.

3. I don't know if (their, they're) joining us or not.

4. If (theirs, there's) anything you need, let the server know.

5. (Whose, Who's) going to pay for this meal?

6. Do you know if (your, you're) going to order pancakes?

7. This bill must be (theirs, there's).

8. (Whose, Who's) orange juice is this?

9. (Its, It's) mine.

Apostrophes with Certain Plurals

To prevent confusion, certain items form their plurals by adding *'s*.

27 A.10 Add **'s** to form the plural of lowercase letters, some capital letters, and words that are used as words.

Sue's *i***'s** and *e***'s** look similar.

Jon's report card has two *A***'s**.

Without the apostrophe, *i*'s would be confused with the word *is,* and *A*'s would be confused with the word *As.*

The plurals of most other letters, symbols, numerals, and words used as words can be formed by adding *s*.

My little sister writes *3***s** for *E***s**.

Why did you put two *!***s** after that sentence?

This composition has too many *and***s**.

Notice the number *3,* the letter *E,* the exclamation point, and the word *and* are italicized. However, the *s* or the apostrophe is *not* italicized.

Some writers prefer to add *'s,* instead of just *s,* to form the plural of all letters, symbols, numerals, and words used as words.

Apostrophes with Certain Dates

An apostrophe is used when numbers are dropped from a date.

27 A.11   Use an apostrophe to show that numbers have been omitted from a date.

> We moved here in '01. (2001)
>
> My grandfather joined the army in '41. (1941)

● Practice Your Skills

Using Apostrophes

If a sentence is missing one or more apostrophes, write **I** for incorrect. If a sentence is correct, write **C**.

(1) Have you ever tried to read documents from early America? **(2)** Many times the *s*s look like *f*s. **(3)** The numbers can also be hard to read. **(4)** The *1*s, *9*s, and *6*s all look different than ours today. **(5)** When the years are written without the first digits, such as *04* or *76*, it's hard to know in what year the document was produced. **(6)** Take a look at an original draft of the Declaration of Independence. **(7)** Some of Jefferson's letters look very strange to our modern eyes. **(8)** His cursive *t*s and *r*s are formed differently than ours. **(9)** If you look at an earlier document like the Magna Carta, which was written in 1215, you can recognize some letters, such as *a*s, *n*s, and *c*s. **(10)** However, it's difficult for modern Americans to read the original Magna Carta because it's written in Latin!

✔ *Check Point:* Mixed Practice

Write correctly the eight words that need an apostrophe.

Has a moth ever turned one of your favorite sweaters into a tasty meal for itself? If so, you might be able to prevent future feasts by knowing the difference between a moth and a butterfly. Recognizing the difference wont be easy. First, look at the insects feelers. If theyre thin, they belong to a butterfly. A moths feelers are usually broad and feathery. Next, observe the insect in question when its resting. Butterflies wings are folded in when they are at rest. A moths wings lie flat when its not flying.

27 B The **semicolon (;)** is used to join the clauses of some compound sentences and to avoid confusion in some compound sentences and in some series.

Independent clauses in a compound sentence can be joined by a conjunction and a comma.

> Josh's favorite animal is the tiger, **but** mine is the bear.

The clauses in a compound sentence can also be joined by a semicolon.

> Josh's favorite animal is the tiger; mine is the bear.

27 B.1 Use a semicolon between the clauses of a compound sentence that are not joined by a conjunction.

Use a semicolon only if the clauses are closely related.

> **Incorrect** Eagles usually nest in pairs; wolves hunt for prey.
>
> **Correct** Eagles usually nest in pairs; wolves travel in packs.

You can find out more about independent clauses on page 642.

➤ Semicolons with Conjunctive Adverbs and Transitional Words

The clauses in a compound sentence can be joined by a semicolon and certain conjunctive adverbs and transitional words.

Notice in the following examples that the conjunctive adverbs *nevertheless* and *thus* and the transitional phrase *as a result* are preceded by a semicolon and followed by a comma.

> Giraffes are not hunters; **nevertheless,** they manage to get plenty of food.
>
> Giraffes can close their nostrils; **thus,** they can keep out sand and dust.
>
> Their necks are very long; **as a result,** they can reach the leaves of very tall trees.

27 B.2 In a compound sentence, use a semicolon between clauses that are joined by certain conjunctive adverbs or transitional words.

The following lists contain conjunctive adverbs and transitional words and phrases that, with a semicolon, can be used to combine the clauses of a compound sentence.

COMMON CONJUNCTIVE ADVERBS				
accordingly	consequently	hence	otherwise	therefore
also	finally	however	nevertheless	thus
besides	furthermore	instead	still	yet
COMMON TRANSITIONAL WORDS AND PHRASES				
as a result		in addition		in other words
for example		in fact		on the other hand

Some of the conjunctive adverbs and transitional phrases listed in the preceding boxes can also be used as parenthetical expressions within a single clause.

Joining Clauses   The hippopotamus is related to the hog; **however,** it looks very different.

Within a Clause   The hippopotamus, **however,** has a huge mouth.

You can learn more about parenthetical expressions on pages 858–859.

● **Practice Your Skills**

Using Semicolons and Commas with Compound Sentences

Rewrite each sentence, correcting any errors in the use of semicolons and commas. If the sentence is correct, write **C.**

1. Many plants are good for humans and animals, and some have no effect at all.

2. Plants are necessary to life on Earth, however, many of these plants are harmful to us.

3. Some plants will simply make a person sick, others can kill a human.

4. The precatory pea has a beautiful red seed, but just one of these seeds can kill an adult human.

5. A plant known as fiddleneck is fatal to horses, it can also kill cows and pigs.

6. In small doses, St. John's wort is safe for humans, however, it can kill rabbits and cause sheep to lose their wool.

Power Your Writing: Catch and Release

You can think of a semicolon as a hybrid of comma and period. The comma part joins two closely related sentences (*catches* them); the period part separates them grammatically (*releases* them). Look at the following example from "The Future of Happiness" (pages 211–212) and think about why the semicolon is appropriate.

> 80% of the youth polled said that having lots of close friends is very or somewhat important; 23% said that when they go out with friends, they stop feeling unhappy.

The writer could have used two separate sentences. By using only the semicolon the writer lets the reader supply the connecting idea. In this way, the semicolon helps create an engaging style.

➤ Semicolons to Avoid Confusion

Sometimes a semicolon is used to take the place of a comma between the clauses of a compound sentence.

27 B.3   Use a semicolon, instead of a comma, between the clauses of a compound sentence connected with a coordinating conjunction if there are commas within a clause.

To get to Maine from New York, we travel through Connecticut, Massachusetts, and New Hampshire; but the trip takes us only four hours.

27 B.4   Use a semicolon instead of a comma between the items in a series if the items themselves contain commas.

I have relatives in Hartford, Connecticut; in Boston, Massachusetts; and in Portsmouth, New Hampshire.

You can find out more about using commas on pages 848–864.

Using Semicolons to Avoid Confusion

Rewrite each sentence, correcting any errors in the use of semicolons and commas. If the sentence is correct, write **C.**

1. Popular tourist attractions around the world include Parliament in London, England, the Eiffel Tower in Paris, France, and the Coliseum in Rome, Italy.

2. The white marble exterior of the Taj Mahal in Agra, India, is inlaid with semiprecious stones, floral designs, and arabesques.

3. Three sites in the United States that many Europeans like to visit are the Grand Canyon in Arizona, Las Vegas, Nevada, and San Francisco, California.

4. Most travelers make the choice of flying, driving, or taking a train, but some people still choose to travel by ship.

5. Copenhagen is a major port, cultural center, and the capital of Denmark, and so it is a popular place to visit.

● *Connect to Writing:* **Persuasion**

Using Semicolons

Your family has won a two-week vacation. All of you must decide where you will go. Your mother has asked you to choose three places, anywhere in the world, that you would like to visit.

Write a paragraph about each of the destinations you have chosen, emphasizing why your family should visit each place. Order your paragraphs so that you write about your least favorite first and your most favorite last. Use semicolons at least three times in your writing.

27 C A **colon (:)** is used to introduce a list of items, to introduce quotations, to separate hours and minutes, between Biblical chapters and verses, and in business letters.

Colons to Introduce Lists

27 C.1 Use a colon (:) before most lists of items, especially when the list comes after the expression *the following.* Commas should separate the items in the list.

All students will need the following: a pen, a sheet of paper, and a dictionary.

There are five stages in the writing process: prewriting, drafting, revising, editing, and publishing.

Three common prewriting strategies are these: lists, outlines, and graphic organizers.

27 C.2 Never use a colon directly after a verb or a preposition.

Incorrect	My three favorite authors are: Charles Dickens, Jane Austen, and Thomas Hardy.
Correct	My three favorite authors are Charles Dickens, Jane Austen, and Thomas Hardy.
Correct	These are my three favorite authors: Charles Dickens, Jane Austen, and Thomas Hardy.

Other Uses of Colons

Colons are also used in a few other situations.

27 C.3 Use a colon to introduce a long, formal quotation.

Catherine Drinker Bowen once had this to say about writing: "Writing, I think, is not apart from living. Writing is a kind of double living. The writer experiences everything twice. Once in reality and once in that mirror which waits always before or behind."

You can learn more about writing long quotations on page 883.

27 C.4 Use a colon between hours and minutes, between Bible chapters and verses, and in business letters.

Hours and Minutes	5:30 AM
Biblical Chapters and Verses	John 3:16
Salutations in Business Letters	Dear Sir or Madam:

● **Practice Your Skills**

Using Colons

Rewrite each sentence, correcting any errors in the use of colons. If the sentence is correct, write **C**.

1. My three favorite books by Dickens are: *A Christmas Carol, Great Expectations,* and *A Tale of Two Cities.*

2. In *A Christmas Carol,* the spirit of Jacob Marley warns Scrooge that a ghost will visit him at 1;00 AM.

3. Thomas Hardy wrote many controversial novels, including his masterpieces *Jude the Obscure* and *Tess of the d'Urbervilles.*

4. He also wrote *The Dynasts:* an epic historical drama in verse.

5. Three of Hardy's most memorable characters are the following: Bathsheba Everdene, Gabriel Oak, and Michael Henchard.

6. My favorite books of this period are: *Northanger Abbey, The Mayor of Castorbridge,* and *Nicholas Nickleby.*

✔ *Check Point:* **Mixed Practice**

Write the following paragraph, adding apostrophes, semicolons, and colons where needed.

(1) Whos the worlds champion jumper? (2) If youre thinking of a person, youre wrong. (3) The kangaroo lays claim to this title. (4) This curious-looking Australian mammal cannot walk however, it certainly can jump. (5) It can easily hop over a parked car it can also travel over 39 miles per hour.

(6) The kangaroo has some quite unusual physical characteristics a small head, large pointed ears, very short front limbs, and hindquarters the size of a mules. (7) Its feet sometimes measure ten inches from the heel to the longest toe. (8) The kangaroos thick tail is so strong that it can use the tail as a stool. (9) The kangaroo is strictly a vegetarian it will not eat another animal.

27 D   Though the principal use of a **hyphen (-)** is to divide a word at the end of a line, hyphens are also used when writing numbers and fractions, to separate parts of some compound nouns, and after certain prefixes.

Hyphens to Divide Words

Whenever possible, avoid dividing words in your writing. Sometimes, however, it is necessary to divide words in order to keep the right-hand margin of a composition or story fairly even.

27 D.1   Use a hyphen to divide a word at the end of a line.

GUIDELINES FOR DIVIDING WORDS

Using the following six guidelines will help you divide words correctly.

1. **Divide words only between syllables.**

   gym-nastics or gymnas-tics

2. **Never divide a one-syllable word.**

   myth   rhyme   strength

3. **Never separate a one-letter syllable from the rest of the word.**

   Do Not Break e·vent, sleep·y, o·boe, i·tem.

4. **A two-letter word ending should not be carried over to the next line.**

   Do Not Break cred·it, hang·er, part·ly.

5. **Divide hyphenated words only after the hyphens.**

   mother-in-law   maid-of-honor   attorney-at-law

6. **Do not divide a proper noun or a proper adjective.**

   Beckerman   Memphis   Atlantic   Indian

If you are unsure how to divide a word, check a dictionary.

Using Hyphens to Divide Words

Write each word, adding a hyphen or hyphens to show where the word can be correctly divided. If a word should not be divided, write *no*.

1. event	**6.** amazement	**11.** gathering
2. hamster	**7.** action	**12.** Timothy
3. growth	**8.** jury	**13.** forgery
4. invoice	**9.** syllable	**14.** flip-flop
5. son-in-law	**10.** Cairo	**15.** avoid

➤ Other Uses of Hyphens

In addition to dividing words, hyphens have other important uses.

Hyphens with Numbers

Hyphens are needed with certain numbers.

27 D.2   Use a hyphen when writing out the numbers twenty-one through ninety-nine.

There are thirty-one students in this class.

Our teacher asked us to find twenty-five soil samples for the experiment.

Hyphens with Compound Nouns

Some compound nouns need one or more hyphens.

27 D.3   Use one or more hyphens to separate the parts of some compound nouns.

Our teacher is my great-uncle.

His son-in-law is my favorite relative.

Hyphens with Certain Adjectives

Hyphens are needed with fractions used as adjectives and with some compound adjectives.

27 D.4 Use a hyphen when writing out a fraction used as an adjective. Also use one or more hyphens between words that make up a compound adjective in front of a noun.

Compound Adjective

I found some **dark-brown** soil in our backyard.

It was **foul-smelling** dirt.

A hyphen is used only when a fraction is used as an adjective, not when it is used as a noun.

Fraction Used as an Adjective

Our soil samples should measure at least **one-quarter** cup.

Fraction Used as a Noun

We put **one half** of the soil sample in the beaker.

A hyphen is used only when a compound adjective comes before a noun, not when it follows a linking verb and comes after the noun it describes.

Adjective Before a Noun

Our science teacher insists on **well-written** lab reports.

Adjective After a Noun

I always try to make sure that my lab reports are **well written.**

Hyphens with Prefixes

27 D.5 Use a hyphen after certain prefixes and before the suffix -*elect*.

HYPHENS USED WITH PREFIXES AND SUFFIXES

Use hyphens in the following situations:

1. between a prefix and a proper noun or proper adjective

all=American   mid=Atlantic   pre=Columbian

2. after the prefix *self-*

self=righteous   self=satisfied

3. after the prefix *ex-* **when it means "former" or "formerly"**

ex=mayor   ex=governor   ex=senator

4. after a person's title when it is followed by the suffix *=elect*

president=elect   mayor=elect

● Practice Your Skills

Using Hyphens

Write *a* or *b* to indicate the letter of the correctly written word in each of the following pairs.

1. a. seventy seven
   b. seventy-seven

2. a. self-assured
   b. self assured

3. a. governor elect
   b. governor-elect

4. a. four-teen
   b. fourteen

5. a. ex-husband
   b. exhusband

6. a. mid-Pacific
   b. mid Pacific

7. a. one-quarter teaspoon
   b. one quarter teaspoon

8. a. mother in law
   b. mother-in-law

9. a. jack in the box
   b. jack-in-the-box

10. a. one quarter of the pie
   b. one-quarter of the pie

CHAPTER 27

● *Connect to Writing:* **Editing**

Using Hyphens

Correctly write each word that should be hyphenated. If none of the words in a sentence needs a hyphen, write **C** for correct.

1. I will enjoy having a new sister in law when my brother finally marries.

2. My brother is going to marry my friend's stepsister in June.

3. She is twenty seven years old.

4. Her mother, May Meriwether, is the mayor elect of our city.

5. She beat the ex mayor by the narrow margin of only ninety two votes.

6. My brother and his fiancée have invited seventy five people to the wedding.

7. One half of the guests are our relatives.

8. I will serve as the bride's maid of honor.

● *Connect to Writing:* **The Writer's Craft**

Analyzing the Use of Hyphens

Writers of poetry and prose often use hyphenated adjectives before nouns. Read the following excerpt from Li-Young Lee's poem "Furious Versions" and answer the questions that follow.

It was a tropical night.
It was a half a year of sweat and fatal memory.
It was one year of fire
out of the world's diary of fires,
flesh-laced, mid-century fire,
teeth and hair infested,
napalm-dressed and skull-hung fire,
and imminent fire, an elected
fire come to rob me
of my own death, my damp bed
in the noisy earth,
my rocking toward a hymn-like night.
—Li-Young Lee, "Furious Versions"

List all the hyphenated words in the excerpt.

Why are these words hyphenated?

How does Lee's use of these hyphenated words affect the rhythm of the poem?

Would the poem have the same effect without the hyphenated words? Explain your answer.

27 E **Dashes (—)** and **parentheses ( )** are used like commas in some situations to separate certain words or groups of words from the rest of the sentence.

Although dashes and parentheses separate words or phrases, they are not interchangeable with commas. Each of these punctuation marks has a specific function.

Dashes

Dashes indicate a greater pause between words than commas do. They can be used in the following situations.

27 E.1 Use dashes to set off an abrupt change in thought.

Mr. Becker—at least I think that's his name—is the drivers' education teacher.

"Where's the —?" Dana began and then hesitated when she saw the car.

The Drivers' Ed car—it's old and dented—is parked in the next lot.

27 E.2 Use dashes to set off an appositive that is introduced by words such as *that is, for example,* or *for instance.*

Certain traffic laws—for instance, making a right turn on a red light—vary from state to state.

27 E.3 Use dashes to set off a parenthetical expression or an appositive that includes commas.

Driving a car—like taking a test, performing in a play, or singing a song—requires concentration.

If you do not know how to make a dash on the computer, you can use two hyphens together. Do not leave a space before or after a dash.

You can find out more about appositives on pages 617–618.

You can find out more about parenthetical expressions on pages 858–859.

➡ **Parentheses**

Always remember that parentheses come in pairs.

27 E.4 Use parentheses to enclose information that is not related closely to the meaning of the sentence.

To decide whether or not you should use parentheses, read the sentence without the parenthetical material. If the meaning and structure of the sentence are not changed, then add parentheses. Just keep in mind that parenthetical additions to sentences slow readers down and interrupt their train of thought. As a result, you should always limit the amount of parenthetical material that you add to any one piece of writing.

> During the late teen years **(**16–19**)**, many drivers pay higher rates for car insurance.

When the closing parenthesis comes at the end of a sentence, the end mark usually goes outside the parenthesis. The end mark goes inside the parenthesis if the end mark actually belongs with the parenthetical material.

End Mark Within Parenthesis	Take your written driver's exam in pencil. **(**Be sure to use a number 2 pencil.**)**
End Mark Outside Parenthesis	To earn your driver's license, you must pass both tests **(**with a score of 70 or better**)**.

Using Dashes and Parentheses

Rewrite each sentence, changing commas to dashes or parentheses where needed. If the sentence is correct, write **C.**

1. Three rules of the road, courtesy to others, respect for pedestrians' right-of-way, and careful driving, should always be followed.

2. Motor vehicles, such as cars and trucks, can be difficult to control on icy streets.

3. Certain privileges, like driving at night, should not be granted to novice drivers.

4. Use your blinker, located on the steering column by your right hand, to signal a turn.

5. Certain states, like Texas, will take away a teenager's license if he or she commits a crime.

6. During the first days of automobiles, the early twentieth century, drivers weren't required to be licensed.

7. Some innovations, like automatic transmission and power steering, have made cars easier to drive.

Connect to Writing: **The Writer's Craft**

Analyzing the Use of Dashes

Emily Dickinson is one poet who made liberal use of dashes in her poetry. Read the following poem by her and then follow the directions.

> He ate and drank the precious Words—
> His spirit grew robust—
> He knew no more that he was poor,
> Nor that his frame was Dust—
> He danced along the dingy Days
> And this Bequest of Wings
> Was but a Book—What Liberty
> A loosened spirit brings—
> —Emily Dickinson

Read the poem aloud, ignoring all the punctuation marks. Next, read the poem aloud, making long pauses only where the dashes are. You should pause briefly at the comma.

How did your readings of the poem differ? Would any other punctuation marks have served the purpose of these dashes? If so, which ones? Explain your answer. Why do you think Dickinson chose to use dashes?

✓ *Check Point:* **Mixed Practice**

Rewrite the following paragraph, adding hyphens, dashes, and parentheses where needed.

Humphrey Bogart 1899–1957 was voted the greatest screen legend male screen legend, that is, by the American Film Institute AFI in 1999. Bogart who is my favorite movie star was a stage actor at the beginning of his career. His movie credits include *The Maltese Falcon* 1941 and *Casablanca* 1942. In 1951, he won an Oscar for his role in *The African Queen*. In this award winning role, he played opposite Katharine Hepburn who, by the way, was the AFI pick for the greatest female screen legend.

Assess Your Learning

■ Using Punctuation Correctly

Write each sentence, adding punctuation where needed. If a sentence is punctuated correctly write **C.**

1. Rattlesnakes don't lay eggs they bear live young.

2. The worlds largest gem is a 596 pound topaz.

3. The soybean is a versatile vegetable for example, 40 different products can be made from it.

4. Greg wont be satisfied until hes totally self sufficient.

5. The following famous people had red hair George Washington, Thomas Jefferson, and Mark Twain.

6. Lenny Burns received a two thirds majority vote in this years mayoral election.

7. When Snuffys leash broke, he jumped the neighbors fence and dove into their pool.

8. The Hindi term for the Republic of India is not *India* it is *Bharat*.

9. My brother in law is president elect of the club.

10. Salt is found in the earth in three basic forms salt water, brine deposits, and rock salt crystals.

11. The rarely seen Indian sea snake is the most poisonous snake in the world.

12. The poet H.D.s real name is Hilda Doolittle.

13. The people on the panel included Terry Hayden, an editorial writer Thelma Casey, a fashion consultant and Judith Howe, a high school teacher.

14. Today, there are more than 7,000 varieties of apples nevertheless only 20 varieties are widely grown.

15. Twenty two people how could we have invited so many! are supposed to arrive for dinner at 630 PM.

■ Editing for Correct Punctuation

Write the paragraph, adding apostrophes, semicolons, colons, and hyphens where needed.

Everyone has heard of the Nobel Prizes but most people havent heard about Alfred Nobel, the man who established the prizes. He was born in Sweden in 1833. Thirty three years later, he invented dynamite. This invention made him very rich it also made him feel very guilty later on. As a result, his will set up a trust fund that annually awards prizes to people throughout the world who excel in the following categories literature, physics, chemistry, medicine, and peace. Now, every December 10, the anniversary of Nobels death, each winner receives up to $959,070.

■ Writing Sentences

Write ten sentences that follow the directions below.

Write a sentence that . . .

1. includes the possessive form of the nouns *uncle* and *dollars*.

2. includes the possessive form of the pronouns *it* and *no one*.

3. includes the joint ownership of something.

4. includes the plural of *no*.

5. includes the word *nevertheless* between two independent clauses in a compound sentence.

6. includes a series of dates.

7. includes a specific time.

8. includes *three fourths* as an adjective.

9. includes a dash.

10. includes parentheses.

Other Punctuation: Posttest

Directions

Write the letter of the answer that correctly punctuates the underlined part in each sentence. If the underlined part contains no error, write **D**.

(1) There has been a huge increase in the number of treadmill <u>users in fact,</u> while only 4.4 million used treadmills in 1987, 37.1 million used them in 1998. (2) The second most popular machine is <u>the stair climber.</u> (3) There are several reasons for the treadmill's <u>popularity it keeps</u> you fit, it is easy to use, and it is safe and reliable. (4) The treadmill is a <u>home exercisers dream.</u> (5) When it rains outside, you can <u>still exercise there</u> is no excuse for slacking off. (6) For some people <u>those who love exercise</u> that is reason enough to own a treadmill. (7) Some people <u>dont like the treadmill</u> because they find it boring. (8) For them, <u>its difficult</u> to stay motivated. (9) Even the <u>self motivated</u> can get bored doing the same exercise day after day. (10) One <u>answer (though it's not</u> for everyone) is to place the treadmill in front of a television.

1. **A** users—in fact
   B users; in fact,
   C users: in fact
   D No error

2. **A** the stair, climber
   B (the stair climber)
   C the stair-climber
   D No error

3. **A** popularity: it keeps
   B popularity; it keeps
   C popularity—it keeps
   D No error

4. **A** home-exerciser's dream
   B home-exercisers' dream
   C home exercisers' dream
   D No error

5. **A** still exercise: there
   B still exercise—there
   C still exercise; there
   D No error

6. **A** (those who love exercise)
   B those who love exercise;
   C those who love exercise:
   D No error

7. **A** dont' like the treadmill
   B don't like the treadmill
   C do'nt like the treadmill
   D No error

8. **A** it's difficult
   B its' difficult
   C its: difficult
   D No error

9. **A** (self motivated)
   B self; motivated
   C self-motivated
   D No error

10. **A** answer, though, it's not
    B answer: though it's not
    C answer; though it's not
    D No error

Writer's Corner

Snapshot

27 A An **apostrophe** (') is used to show ownership or relationship, to represent missing letters in contractions, and with certain plurals and some dates. (pages 894–903)

27 B The **semicolon (;)** is used to join the clauses of a some compound sentences and to avoid confusion in some compound sentences and in some series. (pages 904–907)

27 C A **colon (:)** is used to introduce a list of items; to introduce a quotation; to separate hours and minutes; and it is used between Biblical chapters and verses and in business letters. (pages 908–909)

27 D A **hyphen (-)** is used to divide a word at the end of a line, to divide some numbers and fractions, to separate parts of some compound nouns and some compound adjectives, and to set off certain prefixes. (pages 910–914)

27 E **Dashes (—)** and **parentheses ( )** are used like commas to separate certain words or groups of words from the rest of the sentence. (pages 915–916)

Power Rules

 Check for **run-on sentences** and fix them by adding a conjunction and/or punctuation. (pages 672–674)

Before Editing	**After Editing**
Laura's favorite city is Paris, mine is Rome.	Laura's favorite city is Paris; mine is Rome.
We visited the Coliseum while we were in Rome, it's one of the greatest ancient architectural works.	We visited the Coliseum while we were in Rome. It's one of the greatest ancient architectural works.

 Use standard ways to make **nouns possessive.** (pages 895–897)

Before Editing	**After Editing**
My *brothers* teacher lives next door.	My *brother's* teacher lives next door.
I walk several of the *neighbors* dogs.	I walk several of the *neighbors'* dogs.

Editing Checklist

Use this checklist when editing your writing.

- ✓ Did I correctly use apostrophes to show possession? (See pages 894–900.)
- ✓ Did I use semicolons to join independent clauses? (See page 904.)
- ✓ Did I use colons to introduce lists and long quotations? (See pages 908–909.)
- ✓ Did I use hyphens to break words at the end of lines and to separate compound nouns and adjectives? (See pages 910–914.)
- ✓ Did I use dashes to set off a parenthetical expression or an appositive that includes commas? (See page 915.)
- ✓ Did I use parentheses to enclose information that is not closely related to the meaning of the sentence? (See page 916.)

Use the Power

Use these graphics to help you understand the importance of punctuation in everyday life.

Apostrophe '	Are you going to Gabrielle's house to study?
Dash —	Her brother Jackson——he's majoring in English at Indiana University——is going to help us study for the exam.
Semicolon ;	Before choosing to go to school in Indiana, Jackson visited schools in Evanston, Illinois; Grand Rapids, Michigan; and Madison, Wisconsin.
Colon :	This semester, he's studying the following authors: Ernest Hemingway, F. Scott Fitzgerald, and William Faulkner.
Hyphen -	He'll graduate when he's twenty-one.
(Parentheses)	The professor assigned chapter 2 (pages 56–89) for homework.

Spelling Correctly

How can you communicate your message effectively by using accurate spelling?

Spelling Correctly: Pretest 1

The first draft below contains several spelling errors. One of the errors has been corrected. How would you correct the remaining errors?

Most high ~~scools~~ *schools* do not have room or funds for musick studioes. However, music teachers themselfs continue to teach the fundamentalls of reading musick to intrested students. The notes for music are positioned on a set of lines and spaces called a staff. The stafves always apear together, one above the other. Each one is markked with a clef. The cleffs tell what notes the lines and spaces stand for. The high notes played by piccaloes or sung by sopranoes are on the top staff. The low notes played by celloes and sung by bases are on the bottomm staff.

Spelling Correctly: Pretest 2

Directions

Read the passage. Write the letter of the choice that correctly spells each underlined word. If the word contains no error, write *D.*

In history class we read some **(1)** correspondance between pioneers and their **(2)** familys back home. As they **(3)** proceded on their **(4)** journies, these pioneers often stopped at trading posts. There they were **(5)** ocasionally able to post letters to relatives. These tales of **(6)** inconceivable hardship and **(7)** couragous actions can teach us today. Reading the actual words of our ancestors helps us relate to the **(8)** lonelyness, terrors, and everyday joys of pioneer life. We delight in their innocent **(9)** beleif in a better life, and we recall that **(10)** heros start out as ordinary people.

1. A corespondance
   B correspondence
   C correspondants
   D No error

2. A familyes
   B familes
   C families
   D No error

3. A proceeded
   B proseded
   C preceeded
   D No error

4. A journys
   B journeys
   C journeyses
   D No error

5. A ocasionaly
   B occasionally
   C occassionally
   D No error

6. A inconcievable
   B inconceiveable
   C inconcevable
   D No error

7. A courageous
   B couragious
   C couraggous
   D No error

8. A lonlyness
   B lonelynes
   C loneliness
   D No error

9. A belief
   B beleef
   C beleiv
   D No error

10. A heroses
    B hero
    C heroes
    D No error

Strategies for Learning to Spell

Learning to spell involves a variety of senses. You use your senses of hearing, sight, and touch to spell a word correctly. Here is a five-step strategy that many people have used successfully as they learned to spell unfamiliar words.

1 Auditory

Say the word aloud. Answer these questions.

- Where have I heard or read this word before?
- What was the context in which I heard or read the word?

2 Visual

Look at the word. Answer these questions.

- Does this word divide into parts? Is it a compound word? Does it have a prefix or a suffix?
- Does this word look like any other word I know? Could it be part of a word family I would recognize?

3 Auditory

Spell the word to yourself. Answer these questions.

- How is each sound spelled?
- Are there any surprises? Does the word follow spelling rules I know, or does it break the rules?

4 Visual/Kinesthetic

Write the word as you look at it. Answer these questions.

- Have I written the word clearly?
- Are my letters formed correctly?

5 Visual/Kinesthetic

Cover up the word. Visualize it. Write it. Answer this question.

- Did I write the word correctly?
- If the answer is no, return to step 1.

Spelling Strategies

Spelling is easier for some people than it is for others, but everyone needs to make an effort to spell correctly. Misspellings are distracting for the reader, and they make writing hard to read. Here are some strategies you can use to improve your spelling.

Use a dictionary. If you are not sure how to spell a word, or if a word you have written doesn't "look right," check the word in a dictionary.

Proofread your writing carefully. Be on the lookout for misspellings and for words you are not sure you spelled correctly. One way to proofread your writing for misspellings is to start at the end of your paper and read backward. That way misspellings should pop out at you.

Be sure you are pronouncing words correctly. "Swallowing" syllables or adding extra syllables can cause you to misspell a word.

Make up mnemonic devices. A phrase like "My niece is nice" can help you remember to put *i* before *e* in *niece*. A device like "2 *m*'s, 2 *t*'s, 2 *e*'s" can help you remember how to spell *committee*.

Keep a spelling journal. Use it to record the words that you have had trouble spelling. Here are some steps for organizing your spelling journal.

- Write the word correctly.
- Write the word again, underlining or circling the part of the word that gave you trouble.
- Write a tip to help you remember how to spell the word.

weird   weird   Weird is weird. It doesn't follow the i before e rule.

Knowing common spelling patterns, such as the choice between *ie* and *ei*, can help you spell many words.

28 A   **Spelling patterns—such as *i* before *e* except after *c*—apply to many words and can help you spell many different words correctly.**

Words with *ie* and *ei*

28 A.1   When you spell words with *ie* or *ei*, *i* comes before *e* except when the letters follow *c* or when they stand for the long *a* sound.

IE AND *EI*			
Examples	*ie*	believe	field
	ei after *c*	ceiling	receive
	sounds like *a*	neighbor	weigh
Exceptions	ancient	efficient	neither seize
	conscience	species	height weird
	sufficient	either	leisure foreign

The *ie* and *ei* generalization applies only when the letters occur in the same syllable and spell just one vowel sound. It does not apply when *i* and *e* appear in different syllables.

IE AND *EI* IN DIFFERENT SYLLABLES			
be ing	re imburse	re issue	cri er

Words Ending in *–sede*, *–ceed*, and *–cede*

28 A.2   Words ending with a syllable that sounds like "seed" are usually spelled with *–cede*. Only one word in English is spelled with *–sede*, and only three words are spelled with *–ceed*.

–SEDE, –CEED, AND *–CEDE*			
Examples	concede	precede	recede secede
Exceptions	supersede	exceed	proceed succeed

Practice Your Skills

Using Spelling Patterns

Write each word correctly, adding *ie* or *ei*. Use a dictionary to check your work.

1. th ▦ f

2. n ▦ ce

3. y ▦ ld

4. w ▦ gh

5. h ▦ ght

6. bel ▦ f

7. c ▦ ling

8. rec ▦ pt

9. gr ▦ ve

10. ▦ ght

11. p ▦ ce

12. r ▦ ns

13. n ▦ ther

14. dec ▦ ve

15. rel ▦ ve

16. br ▦ f

17. rec ▦ ve

18. retr ▦ ve

19. n ▦ ghbor

20. l ▦ sure

Practice Your Skills

Using Spelling Patterns

Write each word correctly, adding *–sede, –ceed,* or *–cede.* Use a dictionary to check your work.

1. re ▦

2. ex ▦

3. ac ▦

4. se ▦

5. suc ▦

6. con ▦

7. pre ▦

8. pro ▦

9. super ▦

10. inter ▦

Connect to Writing: Editing

Using Spelling Patterns

Write and correct the misspelled words in this paragraph. There are nine misspelled words. Use a dictionary to check your work.

> For the state of Kentucky, the War Between the States was truly a civil war. Kentucky did not sesede from the Union, as did the nieghboring states of Tennessee and Virginia. Officially Kentucky supported niether the Union nor the Confederacy. Kentucky proceded to declare neutrality on May 16, 1861, but Kentuckians did not succeed in staying out of the conflict. The number of Kentuckians who fought for the Confederacy exceeded 30,000, and twice that number joined the Union Army. Neighbors, freinds, and families were greivously divided in thier loyalties. President Lincoln concedeed that Kentucky was one of the country's "troubling stepchildren" because its location bordered Union states, but many residents supported the Confederacy.

Plurals Lesson 2

28 B Most nouns form their plural form by adding -s or -es to the singular form. Some nouns form their plurals in other ways.

Forming the plural of a noun becomes easier when you remember to use the following generalizations.

Regular Nouns

28 B.1 To form the plural of most nouns, simply add s.

MOST NOUNS				
Singular	artist	symbol	maze	sardine
Plural	artists	symbols	mazes	sardines

28 B.2 If a noun ends with s, ch, sh, x, or z, add es to form the plural.

S, CH, SH, X, AND Z				
Singular	loss	church	dish	fox
Plural	losses	churches	dishes	foxes

Nouns Ending in y

28 B.3 Add s to form the plural of a noun ending with a vowel and y.

VOWELS AND Y				
Singular	day	display	journey	toy
Plural	days	displays	journeys	toys

28 B.4 Change the y to i and add es to a noun ending in a consonant and y.

CONSONANTS AND Y				
Singular	memory	trophy	lady	society
Plural	memories	trophies	ladies	societies

Nouns Ending with *o*

28 B.5 Add *s* to form the plural of a noun ending with a vowel and *o*.

VOWELS AND *O*			
Singular	ratio	studio	rodeo	igloo
Plural	ratios	studios	rodeos	igloos

28 B.6 Add *s* to form the plural of musical terms ending in *o*.

MUSICAL TERMS WITH *O*			
Singular	alto	duo	piano	cello
Plural	altos	duos	pianos	cellos

28 B.7 The plurals of nouns ending in a consonant and *o* do not follow a regular pattern.

CONSONANTS AND *O*			
Singular	echo	veto	silo	ego
Plural	echoes	vetoes	silos	egos

When you are not sure how to form the plural of a word that ends in *o*, consult a dictionary. If no plural form is listed, the plural is usually formed by adding *s*.

Nouns Ending in *f* or *fe*

28 B.8 To form the plural of some nouns ending in *f* or *fe*, just add *s*.

F AND *FE*			
Singular	belief	gulf	chef	fife
Plural	beliefs	gulfs	chefs	fifes

28 B.9 For some nouns ending in *f* or *fe*, change the *f* or *fe* to *v* and add *es*.

F AND *FE* TO *V*			
Singular	half	shelf	leaf	knife
Plural	halves	shelves	leaves	knives

Consult a dictionary to check the plural form of a word that ends with *f* or *fe*.

Forming Plurals

Write the plural form of each noun. Check a dictionary to be sure you have formed the plural correctly.

1. radio	**5.** potato	**9.** tariff	**13.** waltz
2. theory	**6.** taco	**10.** apology	**14.** issue
3. shampoo	**7.** reflex	**11.** calf	**15.** crash
4. stitch	**8.** roof	**12.** valley	**16.** self

Compound Nouns

28 B.10 Most compound nouns are made plural in the same way as other nouns. The letter *s* or *es* is added to the end of the word. But when the main word in a compound noun appears first, that word becomes plural.

COMPOUND NOUNS			
Examples	snowflake	lunchbox	hallway
	snowflake**s**	lunchbox**es**	hallway**s**
Exceptions	passerby	editor-in-chief	mother-in-law
	passer**s**by	editor**s**-in-chief	mother**s**-in-law

Numerals, Letters, Symbols, and Words as Words

28 B.11 To form the plurals of numerals, letters, symbols, and words used as words, add an *s*. To prevent confusion, it is best to use an apostrophe and *s* with lowercase letters, some capital letters, such as *A, I, O, U* and some words used as words.

Examples   Those *G*s look like *6*s.

Swing dancing from the 1940s is back.

Use ***s to mark footnotes.

Don't give me any *if*s, *and*s, or *but*s.

Exceptions   There are four *i*'s and four *s*'s in *Mississippi*.

Name five foods that are shaped like *O*'s.

We need an equal number of *he*'s and *she*'s.

CHAPTER 28

Practice Your Skills

Forming Plurals

Write the plural form of each item. Use a dictionary if you need help.

1. attorney-at-law
2. bystander
3. '90
4. sergeant-at-arms
5. hummingbird
6. *?*
7. sister-in-law

8. *z*
9. *&*
10. mousetrap
11. toothache
12. runner-up
13. *S*
14. pen pal

15. 1900
16. maid-of-honor
17. *in* and *out*
18. classroom
19. *X* and *O*
20. *ABC*

Connect to Writing: Editing

Spelling Plural Nouns

Write each sentence, changing the underlined items from singular to plural.

1. In the <u>1960</u>, the alligator was classified as an endangered species.

2. Before the end of the <u>'70</u>, however, alligators made a comeback, and they were reclassified as a threatened species.

3. There are two <u>*l*</u> in the word *alligator*.

4. Write about the animals in your observation log, and put <u>*?*</u> beside spellings you are unsure of.

5. <u>Hummingbird</u> are always seen in flight because their weak feet cannot support them on flat surfaces.

6. <u>Man-o'-war bird</u> can soar motionless for hours, but they are awkward on land and their feathers get waterlogged in the water.

7. People used to use <u>lily of the valley</u> as a heart medicine.

8. The dried roots of the <u>butterfly bush</u> have been used as a medicine to prevent spasms.

9. The fuzzy brown spikes are actually the fruits of <u>cattail</u>.

10. Some kinds of <u>firefly</u> lay eggs that glow just as the adult insects do.

Other Plural Forms

28 B.12   Irregular plurals are not formed by adding *s* or *es*.

IRREGULAR PLURALS					
Singular	tooth	foot	mouse	child	woman
Plural	teeth	feet	mice	child**ren**	wom**en**
Singular	goose	ox	man	die	
Plural	geese	ox**en**	men	**dice**	

28 B.13   Some nouns have the same form for singular and plural.

SAME SINGULAR AND PLURAL			
Vietnamese	Sioux	salmon	headquarters
Japanese	deer	species	measles
Swiss	moose	scissors	politics

Words from Latin and Greek

28 B.14   Some nouns from Latin and Greek have plurals that are formed as they are in the original language. For a few Latin and Greek words, there are two ways to form the plural.

FOREIGN WORDS				
Examples	alumnus	memorandum	crisis	thesis
	alumni	memoranda	crises	thes**es**
Exceptions	hippopotamus		formula	
	hippopotam**uses**		formula**s**	
	or hippopot**ami**		or formul**ae**	

Check a dictionary when forming the plural of words from Latin and Greek. When two forms are given, the first one is preferred.

Practice Your Skills

Forming Plurals

Write the plural form of each noun. Check a dictionary if you are not sure of the preferred form.

1. mouse	**6.** woman	**11.** hypothesis	**16.** deer
2. child	**7.** synopsis	**12.** appendix	**17.** Swiss
3. tooth	**8.** octopus	**13.** spectrum	**18.** pliers
4. foot	**9.** stylus	**14.** analysis	**19.** corps
5. louse	**10.** vacuum	**15.** salmon	**20.** trout

Connect to Writing: Editing

Forming Plurals

Decide if the underlined plurals are formed correctly. If any are incorrect, write the correct form.

(1) Deer and Canada (2) gooses have become a serious nuisance in many communities, according to the news (3) mediums. Various (4) hypothesises have been put forth, but apparently a major cause of the problem is (5) demographicses. According to the latest (6) analyses, people are living in areas that used to be wilderness. Places that in the 1940s were home to many (7) specieses of wild animals are suburban neighborhoods now. (8) Deers, with no other place to forage, devour gardens and shrubbery and ruin lawns with their sharp, pointed (9) feet. (10) Geese foul lawns and parks and can turn aggressive toward (11) men, (12) womans, and (13) childs who try to shoo them away.

Check Point: Mixed Practice

Write the plural form of each word. Use a dictionary whenever necessary.

1. antenna	**6.** hero	**11.** belief	**16.** lamb
2. synopsis	**7.** hoof	**12.** 100	**17.** appendix
3. scissors	**8.** echo	**13.** opus	**18.** stadium
4. ox	**9.** 1980	**14.** X	**19.** lexicon
5. cello	**10.** buffalo	**15.** valley	**20.** *why*

Use the following generalizations when writing numbers.

28 C **Some numbers are written as numerals while other numbers are written as words.**

Numerals or Number Words

28 C.1 Spell out numbers that can be written in one or two words. Use numerals for other numbers. Always spell out a number that begins a sentence.

The election was held **ten** days ago.

The final vote was **563** for and **1067** against.

Six hundred thirty people came out to vote.

When you have a series of numbers, and some are just one or two words while others are more, use numerals for them all.

In the "Favorite Ice Cream Flavor Poll," **347** young people said chocolate was their favorite flavor; **158** liked brownie fudge; **121** liked chocolate chip; and **40** liked vanilla best.

Ordinal Numbers

28 C.2 Always spell out numbers used to tell order of events or the placement in a series.

He promised to be here **first** thing in the morning.

Andrea wanted to finish **first,** but she came in **third.**

Numbers in Dates

28 C.3 Use a numeral for a date when you include the name of the month. Always use numerals for the year.

Examples	Dr. Seuss's birthday is March 2.
	He was born in 1904.
Exception	Did you know my birthday is the twenty-ninth of February?
	(Always spell out ordinal numbers.)

Practice Your Skills

Spelling Numbers

Write the correct form of the number in parentheses to complete each sentence.

1. (9)   This year's marathon was scheduled for October ▧.

2. (2)   The deadline for entering the race was ▧ weeks before, on September 17.

3. (15th) On the ▧ of September, organizers were disappointed by the lack of interest.

4. (58)   Only ▧ people had signed up for the race.

5. (1996) That was very different from the first marathon the town held in ▧.

Connect to Writing: Editing

Writing Numbers Correctly

Rewrite this paragraph, correcting any mistakes in writing numbers.

> The marathon race was first included in the Olympic Games in Athens in 1896. Just 1 year later, in 1897, the very first Boston Marathon was run. Originally called the American Marathon Race, the Boston Marathon has been held every year, except 1918, for more than 100 years. The very first winner of the race was John J. McDermott of New York City, who finished the race in two hours, 55 minutes, and ten seconds. For finishing 1st, McDermott received a laurel wreath and a pot of beef stew.

28 D **A prefix** is placed in front of a base word to form a new word. A **suffix** is placed after a base word to create a new word.

When you add a prefix, the base word does not change, but the meaning often changes.

PREFIXES		
in + accurate = **in**accurate	**ir** + regular = **ir**regular	**mis** + use = **mis**use
pre + arrange = **pre**arrange	**re** + tell = **re**tell	**un** + able = **un**able
dis + satisfied = **dis**satisfied	**over** + do = **over**do	**il** + legal = **il**legal
re + evaluate = **re**evaluate		

Suffixes –*ness* and –*ly*

28 D.1 The suffixes –*ness* and –*ly* are added to most base words without any spelling changes.

–*NESS* AND –*LY*	
open + **ness** = open**ness**	cruel + **ly** = cruel**ly**
plain + **ness** = plain**ness**	real + **ly** = real**ly**

Words Ending in *e*

28 D.2 Drop the final *e* in the base word when adding a suffix that begins with a vowel.

SUFFIXES WITH VOWELS		
Examples	drive + **er** = driver	isolate + **ion** = isolat**ion**
Exceptions	courage + **ous** = courage**ous**	pronounce + **able** = pronounce**able**

28 D.3 Keep the final *e* when adding a suffix that begins with a consonant.

SUFFIXES WITH CONSONANTS		
Examples	care + **ful** = care**ful**	price + **less** = price**less**
	like + **ness** = like**ness**	state + **ment** = state**ment**
Exceptions	argue + **ment** = argu**ment**	true + **ly** = tru**ly**

When adding -*ly* to a word to make the word an adverb, add the suffix to the correct word. Two adverbs that are often confused are *respectively* and *respectfully*.

respectively—[respective + ly] in the order given. The postal abbreviations for Nebraska and Nevada are *respectively* NE and NV.

respectfully—[respectful + ly] in a polite or courteous manner. He answered his grandmother's curious questions *respectfully*.

Words Ending with *y*

28 D.4 To add a suffix to most words ending with a vowel and *y*, keep the *y*.

SUFFIXES WITH VOWELS AND *Y*		
Examples	enjoy + **able** = enjoy**able**	joy + **ful** = joy**ful**
Exceptions	day + **ly** = dai**ly**	gay + **ly** = gai**ly**

28 D.5 To add a suffix to most words ending in a consonant and *y*, change the *y* to *i* before adding the suffix.

SUFFIXES WITH CONSONANTS AND *Y*		
Examples	easy + **ly** = easi**ly**	happy + **ness** = happi**ness**
Exceptions	shy + **ness** = shy**ness**	sly + **ly** = sly**ly**

Doubling the Final Consonant

28 D.6 Sometimes the final consonant in a word is doubled before an ending is added. This happens when the ending begins with a vowel and the base word satisfies both these conditions: (1) It has only one syllable or is stressed on the final syllable, and (2) it ends in one consonant preceded by one vowel.

DOUBLE CONSONANTS		
One-Syllable Words	hum + er = hum**m**er	man + ish = man**n**ish
	fad + ist = fad**d**ist	red + est = red**d**est
Final Syllable Stressed	begin + er = begin**n**er	regret + able = regret**t**able
	refer + al = refer**r**al	remit + ance = remit**t**ance

Practice Your Skills

Adding Suffixes

Combine the base words and suffixes. Remember to make any necessary spelling changes. Use a dictionary to check your work.

1. regret + able

2. play + ful

3. repel + ent

4. rely + able

5. mercy + less

6. slug + ish

7. grumpy + ly

8. deter + ent

9. sly + ness

10. defy + ant

11. note + able

12. pig + ish

Connect to Writing: Editing

Correcting Misspelled Endings

Rewrite this dialogue, correcting the words that are spelled incorrectly. Use a dictionary to check your work.

"Mine is not an envyable duty," Inspector Fields began, struggling to overcome his shyness, "but I must ask you, Lady Penelope, where you were when this regretable crime was commited."

"It was midnight," Lady Penelope said huffyly. "I was where I ordinarily am at that hour–asleep in bed."

"What would you say if I told you that a relyable witness has testified that he saw you in the garden?"

"I would be compeled to question the truthfullness of your witness's account," Lady Penelope replyed with icy haughtyness.

Check Point: Mixed Practice

Add the prefix or suffix to each base word, and write the new word.

1. pre + determine

2. move + able

3. prepare + ation

4. gay + ly

5. open + ness

6. timid + ity

7. il + logical

8. create + ive

9. like + ly

10. play + ful

11. believe + able

12. mis + spell

13. lonely + ness

14. pre + occupied

15. likely + hood

Words to Master

Make it your goal to learn to spell these 50 words this year. Use them in your writing and practice writing them until spelling them correctly comes automatically.

achievement	gracious	preferred
acknowledgment	happiness	preparation
actually	ignorance	proceed
argument	indispensable	readily
beginning	insurance	reasonably
believe	interesting	removal
chief	judgment	requirement
conceivable	leisure	resistance
continuous	loneliness	ridiculous
correspondence	marriage	separate
courageous	mileage	succeed
curiosity	naturally	successful
eighth	niece	truly
exceedingly	noticeable	unfortunately
excellent	occasionally	unnecessary
excitable	occurrence	weird
glorious	precede	

● *Connect to Reading and Writing:* **Classroom Vocabulary**

English Vocabulary and Spelling

This chapter has introduced you to new terms that will be used often in your study of English grammar. To keep track of these new words, such as *plurals, prefixes,* and *suffixes,* make a booklet that lists and tells about them. Include all the rules that apply and give your booklet a title.

Assess Your Learning

Applying Spelling Rules

Write the letter of the misspelled word in each group. Then write the word, spelling it correctly. Use a dictionary to check your work.

1. (a) niece   (b) ratios   (c) happyness
2. (a) intercede   (b) foriegn   (c) innumerable
3. (a) embarass   (b) seize   (c) engagement
4. (a) offered   (b) criticize   (c) atheletics
5. (a) conceit   (b) branches   (c) niether
6. (a) accidentally   (b) thinness   (c) tomatos
7. (a) peaceful   (b) immediatly   (c) misstep
8. (a) twentieth   (b) rideing   (c) argument
9. (a) journies   (b) rained   (c) proceed
10. (a) trapped   (b) knives   (c) permited
11. (a) mispell   (b) relieve   (c) patios
12. (a) immobile   (b) occuring   (c) betrayal
13. (a) forcible   (b) spying   (c) mathmatics
14. (a) surprised   (b) reign   (c) ridiculeous
15. (a) realy   (b) stepping   (c) valleys
16. (a) passersby   (b) leafs   (c) holidays
17. (a) caring   (b) decieve   (c) studying
18. (a) receipt   (b) beliefs   (c) easyly
19. (a) echos   (b) misguided   (c) geese
20. (a) joyful   (b) seperate   (c) interfere
21. (a) biggest   (b) delaying   (c) liesure
22. (a) generaly   (b) boxes   (c) roofs
23. (a) pettiness   (b) disatisfied   (c) writer
24. (a) anonymous   (b) likeness   (c) dayly
25. (a) editors-in-chief   (b) grammer   (c) eighth

Spelling Correctly: Posttest

Directions

Read the passage. Write the letter of the choice that correctly spells each underlined word. If the word contains no error, write *D*.

P. T. Barnum began his life of odd **(1)** <u>acheivements</u> with the opening of his American Museum in 1842. When **(2)** <u>passersby</u> were treated to advertisements promising "The **(3)** <u>Eigth</u> Wonder of the World" and the like, it is little wonder that **(4)** <u>curiousity</u> brought the public in by the **(5)** <u>1000s</u>. Barnum went on to manage the **(6)** <u>outragously</u> **(7)** <u>successfull</u> tour of Swedish singer Jenny Lind. In 1871, he opened "The Greatest Show on Earth," designed to put all other **(8)** <u>circusses</u> to shame. **(9)** <u>Featureing</u> everything from men swallowing **(10)** <u>knifes</u> to the best of European acrobats, the circus merged with its major competitor in 1881 and was subsequently known as "Barnum & Bailey."

1. **A** achevements
   B achievements
   C achiefments
   D No error

2. **A** passerbys
   B passerbyes
   C passers by
   D No error

3. **A** 8th
   B Eight
   C Eighth
   D No error

4. **A** curiosity
   B curiusity
   C curiousty
   D No error

5. **A** 1000's
   B 1000
   C thousands
   D No error

6. **A** outrageously
   B outragousally
   C outragely
   D No error

7. **A** successful
   B sucesfull
   C succeful
   D No error

8. **A** circusies
   B circi
   C circuses
   D No error

9. **A** Featurring
   B Featuring
   C Featureng
   D No error

10. **A** kniffes
    B knives
    C knife
    D No error

Writer's Corner

Snapshot

28 A **Spelling patterns**—such as *i* before *e* except after *c*—apply to many words and can help you spell many different words correctly. (pages 928–929)

28 B To form the **plural** of most nouns, add *s* or *es*. Some nouns form their plurals in other ways. (pages 930–935)

28 C Some **numbers** are written as numerals while other numbers are written as words. (pages 936–937)

28 D A **prefix** is placed in front of a base word to form a new word. A **suffix** is placed after a base word to create a new word and often a new spelling. (pages 938–940)

Power Rules

Homophones are **words that sound alike** but have different meanings. Use the word with your intended meaning. (pages 726–727 and 746)

Before Editing

What is *you're* favorite movie? (*you're* is a contraction of *you are*)

Their exhausted today. (*their* is the possessive form of *they*)

Its too bad you don't like mysteries. (*its* is the possessive form of *it*)

After Editing

What is *your* favorite movie? (*your* is the possessive form of *you*)

They're exhausted today. (*they're* is a contraction of *they are*)

It's too bad you don't like mysteries. (*it's* is a contraction of *it is*)

When you write, avoid misusing or misspelling these **commonly confused words.** (pages 796–809 and 941)

Before Editing

Ray *complemented* Al's tie. (a *complement* completes something else)

Wanda will arrive *latter*. (*latter* refers to "the second item mentioned")

Bekka needs to *altar* her dress. (*altar* is used in religious ceremonies)

After Editing

Ray *complimented* Al's tie. (*compliment* means *to praise*)

Wanda will arrive *later*. (*later* is the comparative form of *late*)

Bekka needs to *alter* her dress. (*alter* means *to change*)

Editing Checklist

Use this checklist when editing your writing.

- ✓ Did I pay attention to spelling patterns in my writing? (See pages 928–929.)
- ✓ Did I correctly form plurals of regular and irregular nouns? (See pages 930–935.)
- ✓ Did I use spelling generalizations to form plurals of compound words, foreign words, and other plurals? (See pages 932–934.)
- ✓ Did I use a dictionary to check words I wasn't sure how to spell? (See page 927.)
- ✓ Did I change the spelling of base words if needed when adding suffixes? (See pages 938–940.)
- ✓ Did I carefully edit my writing for misspelled words? (See pages 927 and 941.)

Use the Power

Some words or word parts sound the same but are spelled differently. Use a mnemonic device to help you remember how to spell difficult words.

WORD	MNEMONIC DEVICE
achIEve, recEIpt, percEIve, chIEf	**i** before **e** except after **c** (unless n**E**Ither apply)
their/there	**Their** feet take them **here** and **there**. (*Here* and *there* indicate places.)
affect/effect	**R** emember **A** ffect **V** erb **E** ffect **N** oun
desert/deSSert	Two sugars please—for two *SS*'s in de**SS**ert
personAL/personnEL	A person**AL** matter was handled in the personn**EL** office. (*a before e*)
stationAry, stationEry	Station**A**ry is p**A**rked c**A**rs; station**E**ry is **E**nvelopes and p**E**ns.
hEAR/here	You h**EAR** with your **EAR**.

Language QuickGuide

QUICKGUIDE

The Power Rules

Researchers have found that certain patterns of language used offend educated people more than others and therefore affect how people perceive you. Since these patterns of language use have such an impact on future success, you should learn how to edit for the more widely accepted forms. The list below identifies ten of the most important conventions to master the Power Rules. Always check for them when you edit.

 1. Use only one negative form for a single negative idea. (See pages 789–790.)

Before Editing	After Editing
They won't bring *nothing* to the picnic.	They won't bring *anything* to the picnic.
There wasn't *nothing* we could do.	There wasn't *anything* we could do.

 2. Use mainstream past tense forms of regular and irregular verbs. (See pages 684–703.) It's a good idea to memorize the parts of the most common irregular verbs.

Before Editing	After Editing
I already *clean* my room.	I already *cleaned* my room.
Yesterday he *come* to study with me.	Yesterday he *came* to study with me.
She *brung* her new album with her.	She *brought* her new album with her.
I should have *went* along with them.	I should have *gone* along with them.

 3. Use verbs that agree with the subject. (See pages 750–767.)

Before Editing	After Editing
He/she/it *don't* make sense.	He/she/it *doesn't* make sense.
Carlos always *reach* for the top.	Carlos always *reaches* for the top.
The sisters or Elena *sing* next.	The sisters or Elena *sings* next.
Either Maya or her friends *knows* what happened.	Either Maya or her friends *know* what happened.

4. Use subject forms of pronouns in subject position. Use object forms of pronouns in object position. (See pages 716–725.)

Before Editing	After Editing
Her and Morgan always show up together.	*She* and Morgan always show up together.
Him and Jamal went to the same college.	*He* and Jamal went to the same college.
Her and *me* are going to the movies.	*She* and *I* are going to the movies.

5. Use standard ways to make nouns possessive. (See pages 895–897.)

Before Editing	After Editing
Do you have the *coach* jacket?	Do you have the *coach's* jacket?
Is that *Deidres* book?	Is that *Deidre's* book?
Josh wrote the *committees* report.	Josh wrote the *committee's* report.
All the *kids* ideas are important.	All the *kids'* ideas are important.

6. Use a consistent verb tense except when a change is clearly necessary. (See pages 693–703.)

Before Editing	After Editing
The lake level *rises* when it rained.	The lake level *rose* when it rained.
After she forgot her lines, she *doesn't* want to be in the play.	After she forgot her lines, she *didn't* want to be in the play.

7. Use sentence fragments only the way professional writers do, after the sentence they refer to and usually to emphasize a point. Fix all sentence fragments that occur before the sentence they refer to and ones that occur in the middle of a sentence. (See pages 666–671.)

Before Editing	After Editing
One day. The rain finally stopped.	*One day,* the rain finally stopped.
Driving in the city can be difficult. *During the evening rush hour.* So we try to avoid it.	Driving in the city can be difficult *during the evening rush hour,* so we try to avoid it.
I missed the bus today. *The reason being that I took too long at lunch.*	I missed the bus today *because* I took too long at lunch.

8. Use the best conjunction and/or punctuation for the meaning when connecting two sentences. Revise run-on sentences. (See pages 672–674.)

Before Editing

We went to the *store we* decided to buy ice cream.

Micah drove the *car, Inez* gave him directions from her map.

Then Inez drove for a *while,* Micah slept in the back seat.

After Editing

When we went to the store, we decided to buy ice cream.

While Micah drove the car, Inez gave him directions from her map.

Then Inez drove for a while, *and* Micah slept in the back seat.

9. Use the contraction *'ve* not *of* when the correct word is *have*, or use the full word *have*. Use *supposed* instead of *suppose* and *used* instead of *use* when appropriate. (See pages 801, 805, and 808.)

Before Editing

You should *of* finished your homework.

We might *of* missed the whole show.

Reggie could *of* let me know.

Jack was *suppose* to call me.

Reggie *use* to be on the team.

After Editing

You should *have* finished your homework.

We might *have* missed the whole show.

Reggie could *have* let me know.

Jack was *supposed* to call me.

Reggie *used* to be on the team.

10. For sound-alikes and certain words that sound almost alike, choose the word with your intended meaning. (See pages 796–811.)

Before Editing

Mia went *too* her violin lesson.
   (*too* means *also* or *in addition*)

She practiced *to* times today.
   (*to* means *in the direction of*)

Are these *you're* tickets? (*you're* is a contraction of *you are*)

They're new school is very modern.
   (*they're* is a contraction of *they are*)

I put your books over *their*. (*their* is the possessive form of *they*)

Its not a good time to bring up that problem. (*its* is the possessive form of *it*)

After Editing

Mia went *to* her violin lesson.
   (*to* means *in the direction of*)

She practiced *two* times today.
   (*two* is a number)

Are these *your* tickets? (*your* is the possessive form of *you*)

Their new school is very modern.
   (*their* is the possessive form of *they*)

I put your books over *there*.
   (*there* means *in that place*)

It's not a good time to bring up that problem. (*it's* is a contraction of *it is*)

Nine Tools for Powerful Writing • • • • • • • • • • • • • •

Besides using the Power Rules to help you avoid errors, you can also use the following nine tools to turn your good writing into excellent writing.

1. **Set the scene** with adverbial phrases. (See page 272.)

Give your reader the gift of detail. An adverbial phrase is a prepositional phrase that adds detail by modifying a verb, adjective, or adverb. When one of these phrases begins a sentence, it can "set the scene" by offering important details early.

Under a single spotlight in the dark auditorium, she began to sing.

2. Add variety to your sentences by using **adjectives come lately.** (See page 157.)

Adjectival phrases add detail by modifying nouns and pronouns. They often have the most impact when placed after the word or words they modify.

Under a single spotlight in the dark auditorium, she began to sing, **her voice charged with a familiar, quiet power.**

3. Create emphasis by **dashing it all.** (See page 314.)

When you are writing informally, dashes can create abrupt breaks that emphasize a word or group of words. Use one dash to set off words at the end of a sentence. Use a pair of dashes to set off words in the middle of a sentence.

Halfway into the first set she delivered something entirely new—**a series of lively dance tunes.**

This new music—**a series of lively dance tunes**—transformed the room's atmosphere.

4. **Get into the action** with participial phrases. (See page 57.)

You can pack a lot of action into your sentences if you include an *–ing* verb, or "*–ing* modifier." Formally called a *present participial phrase,* these -*ing* modifiers describe a person, thing, or action in a sentence.

The crowd absorbed every lyric and note of the new music, **clapping and moving to its irresistible beat.**

5. Elaborate by **explaining who or what with appositives.** (See page 127.)

Details that elaborate on a person, place, or thing that may be unknown to your reader will strengthen your writing. You can add such details in the form of an appositive. An appositive is a noun or pronoun phrase that identifies or adds identifying information to the preceding noun.

The singer, **a tiny woman,** flashed a huge smile.

6. **Tip the scale** with adverbial clauses. (See page 370.)

In persuasive writing, you can use subordinate clauses to acknowledge an opposing viewpoint. This will tip the scale toward your own viewpoint, which remains in the main clause. Start the clause with a subordinating word like *when, if, because, until, while,* or *since.*

> **While a consistent style may please some fans,** bold new directions are often the mark of a true artist.

7. **Catch and release** related sentences with a semicolon. (See page 223.)

The semicolon combines a comma and a period. The period "catches" the idea in the words before the semicolon, signaling its end. The comma "releases" it and relates it to another idea. Semicolons invite the reader to supply the words or idea that connects what could be two separate sentences.

> Then, as she sang her final note, she pointed to her band; **it was their time to shine.**

8. Use the **power of 3s** to add style and emphasis with **parallelism.** (See page 89.)

One way to add power is to use a writing device called parallelism. Parallelism is the use of the same kind of word or group of words in a series of three or more.

> Her **simple melodies, original lyrics,** and **powerful voice** attract fans of all ages.

9. Write with variety and coherence and **let it flow.** (See page 184.)

Vary the length, structure, and beginnings of your sentences and use connecting words to help your writing flow smoothly.

> As the singer stood under a single spotlight in the dark auditorium, her voice, lyrical and plaintive, touched the hearts of her listeners. But this mood was short-lived. Halfway into the first set she delivered something entirely new—a series of lively dance tunes. While a consistent style may please some fans, bold new directions are often the mark of a true artist. Last night's audience seemed to agree. They absorbed every lyric and note of the new music, clapping and moving to its irresistible beat. The singer, a tiny woman, flashed a huge smile. Then, as she sang her final note, she pointed to her band; it was their time to shine. A full three minutes of their sheer energy brought the set to its thrilling conclusion.

Grammar QuickGuide ....

This section presents an easy-to-use reference for the definitions of grammatical terms. The number on the colored tab tells you the chapter covering that topic. The page number to the right of each definition refers to the place in the chapter where you can find additional instruction, examples, and applications to writing.

12 Nouns and Pronouns

How can you use nouns and pronouns to create lively and precise prose?

Nouns

Pronouns

QUICKGUIDE

13 Verbs

How can you make your writing sing by adding just the right verbs?

Action Verbs

Transitive and Intransitive Verbs

Linking Verbs

14 Adjectives and Adverbs

How can you add interest and detail to your writing with adjectives and adverbs?

Adjectives

Adverbs

15 Other Parts of Speech

How can prepositions, conjunctions, and interjections help you add detail, fluency, and variety to your writing?

Prepositions

Conjunctions

Interjections

16 The Sentence Base

How can you use a variety of sentences to increase fluency in your writing?

Recognizing Sentences

Subjects and Predicates

QUICKGUIDE

Complements

17 Phrases

How can you add precision and variety to your writing with phrases?

Prepositional Phrases

QUICKGUIDE

18 Clauses

How can you connect related ideas with clauses?

Independent and Subordinate Clauses

18 A A **clause** is a group of words that is part of a sentence that has a subject and a verb. 642

> **18 A.1** An **independent (main) clause** can stand alone as a sentence because it expresses a complete thought. 642
>
> **18 A.2** A **subordinate (dependent) clause** cannot stand alone as a sentence because it does not express a complete thought. 643

Uses of Subordinate Clauses

18 B A subordinate clause can function as an adverb, an adjective, or a noun. 644

> **18 B.1** An **adverbial clause** is a subordinate clause that is used like an adverb to modify a verb, an adjective, or an adverb. 644
>
> **18 B.2** All adverbial clauses begin with a **subordinating conjunction.** 645
>
> **18 B.3** An **adjectival clause** is a subordinate clause that is used like an adjective to modify a noun or a pronoun. 647
>
> **18 B.4** A **relative pronoun** relates an adjectival clause to its antecedent—the noun or pronoun it modifies. 647
>
> **18 B.5** A **restrictive (essential) clause** contains information that is essential to identifying a person, place, or thing in a sentence and answers the question "Which one?" Do not use commas to set off an essential clause. 649
>
> **18 B.6** A **nonrestrictive (nonessential) clause** adds additional information and can be removed without changing the main information of a sentence. A nonrestrictive clause answers the question "What kind?" Use a comma or commas to set off a nonrestrictive clause. 650
>
> **18 B.7** A clause that is too far away from the word it modifies is called a **misplaced modifier.** 651
>
> **18 B.8** A **noun clause** is a subordinate clause that is used like a noun. 651

Kinds of Sentence Structure

18 C There are four kinds of sentences: **simple, compound, complex,** and **compound-complex**. The kind of sentence depends on the type and number of clauses in it.   654

> **18 C.1** A **simple sentence** consists of one independent clause.   654

> **18 C.2** A **compound sentence** consists of two or more independent clauses.   654

> **18 C.3** A **complex sentence** consists of one independent clause and one or more subordinate clauses.   655

> **18 C.4** A **compound-complex sentence** consists of two or more independent clauses and one or more subordinate clauses.   655

19 Sentence Fragments and Run-ons

How can you clarify your meaning by fixing unintended sentence fragments and run-ons?

Sentence Fragments

19 A A **sentence fragment** is a group of words that does not express a complete thought.   666

Other Kinds of Sentence Fragments

19 B Phrases and clauses punctuated as sentences are also fragments.   668

> **19 B.1** When phrases are written alone, they are called **phrase fragments.**   668

> **19 B.2** When a subordinate clause stands alone, it is known as a **clause fragment.**   670

Run-on Sentences

19 C A **run-on sentence** is two or more sentences that are written together and are separated by a comma or no mark of punctuation at all.   672

This section presents an easy-to-use reference for the explanations of how various grammatical elements are and should be used. The number on the colored tab tells you the chapter covering that topic. The page number to the right of each definition refers to the place in the chapter where you can find additional instruction, examples, and applications to writing. You can also refer to the Writer's Glossary of Usage (pages 796–809) for help with commonly confused usage items.

20 Using Verbs

How can you use verbs to improve your writing?

The Principal Parts of a Verb

20 A   The **principal parts of a verb** are the **present**, the **present**   684
participle, the **past**, and the **past participle**.

  20 A.1   A **regular verb** forms its past and past participle by adding   684
  –ed or *–d* to the present.

  20 A.2   An **irregular verb** does not form its past and past participle   685
  by adding *–ed* or *–d* to the present form.

Six Problem Verbs

20 B   The verbs *lie* and *lay, rise* and *raise,* and *sit* and *set* are often confused.   691

  20 B.1   *Lie* means "to rest or recline." *Lie* is never followed by a direct   691
  object. *Lay* means "to put or set (something) down." *Lay* is
  usually followed by a direct object.

  20 B.2   *Rise* means "to move upward" or "to get up." *Rise* is never   691
  followed by a direct object. *Raise* means "to lift (something)
  up," "to increase," or "to grow something." *Raise* is usually
  followed by a direct object.

  20 B.3   *Sit* means "to rest in an upright position." *Sit* is never followed by   691
  a direct object. *Set* usually means "to put or place (something)."
  Set is usually followed by a direct object.

Verb Tenses

20 C   The time expressed by a verb is called the **tense** of a verb.   693

QUICKGUIDE

Active and Passive Voice

Mood

21 Using Pronouns

Why is it important to avoid unclear, missing, or confusing pronoun references?

The Cases of Personal Pronouns

QUICKGUIDE

21 A.2 A **predicate nominative** is a noun or a pronoun that follows a linking verb and identifies or renames the subject. Pronouns used as predicate nominatives are always in the nominative case. 720

21 A.3 **Object pronouns** are used as direct objects, indirect objects, and objects of prepositions. 722

21 A.4 An **object of a preposition** is always a part of a prepositional phrase. A pronoun used as the object of a preposition is in the objective case. 723

21 A.5 The **possessive case** is used to show ownership or possession. 726

Pronoun Problems

21 B Common pronoun problems include the misuse of *who* and *whom* and incomplete comparisons. 729

21 B.1 The correct case of *who* is determined by how the pronoun is used in a question or a clause. 729

21 B.2 Forms of *who* are often used in questions. Use *who* when the pronoun is used as a subject. Use *whom* when the pronoun is used as a direct object or object of the preposition. 729

21 B.3 The form of *who* you use depends on how the pronoun is used within the clause. Use *who* when the pronoun is used as the subject of the clause. Use *whom* when the pronoun is used as a direct object or object of the preposition in the clause. 730

21 B.4 In an **elliptical clause,** use the form of the pronoun you would use if the clause were completed. 733

Pronouns and Their Antecedents

21 C A pronoun must agree in **number** and **gender** with its antecedent. 736

21 C.1 **Number** is the term used to indicate whether a noun or pronoun is singular or plural. Singular indicates one, and plural indicates more than one. **Gender** is the term used to indicate whether a noun or a pronoun is masculine, feminine, or neuter. 736

21 C.2 If two or more singular antecedents are joined by *or, nor, either/ or,* or *neither/nor,* use a singular pronoun to refer to them. 736

21 C.3 If two or more singular antecedents are joined by *and* or *both/ and,* use a plural pronoun to refer to them. 737

21 C.4 Use a singular pronoun if the antecedent is a singular indefinite pronoun. 738

22 Subject and Verb Agreement

How can you make your subjects and verbs work together so that your ideas are clear?

Agreement of Subjects and Verbs

Common Agreement Problems

23 Using Adjectives and Adverbs

How can you create colorful prose with adjectives and adverbs?

Comparison of Adjectives and Adverbs

Problems with Comparisons

Problems with Modifiers

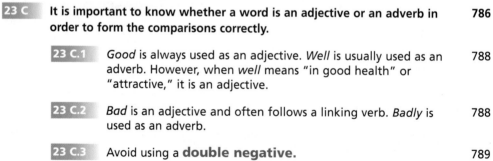

This section presents an easy-to-use reference for the mechanics of writing: capitalization, punctuation, and spelling. The number on the colored tab tells you the chapter covering that topic. The page number to the right of each definition refers to the place in the chapter where you can find additional instruction, examples, and applications to writing.

24 Capital Letters

How can you use capital letters to clarify your meaning when you write?

Capitalization

24 A Capitalize first words and the pronoun *I*. 816

> **24 A.1** Capitalize the first word of a sentence and of a line of poetry. 816

> **24 A.2** Capitalize the first word in the greeting of a letter and the first word in the closing of a letter. 816

> **24 A.3** Capitalize the first word of each item in an outline and the letters that begin major subsections of the outline. 817

> **24 A.4** Capitalize the pronoun *I*, both alone and in contractions. 817

Proper Nouns

24 B Capitalize proper nouns and their abbreviations. 819

> **24 B.1** Names of persons and animals should be capitalized. Also capitalize initials that stand for people's names. 819

> **24 B.2** Geographical names, which include particular places and bodies of water and their abbreviations, initials, and acronyms, are capitalized. 819

> **24 B.3** Capitalize historically important nouns, which include the names of historical events, periods, and documents and their associated initials and acronyms. 821

> **24 B.4** Names of groups, such as organizations, businesses, institutions, government bodies, teams, and political parties, should be capitalized. 822

> **24 B.5** Specific time periods and events, including the days of the week, the months of the year, civil and religious holidays, and special events, should be capitalized. 822

25 End Marks and Commas

How can you create meaning through the careful use of end marks and commas?

Kinds of Sentences and End Marks

QUICKGUIDE

26 Italics and Quotation Marks

How can you create voice in your writing with italics and quotation marks?

Italics (Underlining)

26 A   **Italics** are printed letters that slant to the right. Italics are used for long   872
titles, foreign words, and words or numbers used as words. When you are
writing by hand, underline words that should be in italics.

26 A.1   Italicize (underline) letters, numbers, and words when they are   872
used to represent themselves. Also italicize (underline) foreign
words that are not generally used in the English language.

26 A.2   Italicize (underline) the titles of long written or musical works   873
that are published as a single unit. Also italicize (underline) the
titles of periodicals, movies, radio and television series, paintings
and sculptures, and the names of vehicles. All words in the title
should be italicized.

Quotation Marks

26 B   **Quotation marks** always come in pairs. They are placed at the   875
beginning and at the end of certain titles and uninterrupted quotations.

26 B.1   Use quotation marks to enclose the titles of chapters, articles,   875
stories, one-act plays, short poems, and songs. The entire title
should be in quotation marks.

26 B.2   Use quotation marks to enclose a person's exact words.   877

26 B.3   Begin each sentence of a direct quotation with a capital letter.   878

26 B.4   Use a comma to separate a direct quotation from a speaker tag.   879
Place the comma inside the closing quotation marks.

26 B.5   Place a period inside the closing quotation marks when the end   880
of the quotation comes at the end of the sentence.

26 B.6   Place a question mark or an exclamation point inside the closing   880
quotation marks when it is part of the quotation.

26 B.7   When a question mark or exclamation mark is part of the whole   880
sentence, it is placed *outside* the closing quotation marks.

26 B.8   When writing dialogue, begin a new paragraph each time the   882
speaker changes.

27 Other Punctuation

How can you use apostrophes, semicolons, colons, hyphens, and other punctuation to communicate precisely and enhance your writing style?

Apostrophes

Semicolons

Colons

Hyphens

28 Spelling Correctly

How can you communicate your message effectively by using accurate spelling?

Spelling Numbers

Prefixes and Suffixes

28 D.1	The suffixes *–ness* and *–ly* are added to most base words without any spelling changes.	938
28 D.2	Drop the final *e* in the base word when adding a suffix that begins with a vowel.	938
28 D.3	Keep the final *e* when adding a suffix that begins with a consonant.	938
28 D.4	To add a suffix to most words ending with a vowel and *y*, keep the *y*.	939
28 D.5	To add a suffix to most words ending in a consonant and *y*, change the *y* to *i* before adding the suffix.	939
28 D.6	Sometimes the final consonant in a word is doubled before an ending is added. This happens when the ending begins with a vowel and the base word satisfies both these conditions: (1) It has only one syllable or is stressed on the final syllable, and (2) it ends in one consonant preceded by one vowel.	939

Glossary

English	Español

A

abbreviation shortened form of a word that generally begins with a capital letter and ends with a period

abreviatura forma reducida de una palabra que generalmente comienza con mayúscula y termina en punto

abstract summary of points of writing, presented in skeletal form

síntesis resumen de los puntos principales de un texto, presentados en forma de esquema

abstract noun noun that cannot be seen or touched, such as an idea, quality, or characteristic

austantivo abstracto sustantivo que no puede verse ni tocarse, como una idea, una cualidad o una característica

acronym an abbreviation formed by using the initial letters of a phrase or name (CIA—Central Intelligence Agency)

acrónimo abreviatura que se forma al usar las letras iniciales de una frase o de un nombre (CIA—Central Intelligence Agency [Agencia Central de Inteligencia])

action verb verb that tells what action a subject is performing

verbo de acción verbo que indica qué acción realiza el sujeto

active voice voice the verb is in when it expresses that the subject is performing the action

voz activa voz en que está el verbo cuando expresa que el sujeto está realizando la acción

adequate development quality of good writing in which sufficient supporting details develop the main idea

desarrollo adecuado cualidad de un texto bien escrito, en cual suficientes detalles de apoyo desarrollan la idea principal

adjectival clause subordinate clause used to modify a noun or pronoun

cláusula adjetiva cláusula subordinada utilizada para modificar a un sustantivo o a un pronombre

adjectival phrase prepositional phrase that modifies a noun or a pronoun

frase adjetiva frase preposicional que modifica a un sustantivo o a un pronombre

adjective word that modifies a noun or a pronoun

adjetivo palabra que modifica a un sustantivo o a un pronombre

English	Español
adverb word that modifies a verb, an adjective, or another adverb	**adverbio** palabra que modifica a un verbo, a un adjetivo o a otro adverbio
adverbial clause subordinate clause that is used mainly to modify a verb	**cláusula adverbial** cláusula subordinada que se utiliza principalmente para modificar a un verbo
adverbial phrase prepositional phrase that is used mainly to modify a verb	**frase adverbial** frase preposicional que se utiliza principalmente para modificar a un verbo
aesthetics study of beauty and artistic quality	**estética** estudio de la belleza y de las características del arte
alliteration repetition of a consonant sound at the beginning of a series of words	**aliteración** repetición de un sonido consonántico al comienzo de una serie de palabras
allusion reference to persons or events in the past or in literature	**alusión** referencia a personas o sucesos del pasado o de la literatura
analogy logical relationship between a pair of words	**analogía** relación lógica entre una pareja de palabras
analysis the process of breaking a whole into parts to see how the parts fit and work together	**análisis** proceso de separación de las partes de un todo para examinar cómo encajan y cómo funcionan juntas
antecedent word or group of words to which a pronoun refers	**antecedente** palabra o grupo de palabras a que hace referencia un pronombre
antithesis in literature, using contrasting words, phrases, sentences, or ideas for emphasis: *She was tough as nails and soft as spun sugar.*	**antítesis** en literatura, el uso de palabras, frases, oraciones o ideas contrastantes para producir énfasis: *Era dura como una piedra y con un corazón de oro.*
antonym word that means the opposite of another word	**antónimo** palabra que significa lo opuesto de otra palabra
appositive noun or pronoun that identifies or explains another noun or pronoun in a sentence	**aposición** sustantivo o pronombre que especifica o explica a otro sustantivo o pronombre en una oración

English	Español
article the special adjectives *a, an, the*	**artículo** adjetivos especiales *a (un/una), an (un/una) y the (el/la/los/las)*
assonance repetition of a vowel sound within words	**asonancia** repetición de un sonido vocálico en las palabras
audience person or persons who will read your work or hear your speech	**público** persona o personas que leerán tu trabajo o escucharán tu discurso
autobiography account of a person's life, written by that person	**autobiografía** relato de la vida de una persona, escrito por esa misma persona

B

English	Español
ballad a narrative song or poem. A *folk ballad* may be passed down by word of mouth for generations before being written down. A *literary ballad* is written in a style to imitate a folk ballad but has a known author.	**balada** canción o poema narrativo. Una *balada folclórica* puede transmitirse oralmente de generación en generación antes de que se ponga por escrito. Una *balada literaria* está escrita en un estilo que imita a la balada folclórica, pero se sabe quién es su autor.
bandwagon statement appeal that leads the reader to believe that everyone is using a certain product	**enunciado de arrastre** enunciado apelativo que lleva al lector a creer que todos usan cierto producto
bibliographic information information about a source, such as author, title, publisher, date of publication, and Internet address	**información bibliográfica** datos sobre una fuente: autor, título, editorial, fecha de publicación, dirección de Internet, etc
body one or more paragraphs composed of details, facts, and examples that support the main idea	**cuerpo** uno o más párrafos compuestos de detalles, hechos y ejemplos que apoyan la idea principal
brackets punctuation marks [ ] used to enclose information added to text or to indicate new text replacing the original quoted text; always used in pairs	**corchetes** signos de puntuación [ ] utilizados para encerrar la información añadida al texto o para indicar el texto nuevo que reemplaza al texto original citado; siempre se usan en parejas

brainstorming prewriting technique of writing down ideas that come to mind about a given subject

intercambio de ideas técnica de preparación para la escritura que consiste en anotar las ideas que surgen sobre un tema

business letter formal letter that asks for action on the part of the receiver and includes an inside address, heading, salutation, body, closing, and signature

carta de negocios carta formal que solicita al destinatario que realice una acción e incluye dirección del destinatario, membrete, saludo, cuerpo, despedida y firma

C

case form of a noun or a pronoun that indicates its use in a sentence. In English there are three cases: the nominative case, the objective case, and the possessive case.

caso forma de un sustantivo o de un pronombre que indica su uso en una oración. En inglés hay tres casos: nominativo, objetivo y posesivo.

cause and effect method of development in which details are grouped according to what happens and why it happens

causa y efecto método de desarrollo en cual los detalles están agrupados según lo que sucede y por qué sucede

central idea the main or controlling idea of an essay

idea central idea principal o fundamental de un ensayo

characterization variety of techniques used by writers to show the personality of a character

caracterización varias técnicas utilizadas por los escritores para mostrar la personalidad de un personaje

chronological order the order in which events occur

orden cronológico orden en el que ocurren los sucesos

citation note that gives credit to the source of another person's paraphrased or quoted ideas

cita nota que menciona la fuente de donde se extrajeron las ideas, parafraseadas o textuales, de otra persona

claim in a persuasive speech or essay, a main position or statement supported with one or more examples and warrants

afirmación en un discurso o ensayo persuasivo, punto de vista o enunciado principal fundamentado con uno o más ejemplos y justificaciones

clarity the quality of being clear

claridad cualidad de un texto de ser claro

GLOSSARY

English	Español
classics literary works that withstand the test of time and appeal to readers from generation to generation and from century to century	**clásicos** obras literarias que superan la prueba del tiempo y atraen a los lectores de generación en generación y de un siglo a otro
classification method of development in which details are grouped into categories	**clasificación** método de desarrollo en el que los detalles están agrupados en categorías
clause fragment subordinate clause standing alone	**fragmento de cláusula** cláusula subordinada que aparece de forma independiente
clause group of words that has a subject and verb and is used as part of a sentence	**cláusula** grupo de palabras que tiene sujeto y verbo y se utiliza como parte de una oración
cliché overused expression that is no longer fresh or interesting to the reader	**cliché** expresión demasiado usada que ya no resulta original ni interesante para el lector
close reading reading carefully to locate specific information, follow an argument's logic, or comprehend the meaning of information	**lectura atenta** lectura minuciosa para identificar información específica, seguir un argumento lógico o comprender el significado de la información
clustering visual strategy a writer uses to organize ideas and details connected to the subject	**agrupación** estrategia visual que emplea un escritor para organizar las ideas y los detalles relacionados con el tema
coherence logical and smooth flow of ideas connected with clear transitions	**coherencia** flujo lógico de ideas que discurren conectadas con transiciones claras
collaboration in writing, the working together of several individuals on one piece of writing, usually done during prewriting, including brainstorming and revising	**colaboración** en el ámbito de la escritura, el trabajo en común de varios individuos en un texto, usualmente durante la etapa de preparación para la escritura, incluida la técnica de intercambio de ideas y la tarea de revisión

English

collective noun noun that names a group of people or things

colloquialism informal phrase or colorful expression not meant to be taken literally but understood to have particular non-literal meaning

common noun names any person, place, or thing

comparative degree modification of an adjective or adverb used when two people, things, or actions are compared

comparison and contrast method of development in which the writer examines similarities and differences between two subjects

complement word or group of words used to complete a predicate

complete predicate all the words that tell what the subject is doing or that tell something about the subject

complete subject all the words used to identify the person, place, thing, or idea that the sentence is about

complex sentence sentence that consists of a dependent and an independent clause

composition writing form that presents and develops one main idea

compound adjective adjective made up of more than one word

Español

sustantivo colectivo sustantivo que designa un grupo de personas o cosas

coloquialismo frase informal o expresión pintoresca que no debe tomarse literalmente, pues tiene un significado figurado específico

sustantivo común designa cualquier persona, lugar o cosa

grado comparativo forma de un adjetivo o adverbio que se usa cuando se comparan dos personas, cosas o acciones

comparación y contraste método de desarrollo en cual el escritor examina las semejanzas y las diferencias entre dos temas

complemento palabra o grupo de palabras utilizadas para completar un predicado

predicado completo todas las palabras que expresan qué hace el sujeto o dicen algo acerca del sujeto

sujeto completo todas las palabras utilizadas para identificar la persona, el lugar, la cosa o la idea de la que trata la oración

oración compleja oración que consiste de una cláusula dependiente y una independiente

composición tipo de texto que presenta y desarrolla una idea principal

adjetivo compuesto adjetivo formado por más de una palabra

English	Español
compound noun a single noun comprised of several words	**sustantivo compuesto** sustantivo individual formado por varias palabras
compound sentence consists of two simple sentences, usually joined by a comma and the coordinating conjunction *and, but, or,* or *yet*	**oración compuesta** consiste de dos oraciones simples, unidas generalmente por una coma y la conjunción coordinante and (y), but (pero), or (o) y yet (sin embargo)
compound subject two or more subjects in a sentence that have the same verb and are joined by a conjunction	**sujeto compuesto** dos o más sujetos en una oración que tienen el mismo verbo y están unidos por una conjunción
compound verb two or more verbs in one sentence that have the same subject and are joined by a conjunction	**verbo compuesto** dos o más verbos en una oración que tienen el mismo sujeto y están unidos por una conjunción
compound-complex sentence two or more independent clauses and one or more subordinate clauses	**oración compuesta-compleja** dos o más cláusulas independientes y una o más cláusulas subordinadas
concluding sentence a strong ending added to a paragraph that summarizes the major points, refers to the main idea, or adds an insight	**oración conclusiva** un final que se añade a un párrafo y que resume los puntos principales, se refiere a la idea principal o añade una reflexión.
conclusion a strong ending added to a paragraph or composition that summarizes the major points, refers to the main idea, and adds an insight	**conclusión** un final fuerte que se añade a un párrafo o a una composición y que resume los puntos principales, se refiere a la idea principal y añade una reflexión
concrete noun person, place, or thing that can be seen or touched	**sustantivo concreto** una persona, un lugar o una cosa que puede verse o tocarse
conflict struggle between opposing forces around which the action of a work of literature revolves	**conflicto** lucha entre fuerzas opuestas alrededor de cual gira la acción de una obra literaria

English	Español
conjunction word that joins together sentences, clauses, phrases, or other words	**conjunción** palabra que une dos oraciones, cláusulas, frases u otras palabras
conjunctive adverb an adverb used to connect two clauses	**adverbio conjuntivo** adverbio utilizado para conectar dos cláusulas
connotation meaning that comes from attitudes attached to a word	**connotación** significado que proviene de los valores vinculados a una palabra
consonance repetition of a consonant sound, usually in the middle or at the end of words	**consonancia** repetición de un sonido consonántico, usualmente en el medio o al final de las palabras
context clue clues to a word's meaning provided by the sentence, the surrounding words, or the situation in which the word occurs	**clave del contexto** pistas sobre el significado de una palabra proporcionadas por la oración, las palabras que la rodean o la situación en la que aparece la palabra
contraction word that combines two words into one and uses an apostrophe to replace one or more missing letters	**contracción** palabra que combina dos palabras en una y utiliza un apóstrofo en lugar de la(s) letra(s) faltante(s)
contradiction in a persuasive speech or essay, a logical incompatibility between two propositions made by the author	**contradicción** en un discurso o ensayo persuasivo, incompatibilidad lógica entre dos proposiciones hechas por el autor
controlling idea the main idea or thesis of an essay	**idea dominante** idea principal o tesis de un ensayo
cooperative learning strategy in which a group works together to achieve a common goal or accomplish a single task	**aprendizaje cooperativo** estrategia mediante cual los miembros de un grupo trabajan juntos para alcanzar una meta en común o llevar a cabo una tarea
coordinating conjunction single connecting word used to join words or groups of words	**conjunción coordinante** palabra de conexión usada para unir palabras o grupos de palabras

correlative conjunction pairs of conjunctions used to connect compound subjects, compound verbs, and compound sentences

conjunción correlativa pares de conjunciones usadas para conectar los sujetos compuestos, los verbos compuestos y las oraciones compuestas

count noun a noun that names an object that can be counted (*grains of rice, storms, songs*)

sustantivo contable sustantivo que designa un objeto que se puede contar (granos de arroz, tormentas, canciones)

counter-argument argument offered to address opposing views in a persuasive composition

contraargumento argumento que se ofrece para tratar las opiniones contrarias en una composición persuasiva

creative writing writing style in which the writer creates characters, events, and images within stories, plays, or poems to express feelings, perceptions, and points of view

escritura creativa estilo de escritura en cual el escritor crea los personajes, los sucesos y las imágenes de cuentos, obras de teatro o poemas para expresar sentimientos, percepciones y puntos de vista

critique a detailed analysis and assessment of a work such as a piece of writing

crítica análisis detallado y evaluación de una obra, como un texto escrito

D

dangling modifier phrase that has nothing to describe in a sentence

modificador mal ubicado frase que no describe nada en una oración

dash punctuation mark that indicates a greater separation of words than a comma

raya signo de puntuación que indica una separación mayor entre las palabras que una coma

declarative sentence a statement or expression of an opinion. It ends with a period.

oración enunciativa enunciado o expresión de una opinión. Termina en punto.

definition method of development in which the nature and characteristics of a word, object, concept, or phenomenon are explained

definición método de desarrollo en cual se explican la naturaleza y las características de una palabra, objeto, concepto o fenómeno

GLOSSARY

demonstrative pronoun word that substitutes for a noun and points out a person or thing

pronombre demostrativo palabra que está en lugar de un sustantivo y señala una persona o cosa

denotation literal meaning of a word

denotación significado literal de una palabra

descriptive writing writing that creates a vivid picture of a person, an object, or a scene by stimulating the reader's senses

texto descriptivo texto que crea una imagen vívida de una persona, un objeto o una escena estimulando los sentidos del lector

developmental order information that is organized so that one idea grows out of the preceding idea

orden de desarrollo información que está organizada de tal manera que una idea surge de la precedente

Dewey decimal system system by which nonfiction books are arranged on shelves in numerical order according to ten general subject categories

Sistema decimal de Dewey sistema por cual los libros de no ficción se ubican en los estantes en orden numérico según diez categorías temáticas generales

dialect regional variation of a language distinguished by distinctive pronunciation and some differences in word meanings

dialecto variación regional de un idioma caracterizada por una pronunciación distintiva y algunas diferencias en el significado de las palabras

dialogue conversation between two or more people in a story or play

diálogo conversación entre dos o más personas en un cuento o en una obra de teatro

direct object noun or a pronoun that answers the question *What?* or *Whom?* after an action verb

objeto directo sustantivo o pronombre que responde la pregunta ¿Qué? *(What?)* o ¿Quién? *(Whom?)* después de un verbo de acción

direct quotation passage, sentence, or words stated exactly as the person wrote or said them

cita directa pasaje, oración o palabras enunciadas exactamente como la persona las escribió o las dijo

documentary a work composed of pieces of primary source materials or first-hand accounts such as interviews, diaries, photographs, film clips, etc.

documental obra compuesta por fragmentos de fuentes primarias o relatos de primera mano, como entrevistas, diarios, fotografías, fragmentos de películas, etc.

English	Español
double negative use of two negative words to express an idea when only one is needed	**negación doble** uso de dos palabras negativas para expresar una idea cuando sólo una es necesaria
drafting stage of the writing process in which the writer expresses ideas in sentences, forming a beginning, a middle, and an ending of a composition	**borrador** etapa del proceso de escritura en la cual el escritor expresa sus ideas en oraciones que forman el principio, el medio y el final de una composición

E

English	Español
editing stage of the writing process in which the writer polishes his or her work by correcting errors in grammar, usage, mechanics, and spelling	**edición** etapa del proceso de escritura en la cual el escritor mejora su trabajo y corrige los errores de gramática, uso del lenguaje, aspectos prácticos y ortografía
elaboration addition of explanatory or descriptive information to a piece of writing, such as supporting details, examples, facts, and descriptions	**explicación** agregar información explicativa o descriptiva a un texto, como detalles de apoyo, ejemplos, hechos y descripciones
electronic publishing various ways to present information through the use of technology. It includes desktop publishing (creating printed documents on a computer), audio and video recordings, and online publishing (creating a Web site).	**publicación electrónica o Ciberedición** varias maneras de presentar la información por el uso de la tecnología. Incluye la autoedición (crear documentos impresos en una computadora), las grabaciones de audio y video y la publicación en línea (crear un sitio web).
ellipses punctuation marks (. . .) used to indicate where text has been removed from quoted material or to indicate a pause or interruption in speech	**puntos suspensivos** signos de puntuación (. . .) utilizados para indicar dónde se ha quitado parte del texto de una cita o para indicar una pausa o una interrupción en el discurso
elliptical clause subordinate clause in which words are omitted but understood to be there	**cláusula elíptica** cláusula subordinada en cual se omiten palabras, pero se comprende que están implícitas

e-mail electronic mail that can be sent all over the world from one computer to another

emoticons symbols used by e-mail users to convey emotions

encyclopedia print or online reference that contains general information about a variety of subjects

endnote complete citation of the source of borrowed material at the end of a research report

essay composition of three or more paragraphs that presents and develops one main idea

essential phrase or clause group of words essential to the meaning of a sentence; therefore, not set off with commas

etymology history of a word, from its earliest recorded use to its present use

evidence facts and examples used to support a statement or proposition

exclamatory sentence expression of strong feeling that ends with an exclamation point

expository writing prose that explains or informs with facts and examples or gives directions

correo electrónico mensaje electrónico que puede enviarse a cualquier lugar del mundo desde una computadora a otra

emoticonos símbolos utilizados por los usuarios del correo electrónico para transmitir emociones

enciclopedia obra de referencia, impresa o en línea, que contiene información general sobre varios temas

nota final cita completa de la fuente de la que se tomó información, colocada al final de un informe de investigación

ensayo composición de tres o más párrafos que presenta y desarrolla una idea principal

frase o cláusula esencial grupo de palabras esencial para el significado de una oración; por lo tanto, no está encerrado entre comas

etimología historia de una palabra, desde su uso registrado más antiguo hasta su uso actual

evidencia hechos y ejemplos utilizados para fundamentar un enunciado o proposición

oración exclamativa expresión de sentimiento intenso que termina con signo de exclamación

texto expositivo texto en prosa que explica o informa con hechos y ejemplos o da instrucciones

English	Español
external coherence organization of the major components of a written piece (introduction, body, conclusion) in a logical sequence and flow, progressing from one idea to another while holding true to the central idea of the composition	**coherencia externa** organización de las partes principales de un trabajo escrito (introducción, cuerpo, conclusión) en una secuencia lógica que presenta fluidez y avanza de una idea a otra, pero sustentando la idea central de la composición

F

English	Español
fable story in which animal characters act like people to teach a lesson or moral	**fábula** relato en cual los personajes son animales que actúan como personas para enseñar una lección o una moraleja
fact statement that can be proven	**hecho** enunciado que puede probarse
feedback written or verbal reaction to an idea, a work, a performance, and so on, often used as a basis for improvement	**realimentación** reacción escrita u oral respecto de una idea, obra, representación, etc., que suele utilizarse como base para mejorarla
fiction prose works of literature, such as short stories and novels, which are partly or totally imaginary	**ficción** obras literarias en prosa, como cuentos y novelas, que son parcial o totalmente imaginarias
figurative language language that uses such devices as imagery, metaphor, simile, hyperbole, personification, or analogy to convey a sense beyond the literal meaning of the words	**lenguaje figurado** lenguaje que emplea recursos tales como imágenes, metáforas, símiles, hipérboles, personificación o analogía para transmitir un sentido que va más allá del sentido literal de las palabras
flashback an interruption of the normal chronological order of the plot to narrate events that occurred earlier	**flash-back** interrupción del orden cronológico normal del argumento para narrar sucesos que ocurrieron anteriormente
folktale story that was told aloud long before it was written	**cuento folclórico** relato que se contaba en voz alta mucho antes de que fuera puesto por escrito

English	Español
footnote complete citation of the source of borrowed material at the bottom of a page in a research report	**nota al pie** cita completa de la fuente de la que se tomó información, colocada en la parte inferior de una página de un informe de investigación
foreshadowing the use of hints or clues about what will happen later in the plot	**presagio** uso de pistas o claves sobre lo que sucederá posteriormente en el argumento
formal English conventional rules of grammar, usage, and mechanics	**inglés formal** reglas convencionales de gramática, uso del lenguaje y aspectos prácticos de la escritura
format (page) the way in which page elements, such as margins, heads, subheads, and sidebars, are arranged	**formato (página)** forma en que están organizados los elementos de la página, como los márgenes, encabezados, subtítulos y recuadros
fragment group of words that does not express a complete thought	**fragmento** grupo de palabras que no expresa un pensamiento completo
free verse poetry without meter or a regular, patterned beat	**verso libre** poesía sin metro fijo o patrón rítmico regular
freewriting prewriting technique of writing freely without concern for mistakes made	**escritura libre** técnica de preparación para la escritura que consiste en escribir libremente sin preocuparse por los errores cometidos
friendly letter writing form that may use informal language and includes a heading, greeting (salutation), body, closing, and signature	**carta amistosa** tipo de texto que puede usar un lenguaje informal e incluye membrete, saludo, cuerpo, despedida y firma

G

English	Español
generalization a conclusion based on facts, examples, or instances	**generalización** conclusión basada en hechos, ejemplos o casos
generalizing forming an overall idea that explains something specific	**generalizando** formar una idea general que explica algo específico

GLOSSARY

English	Español
genre (1) a distinctive type or category of literature such as the epic, mystery, or science fiction; (2) a distinctive type or category of text, such as personal narrative, expository essay, or short story	**género** (1) tipo distintivo o categoría literaria, como la épica, las novelas de misterio, o la ciencia ficción; (2) tipo distintivo o categoría de texto, como la narración personal, el ensayo expositivo o el cuento
gerund verb form ending in –*ing* that is used as a noun	**gerundio** forma verbal que termina en –*ing* y puede usarse como sustantivo
gerund phrase a gerund with its modifiers and complements working together as a noun	**frase de gerundio** un gerundio con sus modificadores y complementos, que funcionan juntos como un sustantivo
glittering generality word or phrase that most people associate with virtue and goodness that is used to trick people into feeling positively about a subject	**generalidad entusiasta** palabra o frase que la mayoría de la gente asocia con la virtud y la bondad, y que se utiliza con el fin de engañar a las personas para que tengan una reacción positiva respecto de cierto tema
graphic elements (in poetry) in poetry, use of word position, line length, and overall text layout to express or reflect meaning	**elementos gráficos (en la poesía)** en poesía, el uso de la ubicación de las palabras, la extensión de los versos y la disposición general del texto para expresar o mostrar el significado

H

English	Español
helping verb auxiliary verb that combines with the main verb to make up a verb phrase	**verbo auxiliar** verbo que se emplea junto con el verbo principal para formar una frase verbal
homographs words that are spelled alike but have different meanings and pronunciations	**homógrafos** palabras que se escriben de igual manera, pero tienen significados y pronunciaciones diferentes
homophones words that sound alike but have different meanings and spellings	**homófonos** palabras que suenan de igual manera, pero tienen significados diferentes y se escriben de manera distinta

GLOSSARY

English	Español
hyperbole use of exaggeration or overstatement	**hipérbole** uso de la exageración o amplificación
hyphen punctuation mark used to divide words at the end of a line	**guión** signo ortográfico usado para separar las palabras al final de un renglón

I

English	Español
idiom phrase or expression that has a meaning different from what the words suggest in their usual meanings	**modismo** frase o expresión que tiene un significado diferente de lo que sugieren habitualmente las palabras que la forman
imagery use of concrete details to create a picture or appeal to senses other than sight	**imaginería** uso de detalles concretos para crear una imagen o apelar a los otros sentidos además de la vista
imperative mood verb form used to give a command or to make a request	**modo imperativo** forma verbal usada para dar una orden u hacer un pedido
imperative sentence a request or command that ends with either a period or an exclamation point	**oración imperativa** pedido u orden que termina en punto con signo de exclamación
indefinite pronoun word that substitutes for a noun and refers to unnamed persons or things	**pronombre indefinido** palabra que sustituye a un sustantivo y alude a personas o cosas que no han sido identificadas
independent clause group of words that can stand alone as a sentence because it expresses a complete thought	**cláusula independiente** grupo de palabras que pueden formar por sí solas una oración porque expresan un pensamiento completo
indicative mood verb form used to state a fact or to ask a question	**modo indicativo** forma verbal usada para enunciar un hecho o hacer una pregunta
indirect object noun or a pronoun that answers the question *To or from whom?* or *To or for what?* after an action word	**objeto indirecto** nombre o pronombre que responde la pregunta ¿A quién o para quién? (*To or from whom?*) o ¿A qué o para qué? (*To or for what?*) después de una palabra de acción

English	Español
inference a reasonable conclusion drawn by the reader based on clues in a literary work	**inferencia** conclusión razonable que saca el lector basándose en las pistas de una obra literaria
infinitive verb form that usually begins with *to* and can be used as a noun, adjective, or adverb	**infinitivo** forma verbal que generalmente empieza con *to* y se puede usar como sustantivo, adjetivo o adverbio
informative writing writing that explains with facts and examples, gives directions, or lists steps in a process	**texto informativo** texto que explica algo con hechos y ejemplos, da instrucciones o enumera los pasos de un proceso
inquiring a prewriting technique in which the writer asks questions such as *Who? What? Where? Why?* and *When?*	**indagar** técnica de preparación para la escritura en cual el escritor hace preguntas como ¿Quién? (*Who?*), ¿Qué? (*What?*), ¿Dónde? (*Where?*), ¿Por qué? (*Why?*) y ¿Cuándo? (*When?*)
intensive pronoun word that adds emphasis to a noun or another pronoun in the sentence	**pronombre enfático** en una oración, palabra que añade énfasis a un sustantivo o a otro pronombre
interjection word that expresses strong feeling	**interjección** palabra que expresa un sentimiento intenso
internal coherence in a written piece, organization of ideas and/or sentences in a logical sequence and with a fluid progression	**coherencia interna** en un texto escrito, la organización de las ideas y/o de las oraciones en una secuencia lógica y con un desarrollo fluido
Internet global network of computers that are connected to one another with high speed data lines and telephone lines	**internet** red mundial de computadoras que están conectadas entre sí con líneas de datos y líneas telefónicas de alta velocidad
interrogative pronoun pronoun used to ask a question	**pronombre interrogativo** pronombre utilizado para hacer una pregunta
interrogative sentence a question. It ends with a question mark.	**oración interrogativa** pregunta. Empieza y termina con signos de interrogación en español y termina con signo de interrogación en inglés.

English	Español
intransitive verb action verb that does not pass the action from a doer to a receiver	**verbo intransitivo** verbo de acción que no transfiere la acción del agente a un receptor
introduction one or more paragraphs in a composition or an essay that introduce a subject, state or imply a purpose, present a main idea, and catch the reader's attention	**introducción** en un ensayo, uno o más párrafos que presentan un tema, enuncian o sugieren un propósito, presentan una idea principal y capta la atención del lector
inverted order condition when the subject follows the verb or part of the verb phrase	**orden invertido** circunstancia en la que el sujeto sigue al verbo o a una parte de la frase verbal
irony a recognition and heightening of the difference between appearance and reality. *Situational irony* occurs when events turn out differently from what is expected; *dramatic irony* occurs when the audience has important information that a main character lacks.	**ironía** reconocimiento e intensificación de la diferencia entre la apariencia y la realidad. La *ironía situacional* ocurre cuando los sucesos resultan de manera diferente de lo esperado; la *ironía dramática* ocurre cuando el público tiene información importante de la que carece el personaje principal.
irregular verb verb that does not form its past and past participle by adding *–ed* or *–d* to the present tense	**verbo irregular** verbo que no forma el pasado o el participio pasado al agregar *–ed* o *–d* al tiempo presente

J

jargon specialized vocabulary used by a particular group of people	**jerga** vocabulario especializado usado por un grupo específico de personas
journal daily notebook in which a writer records thoughts and feelings	**diario** cuaderno en el que un escritor anota cada día sus pensamientos y sentimientos
juxtaposition two or more things placed side by side, generally in an unexpected combination	**yuxtaposición** dos o más cosas ubicadas una junto a la otra, generalmente en una combinación inesperada

GLOSSARY

English	Español

L

linking verb verb that links the subject with another word that renames or describes the subject

listening the process of comprehending, evaluating, organizing, and remembering information presented orally

literary analysis interpretation of a work of literature supported with appropriate details and quotations from the work

loaded words words carefully chosen to appeal to one's hopes or fears rather than to reason or logic

verbo copulativo verbo que conecta al sujeto con otra palabra que vuelve a nombrar o describe al sujeto

escuchar proceso de comprender, evaluar, organizar y recordar la información presentada oralmente

análisis literario interpretación de una obra literaria fundamentada con detalles apropiados y citas de la obra

palabras tendenciosas palabras escogidas cuidadosamente para apelar a las esperanzas o los temores del destinatario, en lugar de la razón o la lógica

M

memo short for *memorandum*, a concise form of communication used to disseminate decisions, plans, policies and the like; used frequently in business settings

metaphor figure of speech that compares by implying that one thing is another

meter rhythm of a specific beat of stressed and unstressed syllables found in many poems

memo abreviatura de *memorándum*, forma concisa de comunicación usada para difundir decisiones, planes, políticas y cuestiones similares; utilizada frecuentemente en el ambiente de los negocios

metáfora figura retórica que hace una comparación implícita entre dos cosas

metro ritmo con una cadencia específica de sílabas tónicas (acentuadas) y átonas (inacentuadas) que se halla en muchos poemas

misplaced modifier phrase or a clause that is placed too far away from the word it modifies, thus creating an unclear sentence

modifier word that makes the meaning of another word more precise

mood overall atmosphere or feeling created by a work of literature

multimedia the use of more than one medium of expression or communication such as a presentation composed of visual images and audio soundtrack

N

narrative writing writing that tells a real or an imaginary story with a clear beginning, middle, and ending

narrator the person whose voice is telling the story

network a system of interconnected computers

noncount noun a noun that names something that cannot be counted (*health, weather, music*)

nonessential phrase or clause group of words that is not essential to the meaning of a sentence and is therefore set off with commas (also called *nonrestrictive phrase or clause*)

nonfiction prose writing that contains facts about real people and real events

modificador mal colocado frase o cláusula ubicada demasiado lejos de la palabra que modifica, por lo que crea una oración poco clara

modificador palabra que hace más preciso el significado de otra palabra

atmósfera clima o sentimiento general creado por una obra literaria

multimedia uso de más de un medio de expresión o comunicación, como una presentación compuesta por imágenes visuales y una banda sonora de audio

texto narrativo texto que relata una historia real o imaginaria con un principio, un medio y un final

narrador persona cuya voz cuenta la historia

red sistema de computadoras interconectadas

sustantivo no contable sustantivo que designa algo que no se puede contar (la salud, el clima, la música)

frase o cláusula incidental grupo de palabras que no es esencial para el significado de una oración y, por lo tanto, está encerrada entre comas (también llamada *frase o cláusula no restrictiva*)

no ficción texto en prosa que contiene hechos sobre gente real y sucesos reales

GLOSSARY

English	Español
nonstandard English less formal language used by people of varying regions and dialects; not appropriate for use in writing	**inglés no estándar** lenguaje menos formal utilizado por personas de diversas regiones y dialectos; inapropiado para usarlo en la escritura
noun a word that names a person, place, thing, or idea. A common noun gives a general name. A proper noun names a specific person, place, or thing and always begins with a capital letter. Concrete nouns can be seen or touched; abstract nouns cannot.	**sustantivo** palabra que designa una persona, un lugar, una cosa o una idea. Un sustantivo común expresa un nombre general. Un sustantivo propio nombra una persona, un lugar o una cosa específica y siempre comienza con mayúscula. Los sustantivos concretos designan cosas que pueden verse o tocarse, mientras que los sustantivos abstractos no lo hacen.
noun clause a subordinate clause used like a noun	**cláusula nominal** cláusula subordinada usada como sustantivo
novel a long work of narrative fiction	**novela** obra extensa de ficción narrativa
nuance a small or subtle distinction in meaning	**matiz** diferencia de significado pequeña o sutil

O

English	Español
object word that answers the question *What?* or *Whom?*	**objeto** palabra que responde la pregunta ¿Qué? *(What?)* o ¿Quién? *(Whom?)*
object pronoun type of pronoun used for direct objects, indirect objects, and objects of prepositions	**pronombre objeto** tipo de pronombre utilizado para los objetos directos, objetos indirectos y objetos de preposiciones
objective not based on an individual's opinions or judgments	**objetivo** no basado en las opiniones o juicios de un individuo
objective complement a noun or an adjective that renames or describes the direct object	**complemento objetivo** sustantivo o adjetivo que vuelve a nombrar o describe al objeto directo

English	Español
observing prewriting technique that helps a writer use the powers of observation to gather details	**observación** técnica de preparación para la escritura que ayuda a un escritor a usar su capacidad de observación para reunir detalles
occasion motivation for composing; the factor that prompts communication	**ocasión** motivación para componer; factor que da lugar a la comunicación
online connected to the Internet via a line modem connection	**en línea** conectado a la Internet a través de una conexión de módem
onomatopoeia the use of words whose sounds suggest their meaning	**onomatopeya** uso de palabras cuyos sonidos sugieren su significado
opinion a judgment or belief that cannot be absolutely proven	**opinión** juicio o creencia que no se puede probar completamente
oral interpretation performance or expressive reading of a literary work	**interpretación oral** representación o lectura expresiva de una obra literaria
order of importance or size way of organizing information by arranging details in the order of least to most (or most to least) pertinent	**orden de importancia o tamaño** manera de organizar la información poniendo los detalles en orden de menor a mayor (o de mayor a menor) pertinencia
outline information about a subject organized into main topics and subtopics	**esquema** información sobre un tema organizada en temas principales y subtemas

P

English	Español
paragraph group of related sentences that present and develop one main idea	**párrafo** grupo de oraciones relacionadas que presentan y desarrollan una idea principal
parallelism repetition of two or more similar words, phrases, or clauses creating emphasis in a piece of writing and easing readability	**paralelismo** repetición de dos o más palabras, frases o cláusulas similares que crea énfasis en un texto escrito y facilita su lectura

paraphrase restatement of an original work in one's own words

parentheses punctuation marks ( ) used to enclose supplementary information not essential to the meaning of the sentence; always used in pairs

parenthetical citation source title and page number given in parentheses within a sentence to credit the source of the information

parody humorous imitation of a serious work

participial phrase participle that works together with its modifier and complement as an adjective

participle verb form that is used as an adjective

parts of speech eight categories into which all words can be placed: noun, pronoun, verb, adjective, adverb, preposition, conjunction, and interjection

passive voice the voice a verb is in when it expresses that the action of the verb is being performed upon the subject

peer conference a meeting with one's peers, such as other students, to share ideas and offer suggestions for revision

personal narrative narrative that tells a real or imaginary story from the writer's point of view

paráfrasis reescritura de una obra original con las propias palabras

paréntesis signos de puntuación ( ) utilizados para encerrar información adicional que no es esencial para el significado de la oración; se usan siempre en parejas

cita parentética título de la fuente y número de página escritos entre paréntesis dentro de una oración para dar a conocer la fuente de la información

parodia imitación humorística de una obra seria

frase participial participio que funciona junto con su modificador y su complemento como adjetivo

participio forma verbal que se utiliza como adjetivo

categorías gramaticales ocho categorías en las que pueden clasificarse todas las palabras: sustantivo, pronombre, verbo, adjetivo, adverbio, preposición, conjunción e interjección

voz pasiva voz en que está el verbo cuando expresa que la acción del verbo se realiza sobre el sujeto

conferencia de pares reunión con los propios pares, como otros estudiantes, para compartir ideas y ofrecer sugerencias de corrección

narración personal narración que cuenta una historia real o imaginaria desde el punto de vista del escritor

personal pronoun type of pronoun that renames a particular person or group of people. Pronouns can be categorized into one of three groups, dependent on the speaker's position: first person (*I*), second person (*you*), and third person (*she/he/it*).

pronombre personal tipo de pronombre que vuelve a nombrar a una persona o grupo de personas en particular. Los pronombres se pueden clasificar en tres grupos, según la posición del hablante: primera persona (*I* [yo]), segunda persona (*you* [tú]) y tercera persona (*she/he/it* [ella/él]).

personal writing writing that tells a real or imaginary story from the writer's point of view

narración personal texto que cuenta una historia real o imaginaria desde el punto de vista del escritor

personification giving human qualities to non-human subjects

personificación atribuir cualidades humanas a sujetos no humanos

persuasive writing writing that expresses an opinion and uses facts, examples, and reasons in order to convince the reader of the writer's viewpoint

texto persuasivo texto que expresa una opinión y emplea hechos, ejemplos y razones con el fin de convencer al lector del punto de vista del escritor

phrase group of related words that functions as a single part of speech and does not have a subject and a verb

frase grupo de palabras relacionadas que funciona como una sola categoría gramatical y no tiene un sujeto y un verbo

phrase fragment phrase written as if it were a complete sentence

fragmento de frase frase escrita como si fuera una oración completa

plagiarism act of using another person's words, pictures, or ideas without giving proper credit

plagio acción de usar las palabras, fotografías o ideas de otra persona sin reconocer su procedencia apropiadamente

play a piece of writing to be performed on a stage by actors

obra de teatro texto escrito para que los actores lo representen en un escenario

plot sequence of events leading to the outcome or point of the story; contains a climax or high point, a resolution, and an outcome or ending

argumento secuencia de sucesos que lleva a la resolución del relato o propósito del mismo; contiene un clímax o momento culminante y una resolución o final

plural form of a noun used to indicate two or more

poem highly structured composition that expresses powerful feeling with condensed, vivid language, figures of speech, and often the use of meter and rhyme

poetry form of writing that uses rhythm, rhyme, and vivid imagery to express feelings and ideas

point of view vantage point from which a writer tells a story or describes a subject

portfolio collection of work representing various types of writing and the progress made on them

positive degree adjective or adverb used when no comparison is being made

possessive pronoun a pronoun used to show ownership or possession

predicate part of a sentence that tells what a subject is or does

predicate adjective adjective that follows a linking verb and modifies, or describes, the subject

predicate nominative noun or a pronoun that follows a linking verb and identifies, renames, or explains the subject

plural forma del sustantivo utilizada para indicar dos o más personas o cosas

poema composición muy estructurada que expresa un sentimiento intenso mediante un lenguaje condensado y vívido, figuras retóricas y, frecuentemente, el uso de metro y rima

poesía tipo de texto que utiliza ritmo, rima e imágenes vívidas para expresar sentimientos e ideas

punto de vista posición de ventaja desde cual un escritor narra una historia o describe un tema

carpeta de trabajos colección de obras que representan varios tipos de textos y el progreso realizado en ellos

grado positivo adjetivo o adverbio usado cuando no se realiza una comparación

pronombre posesivo pronombre utilizado para indicar propiedad o posesión

predicado parte de la oración que indica qué es o qué hace el sujeto

adjetivo predicativo adjetivo que sigue a un verbo copulativo y modifica, o describe, al sujeto

predicado nominal sustantivo o pronombre que sigue a un verbo copulativo e identifica, vuelve a nombrar o explica al sujeto

GLOSSARY

English

prefix one or more syllables placed in front of a base word to form a new word

preposition word that shows the relationship between a noun or a pronoun and another word in the sentence

prepositional phrase a group of words made up of a preposition, its object, and any words that describe the object (modifiers)

prewriting invention stage of the writing process in which the writer plans for drafting based on the subject, occasion, audience, and purpose for writing

principal parts of a verb the present, the past, and the past participle. The principal parts help form the tenses of verbs.

progressive verb form verbs used to express continuing or ongoing action. Each of the six verb tenses has a progressive form.

pronoun word that takes the place of one or more nouns. Three types of pronouns are *personal, reflexive,* and *intensive.*

proofreading carefully rereading and making corrections in grammar, usage, spelling, and mechanics in a piece of writing

Español

prefijo una o más sílabas colocadas adelante de la raíz de una palabra para formar una palabra nueva

preposición palabra que muestra la relación entre un sustantivo o un pronombre y otra palabra de la oración

frase preposicional grupo de palabras formado por una preposición, su objeto y todas las palabras que describan al objeto (modificadores)

preescritura etapa de invención del proceso de escritura en la cual el escritor planea un borrador basándose en el tema, la ocasión, el público y el propósito para escribir

partes principales de un verbo presente, pasado y participio pasado. Las partes principales ayudan a formar los tiempos verbales.

forma verbal progresiva verbos usados para expresar una acción que continúa o está en curso. Cada uno de los seis tiempos verbales tiene una forma progresiva.

pronombre palabra que está en lugar de uno o más sustantivos. Entre los tipos de pronombres están los pronombres personales, reflexivos y enfáticos.

corregir relectura atenta de un texto y corrección de la gramática, del uso del lenguaje, de la ortografía y de los aspectos prácticos de la escritura

proofreading symbols a kind of shorthand that writers use to correct their mistakes while editing

símbolos de corrección de textos tipo de taquigrafía que usan los escritores para corregir sus errores cuando revisan un texto

propaganda effort to persuade by distorting and misrepresenting information or by disguising opinions as facts

propaganda intento de persuadir distorsionando y tergiversando la información o disfrazando de hechos las opiniones

proper adjective adjective formed from a proper noun

adjetivo propio adjetivo formado a partir de un sustantivo propio

protagonist the principal character in a story

protagonista personaje principal de un relato

publishing stage of the writing process in which the writer may choose to share the work with an audience

publicar etapa del proceso de escritura en la cual el escritor puede escoger dar a conocer su trabajo a un público

purpose reason for writing or speaking on a given subject

propósito razón para escribir o hablar sobre un tema dado

Q

quatrain four-line stanza in a poem

cuarteta en un poema, estrofa de cuatro versos

R

reader-friendly formatting page elements such as fonts, bullet points, line length, and heads adding to the ease of reading

formato de fácil lectura elementos que se agregan a la página escrita, como tipo de letra, viñetas, extensión de los renglones y encabezados para facilitar la lectura

Readers' Guide to Periodical Literature a print or online index of magazine and journal articles

Guía para el lector de publicaciones periódicas índice impreso o en línea de artículos de diarios y revistas

reflecting act of thinking quietly and calmly about an experience

reflexionar acción de pensar en silencio y con calma sobre una experiencia

English

reflexive pronoun pronoun formed by adding *–self* or *–selves* to a personal pronoun; it is used to refer to or emphasize a noun or pronoun

regular verb verb that forms its past and past participle by adding *–ed* or *–d* to the present

relative pronoun pronoun that begins most adjectival clauses and relates the adjectival clause to the noun or pronoun it describes

repetition repeat of a word or phrase for poetic effect

report a composition of three or more paragraphs that uses specific information from books, magazines, and other sources

research paper a composition of three or more paragraphs that uses information drawn from books, periodicals, media sources, and interviews with experts

resolution the point at which the chief conflict or complication of a story is worked out

restrictive phrase or clause group of words essential to the meaning of a sentence; therefore, not set off with commas (also called *essential phrase or clause*)

résumé summary of a person's work experience, education, and interests

Español

pronombre reflexivo pronombre que se forma al agregar *–self* o *–selves* al pronombre personal; se usa para aludir a un sustantivo o a un pronombre o enfatizarlos

verbo regular verbo que forma el pasado o participio pasado al agregar *–ed* o *–d* al tiempo presente

pronombre relativo pronombre con el que comienza la mayoría de las cláusulas adjetivas y que relaciona la cláusula adjetiva con el sustantivo o pronombre que describe

repetición repetir una palabra o frase para lograr un efecto poético

informe composición de tres o más párrafos que emplea información específica extraída de libros, revistas y otras fuentes

artículo de investigación composición de tres o más párrafos que utiliza información obtenida en libros, publicaciones periódicas, medios de comunicación y entrevistas con expertos en el tema

resolución momento en el que se resuelve el conflicto principal o complicación de un cuento

frase o cláusula restrictiva grupo de palabras esencial para el significado de una oración; por lo tanto, no está encerrado entre comas (también llamada *frase o cláusula esencial*)

currículum vítae resumen de la experiencia laboral, educación e intereses de una persona

revising stage of the writing process in which the writer rethinks what is written and reworks it to increase its clarity, smoothness, and power

rhetorical device (1) a technique used to influence or persuade an audience; (2) a writing technique, often employing metaphor and analogy, designed to enhance the writer's message

rhyme scheme regular pattern of rhyming in a poem

rhythm sense of flow produced by the rise and fall of accented and unaccented syllables

root the part of a word that carries its basic meaning

run-on sentence two or more sentences that are written as one sentence and are separated by a comma or have no mark of punctuation at all

S

sarcasm an expression of contempt, often including irony

scheme a figure of speech, such as parallelism, that changes the normal arrangement of words

script the written form of a dramatic performance, written by a playwright

revisar etapa del proceso de escritura en la cual el escritor vuelve a pensar en lo que ha escrito y lo adapta para mejorar su claridad, fluidez y contundencia

recurso retórico (1) técnica usada para influir o persuadir al público; (2) técnica de escritura, que suele emplear metáforas y analogías, destinada a realzar el mensaje del escritor

esquema de rima en un poema, patrón regular de rima

ritmo sensación de fluidez producida por el ascenso y descenso de sílabas tónicas (acentuadas) y átonas (inacentuadas)

raíz parte de una palabra que lleva en sí lo esencial del significado de la palabra

oración sin final dos o más oraciones escritas como una sola oración y separadas por una coma o escritas sin ningún signo de puntación

sarcasmo expresión de desprecio que suele incluir ironía

esquema figura retórica, como el paralelismo, que modifica la disposición normal de las palabras

guión forma escrita de un espectáculo dramático, realizada por un dramaturgo

English

sensory details descriptive details that appeal to one of the five senses: seeing, hearing, touching, tasting, and smelling

sentence group of words that expresses a complete thought

sentence base a subject, a verb, and a complement

sentence combining method of combining short sentences into longer, more fluent sentences by using phrases and clauses

sentence fragment group of words that does not express a complete thought

sequential order the order in which details are arranged according to when they take place or when they are done

setting the place and time of a story

short story well-developed story about characters facing a conflict or problem

simile figure of speech comparing two objects using the words *like* or *as*

simple predicate the main word or phrase in the complete predicate

simple sentence a sentence that has one subject and one verb

simple subject the main word in a complete subject

Español

detalles sensoriales detalles descriptivos que apelan a uno de los cinco sentidos: vista, oído, tacto, gusto y olfato

oración grupo de palabras que expresa un pensamiento completo

base de la oración un sujeto, un verbo y un complemento

combinación de oraciones método de combinar oraciones breves para formar oraciones más largas y fluidas mediante el uso de frases y cláusulas

fragmento de oración grupo de palabras que no expresa un pensamiento completo

orden secuencial orden en que están organizados los detalles de acuerdo con el momento en que tienen lugar o cuándo se realizan

ambiente lugar y tiempo de un relato

relato corto relato bien desarrollado sobre personajes que se enfrentan a un conflicto o problema

símil figura retórica que compara dos objetos usando la palabra como (*like* or *as*)

predicado simple la palabra o la frase principal en el predicado completo

oración simple oración que tiene un sujeto y un verbo

sujeto simple la palabra principal en un sujeto completo

slang nonstandard English expressions that are developed and used by particular groups

argot expresiones propias del inglés no estándar desarrolladas y usadas por grupos específicos

sonnet a lyric poem of fourteen lines, usually in iambic pentameter, with rhymes arranged according to certain definite patterns

soneto poema lírico de catorce versos, usualmente en pentámetro yámbico, con rimas dispuestas según ciertos patrones definidos

sound devices ways to use sounds in poetry to achieve certain effects

recursos sonoros en poesía, formas de usar los sonidos para lograr ciertos efectos

spatial order the order in which details are arranged according to their physical location

orden espacial orden en el cual los detalles se organizan de acuerdo con su ubicación física

speaker tag in dialogue, text that indicates who is speaking; frequently includes a brief description of the manner of speaking

identificador del interlocutor en un diálogo, el texto que indica quién habla; suele incluir una breve descripción de la manera de hablar

speech an oral composition presented by a speaker to an audience

discurso composición oral presentada por un orador ante un público

standard English proper form of the language that follows a set pattern of rules and conventions

Inglés estándar forma correcta del lenguaje que sigue un patrón establecido de reglas y convenciones

stanza group of lines in a poem that the poet decides to set together

estrofa en un poema, grupo de versos que el poeta decide colocar juntos

stereotype simplified concept of the members of a group based on limited experience with the group

estereotipo concepto simplificado de los miembros de un grupo que se basa en una experiencia limitada con el grupo

story within a story a story that is told during the telling of another story

relato dentro de un relato relato que se cuenta durante la narración de otro relato

style visual or verbal expression that is distinctive to an artist or writer

estilo expresión visual o verbal que es propia de un artista o escritor

subject (composition) topic of a composition or essay

tema idea principal de una composición o ensayo

GLOSSARY

English

subject (grammar) word or group of words that names the person, place, thing, or idea that the sentence is about

subject complement renames or describes the subject and follows a linking verb. The two kinds are predicate nominatives and predicate adjectives.

subjunctive mood words such as *if, as if,* or *as though* that are used to express a condition contrary to fact or to express a wish

subordinate clause group of words that cannot stand alone as a sentence because it does not express a complete thought

subordinating conjunction single connecting word used in a sentence to introduce a dependent clause which is an idea of less importance than the main idea

subplot a secondary plot line that reinforces the main plot line

subtle meaning refined, intricate, or deep meaning, sometimes not noticed during the first encounter with a work of art

suffix one or more syllables placed after a base word to change its part of speech and possibly its meaning

summary information written in a condensed, concise form, touching only on the main ideas

Español

sujeto palabra o grupo de palabras que nombran la persona, el lugar, la cosa o la idea de la que trata la oración

complemento predicativo subjetivo vuelve a nombrar o describe al sujeto y está a continuación de un verbo copulativo. Los dos tipos son los predicados nominales y los adjetivos predicativos.

modo subjuntivo palabras como *if* (si), *as if* (como si) o *as though* (como si) que se usan para expresar la subjetividad o un deseo

cláusula subordinada grupo de palabras que no puede funcionar por sí solo como una oración porque no expresa un pensamiento completo

conjunción subordinante palabra de conexión usada en una oración para introducir una cláusula dependiente que expresa una idea de menor importancia que la idea principal

subargumento argumento secundario que refuerza la línea argumental principal

significado sutil significado delicado, intrincado o profundo que a veces no se nota durante el primer encuentro con una obra de arte

sufijo una o más sílabas colocadas después de la raíz de una palabra para modificar su categoría gramatical y, posiblemente, su significado

resumen información escrita en forma condensada y concisa, que incluye sólo las ideas principales

English

superlative degree modification of an adjective or adverb used when more than two people, things, or actions are compared

supporting sentence sentence that explains or proves the topic sentence with specific details, facts, examples, or reasons

suspense in drama, fiction, and nonfiction, a build-up of uncertainty, anxiety, and tension about the outcome of the story or scene

symbol an object, an event, or a character that stands for a universal idea or quality

synonym word that has nearly the same meaning as another word

synthesizing process by which information from various sources is merged into one whole

T

tense the form a verb takes to show time. The six tenses are the *present, past, future, present perfect, past perfect,* and *future perfect.*

testimonial persuasive strategy in which a famous person encourages the purchase of a certain product

theme underlying idea, message, or meaning of a work of literature

Español

grado superlativo forma de un adjetivo o adverbio que se usa cuando se comparan más de dos personas, cosas o acciones

oración de apoyo oración que explica o prueba la oración principal con detalles específicos, hechos, ejemplos o razones

suspenso en las obras de teatro, de ficción y de no ficción, acumulación de incertidumbre, ansiedad y tensión acerca de la resolución de la historia o escena

símbolo objeto, suceso o personaje que representa una idea o cualidad universal

sinónimo palabra que significa casi lo mismo que otra palabra

sintetizar proceso por cual se integra en un todo la información proveniente de varias fuentes

tiempo verbal forma que toma un verbo para expresar el tiempo en que ocurre la acción. Los seis tiempos verbales son: presente, pasado, futuro, presente perfecto, pretérito perfecto y futuro perfecto

testimonial estrategia persuasiva en cual una persona famosa alienta a comprar un cierto producto

tema idea, mensaje o significado subyacente de una obra literaria

English	Español
thesaurus online or print reference that gives synonyms for words	**tesauro** (Diccionario de sinónimos) material de referencia en línea o impreso que ofrece alternativas para las palabras
thesis statement statement of the main idea that makes the writing purpose clear	**enunciado de tesis** enunciado de la idea principal que pone en claro el propósito para escribir
tired word a word that has been so overused that it has been drained of meaning	**palabra gastada** palabra que se ha usado tanto que se ha vaciado de significado
tone writer's attitude toward the subject and audience of a composition (may also be referred to as the writer's *voice*)	**tono** actitud del escritor hacia el tema y destinatario de una composición (también puede denominarse voz del escritor)
topic sentence a sentence that states the main idea of the paragraph	**oración principal** oración que enuncia la idea principal del párrafo
transitions words and phrases that show how ideas are related	**elementos de transición** palabras y frases que muestran las ideas cómo están relacionadas
transitive verb an action verb that passes the action from a doer to a receiver	**verbo transitivo** verbo de acción que transfiere la acción de un agente a un destinatario
trope in literature, a common or overused theme, motif, figure of speech, plot device, etc.	**tropo** en literatura, un tema, motivo, figura retórica, recurso argumental, etc. muy común o muy usado

U

English	Español
understatement an expression that contains less emotion than would be expected	**minimización** expresión que contiene menos emoción que la esperada
understood subject a subject of a sentence that is not stated	**sujeto tácito** sujeto de una oración que no está explícito
unity combination or ordering of parts in a composition so that all the sentences or paragraphs work together as a whole to support one main idea	**unidad** combinación u ordenamiento de las partes de una composición de tal manera que todas las oraciones o párrafos funcionen juntos como un todo para fundamentar una idea principal

English	Español
V	
verb word used to express an action or state of being	**verbo** palabra usada para expresar una acción o un estado del ser
verb phrase main verb plus one or more helping verbs	**frase verbal** verbo principal más uno o más verbos auxiliares
verbal verb form that acts like another part of speech, such as an adjective or noun	**verbal** forma del verbo que funciona como otra categoría gramatical, tal como un adjetivo o un sustantivo
voice the particular sound and rhythm of the language the writer uses (closely related to *tone*)	**voz** sonido y ritmo particular del lenguaje que usa un escritor (estrechamente vinculado al tono)

W

English	Español
warrant in a persuasive speech or essay, connection made between a claim and the examples used to support the claim	**justificación** en un discurso o ensayo persuasivo, conexión que se hace entre una afirmación y los ejemplos usados para fundamentarla
wordiness use of words and expressions that add nothing to the meaning of a sentence	**palabrería** uso de palabras y expresiones que no añaden nada al significado de una oración
working thesis statement that expresses the possible main idea of a composition or research report	**hipótesis de trabajo** enunciado que expresa la posible idea principal de una composición o de un informe de investigación
works-cited page alphabetical listing of sources cited in a research paper	**página de obras citadas** lista alfabética de las fuentes citadas en un artículo de investigación
World Wide Web network of computers within the Internet capable of delivering multimedia content and text over communication lines into personal computers all over the globe	**red mundial de comunicación** red de computadoras dentro de la Internet capaz de transmitir contenido multimedia y textos, a través de líneas de comunicación, a las computadoras personales de todas partes del mundo

GLOSSARY

writing process recursive stages that a writer proceeds through in his or her own way when developing ideas and discovering the best way to express them

proceso de escritura etapas recurrentes que un escritor sigue a su manera cuando desarrolla ideas y descubre la mejor manera de expresarlas

Index

Note: Italic locators (page numbers) indicate skill sets

Note: Italic locators (page numbers) indicate skill sets

INDEX

Note: Italic locators (page numbers) indicate skill sets

INDEX

C

Call number, 343

Can, may, 800

Capitalization, 816-839, 953, 965-966, 972
    exercises, *814-815, 818, 820-821, 823-824, 826-828, 830-837*

Captions, 479

Case forms, of pronouns, 716-728, 960-961
    nominative, 716-721, 960
    objective, 716, 722-725, 961
    possessive, 716, 726-728, 961

Catch, principal parts, 686

Category, 220

Cause-and-effect reasoning, 392

Cause-and-effect text, 250-251

Characterization
    developing characters, 173, 178-180, 185, 188, 196-197
    imaging, 180
    inference chart, 302
    model, 178-179
    prewriting, 177
    sharpening, 188

Chat, Internet, 490

Chicago Manual of Style, The, 30, 378-379
    style guidelines, 379, 381

Choose, principal parts, 687

Chronological order, 84, 126, 221, 308

Citations
    parenthetical, 373, 377-378
    works-cited page, 379-381

Claim, 228-230, 260, 263, 268, 269

Clarity, 24, 109, 134, 232, 277

Classics, 298

Classifying, 20, 220, 365-366

Clause, 640-663. *See also* Independent clause; Subordinate clause.
    adjectival, 647-650
    adverbial, 370, 644-646, 951, 957
    defined, 642, 957
    diagramed, 657-658
    elliptical, 733-735, 961
    essential (restrictive), 649, 862-863, 957, 967

    fragment, 670-671, 959
    independent (main), 642, 851, 904, 957-958
    misplaced modifier, 651, 957
    nonessential (nonrestrictive), 650, 862, 957, 967
    noun, 651-653, 957
    punctuation with, 645, 654, 851, 904-906, 967
    with relative pronoun, 647-650
    and sentence structure, 654-656, 660
        complex, 655-656
        compound, 654, 656
        compound-complex, 655-656
        simple, 654, 656
    in a series, 848
    subordinate (dependent), 643-653, 659, 951, 957
    with subordinating conjunction, 645
    with *who* and *whom*, 730-733
    wordy, 65-66

Cliché, 52

Close reading, 296

Climax, as literary element, 172

Closing, in a letter, 441, 443, 816, 854, 967

Clustering, 18-19, 179, 196, 202, 217, 265

Coherence, 84-88, 109, 134, 230
    checking for, 134, 230, 232, 277
    chronological order, 84
    defined, 84, 109
    order of importance, 85
    sequential order, 86
    spatial order, 85
    strategies, 84, 230
    transitions, 86

Collaboration, 13, 17, 27, 162, 424

Collective noun, 504-505, 764-765, 952, 963

Colloquialism, defined, 44

Colon, 402, 908-909, 970
    exercises, *909*

Combining sentences
    by coordinating, 58
    exercises, *56, 58-59, 61, 133, 566, 587*
    with phrases, 55-56

    by subordinating, 59

Come, principal parts, 689

Comma splice, 672

Commas
    adjective before a noun, 850
    with adverbial clauses, 645
    with adverbial phrases, 613
    with appositives and appositive phrases, 617, 860-861, 967
    commonly used
        dates and addresses, 854, 967
        letters, 854, 967
    with compound sentences, 654-655, 851-852, 904, 967
    contrasting expressions, 859, 967
    defined, 848
    direct address, 857-858, 967
    with direct quotations, 879
    exercises, *840, 849-853, 855-856, 858-859, 861, 863-867, 879, 905, 907*
    after introductory structures, 852-853, 967
    with items in a series, 848-849, 967
    with nonrestrictive clauses, 650, 862-863, 967
    parenthetical expressions, 858-859, 967
    with participial phrases, 622, 967
    replaced with semicolon, 906-907
    in run-on sentences, 672
    splice, 672
    with two adjectives, 540, 967

Common noun, defined, 503, 952

Comparative degree, 776-785

Compare-and-contrast text
    defined, 244
    model, 244-246
    outline, 247
    patterns of organization
        AABB, 245, 248
        ABAB, 246, 248
    QuickGuide for writing, 249
    Venn diagram, 244

Comparison
    of adjectives and adverbs
        comparative degree, 776-785, 963-964

Note: Italic locators (page numbers) indicate skill sets

Note: Italic locators (page numbers) indicate skill sets

Note: Italic locators (page numbers) indicate skill sets

Note: Italic locators (page numbers) indicate skill sets

E

INDEX

Note: Italic locators (page numbers) indicate skill sets

Information (*continued*)
evaluating, 335-336
Information sources
almanacs, 350, 355
atlases, 350, 355
audiovisual, 358
biographical references, 343-344, 350, 353-354
CD-ROMs, 358
database, 342, 346, 350-354, 356-358
dictionary, 356, 429-433
encyclopedia, 342, 350, 352-353, 358
evaluating, 335-336
government documents and historical records, 357
handbooks, 30, 377-381
Internet and media center, 358-361
language references, 42-45
library, 342-349
library catalog, 14, 344-348
literary sources, 354
magazines, 350-352
microforms (microfilm and microfiche), 351-352
newspapers, 342, 350-352
nonprint resources, 350-361
periodicals, 350-352
primary sources, 332-333
Readers' Guide to Periodical Literature, 352
reference books, 343, 350
research report, 386-387
specialized, 356
thesaurus, 356, 437
vertical file, 357
World Wide Web and online services, 358-361
yearbooks, 350
Informative messages
organizing, 460
preparing, 458-461
presenting, 462
Informative presentations
evaluating presentations of peers, public figures, and media, 462-464

Informative writing, 210, 214-237. *See also* Literary analysis; Research report.
analyzing, 225
audience, 213-215
body, 228-230
capturing attention, 225-226
cause-and-effect writing, 250-251
checklist, 232
claims, 228-230
clarity, 232
coherence, 230, 232
compare-and-contrast texts, 244-249
conclusion, 231
defined, 210
definition texts, 252-253
deleting, 233
details, 217-222, 227-228, 231, 233
discovering and choosing a subject, 214
drafting, 224-231
editing, 235
elaborating, 233
evaluating, 219
exercises, *238-239*
exploring and refining the subject, 217-219
facts and examples, 217, 233
feature story, 211-212
5W-How? questions, 19
gathering and organizing details, 217
getting the subject right, 214-216
graphic organizer, 241, 243, 248, 251, 253
grouping information into categories, 220
how-it-works texts, 242-243
how-to or procedural, texts, 240-241
human interest, 211-212
introduction, 224-227
limiting and focusing a subject, 215-216
logical development, 228-229
logical order, 221

model, 217, 220, 222, 226, 231, 234, 240, 242, 244-247, 250, 252
news story, 211-212
organizing your essay, 220-223
outlining, 222, 247
paragraph and essay structure, 221-222, 233
presentations, 213, 237
prewriting, 214-223
publishing, 213, 237
qualities of, 232
QuickGuide, 241, 243, 249, 251, 253
rearranging, 233
relevance, 219
revising, 232-234
rubric, 236
semicolons, 223
strategies, 214, 216, 230-231, 233
steps in the process, 217-218
substituting, 233
supporting points, 228-229
thesis statement, 217-218, 224-225
title, 231
topic sentence, 222, 224
transitions, 228, 230
types of order, 221-222
unity, 232
uses, 213
valid inferences, 229-230
Venn diagrams, 244
verb tense, 235
warrants, 229
workshops, 240-253
A Writer's Guide, 417-421
Inquiring, 19, 121, 175, 196, 202
Insert editing, of video, 485
Inside address, business letter, 443-444
Instructions, writing, 449
Intensive pronoun, 509, 952
Interest inventory, 13
Interfaces, on Web site, 486, 489-490
Interjection
common, 568
defined, 502, 568, 954

Note: Italic locators (page numbers) indicate skill sets

INDEX

Note: Italic locators (page numbers) indicate skill sets

Note: Italic locators (page numbers) indicate skill sets

INDEX

Note: Italic locators (page numbers) indicate skill sets

Mood, of a verb (*continued*)
indicative, 706, 960
subjunctive, 707-708, 960
Multimedia, 164, 386-387, 473-487
Multiple-choice questions, in tests,
411-412

N

Narrative writing, 90-91, 116-139
audience, 124
body, 130
conclusion, 90, 131
defined, 116
drafting, 128-132
editing, 135-136
e-mail, 209
evaluating, 134, 136
exercises, *91, 122, 124-127, 129,
131-139, 811*
introduction, 128-129
model, 90, 117-122, 129-131
paragraph, 90
prewriting, 121-127
prompt, 414-415
publishing, 137
purpose, 5-6, 124
revising, 133-134
structure, 90
subject, 121-124
supporting sentences, 90, 130
tone, 128-129
topic sentence, 90, 130
Narrator, 121-122, 173-174, 177, 181
Natural order of sentences, 588-590,
730, 762, 955
Negative words, 789
Net, defined, 491
Netiquette, 491, 496-497
Network, on Internet, 488-492
Newsgroups, 496-497
Newspaper
online, 351-352
punctuation of titles, 831-832,
873
as research tool, 332-333, 342,
351-352
and word choice, 54
Nine Tools for Powerful Writing,
950-951

Nominative case, 716-721,
729-731, 960. *See also* Predicate
nominative; Pronoun; Subject of
a sentence.
exercises, *719-721*
Nonessential clause or phrase,
617-618, 622, 649-650, 957, 967
Nonfiction
arrangement of in library, 343
defined, 343
Nonrestrictive clause or phrase. *See*
Nonessential clause or phrase.
Nonverbal communication, 422,
461-463, 467
strategies, 461-462
Note cards, 304-307, 337-339, 460
Note-taking
graphic organizer, 97, 241, 243,
269, 271, 397-398
informal outline, 397-398
model, 338
note cards, 304-307, 337-339, 460
in presentations, 467-468
quotations, 377
for research report, 337-339
for speeches, 460
strategies, 399
as study skill, 397-399
summary, 397-398
Noun, 502-506
abstract, 502-503, 952
collective, 504-505, 764-765, 952
common, 503-504, 952
compound, 504-505, 932, 952
concrete, 502-503, 952
defined, 502, 952
of direct address, 829-830,
857-858, 967
exercises, *500-501, 503-506,
515-517, 895-897, 932-933,
935*
gerund as, 623
gerund phrase as, 624-625
infinitive as, 626
infinitive phrase as, 628
plurals, forming, 930-935, 948,
972
possessive case, 279, 518,
894-897, 948
proper, 503-504, 542, 819-827,
952, 965

used as adjective, 543-544, 828
Noun clause, 651-653, 957
Number. *See also* Plurals.
agreement of pronoun and
antecedent, 736-740
agreement of subject and verb,
748-773
defined, 736, 750
of nouns and pronouns, 750
plural, 750-754, 760-761
singular, 750-754, 760-761
of verbs, 751-752
Numbered list, 476
Numbers
fractions, 912
with hyphens, 911
and italics, 872
plural, 902
spelling
in dates, 936-937, 972
ordinals, 936, 972
words or numerals, 936, 972

O

Object of preposition, 562, 623-624,
649, 652, 723-725, 961
Object of verb. *See* Direct object;
Indirect object.
Object pronoun, 722, 961
Objection, 264
Objective case, 638, 716, 722-725,
729-731, 961
Observation
objective, 155
subjective, 155
Occasion
defined, 15
writing process, 15
Old English, 426
Online catalog
explained, 344-348, 350-361
item information entry, 346
limiting search, 347
record, 345
search by author's name, 347
search by keyword, 347, 359
search by subject, 347
search by title, 347
strategies for use, 347

Note: Italic locators (page numbers) indicate skill sets

Note: Italic locators (page numbers) indicate skill sets

INDEX

Note: Italic locators (page numbers) indicate skill sets

Note: Italic locators (page numbers) indicate skill sets

Note: Italic locators (page numbers) indicate skill sets

Purpose (*continued*)

audiovisual production, 480

for communicating, 422, 439

composition, 99

creative writing, 15, 172

describe, 5-6, 150

entertain, 15, 172, 459

explain, 5-6, 15, 124, 225

express, 15

group discussion, 468-470

inform, 5, 15, 225, 459

letters, 440-453

list of, 5-6, 15

literary analysis, 303

narrative, 5-6, 124

persuade, 5-6, 15, 265, 459

reflect, 15, 121

research report, 382

self-expressive, 15

speeches, 458-459

story, 172

voice, 6

Web site, 486

of writing, 5-6, 15, 116-321

Put, principal parts, 685

Q

Quatrain, 207

Question mark, 843, 880, 967

Questions. *See also* Interrogative sentence; Tests.

essay tests, 414-421

5W-How?, 19

inquiring, 19

inverted order, 589, 762

punctuation, 843, 880

research, 331

standardized tests, 401-413

Quotation marks, 311, 875-886, 968-969

and citations, 337, 378

and commas, 878-879, 968

for dialogue, 185-187, 882, 968

for direct quotations, 311, 877-881

and end marks, 880-881

and exclamation points, 881, 968

indirect quotation, 877

long passages, 883, 969

and periods, 878, 880, 968

and question marks, 880, 968

quotations within quotation, 884, 969

to show irony or sarcasm, 884-886, 969

for titles, 875-876, 968

using, 875-886

Quotations

capitalizing, 878-879

credit for, 377-378

direct, 311-312, 877

and ellipses, 312

indirect, 877

literary analysis, 311-313

and quotation marks, 877-881

taking notes, 337-339

R

Raise, principal parts, 691, 805

Rambling sentences, 63

Reaction shot, in video production, 484

Reading

comprehension, 406-409

as prewriting strategy, 14

Reading skills

adjusting reading rate to purpose, 395-396

close reading, 395

scanning, 395

skimming, 395

SQ3R study strategy, 395-396

analyzing, 103, 146-149, 172-174, 260-263, 392

interpreting, 123

relationships among details, 392, 397

Real time, defined, 491

Reasoning

analogy, 402-404

cause-and-effect, 392

counter-argument, 264

critical thinking, 392-421

deductive, 392

fact, 261-236

generalization, 274

inductive, 392

opinion, 261-263

sound, 392-393

technique, pillar, 271

using, 392

Reciprocal pronoun, 513-514, 952

Redundancy, 64-66

Reference materials. *See* Information sources.

Reflecting

on experience, 124

writing aim, 156

Reflexive pronouns, 509-510, 952

Regional dialects, 42

Regular adjectives, 597

Regular comparison of modifiers, 778-780

Regular nouns, 930

Regular verbs, 684-685, 947, 959

Relative pronouns, 59, 647-650, 957

Relevance, evaluating information for, 219

Relevant sources, finding, 332-334

Repetition

as sound device, 203

unnecessary, 64

Request letter, 445-446

Research companion, 342-361

library or media center, 342-349

print and nonprint reference materials, 350-358

using the Internet for research, 358-361

Research report, 324-389

accuracy, checking for, 382

audience, 328

body, 363, 372-379

citations, 363, 373, 376-381

conclusion, 363, 375

defined, 324

drafting, 371-381

editing, 384

elements of, 363

exercises, *325, 328-330, 336, 339-341, 349, 357, 361, 364, 366-367, 369-371, 376, 380, 383-389*

footnotes and endnotes, 378-379

gathering information, 332-361

introduction, 363, 371, 373

model, 325-327, 338, 365-366, 368-369, 373-376

Note: Italic locators (page numbers) indicate skill sets

INDEX

Sentence (*continued*)

compound, 654, 662, 852, 958

compound-complex, 654-655, 662, 958

concise, 63-66

concluding, 75, 78-79, 89, 92, 94, 96, 99, 109

correcting, 11, 31, 62, 135, 411-412, 666-667, 669, 670, 672-673, 678-679

declarative, 842, 868, 966

defined, 578, 606, 954

diagramed, 599-602, 631-634, 657-658

end marks, 845-846, 877-878, 880

exclamatory, 842-843, 868, 966-967

fluency, 55-62, 184, 579, 586, 951, 954

fragment, 62, 578, 662, 666-671, 678, 838, 890, 948, 958

imperative, 842, 868, 966-967

interrogative, 842-843, 868, 966-967

inverted order, 588-589, 762, 963

kinds of sentences, 842-844

natural order, 588-589, 762

numbers, 936

patterns, 60-66

punctuating, 135, 157, 613, 617, 622, 645, 654, 877-878, 880, 894, 904-906

rambling, 63

recognizing, 578-579, 954

rubric, 67

run-on, 135, 606, 672-674, 678, 838, 922, 949, 958

semicolon in, 135, 223, 904-907, 922

simple, 370, 654, 958

structure, 61, 184, 279, 654-656, 662, 951, 958

supporting, 75, 77-78, 80, 82, 89, 92, 94, 96, 99, 105

topic, 75-77, 80, 82, 89, 92, 94, 96, 99, 105, 109, 130

variety, 55-62, 950-951

write in complete, 225, 303, 370, 580, 662, 890

Sentence base, 576-607

Sentence fragment, 9, 62, 578, 638, 662, 666-671, 678-679, 838, 890-891

appositive phrase, 638

clause fragment, 670, 678

correcting, 9, 62, 638, 662, 666-667, 669-671, 678-679, 838

defined, 578, 666, 678

exercises, *579, 667, 669, 671*

phrase fragment, 668, 678

subordinate clause fragment, 670-671

used for emphasis (effect), 62, 885, 890-891

Sentence parts

complement, 592-598, 606

predicate, 580-591, 606

subject, 580-591, 606

Sentence structure, 61, 576-607, 654-656, 662, 762, 852-853

complex, 654-655, 662

compound, 654, 662

compound-complex, 654-655, 662

creating, 654-655

identifying, 654-655

introductory, 852-853

inverted order, 588-589, 762

kinds, 654-656, 662

natural order, 588-589, 762

simple, 654, 662

varying, 61

Sentence style

concise sentences, 63-66

varying beginnings, 60, 184, 233, 588-589

varying length, 55-59, 184, 233, 654-655, 662

varying structure, 61, 184, 233, 654-656

Sequential order, 86, 156, 451, 482

Series of items. *See* Items in a series.

Server, defined, 491

Set, principal parts, 685, 805

Setting

creating, 181, 185, 197

defined, 173

details, 181, 188, 297-298

as literary element

of drama, 297

of fiction, 296

model, 181

play, 195, 197

prewriting, 177, 181-182

short story, 173, 181-182, 185, 188, 197

Shall, will, 805

Shape, as a literary element, 296

Share, principal parts, 684

Short story

analyzing, 172-174

beginning, 172

characters, 173, 178-180

chronological order, 172, 183, 185, 187

climax, 172

conclusion, 174

conflict, 172

defined, 172

description, 172

details, 175-176, 178-179, 181, 185, 188

devices for enhancing the plot, 187

dialogue, 185-186

dialogue and plot techniques, 187

drafting, 185-187

strategies, 185

editing and publishing, 190

elements of, 172-174

ending, 172

evaluation checklist, 189

events, 172-176, 180, 183, 185, 187

examples for using dialogue, 186

flashback, 187

fluency, 184

foreshadowing, 187

framing your story, 181-182

ideas, 175

imaging, 180

juxtaposition, 187

main idea, 174

Note: Italic locators (page numbers) indicate skill sets

Note: Italic locators (page numbers) indicate skill sets

Note: Italic locators (page numbers) indicate skill sets

Subject of a sentence (*continued*)
  compound, 586, 654, 758-759,
    772, 955, 962-963
  defined, 580, 606, 954
  diagramed, 599-601
  identifying, 580-583
  inverted order, 588-591, 762, 955,
    962-963
  natural order, 588-591, 762, 955
  nominative case, 716
  plural, 752-753
  position in sentence, 60
  pronouns used as, 9, 108, 518,
    649, 716-719, 746, 760-761
  simple, 581, 954
  singular, 752-753
  understood, 590-591, 955
  and varying sentence beginnings,
    60, 588-590
Subject-area assignments, 399-400
Subjective details, 155
Subjective observation, 155
Subject-verb agreement. *See*
  Agreement, subject-verb.
Subjunctive mood, 707-708, 960
Subordinate clause, 370, 643-653,
  957
Subordinating conjunction, 645-646,
  957
  combining sentences, 59
  common, 645
  defined, 645
  identifying, 645-646
Subplot, 187
Suffixes
  common, 436
  defined, 435, 938
  doubling final consonant, 939
  exercises, *436, 940*
  and hyphens, 913
  -ness, -ly, 938
  spelling rules for, 938-939,
    972-973
  as word parts, 435-436, 938-939
  for words ending in *e*, 938
  for words ending in *y*, 939
Summarizing
  defined, 337
  how to, 337-338
  model, 338

as note-taking skill, 397
Summary
  in conclusion, 260, 273
  for note-taking, 338, 397
Superlative degree of comparison,
  776, 778-779, 781, 783, 963-964
Superscript, 378
Supporting details
  defined, 18
  developing a subject, 18-19, 146
  developing main idea, 80, 105,
    133, 228, 233, 311
  gathering evidence, 304
  ordering, 20
  outline, 222, 273, 368
  reading comprehension tests, 406
  taking essay tests, 416, 419
  taking notes, 397
Supporting information, 229, 267
Supporting paragraphs
  descriptive writing, 146
  expository writing, 222
  personal narrative writing, 125,
    130
  writing compositions, 99, 105
  writing to persuade, 260
Supporting sentences
  defined, 77
  in descriptive writing, 92
  in expository writing, 94
  and implied main idea, 75, 77-78,
    80
  model, 78, 90, 92, 94, 96
  in narrative writing, 90
  and paragraph unity, 82
  in persuasive writing, 96
  writing compositions, 99, 105
Surf, 227, 429, 492
Swim, principal parts, 689
Syllable
  count in poetry, 201, 203, 296
  word division, 431-432, 435,
    778-779, 910, 927-928, 939
Symbols
  accent marks, 347, 432
  diacritical marks, 432
  figurative language (figures of
    speech), 205
  graphic, 480

phonetic, 431-432
  for revising and proofreading, 11,
    30-31, 420
  rhetorical device, 310
  writing a poem, 205
  writing to persuade, 276
  visual, 480
Synonyms
  defined, 437
  in dictionaries, 432, 437
  and meaning of a word, 432, 437
  recognizing, 356, 432, 437
  reference books, 356, 432, 437
  in thesaurus, 356, 437
Syntax. *See* Clause; Complement;
  Phrase; Predicate; Sentence;
  Subject of a sentence.
Synthesize, for summary, 301, 367

T

Table of contents, as research tool,
  349
Take, principal parts, 687
Taking notes. *See* Note-taking.
Task groups, 470
Teach, principal parts, 686
Tear, principal parts, 689
Technological terms, 825
Technology
  creating texts, 473-478
  editing texts, 473-474
  publishing texts, 473-480
  revising texts, 473-474
Tell, principal parts, 686
Tense, 693-703
  conjugation, 695
  defined, 693
  exercises, *698-699, 701-703*
  future, 694
  future perfect, 694
  past, 693
  past perfect, 694
  present, 693
  present perfect, 694
  progressive form, 699-701
  shifts in, 702-703
Testimonial, 274, 276
Tests
  analogy, 402-404

Note: Italic locators (page numbers) indicate skill sets

Note: Italic locators (page numbers) indicate skill sets

Usage labels, in dictionary, 432
Usage QuickGuide, 959-964
Use to, used to, 808

Valid inference, 229-230
Variety in sentences
  varying sentence beginnings,
    60-61, 184, 951
  varying sentence length, 55-59,
    61, 184, 579, 951
  varying sentence structure, 61,
    579, 951
Venn diagram, 244, 249
Verb
  action, 522-525, 529-530,
    534-535, 592-595, 722, 786,
    953, 955
  active voice, 6, 704-705, 712-713,
    960
  agreement with subject, 9, 317,
    534, 606, 712, 748-773, 947,
    962-963
  auxiliary, 522, 584, 953, 955
  common helping, 522, 584, 754
  common linking, 527-528, 582
  complete predicate, 582, 955
  compound, 58, 588, 592, 654,
    851, 955
  conjugation, 695-699, 960
  defined, 502, 522, 534, 953
  diagramed, 599-601, 633-634, 657
  exercises, *523-526, 528-530,*
    685-686, 688, 690, 692, 698,
    701-703, 705, 708
  helping, 522, 584, 684-685,
    693-694, 754, 962
  intransitive, 525, 534, 953
  irregular, 8, 190, 947
  linking, 527-530, 534, 540, 582,
    595, 597, 720, 766, 786, 788,
    912, 953, 955, 961, 964
  mood, 706-708, 712
  number, 750, 962
  passive voice, 704-705, 712-713,
    960
  position in sentence, 588-589, 955
  principal parts, 431, 684-690,
    713, 959
    irregular verb, 684-685, 959
    regular verb, 685-690, 959

problem verbs, 691-692, 959
progressive form, 696, 699-701
regular, 8, 190, 947
simple predicate, 582, 955
specific, 46
tense, 748, 693-694, 713, 960
transitive, 525-526, 534, 953
used as adjective, 619, 621,
  623-624, 626, 956
verb phrase, 522, 584-586, 953,
  955
vivid, 46
Verb phrase
  defined, 522, 584, 953, 955
  identifying, 531
  order, 588, 955
  parallelism, 89, 673, 951
  in questions, 585
  using, 754
Verb tense
  consistent, 9, 235, 318, 702, 748,
    948
  future, 693-696, 960
  future perfect, 693-694, 696-697,
    960
  future perfect progressive, 699-700
  future progressive, 699-700
  past, 693, 713, 960
  past perfect, 693-694, 696-697,
    960
  past perfect progressive, 699-700,
    702
  past progressive, 699-700
  present, 693, 695-697, 960
  present perfect, 693-694,
    696-697, 960
  present perfect progressive, 699
  present progressive, 699
  principal parts, 431, 684-690,
    713, 959
  progressive form, 699-701, 960
  shifts in, 702-703, 960
  uses of, 693-703
Verbal phrase, 621-622, 624-625,
  627-629, 956
  and comma, 622
  gerund phrase, 624-625, 639, 956
  identifying, 635-636
  infinitive phrase, 627-628, 639,
    956

participial phrase, 621-622, 627,
  639, 956
Verbals
  defined, 619, 638
  gerunds, 623-624, 638, 956
  infinitives, 626-627, 638, 956
  participle, 619-621, 638, 956
Verb-subject agreement. *See*
  Agreement, subject-verb.
Vertical file, 357
Video files, on Web site, 494
Video production
  assemble editing, 485
  audio tasks, 481
  background music, 485
  brief, 480
  camera moves, 482-483
  camera shots, 482-483
  camera techniques, 483
  computer editing, 485
  concept outline, 480
  cutaway shot, 484
  cuts, 483
  dissolve, 485
  establishing shot, 484
  fade, 485
  final cut, 485
  forms, 480
  in-camera editing, 485
  insert editing, 485
  panning, 483
  post-production, 485
  pre-production, 480-482
  pre-production checklist, 481
  pre-production tasks, 481
  reaction shot, 484
  script, 481
  special effects, 482, 484
  storyboard, 481
  titles, 485
  tracking, 483
  treatment, 480-481
  video editing programs, 485
  video production schedule, 482
  video tasks, 481
  voiceover narration, 485
  zooming, 483

INDEX

Note: Italic locators (page numbers) indicate skill sets

INDEX

Note: Italic locators (page numbers) indicate skill sets

Image Credits

Every reasonable effort has been made to contact all copyright holders. If we have omitted anyone, please let us know and we will include a suitable acknowledgement in subsequent editions.

Corbis: pp. 122 © BEMBARON JEREMY / CORBIS SYGMA, 198 © Comstock Select / Corbis, 608 © Bettmann / CORBIS, 626 © Bettmann / CORBIS, 664 © Melissa Moseley / Sony Pictures / Bureau L.A. Collection / Corbis, 690 © Visuals Unlimited/Corbis, 918 © Bettmann / CORBIS

Dreamstime: pp. 7, 14, 15, 18, 21, 23, 76, 82, 84, 93, 103, 108, 112, 128, 146, 151, 155, 157, 162, 164, 177, 219, 227, 282, 310, 319, 320, 323, 334, 358, 388, 492, 499, 505, 539, 558, 576, 587, 619, 655, 663, 681, 706, 744, 747, 777, 785, 834, 914, 924, 937, 945, 951,

Getty Images: pp. 847 Ben Edwards / Stone / Getty Images

iStockphoto: pp. 3, 4, 8, 31, 33, 34, 42, 43, 57, 60, 68, 83, 94, 95, 107, 115, 126, 132, 145, 158, 163, 164, 178, 180, 182, 201, 224, 225, 226, 233, 237, 238, 246, 249, 258, 262, 292, 328, 332, 337, 339, 340, 363, 391, 520, 536, 557, 570, 607, 616, 663, 673, 674, 699, 713, 714, 748, 774, 813, 814, 856, 859, 863, 864, 870, 884, 892, 907, 912, 916,

Jupiter Images: pp. 50, 80, 138, 188, 189, 215, 220, 228, 242, 248, 250, 252, 282, 314, 340, 400, 412, 417, 423, 424, 450, 472, 484, 506, 523, 596, 636, 640, 648, 662, 676, 682, 687, 695, 794

Library of Congress: pp. 348, 500, 618, 630, 840

Wikimedia Commons: p. 622

Text Credits

"A Day's Wait" from THE SHORT STORIES OF ERNEST HEMINGWAY by Ernest Hemingway. Reprinted with the permission of Simon & Schuster, Inc. Copyright © 1933 by Charles Scribner's Son. Copyright renewed © 1961 by Mary Hemingway. All rights reserved.

Excerpt from "Living Like Weasels" from TEACHING A STONE TO TALK: EXPEDITIONS AND ENCOUNTERS by Annie Dillard. Copyright © 1982 by Annie Dillard. Reprinted by permission of HarperCollins Publishers.

"Say it with Flowers" from YOKOHAMA, CALIFORNIA by Toshio Mori. © 1985 by Caxton Printers Ltd. Reprinted by permission of Caxton Press, a division of The Caxton Printers Ltd.

WHEN HEAVEN AND EARTH CHANGED PLACES by Le Ly Hayslip, copyright © 1989 by Le Ly Hayslip and Charles Jay Wurts. Used by permission of Doubleday, a division of Random House, Inc.